# TON-UP LANCS

# TON-UP LANCS

A photographic record of the thirty-five RAF Lancasters
that each completed one hundred sorties

Norman Franks

GRUB STREET • LONDON

First published in 2005
Grub Street
4 Rainham Close
London
SW11 6SS

Copyright © 2005 Grub Street
Text copyright © 2005 Norman Franks

This edition first published 2015

**British Library Cataloguing in Publication Data**
Franks, Norman L. R.
   Ton-up Lancs : a photographic record of the thirty-five RAF
   Lancasters that each completed one hundred sorties. – Rev. ed.
   1.Great Britain. Royal Air Force. Bomber Command – History
   2.World War, 1939-1945 – Aerial operations, British
   3.Lancaster (Bombers)
   I.Title
   940.5'44'941

   **ISBN 9781909808263**

Designed by Roy Platten, Eclipse. roy.eclipse@btopenworld.com

Updated and expanded from *Claims to Fame – The Lancaster,*
Arms & Armour, 1994

**Author's note:**
Awards without brackets have been already presented, while those
with brackets denote awards which came later.

Printed and bound in India by Replika Press Pvt. Ltd.

# Contents

# Introduction

As with so many of my books, information continues to come in long after publication, often prompted by readers, or simply through new avenues of research suddenly opening up. In my original book which came out in 1994, under the title The Lancaster, part of what was supposed to be a series of books on famous aircraft under a general heading of 'Claims to Fame' I covered the stories of 34 Avro Lancasters, each of which flew 100 or more operations during World War Two.

Over the last ten years I have been able to add information and recollections from several aircrew members who flew in these Lancasters, and have managed to clarify some events that may have been obscure. There were a few suggestions that other Lancasters achieved 100 ops, but in the end I have only been able to confirm one more, that being PA990 of 626 Squadron. I am happy, therefore, to say that there were 35 Lancasters that were able to be named in the 'Ton-Up' Club. Its history is included in this book. There may still be others whose records are incomplete. People are working on one or two other Lancasters that may have topped the 100 mark, one being Alan Chambers who, in addition, is studying all Bomber Command raids during the war.

The Lancaster is the RAF's most famous four-engined heavy bomber of World War Two. Its very name is enough to conjure up all sorts of images, not only to the men who flew them and flew in them; to the men and women who helped to build them and service them; or who had friends or relatives who may have died operating them, but to people of other generations who have an interest in any famous aeroplane. The Lancaster is so well known that sometimes it is easy to forget or ignore the statistics relating to this sturdy machine which helped take Bomber Command's war to targets all over Germany and its occupied territories between 1942 and 1945. Because this book deals with just a handful of these aeroplanes, these statistics become a highlight.

A total of 7,366 Lancasters were built, of which 3,400 were lost on operations and a further 200 plus were destroyed or written-off in crashes[1]. They undertook approximately 156,000 operational sorties and carried over 600,000 tons of bombs.

Some 125,000 aircrew served in Bomber Command in World War Two, of whom 73,700 became casualties – a staggering 60 per cent. Of this total 63,750 occurred on operations, the others suffering during training or associated flying duties. In all 55,000 died, over 47,000 of them on operational sorties; over 9,800 others were taken prisoner. The other 8,400 or so were those who returned wounded or were injured in accidents, divided almost exactly by those 'on ops' and those on other duties.

Of those who died, nearly 38,500 were members of the Royal Air Force (RAF), almost 10,000 Royal Canadian Air Force (RCAF), over 4,000 Royal Australian Air Force (RAAF), while some 1,700 were Royal New Zealand Air Force (RNZAF); men from Poland, France, South Africa and other European or Dominion countries made up the balance.

For a bomber crew to complete a tour of operations (a tour of duty) they had to carry out a set number of sorties against hostile targets. The number varied, but was generally 30, although sometimes it was 25 and at others it went up to 35. Different squadron commanders occasionally varied these even further, so that if a crew completed a particularly hazardous few trips towards the end of their tour he may allow them to finish on 29 or even 28. By the same token, if casualties had been heavy and a need to mount a 'Maximum Effort' was called for, a crew might be asked to do an extra one. Some keen 'press-on types' may even have gone on to do 32 or 33, especially if a crew member had missed one or two and the others wanted them all to finish together.

However, with each raid having the potential of being their last, few really chanced their arm, and as soon as they were allowed to finish, finish they did. But the aeroplanes went on. As long, that is, as they performed well, didn't get too badly damaged and passed the regular maintenance service.

Having read the statistics above one can appreciate that neither the crew nor the aeroplane had a particularly good chance of finishing a set number of bombing missions, and a crew could just as easily go missing on their first trip as on their 30th – and often did. The chances of any Avro Lancaster completing a large number of raids was even less likely, for as one crew ended a tour (or were lost in another aeroplane), their usual machine had to keep on going until it too 'failed to return', was damaged beyond repair or simply became worn out.

One cannot say with any real accuracy just how many Lancasters flew on operations, but it had to be around 6,500. Yet of this supposed total, only 35 – a mere 1.9 per cent – managed to complete 100 or more ops. The highest number of operations flown by a Lancaster was a miraculous 140.

To know how many operations a particular aeroplane flew is one thing, to know what these operations were, when they were flown, and just as importantly, who flew them, is the reason for this book. So, whether you flew them, flew in them, helped to build or service them or just have an interest in them, the record of these 35 very gallant 'ladies' is here for all to see. It is their claim to fame.

For this revised edition I wish to thank the following for their generous help:

Steve Bethel, Robert Stone, Michel Evrard, Inge Gustafsson Ph.D, Jack Mathers, Norman Owen DFM, J R O'Hanlon, Dennis Baldry, Donald Lawson, Frank Phripp DFC, Richard B Revill, Arthur Laflamme, Royan Yule DFC, Alan R Witty, Harry Hayton, Douglas Crowe, David Stapleton, Ted Willoughby, Douglas Joss, Ivor Billinge, H Davy, Bob Bennet Jr, Pat Walkins, Peter Green, R G Robinson, Peter Renshaw, Molly Would, Carol Sawbridge, Howard Sandall, Alan Chambers and the late Stuart Howe.

For the pictures of PA474 I have to thank Martin Bowman, Richard Paver and the Battle of Britain Memorial Flight.

---

[1]Figures do vary depending on which source is used so I have used approximate figures which still make the points required.

# The Avro Lancaster

The Lancaster, which was developed from the disappointing Avro Manchester, began to equip Bomber Command squadrons in 1942, the first being 44 (Rhodesia) Squadron at RAF Waddington, Lincolnshire, followed by 97 Squadron at nearby Woodhall Spa. By 1945 there were 56 squadrons flying them and over 1,000 of the type were either in these squadrons or on the strength of training or operational conversion units (OCUs).

The aircraft achieved many 'firsts': first to fly Pathfinder missions, in August 1942; first to carry 8,000 lb bombs, in April 1943; first to carry a 12,000 lb bomb, in September 1943, followed by the 12,000 lb deep penetration bomb – the Tallboy – in June 1944; then finally the mammoth 22,000 lb Grand Slam bomb, in March 1945.

It also achieved recognition in other ways: the famous raid on the Ruhr dams by the specially formed 617 Squadron in May 1943, and the sinking of the *Tirpitz* by 9 and 617 Squadrons in November 1944. It played a major part in the important raid on the German experimental rocket base at Peenemünde in August 1943 which resulted in severe delays to the V1 and V2 flying bombs and rocket programme. Of the 32 awards of the Victoria Cross awarded to men of the RAF in World War Two, ten were given to men who flew in the Avro Lancaster.

Some more facts. Empty, the Lancaster weighed 36,900 lbs (16.5 tons), while fully loaded it was 68,000 lbs (30 tons). Bomb loads could and did vary, but the average weight was 14,000 lbs (6.25 tons). With this figure it had a range of 1,600 miles and a service ceiling of 24,500 feet. Four 1,460 hp Merlin 20 or 22 (or 1,640 hp Merlin 24) engines hauled this vast load into the sky, together with a seven-man crew – sometimes eight.

For those unfamiliar with fuel loads the figures in the table below will seem even more fantastic. These are figures for actual raids with accurate bomb loads in 1943.

Anyone who fills their car up each week with, say, 15 gallons of petrol will easily calculate that the bomber that went to Milan carried enough fuel to fill up his or her car for 137 weeks – two and a half years! Multiply that by the number of aircraft that went to Milan that August night – 504 – and the total comes to 1,039,248 gallons (with which the family car would be supplied for 1,330 years).

| Target | Date | Fuel load | Bomb Load |
|---|---|---|---|
| Hamburg | 24/25 Jul | 1,500 galls | 1 x 4,000 lb bomb, 3 x 1,000 lb bombs and 540 x 4 lb incendiaries |
| Essen | 25/26 Jul | 1,500 galls | 1 x 4,000 lb bomb, 3 x 1,000 lb bombs and 540 x 4 lb incendiaries |
| Nürnberg | 10/11 Aug | 1,800 galls | 1 x 4,000 lb, 1 x 1000 lb, 1 x 500 lb and 690 x 4 lb incendiaries |
| Milan | 12/13 Aug | 2,062 galls | 1 x 4,000 lb, 540 x 4 lb and 48 x 30 lb incendiaries |
| Berlin | 23/24 Aug | 1,743 galls | 1 x 4,000 lb, 2 x 1000 lb, 690 x 4 lb incendiaries and 48 x 30 lb incendiaries |
| Berlin | 31 Aug/1 Sep | 1,900 galls | 1 x 4,000 lb, 1 x 1,000 lb and 90 x 4 lb incendiaries |
| Berlin | 3/4 Sep | 2,062 galls | 1 x 4,000 lb, 630 x 4 lb and 48 x 30 lb incendiaries |

And that was just one night, with another 152 bombers going to Turin as well.

The pure logistics of the amount of aviation fuel needed to sustain not only Bomber Command, but Coastal and Fighter Command too, plus training, transport, communications aircraft et al, not to mention the massive US 8th Air Force operating in Britain, is almost incomprehensible.

The Lancaster crew probably didn't concern themselves with this mind-boggling statistic. One of them could be trying to work out how he might get hold of just two gallons of petrol for his own car in order to see his girlfriend the next night – if he got back from Milan that is. What concentrated the mind of the Lancaster pilot, of course, was that his skill was needed to get this powerful but heavily laden beast off the ground.

He and his six crewmen were fully aware of the potential death-trap they were flying; a huge metal tomb stuffed with high-explosives, incendiaries, 2,062 gallons of high octane fuel, not to mention several thousand rounds of .303 ammunition for the Lancaster's eight machine guns.

Bomb loads varied because of either the target or the distance to that target. Less fuel meant a higher bomb load, while longer range, i.e. more fuel, generally resulted in a smaller bomb load. By 1943 the Lancaster was really into its stride, the usual bomb load would be one 4,000 lb 'cookie', another 2,000 lbs of High Explosive (HE) – either two 1,000 pounders or four 500 pounders, plus a selection of 4 lb and or 30 lb incendiaries, depending on room, load capacity and target. The idea was that the bombs blasted the targets, while the burning incendiaries set it on fire.

# Researching this Book

It was necessary, when compiling this book, to plough through the squadron diaries (Forms 540 and 541) to list each occasion a particular Lancaster flew an operational sortie. If originally I thought this was just a time-consuming chore I was soon to discover that it was fraught with all sorts of difficulties.

Anyone reading through the old wartime diaries will know that they are only as accurate as the men – or perhaps women – who compiled them. They range from the excellent to the very poor. If a squadron had, say, a former journalist as its diary compiler then the diary could be not only interesting but well kept and well documented as well as accurate. If, on the other hand, someone who could type with at least one finger was 'volunteered' and was far more interested in getting down to the NAAFI, or trying to get away with the minimum amount of information he knew his CO would be happy with – and sign, (if the CO signed at all and didn't leave the formality to his adjutant) – those records could be poor, inaccurate and sometimes downright untrustworthy.

With bomber operations happening almost every night, the orderly room staff's daily task of typing up everything from 12 to 22 Lancaster serial numbers, along with the seven crewmen's names, plus flying times and comments, has to be riddled with typing errors as well as errors of fact. On several occasions I found the same aircraft serial number flying at the same time with two different crews – an obvious error. Other times it was obvious the clerk typed the serial number of the aircraft a crew usually flew without checking if they had actually flown in it that night.

What was less obvious of course, was when the aircraft I was researching flew and the serial was typed out incorrectly or listed with a fictitious serial number. Aircraft were often referred to by their fuselage letter, eg: A-Able. If this aircraft was lost or sent away for major repair, and a new A-Able arrived, sometimes the old serial number was typed out instead of the new one.

On occasions the copy page I was reading was a very poor carbon copy – almost illegible. Crews might be listed wrongly, misspelt, or a last minute crew change, where say a crew member went sick and was replaced by a spare bod, wasn't noted in the records. That would show a man taking part in a sortie when in reality he was in bed with two aspirins.

What is recorded is the best of the surviving evidence, which is fairly accurate, although I would not be able to vouch that it is 100 per cent so. However, what is produced will give a pretty accurate picture of what each of these 35 Lancasters did and who flew them.

Another problem I found was that where publicity had occurred when a particular Lancaster reached its 100th op, it often proved very difficult to reconcile this to the records. All sorts of things could have happened, of course, and one can picture the scene.

A flight commander happens to mention to the CO that A-Able is nearing its 100th op, according to the bomb tally painted on the side of the cockpit. The CO appears interested and asks for a full breakdown of the sorties flown. The flight commander in turn tells the adjutant, say, who gives the task to a corporal clerk who is about as interested in the job as he is of being away from his bride of two months, who lives 300 miles away from where he is based. So he swiftly, and grudgingly, runs through the Form 541 pages and quickly lists the ops; this list eventually goes back up the chain to the CO.

Thus on such-and-such a night, A-Able flies its 100th sortie. However, what the corporal clerk failed to see, was that one sortie was aborted right after take-off and not counted, and that another was listed as being flown when in fact the aircraft was being serviced. Thus its 100th op was in reality only its 98th! That it eventually went on to fly 109 sorties, is one thing, but because there was now a definite record of its 100th op date, counting forward from that, the record shows that A-Able flew 111 in total.

In any event, it was the aircraft's ground crew who painted the bomb symbols on the nose – it had little to do with the aircrew other than being of interest if it was 'their' particular aircraft for a period of time. The ground crew looked after it, serviced it, repaired minor battle damage, changed the engines from time to time, and so on. They took pride in it. Few of the flyers, if any , took the trouble to check totals, especially if they returned from a short leave, saw that some more bombs had gone up and assumed the aircraft had done additional trips in their absence. Their main preoccupation was staying alive and finishing their tour.

The difficulty was the interpretation the ground crew put on a sortie, and that may be different from the record keepers. That is not to say the ground crew were taking liberties, far from it, but merely being proud of their aircraft and if they understood it had flown an op, then up went another bomb. The only problem comes later, when the actual bomb symbols do not easily tally with the records, and a photograph of the bomb tally *must* be accurate in terms of ops flown!

As in all things, once a fact, however inaccurate, becomes established it is difficult to reconcile or change it. Therefore the reader will find in some of the aircraft biographies that follow, an occasional reference to total sorties being different – in dispute if you like – to some long-assumed established 'fact'.

Mentioning aborted missions, these too caused problems, in that sometimes they were counted as ops, sometimes not. Obviously if a Lancaster lost an engine right after take-off and the pilot went round and landed again, then the mission was not counted. If on another raid, the Master Bomber called off the raid near or even over the target, the raid might be abandoned but the op counted – quite naturally.

Ron Clark, who flew EE139 with 100 Squadron in 1943 (see **The Tour**) was asked about aborts and the like. He says:

'The issue of aborts in 1943 was a grey area and sometimes these were credited or half credited or not credited, depending on the circumstances.

'The decision to abort was not easy, it was a terrific anti-climax and a lot of trouble had gone in for nothing. One had the feeling of letting the side down. We aborted our trip to Oberhausen on 14 June because of rear turret failure before reaching the coast. The CO criticised my decision and probably thought a pep-talk was in order as I was a new boy. The night fighter usually approached

from the rear and below and Geoff Green in the defective turret would still have had the chance to detect it. Of course, the enemy had tremendous advantage in fire-power and the ability to pick up the glare of a bomber's exhausts. It might have been impossible for Geoff to bale out in an emergency though.

'After having an engine fail on the Nürnberg trip on 27 August, we decided to press on but we gradually lost height and rather than stress the remaining engines for such a long flight we dropped the bombs in the Channel and returned to base. At the debriefing I was taken aback when the ground engineer officer threatened me with a court-martial after I said that I wanted a new engine instead of another re-conditioned one. As I walked away I glanced at "Dinger" Bell, the Flight Commander, who seemed equally surprised. Neither trip was credited of course.'

Bomber Command set up a bomb-line later in the war – a line at which by flying past it the sortie counted towards a crew's tour, but by aborting on the near side of it, it didn't. For obvious reasons, the 'line' was not advertised and in any event it changed from time to time. It has not been clear anywhere in the Form 541s whether each and every raid was made official or not when aborts occurred. The reader will have to pick his own way through that minefield as he reads the raid lists. At this distance I am certainly not going to make decisions of that nature. Ron Clark remarks on this bomb-line:

'My rear gunner, Geoff Green, who operated his second tour in 1944, tells me that the 'Bombing Line' was instituted after the Invasion of Europe to protect the Allied forces from our own bombs. This line fluctuated with the rapid advance and was the cause of some misunderstandings and casualties on the ground. Geoff recalls some awkward moments with Canadian soldiers in a bar in Paddington. They had taken casualties in this way but they ended up by buying him a pint.'

As author of this book I have not, by the same token, set out to prove any points, merely to record the details of these 35 'above-average' Lancasters – centenarians – whose rise to fame was in the number of ops they flew. In some cases, where in the past a certain number of ops have been credited to them, the total figure is a problem. Others are not so problematic, but all went on to, or over, the 100. Some squadrons claimed credits for sorties flown during the food-dropping missions to Holland in 1945 – Operation Manna, while others also gave credit to trips flown during Operation Exodus – the return of released Allied prisoners of war by air.

Where these occurred they have been noted, but it will be up to the reader if he wishes to think whether a Lancaster which flew 109 bombing raids plus two Manna trips and two Exodus trips made a total of 113 sorties or not. That is not germane to the aims of this book. All I might say is that what is good for one Lanc should be good enough for another!

By and large a pattern does emerge when looking at the life of almost any Lancaster during World War Two. It arrived on a squadron, was checked over by the ground crew and assigned to a flight. Unless it was specifically a replacement for a crew's Lancaster which had been seriously damaged a night or so before, then the new bomber was available to any crew who needed an aeroplane. As there were usually more crews than available/serviceable machines, one or two crews regularly shared a Lancaster. From time to time it then became the more or less permanent aeroplane for one specific crew. After a few ops the Lanc was taken from the Availability State for a couple of days while it was looked over by the maintenance section – something like a family car's first 1,000 mile service.

Once back in action, its usual crew would generally continue with it, but then for a couple of nights another crew might take it, this occurring as the regular crew took a 48-hour leave or some such break period. On their return they would take over the machine again until the end of their tour – or they would fail to return while flying another machine. In between times, of course, anything could happen, from slight damage to an engine failure which would take the bomber out of the line for a few days. A Lancaster might have an many as eight or nine engine changes on a squadron. The RAF's accident damage categories referred to in the text need a little explanation: Cat AC = minor damage; Cat E = write off.

Then the regular crew may be lucky enough to finish their tour. The Lancaster then seems to be in a sort of limbo while two or three other crews – probably new crews – start their tours. Suddenly one finds that once

again a more or less regular crew is flying it on most ops. This continued until the bomber had another major service, or, as the ops mounted up, it might go away from the squadron – even back to the makers – for a complete refit and overhaul. If it returned to the same squadron it would continue although it could just as easily be reassigned to another squadron.

One might also imagine there were many aspects to flying these Lancs, which had now become veterans, with 60, 70 or 80 missions completed. Not everyone was keen to fly them. On the one hand they were getting old and had perhaps lost some of their sprightliness. Why should a crew choose to fly an old crock when it may have the chance to fly a brand new machine?

Then again, as superstition and luck – real or imagined – played a very large part in any air force crew's flying, one would obviously start thinking that this particular Lancaster with its 80-plus-ops was living on borrowed time. Its luck must surely be running out soon and one did not want to be flying it over Germany when it did. A few Lancasters got into the 90s before they were lost, one even going down on its 99th sortie. Other crews might feel that this particular Lancaster had led a charmed life and would always come home. It is also a fact that some squadrons did not like to add any nose art-work and even bomb symbols to their aircraft; another form of not wanting to invite bad luck.

It should also be kept in mind that when most of these Lancasters were operating, the crews were able to fly many more short-haul trips, especially during the invasion period of 1944. In 1943 bomber crews flew deep into Germany whereas the generation of crews flying in 1944 could get through a tour with far more short-haul operations just across the Channel. At one stage in late 1944 some crews were having to fly 36 ops to complete a tour. Nevertheless, while the trips may have been shorter, they were no less dangerous and a crew could be lost flying against a V1 site in northern France just as easily as going to Berlin.

The bulk of this book is a brief account of each of the 35 known Lancasters that became centenarians, and continues their story until either they were 'retired', the war ended, or they were shot down – or in the language of the time, simply 'failed to return'.

# Understanding the Lists

For the most part, the operational sortie lists at the end of each Lancaster history are self-explanatory, with date, target, the times the aircraft took off and landed back, and the crew as listed in the Form 541.

Where a crew's subsequent sortie in an aircraft was made, then merely the name of the captain is recorded. Where there has been a crew change, then the new name is noted as 'in' and the missing man as 'out'. These will not be completely accurate due to human error; what is shown here is what is recorded in the 541s.

The addition of a second pilot (2P) is generally a new pilot who was required to fly at least one, sometimes two, trips with a seasoned pilot and crew, to get the feel of operations, prior to taking his own crew out. Sometimes the second pilot would be a senior officer, who decided to go along for the ride. In some squadrons it became the custom to have navigators, bomb aimers and even air gunners do a practice trip or two, hence occasionally these will be listed, e.g: (2BA), (2N) etc. However, on some sorties and in some squadrons, a second navigator would be part of the crew to operate and monitor the H²S radar. On 101 Squadron special operators made up the eighth crew position and are recorded as SO in the lists.

Crew positions/duty have not always been possible to record accurately. Some records simply do not show what duty a man performed. However, most squadrons did note the seven men down in their crew position in a specific way. That is to say that if they recorded them as, pilot (P), navigator (N), bomb aimer (BA), flight engineer (FE), wireless operator (WOP), mid-upper (MU), and rear gunner (RG), then they always (mostly) listed them in that order. In the majority of cases, I have listed the crew in the way it was generally done, so one can assume that subsequent crews show the same positions. At one period some units carried a third gunner to man an 'under gun'.

In any event, the pilot was always first, and generally the two gunners were listed last, but not always. At least one squadron listed the flight engineer last. Hopefully, at some stage, the squadron's way of listing them has been shown.

Occasionally squadrons going to the same target will record a different name. The main reason for this appears to be that one unit might record the general target area, while another its specific aiming point. I have chosen generally to record the target as it appears in the squadron records. Any reader wishing to tie-up these targets could cross-check them with either Martin Middlebrook's excellent reference book *The Bomber Command War Diaries* or the list of Bomber Command targets in Air-Britain's *The Lancaster File* by J J Halley.

## GLOSSARY OF RANK ABBREVIATIONS USED IN THE LISTS

| | | | |
|---|---|---|---|
| Sgt | Sergeant | FO | Flying Officer |
| FS | Flight Sergeant | FL | Flight Lieutenant |
| WO | Warrant Officer | SL | Squadron Leader |
| PO | Pilot Officer | WC | Wing Commander |
| GC | Group Captain | | |

The ranks of officers on detachment from the US 8th Air Force to RAF Bomber Command are abbreviated in the lists as follows:

| | | | |
|---|---|---|---|
| T/Sgt | Technical Sergeant | 1/Lt | First Lieutenant |
| Flt Off | Flight Officer | 2/Lt | Second Lieutenant |

# The Tour

Whilst researching this book I was in contact with Ron Clark DFC who had completed a tour of operations in 1943, flying for the most part Lancaster EE139 *Phantom of the Ruhr*. He and his crew were with 100 Squadron, although their last operational sortie was with 625 Squadron, which had been formed from C Flight of 100 Squadron on 1 October of that year.

Although all I really needed was a couple of stories about EE139, what he produced was so good and rich in detail that it really could not be cut, so it has been reproduced here in its entirety. In this way the reader can hopefully gain some insight into what it meant to fly on operations during World War Two and be part of a bomber crew.

In reading his words one will begin to appreciate the stories of the 35 Lancasters that are featured in this book and remember that whatever the aircraft itself achieved, there were seven, sometimes eight, men taking it on operations.

'At the end of May 1943 after two years training in my case, my new crew and I were posted to 100 Lancaster Squadron based at Waltham, near Grimsby. This was it! I had a total of 437 hours, 45 minutes flying time in my log-book.

'RAF Waltham seemed strangely quiet after the bustle of RAF Lindholme where we had completed our crew training and we spent the next 10 days doing local flying. On 2 June we became acquainted with EE139 for the first time. After some local flying details and a X-country flight we began to realise that EE139 was ours.

'Settling into the squadron routine we visited the aircraft every morning, then sat in the Flight Office – always a snappy salute when entering – got to know the other crews and then took tea and toast with the two charming ladies who kept the village Post Office over the hedge from the aircraft disposal. As a crew we had a Nissen hut to ourselves and sometimes the ground crew

Ron Clark DFC, 100 Squadron, took EE139 *Phantom of the Ruhr* on her first sortie, 11/12 June 1943.

dropped in. Occasionally we carried out a 'low-level' on Grimsby, some more occasionally than others.

'We were a seven-man crew, all NCOs. Harold "Ben" Bennett the flight engineer was a Lancastrian from Preston and a regular, an ex-brat from Halton. He had joined the crew at the Heavy Conversion Unit at Lindholme, where we had flown Halifaxes, then finishing on Lancasters. His expertise stood us in good stead.

'Jim Siddell, navigator, was a strong-minded Yorkshireman whose job was to keep us on track although he had little to go on when the Gee navigation system was jammed. The Station routine had little attraction for him and his Flight Office was not often graced with his presence, for which I had some explaining to do. Jim, as the only married man in the crew, was shot down and killed in a Mosquito aircraft over Holland later in the war.

'Lishman "Lish" Easby was the wireless operator. Some of the crew were tickled by his North Riding accent, now considerably modified after post-war years in the Civil Service.

'At 29 years-old, Les Simpson, the mid-upper gunner, was the Daddy of the crew. He had recourse to the sick bay once or twice, one occasion being after falling off the top of the fuselage after giving his turret perspex an extra polish. By then we were all a bit touchy about these details, especially if the aircraft had been used by another crew whilst we were on leave. Occasionally, on our early trips, Les, no doubt half frozen, had inadvertently fired a burst from his twin Brownings and sometimes saw things which weren't there. Gleefully, and I suspect mainly by his fellow Londoner, Doug Wheeler our bomb aimer, Les was dubbed "Trigger" after these unwelcome interruptions. Les secretly revelled in this soubriquet as it marked him out as the veteran gunner he was becoming.

'If there was any escapade in the offing, Geoff Green, our rear gunner from King's Lynn, was sure to be involved. On one occasion after we had paid a visit to the Marquis of Granby, we saw Geoff hobbling down the street on somebody's crutches. He was a sartorial example to the rest of the crew and at our first meeting we noticed with approval his custom-made uniform. Geoff went on to complete a second tour of ops on Lancasters, and was awarded a DFC for shooting down a jet fighter. After a permanent commission, he retired years later as a squadron leader.

'Finally on 11 June we were posted for operations for that coming night. The Station became more active, the heavy chain was locked around the telephone kiosk [to prevent people making calls during operations, for security reasons] and we waited in anticipation for the briefing. Our EE139 was at the bottom of the Battle Order but all eyes were on the tapes pinned to the map of Europe. "Gentlemen, the target for tonight is Düsseldorf," said the Squadron Commander. "Happy Valley again," muttered the older hands as the Station Commander, the CO, and finally the Intelligence Officer had their say.

'A welter of crews with their equipment and parachutes boarded the crew buses which dropped us off at the aircraft. The long bomb-trolleys and belts of ammunition of the armourers were on hand as we greeted the ground crew and checked over EE139. No tea at the Post Office tonight!

'Finally settled we could hear Merlin engines spluttering into life as we awaited our turn. The gunners were wedged into the turrets with thick electrically-heated suits and fur-lined boots. The rest of us wore normal battledress on the adequately heated flight-deck. In my case I had on army boots and neck scarf, with emergency rations and shaving kit stuffed into my battledress pockets. Later one had to decide when to consume the bar of chocolate and the can of orange juice which was an aircrew concession.

'Strapped into the pilot's seat with the Mae West and parachute harness, one became conscious that the Elsan toilet was located right at the back of the aircraft, so I could see a problem looming. Ben Bennett solved it by attaching a tube to an empty can with an empty orange juice tin on the other end. We passed this contraption round the crew like the port at a mess dinner. This was rarely used after the first couple of trips, probably because on those early sorties the added tension resulted in more frequent calls.

'I settled into my seat. I had already noticed that on the square of armour plate situated behind the pilot's head (later removed to save weight) somebody in the Avro factory had pencilled, "May good luck follow you everywhere." We would certainly need it.

'The aircraft in the first wave were taxying out of their dispersal points and we signalled the ground crew to stand-by for start-up. We always did this in the same sequence to bring in certain services powered by the engines. With strict radio silence being maintained, we waved the chocks away and taxied out to join the queue. The line of well-groomed purposeful Lancasters were a brave sight with their big props flicking over. Although each aircraft had six machine guns facing aft, there was a solitary Bren gun mounted on a pick-up truck guarding the approach to the runway in case an intruder showed up.

'One by one the heavily laded Lancasters swept down the runway to climb lazily over the bungalows of Waltham village and head for the rendezvous point on the coast above Mablethorpe. Finally it was our turn. The Aldis lamp winked green and we taxied onto the main runway. A final check with the crew and I opened the throttle to full power. This had to be done asymmetrically along with coarse use of the rudder to keep the aircraft straight, cancelling out the effect of the torque from the propellers and any cross-wind until the tail came up as the speed increased. With the speed now rapidly increasing and with the high pitched crescendo of sound from the Merlins, ears alert for engine failure before the critical speed, the end of the runway was coming up fast.

'The ASI needle flickered to flying speed and I heaved back on the control column. As the rumble of the wheels ceased, EE139 was airborne for her first operation. Landing gear up quickly, increase speed to prevent stalling as the flaps came up and then reduce power when they were retracted. Turn onto course and do the after take-off checks.

'We arrived at the coast and circled to gain height until it was time to set course across the North Sea. A rate-one 360 degree turn took two minutes and the aim was to depart right on time and maintain the density of the stream of aircraft. Darkness rapidly fell as we set course, flying away from the sun, but that was no signal to switch on the navigation lights.

'We kept a good look-out but there was the occasional sickening lurch as we encountered the slipstream of an unseen bomber. One thought of the people at home who would read tomorrow about the raid and also the casualties in the morning newspapers, then we were on our way.

'As we approached the Dutch coast the tension increased and the crew kept in contact by intercom, especially with Geoff in the rear turret. I soon abandoned the gently weaving technique so as not to disorientate the gunners. As we were in the last wave, the target came into view early as the attack had started. It reminded me of the glow of the steelworks near my home-town in West Cumberland. Soon one could see what looked like sparks high above the target. Then with the final turn-in, we were exposed to the inferno below.

'The tracer fire had now become large puffs of smoke from the flak barrage. The widespread fires augmented by the flashes of the guns, exploding bombs, photographic flares dropped from aircraft, coupled with the probing searchlights, and an occasional stream of tracer bullets created a terrifying picture. We were unprepared for this but Doug, lying on his stomach, with his parachute pack beneath him, was already guiding us to the target markers dropped by the Pathfinders.

'An aircraft not far away was coned in the searchlights. It appeared as a bright object in the middle of a colossal web of light. The flak turned its attention to this visual target and the unfortunate bomber (and crew) were soon enveloped in the shell bursts. Before long one could see the bobbles of tracer fire from the night fighters and then the aircraft exploded. As the searchlights were looking for further prey, Doug was lining up his bomb-sight and ordered, "Bomb-doors open."

'This was the most testing part of the operation as it meant holding steady for 15 seconds whilst following his instructions minutely. "Left ... left ... right a bit ... steady ..." Could we avoid that column of smoke, often a feature for the last wave? Another aircraft was reported above us, its bomb-doors open.

'"Bombs gone!" What relief! A quick turn onto the course out as the bomb-doors closed just as the 4,000 lb 'cookie' from the aircraft above plunged downwards. Lightened of her load EE139 was much livelier and gradually the target receded and we climbed to take advantage of favourable winds.

Some of Ron Clark's crew with the Post Office ladies: Geoff Green, Ron Clark, Les Simpson, Ben Bennett, Lish Easby.

'We were not sure of our position as we neared the English coast and called "Darkie" [radio code for emergency]. Do we need any help? No thanks, just confirm our position. We landed safely at base. Over the egg and bacon after de-briefing we pondered momentarily about our future; 29 more ops?

'The next night it was operations to Bochum, again the Ruhr – the Happy Valley. Over the target it was our turn to be "Buggins" [caught out] as we were coned in the searchlights. I immediately kicked the Lancaster into a steep diving turn – no time to warn the crew; they knew what to expect. The Elsan would shoot its contents into the roof. We slid into comparative darkness and breathed again with only slight flak damage.

'The Battle of the Ruhr wore on but on 12 July we were surprised to see the tape leading to Turin – something new! There was a long detour over

the Bay of Biscay on the way back in order to avoid flying over enemy territory in daylight. We were promised fighter escort at dawn and a diversionary airfield in Cornwall was nominated in case we ran short of fuel.

'Compared to the German targets there was only token resistance over Turin and we headed for home. As dawn broke over the Bay of Biscay there was no fighter escort to be seen. In fact there was nobody to be seen at all and we plotted a solitary course to Cornwall. Any marauding Ju88 would have got a hot reception but we were glad to see the coast and Ben said we had just enough petrol to reach Waltham. People were going to work as we skimmed over Cleethorpes.

'I picked out the runway through bleary eyes and suddenly – bang! Everything in the aircraft rattled and what a bounce. With the Lancaster, one bounce usually meant more – very undignified in daylight – so I opened the throttles and went round again. Ben squeezed the last drops of fuel out of the tanks and I was wide awake enough to make a normal landing after being 11 hours in the air strapped to the pilot's seat.

'On all RAF stations there was a sprinkling of Commonwealth aircrews. The Australians in dark blue; the New Zealanders and Canadians in RAF blue but different; the South Africans with their army ranks and khaki uniforms plus a few Americans in the RCAF who usually changed into US uniforms which improved their pay prospects. To serve with them was one of the privileges of being in the RAF and many of them stayed on to fly in the airlines after the war.

'Although we were an all-English crew, some of the gunners in the squadron were French-Canadian and at about this time they all moved from the sergeants' mess to the officers' quarters through their government's policy. The RAF sergeant pilots were given accelerated promotion and within a few months I moved from sergeant through flight sergeant to warrant officer. The other crew members remained sergeants.

'I was not offered a commission but when I applied, it seemed a formality and it was promulgated just before my last operation of the tour. The others were commissioned after they finished their tour except for Ben who became a warrant officer. The Uxbridge Syndrome was apt to break out now and then. The CO asked me how my relations with the crew would be affected if I was commissioned. I suppose he had to ask something and what could I say? Not much!

'On 24 July the assault on Hamburg began and during the next nine nights we carried out, with EE139, four operations, interspersed with one to Essen and another to Remscheid, where our good photograph of the aiming point showed a town of roofless buildings.

'The weather on our trip of 2 August was very bad and after avoiding thunderstorms we found ourselves off track in the middle of a heavy flak barrage over what was probably Bremen. We dropped the bombs and returned, being credited with half a trip for our pains. Fortunately aborts were infrequent, with our well-maintained aircraft.

'By the third trip to Hamburg the Germans had considerably strengthened the defences and a veritable forest of searchlights stretched along the Elbe. Fortunately with the introduction of window, the radar element was neutralised. Lish Easby spent a lot of his time stuffing packets of window – aluminium foil strips – down the flare-chute.

'Normally, if the pilot was incapacitated, the flight engineer would do his best to fly the aircraft, there being no co-pilot of course. In our case I thought it best to nominate Doug Wheeler for the job as he had received some pilot training and he sometimes flew the aircraft when we carried out local exercises. Ben kept his counsel about this but in an emergency he would have had his hands full in any case without flying the aircraft.

'Ben had already painted the *Phantom of the Ruhr* on the nose of the aircraft. As a skeleton in a shroud, clutching a bomb in each bony fist it had rather a grim appearance despite the sardonic grin on its face. There was also a line of small bombs depicting the German targets and an ice-cream cornet for the Turin trip, shortly to be followed by one for Milan.

'After ops to Nürnberg and Milan we entered the briefing room on 15 August to see the tape running along the Baltic coast but couldn't make out the target. A terse message read out by the C-in-C, universally known amongst the crews as "Butch" Harris, said that if we did not destroy the missile plant at Peenemünde this night we would have to repeat the process until we did. As the bombing height was only 8,000 feet it all sounded pretty interesting.

'We had moved up the Battle Order and being now in the first wave we could see the usual flak over Flensburg on the way in and arrived over the target just as the markers were going down. The people on the ground must have been surprised and the night fighters had been lured to Berlin as the likely destination. However, there was the usual spirited defence with a flak-ship just off the coast taking part on this occasion.

'In brilliant moonlight I thought it would be a good idea to have a closer look at the enemy and our substitute mid-upper, Flying Officer Wilson, was enthusiastic, so after the bombing I pushed the nose down and we were soon belting over the flat Pomeranian countryside at about 200 feet. Geoff quibbled a bit about opening up on civilian targets and I said without a lot of conviction, "Oh, they're all Germans." He scored hits on a large building to which I alerted him as we flashed past while the other gunner was enjoying himself. There was not a light to be seen and no retaliation so we climbed and headed for home.

'The "Master of Ceremonies" Squadron Leader John Searby, was the hero of that night as he circled the target seven times redirecting the attack by radio as the markers were tending to drift off. But who knows what dramas were played out in the 40 aircraft that were lost after the night fighters redeployed.

'On 25 August 1943 a frisson ran through the briefing room when the Big City appeared on the map, although this was not totally unexpected with the longer nights having arrived. This was the first of three trips we carried out to Berlin with EE139. The Station Commander was present at debriefing. His smart attire was in stark contrast to the dishevelled state of the crews, without a trouser crease between us. I always got the impression that he disliked my scarf; but perhaps he liked it.

'I was detailed to take Sergeant Cook and his crew in EE139 on their first operation on 22 September, which was to Hannover. They were a good crew and they reminded me of our first operation. The next night we went to Mannheim – a well defended target judging from our previous visit. Over the target we were coned and this time they held on and the aircraft was badly damaged by flak and a night fighter. Ben Bennett was awarded the DFM for his cool action under heavy fire.

'This operation put EE139 into the workshops. We said a fond farewell to *Phantom of the Ruhr* the next day as she stood stricken but defiant in the big hangar. She was to haunt the skies of Europe again and completed 121 operations before being retired for crew training.

'A week later we were "top of the bill" to Hagen and we completed our tour in JA714 after taking her to help form 625 Squadron at Kelstern. The Flight Commander asked if we would like to space-out the last few trips but the others wanted to finish quickly. The odds were lengthening against us now, always top of the Battle Order, usually we were first off and first back. It was preferable to be ahead of about 20 aircraft approaching the same airfield at night with navigation lights off.

'With thumb hovering over the transmitter button to get the first call in, the WAAF operator in the control tower came straight back almost before I had finished – "Join circuit R for Roger." Was that a sound of relief in her voice? She would know us by now.

'Our first and last operation with 625 Squadron was yet again to Hannover and we had a brand new pilot on his first sortie. He must have thought he was pushing his luck. Arriving at dispersal everything was behind time. After all the others had taken off I stopped the bombing-up, cleared all the equipment away and hurriedly started the engines. We broke radio silence to request permission to taxi down the deserted runway to save time after pondering a down-wind take-off. We thundered down the runway into the empty sky and 625 had achieved the maximum effort.

'A few mornings later the crew parted at the local railway station to go our separate ways. We were grey-faced but a load had been lifted. I saw Doug Wheeler several times at Lindholme where I was a flying instructor and once met him by chance in the Strand after the war. I also met Ben one day on a train when he was with an aeronautical company. Les worked at Heathrow airport for a while and I met him occasionally.

'Years after the war, Geoff, Lish and I regained contact and later Ben too, through a magazine article he had written. I expect that in our retirement our thoughts turn back to those heady days and the bond that has been forged between us.'

\*\*

What Ron did not mention was that on the same operation which resulted in Harold "Ben" Bennett receiving the DFM, Ron was awarded the DFC. Their citations read:

'Warrant Officer Clark and Sergeant Bennett were captain and flight engineer of an aircraft detailed to attack Mannheim and Ludwigshafen one night in September 1943. Whilst over the target area, the bomber was illuminated by the searchlights and subjected to heavy fire from the ground defences. In spite of this, Warrant Officer Clark executed a successful bombing-run. The aircraft was hit by anti-aircraft fire, however, and one shell, which passed through the structure, almost severed an aileron control rod. The bomber immediately went into a steep dive. As Warrant Officer Clark, assisted by the flight engineer, battled to pull the aircraft out of the dive, the aileron control snapped. An enemy fighter then came in to attack, causing further damage by its cannon fire. Despite this, control was regained, the fighter evaded and ultimately, Warrant Officer Clark flew the crippled bomber to base. In the face of a perilous situation, these airmen displayed great gallantry, skill and resource, setting an example worthy of great praise.'

*The Phantom of the Ruhr* – EE139.

'During the attack on Mannheim and Ludwigshafen on the night of 23rd September 1943, Sergeant Bennett was flight engineer of a Lancaster which was coned by innumerable searchlights and hotly engaged by heavy flak in the target area. Despite such intense opposition which would have deterred a less gallant crew, the bombing-run was continued and the bombs were not released until the centre of the target was in the bombsight. In the course of this sharp engagement, the aircraft was severely damaged by flak, one shell passing right through the aircraft, nearly severing the starboard aileron control rod and causing the aircraft to go into a deep spiral dive when the aileron control jammed. Sergeant Bennett assisted the captain in pulling the control column central but in doing so, the aileron control snapped resulting in severe wing flutter and juddering of the whole aircraft. In this perilous situation and whilst still illuminated by searchlights, they were attacked by a night fighter which scored hits with cannon shells, inflicting further damage. Throughout this ordeal, Sergeant Bennett showed exceptional fighting qualities and resourcefulness in that he decided to cut away the trimmer tabs to the starboard aileron in the belief that this would cure the wing flutter. His action proved to be right and the aircraft became more controllable which enabled his captain to avoid further attacks from the hostile fighter. The successful completion of this operational flight was to the resourcefulness of this NCO. It is recommended that such sustained courage and unusual initiative be recognised by the award of an Immediate Conspicuous Gallantry Medal.'

This was not awarded but the DFM was.

# R5868
# QUEENIE/SUGAR

Lancaster R5868 'Q' in May 1943 whilst with 83 Squadron, showing 58 bomb symbols and the Devils of the Air insignia. Rick Garvey is in the cockpit; the others are, from left to right: Bill Webster, Len Thomas, C Turner, Jimmy Sukthanker, Jack Cooke and Hugh Ashton.

The book starts with this Lancaster as it has become famous as the one credited with the highest number of raids to survive to the present day. The machine as a whole is preserved and on permanent display at the Royal Air Force Museum at Hendon, North London, although due to battle damage, repairs and maintenance, much of what one sees of the aeroplane today cannot possibly be the same as was observed in its hey day during World War Two.

Built by Metro Vickers at Trafford Park, Mosley Road, Manchester, as part of Contract 982866 (1939), R5868 was a Mark I, being the 27th off the Lancaster production line. Once built and equipped with four Merlin XX engines the

aircraft was delivered to Avro's at Woodford for the final assembly and tests on 20 June 1942.

On 29 June R5868 was delivered to 83 Squadron at Scampton, Lincolnshire, assigned to B Flight and given the squadron code letters OL and its individual letter Q-Queenie. After 83's ground personnel worked on it a few days to bring the new bomber up to squadron specifications, it was put on the operational strength and deemed ready for ops. The men who looked after her on the ground during its time with 83 were Sergeants Jim Gill and Harry Taylor, and Leading Aircraftmen Arthur Paget and Ron Pollard.

Her first captain and crew were not 'freshers' but an

experienced bomber crew; captain Squadron Leader R Hilton DFC, the B Flight commander, had already flown with 214 Squadron in 1941 before joining 83. His first tour covered 34 ops, 27 being flown with 83. Ray Hilton was now back with 83 on his second tour.

It was he who took *Queenie* to Wilhelmshaven on the night of 8/9 July 1942. The aircraft's load comprised 1,260 x 4 lb incendiaries, which the bomb aimer, Sergeant C H Crawley dropped from 16,000 feet, all falling in the target area in the early hours of the morning. The crew took *Queenie* to Danzig harbour two nights later to lay mines.

On the 14/15th, Pilot Officer J E Partridge took R5868 on a mining trip to Bordeaux, then on the 18th came a daylight raid on the Krupps works at Essen in the Ruhr valley, not something Lancasters did too often. Ray Hilton was again at the controls and it resulted in him receiving a Bar to his DFC. Not only that, but John Partridge received a Bar to his DFC and his navigator, Reg Kleemans, won the DFM. What was remarkable was that Partridge had only just been recommended for the DFC following a raid on the submarine pens at Danzig which took place on the 11th, so this Bar to the DFC was for an operation just a week later! What Hilton and the others discovered after crossing the enemy coast was that the expected cloud cover had disappeared but they carried on to the Ruhr. They eventually found the cloud and bombed on Gee. On the way back Partridge was attacked by fighters but they got away without too much damage.

Sergeant Harry Lavey was the rear gunner in *Queenie* on that daylight mission and recalled seeing the German fighters on the port quarter. He was so startled that when he warned of the danger over the intercom, his words came out like mumbo-jumbo, but the mid-upper had also seen them and began firing, Hilton managing to find some cloud into which they flew. Lavey too later won the DFM after 31 missions and went on to fly with the Pathfinders, while the mid-upper, Alexander MacQueen, received the DFC in the new year.

On the night of 25/26 July night fighters did attack but Hilton evaded two attempts by FW190s and a Me110 to get at them. On 5/6 August the squadron CO, Wing Commander D Crichton-Biggie, took *Queenie* on a mining trip to the Gironde river when the Lanc was slightly damaged by flak.

Hilton complained that *Queenie* always seemed to fly one wing low and despite several attempts by the ground crew to rectify it, they never succeeded. Nevertheless, he

Neale McClelland and crew in front of R5868, 467 Squadron RAAF. The original bomb log has been painted out and started again with a kneeling nude holding a bomb. After the first few bombs were marked, they were not carried on until nearing the 100th operation. Standing, from left to right: Wally Booth, Steve Bethell, Ken Warden, Albert Martin. In front, from left to right: Bill Griffin, McClelland, Stan Bray.

took *Queenie* on 18 raids during his second tour which he concluded in February 1943, being promoted to Wing Commander. Among them was 83's first Pathfinder mission on 18/19 August. There was also the occasion Hilton's wireless operator, Flight Sergeant H Kitto, was slightly wounded, apparently by fire from another Lancaster which they had just overtaken.

*Queenie* went to Italy for the first time on 6/7 November, the target Genoa. Italy was always a long haul with the Alps to cross. Fifteen crews from 83 took part, two going down over the target, and *Queenie* had to land at Mildenhall on its return. Flight Lieutenant J Hodgson DFC took Queenie on her 30th trip on 21/22 December, to Munich, and then Hilton took her on her first trip to Berlin, on 16/17 January. On this sortie Hilton carried Target Indicator (TI) markers and flares for the first time. Trying to ensure the target was marked accurately, he spent 25 minutes over the Big City that night, but finally haze and broken cloud beat them and they had to bring their markers back. *Queenie* did not operate again for

McClelland and crew, and *Queenie's* ground crew, 83 Squadron.

Neale McClelland DFC,
467 Squadron.

four weeks, probably due to a service and being fitted with Merlin 22 engines. On 11/12 February, another Partridge – Flight Sergeant H A – took her to Wilhelmshaven with a mixed load of TIs, bombs and flares. He and his crew were lost on 5/6 March, shot down by a night fighter during a raid on Essen in W4847.

Hilton, now a staff officer at Group HQ, returned to fly one last sortie on 19 February, strangely enough a raid on Wilhelmshaven, where he had taken *Queenie* on her first mission. Some of Hilton's crew flew with Squadron Leader D A J McClure DFC and were lost with him over Essen on 12/13 March: O R Waterbury DFC, A F MacQueen DFC and P J Musk DFM.

Flying Officer F J Garvey and crew now began to fly R5868 that month and soon became her regular crew. Over Cologne on 26 February flak damaged the bomb-doors and they had to fly home with them partially open. The 4,000 lb 'cookie' fell on them and prized them apart sufficiently for the bomb to drop. Minor flak damage occurred on 1 March, again over Berlin, the pilot this time being Pilot Officer V S Moore. Valentine Moore had won his DFM with 57 Squadron in the summer of 1942. At the end of June he had to ditch his Wellington in the North Sea and only he and two others survived to be rescued by ASR launch. Commissioned and then serving with 83 Squadron he was to win the DSO, and then the DFC with 692 Squadron in 1944. All his crew in 83 Squadron were decorated with either DFCs or DFMs.

24

Harry Lavey flew his 45th and last sortie in *Queenie* – to Nüremberg – on 8/9 March. Not satisfied with this, Lavey later volunteered again and completed another 33 ops on B25 Mitchell bombers.

More excitement came over Berlin on 29/30 March. For 12 minutes Garvey was chased by a FW190 then a Me110 night fighter. Frederick "Rick" Garvey flew *Queenie* to Cologne on 3/4 July, recorded as her 60th op. On the 8/9th Pilot Officer Hugh Ashton, Garvey's rear gunner, completed his 30th sortie and received the DFC at the end of his first tour.

Squadron Leader R J Manton flew *Queenie* to Hamburg on 24/25 July, the first time the aircraft carried

PO J W McManus RAAF in *Sugar*, the bomb tally standing at 98. Note the ribbons of the DSO and two DFCs, and Göring's famous boast.

'window', bundles of thin aluminium foil strips to jam and confuse German radar. This was the start of the Battle of Hamburg. The following night Garvey took Brigadier-General F L Anderson of the US 8th Air Force to Essen as an observer, together with the Group's Navigation Officer, Squadron Leader A Price. Garvey took Anderson to Hamburg two nights later.

Garvey, a Canadian in the RAF, completed some 19 ops in *Queenie*. He was the son of a sports editor with the *Vancouver Province* newspaper, Rick himself having started his career with the same paper. Working his way to England on a ship to join the RAF he was the first RAF pilot to complete 60 bomber ops straight through without a stop. He received the DFC and then the DSO after completing his second tour, but sadly he was to lose his life at RAF Cottesmore. Testing an Oxford following repairs to its wing, the machine broke up in the air.

Awards to crewmen who had flown in *Queenie* included DFCs to Garvey, Hugh A Ashton, Pilot Officer Shailendra E Sukthanker, Garvey's navigator, and a DFM to Garvey's bomb aimer, John A Cook, whose last op in *Queenie* had been his own 35th. In Hilton's crew DFCs went to Orville R Waterbury (N), Alexander F MacQueen (MU), while Roy Beavan, the flight engineer, received the DFM. Sadly Waterbury and MacQueen were killed in 1943 flying with S/L D A J McClure DFC over Essen on 12/13 March. Wing Commander Hilton himself was lost over

Berlin on 23/24 November in JB284. He had flown over 60 bomber ops.

Garvey's last ops in *Queenie* in mid-August 1943 brought her score to 68 sorties, but they were her last with 83 Squadron. She had run up a total of 368 operational flying hours and now needed a major overhaul. Following this service she was sent to 467 Squadron RAAF (B Flight) at Bottesford, Leicester, then moving to Waddington, Lincolnshire in November. With 467 Squadron she changed her codes to PO and became S-Sugar. She replaced the previous *Sugar* (JA981) that had moved to 617 Squadron.

When R5868 arrived on 467, Ted Willoughby made his way to dispersal to see the new aircraft arrive. As he watched the Lancaster coming in to land and as the pilot touched down, it bounced 100 feet back up into the air. Three times it did that, Ted recalls, but finally the pilot got it down and taxied round. He spotted Ted and asked him to guide him into the aircraft's dispersal point. This pilot was not at all happy with the aircraft.

When Neale McClelland took it up on some Night Flying Tests (NFTs) he wasn't happy either, and Stan Poole, another of *Sugar's* ground crew, put it down to the trimmers. The next day, McClelland, with Ted in the Lanc too, found he couldn't get the thing down at all and finally had to land it on the grass. Stan Poole then found that some bolts in the bomb compartment had sheared off. Ted decided that 83 Squadron had put it out to grass and someone had said – 'bung it to the Aussies'!

Now we have an example of poor record keeping. As a replacement aircraft, the recording staff continued to note that aircraft 'S' was still JA981 long after that aircraft had left and R5868 was now the squadron's S-Sugar. Thus in the Form 541 for 27/28 September 1943, JA981 is shown as that flying to Hannover, whereas (a) it was R5868, and (b) JA981 had by this time been lost on ops with its new squadron. Not that its new owners were over-pleased with the overhauled R5868 and Pilot Officer A M Finch who took it to Hannover later reported that it was unreliable for ops! This obviously did not phase anyone particularly for R5868 went to Bochum on the night of the 29th with Pilot Officer N M McClelland at the controls.

Three different pilots flew *Sugar* in early October then she flew on one raid with 207 Squadron, at RAF Langar, just a few miles to the south-west of Bottesford. On 8/9 October, Pilot Officer C W Barnett of that squadron raided

Hannover, but she was back with 467 for McClelland to take her back to that target on the 18/19th, although McClelland again reported that he felt *Sugar* was only fit for service with a conversion unit. Obviously his suggestion did not find favour and he took her to Düsseldorf on 3/4 November, and then to Berlin on the 18/19th, and back to the German capital three days later for R5868's 80th operation, the 81st being Berlin again the following night. Again records indicate other serial numbers but log-books of crew members note R5868. When 467 moved to Waddington, McClelland was the pilot who flew her there.

The Battle of Berlin began on the night of 18/19 November; McClelland taking a second pilot for experience. Steve Bethell, the crew's mid-upper, recalls they were part of the first wave of the main force and were shot-up by flak over Bonn, but the aircraft was repaired and ready for Berlin again on the 22nd. Neale McClelland received the DFC after this trip. McClelland was to survive the war and upon his return to Australia he

R5868's cockpit.

Loading up for an operation on 10 May 1944.

joined Quantas Airways flying Lancastrians from Sydney to Karachi. However, he was lost over the Indian Ocean on 23 March 1946.

Jack Colpus now took *Sugar* on a couple of raids, during one of which she was damaged, the night of 26/27 November. Coned by searchlights on another Berlin trip Colpus took evasive action but another Lanc (61 Squadron) came from the port quarter, losing height, and the two aircraft collided. *Sugar* fell away to port in a dive, Colpus applying full rudder and aileron to control the aircraft but then found he could only get 140 mph out of it, so he lightened the load on the port side by ordering the engineer to run all four engines off the port outer fuel tank. They got back but landed at Tholthorpe, Yorkshire, although Colpus had to keep on full right rudder for four hours, assisted by the engineer down in the bomb aimer's compartment holding the rudder with a strap. John Colpus was later to receive the DFC. *Sugar* had lost five feet of wing-tip and suffered other damage and was sent away to the manufacturers for repairs. Jack Colpus cycled out to dispersal when he got back to Waddington to tell Ted Willoughby that he had busted 'his' precious *Sugar*.

*Sugar* was away being worked on – including a completely new port outer wing – until well into the new year, Pilot Officer J W McManus then becoming her regular pilot. He started her 1944 log with another trip to Berlin on 15/16 February following a gap of over three months since her last trip. The trip had a hairy start,

*Sugar* twice swinging on take-off but he got her off on the third attempt. His rear gunner, Cliff Fudge, would remember this trip as he celebrated his 21st birthday over the German city. John McManus later received the DFC. By now, of course, *Sugar's* total raids was approaching 100.

\*\*

At first, *Queenie's* nose artwork was a red devil thumbing its nose whilst dancing in some flames. This was Mephistopheles – to whom Faust had sold his soul in German legend. The motto over the flames was 'Devils of the Air'. A picture of Garvey and his crew clearly shows this, along with 58 bomb symbols, so it would have been taken about June 1943. All this must have been painted out prior to its arrival at 467. Then appeared a nude female kneeling in front of a bomb, just aft of the front turret, on the port side. This was painted on by Sergeant A W Martin, McClelland's flight engineer, and Stan Poole. Two small rows of five bombs each were also painted on but it seems that these were not added to and remained unchanged until *Sugar's* ops were well into the 90s.

With some obvious publicity coming up, the Station Commander, Group Captain D Bonham-Carter, one day came out to the dispersal when Ted Willoughby was there and said that the nude would have to go, "because it's rude and *Sugar* will be publicised so much, it will upset the Archbishop of Canterbury." McManus and his crew said it should be replaced with something appropriate

FO T N Scholefield after *Sugar's* reported 100th op, but in fact it was her 91st (12 May 1944). From left to right: Scholefield, I Hamilton, R T Hillas, F E Hughes, R H Burgess, K E Stewart and J D Wells.

and a couple of days later Ted saw an article in the *Reader's Digest* relating to Hermann Göring's boast about no enemy aircraft flying over Germany, and it was decided this, along with an updated bomb tally should be painted on. After some discussion with the Station Commander concerning the political connotations, permission was given and Ted set to work. He had *Sugar* towed to No.3 hangar, and helped by a trained pre-war sign-writer (Flight Sergeant Dan Smith), Ted worked all night marking the required number of bombs in rows of 12, and the famous legend *"NO ENEMY PLANE WILL FLY OVER REICH TERRITORY,* Herman Goering". With the addition of an 'S' just aft of the front gun turret, she was ready for the press – if she made the hundred. Someone noted that Herman should be spelt Hermann, but it was never altered.

*Sugar* was now showing signs of age. Coming back from Frankfurt on 22/23 March all four engines began to splutter and the Lanc lost height to 10,000 feet. However, some switch-juggling caused them to pick up again. Just as well for the WOP, Sergeant M Williams, had forgotten his parachute! On landing the tail wheel tyre burst.

The next trip was to Berlin again, but the op was not completed as the port outer failed and there was an oil leak from the port inner, causing them to turn back. A night fighter trailed them for 15 minutes but was finally lost in cloud and by evasive tactics. The next night the port outer failed on the bomb-run over Aulnoye and coming back at 5,000 feet only just made Tangmere, the RAF fighter airfield on the Sussex coast. Fortunately it had been a French target.

Following a few days of service, *Sugar* was taken over by Pilot Officer A B L Tottenham RAAF, who took it on seven straight raids without a hitch. In early May Pilot Officer T N Scholefield RAAF became skipper. With the invasion coming up, targets were now mostly French, which included V1 flying bomb sites, gun positions, and all manner of transport centres, both rail and road. Anthony Tottenham later went to 463 Squadron and won the DFC. Tom Scholefield later flew with 97 Squadron and won the DFC and Bar.

On the night of 11/12 May, Bourg Léopold was the target for *Sugar's* 100th raid with Scholefield at the controls. Officially that is, but due to various mix-ups in the records it was only the Lanc's 91st. In any event it was not an auspicious occasion. Haze made it impossible for the target to be identified so the attack was called off. Then two Ju88 night fighters made several determined attacks over a 10-minute period, the gunners claiming one of them damaged. The bombs were jettisoned over the sea. However, having returned, there were celebrations outside the watch office and later LAC Poole painted on the 100th bomb symbol. *Sugar* herself was 'awarded' a DSO and two DFCs during her war service, the ribbons being depicted beneath her bomb tally.

*Sugar* now had a break until D-Day, Flying Officer I Fotheringham taking her out on 5/6 and 6/7 June, then again on 8/9th. More raids followed into July including the Caen operation on the 18th. Next night she went to Révigny, and then she apparently visited Courtrai, bombing the rail yards there. This is not recorded in the 541, probably because Wing Commander G G Petty DSO DFC flew her. She was then sent off for another major refit, but the reason given in an RAF Bulletin dated 2 August gives us a clue. This stated that on her last raid in trying to evade a night fighter several wing rivets were

sprung. The war diary makes no mention of this nor is it clear if the 'last raid' was the one recorded to Révigny or the one not recorded to Courtrai. One suspects it would be the latter. The Bulletin also noted that it had been R5868's 114th operation.

On 3 August 1944 (or perhaps earlier, on 26 July), R5868 was sent off to RIW – Repair Inspection Works – in Lincolnshire. There are photographs of *Sugar* taken here, one showing the whole of the forward cockpit area missing as well as all four engines, and close by the nose itself on the ground. The RIW maintenance crew – No.16 party – stand in front of the bomb tally, which clearly shows 114 bombs. If, therefore, its 100th raid was in fact its 91st, then one should suppose that its last mission on 20 July was its 106th!? (This also assumes that the final bomb symbol was painted on her before leaving the squadron.)

Writing '100 NOT OUT' on a 'cookie' is Ted Willoughby, one of *Sugar's* faithful ground crew, for the 12 May sortie. Standing right is Air Commodore A Hesketh, OC 53 Base, which included RAF Waddington.

Once repaired and overhauled, plus having H²S fitted, *Sugar* was returned to 467 on 3 December. Various crews operated in the aircraft during that month, including Flight Lieutenant M G Johnson who had flown her on her last July mission. Even in 1945 there was no set crew flying *Sugar* although Flying Officer L W Baker RAAF took it on most of her final trips, including one to Czechoslovakia on 18/19 April and the final raid to the U-Boat pens at Flensburg on 23 April – Laurie Baker and crew's own 21st sortie.

*Sugar* also took a breather by being taken on a goodwill tour of the 8th USAAF bases in England, captained by Wing Commander F M Osborn DFC from RAF Coningsby, the crew being representatives from various 5 Group units, plus three members of the ground crew. In all 36 US bases were visited. *Sugar* returned to ops with a trip to Würzburg on 16/17 March.

One trip to Brux, 16/17 January, was flown by Flight Lieutenant F Lawrence DFC DFM, whose flight engineer was Sergeant D R Baldry. Frank Lawrence had won his DFC and DFM with 460 Squadron. This crew flew two ops in *Sugar*, Dennis Baldry recalling the one to Brux:

'As regards the two trips we did in *Sugar*, the first to Brux was I believe the longest flight carried out by *Sugar*. The defences were very heavy all the way and on the bombing-run flak penetrated the bomb aimer's blister and Perce Garvey was hit on the forehead. I remember him coming up to the cockpit with blood running down his face. I think he was rather proud of his wound, which fortunately was not serious.

'The trip to Siegen [1/2 February] I've just recorded "moderate light and heavy flak, easy." Frank Lawrence was our second skipper. We lost our first under very unhappy circumstances and we also got a new rear gunner. When Frank joined us at 467 Squadron, Waddington, he was a flight lieutenant, later promoted to squadron leader. We moved to 460 Squadron at Binbrook where Frank took over a flight.'

It is still difficult to reconcile *Sugar's* total ops exactly. In addition to the ones I recorded in the first edition of this book, a few more have come from various sources. That sortie flown with 207 Squadron is one, 8/9 October 1943. One I missed was 24/25 June 1944. *Sugar* was the spare

*Sugar* now sporting 107 bomb symbols. The Duke of York, third from the left, standing between Waddington's Station Commander (left) and the CO of 467 Squadron.

aircraft and because another went u/s, Flying Officer Skelton and crew took her, possibly because her usual skipper was on leave. There is apparently another on 20 July 1944 which is not in the 541, flown by Wing Commander G G Petty DSO, to Courtrai. This came from the log-book of the flight engineer Stanley W Archer DFM. It is no secret that some senior officers flew missions and made sure they were not recorded officially so as not to upset anyone at Group HQ! Flying Officer R H Melville RAAF flew on another to Bergen, Norway, on 28 October 1944 – according to Stan Archer's log, although he brought his bombs back as the target could not be identified, landing back at Marston Moor. The 541 records this was flown in NF910 but that is in doubt. Finally, Wing Commander I H A Hay flew an Exodus sortie from Brussels to Westcott with 24 ex-PoWs on 26 April 1945. This again came from Stan Archer's log-book.

R5868 left 467 Squadron on 23 August 1945 to go to 15 Maintenance Unit (MU) where it became non-effective in August 1947. Struck off Charge as an 'Exhibition Aircraft' on 22 February 1956, it became part of the Historic Aircraft Collection at 13 MU, Wroughton, on 16 March 1956. On 24 November 1970, after some years as Gate Guard at RAF Scampton, commencing in 1959, the Lanc went to 71 MU, Bicester, for refurbishment before going to the RAF Museum on 12 March 1972. She is still there.

## 83 SQUADRON
## 1942

**8/9 July** *0007-0420*
*WILHELMSHAVEN*
SL R Hilton DFC
PO O R Waterbury RCAF (N)
Sgt R Beavan (FE)
FS H Kitto (WOP)
Sgt C H Crawley (BA)
PO A F MacQueen (MU)
Sgt H Lavey (RG)

**11/12 July** *2306-0257*
*GARDENING – DANZIG*
SL R Hilton and crew
FO H Barber (2P)

**14/15 July** *2306-0644*
*BORDEAUX (MINING)*
PO J Partridge DFC
FS R W Kleeman (N)
Sgt R Scott (FE)
Sgt J H Ridd (WOP)
Sgt J Allen (BA)
Sgt A Ireland (MU)
Sgt E Mills (RG)

**18 July** *1050-1450*
*ESSEN*
SL R Hilton and crew
Sgt D R Gilchrist in,
Sgt Crawley out

**19/20 July** *2357-0557*
*VEGESACK*
FS C D Calvert
Sgt D Dunmore
PO R M Rees
Sgt H A Hatfield
Sgt L A Connett
Sgt W D Henderson
Sgt T W Strong

**21/22 July** *2356-0337*
*DUISBURG*
SL R Hilton and crew

**23/24 July** *0053-0450*
*DUISBURG*
FS L T Goodfellow
PO E H Penfree
Sgt J J Mathieson
Sgt E Webster
Sgt F M Tutton
Sgt C H J Byrd
Sgt D L Howe

**25/26 July** *0034-0406*
*DUISBURG*
SL R Hilton and crew

**26/27 July** *2303-0411*
*HAMBURG*
PO J E Partridge and crew
Sgt H Lavey in, Sgt Ridd out

**5/6 Aug** *2227-0541*
*GIRONDE (MINING)*
WC D Crichton-Biggie
PO H L Mazengarb
FS D J Calderwood
Sgt Chaster
Sgt P J Musk (DFM)
Sgt J Rogers
Sgt C J Millard

**6/7 Aug** *0053-0456*
*DUISBURG*
PO J Marchant RAAF
PO F C Oldmeadow
Sgt L Edwards
Sgt F C Milton
Sgt J Phipps
Sgt R L Romig
Sgt J E Smith

R5868 having a major refit in late 1944. The whole nose section has been taken off and sits on the ground. The workers are under Cpl H Smith (second from right), others are Cpl Cox, LACs Symonds, Pursglove, McCombie and AC2 Mitchell.

**9/10 Aug** *0012-0409*
*OSNABRÜCK*
SL R Hilton and crew
Sgt D G Lovell in,
Sgt Gilchrist out

**10/11 Aug** *2246-0424*
*MAINZ*
PO J Hodgson
Sgt W A Hamilton
Sgt D N McCartney
Sgt A B Smart
FS G R Phelby
Sgt T Williams
Sgt S A Hathaway

**18/19 Aug** *2110-0215*
*FLENSBURG*
SL R Hilton and crew

**24/25 Aug** *2050-0235*
*FRANKFURT*
SL R Hilton and crew

**8/9 Sep** *2106-0230*
*FRANKFURT*
FS L T Jackson
Sgt D Smith
PO J McMillan
Sgt K C Taylor
FS B E Hargrove
Sgt L R Brettle
Sgt D Crossthwaite

**13/14 Sep** *2303-0326*
*BREMEN*
SL R Hilton and crew

**14/15 Sep** *2011-0017*
*WILHELMSHAVEN*
SL R Hilton and crew

**2/3 Oct** *1925-2305*
*KREFELD*
SL R Hilton and crew
PO B Becker and FS P Musk in,
Sgt Kitto and Beavan out

**5/6 Oct** *1915-0100*
*AACHEN*
FL J E Partridge and crew
Sgt D L Coen in,
Sgt Allen out

**6 Oct** *1915-2340*
*OSNABRÜCK*
SL R Hilton and crew
WC D Crichton-Biggie (2P)
Sgt A MacFarlane in,
Sgt Becker out

**13 Oct** *1815-2340*
*KIEL*
SL R Hilton and crew

**6/7 Nov** *2125-0645*
*GENOA*
SL R Hilton and crew

**7/8 Nov** *1800-0110*
*GENOA*
SL J K M Cooke DFC
Sgt T Milton
FL D G M Ransome
Sgt W L Gibbs
Sgt T R Cairns
Sgt S A Hathaway
Sgt H Plant

**9 Nov** *1725-2245*
*HAMBURG*
SL R Hilton and crew
FL E R Simpson DFM in,
Sgt Warren out

**13/14 Nov** *1810-0230*
*GENOA*
SL R Hilton and crew,
Sgt Warren back

**15/16 Nov** *1810-0130*
*GENOA*
PO R N H Williams DFM
FS T R Armstrong
FS G L Davies
FS C H Crawley

FS G H Bishop
FS J R Buchby
FS C C Y Lambert

**29/30 Nov** *0050-0815*
*TURIN*
FS H A Partridge
Sgt R O Fulton RCAF
PO L W Sprackling
Sgt J M Freshwater
Sgt H Fell
Sgt A D Finnie
Sgt J L Organ

**3 Dec** *0205-0800*
*FRANKFURT*
PO J Marchant DFC RAAF and crew

**21/22 Dec** *1756-0103*
*MUNICH*
FL J Hodgson DFC and crew
Sgt C W Candlin and
FS C F J Sprack in, Sgt McCartney and
Hathaway out

## 1943

**16/17 Jan** *1655-0015*
*BERLIN*
SL R Hilton and crew

**11 Feb** *1747-2310*
*WILHELMSHAVEN*
FS H A Partridge and crew

**13 Feb** *1830-2310*
*LORIENT*
FS H A Partridge and crew

**14/15 Feb** *1911-0246*
*MILAN*
SL J K M Cooke DFC and crew,
FS A B Smart in, Sgt Milton out

**16 Feb** *1916-2338*
*LORIENT*
SL S Robinson DFM

FS A B Smart
PO D Norrington DFM
FS J H Henderson
Sgt M B W Hambrook
FS C F J Sprack
Sgt W A Rings
(all but Smart were killed
in 1943, five on 26 Feb,
Sprack DFM on 13 June)

**18 Feb** *1846-2308*
*WILHELMSHAVEN*
FO F J Garvey
Sgt R B Hicks (FE)
SL R Anderson (N)
Sgt C E Turner (WOP)
Sgt J A Cook (BA)
FS R O Fulton (MU)
Sgt H A Ashton (RG)

**19 Feb** *1811-2218*
*WILHELMSHAVEN*
WC R Hilton DFC and crew
FS J Rodgers in, Warren out

**25/26 Feb** *2032-0256*
*NÜRNBERG*
FO F J Garvey and crew
Sgt S Sukthanker and
Sgt L L J Thomas in,
SL Anderson and FS Fulton out

**26 Feb** *1940-2304*
*COLOGNE*
FO F J Garvey and crew
Sgt D B Bourne and
Sgt J Goldie DFM
in, Sgts Hicks and Ashton out

**28 Feb** *1838-2312*
*ST NAZAIRE*
PO V S Moore DFM
Sgt J H Wright (FE)
FO G H Wilson
FO D L Giggory RCAF
Sgt D L Coen (BA)
Sgt G K Finnie RCAF
FO D H Luck

**1/2 Mar** *1910-0125*
*BERLIN*
PO V S Moore and crew

**8/9 Mar** *1957-0244*
*NÜRNBERG*
FO F J Garvey and crew
FS H Lavey in, Sgt Goldie out
(45th op for Lavey)

**11/12 Mar** *2010-0147*
*STUTTGART*
FO F J Garvey and crew
FO N C Johnson and
Sgt H A Ashton in,
Sgt Bourne and FS Lavey out

**12 Mar** *1928-2336*
*ESSEN*
FO F J Garvey and crew
Sgts Bourne and J A Cook in,
FO Johnson and Sgt Coen out

**27/28 Mar** *2009-0305*
*BERLIN*
FO F J Garvey and crew

**29/30 Mar** *2126-0434*
*BERLIN*
FO F J Garvey and crew
Sgt W L Webster in,
Sgt Bourne out

**2/3 Apr** *2009-0045*
*ST NAZAIRE*
FS G A McNichol RCAF
Sgt G C Mott
PO H H F Beupre RCAF
Sgt G S MacFarlane

R5868 minus engines and nose.

PO T W Lewis RCAF
Sgt H R Willis
FS C E Hobbs RCAF
(PO McNichol killed 17 April
returning on two engines; crew
all taken prisoner)

**23/24 May** *2247-0319*
*DORTMUND*
FO F J Garvey and crew

**25/26 May** *0007-0415*
*DÜSSELDORF*
FO F J Garvey and crew

**27/28 May** *2247-0343*
*ESSEN*
FS R King RAAF
Sgt K E L Farmelo
FS D E Curtin
Sgt D J Phelan
Sgt H Samme
Sgt R A Adams
Sgt E D McPherson
(Farmelo, Adams DFM, and
McPherson DFM, all killed 20
Jan 1944; FL King DFC was
wounded and taken prisoner)

**29/30 May** *2232-0320*
*WUPPERTAL*
FO M R Chick
FS A W Hicks (FE)
Sgt J W Slaughter (N)
Sgt B Turner (WOP)
PO C A S Drew (BA)
Sgt L P Howell (MU)
Sgt A Ellwood (RG)

**11/12 June** *2335-0427*
*MÜNSTER*
FO M R Chick and crew
FS S T Stacey in, Sgt Howell out

**12/13 June** *2327-0403*
*BOCHUM*
FO M R Chick and crew
Sgt Howell back

**16/17 June** *2304-0311*
*COLOGNE*
FS M K Cummings RAAF

Sgt H W Luker RAAF
Sgt F W Wilcox
Sgt H W Cheshire
Sgt J Roughley
Sgt N Woodcock
Sgt R A Taylor RCAF
(all lost 18 June in another
Lancaster – training flight)

**19/20 June** *2243-0228*
*MONTCHANIN*
PO H Mappin
FS C E Wiggett
Sgt A J Boar
Sgt A A Crank
Sgt G A Livett
Sgt W Anderson
Sgt F W Turner
(all lost 21/22 June)

**21/22 June** *2349-0407*
*KREFELD*
FO M R Chick and crew

**22/23 June** *2309-0316*
*MÜLHEIM*
FL F J Garvey and crew

**24/25 June** *2302-0326*
*ELBERFELD*
FL F J Garvey and crew
SL R J Manton (2P)
Sgt J A P Logan in,
FS Thomas out

**28/29 June** *2304-0323*
*COLOGNE*
FL F J Garvey and crew

**3/4 July** *2322-0407*
*COLOGNE*
FL F J Garvey and crew

**8/9 July** *2255-0344*
*COLOGNE*
FL F J Garvey and crew

**12/13 July** *2246-0816*
*TURIN*
FO W R Thompson
Sgt A W Belton
Sgt D E Potts

Sgt A Wilkes
Sgt P Henratty
Sgt R B Hicks
Sgt J H Tolman

**24/25 July** *2216-0427*
*HAMBURG*
SL R J Manton
Sgt F S Chadwick
SL A G A Cochrane DFC
Sgt A E Evans
Sgt C Taylor
WO S T Stacey
FO A J Ellis RCAF
(Manton, Cochrane, Evans,
Stacey DFC and Ellis all killed
in late 1943)

**25/26 July** *2228-0307*
*ESSEN*
FL F J Garvey DFC
Brig-Gen F L Anderson USAAF
SL A Price (N)
FS W L Webster (FE)
FS B H Turner (WOP)
FS J A Cook (BA)
FS L L J Thomas
PO H A Ashton (RG)

**27/28 July** *2235-0409*
*HAMBURG*
FL F J Garvey DFC and crew
Brig-Gen F L Anderson USAAF
FS D E Potts (N) in, SL Price out

**29/30 July** *2214-0356*
*HAMBURG*
SL R J Manton and crew

**12/13 Aug** *2130-0517*
*MILAN*
FL F J Garvey and crew
SL G F Georgeson DFC in,
Sgt Potts out

**14/15 Aug** *2127-0534*
*MILAN*
FL F J Garvey DFC
FS S J Davis (2P)
SL N A Burt
FS W L Webster

FS B H Turner
FS J A Cook
FS L L J Thomas
FS H Sykes

## 467 SQUADRON RAAF

**27 Sep** *1927-2050*
*HANNOVER*
PO A M Finch
Sgt V L Johnson (FE)
Sgt J W Nedwich (BA)
FO H C Ricketts (N)
FS G G Johnson (WOP)
FS R Smibert (MU)
FS R H Mark (RG)

**29 Sep** *1800-2250*
*BOCHUM*
PO N M McClelland
FO J A Colpus (2P)
Sgt A W Martin (FE)
FO McCarthy (BA)
PO W Booth (N)
Sgt S Bray (WOP)
Sgt S G W Bethel (MU)
Sgt K L Worden (RG)

**2/3 Oct** *1815-0232*
*MUNICH*
FL H B Locke
Sgt W G Holt (FE)
FS F F Townsend (BA)
Sgt H Hassell (N)
Sgt L Butler (WOP)
Sgt T Brooks (MU)
FS T Munro (RG)

**3/4 Oct** *1836-0047*
*KASSEL*
FO J A Colpus
Sgt K Smith (FE)
Sgt S T Bridgewater (BA)
FO D J Stevens (N)
Sgt P MacDonald (WOP)
Sgt J L Brooks (MU)
Sgt F A Rutt (RG)

## 207 SQUADRON

**8/9 Oct** *2247-0420*
*HANNOVER*
PO C W Barnett
Sgt P C Lambert
PO E J Anderson
Sgt D Frisky
Sgt F H Hazel
Sgt A Burton
Sgt A Bruce

## 467 SQUADRON RAAF

**18 Oct** *1726-2241*
*HANNOVER*
PO N M McClelland and crew
PO H Griffin in, FO McCarthy out

**3 Nov** *1701-2241*
*DÜSSELDORF*
PO N M McClelland and crew
Sgt C C Schomberg (2P)

**10/11 Nov** *2056-0431*
*MODANE*
PO A Fisher
Sgt S L Smith (FE)
FS H McGallaway (BA)
FS M H Rooney (N)
FS T H Ronaldson (WOP)
Sgt J H Rayns (MU)
FS F Beamish (RG)

**18/19 Nov** *1715-0136*
*BERLIN*
PO N M McClelland and crew
FS D L Gibbs (2P)

**22 Nov** *1641-2312*
*BERLIN*
PO N M McClelland and crew
FS F A Connolly (2P)
Sgt Martin out, Sgt F Miller in

**23 Nov** *1653-2324*
*BERLIN*
PO N M McClelland and crew
Martin back, Miller out

**26/27 Nov** *1713-0059*
*BERLIN*
FO J A Colpus and crew
Sgt L M Jackson in,
Sgt Brooks out

## 1944

**15/16 Feb** *1737-0025*
*BERLIN*
PO J W McManus
Sgt J B McNab (FE)
Sgt I Stapleton (BA)
FS A R T Boys (N)
Sgt M Williams (WOP)
FS L C Vaughan (MU)
Sgt C K Fudge (RG)

**19/20 Feb** *2342-0707*
*LEIPZIG*
PO J M McManus and crew
Sgt H Feltham in, Sgt McNab out

**20/21 Feb** *2349-0136*
*STUTTGART*
PO J M McManus and crew
FS A Summers in, Sgt Fudge out

**24/25 Feb** *1832-0204*
*SCHWEINFURT*
PO J W McManus and crew
McNab and Fudge back

**25/26 Feb** *1830-0215*
*AUGSBURG*
PO J W McManus and crew

**1/2 Mar** *2311-0719*
*STUTTGART*
PO J W McManus and crew
FO E G Strom in, FS Boys out

**18/19 Mar** *1857-0055*
*FRANKFURT*
PO J W McManus and crew

**22/23 Mar** *1912-0024*
*FRANKFURT*
PO J W McManus and crew
FS Boys back, FO Strom out

**24 Mar** *1852-2211*
*BERLIN*
PO J W McManus and crew

**25/26 Mar** *1920-0035*
*AULNOYE*
PO R E Llewelyn
Sgt L H Dixon
PO G W Venables
Sgt W Prest
FS K Overy
Sgt F W Hammond
Sgt K W Ward

**11/12 Apr** *2025-0036*
*AACHEN*
PO A B L Tottenham
Sgt R J Taylor
Sgt S Adam
FS J G Walsh
FS H A Cummins
Sgt T A Stevens
FS G G Podsky

**18/19 Apr** *2111-0126*
*PARIS / JUVISY*
PO A B L Tottenham and crew

**20/21 Apr** *2333-0350*
*PARIS / LA CHAPELLE*
PO A B L Tottenham and crew

**22/23 Apr** *2328-0455*
*BRUNSWICK*
PO A B L Tottenham and crew

**24/25 Apr** *2051-0630*
*BRUNSWICK*
PO A B L Tottenham and crew

**26/27 Apr** *2129-0627*
*SCHWEINFURT*
PO A B L Tottenham and crew

**28/29 Apr** *2326-0655*
*ST MÉDARD*
PO A B L Tottenham and crew

**3/4 May** *2150-0323*
*MAILLY-LE-CAMP*
PO T N Scholefield
Sgt R H C Burgess (FE)
FS F Hughes
FO I Hamilton
FS R T Hilas
Sgt J D Wells
FS K W Stewart (RG)

**6/7 May** *0035-0521*
*SABLE-SUR-SARTHE*
PO T N Scholefield and crew

**10/11 May** *2205-0133*
*LILLE (M/YARDS)*
PO T N Scholefield and crew

**11/12 May** *2216-1052*
*BOURG LÉOPOLD*
PO T N Scholefield and crew

**6 June** *0253-0705*
*ST PIERRE DU MONT*
FO I Fotheringham
Sgt P A Scratchley
Sgt G R S Miller
FO J M Beaton
FS F J Pottinger
Sgt C R Knapman
FO C A Phillips
(FO Fotheringham and crew
lost 28/29 July)

**6/7 June** *2353-0352*
*ARGENTAN*
FO I Fotheringham and crew

**8/9 June** *2307-0518*
*RENNES*
FO I Fotheringham and crew

**12/13 June** *2218-0518*
*POITIERS*
FS K V Millar
Sgt J H Barnes
FS A M Hughes
WO K A McKay
FS A M Meggs
FS A J Perkins
FS B Bronilow

**14/15 June** *2246-0321*
*AUNAY-SUR-ODON*
FO I Fotheringham and crew

**24/25 June** *2247-0209*
*PROUVILLE – V1 SITE*
FO G C Skelton
Sgt L N Furlong
FS C S Birks
WO E E S Vidal (N)
FS N J Morrison
FS W A Leschen
Sgt L McKenzie

**27/28 June** *2201-0532*
*VITRY*
FO I Fotheringham and crew

**29 June** *1209-1534*
*BEAUVOIR*
FS M G Johnson
Sgt P Hounslow
FS R Dunn
FS N J Palfrey
FS J C Whitelaw
FS F S Cavanagh
FS E C Evans

**4/5 July** *2313-0336*
*ST LEU D'ESSERENT*
FO W R Williams
Sgt A J Goodwin
Sgt D J MacDonald
Sgt L F C Weeks
FS J J Murray
FO J H Kitt
Sgt A H Cooper

**7/8 July** *2223-0312*
*ST LEU D'ESSERENT*
PO M G Johnson and crew

**14/15 July** *2211-0455*
*PARIS / VILLENEUVE*
PO M G Johnson and crew

**18 July** *0357-0727*
*CAEN*
FS I R Cowan
Sgt F G W Mills
Sgt E E Warrender
Sgt B S Cox
FS C F Curtis
FS S Murphy
FS F K White

**18/19 July** *2304-0418*
*RÉVIGNY*
PO M G Johnson and crew

**20 July** *– night*
*COURTRAI*
WC G G Petty DSO DFC
(crew and raid not listed in 541)
(damaged by night fighter?)

**17/18 Dec** *1653-0142*
*MUNICH*
SL E LeP Langlois DFC
FS J Scott
FO L W E Baines
FO A F Reid (DFC)
FO E C Patten (DFC)
FO C J Cameron
FL E C Ellis
(Langlois, Scott, Reid, Patten
Cameron were lost on
4 March 1945, Langlois as
WC and CO of 467 Sqn)

**18/19 Dec** *1720-0239*
*GDYNIA*
FO P K Shanahan
Sgt H C Compton
FS B T Stephens
FS L A Smith
FS A R Price
FS J H Schluter
FS R Schlenker

**21/22 Dec** *1644-0335*
*PÖLITZ*
FO G H Stewart
Sgt F Baker
FS R Calov
FO R C Faulks
WO M J H West
FS D J Morland
FS R H Skuthorp

**27 Dec** *1220-1713*
*RHEYDT*
FL M G Johnson and crew

Frank Lawrence and crew: Perce Garvey, Dennis Baldry, R E Chaplin, Eddie Durrant, Mac McCarthy, Lawrence, and Ian Hodgson.

## 1945

**1/2 Jan 1706-2344**
*GRAVENHORST / MITTELAND CANAL*
FL W K Boxsell DFC
Sgt R J Bauchop
FS R L Pegler
FS V E Auborg
FS H H Leach
FS J R Stokes
Sgt W J Turnbull

**5 Jan 0112-0719**
*ROYAN*
FO L W Baker
Sgt H V Price (FE)
FS P E Vertigan (BA)
FS A J Johnson (N)
FS R O Sayer (WOP)
FS A F Wallace (MU)
FS G J Collins (RG)

**13/14 Jan 1634-0244**
*PÖLITZ*
SL E LeP Langlois and crew

**14/15 Jan 1629-0140**
*LEUNA-MERSEBURG*
FO J J J Cross
Sgt K M Pope
FO R H Thomas
WO D F Edwards
FS W V Maurer
FS W K Perry
PO J E Brunskell

**16/17 Jan 1812-0355**
*BRUX*
FL F Lawrence DFC DFM
Sgt D R Baldry (FE)
WO P K Garvey (BA)

WO J S Hodgson (N)
FS V J M McCarthy (WOP)
Sgt E W Durrant (MU)
DO R F Chaplin (RG)

**1 Feb 1621-2232**
*SIEGEN*
FL F Lawrence and crew

**2/3 Feb 1950-0254**
*KARLSRUHE*
SL E LeP Langlois and crew

**16/17 Mar 1754-0134**
*WÜRZBURG*
FL K P Shanahan and crew

**20/21 Mar 2333-0752**
*BÖHLEN*
FO L W Baker and crew
Sgt N W Teggart and
FO N B Ridings in, Sgt Price
and FS Vertigan out

**22 Mar 1113-1632**
*BREMEN*
WC I H A Hay
FS W V Ward (FE)
FO N B Ridings (BA)
FO A R T Boys (N)
Sgt G H Wing (WOP)
Sgt C W Carter (MG)
Sgt P G Sanday (RG)

**23/24 Mar 1919-0051**
*WESEL*
FO L W Baker and crew
FO R H Thomas in,
FO Ridings out

**27 Mar 1013-1456**
*FARGE*

FO L W Baker and crew
Vertigan back, Thomas out

**4 Apr 0558-1307**
*NORDHAUSEN*
WC I H A Hay
FO C H Nissen (2P)
FS L G W Barnes
FO L A Tabor
FS M J Miller
FO F G Bourke
FS A J Smith
FS A H Thomas

**6 Apr 0813-1131**
*IJMUIDEN*
SL W M Kynock DFC
Sgt D B Easton
FO R H Darwin
FO S Harwood
WO K R Morris
FS W T J George
WO R Watts
(mission aborted due to Allied troops
taking occupation)

**9 Apr 1419-1937**
*HAMBURG*
WC I H A Hay and crew (see
22 March raid)

**16/17 Apr 2335-0817**
*PILSEN*
FO R A Swift
Sgt G W Wrightson (FE)
FS J R Lewis (BA)
FS C M Wasson (N)
FS H S Stubbs (WOP)
FS T R King (MU)
FS K M Symonds (RG)

**18/19 Apr 2336-0744**
*KOMOTAU*
FL L W Baker and crew
FO Ridings in, Vertigan out

**23 Apr 1508-2032**
*FLENSBURG*
FO L W Baker and crew
(aborted, ordered not to bomb
by Deputy Leader)

**24 Apr – day**
*EXODUS – BRUSSELS*
WC I H A Hay and crew

**26 Apr – day**
*EXODUS – BRUSSELS*
WC I H A Hay and crew

**4 May – day**
*EXODUS – JUVINCOURT*
WC I H A Hay and crew

**6 May – day**
*EXODUS – JUVINCOURT*
FL M G Bache and crew

**12 May – day**
*EXODUS – BRUSSELS*
FO L W Baker and crew

# W4964
# JOHNNY WALKER

This Mark I Lancaster, built at the Metropolitan Vickers plant at Trafford Park, Manchester, with four Merlin XX engines, left the A V Roe factory on 12 April 1943 with the serial number W4964. After some quick work at an MU she was assigned to 9 Squadron at RAF Bardney, Lincolnshire.

The aircraft was given the squadron code letters of WS and the individual letter J-Johnny, the latter led to its famous nose-art painting of the Johnny Walker whisky symbol with the firm's equally famous motto 'Still Going Strong' written beneath it.

Its first operational sortie was to Stettin on the night of 20/21 April 1943, just eight days after leaving the factory. However, ops then came slowly at first, her next not being until early May. Her eighth, to Düsseldorf on the night of 11 June, gave her skipper, Sergeant T H Gill, and his crew some anxious moments over the target. Just after the bombs had gone down and Gill was sweating out those few moments flying straight and level for the bombing photo to be taken, the bomber received a flak hit. The hydraulic pipe-line was fractured so that the bomb-doors could not be closed. Flying home, the emergency bottle was used for landing to put down the undercarriage and flaps. Further problems ensued the next night when the 4,000 lb 'cookie' did not release over Bochum, it was eventually jettisoned over Münster on the way home. Gill was later commissioned but he and his crew failed to return from a raid on Mannheim in ED666 on 5/6 September.

J-Johnny had a couple of minor problems during its first dozen sorties: an unserviceable rear turret caused an abort on 23 May and an intercom failure on 25 July followed by an electrical failure to the mid-upper turret, resulted in another. It had already been sent back to ROS at Avro's for a major service and then in August it was made Cat AC – cause unknown – the day after going on the famous raid to the experimental rocket plant at Peenemünde. W4964 returned a month later ready to carry on.

*Johnny* slowly began accumulating missions, including 12 ops to the German capital during the Battle of Berlin over the winter of 1943-44. A trip on 2 January had to be aborted because the air-speed indicator (ASI) iced-up and the starboard-inner engine over-heated. Her main skipper during this period was Pilot Officer C P Newton. Charles Newton was later awarded the DFC, and during his tour flew 16 raids in *Johnny*. His engineer, John H Turner, WOP, James Ryan, mid-upper, William J Wilkinson, and rear gunner, Robert H McFerran, each won the DFM. Turner's citation noted:

> 'As Flight Engineer, this NCO has completed 28 highly successful operational trips. It is due in no small measure to the conscientious care which he has always given to his engines and airframe both on the ground and in the air that his Captain has never been under the necessity of returning from a sortie for technical or other reasons.'

Another skipper, who took *Johnny* to Stettin on 5/6 January 1944, had the misfortune of going missing on 22/23 March in another Lancaster (LM430), but on board was Bardney's Station Commander, Group Captain N C Pleasance. It was Flying Officer Albert Manning's 20th op, but experience is no guarantor that luck will not run out.

The crew of W4964 after a raid on Stettin – believed to be that flown on 5/6 January 1944. If correct it is the crew of FO A E Manning.

*Johnny Walker* following the 104th operation. The 100th was denoted by an extra large bomb at the right end of the lower row of bombs. Note the kangaroo insignia below the navigator's window and the various markings for medals awarded to crew members, wound stripes, a searchlight shot out and one enemy plane shot down.

Only one man survived (not one who had earlier flown in *Johnny)*.

Sergeant P E Plowright next took over *Johnny* and did 18 trips between December 1943 and May 1944. He was commissioned and received the DFC. Crewmen Robert P Allen RCAF and Norman Lucas were also commissioned.

On 19 May Philip Plowright took Pilot Officer J D Melrose to Tours as second pilot. James Melrose later took over W4964 and flew 22 more sorties with it – including its 100th. By that time Melrose was a Flight Lieutenant with the DFC.

By D-Day, *Johnny* had completed some 70 sorties and flew on the night of this famous day itself, marked as sortie No.71 on the nose, the bomb symbol having the letter 'D' painted on it to denote the occasion. *Johnny* became Cat AC again on 30 July, going back to ROS, but returned to the squadron on 4 August. By the time the Lancaster was nearing its 100th operation the squadron was given a most important task, that of attacking the German battleship *Tirpitz* in Kaa Fjord, Norway. The Lancaster force from 9 and 617 Squadrons would carry 12,000 lb Tallboy bombs.

In order to make the attack, the two squadrons flew to Yagodnik, Russia, via Lossiemouth in Scotland, heading out on 11 September. Two crews on this transit flight who had flown W4964 made force landings in Russia in other Lancs. From Yagodnik, via Archangel, the Lancaster force made the attack on 15 September – including Melrose in J-Johnny. One Tallboy, later considered to be that dropped by *Johnny*, hit the battleship, while some near misses caused further damage. For *Johnny* it meant that 100 ops had now been recorded. Melrose later received a Bar to his DFC, while Stuart Morris (bomb aimer) received the DFC.

*Johnny's* last six operations were flown during September and early October 1944 and then the veteran was rested from war duties. It was eventually struck off charge (SOC) on 2 November 1949.

This Lancaster had several other interesting markings on its nose, apart from the very distinctive figure of Johnny Walker. As the members of its early crews received decorations so the relevant ribbons were painted in a vertical line. Two DFMs then two DFCs with the recipients' initials beneath them. The aircraft also carried three wound stripes for damage received, a chevron representing a year's duty on active service, the ribbon of the 1939-45 Star, then a swastika which presumably was meant to represent a German aircraft, although no record of any claim seems to have survived. A searchlight represented the time an under-gunner (which 9 Squadron had for a brief period) shot out a searchlight beam flying back at low level, then two more award ribbons, both DFMs. There is also a star – undoubtedly a red star denoting the trip to Russia.

Also at some stage a kangaroo was painted by the navigator's window just aft of the cockpit canopy (port side) denoting an Australian – in fact Flying Officer Jimmy W Moore, the Aussie navigator in Melrose's crew. James Melrose also said there was another kangaroo by the wireless operator's window for his Aussie WOP, Flying Officer R G Woolf.

To give the reader some indication of the attrition rate in Bomber Command during 1943-45 when these Lancasters were operating, James Melrose noted that of the nine crews who joined 9 Squadron at the time he arrived, his was the only one left two months later.

James Melrose and crew. From left to right: Melrose, S A Morris, E C Selfe, J W Moore, E E Staley, E Hoyle and R G Woolf.

## 9 SQUADRON
### 1943

**20/21 Apr** 2147-0524
*STETTIN*
WO W E Wood
Sgt C E Clayton
Sgt Chipperfield
PO T Mellard
Sgt G T M Gaines
Sgt H G Watson
Sgt W R Barker

**4/5 May** 2202-0410
*DORTMUND*
Sgt J D Duncan
Sgt S G Bluntern
FS H T Brown
Sgt G Bartley
Sgt S Hughes
Sgt L G Warner
Sgt D B McMillan

**12/13 May** 2345-0441
*DUISBURG*
Sgt G H Saxon
Sgt D C Ferris
Sgt W C McDonald
Sgt R M Morris
Sgt J Reddish
Sgt J C Owen
Sgt J Buntin

**13/14 May** 2134-0540
*PILSEN*
WO W E Wood and crew
Sgt E L Crump in, Sgt Chipperfield out

**23/24 May** 2237-0205
*DORTMUND*
Sgt G E Hall
Sgt L Field
Sgt W D Evans
Sgt E Colbert
Sgt O J Overington
Sgt K Chalk
Sgt H G Williams

**25/26 May** 2311-0412
*DÜSSELDORF*
Sgt T H Gill
Sgt M McPherson
Sgt R V Gough
Sgt B P Revine
Sgt W A Morton
Sgt K McDonagh
Sgt R McKee

**27/28 May** 2201-0305
*ESSEN*
Sgt T H Gill and crew

**11/12 June** 2330-0448
*DÜSSELDORF*
Sgt T H Gill and crew

**12/13 June** 2240-0345
*BOCHUM*
Sgt T H Gill and crew

**14/15 June** 2247-0336
*OBERHAUSEN*
Sgt J A Aldersley
Sgt P Hall
Sgt P Webster
Sgt H Popplestone
Sgt G J Sinclair
Sgt H F Poynter
Sgt D G Fremblay

**24/25 July** 2313-0415
*HAMBURG*
Sgt C P Newton (DFC)
Sgt J H Turner (FE)
Sgt P Hall
Sgt E J Duck
Sgt J Ryan (WOP) (DFM)
Sgt W J Wilkinson (MU) (DFM)

Sgt R McFerran (RG) (DFM)

**25/26 July** 2159-0044
*ESSEN*
FS G A Graham RCAF
Sgt W G Statham (FE)
PO D J Macdonald RCAF
Sgt R McK Innes
Sgt A F Williamson
Sgt H F Altus RAAF (MU)
Sgt K Mellor (RG)
(aborted due to intercom
failure, MU electrical failure;
jettisoned 'cookie' safe)
(all lost over Berlin, 18 Nov 43)

**27/28 July** 2303-0357
*HAMBURG*
FS G A Graham and crew

**29/30 July** 2242-0400
*HAMBURG*
FS G Ward
Sgt J Sutton
Sgt E D Keene
Sgt G L James
Sgt G F K Bedwell
Sgt N R Nixon
Sgt W L Doran RCAF
(all lost, Berlin, 2 Jan 44)

**3 Aug** 0015-0455
*HAMBURG*
PO C P Newton and crew

**10/11 Aug** 2216-0610
*NÜRNBERG*
PO C P Newton and crew

**12/13 Aug** 2154-0620
*MILAN*
Sgt R A Knight
Sgt T Bradford
Sgt G A Munro
Sgt J W Noble
Sgt D G Connor
Sgt R E Jones
Sgt R G Nelson

**15/16 Aug** 2036-0433
*MILAN*
Sgt G E Hall and crew
Sgt R A Chorley in, Sgt Chalk out

**17/18 Aug** 2124-0451
*PEENEMÜNDE*
PO C P Newton and crew

**1/2 Oct** 1841-0001
*HAGEN*
PO C P Newton and crew

**2/3 Oct** 1847-0252
*MUNICH*
PO C P Newton and crew

**4/5 Oct** 1842-0052
*FRANKFURT*
PO C P Newton and crew

**7/8 Oct** 2059-0305
*STUTTGART*
PO C P Newton and crew

**8/9 Oct** 2303-0356
*HANNOVER*
FS G Ward and crew

**18 Oct** 1718-2236
*HANNOVER*
FS G Ward and crew

**20/21 Oct** 1726-0038
*LEIPZIG*
FS G Ward and crew

**22/23 Oct** 1806-0029
*KASSEL*
FS M J Smythe
Sgt Whiting
Sgt E Hubbert

PO J C Doughty
Sgt Cattley
Sgt Sorge
Sgt J Heron

**3 Nov** 1654-2120
*DÜSSELDORF*
PO C P Newton and crew

**10/11 Nov** 2053-0508
*MODANE*
PO W M Reid
Sgt S W Richards
FO R D H Parker
Sgt D G Moir
Sgt B Harthill
Sgt C J Wilheim
Sgt G Brown

**18/19 Nov** 1742-0150
*BERLIN*
PO W M Reid and crew

**22 Nov** 1648-2317
*BERLIN*
FO C P Newton and crew
Sgt L T Fairclough in, Sgt Duck out

**23 Nov** 1656-2350
*BERLIN*
FO C P Newton and crew
FS Allen in, Sgt Fairclough out

**2 Dec** 1644-2329
*BERLIN*
FO C P Newton and crew
PO H S Sandy (2P)
FL G Bell in, FS Allen out

**3 Dec** 0031-0803
*LEIPZIG*
Sgt P E Plowright (DFC)
Sgt W C Lewis
Sgt N H B Lucas
FS R P Allen RCAF
Sgt H Hannah
Sgt F Corr
Sgt N F Wells

**16 Dec** 1639-2355
*BERLIN*
FO C P Newton and crew
Duck back, Bell out

**23 Dec** 0024-0731
*BERLIN*
FO C P Newton and crew

**29/30 Dec** 1657-0019
*BERLIN*
Sgt D P Proud
Sgt F Harman
Sgt D Carlick
Sgt L T Fairclough
Sgt W H Shirley
Sgt S L Jones
Sgt R L Biers

### 1944

**2 Jan** 0013-0820
*BERLIN*
Sgt D P Proud and crew

**2/3 Jan** 2349-0227
*BERLIN*
PO D H Pearce
Sgt C W Howe
FO J E Logan
FO W E Pearson
Sgt W R Doran
Sgt S L Jones
FS E A Thomas
(aborted with iced-up ISA
and std-inner overheating)

**6 Jan** 0019-0835
*STETTIN*
FO A E Manning

Sgt N Burkitt (FE)
FO J W Hearn (N)
FS P Warywodo RCAF (BA)
FL A G Newbond (WOP)
Sgt J J Zammit (MU)
FS R C Hayter (RG)

**14 Jan** 1640-2213
*BRUNSWICK*
FO C P Newton and crew
PO H C Clark (2P)

**20 Jan** 1639-2338
*BERLIN*
Sgt D P Proud and crew

**21/22 Jan** 2027-0311
*MAGDEBURG*
Sgt D P Proud and crew

**27/28 Jan** 1732-0158
*BERLIN*
FO C P Newton and crew

**1/2 Mar** 2331-0740
*STUTTGART*
Sgt P E Plowright and crew

**15/16 Mar** 1914-0258
*STUTTGART*
Sgt P E Plowright and crew
Sgt W S Richardson in, Sgt Lucas out

**18/19 Mar** 1913-0124
*FRANKFURT*
FS W R Horne
Sgt T W Powell
FS J J Shirley
Sgt J T Johnson
Sgt J H McReery
Sgt R A Morton
Sgt J S Parker

**22/23 Mar** 1902-0033
*FRANKFURT*
Sgt P E Plowright and crew
Sgt Lucas back

**25/26 Mar** 1921-0035
*AULNOYE*
FL J F Ineson
Sgt L C Margetts
FS H F MacKenzie RCAF
FP T L M Porteous RNZAF
Sgt R H Warren
Sgt H S Chappell
Sgt J Wilkinson
(lost 3/4 May; Porteous PoW,
Chappell evaded, others killed)

**26/27 Mar** 2004-0101
*ESSEN*
Sgt P E Plowright and crew

**30/31 Mar** 2224-0619
*NÜRNBERG*
Sgt P E Plowright and crew

**10/11 Apr** 2255-0525
*TOURS*
WC E L Porter DFC and Bar
Sgt C E Bowyer
PO J Waterhouse
FO J McMaster (DFC)
FS B Owen
FS J Michael
FS C R Bolt RCAF
(reached target but could not i/d
aiming point so did not bomb)

**11/12 Apr** 2033-0043
*AACHEN*
FL J F Ineson and crew

**18/19 Apr** 2051-0135
*JUVISY*
PO P E Plowright and crew
Lucas now PO, Allen now WO

W4964 did several trips to Berlin. This picture shows the Big City in the summer of 1945.

**20/21 Apr** *2316-0347*
LA CHAPELLE
PO P E Plowright and crew

**24/25 Apr** *2059-0710*
MUNICH
PO P E Plowright and crew

**28/29 Apr** *2255-0640*
ST MÉDARD-EN-JALLES
PO P E Plowright and crew
(sqn ordered not to bomb due
to smoke and haze)

**29/30 Apr** *2228-0554*
ST MÉDARD-EN-JALLES
PO P E Plowright and crew

**1/2 May** *2141-0518*
TOULOUSE
PO P E Plowright and crew

**3/4 May** *2203-0231*
MAILLY-LE-CAMP
PO P E Plowright and crew

**8/9 May** *2137-0231*
BREST / LANVEOC
PO P E Plowright and crew

**10/11 May** *2206-0135*
LILLE
PO P E Plowright and crew

**11/12 May** *2229-0156*
BOURG LÉOPOLD
PO P E Plowright and crew
(ordered to abort near target
area due to haze)

**19/20 May** *2221-0339*
TOURS
PO P E Plowright and crew
PO J D Melrose (2P)

**21/22 May** *2251-0309*
DUISBURG
PO P E Plowright and crew

**22/23 May** *2242-0520*
BRUNSWICK
PO J D Melrose (DFC)
Sgt E C Selfe (FE)
FO J W Moore RAAF (N)
FO S A Morris (BA) (DFC)
FO R G Woolf RAAF (WOP)
Sgt E Hoyle (MU)
Sgt E E Staley (RG)

**24/25 May** *2313-0208*
EINDHOVEN
PO H C Clark and crew
(ordered to abort due
to poor visibility)

**27/28 May** *2258-0355*
NANTES
PO J D Melrose and crew

**3/4 June** *2315-0236*
CHERBOURG
PO R S Gradwell
Sgt T Lynch
FO P E Arnold
FO R B Atkinson RCAF
Sgt J T Price
Sgt W F Best RCAF
Sgt L Sutton

**6 June** *0311-0716*
ST PIERRE-DU-MONT
FO P D Blackham
Sgt J D Murrie
FO J Wenger RCAF
FO J D Elphick RCAF
FO G A White RCAF
Sgt V G Stokes
Sgt J McHickey RCAF

**6/7 June** *2334-0325*
ARGENTAN
FO J D Melrose and crew

**8/9 June** *2306-0517*
RENNES
FO J D Melrose and crew

**10/11 June** *2205-0335*
ORLÉANS
FO J D Melrose and crew

**14/15 June** *2243-0320*
AUNAY-SUR-ODON
FO J D Melrose and crew

**21/22 June** *2312-0350*
GELSENKIRCHEN
FO J D Melrose and crew

**23/24 June** *2241-0518*
LIMOGES
FO J D Melrose and crew

**24/25 June** *2246-0228*
PROUVILLE – V1 SITE
FO P D Blackham and crew

**27/28 June** *2158-0519*
VITRY LE FRANÇOIS
FO J D Melrose and crew

**29 June** *1215-1520*
BEAUVOIR – V1 SITE
FO J D Melrose and crew

**4/5 July** *2325-0325*
CREIL
FO D J Melrose and crew

**7/8 July** *2240-0315*
ST LEU D'ESSERENT
FO J D Melrose and crew

**12/13 July** *2157-0635*
CULMONT-CHALANDREY
FO J D Melrose and crew

**18 July** *0407-0735*
CAEN
FO A M Morrison
Sgt A Aitkenhead
Sgt J F Reid RCAF
FS L L Westmore RCAF
WO F Black RAAF
Sgt B Strachen
Sgt F Hooper
(this crew force-landed LL884
in Russia 12 Sep on transit flt;
no injuries)

**20/21 July** *2318-0244*
COURTRAI
FS W D Tweedle

Sgt C G Heath
FS E Shields
Sgt J W Singer RCAF
Sgt A Carson
Sgt J A Foot
Sgt K Mallinson

**23/24 July** *2300-0456*
KIEL
FO J D Melrose and crew

**25 July** *1754-2151*
ST CYR AIRFIELD
FO J D Melrose and crew

**26/27 July** *2128-0613*
GIVORS
FO J D Melrose and crew

**28/29 July** *2201-0607*
STUTTGART
FO C B Scott
Sgt J E Simkin
Sgt L A Harding
Sgt L W Langley
Sgt E M Hayward
Sgt F A Saunders
Sgt L J Hambly
(lost 23/24 Sep; all killed
except Langley – PoW)

**30 July** *0632-1147*
CAHAGNES
FO D McIntosh
Sgt R V Cosser
Sgt N A Hawkins
Sgt P J Ramwell
Sgt P E Tetlow
Sgt J A Wood
Sgt G Owen
(ordered to abort due to
cloud covering target)

**13 Aug** *0833-1302*
BREST
FL J D Melrose and crew

**14 Aug** *0832-1300*
BREST
FL J D Melrose and crew

**15 Aug** *0958-1321*
GILZE-RIJEN AIRFIELD
FO B Taylor
Sgt D J Doherty
Sgt A L Cunningham
Sgt A M Holmes RCAF
FS K Burns
Sgt G C Freeman RCAF
Sgt G M Young RCAF

**16 Aug** *1124-1742*
LA PALLICE
FL G C Camsell RCAF
Sgt W Andrews
Sgt P R Aslin
FO R H Thomas
Sgt D Beevers
Sgt W J Hebert RCAF
FS A E Boon RCAF
(this crew force-landed in Russia on
12 Sep (PD211); no injuries)

**24 Aug** *1239-1531*
IJMUIDEN
FL G C Camsell and crew

**27 Aug** *1418-1844*
BREST
FO K S Arndell RAAF
Sgt P H Jones
FS P E Campbell RNZAF
FO H W Porter
Sgt R Meads
Sgt J Brown
Sgt L J Richards

**15 Sep** *0950-1705*
TIRPITZ
FL J D Melrose and crew

**23/24 Sep** *1907-0101*
MÜNSTER
FL J D Melrose and crew

**27 Sep** *0120-0737*
KARLSRUHE
FO K S Arndell and crew

**27/28 Sep** *2150-0422*
KAISERSLAUTERN
FO K S Arndell and crew

**5 Oct** *0750-1307*
WILHELMSHAVEN
FO E C Redfern
Sgt J W Williams
Sgt R W Cooper
FO O P Hull
Sgt L G Roberts
Sgt W Brand
Sgt D Winch

**6 Oct** *1747-2230*
BREMEN
FO A E Jeffs
Sgt C V Higgins
Sgt K C Mousley
Sgt H A Fisher RCAF
Sgt C M McMillan
Sgt W Thomas
Sgt G J Symonds

# DV245
# The Saint

This machine was assigned to 101 Squadron at Ludford Magna, in Lincolnshire, on 19 September 1943, after being built at Metropolitan Vickers works, Manchester. It was a Mark III equipped with four Merlin 28 engines. From the factory it had gone to 32 MU at the end of August before being assigned to its squadron.

Coded SR, with individual letter 'S for Sugar' it became known as *The Saint*, and made its first raid on the night of 7/8 October, to Stuttgart, with Flying Officer R R Leeder. While a variety of crews flew DV245 during the final months of 1943, Roy Leeder was the aircraft's most usual skipper. He completed 16 ops (of their tour of 30) between October and 24 February 1944, at which time Leeder, now a Flight Lieutenant, completed his tour and was posted to 1 Lancaster Finishing School (LFS). It was in fact his crew that suggested naming the aircraft *The Saint* from the books by Leslie Charteris, and the radio programme of the same name. Eric Bickley, the rear gunner, supplied a sketch for the ground crew artist featuring the yellow saint astride a red bomb. At the end of their tour Leeder and James Turner received DFCs; Geoff Smith, Roy Brown, Percy Drought and Eric Bickley DFMs.

Roy Leeder recalled the occasion DV245 was used to fly for an experiment at Farnborough on 1 January 1944, taking up a lady boffin:

'In fact we flew with two boffins, Mrs Pearce and Mr McClellan. The purpose of the flight was to investigate the practicability of passing nitrogen – an inert gas – over the petrol in the fuel tanks in order to preclude the likelihood of fire in the event of the tanks being penetrated by flak or incendiary bullets.

'The question of valves freezing up was also involved and presumably that is why on the flight we endeavoured to get as high as possible to see if this would happen. [They reached 29,000 feet!] In the event we heard nothing more of this experiment, so the idea must have been impracticable.

'All our shakiest do's were caused by appalling weather on return to England. In "S for Sugar" we frequently experienced difficulty from the closing down of the weather on our return from an operation. The fact that we survived can, I think, largely be attributed to the fact that *Sugar* must have been a remarkably stable aircraft. I can recall an occasion when I was trying in vain, to visually identify our airfield through low cloud, when over the intercom I heard Jim Turner, our navigator, screaming: "Watch your airspeed, skipper!" I must have inadvertently been pulling back on the stick, for the airspeed had sunk to well

Roy Leeder (DFC) took DV245 on her first sortie, 7/8 October 1943.

below stalling speed. I pushed desperately forward on the stick and our airspeed slowly built up. In theory we should have spun into the ground.'

Eric Bickley recalled the staggering flight up to 29,000 feet at Farnborough, and that they were unable to reach the hoped-for 30,000 feet. He also remembered that they should have been at Farnborough for three days but as they accidentally hit some scaffolding with a wing-tip whilst taxying, they were there for a week. Eric later began another tour with 207 Squadron in 1945.

Once more a variety of crews flew DV245, before Flying Officer Harold Davies DFC emerged as the Lanc's more regular pilot – with 13 ops on her. "Dave" Davies' bomb aimer was Jack Kemp, who was to receive the DFM.

'The Nürnberg trip of 30 March 1944 was probably one of our most gruelling operations. We *saw* more aircraft shot down than on any other sortie; at one point they were going down on either side of us, each no more than 400 yards away, in less than a minute, but *Sugar* brought us back safely.

'Returning from Brunswick on 22 May somewhere east of the Ruhr, a cone of searchlights snapped on dead ahead. Dave turned instinctively to starboard so he could see it, with the intention of sneaking past it, when a second cone sprang up requiring further deviation to starboard. This brought howls of protest from the navigator, "Ted" Barlow, who wanted us to make a port turn of 30 degrees. In all there were at least five cones in a line and we were heading about 330-345 degrees.

'Ted's protests went on until he was advised (!) to "have a look". He did and he was very quiet after that! To my knowledge he never looked out again on any raid.

'We decided to maintain the northerly heading and I was able to get a good fix on the coast. From this and the air-plot, the wind was found to be 180 degrees out from the forecast. I believe a correction had been broadcast but we missed it as did many others. I heard that several aircraft ran out of fuel. The enemy searchlights brought us home that night.

'Two nights later we were going to Aachen. It was a warm night and facing downwind on the

Eric Bickley was Roy Leeder's rear-gunner and won the DFM.

perimeter track, the engines were over-heating. On take-off three engines returned to normal but the starboard-outer radiator gauge went up to the stop. At 500 feet, Bill Lees and Dave decided to shut it down, although a couple of attempts to restart it were made over the North Sea, but the vibration caused us more anxiety than the knowledge that we were on three engines, so we completed the trip like that.'

101 Squadron, of course, was a little out of the ordinary because by the autumn of 1943 its Lancasters were being equipped with ABC (Airborne Cigar) apparatus that could search out and then jam enemy R/T frequencies. Often an eighth crew member was carried to operate ABC, generally a specially trained German-speaking operator. These Lancasters usually carried a normal bomb load only slightly reduced due to the weight of the extra man and his apparatus; the ABC-equipped Lancasters being distinguishable from others by their two large dorsal masts atop the fuselage.

DV245 operated during the Battle of Berlin over the winter of 1943-44, taking off nine times for the 'Big City', but had to abort twice through mechanical problems, on 2 and 16 December. It also flew on the night of D-Day on a Special Duties patrol but had to abort as its engines began to overheat. Overall this was rare for *Sugar*, as its aborts due to mechanical problems were few.

By August 1944 *Sugar* had notched up over 50 trips. Then Sergeant Stanley Bowater took over, going on to fly 22 more in it. He won the DFC and survived the war but died in a Shackleton crash, flying with 205 Squadron (co-pilot) on an anti-piracy patrol over the South China Sea in December 1958. He had received the AFC in 1952 flying a Sunderland during an expedition to Greenland.

His bomb aimer was Gerry Murphy, who remembered:

'After our third op on 101, we were told *The Saint* was to be our aircraft. I had mixed feelings because it had completed over 50 trips and it appeared to be a lucky aircraft, but it could be that its luck was due to run out.

'Like other crews we became very attached to our Lancaster. We did not like flying in another aircraft when she was in for service and we did not like other crews flying her when we were on leave. I think that she had only one vice: a reluctance to lose height, as the skipper soon discovered. She

Three of Leeder's crew: Geoff Smith, Roy Brown and Percy Drought. All three men received DFMs.

did not want to come down!

'We had no shattering experiences while flying *The Saint* but like most Lancasters she was holed by flak from time to time. On one occasion "Bow" Bowater nearly bought it when a piece of shrapnel came up through the floor and took away the oxygen mask clip on the side of his helmet. Another fraction of an inch and he would have gone. On another night we brought her back well holed and our ground crew were disgusted. They almost regarded her as their personal property which they had lent to us!

'There were amusing incidents. One night on a bomb-run, the target was not quite in the bomb-sight and I automatically called, "Dummy run!" There was no response for a moment and then I heard the voice of the rear-gunner over the intercom: "Who is the dim-witted b....... who just called dummy run?" This was followed by ribald comments and improper suggestions by other members of the crew.

'A couple of nights later during an op the skipper called me on the intercom and did not receive a reply. My oxygen tube had got fouled. The skipper realised what might have happened, asked the engineer to check and then the comments started: "Leave him and we'll have no more dummy runs!" "'Let the b...... die and we'll live longer."

'Thirty-five years later, when we met again for the first time since 1944, we were parking our cars and being the last to arrive I had some difficulty finding a space in the car park. Watched by the crew, I drove around and on my third circuit, Ted Reeves shouted, "I see you are still doing dummy runs!"

In the autumn, *Sugar* began to vie with another Lancaster on the squadron – DV302 H-Harry – as to which would reach the century mark first. In the end, although it seemed *Harry* would get there first, several raids were aborted, so *Sugar* got there with *Harry* still on 98.

*Sugar* completed her 100th operational sortie on the night of 5/6 January 1945 with a raid on Hannover. It was flown by a Canadian from Regina, Saskatchewan, Flying Officer R P Paterson. In a typical wartime propaganda press release at the time of the 100th trip, Paterson was reported as saying: 'Give me *Sugar* any time and I'll fly her. Despite its age it can do as well as any aircraft I know and I think it climbs better than most. I don't think it's been hit by heavy flak. I'd be content to finish my tour in it.'

In spite of his remarks, the sortie to Hannover was only Paterson's second trip in *Sugar* (the first being in early December!) and he only flew it once more – in March. DV245's usual skipper towards the end of its days was Flight Lieutenant K Hanney and his crew, who had taken the aircraft out on 15 raids between December 1944 and April 1945. By the time *Sugar* reached its century it had had several engine changes and its operational flying time stood at over 720 hours.

Over Pforzheim on 23 February, a twin-engined jet aircraft approached – probably a Me262. The bomb aimer in the front turret fired three bursts at it and it caught fire, crashed and exploded. This was John R Drewery RCAF who was awarded the DFC. His citation read:

B G Lyall with Roy Brown and Percy Drought.

'Flying Officer Drewery has participated in many sorties as an air bomber and has at all times displayed a high standard of ability and determination.

'One night in February, 1945, he was detailed to take part in an attack against Pforzheim. When over the target area, an enemy fighter was sighted. Flying Officer Drewery promptly manned the front gun turret, gave his pilot the necessary combat manoeuvres and then opened fire. His bullets struck the enemy aircraft which caught fire, and dived towards the ground where it exploded on impact. By his vigilance, promptitude and good shooting, this officer contributed in good measure to the safety of his aircraft. Flying Officer Drewery is a most devoted and fearless member of aircraft crew.'

His pilot George Withenshaw later received the DFC too. Meantime, Hanney continued to fly ops in DV245 into March, along with others. Fortunately for Hanney he was not flying *The Saint* on 23 March, during a raid by 128 Lancasters from 1 and 5 Groups, attacking railway bridges at Bremen and Bad Oeynhausen. Two Lancs were lost on the Bremen sortie – one being DV245 – on trip number 119. It was a daylight sortie and the Lancaster was attacked and shot down by another Me262 jet. Flying

Officer Ralph Robert Little RCAF (an American) and his crew were all killed. The bomber crashed near Stöttinghausen, SE of Twistringen at 10.30. By one of those strange coincidences, the rank and initials of her first operational skipper were exactly the same as its last. Another coincidence is that Paterson, who flew the 100th trip, was the pilot of the other Lanc lost this date (LL755), although he and two of his crew survived as prisoners of war.

(While the Squadron diary reflects the above, it has been recorded elsewhere that these two pilots were each flying the other aircraft.)

Although a poor picture, it does depict the 'Saint' insignia and 40 bomb symbols.

Stan Bowater (front) and crew. From left to right: Gerry Murphy, Ted Reeves, Hugh Dickie, Ken Dickinson, Andy Oliver and Freddie Campbell.

## 1943
## 101 SQUADRON

**7/8 Oct** *2025-0335*
*STUTTGART*
FO R R Leeder (DFC)
Sgt G F Smith (FE) (DFM)
PO J A Turner (N) (DFC)
Sgt R S Brown (WOP) (DFM)
Sgt B G Lyall (BA)
Sgt P J Drought (MU) (DFM)
Sgt E W Bickley (RG) (DFM)
WO D M Windle (SO)

**8/9 Oct** *2240-0415*
*HANNOVER*
FO R R Leeder and crew

**18/19 Oct** *1710-2225*
*HANNOVER*
SL J F Dilworth
Sgt F Brookes
FL F L South
WO W W Mitchell
FS H I Howard
Sgt H James
FS W G Osmotherly
FS L H Fox

**20/21 Oct** *1755-0015*
*KASSEL*
FO R R Leeder and crew

**3/4 Nov** *1705-2130*
*DÜSSELDORF*
FO R R Leeder and crew

**18/19 Nov** *1705-0155*
*BERLIN*
FO R R Leeder and crew

**22 Nov** *1650-2325*
*BERLIN*
FO R R Leeder and crew

**26/27 Nov** *1705-0005*
*STUTTGART*
FO N A March
Sgt F C G DeBrook

Sgt C G Kaye
Sgt D W Ince
PO K R Middleton
Sgt D R Glendinning
FS F H Quick
Sgt O Fischl

**16/17 Dec** *1610-1945*
*BERLIN*
FO R R Leeder and crew
(aborted due to std-outer
overheating, jettisoned bombs)

**20 Dec** *1729-2235*
*FRANKFURT*
FO R R Leeder and crew

**24 Dec** *0025-0740*
*BERLIN*
FO R R Leeder and crew

## 1944

**14 Jan** *1645-2215*
*BRUNSWICK*
FO R R Leeder and crew

**20 Jan** *1630-2325*
*BERLIN*
FO R R Leeder and crew

**21/22 Jan** *2000-0250*
*MAGDEBURG*
FO R R Leeder and crew

**27/28 Jan** *1730-0150*
*BERLIN*
FS E T Holland RAAF
Sgt T Haycock
FS H Scott RAAF
FS A P Farquharson
FS I R Smith RAAF
FS F M McCarthy RAAF
Sgt V G Smith
FO H L Croisette

**30 Jan** *1715-2335*
*BERLIN*
FO R R Leeder and crew

**15/16 Feb** *1717-0005*
*BERLIN*
PO N A Marsh and crew
FS W S Ricketts RAAF in,
FS Quick out; Sgt Fischl out,
FL F C Bertlesham RCAF in

**19/20 Feb** *2352-0718*
*LEIPZIG*
FO R R Leeder and crew
Sgt R M McLeod in, Sgt
Lyall out; Sgt J Davidson in,
WO Windle out

**20/21 Feb** *2336-0658*
*STUTTGART*
FL R R Leeder and crew
Sgt Davidson out, WO Windle back

**24/25 Feb** *1818-0213*
*SCHWEINFURT*
FL R R Leeder and crew
(last but one op for Leeder,
tour expired end of Feb)

**15/16 Mar** *1917-0150*
*STUTTGART*
WO T J Drew
Sgt S J Rodway
PO I M Bremner
Sgt C G Dudley
Sgt H N Merrion
Sgt J M Davies
Sgt F G Walter
(aborted, port-inner failed)

**18/19 Mar** *1910-0105*
*FRANKFURT*
FS J King
Sgt D H Perrett
FO W D Menger RCAF
Sgt A W Worts
FL H J Moore RCAF
Sgt T Bathgate
FS R L Williams RAAF
Sgt W J Childs

**22/23 Mar** *1830-0005*
*FRANKFURT*

FO H Davies (DFC)
Sgt W E Lees (FE)
FS E Barlow RNZAF (N)
FS R Pritchard RAAF (WOP)
Sgt J H Kemp (BA) (DFM)
Sgt M G Smith (SO)
Sgt R E Stace RAAF (MU)
Sgt T Jones (RG)

**24/25 Mar** *1840-0220*
*BERLIN*
FO H Davies and crew

**26/27 Mar** *1930-0130*
*ESSEN*
FO H Davies and crew
Sgt A H Grainger in, Sgt
Smith out

**30/31 Mar** *2210-0130*
*NÜRNBERG*
FO H Davies and crew
Sgt F W Balge RCAF in, Sgt
Grainger out
(101 Sqn lost seven aircraft
on this disastrous raid)

**9/10 Apr** *2100-0210*
*VILLENEUVE ST GEORGES*
FL J A Keard
Sgt R Webster
FO A M Shannon RCAF
Sgt R J Crawford
Sgt J R Spowart
Sgt A Clarence
Sgt J E Worsford

**10/11 Apr** *2320-0435*
*TOURS*
FO H Davies and crew
Sgt Smith out (no 8th man)

**18/19 Apr** *2200-0245*
*ROUEN*
FO H Davies and crew

**20/21 Apr** *2325-0405*
*COLOGNE*
FO H Davies and crew

Sgt F W Balge RCAF in (SO)

**22/23 Apr** *2245-0350*
*DÜSSELDORF*
FO H Davies and crew

**24/25 Apr** *2142-0500*
*KARLSRUHE*
FO H Davies and crew

**27/28 Apr** *2145-0610*
*FRIEDRICHSHAFEN*
FL J A Keard and crew
PO D C Frazer in (SO)

**30 Apr/1 May** *2140-0235*
*MAINTENON*
PO R R Waughman
Sgt J Ormerod
PO A Cowan
Sgt I Arndell
FS N Westby
Sgt T Dewsbury
FS H S Nunn RCAF

**9/10 May** *2250-0120*
*MARDYCK*
PO J N Brown
Sgt J W Offord
FO W R Cuthbertson
Sgt T Lyth
FS J Pritchard RAAF
Sgt D Urquhart RCAF
Sgt A T Couch RCAF
Sgt C V King RAAF

**11/12 May** *2150-0130*
*HASSELT*
FO H Davies and crew

**22/23 May** *2220-0410*
*BRUNSWICK*
FO H Davies and crew

**24/25 May** *2250-0305*
*AACHEN*
FO H Davies and crew
(flew sortie on 3 engines)

**2/3 June** *2340-0305*
*BERNEVAL LE GRAND*
FO H Davies and crew

**5/6 June** *2250-0400*
*SPECIAL DUTIES PATROL*
PO J N Brown and crew
(eventually aborted due to
engines overheating)

**7/8 June** *2345-0410*
*FORÊT DE CERISY*
PO J N Brown and crew

**11/12 June** *0110-0530*
*ÉVREUX*
FL N S Wedderburn
FS R Schofield
FO R Sidwell
FO W Patrick
FO E Hunter RCAF
Sgt H W Armishaw RCAF
PO R P Booth

**14/15 June** *2055-0115*
*LE HAVRE*
PO J Harvey
Sgt J P Irvine
Sgt W R Osadchy RCAF
Sgt J L Sime
Sgt I M Hanon RCAF
Sgt A Wilson
Sgt F R Leveridge
Sgt W T Cooper
(bombs failed to release,
eventually jettisoned HEs)

**15/16 June** *2120-0025*
*BOULOGNE*
PO J Harvey and crew

**24 June** *1555-1920*
*LES HAYONS – V1 SITE*
FS P J Hyland
Sgt J Hodgson
Sgt C E Smith
Sgt J T V Moore
Sgt T Crane
Sgt E R Brown
Sgt A W Tuuri RCAF
Sgt W H Engelhardt
(all lost 28/29 July)

**27/28 June** *2149-0538*
*VITRY LE FRANÇOIS*
PO J Harvey and crew

**31 Jul/1 Aug** *2154-0118*
*FORÊT DE NIEPPE – V1 SITE*
FO L Bursell RNZAF
Sgt P J Clifford
Sgt F L S Sharp
Sgt E Reeves
Sgt W Woodbridge
FS C W Austin RCAF
FS C L Robinson RCAF
PO R J Hardacre RCAF

**3 Aug** *1145-1635*
*TROSSY-ST-MAXIMIN*
FO G M Ayatso RCAF
Sgt C T Keeling
Sgt J W Lovett
Sgt J F Andrews RCAF
FO B L Patterson RCAF
FS C F Pearce RAAF
Sgt D H Balchin RCAF
PO F G D Smith (SO)
(shot down 12/13 Aug; all PoW
except Andrews (KIA) and Smith
who was not with them this night)

**4 Aug** *1335-2140*
*PAUILLAC*
FO G M Ayatso RCAF and crew

**5 Aug** *1430-2225*
*BLAYE*
FO G M Ayatso RCAF and crew
Sgt P D Kaye in, PO Smith out

**7/8 Aug** *2116-0132*
*FONTENAY-LE-MARMION*
FO G M Ayatso RCAF and crew

**26/27 Aug** *2035-0155*
*KIEL*
Sgt S Bowater (DFC)
Sgt A W Oliver (FE)
Sgt F Campbell (N)
Sgt E Reeves (WOP)
Sgt G J H Murphy (BA)
Sgt J W Walsh (SO)
Sgt H Dickie (MU)
Sgt K R Dickinson (RG)

**29/30 Aug** *2126-0622*
*STETTIN*
Sgt S Bowater and crew

**31 Aug** *1347-1729*
*ST RIQUIER*
PO R Totham
Sgt G C Larkman
Sgt H W Emerson
FS H Johnson
Sgt R M Cavill
Sgt H Wynne
Sgt R M McPherson
Sgt W J Childs

**3 Sep** *1548-1903*
*GILZE-RIJEN AIRFIELD*
PO D H G Ireland RCAF
Sgt H J Black
PO J C Munro RCAF
FS F Coulson RCAF
Sgt C E Deatherage
Sgt E A J Davies RCAF

DV245 of 101 Squadron over Cap Gris Nez, 26 September 1944.

Sgt J K Ladley RAAF

**5 Sep** *1616-1948*
*LE HAVRE*
PO D H G Ireland and crew

**6 Sep** *1741-2114*
*LE HAVRE*
PO D H G Ireland and crew
(mission aborted over target
by Master Bomber)

**8 Sep** *0640-1044*
*LE HAVRE*
PO D H G Ireland and crew

**10 Sep** *1716-2045*
*LE HAVRE*
Sgt S Bowater and crew

**15/16 Sep** *2245-0345*
*KIEL*
Sgt S Bowater and crew

**16/17 Sep** *2217-0135*
*STEENWIJK*
Sgt S Bowater and crew

**17 Sep** *1703-1913*
*WESTKAPELLE*
Sgt S Bowater and crew

**20 Sep** *1538-1913*
*CALAIS*
Sgt S Bowater and crew

**25 Sep** *0709-0953*
*CALAIS*
Sgt S Bowater and crew

**26 Sep** *1118-1428*
*CAP GRIS NEZ*
Sgt S Bowater and crew

**3 Oct** *1339-1636*
*WESTKAPELLE*
Sgt S Bowater and crew

**6 Oct** *1739-2206*
*BREMEN*
Sgt S Bowater and crew

**7 Oct** *1212-1632*
*EMMERICH*
Sgt S Bowater and crew

**9 Oct** *1730-2248*
*BOCHUM*
PO F D McGonigle
Sgt J R McDowell (FE)
FS J E Knight RAAF
FS L Collins RAAF
FS R W L Hart RAAF
Sgt R J Beckett
Sgt D Conroy

PO J K Armour RCAF (SO)
(lost 16/17 Jan 1945 with only
Knight surviving as a PoW)

**14 Oct** *0639-1108*
*DUISBURG*
Sgt S Bowater and crew

**15 Oct** *0027-0557*
*DUISBURG*
Sgt S Bowater and crew

**19/20 Oct** *2136-0413*
*STUTTGART*
Sgt S Bowater and crew

**25 Oct** *1305-1732*
*ESSEN*
PO F D McGonigle and crew

**26 Oct** *1335-1845*
*COLOGNE*
PO J W Hunting
Sgt J F Hailstones
FS W A Granger RAAF
FS G S Gayner RAAF
Sgt J Richardson
Sgt A J Clark
Sgt E L Pierson
Sgt J Rees

**29 Oct** *1159-1451*
*DOMBERG*
Sgt S Bowater and crew

**30 Oct** *1746-2339*
*COLOGNE*
Sgt S Bowater and crew

**31 Oct** *1747-2257*
*COLOGNE*
Sgt S Bowater and crew

**2 Nov** *1604-2141*
*DÜSSELDORF*
Sgt S Bowater and crew

**6 Nov** *1124-1632*
*GELSENKIRCHEN*
Sgt S Bowater and crew

**9 Nov** *0845-1323*
*WANNE-EICKEL*
FO R D Gray
Sgt T J Stynes
FS R C Brown RCAF
Sgt J H P Jones
PO W I Strachen RCAF
FS N G Hunt RCAF
FS P J Price RCAF
FS Glick RAAF

**11 Nov** *1545-2135*
*HOESCH-BENZIN*

Sgt S Bowater and crew

**16 Nov** *1240-1728*
*DÜREN*
Sgt S Bowater and crew

**18 Nov** *1558-2117*
*WANNE-EICKEL*
SL T J Warner
Sgt W Hartwill
Sgt R W Palmer
PO D W Weston
FS J H Symonds
Sgt E C Roberts
Sgt J H Jackson
Sgt H Felix

**21 Nov** *1533-2222*
*ASCHAFFENBURG*
PO D H G Ireland and crew
Sgts J W Hodder and E J Hartman in,
Davies and Ladley out

**27 Nov** *1606-2248*
*FREIBERG*
FO J W Hunting and crew
Sgt Rees out

**2/3 Dec** *1750-0017*
*HAGEN*
FO R P Paterson RCAF
Sgt A J Wallis
FO M Ormstein
Sgt W Yeomans
Sgt M Dillon
Sgt A Greenhough
FO W E Thoroldson
RL C T Candy RCAF

**4 Dec** *1650-2305*
*KARLSRUHE*
FO K Hanney
Sgt A R Rogers
FS J L Day RAAF
Sgt H Lyon
FS R Smith
Sgt E Lipscomb
Sgt D Ingham

**5 Dec** *1811-2359*
*SOEST*
FO J W Hunting and crew

**12 Dec** *1638-2234*
*ESSEN*
FO K Hanney and crew

**15 Dec** *1439-2110*
*LUDWIGSHAVEN*
FO K Hanney and crew

**17 Dec** *1525-2257*
*ULM*
FO K Hanney and crew and
Sgt D Cooper (SO)

**28 Dec** *1529-2138*
*BONN*
FO W W Watt
Sgt R E A Winstone (FE)
Sgt S R Allen (N)
Sgt G A Stephens (WOP)
FO A W Stuart (BA)
Sgt J A Slater (MU)
Sgt D Mortimer (RG)
(all lost 23 Feb 1945)

**31 Dec** *1503-2135*
*OSTERFELD*
FO K Hanney and crew

## 1945

**2 Jan** *1520-2337*
*NÜRNBERG*
FL R H H Wilder
Sgt J Dutton
FO J A Blackhall
Sgt K Gough
FO R Elliott
Sgt R J Brown
Sgt L Drill
Sgt A C Neve

**5/6 Jan** *1848-0046*
*HANNOVER*
FO R P Paterson and crew
Sgts D Nelson and R Blitz in,
Sgt Wallis and FL Candy out

**6 Jan** *1559-2206*
*HANAU*
FO H G H Meadows
Sgt D Thornhill
FO J T Burke
FS K Fritton
FS K R Rudge
Sgt R Fisher
Sgt J W Feast

**16/17 Jan** *1746-0133*
*ZEITZ*
FO K E Roberts RAAF
Sgt L Schofield
Sgt S E Adams
WO W Hawke RAAF
Sgt A Lister
Sgt S Arnold
Sgt H Campbell
Sgt O S Cleyn RCAF

**22 Jan** *1600-2249*
*LUDWIGSHAVEN*
FO H I Davis
Sgt A H Woodier (FE)
Sgt S C Campbell
Sgt P Hammond
Sgt M H Pollard
Sgt J McCafferty
Sgt W Paul
Sgt W W Lemke RCAF

**3 Feb** *1635-1824*
*BOTTROP*
FO K Hanney and crew
(aborted)

**7/8 Feb** *1911-0028*
*KLEVE*
FO K Hanney and crew

**13/14 Feb** *2143-0705*
*DRESDEN*
FO K Hanney and crew
PO J Kerr (2P) and Sgt
F Smith in as SO

**14/15 Feb** *2019-0510*
*CHEMNITZ*
FO K Hanney and crew

**20/21 Feb** *2151-0445*
*DORTMUND*
FO K Hanney and crew

**21/22 Feb** *1957-0154*
*DUISBURG*
FO R A Andrew
Sgt A Hammond RCAF
FO E C Lobsinger RCAF
Sgt W Myers
FO E A Hamilton RCAF
FS J Mess RCAF
FS S A LaLonde RCAF
Sgt H van Geffen

**23/24 Feb** *1607-0001*
*PFORZHEIM*
FO G Withenshaw RCAF
Sgt A H Halliday
FL B H Lapointe RCAF
Sgt A Parsons
FO J R Drewery RCAF (BA)
FS W H Robinson RCAF
FS J E Stead
PO E Graumann RCAF (SO)

**2 Mar** *0709-1240*
*COLOGNE*
PO G Withenshaw and crew
PO Graumann out

**5/6 Mar** *1653-0209*
*CHEMNITZ*
FL K Hanney and crew
FS R A Bird in, Rogers out

**7/8 Mar** *1713-0303*
*DESSAU*
FO L W Rodger RCAF
Sgt W A Beach
FO A J Knebel RCAF
PO L A Pool
FO N A Jevne RCAF
FS J V Mills
Sgt R Krull

**8/9 Mar** *1721-0110*
*KASSEL*
FS J A Kell
Sgt J Ness RCAF
WO W Rusby
Sgt E Baines
Sgt C Adams
PO E Marshall
Sgt W West RCAF

**11 Mar** *1152-1655*
*ESSEN*
FL K Hanney and crew

**12 Mar** *1312-1905*
*DORTMUND*
FL K Hanney and crew

**13 Mar** *1745-2329*
*DAHLBURSCH*
FL K Hanney and crew

**16/17 Mar** *1741-0149*
*NÜRNBERG*
FO R P Paterson and crew

**21 Mar** *0207-0702*
*HEIDE*
SL K F Flint (DFC)
Sgt J E Crawford
FO J P Bannister (DFC)
FS I S Sangster
FO A Smith
FS C J Clark
FS E Iles
FO J C Wilson RCAF

**22 Mar** *0058-0655*
*BRUCH STRASSE*
PO G Withenshaw and crew
Sgt L N Lemke in (SO)

**23 Mar** *0658-*
*BREMEN*
FO R R Little RCAF
Sgt A J Clifton (FE)
FO J G Lee RCAF (N)
Sgt H Woodards (WOP)
FO W H Brooks RCAF (BA)
Sgt P S Nelson (MU)
Sgt T Churchill (RG)
(all killed)

DV245 being refuelled and bombed-up in March 1945, shortly before her demise. She was also the last Lancaster lost by 101 Squadron.

# DV302
# HARRY

DV302 was one of 101 Squadron's two centurion Lancasters; its rival being DV245. It was a Metro Vickers-built Lancaster Mark I, completed by A V Roe in September 1943, with four Merlin 22 engines. Sent to 32 MU at St Athan on 1 October, it was then assigned to 101 Squadron based at Ludford Magna, Lincolnshire, on 7 November.

Given the squadron code letters of SR, it became H-Harry when given its personal identity letter, although it was sometimes referred to as H-Howe. Arriving on the squadron during the Battle of Berlin it is not surprising to learn that during the aircraft's first 25 operations over Germany, no fewer than 16 were against the Big City. In fact its first six missions were to Berlin and, of its first 18, 15 were to the German capital.

On 18 November 1943, the aircraft took its first trip, skippered by a New Zealander, Flying Officer D H Todd, later Flight Lieutenant DFC. Douglas Todd and three of his crew had earlier been with 98 Squadron, as fellow New Zealander Vic Viggers recalled:

'Our first operational sortie was with 98 Squadron flying B25 Mitchells, and attacking gun emplacements on the Dutch and French coasts. As volunteer aircrew for heavy bombers were being called for, we applied. After going through 1667 Conversion Unit we went to 101 Squadron and completed our tour of 30 operations – 11 of them to Berlin.

'I do remember Toddy had his aircraft preferences and referred to *Harry* as a very air worthy aircraft backed-up, of course, by a competent and caring ground crew. Sadly Doug Todd was killed in a hit-and-run accident in Palmeston North, New Zealand, in the 1970s.

'Our first special operator, Spafford, decided to change to another crew after our first four trips and was shot down and killed the very next night.'

Doug Todd took DV302 on nine of his first 16 sorties and

at the end of their tour, Viggers, Ken Bardell and Harry Whittle all received DFCs, Stan Powell the DFM. Powell's citation recorded:

FO D H Todd RNZAF took DV302 on her first op, to Berlin, on 18/19 October 1943.

'With ten attacks on Berlin to his credit, Sergeant Powell had completed 27 sorties on his first operational tour as a Flight Engineer with a splendid keenness and efficiency. He has at all times displayed a high degree of skill and initiative to his Captain in emergency. Sergeant Powell sets his mind to the task in hand fearlessly and with a fine spirit of determination which has inspired confidence and been a magnificent example to the crew. The courage and devotion to duty this NCO has displayed is worthy of the highest praise and fully merits this recommendation for an award of the Distinguished Flying Medal.'

DV302's more usual crew then became that of Flight Sergeant (then P/O) E T Holland RAAF who did 20 trips in the aircraft. Flying Officer J Kinman was the next regular skipper for ten trips, although his first in DV302 (as second pilot on his experience trip), was aborted soon after take-off on 12 June 1944, the port outer engine failing. Flight Sergeant A L Plimmer, Kinman's bomb aimer, was later wounded during a daylight sortie on 15 August, although they were not in DV302 on this occasion. Despite a painful wound to his right arm, he continued to direct Kinman and completed an accurate

Todd's wireless operator, Vic Viggers RNZAF. Both he and his pilot won DFCs with 101 Squadron.

bombing attack. For this, Albert Plimmer received the DFM.

Not surprisingly, the reader will find that several crews who flew *The Saint* (DV245) in 101 Squadron, also flew *Harry*, such as Flying Officer H Davies and R E Ireland RCAF. Like *The Saint, Harry* was operated as an ABC-equipped Lancaster, often flying with an eighth aircrew member, the German-speaking ABC operator, whose job it was to locate German R/T wavelengths then confuse night fighter crews and their ground controllers by either jamming the frequencies or giving out fake orders.

DV302 flew on special duties during the night of D-Day followed by attacks on V1 rocket sites throughout that fateful month of June. *Harry* became Cat AC on 5 July 1944 and went to ROS for overhaul but was back on 101's strength ten days later. However, the machine was out of action for most of August, so was most probably having a major service. Pilot Officer Arthur E "Bill"

Netting took over DV302 in late August, flying no less than 29 sorties in it, receiving the DFC. The navigator, Sergeant Ernest Cantwell received the DFM, and recorded recollections of the Lanc – which they called *Howe*:

'Shortly after joining 101 in July 1944 we were invited to take on H-Howe, a veteran of nearly 60 ops. We subsequently looked it over and unanimously decided we would take it in preference to a new one. If sentiment came into our decision it was a wise one, for H-Howe safely took us through 30 ops out of a tour of 32. Our WOP, Cyril Complin, went sick and missed two trips so we [as a crew] did two extra trips in order that he would not have to complete his 30 with a strange crew. That cost him a few pints!

'Our first op was to Stettin, lasting some nine hours during which time we were coned in searchlights over the target. However, the "old boy" responded faithfully to the manoeuvres the skipper asked of him to escape the glare and hostility focused on us. We returned to base feeling that we had well and truly been initiated into what operational flying was all about.

'Another incident still fairly vivid was a daylight to Essen when we were alerted over the target by the mid-upper, that a stick of bombs was falling on us from an aircraft above. One of them struck a glancing blow to the port-inner engine and removed the propeller nose cone. Fortunately little further damage was inflicted and the faithful Merlin continued to function. We were later informed that it had most likely been a tail-fused 1,000 pounder.

'Our base at Ludford Magna was equipped with "Fido" [Fog Investigation Dispersal Operation – burning petrol to light up a runway] and returning on another occasion in thick fog, it was used to aid our landing. It was quite an experience landing between tracks of burning petrol and I recall watching the skipper struggling to control against the turbulence.

'With regard to the fighter painted on the nose of *Howe*, we were told that the previous crew were credited with shooting down the first enemy aircraft with the .5 nose gun-turret fitted on it.

Vic Viggers, Bill O'Dwyer, Doug Todd and Bill Fraser.

FO A E Netting and crew, from left to right: M A Ordway, C H N Complin, E A Cantwell, Netting, P R Gunter, V R Burrill and T C Brown.

RCAF special and Jimmy Harris, the flight engineer, who had crash-landed in England and France respectively while spare-bodding during Christmas week when our skipper was in hospital with tonsillitis.

'As we reached the target three minutes early, we had to do an orbit, always dicey over the target, so as to be on the correct heading to bomb on the sky markers at 17,500 feet. There was ten-tenths cloud.

'Over the target, oxygen to the skipper and engineer cut out and this caused Jimmy to become oxygen-happy on the way home as we climbed to 20,000 feet to clear the front. Then the heating packed up so we all froze with icicles forming on eyebrows and anywhere that breath condensed – one from my mouthpiece extended down for ten inches before breaking off.

'Over Ludford, one under-cart leg would not lock down until we used emergency air. Despite the relatively minor mechanical problems, H-Howe proved its mettle once again by getting its crew home safely after eight hours, 50 minutes in the air.

'F/O A "Woody" Woodhart had joined us as bomb aimer after Col Donaghue, [RAAF] our regular B/A had baled out while spare bod with S/L [T J] Warner on the Boxing Day raid to St Vith, and been taken prisoner. Woody, whose previous crew had broken up following a crash in which several were injured, and now with only 12 more trips to do, was inclined to regret having joined a sprog Aussie crew with only eight up at that time. Munich was our second orbit in the three trips he had done with us. We had been hit by flak over France on the way home from Nürnberg on 2 January by the US (friendly?) anti-aircraft gunners understandably (to all but the crews of the Lancs shot down). We were then diverted to Catfoss where we landed after a little location trouble with the gauges showing empty.

'We had overshot after "Kangaroo" Kurtzer, the skipper, had bounced the kite twice before going round again on return from the Hanau trip on 6 January. Johnnie was an excellent skipper who spoke fluent German as all his grandparents were born there. He excelled in keeping to a pre-

Apparently the crew were entertained by the manufacturers for their gun's first success.'

*Howe*, or *Harry*, went on operating until 30 April 1945, the date it went to 46 MU at Lossiemouth. The aircraft achieved 98 ops by the time *Sugar* had completed her 100th, *Harry's* own 100th coming on 7/8 January 1945, when Pilot Officer J A Kurtzer RAAF (DFC) took it to Munich. In all it is reputed to have flown 121 operational sorties, although the list might indicate at least one more.

One of Johnny Kurtzer's crew was John Fletcher, the wireless operator. He sent me the following account of that 100th trip:

'Our 'plane, C-Charlie, having broken its back when it crashed at Ludford the previous week, with F/O West at the controls, trying to land in a snow storm while on a training flight, we were taking whatever kite was available. Wally Stoney, the outstanding Chiefie responsible for "Charlie", and the rest of our ground crew, were making sure we had a good one to fly.

'January 7, 1945, Munich the target, and we set out at 1805 hours in H-Howe on its 100th trip. We immediately struck a cold front with severe icing until we cleared it at 14,000 feet. Ice forming on the ABC aerials, then breaking away and hitting the roof of the kite with loud bangs was rather trying on the nerves, especially for a relatively new crew in a strange aircraft with Munich the target. This was even more so for both John Fochs, the

arranged plan by flying us out of a blue light controlled cone over Berlin in a spiral dive from 20,000 to 500 feet, pulling out being a three-man effort. They had taken up their positions before the G-force became prohibitive. We had seen too many others caught like a moth in a spider's web to fancy our chances of survival. His one weakness was landing during which some of the crew took up crash positions as he normally bounced at least twice – hence his nickname of Kangaroo – and frequently had to go round again.'

After the 100th sortie there appears to be few regular crews flying the aircraft which may well be a sign of its ageing, but it still achieved some long trips, notably to Chemnitz, Dessau, Nürnberg and an eight-hour sortie to Potsdam on 14/15 April 1945. With 121 bombs painted on its nose, plus a long service medal ribbon applied by its faithful ground crew (and what looks like a Ju88 falling in flames, although there is no surviving reference to any successful combat), DV302 was finally Struck off Charge on 15 January 1947.

DV302 with Sgt M A "Basil" Ordway by his mid-upper turret. Note ABC aerials.

It is understood that one of the aircraft's Merlin engines still survives. A former Lancaster pilot named Mackenzie Hamilton owned a 1930 Rolls-Royce Merlin Competition Roadster, but by 1946 its Kestrel engine was beyond repair. Knowing that Lancasters were being broken up at Lossiemouth, Hamilton went along and managed to obtain DV302's port-inner engine, which he managed to squeeze into the car's chassis. Hamilton was killed in a flying accident in 1965; in 1990 the car was bought by a new owner, for the cost of £48,000, plus commission and VAT!

## 101 SQUADRON
## 1943

**18/19 Nov** *1710-0140*
*BERLIN*
FO D H Todd RNZAF (DFC)
Sgt S Powell (FE) (DFM)
FO W Frazer (N)
FO V C Viggers RNZAF (DFC)
Sgt K H Bardell (BA) (DFC)
Sgt H R Whittle (MU) (DFC)
FS W M O'Dwyer (RG)
FO G L Spafford (SO)

**22 Nov** *1700-2340*
*BERLIN*
FS E J Trotter
Sgt J Rawcliffe
FO D Holder
Sgt J T Broad
Sgt V Pullen
Sgt A Kirton
Sgt K Archibald

**23 Nov** *1700-2329*
*BERLIN*
FL T W Rowland
Sgt R Allison (FE)
FO D G Higgs (N)
Sgt P H Lamprey (WOP)
FS W H Yuill (BA)
Sgt R Bateman (MU)
Sgt H G Clements (RG)
FO B Wilkinson (SO)
(all lost except Wilkinson on
14/15 January 1944)

**26/27 Nov** *1700-0110*
*BERLIN*
FO D H Todd and crew
PO W M Shubic and FO
P J W Raine in, O'Dwyer
and Spafford out

**2/3 Dec** *1657-0027*
*BERLIN*
FS K B Corkhill
Sgt E A F Cole
Sgt K G Thompson
Sgt H Street
Sgt R M Gundy RCAF
Sgt L P Swales
Sgt F G Welsh
Sgt G E H Schultz

**16/17 Dec** *1625-0015*
*BERLIN*
FO D H Todd and crew
O'Dwyer back, Shubic out

**20 Dec** *1720-2325*
*FRANKFURT*
FO D H Todd and crew
FL W F J Hill in, O'Dwyer out

**24 Dec** *0035-0815*
*BERLIN*
FS D Langford
Sgt H Swift
Sgt J E Price
Sgt F Urch
FS H W Davy
Sgt G A Wilby
Sgt H R Riley
Sgt D Hoffman

**29 Dec** *1710-2355*
*BERLIN*
FO D H Todd and crew
O'Dwyer back, Hill out

## 1944

**2 Jan** *0015-0815*
*BERLIN*
FO D H Todd and crew
O'Dwyer out, Sgt P J Drought in

**2/3 Jan** *2345-0650*
*BERLIN*
FO D H Todd and crew
FS R Teitz RAAF in, Sgt Drought out

**14 Jan** *1645-2235*
*BRUNSWICK*
FO D H Todd and crew
O'Dwyer back, Teitz out;
FS P S W Napier RAAF
in, FO Raine out

**20/21 Jan** *1640-0001*
*BERLIN*
FS L Kidd RAAF
FS J Hall (FE)
FS F T Sanderson RAAF (N)
Sgt T M Cavender RAAF (WOP)
FS K F Stanton RAAF (AB)
Sgt J A Watt RAAF (MU)
Sgt R Wilson (RG)
PO O Fischl (SO)

**21/22 Jan** *2010-0310*
*MAGDEBURG*
FS A J Sandford
Sgt A H Smallman
Sgt E Barron
Sgt T D Simpson
Sgt R T Ottewell
Sgt K Bartholomew
Sgt E H Alcock
Sgt E H Manners

**27/28 Jan** *1740-0205*
*BERLIN*
FS K B Corkhill and crew
Sgts H Manser and P N D Skingly
in, Street and Schultz out

**29 Jan** *0020-0835*
*BERLIN*
FO D H Todd and crew
Sgt G T J Heath in,
O'Dwyer out

**30/31 Jan** *1720-0005*
*BERLIN*
FS K B Corkhill and crew

**15/16 Feb** *1730-0000*
*BERLIN*
FS E T Holland RAAF
Sgt T Haycock
FS H Scott RAAF
FS A P Farquharson RAAF
FS I R Smith RAAF
Sgt A M McCartney
Sgt V G Smith RAAF

**20/21 Feb** *2345-0730*
*STUTTGART*
FS E T Holland and crew
and Sgt H Docherty (SO)

**24/25 Feb** *2030-0500*
*SCHWEINFURT*
FS E T Holland and crew

**25/26 Feb** *2120-0440*
*AUGSBURG*
FS E T Holland and crew

**15/16 Mar** *1910-0330*
*STUTTGART*
PO E T Holland and crew
FS R J Hardacre in, Sgt
Docherty out

**18/19 Mar** *1900-0045*
*FRANKFURT*
PO E T Holland and crew
PL L P Whymark in, Sgt
McCartney out

**22/23 Mar** *1825-0010*
*FRANKFURT*
PO E T Holland and crew

**24/25 Mar** *1900-0150*
*BERLIN*

PO E T Holland and crew
Sgt M G Smith (SO) in,
FS Hardacre out

**26/27 Mar** *1940-0025*
*ESSEN*
PO E T Holland and crew
Sgt R W Sharp (2P)

**30/31 Mar** *2215-0635*
*NÜRNBERG*
PO E T Holland and crew
FS Hardacre back, Smith out

**10/11 Apr** *2330-0455*
*AULNOYE*
PO E T Holland and crew
FS Hardacre out

**11/12 Apr** *2020-0020*
*AACHEN*
PO E T Holland and crew
FS Hardacre back

**18/19 Apr** *2145-0155*
*ROUEN*
FS E A Askew
Sgt T B Johnstone
Sgt C W Rolfe
Sgt S N Hewitt
Sgt W S Newman
Sgt E J Delaney RCAF
Sgt S Morford

**20/21 Apr** *2320-0355*
*COLOGNE*
PO E T Holland and crew

**22/23 Apr** *2305-0500*
*BRUNSWICK*
PO D C Rippon
Sgt R A Smith
Sgt R W Snell
Sgt B Whitehead
FO F J Lynam
Sgt R D Stack
Sgt W T R Hunter
PO H H King RCAF
(all except King lost 30
June/1 July)

**24/25 Apr** *2120-0400*
*KARLSRUHE*
PO E T Holland and crew

**26/27 Apr** *2130-0630*
*SCHWEINFURT*
PO E T Holland and crew

**27/28 Apr** *2150-0630*
*FRIEDRICHSHAFEN*
PO K Fillingham
Sgt C D Goodliffe
FO S J Licquorish RCAF
Sgt P R Medway
FO K D Connell RCAF
Sgt J Soulsby
Sgt J Law
FS A M Marks

**3/4 May** *2200-0400*
*MAILLY-LE-CAMP*
PO T A Welsby
Sgt J A Parker
FO F A Pierce
Sgt T R Hurst
Sgt M T Boreham RCAF
Sgt R Cox
Sgt G A Wallace
FS R Laurie RAAF

**21/22 May** *2215-0250*
*DUISBURG*
PO R R Waughman
Sgt J Ormerod
PO A Cowan
Sgt I Arndell
FS N Westby
Sgt T Dewsbury

FS H S Nunn RCAF
Sgt E H Manners

**22/23 May** *2225-0320*
*DORTMUND*
PO R R Waughman and crew

**24/25 May** *2350-0430*
*AACHEN*
PO E T Holland and crew
Sgt W O Ross in, PO
Whymark out

**28 May** *0010-0425*
*AACHEN*
PO E T Holland and crew

**2/3 June** *2340-0335*
*TRAPPES*
PO E T Holland and crew

**5/6 June** *2220-0535*
*SPECIAL DUTIES*
FL R N Knights
Sgt W Ferry
FS B Pinner
FS M E Bromley
FS J O'Regan
Sgt F W Morgan
FS H S Mann RCAF
FO H L Croisette

**8/9 June** *2325-0340*
*FORÊT DE CERISY*
PO E T Holland and crew

**12/13 June** *2245-0255*
*GELSENKIRCHEN*
PO L P Bateman RCAF
Sgt A Fazacherley
WO W E Buie RCAF
FS E Crook
FO F C Brooks RCAF
WO J J Byrne
Sgt J V Browne
Sgt H Docherty

**14/15 June** *2048-0007*
*LE HAVRE*
PO D C Rippon and crew

**24 June** *1605-1930*
*LES HAYONS – V1 SITE*
FO J Kinman
Sgt H Mawson
FS M Gisby
Sgt E E Evans
Sgt A L Pimmer (DFM)
Sgt T Wright
Sgt S C Trevis
Sgt J P Auer

**25 June** *0730-1115*
*LIGESCOURT – V1 SITE*
FO J Kinman and crew

**28 June** *0045-0500*
*VAIRIES*
FO J Kinman and crew

**29 June** *1210-1555*
*SIRACOURT – V1 SITE*
FO J Kinman and crew

**30 June/1 July** *2224-0323*
*VIERZON RAIL YARDS*
FO J Kinman and crew

**4/5 July** *2256-0413*
*VILLENEUVE ST GEORGE*
FO J Kinman and crew

**23/25 July** *2240-0345*
*KIEL*
FO J Kinman and crew

**24/25 July** *2240-0350*
*STUTTGART*
FO J Kinman and crew
(aborted due to u/s rear turret)

**29 July** *0225-0540*
*FORÊT DE NIEPPE*
FO J Kinman and crew

**31 July/1 Aug** *2155-0105*
*FORÊT DE NIEPPE*
FO J Kinman and crew
FL D M MacDonald RCAF in,
Sgt Evans out

**29/30 Aug** *2150-0610*
*STETTIN*
PO A E Netting (DFC)
Sgt T C Brown (FE)
Sgt E H A Cantwell (N) (DFC)
Sgt C H N Complin (WOP)
Sgt P R Gunter (BA)
Sgt M A Ordway (MU)
Sgt V R Burrill RCAF (RG)
Sgt J E C Lodge (SO)

**3 Sep** *1549-2011*
*GILZE-RIJEN AIRFIELD*
PO A E Netting and crew

**6 Sep** *1749-2059*
*LE HAVRE*
PO A E Netting and crew
(abandoned by controller)

**8 Sep** *0647-1048*
*LE HAVRE*
PO R Totham
Sgt R C Larkman
Sgt H W Emerson
FS H Johnson
FS R M Caville
Sgt H Wynne
Sgt R M McPherson
Sgt Hawkins
(abandoned due to weather)

**10 Sep** *1701-2037*
*LE HAVRE*
PO A E Netting and crew

**11/12 Sep** *2108-0241*
*DARMSTADT*
PO A E Netting and crew

**16/17 Sep** *2130-0124*
*HOPSTEN AIRFIELD*
Op Market Garden
PO A E Netting and crew

**20 Sep** *1544-1851*
*CALAIS*
PO A E Netting and crew

**25 Sep** *0651-1044*
*CALAIS*
PO A E Netting and crew
(abandoned due to weather)

**26 Sep** *1059-1353*
*CAP GRIS NEZ*
PO A E Netting and crew

**5/6 Oct** *1850-0116*
*SAARBRÜCKEN*
PO W A McLenaghan RCAF
Sgt C G Vicary (DFM)
PO J K Balcombe RCAF
WO L F Kennedy RCAF
Sgt J D Lamb
Sgt F R Boyd RCAF
Sgt F R Fletcher RCAF
PO E Grauman RCAF
(abandoned; bomb-doors
failed to open over target)
(all PoWs – shot down 23/24 Feb 1945)

**6 Oct** *1746-2215*
*BREMEN*
FO L James
Sgt W G Orr
FS L R Coleman RCAF
FS G H Taylor
FS R S Davies

FS Gordon
FS G Williams RCAF
Sgt L R Hall

**7 Oct** *1216-1643*
*EMMERICH*
FO L James
Sgt A Yorrington
FO R D Irving RCAF
Sgt L L Wright
PO H G Bullock RCAF
Sgt E W Dean RCAF
Sgt A R Walker
Sgt D Burnett

**14 Oct** *0648-1139*
*DUISBURG*
FO R E Ireland RCAF
Sgt H J Black
FS R E Hine RCAF
PO J C Munro RCAF
FS F Coulson RCAF
FS G E Deatherage RCAF
FS K A Davies RCAF
FS J K Ladley RCAF

**14/15 Oct** *2236-0341*
*DUISBURG*
PO A E Netting and crew
Sgt B C Reeves in, Sgt Complin out

**15 Oct** *1731-2145*
*WILHELMSHAVEN*
PO A E Netting and crew

**19/20 Oct** *2132-0415*
*STUTTGART*
PO A E Netting and crew
Complin back, Reeves out

**23 Oct** *1619-2151*
*ESSEN*
PO A E Netting and crew

**25 Oct** *1207-1745*
*ESSEN*
PO A E Netting and crew

**28 Oct** *1327-1835*
*COLOGNE*
PO A E Netting and crew

**30 Oct** *1740-2355*
*COLOGNE*
PO A E Netting and crew

**31 Oct** *1805-2303*
*COLOGNE*
PO A E Netting and crew

**2 Nov** *1601-2144*
*DÜSSELDORF*
SL I McLeod-Selkirk
Sgt F Milton
FO R C Pitman
Sgt A Pringle
FO G W Hess RCAF
Sgt F W Hughes
Sgt R Hurley
Sgt H Van Geffen

**4 Nov** *1713-2202*
*BOCHUM*
PO A E Netting and crew

**6 Nov** *1122-1626*
*GELSENKIRCHEN*
PO A E Netting and crew

**9 Nov** *0746-1301*
*WANNE-EICKEL*
PO A E Netting and crew

**11 Nov** *1601-2143*
*HOESCH / DORTMUND*
PO A E Netting and crew

**16 Nov** *1242-1736*
*DÜREN*
PO A E Netting and crew

# DV302 HARRY

The crew that took DV302 on her 100th op. From left to right: A L Woodhart, J W Fletcher, J S Alexander, J A Kurtzer DFC, J Harris, J C H Dyke and G H Honeysett.

**21 Nov** *1523-2216*
ASCHAFFENBURG
PO A E Netting and crew

**27 Nov** *1621-2308*
FREIBURG
PO R A Lowe RCAF
Sgt E J Rogers
FS B J Brophy RCAF
Sgt W A Perry
FO R G Masters RCAF
Sgt C J Mountjoy
Sgt A J Clutchy RCAF

**29 Nov** *1209-1729*
DORTMUND
PO V W Ashes RAAF
Sgt G Kennedy
FS A Watt
FS W J Gurner RAAF
Sgt A W Robinson
Sgt J P Fellows
Sgt J Pringle

**30 Nov** *1654-2204*
DUISBURG
FO R A W Harrison
Sgt J B Breare
FS R J Swain
FS K E McDonnell
Sgt G H Hillman
Sgt D J Mackay
Sgt S Stephens
Sgt F Smith
(Breare, Swain, Hillman, Mackay and Smith all lost following collision with a 101 Sqn Lanc 1/2 Feb 1945)

**2 Dec** *1736-2348*
HAGEN
FO A E Netting and crew

**4 Dec** *1651-2318*
KARLSRUHE
FO A E Netting and crew

**6/7 Dec** *1645-0035*
LEUNA / MERSEBURG
FO A E Netting and crew
PO H I Davies (2P)

**12 Dec** *1610-2056*
ESSEN
FO A E Netting and crew

**15 Dec** *1425-2056*
LUDWIGSHAVEN
FO A E Netting and crew

**17 Dec** *1518-2326*
ULM
PO K J Brookin
Sgt H J Hadingham
Sgt F Edwards
Sgt J Rogerson
FS V A Maki
Sgt J Brown
Sgt S Borthwick

**28 Dec** *1531-2059*
BONN
WC M H deL Everest
Sgt T Murray
FO A Jeffcoat
Sgt R Whiteford
FO R Shephern
Sgt W H Horner
Sgt J W Holder

**29 Dec** *1508-2110*
SCHOLVEN
FO C G Rogers
Sgt J Gorman

FS R Newnham RAAF
PO R Rowland
Sgt E A Mason
Sgt W J Calvert
Sgt R T Small
PO J McDermott

## 1945

**2 Jan** *1504-2309*
NÜRNBERG
FO W A McLenaghan and crew
FO R Inceberg RCAF and FO S Brookes in, Sgt Lamb and PO Grauman out

**5/6 Jan** *1851-0040*
HANNOVER
FO W A McLenaghan and crew
FO Brookes out

**6 Jan** *1557-2210*
HANAU
FO W A McLenaghan and crew

**7/8 Jan** *1849-0337*
MUNICH
PO J A Kurtzer RAAF (DFC)
Sgt J Harris (FE)
FS G H Honeysett RAAF (N)
FS J W Fletcher (WOP)
FO A L Woodhart (BA)
FS J C H Dyke RAAF (MU)
FS J S Alexander RAAF (RG)
Sgt J O S Fochs RCAF (SO)

**16/17 Jan** *1744-0300*
BRUX
FO W A McLenaghan and crew
Sgt H Felik in

**28/29 Jan** *1940-0309*
STUTTGART
FO W A McLenaghan and crew
Sgt H Wells in, Sgt Felik out

**1 Feb** *1546-2233*
LUDWIGSHAVEN
FO W A McLenaghan and crew
Sgt Wells out

**2 Feb** *1546-2234*
WIESBADEN
FO W A McLenaghan and crew
Sgt Van Geffen in; abandoned at 2127 – Gee u/s

**7/8 Feb** *1905-0031*
KLEVE
PO J D Robinson
Sgt S A Lewis
FS C G Scott RCAF
WO N W Berger RCAF
FO J R Weinfield RCAF
FS S A Spence RCAF
FS J C Spencer RCAF

**14/15 Feb** *2015-0520*
CHEMNITZ
FO H J West
PO K D J Ward
FL W O Mitchell
Sgt R A Kemshall
Sgt H D Budd
Sgt G A Duncan
Sgt R F Milroy
FO H Walker RCAF

**20/21 Feb** *2039-0415*
DORTMUND
FO H I Davies
Sgt A H Woodier (FE)

DV302 with the 'NAAFI Gang' at the end of the war. 121 bomb symbols, one enemy aircraft shot down, and a long service medal ribbon.

FS F Campbell
Sgt F Hammond
FS M H Pollard
Sgt J McCafferty
Sgt W Paul
Sgt L W Lemke RCAF

**21/22 Feb** *1940-0125*
DUISBURG
FO H J West and crew
FO H G Sheath in, FL
Mitchell out

**23 Feb** *1550-2339*
PFORZHEIM
FO H J West and crew

**1 Mar** *1140-1822*
MANNHEIM
FO E W Mackay RCAF
Sgt N H Allpress
FlO G L Hillier RCAF
FS J Kevac RCAF
FO R G Millward RCAF
Sgt R S Hadden
Sgt B Girwing RCAF

**2 Mar** *0647-1219*
COLOGNE
FO R L Black RCAF
Sgt J E McDonald
FS W V McIntyre RCAF
Sgt E S Stanley

FS C E Wade RCAF
FS G Nutkins RCAF
FS C P Rolfe RCAF

**5/6 Mar** *1633-0228*
CHEMNITZ
PO P G L Collett RAAF
FS R Matin
FS W H Horner RAAF
FS A Conden
FS M Hann RAAF
Sgt M Smedley RAAF
PO A W Thompson RAAF
FO C D Ruppell

**7/8 Mar** *1657-0255*
DESSAU
FO W K Weightman
Sgt R D Bond
PO J D Browne
Sgt R Burtaft
PO E Davies
Sgt A P Ainley
Sgt C Amory

**8/9 Mar** *1716-0048*
KASSEL
FO W K Weightman and crew

**13 Mar** *1740-2330*
DAHLBURSCH
FO H I Davies and crew

**15/16 Mar** *1723-0106*
MISBURG
PO P G L Collett and crew
FO J C Wilson RCAF in,
FO Ruppell out

**16/17 Mar** *1730-0210*
NÜRNBERG
FL J R Crooke RCAF
Sgt J G Wheeler
FS F Graham
FS A Atkinson
FO A R Nevin RCAF
Sgt R F Poulson
Sgt R K O'Brien
FS J Engler RCAF

**19 Mar** *0059-0759*
HANAU
PO P G L Collett and crew

**21 Mar** *0211-0774*
HEIDE
FO E W Mackay and crew
FO A L Schaefer RCAF in (SO)

**31 Mar** *0615-1146*
HAMBURG
FL H J West and crew
Sgt C Lambie and FO H G
Sheath in, PO Ward and FL
Mitchell out

**9/10 Apr** *1938-0131*
KIEL
FL H J West and crew

**14/15 Apr** *1824-0305*
POTSDAM
FL H J West and crew

**18 Apr** *1039-1452*
HELIGOLAND
FL H J West and crew

# ED588 GEORGE

A Mark III Lancaster with four Merlin XX engines, ED588 was an Avro-built machine assigned to 97 Squadron at Coningsby, Lincolnshire, on 8 February 1943. However, within two days it had gone Cat AC and was not returned to 97 until 6 March, by which time the unit had moved to Woodall Spa. If anyone thought this poor start an ill-omen they would have been wrong.

The squadron records show its first operational sortie was flown on the night of 26 March with Sergeant K Brown and his crew taking it to Duisburg. Although coded with 97's OF, it is shown as having the individual letter 'E' in the records but by the next night it was being shown as 'H'. In all it completed eight operations with 97 Squadron during March and April, six with Ken Brown (who was to win the DFM) in control, including a trip to Kiel on 4/6 April during which another Lancaster fired a burst at it north of Heligoland. Luckily the air-gunner missed.

On 10/11 April a sortie to Frankfurt was abandoned after about 1½ hours due to engine trouble. After a trip to Italy a couple of nights later, ED588 was re-assigned to 50 Squadron at RAF Skellingthorpe, Lincolnshire, where its new squadron codes became VN, together with a new individual letter – G for George.

Now in the guise of VN-G, ED588 made its first sortie with 50 Squadron on the last night of April with Sergeant D A Duncan, who became its more-or-less regular pilot until August, completing perhaps 16 sorties in it, with some others being aborted due to technical problems. Some of these were noted as 'Not Completed', so one must assume that most of these were not counted or allowed. During this period *George* was hit and damaged by flak on at least two occasions. Douglas Duncan was commissioned and was awarded the DFC.

During the winter, Flying Officer F B M Wilson flew *George* several times, including three ops to Berlin, with the aircraft going to this target on 15 occasions during Bomber Command's Battle of Berlin. One trip – 2/3 December – the mid-upper gunner's oxygen failed and he fell unconscious but recovered later. In early 1944 Flight

FL E Berry DFC. He flew many ops in ED588 in early 1944.

Sergeant E Berry RAAF took *George* regularly to targets in Germany and France – 18 being consecutive during February-April. Ernest Berry was commissioned halfway through this period, and in May and June added a further six trips in *George*. He later received the DFC.

Brian Holmes, Berry's Flight Engineer, recalled the following:

'I was Ernie Berry's Flight Engineer, although for some reason we called him "Bill", but then I was called "Bob"! We did most of our tour in her before going our separate ways. [Brian mentioned

Ernie Berry and crew. From left to right: W Bull, P M N Honeywood, R Phillips, R Hamilton, Berry, Howarth. The aircraft is a Wellington of 29 OTU.

'Bill Enoch and crew took over after I had finished my tour of ops. I took Bill on his first experience trip as second pilot, and I believe he later completed his tour successfully.'

Enoch completed 23 ops of his tour in ED588. They went on leave just before the end of August 1944 and on the very next mission, the aircraft failed to return from a raid on Königsberg on the night of 29/30th, one of four 50 Squadron Lancs that didn't get home. For Flying Officer Tony Carver and his crew, this target proved fatal and the entire crew were killed, all being buried in Sweden. Enoch returned to complete his tour in October, in other Lancs, and received the DFC. Coincidentally, Enoch's navigator's name was George, Flying Officer Andrew George, and he too received the DFC.

During ED588's period on 50 Squadron, it became Cat C twice. Firstly on 1 September 1943 having returned damaged from Berlin, and again on 12 April 1944 after a raid on Aachen. It then had a full overhaul at 58 MU, ROS, but was back on ops again by the 18th of that month.

G-George appears devoid of any nose-artwork other than a steadily increasing number of bomb markings in

that Berry was later killed, but that was not the case.]

'We were engaged on ops from Skellingthorpe from February to June 1944 and completed 25 of our 33 trips in 'G'. I'm not sure of the number of trips that were credited to her on our final op on 14/15 June, to Aunay-sur-Odon, but it couldn't have been far short of 100.

'As a matter of interest, on our trip to Aachen on 11 April, we were hit by an incendiary bomb in the No.2 starboard petrol tank, from one of our bombers overhead, but it didn't go off! (Lucky for 'G' and lucky us.) Anyway, on removal from the aircraft, the bomb was found to be still "live" and by all accounts went off when dropped from a "test wall". We were certainly lucky that night and went on to complete our tour.'

Very much alive, Ernest Berry contacted me from New South Wales and sent me a number of photographs which appear in this book. He was able to be put in touch with Brian Holmes after so many years, who apologised to his old skipper for saying he thought he'd been killed! Flying Officer Howell W T Enoch took over ED588 after Berry, as the latter also confirms:

ED588 after 72 operations.

rows of ten.  After ten such rows, the 100th bomb was added after a trip to St Leu on 4 July 1944.  The 11th and 12th rows were added beneath the cockpit.  One of the last photographs of *George* was taken with 125 bombs marked and it was supposed to have been lost on its 128th op.  *George* gave very little trouble, rarely being aborted through engine or other malfunctions;  it just plodded on until finally it went on one trip too many and failed to get home.  It is now known that the raid on Köningsberg met with heavy night fighter opposition and in all 15 Lancaster bombers were lost, G-George being one of them.  Had it not failed to return, and with several months of the war still to run, ED588 might well have become the Lanc with the most sorties flown.  This bomber's flying hours are recorded as 1,051.45.

**

After the original book came out I had a letter from Inge Gustafsson Ph.D., of Sweden, who was able to update me as to the fate of ED588:

'Lancaster ED588 crashed in the south of Sweden at a place called Höjalen, in the province of Scania, at 23.45 hours local time.  The aircraft had been attacked by a German night fighter based in Denmark, pursuing the aircraft over Swedish territory.

'ED588 crashed burning with a full bomb load into a small hill.  It was totally destroyed on impact and the entire crew were killed instantly.  Their remains were buried at Palsjö churchyard in Helsingborg.  Sergeants Mutch and Bysouth were the only members that could be individually identified.  The other five crew members are resting in a collective grave.  Beside the road, near the crash, local people erected a

FO H W T Enoch began operating ED588 in June 1944.  Enoch is on the left with his crew – and their mascot.  FO A George is third from left holding bear.

Enoch in the cockpit of ED588, the Lancaster now showing 116 ops – August 1944.  She was lost after 128 sorties that same month.

ED860 QR-N and behind her ED588 VN-Q. Two veterans ready for the off.

memorial consisting of one of the damaged propellers placed upon a big vertical log, together with a name plate of the crew. At the crash site is also a small sign indicating the exact point of impact.

'I should add that this night was indeed eventful, as the Luftwaffe had a successful night. Six more Lancasters crashed in the south of Sweden and were totally written off, resulting in a further 19 crew members dead and three missing – probably having parachuted into the Baltic sea. The other crew members parachuted over Sweden and were interned for a period of time. Another Lancaster made a forced landing at the Swedish air force base at Kalmar after being hit by incendiaries from another aircraft over the target, damaging the aircraft and injuring the pilot.

'Finally, three more Lancasters crashed at sea west of Sweden. From those, six crew members are buried at Falkenberg churchyard on the west coast of Sweden and four are buried in Anholt, Denmark. Four airmen were saved by Danish fishermen and taken into captivity. The rest are missing.'

Near the end. ED588 now sports 125 bombs.

## 97 SQUADRON
### 1943

**26 Mar** *1901-2320*
DUISBURG
Sgt K Brown (DFM)
Sgt H Hogg
Sgt F H Alexander
Sgt D H Meade
Sgt J Curry
Sgt J T Sullivan
Sgt L C Boyton

**27/28 Mar** *2026-0304*
BERLIN
Sgt K Brown and crew

**28/29 Mar** *2000-0136*
ST NAZAIRE
Sgt G W Armstrong
Sgt E Bellis (FE)
Sgt J J Mansfield (N)
Sgt David (BA)
Sgt R J Williams (WOP)
Sgt S Blackhurst (MU)
Sgt A Laing (RG)

**29/30 Mar** *2148-0433*
BERLIN
Sgt K Brown and crew

**3 Apr** *1914-2345*
ESSEN
Sgt K Brown and crew
Sgt Freedman in (MU),
Blackhurst out

**4/5 Apr** *2103-0232*
KIEL
Sgt K Brown and crew
Sgt T J Roche in (BA),
FS Broomfield in (MU),
David and Freedman out

**8/9 Apr** *2059-0225*
DUISBURG
Sgt K Brown and crew

**9/10 Apr** *2017-0054*
DUISBURG
FS W McLeod
Sgt F J Horsham
FS Gillespie
Sgt B L May
Sgt J Curry
FO E A Adams
Sgt J Baker

**13/14 Apr** *2043-0708*
LA SPEZIA
Sgt K Brown and crew
Sgt Baker (2P)
Lt D S Watt in (BA)

## 50 SQUADRON

**1 May** *0037-0459*
ESSEN
Sgt D A Duncan (DFC)
Sgt E Poulter
Sgt W J Evans
Sgt R L Hayter
Sgt I C Dooley
Sgt J Fulton
Sgt K D White

**4/5 May** *2233-0359*
DORTMUND
Sgt D A Duncan and crew

**13/14 May** *2201-0458*
PILSEN
Sgt D A Duncan and crew
(damaged by flak)

**23/24 May** *2304-0343*
DORTMUND
Sgt D A Duncan and crew

**25/26 May** *2344-0355*
DÜSSELDORF
Sgt D A Duncan and crew
Sgt Curtis in, White out

**29/30 May** *2257-0325*
WUPPERTAL
FO A N Hollis
Sgt D S Adshead
FO R Palmer
Sgt T G Cheshire
Sgt R G Yates
Sgt R A Kemp
Sgt W Walker

**11/12 June** *2342-0423*
DÜSSELDORF
Sgt D A Duncan and crew

**12/13 June** *2214-0333*
BOCHUM
Sgt D A Duncan and crew

**24/25 June** *2311-0350*
WUPPERTAL
PO R L Hendry
Sgt D D Rhynd
FO K Toner
Sgt P A Chapman
Sgt A McDowall
Sgt A S Cousins
Sgt Dalrymple
(all lost 9/10 July, except
Dalrymple, not on op)

**25/26 June** *2305-0335*
GELSENKIRCHEN
Sgt D A Duncan and crew

**28/29 June** *2335-0416*
COLOGNE
Sgt D A Duncan and crew
Sgt Howie in (2N)

**24/25 July** *2241-0326*
HAMBURG
Sgt W A Duncan and crew
Sgt Page in (2N)

**25/26 July** *2200-0234*
ESSEN
PO K Ruskell
Sgt T S Bradley
FO D H Simpson
FS E E Howell
Sgt J H Blott
Sgt G A Lewes
PO M Dicks

**27/28 July** *2236-0335*
HAMBURG
PO K Ruskell and crew

**29/30 July** *2240-0329*
HAMBURG
FS J W Thompson
Sgt E W Lowe
Sgt S Chapman
Sgt C R Corbett
Sgt A E Nicholson
Sgt J Conlon
Sgt T A Wyllie

**3 Aug** *0013-0534*
HAMBURG
FS J W Thompson and crew

**10/11 Aug** *2153-0543*
NÜRNBERG
Sgt D A Duncan and crew
FS L A J McCleod (2P)

**17/18 Aug** *2151-0422*
PEENEMÜNDE
Sgt D A Duncan and crew

**22/23 Aug** *2120-0149*
LEVERKUSEN
Sgt D A Duncan and crew
FO G M Brown (2P)

**27/28 Aug** *2106-0454*
NÜRNBERG
Sgt D A Duncan and crew

**31 Aug** *0019-0402*
MÜNCHEN-GLADBACH
Sgt D A Duncan and crew

**31 Aug/1 Sep** *2030-0358*
BERLIN
FS J L Heckendorf
Sgt J Henderson
PO K T Dale
Sgt A D Hope
Sgt R C Turner
PO G K Luton
Sgt D Hall
(flak damage)

**23/24 Sep** *1905-0200*
MANNHEIM
FO G M Brown
Sgt G Smith
Sgt T Watson
Sgt B F Tutt
Sgt D Little
Sgt P W Green
Sgt R W Sindon

**27/28 Sep** *1933-0134*
HANNOVER
FO G M Brown and crew

**28 Sep** *1838-2343*
BOCHUM
FO G M Brown and crew

**1 Oct** *1835-2353*
MUNICH
FO G M Brown and crew

**3/4 Oct** *1832-0052*
KASSEL
FO G M Brown and crew

**4/5 Oct** *1830-0050*
FRANKFURT
FO G M Brown and crew

**7/8 Oct** *2040-0310*
STUTTGART
FO G M Brown and crew

**3 Nov** *1720-2144*
DÜSSELDORF
FO F B M Wilson
Sgt H W Felton
PO J B H Billam
Sgt J Short
FS P F J Harrington
FS J W Newman
FS I W Anderson

**10/11 Nov** *2049-0502*
MODANE
FL F B M Wilson and crew
FSs S O Smith and S Proctor
in, Short and Anderson out

**18/19 Nov** *1720-0129*
BERLIN
FO F B M Wilson and crew
Sgts E J Gunn and Bateman
in, Smith and Proctor out

**22 Nov** *1653-2326*
BERLIN
FO F B M Wilson and crew
Sgt L C Green and C Baker
in, Gunn and Bateman out

**23 Nov** *1718-2355*
BERLIN
FO F B M Wilson and crew
Sgt E J Gash and J P Flynn
in, Green and Baker out

**2/3 Dec** *1639-0022*
BERLIN
Sgt R C Thornton
Sgt J Clark
Sgt D R Neal
Sgt J Webb
Sgt L A Taylor
PO C A Maddin
Sgt C Seddon

**16/17 Dec** *1645-0030*
BERLIN
FS R A Leader
Sgt E D Rosenberg
FO A R Candy
FS S J R Lewis
Sgt D R Tupman
PO L Stevens
Sgt T F Coulson

**20 Dec** *1726-2305*
FRANKFURT
FO M J Beetham (DFC)
Sgt E D Moore
FO W F Swinyard
Sgt K Payne
Sgt J C A Rodgers
Sgt A L Bartlett
Sgt F G Ball

**23/24 Dec** *2344-0818*
BERLIN
PO D A Jennings
Sgt I T Stephen
Sgt T R D Carroll
FS G W Hughes
Sgt H C P...?
Sgt E W Turton
Sgt C King

**29/30 Dec** *1717-0016*
BERLIN
FS C Erritt (DFC)
Sgt G Jones
FS N P Delayen
FS F A Taylor
Sgt H W J Lineham
Sgt P A Gleeson (DFC)
FS J McK Williamson
(lost with 83 Sqn 12/13 Aug;
Delayen and Williamson,
PoWs, Lineham not on op)

### 1944

**1/2 Jan** *2350-0810*
BERLIN
FS C Erritt and crew

**2/3 Jan** *2347-0726*
BERLIN
FS C Erritt and crew

**6 Jan** *0006-0919*
STETTIN
FS C Erritt and crew

**14 Jan** *1716-2230*
BRUNSWICK
FS C Erritt and crew

**20/21 Jan** *1634-0010*
BERLIN
Sgt L D Wort
Sgt H R Sinton
Sgt W Jennings
Sgt G H Fry
Sgt D Gapp
Sgt A W Russell
Sgt D R Oliver

**21/22 Jan** *2037-0304*
MAGDEBURG
SL F W Chadwick
FS W J Beesley
WO J Watt
PO A R Verrier
FS G F Graham

FO H A Hughes
FS A M MacDonald

**27/28 Jan** *1734-0244*
*BERLIN*
PO L Creed
Sgt S G Attwood
Sgt D Gressop
Sgt C A Hern
Sgt H R S Elder
Sgt L C Hagben
Sgt I G Evans

**29 Jan** *0050-0816*
*BERLIN*
PO L Creed and crew

**30 Jan** *1725-2349*
*BERLIN*
PO L Creed and crew

**15/16 Feb** *1739-0104*
*BERLIN*
PO W V Amphlett
Sgt K Tonks
FO I G Evans (N)
FS W T Newton
Sgt F W Kendrick
FO A Arnold
FS H Jackson
(Amphlett and Evans KIA
21/22 May flying with others)

**19/20 Feb** *2355-0741*
*LEIPZIG*
FS G A Waugh
Sgt G C Prince
Sgt D A Chaston
Sgt R J Dunn
Sgt D L Sehlin RCAF
Sgt D C Lynch
Sgt R F Thibedeau RCAF
(shot down 30/31 March; Waugh,
Prince, Lynch and Dunn PoWs,
rest killed)

**21 Feb** *0001-0731*
*STUTTGART*
FS G A Waugh and crew

**24/25 Feb** *2030-0510*
*SCHWEINFURT*
FS E Berry RAAF (DFC)
Sgt B R W Holmes (FE)
FS L Howarth (N)
Sgt P M N Honeywood
FS W Bull (BA)
Sgt R Hamilton (MU)
Sgt R Phillips (RG)

**25/26 Feb** *1833-0246*
*AUGSBURG*
FS E Berry and crew

**1/2 Mar** *2334-0752*
*STUTTGART*
FS E Berry and crew

**15/16 Mar** *1934-0316*
*STUTTGART*
FS E Berry and crew

**18/19 Mar** *1816-0104*
*FRANKFURT*
FS E Berry and crew

**22/23 Mar** *1908-0049*
*FRANKFURT*
FS E Berry and crew

**24/25 Mar** *1914-0308*
*BERLIN*
FS E Berry and crew

**26/27 Mar** *2007-0109*
*ESSEN*
PO E Berry and crew

**30/31 Mar** *2232-0543*
*NÜRNBERG*
PO E Berry and crew

**5/6 Apr** *2033-0350*
*TOURS M/YARDS*
PO E Berry and crew

**10/11 Apr** *2319-0501*
*TOURS M/YARDS*
PO E Berry and crew

**11/12 Apr** *2038-0037*
*AACHEN*
PO E Berry and crew

**18/19 Apr** *2106-0156*
*JUVISY M/YARDS*
PO E Berry and crew

**20/21 Apr** *2312-0353*
*PARIS M/YARDS*
PO E Berry and crew

**22/23 Apr** *2325-0523*
*BRUNSWICK*
PO E Berry and crew

**24/25 Apr** *2052-0736*
*MUNICH*
PO E Berry and crew

**26/27 Apr** *2142-0639*
*SCHWEINFURT*
PO E Berry and crew

**28/29 Apr** *2314-0620*
*ST MÉDARD-EN-JALLES*
PO E Berry and crew

**29/30 Apr** *2243-0602*
*ST MÉDARD-EN-JALLES*
PO A Handley
FO T E Archard (N)
Sgt R S Garrod (BA)
Sgt D Bisset (WOP)
Sgt C T Brown (FE)
Sgt C Whitelock (MU)
Sgt G E Gilpin (RG)
(all lost 3/4 May)

**7 May** *0050-0521*
*LOUAILLE*
PO W V Amphlett
Sgt H Snowling (FE)
FO I G Evans (N)
FO D A Bacon (BA)
FS G E Jagger (WOP)
Sgt F W Kendrick (MU)
Sgt D R Oliver (RG)
(all lost 21/22 May)

**10/11 May** *2212-0130*
*LILLE M/YARDS*
PO E Berry and crew

**11/12 May** *2238-0215*
*BOURG LÉOPOLD*
PO E Berry and crew

**19/20 May** *2209-0504*
*TOURS M/YARDS*
PO E Berry and crew

**21/22 May** *2219-0349*
*DUISBURG*
PO E Berry and crew

**22/23 May** *2225-0436*
*BRUNSWICK*
PO E Berry and crew

**12/13 June** *2242-0449*
*POITIERS*
PO L W Pethick
Sgt J Potter
FO J D Bald
Sgt W V Wallace
Sgt L Taylor
Sgt R Marlow
Sgt R T Mackenley

**14/15 June** *2218-0241*
*AUNAY*
PO E Berry and crew

**19/20 June** *2249-0108*
*WATTEN – V1 SITE*
FO H W T Enoch (DFC)
Sgt G Pritchard
FO A George (N)(DFC)
Sgt J Hugh
Sgt E Garstang
Sgt H R Southcott
Sgt E Goymer
(recalled – weather)

**21/22 June** *2314-0350*
*GELSENKIRCHEN*
FO H W T Enoch and crew

**23/24 June** *2240-0535*
*LIMOGES M/YARDS*
FO H W T Enoch and crew

**24/25 June** *2248-0231*
*PROUVILLE – V1 SITE*
FO H W T Enoch and crew

**27/28 June** *2140-0543*
*VITRY*
FO H W T Enoch and crew

**29 June** *1233-1528*
*BEAUVOIR – V1 SITE*
FS T G Curphey RCAF
Sgt I W Lewis (FE)
Sgt D R Allen (N)
FO G E Sholte RCAF (BA)
Sgt H Lambert
FO M L G Lovering RCAF
Sgt J I Fisher
(all lost 28/29 July except
Fisher, not on op)

**4/5 July** *2337-0322*
*ST LEU D'ESSERENT*
FO H W T Enoch and crew

**7/8 July** *2244-0309*
*ST LEU D'ESSERENT*
FO H W T Enoch and crew

**12/13 July** *2205-0558*
*CULMONT*
FO H W T Enoch and crew

**15/16 July** *2207-0532*
*NEVERS*
FO H W T Enoch and crew

**18 July** *0423-0746*
*CAEN*
FO H W T Enoch and crew

**18/19 July** *2300-0428*
*RÉVIGNY*
FO H W T Enoch and crew

**20/21 July** *2314-0223*
*COURTRAI*
FO H W T Enoch and crew

**25 July** *0220-0410*
*DONGES*
PO D L Haynes RAAF
Sgt E H Blackwell (FE)
Sgt G C Remsbery (N)
FS P H Clucas (BA)
FS G D Currey RAAF
Sgt E P Gavin
Sgt W I Warrington RAAF
(all lost 12/13 Aug except
Blackwell, and Gavin – not on op)

**26/27 July** *2125-0639*
*GIVORS*
PO D L Haynes and crew

**28/29 July** *2204-0607*
*STUTTGART*
PO D L Haynes and crew

**30 July** *0559-1031*
*CAHAGNES*
PO D L Haynes and crew

**31 July** *1739-2301*
*JOIGNY*
PO D L Haynes and crew

**1 Aug** *1516-1826*
*SIRACOURT*
PO D L Haynes and crew

**2 Aug** *1425-1945*
*BOIS DE CASSAN*
PO D L Haynes and crew
FS J L Shortal (RG) in, (lost
on 12/13 Aug op), Gavin out

**3 Aug** *1145-1630*
*TROSSY ST MAXIMIN*
PO D L Haynes and crew

**5 Aug** *1050-1540*
*ST LEU D'ESSERENT*
FO H W T Enoch and crew

**7/8 Aug** *2132-0154*
*CHÂTERELLAULT*
FO H W T Enoch and crew

**11 Aug** *1209-1939*
*BORDEAUX*
FO H W T Enoch and crew

**12/13 Aug** *2137-0312*
*RÜSSELSHEIM*
FO H W T Enoch and crew
FS P D A Lorimer RAAF (2P)

**13 Aug** *1635-2347*
*BORDEAUX*
FO H W T Enoch and crew

**14 Aug** *1745-2242*
*BREST*
PO R J Odgers RNZAF
Sgt K Cox
Sgt L Clark
Sgt S D Bartlett
Sgt P Donnelly (WOP)
FS G T Alcock
Sgt E Neville
(shot down 11/12 Sep;
Clark, Donnelly and Bartlett
PoWs, others KIA except
Alcock, not on op)

**16/17 Aug** *2055-0531*
*STETTIN*
FO H W T Enoch and crew

**18 Aug** *1130-1615*
*FORÊT DE L'ISLE ADAM*
FO H W T Enoch and crew

**19 Aug** *0513-1145*
*LA PALLICE*
FO H W T Enoch and crew

**25/26 Aug** *2028-0514*
*DARMSTADT*
FO H W T Enoch and crew

**26/27 Aug** *2039-0719*
*KÖNIGSBERG*
FO H W T Enoch and crew

**29/30 Aug** *2058-*
*KÖNIGSBERG*
FO A H Carver
Sgt R H Clifford (FE)
Sgt F G Plowman (N)
Sgt D A MacDonald RCAF (BA)
Sgt E Mutch (WOP)
Sgt W R Campbell (MU)
Sgt R W Bysouth (RG)
(all lost)

# ED611
# UNCLE JOE

Built by A V Roe as a Mark III with four Merlin 28 engines, ED611 arrived at 5 MU on 14 February 1943 and was then assigned to 44 (Rhodesia) Squadron at Waddington, south of Lincoln, on 5 April. The following month the squadron moved its base to RAF Dunholme Lodge, just to the north of Lincoln. Given the squadron code letters KM, its individual letter was U for Uncle. It is unclear if the aircraft was known merely as U-Uncle, or *Uncle Joe* at this early stage. We know it became *Uncle Joe* later but whether this was due to its change of squadron (to 463), at which time its code letter became JO, has not been confirmed.

Joseph Stalin, the Russian leader, was often referred to as ('kindly') Uncle Joe by the media, and was of course very much in the news during this mid-war period. To those who did not know him, he probably looked a kind and friendly uncle-type. Thus at some stage U-Uncle had Stalin's portrait painted on the nose of the Lancaster, superimposed on a large red star of Russia. Once ED611 began operations, its ground crew began painting not tiny bomb symbols beneath the cockpit but tiny stars: yellow for night sorties, red for day ops.

Looking at photographs it appears that after 55 stars had been painted on the aircraft, in five and a half rows of ten and five, more five-star rows were begun further forward, just aft of the front turret. After nine such rows had been completed, making 45, which brought the tally to 100, the front set of stars were painted over and the earlier rows of ten were extended. This brought the star rows right down to the bomb-doors but it is not certain where further stars were painted, as ED611 eventually completed some 115 operations.

At the time ED611 flew its 100th mission, someone chalked under Stalin's portrait '100 Up Tonight' at which stage there were only 98 stars, confirming that whether bombs or stars were marked on aircraft, they were not religiously painted on after each and every raid. Some people have the impression that a man with a pot of paint and a ladder is ready and waiting to paint these symbols on aircraft even before the crew get out of the aircraft!

Vic Trimble and crew in front of ED611 – in the snow! The bombs denote ops with 44 Squadron, the two stars the first ops flown by 463 Squadron in February 1944. From left to right: Bill Aldworth, Jim Marles, Trimble, Jack Lawrence, Ron Nixon, Arthur Herriott, Roy McNaughton.

A short while later there was another paint or chalk mark – '104 Not Out' – but just why and when is unclear, especially as on the port bomb-door, which hangs down, has been written – 'Good-Bye Old Faithful' – which would seem to indicate ED611 had reached the end of the line. It suggests that reference to the 104 was not washed off and further stars were not painted on – at least, not where they could be seen in a photograph – after the 100.

Its first sortie was a long haul to La Spezia in northern Italy on 13/14 April 1943, with Flying Officer D McN Moodie RCAF in command. Moodie and crew went to 97

Trimble's crew at Castle Bromwich with the MD, Production and Engineering Managers. From left to right: Lawrence, Nixon, McNaughton, Marles, Trimble, Aldworth, and Herriott.

Aldridge finally evaded the enemy aircraft. By superb airmanship, he then succeeded in flying the badly crippled bomber to base. This officer has completed many sorties and his work throughout has been of a high standard.'

*Uncle* was out of action until 18 September, returning to 44 Squadron where it went on to complete a total of 43 ops, but it also continued to have encounters with night fighters during this period. One was on the night of 4/5 October going to Frankfurt. The rear gunner, Sergeant D H Watts, spotted a Ju88 at 300 yards, then he and the mid-upper, Pilot Officer A Rimmer, both opened fire as the pilot, Flying Officer C D Wiggin, put the Lanc into a diving turn to port. Fortunately for the Lanc crew, the night fighter had been burning its navigation lights which quickly went out as the gunners opened up. The Junkers did not return fire and it was last seen diving away to starboard. Another combat occurred on the night of 21/22 January 1944 over Magdeburg. The rear gunner, Sergeant D Chalmers, spotted a Me109 at 700 yards and ordered the pilot to take evasive action. As Pilot Officer R M Higgs did so, the Messerschmitt pilot attacked and both gunners – Flight Sergeant H S Tiller was in the mid-upper position – returned fire. Strikes could be seen on the 109 which was then observed to go underneath with black smoke coming from its engine and was not seen again. Two minutes later another 109 was spotted attacking another Lancaster off to port and the rear gunner opened fire. The other bomber dived and the 109 broke off and headed away and down. David Chalmers and Henry Tiller both received the DFM but Chalmers was later killed in action. Both air gunners' citations recorded that they had been on 25 raids including seven to Berlin.

After taking part in the Battle of Berlin – ten trips – ED611 was assigned to 463 Squadron RAAF at Waddington on 4 February, its new code letter being JO. Some of the early ops recorded for *Uncle* were shown under the serial number ME611, but as there was no such serial number for a Lancaster, this has to be a typing error.

Squadron in July and flew another Lancaster that was to achieve its century – EE176 – on seven of her trips. Duncan Moodie received the DFC with 97.

*Uncle* became Cat AC on 21 August after being damaged by an Me109 attack on the Peenemünde raid of 18/19 August. All its starboard side was shot-up, the starboard-outer engine knocked out which affected the rear turret's hydraulics, the intercom was knocked out and the starboard wheel-tyre was punctured. Later the aircraft came under attack from a Me210 but *Uncle's* pilot, Pilot Officer D R Aldridge, having dived steeply, got the damaged Lanc under control, climbed again and then, with Sammy Holmes the rear gunner coming forward to say his turret was virtually useless, they headed for home, flat out, low over Denmark at 230 knots on three engines. It was their 26th operation and *Uncle's* 24th or 25th. Deryck Aldridge received the DFC for this effort, his navigator, Flying Officer Desmond B F Heslop, collecting one too. Aldridge's citation read:

'On 17th August 1943, this officer piloted an aircraft which attacked Peenemünde. Soon after leaving the target area, the bomber was attacked by an enemy fighter. The rear turret and the intercom and call-light systems were rendered useless, but, in spite of this the attacker was beaten off. Some ten minutes later, the bomber was engaged by another fighter. Much damage was sustained but, by skilful tactics, Pilot Officer

*Uncle* began its second career on 19/20 February with a raid on Leipzig, piloted by Pilot Officer Vic H Trimble RAAF. His flight engineer was Jim Marles who recalled:

'Our crew took *Uncle Joe* on its first trip after being assigned to 463 Squadron, and later completed our tour on her, our last being Frankfurt of 18/19 March.

'ED611 was a wonderful old aircraft but it did have one peculiar habit of the engines refusing to synchronize which caused havoc with our eardrums. I was continually trying to tune them during the flight. When the aircraft came to the squadron it had done 43 trips and they were painted in small bombs forward of Stalin which was already painted within the star, hammer and sickle. I have a photo of our crew standing under the motif. We had done two trips in her and you can see the two stars painted aft of the motif. It was taken while we were clearing snow and was quite exciting for the skipper and rear gunner, Jack Lawrence, both Aussies from Brisbane, as they had not seen snow for real before.

'Chiefy Turrell, who was in charge of ED611, wrote to me after we had left and said that it was coming up for 100 trips.'

*Uncle* had a variety of skippers after this, including one trip by 463's CO, Wing Commander Rollo Kingsford-Smith DFC to Schweinfurt on 26/27 April. Schweinfurt was the home to the ball-bearing factories and this night 21 Lancasters failed to get home. The RAAF Official History states: 'The report of Wing Commander R Kingsford-Smith, cautiously optimistic, is typical of the RAAF assessment of the raid at that time: ".. the bombing appeared to be quite accurate. I cannot assess the markers as no ground detail could be seen. Flak and searchlights over the target offered little opposition …" '

Missing the immediate pre-D-Day night, *Uncle* was taken over by an extraordinary crew on the night of 6/7 June. It would appear that a senior officer wanted to be part of this great day, for the crew comprised a wing commander, a squadron leader, two flight lieutenants, two junior officers and a flight sergeant. From 5 Group Headquarters came Wing Commander George Geoffrey Petty DSO DFC, who had been an RAF apprentice in 1931, commissioned in 1940, awarded the DFC in 1941 and the

W/Cdr G G Petty DSO DFC took ED611 to Argentan during D-Day.

DSO in 1943. One of his earlier sorties had been a daylight to Milan in October 1942. Petty had flown Q-Queenie (R5868) in July 1944, the sortie not being recorded in the records (see the chapter on this Lancaster). In 1953 Petty took the record for a flight from London to Cape Town flying in a Canberra, for which he received the AFC.

During this D-Day period *Uncle's* usual crew was that captained by Pilot Officer N W Sanders RAAF, who had arrived on the squadron on 12 April 1944. On the night of 8/9 June they had a tyre burst on take-off and great difficulty was experienced in getting the laden bomber off the ground but Sanders managed it. Over the target they met heavy ground opposition, causing them to make three dummy bomb-runs before letting the bombs go on the fourth run – on which they were considerably shot-about. Noel Sanders even managed a good landing on one good tyre back at base, and apparently it should have

ED611 about to embark on her 100th trip, September 1944. Note 44 Squadron's bomb symbols have now changed to stars.

ED611 after 104 raids, about to depart for a refit at the end of September 1944. She would return to 463 and complete a few more ops before the war ended.

been their night off! Sanders received the DFC on completion of his tour.

Another crew lost both outer-engines over Brest on 14 August, but Flight Sergeant A G Stutter made an excellent return and landing. However, *Uncle* was now nearing 100 ops, the magic figure being reached (one assumes) on a raid in mid-September. A count through the Form 541s could indicate the 100th op being flown on 12/13 September, but when the aircraft went for a major refit at the end of that month the ground crew chalked that '104 Not Out' on the nose. This would indicate another, with a further nine flown after its return, making 113, but in total 115 have been credited to ED611. There is nothing in the squadron records to identify or even acknowledge the 100th mission.

Having become Cat B at the end of September, *Uncle* went off for a minor refit at Avro's, coming back to 463 Squadron on 15 December. If the total of 115 ops is correct, only nine more can be found after its return, so once again, either the 100th is in question or some of its final sorties are either not recorded or recorded incorrectly. By counting ops below, the 100th does appear to be that flown to Stuttgart on 12/13 September, captained by another of the Lanc's more regular skippers, Pilot Officer T A Perry RAAF, who also later received the DFC.

*Uncle's* last sortie came on 8/9 February 1945, to Pölitz, with Flying Officer M S Wickes RAAF in command. Prior to bombing they were attacked by two Ju88s that resulted in No.1 port fuel tank catching fire and the

hydraulics being severely damaged. The fighters were eventually evaded and being just a few minutes from the target, they carried on and bombed. Immediately afterwards, Milton Wickes had to feather the port-inner engine but the fuel tank was still burning and it stood out like a beacon, attracting another night fighter. Wickes put the Lanc into a corkscrew manoeuvre and while the fire dimmed it did not go out, so he ordered everyone to prepare to bale out. Making one last attempt before the wing burned through, he dived *Uncle* steeply and the fire was finally extinguished.

They were now on three engines heading home and with the bomb-doors hanging down. The artificial horizon was u/s, ten degrees of flap was also shown and the intercom to both gunners had been knocked out. However, the rear gunner had succeeded in shooting down the Ju88 in the second attack, with the aid of the mid-upper. The navigator brought them out over Denmark and because of their fuel shortage they only just made RAF Carnaby, with a very damaged aeroplane that was anything but air worthy. Milton Wickes later received the DFC for this sortie.

It was a sad but gallant finale to *Uncle's* operational tour of duty. The machine now went off to be repaired and, still Cat B on 9 March, went to RIW, then to AW/CN on 22 June, ending up at West Freugh as a hack aircraft with the Bombing Trials Unit. It was finally Struck off Charge on 22 June 1947.

Some time after ED611 left 463 Squadron another JO-U came on the scene. Lancaster RF141, which survived in the RAF until 1948, was named *Uncle Joe Again*, this too carrying a portrait of Stalin on the port side of the nose.

Lancaster RF141 *Uncle Joe Again*, which replaced ED611 in 1945.

## 44 (RHODESIA) SQUADRON
## 1943

**13/14 Apr** *2041-0627*
LA SPEZIA
FO D McN Moodie RCAF (DFC)
Sgt L F Melbourne (FE)
Sgt J T Bundle (N)
Sgt H W N Clausen (BA)
Sgt T E Stamp (WOP)
Sgt L A Drummond
Sgt F A Hughes (RG)
(see also EE176)

**14/15 Apr** *2217-0050*
STUTTGART
Sgt L J Ellis
Sgt R L LePage
PO W A Rollings
Sgt J Brown
Sgt A C Ellis
Sgt R Williams
Sgt S S McClellan
(abort – oil leak)

**16/17 Apr** *2117-0546*
PILSEN
Sgt J O Pennington (DFC)
Sgt D Morrison
Sgt J R Hewitt
Sgt L Hawkes
Sgt D Betts
Sgt W A Harrell
Sgt G B Homewood (DFM)

**18/19 Apr** *2107-0601*
LA SPEZIA
FL R D Robinson (DFC)
Sgt E E C Hayward
FO A A StC Miller (N) (DFC)
Sgt L A T Parsons
Sgt A J Woodgate
PO D Hartung
Sgt G M E Weller
Sgt D S Mindel

**20/21 Apr** *2130-0528*
STETTIN
Sgt G N Stephenson
Sgt J A Robinson
FS E G More
Sgt A R Smith
Sgt D Betts
Sgt S R Hopkins
Sgt W J Beggs

**27 Apr** *0048-0453*
DUISBURG
FS C Shnier
Sgt A N Gibbons
Sgt N Laidler
Sgt H T Wigley
Sgt P C Evans
Sgt D E Croft
Sgt B G Knoeson

**1 May** *0033-0501*
ESSEN
FO W D Rail
Sgt H K Underwood
Sgt A T C Bromwich
Sgt W C Digby
Sgt R C Boardman
Sgt R S A Walker
Sgt G Batty

**4/5 May** *2144-0315*
DORTMUND
Sgt D R Aldridge (DFC)
Sgt T Phillips
FO D B F Heslop (N) (DFC)
Sgt J A Dellow
Sgt R W West
Sgt D J N Palmer
Sgt T S Holmes

**13 May** *0015-0420*
DUISBURG
Sgt D R Aldridge and crew
Sgt D Wolensky in, Sgt
Palmer out

**13/14 May** *2139-0554*
PILSEN
Sgt D R Aldridge and crew
Palmer back

**23/24 May** *2250-0400*
DORTMUND
Sgt D R Aldridge and crew

**25/26 May** *2346-0403*
DÜSSELDORF
Sgt D R Aldridge and crew

**29/30 May** *2257-0402*
WUPPERTAL
Sgt D R Aldridge and crew

**11/12 June** *2332-0407*
DÜSSELDORF
Sgt D R Aldridge and crew

**20/21 June** *2158-0741*
FRIEDRICHSHAFEN
FO D McN Moodie and crew

**8/9 July** *2249-0441*
COLOGNE
PO D R Aldridge and crew

**9/10 July** *2226-0041*
GELSENKIRCHEN
PO D R Aldridge and crew
(abort – std-outer and port-
inner, and M/U turret u/s)

**12/13 July** *2233-0745*
TURIN
Sgt D A Rollin (DFC)
Sgt J C Blackmore
Sgt T B Malia
Sgt E J Tocher
Sgt L Barker
Sgt B J Chew
Sgt R Standing
(all except Barker (PoW)
lost 16/17 Dec)

**24/25 July** *2234-0324*
HAMBURG
PO D R Aldridge and crew

**25/26 July** *2214-0291*
ESSEN
Sgt R M Campbell
Sgt J G Watkins
Sgt J G Poperwell
Sgt A H Thompson
Sgt J Graham
Sgt H C Macannick
Sgt W Phillips

**29/30 July** *2214-0309*
HAMBURG
PO D R Aldridge and crew

**2/3 Aug** *2324-0435*
HAMBURG
PO D R Aldridge and crew

**12/13 Aug** *2150-0635*
MILAN
FS H G Norton
Sgt J H Stevens
Sgt S D Stait
Sgt F Thompson
Sgt E E Greenfield
Sgt R G Martin
Sgt W A Whalley

**15/16 Aug** *2029-0453*
MILAN
PO D R Aldridge and crew

**17/18 Aug** *2132-0458*
PEENEMÜNDE
PO D R Aldridge and crew
(badly damaged by flak
and a Me210 attacked)

**4/5 Oct** *1810-0039*
FRANKFURT
FO C D Wiggin
Sgt A Jones
FO R H Maury
FO C G Rogers
Sgt A Dickson
PO A Rimmer
Sgt D H Watts

**18 Oct** *1709-2228*
HANNOVER
PO D A Rollin and crew

**20/21 Oct** *1709-0043*
LEIPZIG
PO D A Rollin and crew

**3 Nov** *1707-2121*
DÜSSELDORF
PO R L Ash
Sgt G F Ives
PO C G Whitehead
FS H Custom
Sgt B H White
Sgt J Murphy

**18/19 Nov** *1658-0130*
BERLIN
PO R M Higgs (DFC)
Sgt J E Cowan
FS T W Black
Sgt J W Would
Sgt V G Williams
FS H S Tiller RAAF (DFM)
Sgt D Chalmers (DFM)

**22 Nov** *1649-2355*
BERLIN
PO R M Higgs and crew

**26/27 Nov** *1731-0115*
BERLIN
PO R M Higgs and crew

**4 Dec** *0032-0740*
LEIPZIG
PO R M Higgs and crew

**16 Dec** *1628-2348*
BERLIN
PO R M Higgs and crew
Sgt D D Orme in, Cowen out

**20 Dec** *1700-2251*
FRANKFURT
PO N F Lyford
Sgt A Semple
Sgt J R Tijon
FS G Owen
Sgt G A Ford
Sgt H Marrs
Sgt A Wainwright

**24 Dec** *0017-0748*
BERLIN
PO N F Lyford and crew

**29 Dec** *1645-2331*
BERLIN
PO R M Higgs and crew
Cowan back

## 1944

**14 Jan** *1636-2331*
BRUNSWICK
PO R M Higgs and crew
(abort – engine trouble)

**20 Jan** *1634-2327*
BERLIN
PO R M Higgs and crew

**21/22 Jan** *1941-0244*
MAGDEBURG
PO R M Higgs and crew
(combats with Me109s)

**27/28 Jan** *1731-0155*
BERLIN
FS E Barton
Sgt J C Thompson
FO G F Garland
Sgt F H Barnes
Sgt T M Willett
Sgt R W Joy
Sgt L J Hummell

**29 Jan** *0026-0530*
SYLT
FS E Barton and crew
(icing problems, Sylt
secondary target)

**30/31 Dec** *1703-0015*
BERLIN
PO B M Hayes
Sgt J M Ella
Sgt C Dean
FO E Dunn
Sgt W K Walker
Sgt K V Radcliffe
Sgt W G Perrie

## 463 SQUADRON RAAF

**19/20 Feb** *2357-0731*
LEIPZIG
PO V H Trimble RAAF
Sgt A J Marles (FE)
FL A Williams (N)
Sgt B T Aldworth (BA)
Sgt W J Nixon (WOP)
Sgt R McNaughton (MU)
FS J P Lawrence RAAF (RG)

**24/25 Feb** *2041-0445*
SCHWEINFURT
PO V H Trimble and crew
FO A W Herriott in
Williams out

**25/26 Feb** *1840-0208*
AUGSBURG
PO V H Trimble and crew

**1/2 Mar** *2307-0636*
STUTTGART
PO V H Trimble and crew

**15/16 Mar** *1932-0250*
STUTTGART
PO V H Trimble and crew

**18/19 Mar** *1906-0121*
FRANKFURT
PO V H Trimble and crew

**22/23 Mar** *1858-0054*
FRANKFURT
PO B W Giddings
Sgt A Pritchard (FE)
FS W Webb (N)
FS C Clement (BA)
FS R Bethel (WOP)
FO J McGill (MU)
FS W Seale (RG)

**24/25 Mar** *1927-0235*
BERLIN
FO B A Burkham
Sgt W Sinclair (FE)
FO R W Board (N)
FS L F Manning (BA)
FS E L Holden (WOP)
Sgt F Burton (MU)
FS Moorhead (RG)

**10/11 Apr** *2315-0413*
TOURS
PO K H Robertson

Sgt R J Patrick
Sgt D Ball
FO F N Chandler
FS S E W Smith
PO C G Parker
FS N J Bowman

**18/29 Apr** *2053-0211*
*JUVISY*
FS R W Page
Sgt S R Crate
WO W W Fair
FO J Braithwaite
FS E R Brown
Sgt R Guile
FO C H Noakes

**26/27 Apr** *2148-0609*
*SCHWEINFURT*
WC R Kingsford-Smith (DFC)
Sgt R Fairburn
FO N H Kobeike
FS B W Webb
FO M J McLeod
FO J E R Rees
FO R M Croft

**28/29 Apr** *2313-0620*
*ST MÉNARD*
PO N W Saunders RAAF
Sgt D A Brett RAF (FE)
FS M B Greacen (N)
FO E Rosenfeld (BA)
FS E O Davis (WOP)
FO G H Swindells (MU)
Sgt G Elliott (RG)
(abort due to haze)

**1/2 May** *2152-0536*
*TOULOUSE*
PO N W Saunders and crew

**3/4 May** *2153-0316*
*MAILLY-LE-CAMP*
PO N W Saunders and crew

**31 May/1 June** *2351-0502*
*SAUMUR*
PO N W Saunders and crew

**3/4 June** *2312-0252*
*FERME D'URVILLE*
PO A B Tottenham
Sgt R J Patrick
FS D Ball
FO F N Chandler
FS S E W Smith
PO C G Barker
PO N J Bowman

**6/7 June** *2329-0353*
*ARGENTAN*
WC G G Petty DSO DFC
SL Evans
FL Archer
FO D Falgate
FL K M D Lyons
PO Aitken
FS Flood

**8/9 June** *2310-0509*
*RENNES*
PO N W Saunders and crew
(burst tyre on take-off but
carried on; damaged by flak
over target after three runs)

**15/16 June** *2133-0409*
*CHÂTELLERAULT*
PO N W Saunders and crew

**21/22 June** *2315-0351*
*GELSENKIRCHEN*
PO N W Saunders and crew

**23/24 June** *2234-0524*
*LIMOGES*
PO N W Saunders and crew
PO M F Sweeney (2P)

**24/25 June** *2234-0221*
*PROUVILLE*
PO N W Saunders and crew

**27/28 June** *2202-0528*
*VITRY*
PO M J Roe
Sgt W N Hall
Sgt A E Fox
Sgt T F Byrne
FS N S Palmer
FS T R Ryan
Sgt K C Butcher

**29 June** *1218-1532*
*BEAUVOIR – V1 SITE*
PO M J Roe and crew

**4/5 July** *2322-0327*
*ST LEU D'ESSERENT*
PO M J Roe and crew

**7/8 July** *2215-0304*
*ST LEU D'ESSERENT*
PO N W Saunders and crew

**12/13 July** *2152-0555*
*NEVERS*
PO N W Saunders and crew

**15/16 July** *2218-0528*
*CULMONT-CHALINDREY*
PO N W Saunders and crew

**18 July** *0359-0734*
*CAEN*
FS T A Perry (DFC)
Sgt F A England
FS G S Carlton
FS W T Clayton
FS H E Williams
FS C T Forrester
Sgt L Oxley

**18/19 July** *2306-0416*
*RÉVIGNY*
FO D C Gundry
Sgt P O F Wadsworth (FE)
FS E J Sincock (N)
FS E P Fallon (BA)
FS V J Davidson (WOP)
Sgt N M Davidson (MU)
FS E Burke (RG)

**19 July** *1916-2332*
*THIVERNY – V1 SITE*
PO N W Saunders and crew

**20/21 July** *2331-0242*
*COURTRAI*
FO I J Dack
Sgt H E Lee
FS J F Maple
FS J R McWilliam
Sgt A Easton
FS R Coward
Sgt C F Kirby

**26/27 July** *2135-0614*
*GIVORS*
PO N W Saunders and crew

**28/29 July** *2206-0553*
*STUTTGART*
FO M F Sweeney
Sgt H R Carpenter
FS H H Mirtha
FO G T Gill
FS G A Russ
FS W N Robinson
FS R W Palmer

**31 July** *1719-2228*
*RILLY-LA-MONTAGNE*
PO N W Saunders and crew

**1 Aug** *1636-2133*
*MONT CANDON*
PO N W Saunders and crew
(abandoned by MB – fog)

**3 Aug** *1202-1631*
*TROSSY ST MAXIMIN*
PO N W Saunders and crew

**5 Aug** *1040-1542*
*ST LEU D'ESSERENT*
FS A G Stutter (DFC)
Sgt H Walsh RAF (FE)
FS P L Wilkinson (N)
FS P O'Loughlin (BA)
FS D J Browning (WOP)
FS M F Woodgate (MU)
FS H R Holmes (RG)

**6 Aug** *0932-1331*
*BOIS DE CASSAN*
PO N W Saunders and crew

**7/8 Aug** *2120-0200*
*SECQUEVILLE*
PO T A Perry and crew

**9/10 Aug** *2043-0322*
*CHÂTELLERAULT*
PO N W Saunders and crew

**11/12 Aug** *2029-0451*
*GIVORS*
PO N W Saunders and crew

**12/13 Aug** *2115-0451*
*GIVORS*
PO N W Saunders and crew

**14 Aug** *1757-2229*
*BREST*
FS A G Stutter and crew
(lost std-outer over tgt, then
port-outer 50 miles from base)

**15 Aug** *0939-1335*
*GILZE-RIJEN AIRFIELD*
PO T A Perry and crew

**16/17 Aug** *2138-0527*
*STETTIN*
FO M F Sweeney and crew

**18 Aug** *1148-1632*
*L'ISLE ADAM*
PO T A Perry and crew

**25/26 Aug** *2037-0501*
*DARMSTADT*
PO N W Saunders and crew

**29/30 Aug** *2035-0700*
*KÖNIGSBERG*
PO N W Saunders and crew

**31 Aug** *1618-2006*
*ROLLENCOURT*
PO T A Perry and crew

**11 Sep** *0522-0925*
*LE HAVRE*
PO T A Perry and crew

**11/12 Sep** *2058-0238*
*DARMSTADT*
PO T A Perry and crew

**12/13 Sep** *1901-0156*
*STUTTGART*
PO T A Perry and crew

**17 Sep** *0811-1129*
*BOULOGNE*
PO K W Reilly
Sgt R W Jones
FS A R MacKenzie
FO B C Howard
FS R N Hall
Sgt A D Pryer
FS R N Battye

**18 Sep** *1814-2328*
*BREMERHAVEN*
PO K W Reilly and crew

**19/20 Sep** *1901-0001*
*RHEYDT*
PO K W Reilly and crew

**23/24 Sep** *1908-0023*
*DORTMUND-EMS CANAL*
PO T A Perry and crew

**27 Sep** *0059-0704*
*KARLSRUHE*
FO L C Peart
Sgt P Kerns
FS J Palmer
FS A E Parkes
FS K N Brandwood
FS G C Bowler
FS P J Rogers

**27/28 Sep** *2200-0442*
*KAISERSLAUTERN*
FO L C Peart and crew

**27 Dec** *1216-1636*
*RHEYDT*
FO M S Wickes (DFC)
Sgt L R Botting (N)
FO R S Brownlee
WO F K Brett
FS R S Jenkins
Sgt F H Boddy
Sgt L D Cottrell

**31 Dec** *0224-0732*
*HOUFFALIZE*
FL B S Martin and crew
(tgt not seen – abandoned)

## 1945

**1 Jan** *0735-1400*
*DORTMUND-EMS CANAL*
FO M S Wickes and crew

**5 Jan** *0047-0737*
*ROYAN*
FO M S Wickes and crew

**7/8 Jan** *1656-0207*
*MUNICH*
FO M S Wickes and crew

**13/14 Jan** *1639-0335*
*PÖLITZ*
FO G F Lincoln
Sgt J Clift
FS D Pickford
FS W E Hooper
FS D M Stubing
FS Hutchinson
FS W C Faust

**14/15 Jan** *1632-0215*
*MERSEBURG-LEUNA*
FO M S Wickes and crew

**1 Feb** *1617-2237*
*SIEGEN*
PO E Foster
Sgt C Beighton
Sgt D J Starling
Sgt H K Hurst
FS F Pentiman
Sgt H Goode
Sgt G E Howitt

**8/9 Feb** *1655-0300*
*PÖLITZ*
FO M S Wickes and crew
(badly damaged by Ju88
night fighters, one of which
was shot down)

# ED860
# NUTS/NAN

Another A V Roe, Manchester-built Mark III, equipped with four Packard Merlin 28 engines, ED860 was produced in early 1943 and assigned to 156 Squadron at Warboys, Huntingdonshire, on 14 April. Once in the hands of its new ground crew, the Lanc was given the squadron code letter GT and individual letter N for Nuts, also later known as *Nan*. 156 Squadron was part of the new Pathfinder Force and ED860 served with this unit until August 1943, taking part in 23 operations.

Bernard Fitch and crew flew seven ops in ED860. From left to right: A Lyons, Len Whitehead, Les Cromerty, Fitch, Syd Jennings, Johnnie Taylor and C Kershaw.

According to records, it was assigned to 61 Squadron at Syerston, Nottinghamshire, on 20 August, although 156 Squadron still noted the aircraft's last op was on the 22nd, followed by another on the 23rd. This looks too much like an error, the clerk assuming a 'new' aircraft 'N' was still ED860. Therefore its last trip with 156 was to Milan on 15 August and its first with 61 Squadron occurred on the 23rd, as a 156 Squadron combat report dated 27 August notes ED860, while 61 Squadron clearly shows ED860 as operating with them to the same target. Also, the combat report notes the aircraft (it says is ED860) as aircraft 'Y'.

One pilot to fly her in 156 Squadron was Flight Lieutenant R E Young and his crew. They flew her on nine (or ten) trips, being forced to abort one to Cologne on 16/17 June 1944 due to severe icing that froze the front turret and made the R/T u/s. I was sent copies of Tom Evans' log-book by his cousin Peter Renshaw and in reading it found an item of interest. In August 1943, F/Lt Young suddenly becomes S/L Young, obviously promoted to flight commander. He then begins to fly another Lancaster and no longer takes ED860 on ops, although curiously, the new Lancaster (JA975) is noted as 'N'! Perhaps he felt he deserved a newer machine?

Ralph Young, later Wing Commander DFC, had come from 12 Squadron with his crew, where they had begun ops in April. They had flown seven ops before moving to 156 Squadron. Tom Evans records 29 ops with Young by 6 September. Then they go to 7 Squadron PFF, Young still a flight commander, and now Wing Commander, where Tom's ops go up to 46 by the end of December (DFC). Tom called it a day – his daughter was expected – but Young (DSO) continued his second tour and was shot down on 28/29 January 1944. He and two of his crew were captured, the four others were killed. His navigator while with 156, Flight Lieutenant Thomas Burger DFC, was among those who died. Young died in April 1995.

Once with 61 Squadron ED860 certainly had the individual letter retained as 'N' but now called N for Nan; squadron code letters were changed to QR. *Nan* started out with 61 Squadron with a trip to the Big City as the Battle of Berlin was just starting. Once this battle got into its stride, *Nan* went to Berlin on a further 19 occasions, although one was aborted due to engine problems. Few crews flew this Lanc for long, although Flying Officer B C Fitch piloted her on 2/3 September, and then from October operated with her on six more trips. His navigator was Syd Jennings who remembered:

Bernard Fitch DFC.

'Our first trip was a mining sortie off Texel. Despite intense AA fire from flak-ships we dropped our mines from 750 to 1,000 feet but because of our height, the flak came at us horizontally!

'On one of our Berlin trips I was acting as Windfinder, and we had been given a NNE wind at 70 mph, whereas I soon discovered the true winds were 120 mph at 040 degrees. I sent this back to Bomber Command HQ but they just couldn't believe it and only adjusted the wind as 75 mph at 030 degrees. Thus most bombers came back via the Ruhr, and as a result a lot of aircraft were brought down.

'On another occasion our compass was found to be 60 degrees off so I had to get a shot from the astrodome on Polaris and use the astro-compass from then on, but we made it to the target and back.'

Up goes the 100th bomb symbol – for the 29 June 1944 sortie.

Bernard Fitch, who like his navigator would receive the DFC, remembers the windy Berlin trip, as due to the winds they had to do a dummy run over the city and on both runs the headwind was so strong they were practically standing still during the approach. The rear turret became frozen, so when a night fighter came at them the gunner could only order a corkscrew; they lost 4,000 feet. He also recalled the 18/19 November trip to Berlin for another reason:

'We were due to go on leave on Friday 19 November, and I was due to get married in Bedford the next day. The squadron was comfortably established at Syerston, and best uniforms were at the cleaners in nearby Newark. Out of the blue we were moved to Skellingthorpe on the 16th. Things were not back to normal when ops on the 18th turned out to the opening of the Battle of Berlin, which didn't auger well for a stand down (and leave) the next day.

'It was a hell of a rush to get off in time in ED860. Something had to go wrong and we lost our upper escape hatch on take-off, so for most of us the trip was colder than usual. But we made it although it took us 7½ hours.

'Next morning we retired to bed not knowing whether it was leave or ops. Thus we – and I especially – were very relieved on being called as arranged at 2 pm, to learn of a stand down! It took much longer than our flight time to Berlin to travel to Bedford, but at least I got to the church on time, albeit in my working uniform.'

Flying Officer H N Scott RCAF then seemed to fly *Nan* more regularly than anyone else – 21 ops – until Pilot Officer E A Stone took over in early 1944, operating her until May. Henley Scott received the DFC.

Ted Stone flew *Nan* firstly in late January, then regularly at the start of March. In all he piloted her on 21 sorties during his tour, including the disastrous raid on Nürnberg on the night of 30/31 March, the night Bomber Command lost 96 heavy bombers. With *Nan* having taken them through most of their tour, the crew were extremely proud of ED860 and they agreed amongst themselves that the first daughter born to a wife of a crew member would have her christened *Nan* in her honour and memory. Stone's wife in fact became the first later in

Aircrew and ground crew on 30 June 1944. FL B S Turner stands eighth from left.

1944, so the baby was christened Jennifer Nan Stone. In due time Jennifer Nan married and her daughter was named Nanette, thereby continuing the association with this Lancaster. Stone received the DFC at the end of his tour.

As Stone finished his tour, *Nan* had completed 92 ops. The 100th came in early summer 1944, during Flying Officer B S Turner's tour in June. In all Basil Turner flew 14 ops in *Nan* and he too received the DFC on completing his tour.

*Nan* had missed D-Day due to a major servicing but on the night of 18/19 July 1944 she and her crew of Flying Officer D G Bates came under night fighter attacks over Révigny. According to the combat report, the Lancaster was at 8,500 feet, and the time was 0148 hours. After one inconclusive action, the mid-upper gunner, Pilot Officer J Fletcher, saw an aircraft coming in astern, and gave the pilot the order to corkscrew as he opened fire, the rear gunner, Sergeant D Hancock, also blazing away. Bullets were seen to strike the enemy aircraft which burst into flames and dived to the ground where both gunners saw it explode, witnessed too by the pilot and bomb aimer. As the pilot came round to try for another bomb-run, they came under fire from another Lancaster's gunners but luckily suffered no damage. By this time the target

markers were no longer visible and so the attack had to be abandoned. *Nan's* crew were surprised by the initial attack. Ordinarily 'Monica' (a set that picked up airborne radar warning of enemy aircraft in the vicinity) would have alerted the crew but the wireless operator was so engrossed with his radio watch that he failed to spot it.

In August 1944, Flying Officer N E Hoad and his crew, who had commenced their tour in July, began to fly ED860, making six trips in all. Norman Hoad recalled:

'The "honour" of flying ED860 was something of a dubious privilege in that in some respects it was well past its sell-by-date. However, as a new boy on the squadron it was not for me to pick and choose and I had to make the best of it. Both outer engines had a nasty habit of over-heating for which there was no remedy but to throttle back. Apart from having to fly the machine with engines out of sync, the most serious consequence was to trail slowly behind the rest of the [bomber] stream.

'On the submarine pen operation on 11 August [Bordeaux] we were so far behind we attacked virtually on our own. Not wishing to make a lonely way home across enemy-held territory, I took the

Norman Hoad and crew. Standing, from left to right: Bill Ball, "Moosh" Embury, Bill Pullin, Norman England, Wilson and "Lucky" Webb. In front: Hoppy Boyd and Hoad.

decision to drop down to sea level and make the return flight the long way round at wave-top height. Some way out in the Bay of Biscay we encountered a Dornier 14 flying-boat going the other way but both of us chose to ignore the other!

'The last time I flew "N" was, of course, on 29 August in the raid on Königsberg. Here again her foibles were a pain. The Lancaster's auto-pilot was pneumatically operated and on this occasion the aircraft was thrown into a violent pitch every time an attempt was made to engage. This is not the best way to treat a heavily loaded aircraft and the result was that it had to be flown manually for the ten hours, 45 minutes the flight lasted.

'Approaching the target area the fighters were extraordinarily active and though I did not see them myself, I was constantly told by my gunners to corkscrew. The 5 Group corkscrew should, in theory, enable a pilot to maintain a roughly straight track but a continuous series of 60-degree banked turns in either direction, coupled with dives and climbs through 1,000 feet, can and did

lead to some deviation in our route. So much so in this case that I found myself totally out of position to make the bombing-run on the prescribed heading so I decided to go round again rather than waste my bombs.

'It took a certain amount of time and as at Bordeaux, I found myself over the target area more or less alone. At some stage in all this the aircraft sustained various hits, the most serious of which was in the starboard wing-root between the fuselage and the starboard main fuel tank. To this day I do not know whether this was merely flak damage or, as I think more likely, cannon fire from an upward-firing night fighter. At all events I was given a new paddle-bladed Lancaster for my next operations!'

N-Nan became Cat C after this raid, and did not return to serviceability until 18 October. In fact she went on only one more mission and then it was made Cat E on the 28th, to be ingloriously Struck off Charge and scrapped on 4 November 1944, without seeing the victory she had helped to secure. ED860 had flown almost 1,032 hours.

# ED860 NUTS/NAN

Norman Hoad noted in his log-book that the six ops he flew in *Nan* had been numbered as her 118, 119, 120, 121, 124 and 129th, so that its final mission had to be her 130th. ED860 had no special artwork, just two columns of bombs each in five lines of ten for the first 100, then another column in tens starting back under the first one. Curiously there were two swastika markings painted on,

denoting two successes against enemy night fighters, although only the victory on 18/19 July is known for certain. As explained earlier, the combat on 27 August 1943 – the Lancaster crew 'attacking' a Heinkel 111 on their way to Nürnberg – had to be another aeroplane. *Nan* did have encounters with Ju88s over Stuttgart on 7/8 October 1943 but no claims appear to have been made.

Bombing-up ED860. Aircrew from left to right: Ball, Pullin, Embrey, England, Boyd and Webb. Hoad is in cockpit.

## 156 SQUADRON
## 1943

**20/21 Apr** *2135-0455*
STETTIN
PO J M Horan RCAF (DFC)
FS R J Atkin (N) (DFM)
FS E P Fast RCAF (WOP) (DFM)
Sgt J C Chapman (FE) (DFM)
FO D C A Saunders (BA) (DFC)
Sgt G G Forbes (MU) (DFM)
Sgt J R Curtis (RG) (DFM)

**27 Apr** *0035-0435*
DUISBURG
PO J M Horan and crew
FL G L Mandeno (2P) (DFC)

**1 May** *0042-0459*
ESSEN
FL D T Muir
PO H G Innes
Sgt G W Bramley

Sgt H J Folland
Sgt R H Wedd
Sgt M Haslegrave
Sgt W M MacKinley

**4/5 May** *2253-0454*
DORTMUND
FO B F Smith
PO W J Smith
FO R E Goodwin
Sgt B Marshall
FO J A Phillips
Sgt L J Jones
FO S Hayes

**13/14 May** *2210-0532*
PILSEN
Sgt L W Overton (DFC)
Sgt D P Clements
Sgt J A M Arcari
Sgt T Cable
Sgt D M Davies
Sgt F Sunderland
Sgt A Barnett

**23/24 May** *2255-0324*
DORTMUND
FS D L Wallace
Sgt T H Harvey
Sgt W H Moore
Sgt R J Jackson
Sgt R J Twinn
FS D Ross
Sgt H A Lister

**25/26 May** *2350-0424*
DÜSSELDORF
FS D L Wallace and crew

**29/30 May** *2243-0340*
WUPPERTAL
Sgt L W Overton and crew

**11/12 June** *2346-0419*
MÜNSTER
FL R E Young (DSO DFC)
PO T Burger (N) (DFC)
Sgt E G Hodges (WOP)

Sgt J K Calton (FE)
Sgt T H Evans (BA)
Sgt J S Goodman (MU)
Sgt J W Boynton (RG)

**12/13 June** *2331-0352*
BOCHUM
FL R E Young and crew

**16/17 June** *2241-0210*
COLOGNE
FL R E Young and crew
(abort due to severe icing)

**24/25 June** *2314-0341*
ELBERFELD
FL R E Young and crew

**28/29 June** *2306-0340*
COLOGNE
Sgt C W Wilkins
Sgt H Holman
Sgt E S Crabbe
Sgt G E Milton

Sgt A Cloud
Sgt R Lobb
Sgt E J Cahill

**3/4 July** *2247-0328*
*COLOGNE*
FL A L McGrath RNZAF (DFC)
FO R P Wright
FO J Facey
Sgt D L Wilkie
FO C R Johnson
Sgt J Poochera
Sgt G D Aitken

**8/9 July** *2255-0353*
*COLOGNE*
FL R E Young and crew

**24/25 July** *2221-0436*
*HAMBURG*
FL R E Young and crew

**27/28 July** *2201-0359*
*HAMBURG*
FL R E Young and crew

**29/30 July** *2203-0345*
*HAMBURG*
FL R E Young and crew

**2/3 Aug** *2336-0531*
*HAMBURG*
FL R E Young and crew

**7/8 Aug** *2147-0609*
*TURIN*
WO G Denwood DFC
PO F R Kennedy RAAF (N) (DFC)
Sgt E J Cutter
Sgt A L Barlow
FS J C Ross
WO J E Barnham
FS J A O Lovis

**9/10 Aug** *2339-0443*
*MANNHEIM*
WO G Denwood and crew

**10/11 Aug** *2135-0503*
*NÜRNBERG*
WO G Denwood and crew

**15/16 Aug** *2035-0401*
*MILAN*
PO P A Coldham
FO A P Stevens
Sgt A A P Bland
Sgt T E Rees
FS G R Robinson
FS N Warwick
FS G H Pascoe

## 61 SQUADRON

**23/24 Aug** *2030-0401*
*BERLIN*
Sgt M C Lowe
FS J G McAlpine (2P)
Sgt C R Moffitt (FE)
FO R J Clarke (N)
Sgt M W McPhail (BA)
Sgt D A Turner (WOP)
Sgt A W Deardon (MU)
Sgt H A White (RG)

**27/28 Aug** *2102-0429*
*NÜRNBERG*
FS J G McAlpine
Sgt E Vine (FE)
FS H W Harris (N)
Sgt V A Martin (BA)
PO S Heald (WOP)
Sgt H S Oldfield (MU)
Sgt B H Varey (RG)

**31 Aug/1 Sep** *2032-0355*
*BERLIN*
Sgt E Willsher (DFC)

Sgt T J Hurdiss
Sgt J E Gripton
Sgt R C Everest
Sgt B W Bell
Sgt R E Salter
Sgt J Fenswick

**2/3 Sep** *2017-2315*
*GARDENING – TEXEL*
FO B C Fitch (DFC)
Sgt J W Taylor (FE)
FO S A Jennings (N) (DFC)
PO A Lyons (BA)
Sgt C Kershaw (WOP)
FS H W Pronger (MU)
Sgt L W Cromarty (RG)

**3/4 Sep** *2014-0337*
*BERLIN*
Sgt E Willsher and crew

**5/6 Sep** *1953-0220*
*MANNHEIM*
Sgt E Willsher and crew

**6/7 Sep** *1958-0417*
*MUNICH*
PO E Willsher and crew

**22/23 Sep** *1845-0007*
*HANNOVER*
PO E Willsher and crew

**23/24 Sep** *1857-0137*
*MANNHEIM*
PO E Willsher and crew

**27/28 Sep** *1948-0119*
*HANNOVER*
FS J G McAlpine and crew

**29 Sep** *1821-2308*
*BOCHUM*
FS J G McAlpine and crew

**1/2 Oct** *1829-0024*
*HAGEN*
FO H N Scott RCAF (DFC)
Sgt A E Harris
PO S Halliwell
Sgt S R Knight
Sgt W C McDonald
Sgt E F Dunn
Sgt C A Haig

**2/3 Oct** *1840-0258*
*MUNICH*
FO H N Scott and crew
Sgt S P Nicholls in (MU)

**4/5 Oct** *1833-0104*
*FRANKFURT*
PO J F McLean
Sgt W D French
Sgt A Pestell
Sgt B R Greatree
Sgt W Brown
Sgt R T Charles
Sgt R D Murdock

**7/8 Oct** *2026-0312*
*STUTTGART*
FS J G McAlpine and crew
(encounters with 4 Ju88s)

**8/9 Oct** *2249-0413*
*HANNOVER*
FO H N Scott and crew
Sgts F J Davies (N), D B
Chalk (RG) & G Allan (MU) in

**18 Oct** *1729-2301*
*HANNOVER*
FO H N Scott and crew
Sgt F J Peack (N) in,
Haig back

**20/21 Oct** *1730-0101*
*LEIPZIG*
FO B C Fitch and crew

**22/23 Oct** *1810-0024*
*KASSEL*
FO H N Scott and crew

**3 Nov** *1718-2211*
*DÜSSELDORF*
FO B C Fitch and crew

**10/11 Nov** *2026-0516*
*MODANE*
FO H N Scott and crew
Sgt J C Homewood in (N)

**18/19 Nov** *1750-0111*
*BERLIN*
FO B C Fitch and crew
Sgts G R Jeffrey (BA) and
H S Rosher (MU) in

**22 Nov** *1700-2355*
*BERLIN*
FO H N Scott and crew
FL C T Fuller in (N)

**23/24 Nov** *1724-0016*
*BERLIN*
FO H N Scott and crew

**26/27 Nov** *1743-0040*
*BERLIN*
FO H N Scott and crew

**2 Dec** *1652-2121*
*BERLIN*
PO D Paul
Sgt F T Coulter
FS R A Griffin (N)
Sgt D H Millar
Sgt R F Brazier
Sgt S Billington
Sgt P McGibney
(abort, loss of power)

**16 Dec** *1622-2339*
*BERLIN*
FO H N Scott and crew
FS R A Griffin in (N)

**20 Dec** *1717-2256*
*FRANKFURT*
FO B C Fitch and crew

**24 Dec** *0005-0741*
*BERLIN*
FO H N Scott and crew
FL C T Fuller in (N)

**29 Dec** *1654-2338*
*BERLIN*
FO H N Scott and crew

## 1944

**1/2 Jan** *2353-0730*
*BERLIN*
FO H N Scott and crew

**2/3 Jan** *2326-0656*
*BERLIN*
FO B C Fitch and crew
Sgt L C Whitehead in (MU)

**6 Jan** *0001-0837*
*STETTIN*
PO V McConnell
Sgt T Powell
FO A J Watts
Sgt H S Vickers
Sgt W Surgey
Sgt G H Bradshaw
Sgt W J Throsby

**14 Jan** *1647-2207*
*BRUNSWICK*
FO B C Fitch and crew
FS L G Rolton in (BA)

**20 Jan** *1620-2316*
*BERLIN*
FL H N Scott and crew
FL J A McDonald in (BA),
Knight out

**21/22 Jan** *2003-0237*
*BERLIN*
FL H N Scott and crew

**27/28 Jan** *1734-0210*
*BERLIN*
PO A E Stone (DFC)
Sgt A Dick
FS J F Mills
Sgt W J Sinclair
Sgt T Francis
Sgt G E Cunningham
Sgt A Kane

**28/29 Jan** *2345-0738*
*BERLIN*
FL H N Scott and crew
FS G A Leslie in (BA)

**30 Jan** *1738-2324*
*BERLIN*
FL H N Scott and crew

**15 Feb** *1656-2348*
*BERLIN*
FL H N Scott and crew
Sgt J H Eastwood (2P)
McDonald back

**19/20 Feb** *2327-0634*
*LEIPZIG*
FL H N Scott and crew
Leslie back, McDonald
out; FL J Breakey (MU)

**20/21 Feb** *2329-0701*
*STUTTGART*
FL H N Scott and crew
McDonald back,
Sgt W Walker in (MU)

**24/25 Feb** *2045-0414*
*SCHWEINFURT*
FL H N Scott and crew
Leslie in, FS H W Pronger in (MU)

**25/26 Feb** *1822-0203*
*AUGSBURG*
FL H N Scott and crew
(4,000 lb hung up, only
dropped incendiaries)

**1/2 Mar** *2315-0737*
*STUTTGART*
PO A E Stone and crew

**10/11 Mar** *1959-0135*
*CHÂTEAUROUX*
PO A E Stone and crew

**15/16 Mar** *1905-0311*
*STUTTGART*
PO A E Stone and crew

**18/19 Mar** *1915-0042*
*FRANKFURT*
PO A E Stone and crew
PO D Carbutt (2P)

**22/23 Mar** *1857-0042*
*FRANKFURT*
PO A E Stone and crew

**24/25 Mar** *1841-0135*
*BERLIN*
PO A E Stone and crew

**30/31 Mar** *2214-0627*
*NÜRNBERG*
PO A E Stone and crew

**5/6 Apr** *2021-0356*
*TOULOUSE*
PO E H Williams
Sgt A B Woodvine

FS D Bresley
FS A D Anderson
Sgt J L Parker
FS E Parry
Sgt S A Gardner

**10/11 Apr** *2213-0313*
*TOURS M/YARDS*
PO A E Stone and crew

**11/12 Apr** *2037-0014*
*AACHEN*
PO A E Stone and crew

**18/19 Apr** *2105-0119*
*JUVISY M/YARDS*
PO A E Stone and crew

**20/21 Apr** *2308-0355*
*PARIS M/YARDS*
PO A E Stone and crew

**22/23 Apr** *2328-0456*
*BRUNSWICK*
PO A E Stone and crew

**24/25 Apr** *2044-0707*
*MUNICH*
PO A E Stone and crew

**26/27 Apr** *2123-0628*
*SCHWEINFURT*
PO A E Stone and crew
Sgt H W Cooper (2P)
FL R B G Murphy RAAF (N)

**28/29 Apr** *2304-0641*
*ST MÉDARD*
PO A E Stone and crew
PO D Street (2P)
FO R P Keyser in (N)

**29/30 Apr** *2228-0544*
*ST MÉDARD*
PO A E Stone and crew
FL Murphy (N)

**3/4 May** *2204-0311*
*MAILLY-LE-CAMP*
PO A E Stone and crew
FO J H Dyer in (N)

**7 May** *0036-0515*
*LOUAILLES*
PO A E Stone and crew
Mills back

**8/9 May** *2139-0221*
*BREST*
PO A E Stone and crew
FL J Breakey in (MU)

**10/11 May** *2205-0135*
*LILLE*
PO D Street
Sgt C F Waghorn
FS D K Grant
FS T W Boothby
Sgt P F Hadden
Sgt R Gilbert
Sgt T W Brown

**19/20 May** *2229-0430*
*TOURS M/YARDS*
PO A E Stone and crew
Sgt T E Hunt in (FE)

**21/22 May** *2225-0306*
*DUISBURG*
PO A E Stone and crew
Sgt D Dunkley in (FE)

**22/23 May** *2239-0428*
*BRUNSWICK*
PO R J Auckland
Sgt J Slome
PO J Moran
FS D G Patfield
Sgt E V Jackson
Sgt J Miller
Sgt G R Chinery

**24/25 May** *2310-0205*
*EINDHOVEN AIRFIELD*
PO R J Auckland and crew
(recalled)

**27/28 May** *2310-0437*
*NANTES M/YARDS*
FO B S Turner (DFC)
Sgt R Brown
WO G W James RCAF
FO E Jones RAAF
Sgt H Edwards
Sgt G W McDonell RCAF
Sgt N W Pettis RCAF

**31 May/1 June** *2337-0519*
*SAUMUR*
PO H W Cooper
Sgt F E Hardy
FO B A Little
WO G McLaughlin
Sgt K G Merrifield
Sgt J F Blane
Sgt W I Quigley

**19/20 June** *2255-0031*
*WATTEN – V1 SITE*
FO B S Turner and crew
(recalled by MB)

**21/22 June** *2312-0406*
*GELSENKIRCHEN*
FO B S Turner and crew

**23/24 June** *2243-0516*
*LIMOGES M/YARDS*
FO B S Turner and crew

**24/25 June** *2259-0213*
*PROUVILLE – V1 SITE*
FO B S Turner and crew
FL I M Pettigrew in (FE)

**27/28 June** *2138-0538*
*VITRY*
FO B S Turner and crew
Brown back

**29 June** *1200-1525*
*BEAUVOIR – V1 SITE*
FO B S Turner and crew

**4/5 July** *2335-0320*
*ST LEU D'ESSERENT*
FO B S Turner and crew

**14/15 July** *2204-0508*
*VILLENEUVE*
FO B S Turner and crew

**15/16 July** *2228-0532*
*NEVERS*
FO B S Turner and crew

**18 July** *0350-0714*
*CAEN*
FO B S Turner and crew

**18/19 July** *2305-0435*
*RÉVIGNY*
FO D G Bates
Sgt G Farrow
FS A N Hughes
PO G O Cameron
Sgt F W Cotton
PO J Fletcher (MU)
Sgt D Hancock (RG)
(combat – did not bomb -
signals unclear)

**20/21 July** *2307-0225*
*COURTRAI*
FS W R McPherson
Sgt W J Smith
FO P P Brosko RCAF
Sgt R G McMillan RCAF
Sgt G H Postins
Sgt J A McFie
Sgt D T Currie

**24/24 July** *2224-0558*
*DONGES*
FO C N Hill RCAF
Sgt C L Goss
FO D Hayley RCAF
FO G S Machen RCAF
Sgt M R Vagnolini
Sgt G R Mildren
Sgt J V O'Neill

**25 July** *1740-2212*
*ST CYR*
FS A H Harrison RCAF
Sgt E W Walker
Sgt W D Beacon RCAF
Sgt J E Heffernan RCAF
Sgt R L Taylor
Sgt J M Fraser
Sgt J M Stewart
(damaged by flak)

**26/27 July** *2124-0640*
*GIVORS*
FS A H Harrison and crew

**28/29 July** *2213-0556*
*STUTTGART*
FS A H Harrison and crew

**30 July** *0604-1015*
*CAHAGNES*
FS A H Harrison and crew
(aborted by MB)

**31 July** *1725-2220*
*RILLY-LA-MONTAGNE*
FL B S Turner and crew

**1 Aug** *1500-1830*
*SIRACOURT – V1 SITE*
FL B S Turner and crew
(abandoned by MB)

**2 Aug** *1445-1915*
*BOIS DE CASSAN – V1 SITE*
FL B S Turner and crew
FS C Baldwin in (3AG)

**5 Aug** *1045-1525*
*ST LEU D'ESSERENT*
FL B S Turner and crew

**6 Aug** *0940-1425*
*BOIS DE CASSAN – V1 SITE*
FO E R Church
Sgt D Dunkley
FO S A Fleming
WO W Lewis
Sgt T Moffatt
Sgt F Kohut
FS A J Anderson

**7/8 Aug** *2126-0131*
*SECQUEVILLE*
FO N E Hoad
Sgt C S Webb (FE)
FO K W Ball (N)
FO W H Pullen (BA)
Sgt C P Boyd (WOP)
Sgt N England (MU)
Sgt G Anslow (RG)

**9/10 Aug** *2045-0320*
*CHÂTELLERAULT*
FO N E Hoad and crew

**11 Aug** *1201-1939*
*BORDEAUX*
FO N E Hoad and crew
Sgt C V Embury in (RG)

**12/13 Aug** *2130-0315*
*RÜSSELSHEIM*
FO N E Hoad and crew

**14 Aug** *1752-2248*
*BREST*
WO D R Souter RCAF (DFC)
Sgt H J Ockerby

Framed record of ED860's operations,
although the record was broken.

Sgt J F Duncan
Sgt F Carling
Sgt C Darn
Sgt B McCormack
Sgt F Maudesley

**15 Aug** *1008-1341*
*GILZE-RIJEN AIRFIELD*
WO D R Souter and crew

**16/17 Aug** *2114-0505*
*STETTIN*
FO N E Hoad and crew

**18 Aug** *1129-1620*
*BORDEAUX*
FO J S Cooksey (DFC)
Sgt D E Rose
Sgt E P Meaker
Sgt T Stephenson
Sgt S J Scarrett
Sgt A R Marshall
Sgt N W Salter

**19 Aug** *0526-1154*
*LA PALLICE*
FO J S Cooksey and crew

**25/26 Aug** *2056-0535*
*DARMSTADT*
WO D R Souter and crew

**26/27 Aug** *2013-0708*
*KÖNIGSBERG*
WO D R Souter and crew

**29/30 Aug** *2035-0722*
*KÖNIGSBERG*
FO N E Hoad and crew

**23 Oct** *1443-1756*
*FLUSHING*
FO L A Pearce
Sgt J B Murray (FE)
FS R B Pettigrew RAAF (N)
Sgt D A Barker (BA)
Sgt A E Perry (WOP)
Sgt A Barker (MU)
Sgt R Gillanders (RG)

# ED888
# MOTHER/MIKE SQUARED

ED888 came off the production line in early 1943. Built as a Mark III by A V Roe at Manchester, and initially equipped with four Merlin 28 engines, by 20 April it had arrived at 103 Squadron's base at Elsham Wolds, Lincolnshire and been assigned to B Flight.

Given the squadron code letter of PN, it became M-Mother as it received its individual code letter, and the aircraft initially had nothing in the way of nose-art other than a steadily increasing number of bomb symbols. *Mother* flew on 54 ops with 103 Squadron, the aircraft being 'awarded' a DFC after it completed its 50th mission in November 1943.

The early part of ED888's career was fairly routine. The first time something out of the ordinary occurred was during a trip to Nürnberg on 27/28 August. The navigator's oxygen plug was accidentally pulled out as the wireless operator squeezed by his companion's compartment, resulting in the navigator passing out. As he eventually came to, he had lost all track of their position so they were forced to abort, jettisoning their bombs in the Channel.

ED888 flew to Berlin six times with 103 Squadron, being hit by flak on one of them and having to abort another after the starboard outer engine packed up. She also had encounters with night fighters. During a raid on Mannheim on 23/24 September, the mid-upper spotted one with a nose light, but it quickly went out and the fighter disappeared when he fired at it. A FW190 approached them on 20/21 October but again a burst from an alert mid-upper gunner sent the fighter off into the darkness.

*Mother's* regular skipper during her first months with the squadron was Sergeant, later Pilot Officer Denis W Rudge, who flew 23 ops and received the DFC; his navigator, George Lancaster (a good name) was given the DFM. The mid-upper gunner was Charlie Baird:

'We were [at the start] an all-NCO crew so ate, slept, flew and imbibed together, and we had a very good ground crew whom we valued very

ED888's first regular crew. From left to right: Pilot Denny Rudge, Charlie Baird, Chiefy Catton, Jack Fitzpatrick, Trevor Greenwood, George Lancaster and Sid Robinson.

highly. They were Bert Booth, fitter, Bob Draper, rigger, Tom Gean, aircraft hand. They were very protective of ED888 and didn't care to see a few holes in her. We were a very alert crew and were never complacent from start to finish of our tour. We had no idle-chat from take-off to return and when we spoke it was all business. I'm certain this led to our success in surviving.

'On several occasions when I saw an enemy aircraft, immediately Den went into action; he was a great pilot and only 19-years-old. Our theory was that if the German pilot broke off his attack on realising we were awake, then he would go off and look for someone less alert. One night we took a Wing Commander Slater as second "dickie" and on

George Lancaster, Charlie Baird, Trevor Greenwood and Jack Kilpatrick in front of ED888, summer 1944.

landing he told our skipper we were too damned quiet and had no animation. Den told us of his remarks and only said to us: ".. bugger the animation, let's carry on as we are!"

'Very few crews were finishing their 30 ops at this period, many coming off early, a lot going down on their 28th or even 30th. We came to our 30th on 23 August 1943 and we were briefed for the Big City – Berlin! What a hot-bed to finish on; the adrenalin was flowing freely. This is how that evening went.

Fitter Bert Booth and Jack Fitzpatrick, Rudge's Aussie rear-gunner, relax on a 4,000 lb 'cookie'.

'Main meal 7pm, final briefing 7.30, driven out to *Mother of them All*, engines tested and general last minute checks, then shut down engines. It was while we were lying on the hard-standing with the ground crew having a last smoke and idle chatter as other crews were testing their aircraft, that one, about 500 yards from us, had a negative earth and its bombs fell off on trying to start the engines.

'As soon as we saw the first

J R "Blondie" O'Hanlon, WOP/AG in G S Morgan's crew, autumn 1943.

incendiaries catch alight we all dashed for the slit-trench which hadn't been used for some months. I was the first in with all the others on top of me. We were barely in when the aircraft blew up; a hell of a blast of hot air and debris began dropping about us.

'Out we got, skip and engineer ran around checking [ED888] for damage, none apparent, so all aboard. At this time I became aware of a dreadful odour, and there it was; someone had used the trench as a toilet and I had landed on it. So out with knife and I cut the right knee out of my Sidcot flying suit, then gave it the heave-ho down the flare chute.

'By now – 8.25 – we were taking off and were wondering if this was all a bad omen for our last trip. We all had very mixed thoughts. Anyhow, M-Mother took us to Berlin and whilst many aircraft went down around us, we had a charmed run; 50 aircraft were lost on this raid.

'On our return we were all very sad at the thought of never flying ED888 again. All we could do was to give her a pat and while it may sound

Rear gunner Bob Shilling gives the rear-turret that extra polish.

daft, there were lumps in some of our throats.

'Her first op was on 4 May 1943, Nick Ross being the pilot, a Scot like me, and a few weeks later, while we were on leave, another Scottish pilot, Bob Edie, took her on a raid, so she had a good Scots influence during her first 32 trips; a great aircraft. She should be in some museum today, rather than being broken up as she was.'

What turned out to be ED888's last sortie with 103 Squadron – at least in 1943 – was a raid on Berlin on 26/27 November, with Flying Officer G S "Taffy" Morgan bringing the Lanc safely home. Gomer Morgan received the DFC in 1944, but with 576 Squadron (a nucleus of 103 forming 576 in November); 15 of his ops had been flown in *Mother*.

ED888, like Morgan, was part of 103 Squadron which was hived off to become the foundation of the new 576 Squadron, on 25 November. In all 13 crews left 103 and another four came in from 101 Squadron. 576 also operated from Elsham Wolds. ED888's fuselage letters were changed to UL-V, becoming V-Victor, but Morgan still flew her.

With a nominal gender change, the first trip with 576 was another to Berlin and it did a further eight trips to the Big City. On one (23/24th December), ED888 took a Mr (Sergeant) Benjamin Frazier along, a US Army war correspondent. His account of the raid later appeared in the *Yank* magazine. During another Berlin op, the bomber was attacked by a Do217 night fighter on 28/29

January 1944, but its gunners damaged the Dornier and sent it packing. Bob "Blondie" O'Hanlon was Morgan's wireless operator and remembered the trip with the war correspondent:

'On that trip the wireless receiver went off for a while, however, after a look around for the cause it again functioned. When we got back I explained the problem to the Flight Sergeant (Molyneaux) and years later we were still arguing about the cause.

'On another trip to Berlin with one engine u/s and thick fog over Elsham Wolds, we had to fly round and on our last circuit the rear gunner, [R C] "Bob" Shilling nearly collected the red light from the main hangar roof. We were told to fly north and eventually found clear air at Scorton. Control was asked for the runway lights to be lit, when they were, I think everyone grabbed their 'chutes; it was like Blackpool illuminations, very bright red, white and blue. However, we landed safely. One thing we won't forget is that that night we took one of the ground crew with us. We were lucky when we got to the sergeants' mess as we were wearing our flying clothing, so the 'extra crewman' couldn't display any rank. Later, back at Elsham mess, a bill arrived for this gentleman. As far as I know, its still pinned to the notice board!'

During March 1944, ED888 was once more given the letter 'M' – this time becoming *Mike*. In fact, all 576's aircraft were marked with a small '2' beside the individual letter, so it was not long before ED888 became known as *Mike Squared* although it continued to be known by some as *Mother of them All*.

ED888's first recorded trip as $M^2$ was to Essen on 26/27 March but upon crossing the North Sea the starboard inner engine packed up and while the engineer was trying to feather it, he feathered another engine by mistake. Consequently the aircraft lost a lot of height before he got the third engine going again, and once the pilot regained the lost height he decided to continue on to the target. Their troubles were not over for just outside the target area they were attacked by a Ju88 and badly shot-up, but they managed to lose the night fighter. Then they were attacked by another '88 but no more damage was sustained.

Neil Lambell RAAF, Morgan's bomb aimer.

Jock Mearns, Morgan's navigator.

Re-crossing the enemy coast, a second engine failed, but asking for help they were located by a Mosquito that escorted them back across the sea and to the RAF fighter station at West Malling, in Kent, where they landed safely. The pilot, Sergeant Charles G Wearmouth, was later commissioned and received the DFC later in the year.

Back on strength in April, ED888's usual skipper became Pilot Officer J S Griffiths who flew *Mike* on 29 of its 30 operations between then and the end of July – at which time he completed his tour, including *Mike's* 99th op. Jimmy Griffiths, another Scot, soon discovered that ED888 was the oldest, most clapped-out aircraft on the squadron and asked his flight commander if he could get another aircraft. A few days later they received a new one only to experience a problem with it whilst taking off on a raid on 30 April. Hitting a hedge, the new Lanc (LM527) had its underside and wheels damaged, and being unable to jettison the bombs or lock down the wheels, the crew were forced to bale out close to the airfield. Nobody was hurt but they had to return to ED888 and it became 'their' aircraft. In fact nobody else wanted to fly it, even when they were on leave!

Griffiths' rear gunner, a Welshman named D W "Taffy" Langmead, shot down two German night fighters, a

Me410 from point-blank range on 24/25 June, then a Ju88 on their 30th and last trip while on the bomb-run over Révigny marshalling yards on 14/15 July. On this occasion they had just got a message to abort but the bomb aimer, Charlie Bint, had the target in his sights and Jimmy told him to go ahead and bomb. Just then the Ju88 flew right across them and then came in from behind. Taffy and the '88 opened fire at the same time, but the Ju88's fire ceased abruptly and the fighter spun down into some cloud.

Pilot Officer J B Bell was flying with Griffiths this night, ED888's 99th, then took over *Mike*, doing 32 straight ops, including the 100th on 20 July. By October when he completed his tour he, like Jimmy, received the DFC. Shortly after the 100th trip, *Mike* had the ribbon of the DSO painted on the nose by the Station Commander, Group Captain W C Sheen, and by now the aircraft also had those two swastikas up for Langmead's two claims. Above each was the name Taffy.

On the last day of October, *Mike* returned to 103 Squadron. 576 Squadron was being moved to Fiskerton, and ED888 was re-coded PM-M². There were now 131 bomb symbols beneath the cockpit area and it went on to complete another nine back with 103 Squadron.

ED888's 100th op. PO J B Bell and crew, 20 July 1944.

The symbols had been marked in two lots of five x ten bomb rows, then three further ten-bomb rows beneath the medal ribbons. In one photograph there is then a row of six, below that two more, and one more below them, making 139. Where the 140th bomb went is still unclear. One more adornment was that of a rosette on her painted DFC ribbon, denoting a Bar to this decoration.

The last op came on Christmas Eve, Flight Lieutenant S L Saxe RCAF taking *Mike* to Cologne. In fact, after Bell ended his tour, no individual pilot took ED888 on more than one trip, except Flight Lieutenant R A Butts RCAF, who did two. The Lancaster became Cat AC on 26 January 1945 and went to Avros for an overhaul and although it returned to 103 Squadron on 3 February it did not fly on any more ops prior to it becoming Cat B on the 20th. By early August, *Mike* was at 10 MU and finally Struck off Charge on 8 January 1947, and reduced to scrap.

## 103 SQUADRON 1943

**4/5 May** *2202-0302*
DORTMUND
WO N R Ross
FS J A B Cooper
Sgt L McLellan
Sgt G Hickson
Sgt A J S Girling
Sgt T A Platt
FS M R Tuxford

**13 May** *0010-0450*
DUISBURG
Sgt D W Rudge (DFC)
Sgt G Lancaster (N)
Sgt T W Catton (FE)
Sgt H T Greenwood (WOP)
Sgt S T Robinson (FE)
Sgt C R Baird (MU)
Sgt J D Kilpatrick (RG)

**13/14 May** *2336-0521*
BOCHUM
Sgt D W Rudge and crew

**23/24 May** *2250-0358*
DORTMUND
Sgt D W Rudge and crew

**25/26 May** *2339-0447*
DÜSSELDORF
Sgt D W Rudge and crew
Sgt D Williamson in,
Catton out

**29/30 May** *2250-0406*
WUPPERTAL
Sgt D W Rudge and crew
Sgt R P Orme in,
Sgt Williamson out

**11/12 June** *2304-0333*
DÜSSELDORF
Sgt D W Rudge and crew

**12/13 June** *2235-0341*
BOCHUM
Sgt D W Rudge and crew

**14/15 June** *2222-0310*
OBERHAUSEN
Sgt D W Rudge and crew

**16/17 June** *2236-0337*
COLOGNE
Sgt R J Edie
Sgt E H J Suarez
PO J C Maxwell
Sgt W Fawley
Sgt E S Boorman
Sgt E C Benham
Sgt J May

**21/22 June** *2305-0317*
KREFELD
SL T O Prickett DFC (DSO)
FL W C Longstaff
Sgt L Pulfrey
Sgt S Foster
Sgt J Terrans
Sgt W J Miller
FS J L Betty

**22/23 June** *2302-0323*
MÜLHEIM
Sgt D W Rudge and crew

**24/25 June** *2239-0340*
WUPPERTAL
Sgt D W Rudge and crew

**25/26 June** *2244-0328*
GELSENKIRCHEN
Sgt D W Rudge and crew

G/Capt W C Sheen paints the DSO ribbon on ED888 following her 100th sortie, while Jim Bell and Jimmy Griffiths look on.

**28/29 June** *2258-0350*
COLOGNE
WO E J Presland
FS L D Groome
Sgt G Aitken
Sgt S G Staplehurst
Sgt C D Hornby
Sgt E R Foster
FS E E Piper

**3/4 July** *2237-0401*
COLOGNE
Sgt D W Rudge and crew

**8/9 July** *2219-0400*
COLOGNE
Sgt D W Rudge and crew

**9/10 July** *2235-0425*
GELSENKIRCHEN
Sgt D W Rudge and crew

**12/13 July** *2207-0902*
TURIN
Sgt D W Rudge and crew

**24/25 July** *2207-0338*
HAMBURG
Sgt D W Rudge and crew

**25/26 July** *2155-0222*
ESSEN
Sgt D W Rudge and crew

**27/28 July** *2211-0315*
HAMBURG
WO E J Presland and crew

**29/30 July** *2246-0539*
HAMBURG
Sgt H Campbell
Sgt M Hartley
Sgt D J McGrath
Sgt T W Moore
Sgt J J Robslaw
Sgt C O'Neill
Sgt W H Chambers

**2/3 Aug** *2355-0543*
HAMBURG

Sgt H Campbell and crew

**7/8 Aug** *2053-0505*
TURIN
Sgt D W Rudge and crew

**9/10 Aug** *2309-0450*
MANNHEIM
Sgt D W Rudge and crew

**10/11 Aug** *2146-0459*
NÜRNBERG
Sgt D W Rudge and crew

**12/13 Aug** *2108-0548*
MILAN
Sgt D W Rudge and crew

**15/16 Aug** *2001-0423*
MILAN
Sgt D W Rudge and crew

**22/23 Aug** *2101-0408*
LEVERKUSEN
Sgt D W Rudge and crew
FL M McMahon (2P)

**23/24 Aug** *2024-0306*
BERLIN
Sgt D W Rudge and crew

**27/28 Aug** *2132-0201*
NÜRNBERG
FS M McMahon
Sgt W P S Hersham
FO A G MacDonald
Sgt A R Fleming
Sgt H K Grant
Sgt G E Crawford
Sgt T Thompson

**31 Aug/1 Sep** *2029-0428*
BERLIN
FS H Campbell and crew
FO R E Ault and Sgt P W
Alderton in, McGrath and
Robson out (hit by flak)

**5/6 Sep** *2000-0250*
MANNHEIM

FS H Campbell and crew
McGrath back, Ault out

**6/7 Sep** *2006-0405*
MUNICH
FS H Campbell and crew

**22/23 Sep** *1918-0019*
HANNOVER
PO M P Floyd
Sgt R H Mansfield
Sgt E Benroy
Sgt J W Brewster
Sgt C J Fuller
Sgt L Marsh
Sgt W Walters

**23/24 Sep** *1913-0145*
MANNHEIM
Sgt T Gallacher
Sgt T Dixon
FS G Beike
Sgt H Crook
Sgt J A Bonsonworth
Sgt F C Read
Sgt F Child

**27/28 Sep** *1944-0118*
HANNOVER
Sgt T Gallacher and crew

**29 Sep** *1845-2308*
BOCHUM
FL F J Hopps
Sgt R S Imeson
PO N Olsberg
Sgt F J Roberts
Sgt R Thomas
Sgt N James
Sgt R E Black

**1/2 Oct** *1856-0024*
HAGEN
FS M J Graham
Sgt G P Rae
Sgt W J C Keigwinarea
Sgt W J Condick
Sgt P Harris
Sgt D Roberts
Sgt P J Daly

**4 Oct** *1839-2203*
LUDWIGSHAVEN
Sgt B B Lydon
Sgt E Buxton
Sgt E Benroy
Sgt T C Forster
Sgt S J Edwards
Sgt J A Brewster
Sgt A P Collins
(abort – std-outer u/s)

**7/8 Oct** *2041-0315*
STUTTGART
FS H Campbell and crew

**8/9 Oct** *2315-0359*
HANNOVER
FS H Campbell and crew

**18 Oct** *1737-2301*
HANNOVER
FO G S Morgan
Sgt J R Means (N)
FS N A Lambell RAAF
PO E M Graham (FE)
Sgt J R O'Hanlon (WOP)
Sgt S S Greenwood (MU)
Sgt C E Shilling (RG)

**20/21 Oct** *1742-0050*
LEIPZIG
FO G S Morgan and crew
(FW190 attack – no damage)

**22/23 Oct** *1742-0050*
KASSEL
FO G S Morgan and crew
(abort, Nav's oxygen failed)

**3 Nov** *1722-2146*
DÜSSELDORF
FO G S Morgan and crew

**10/11 Nov** *2035-0454*
MODANE
FO G S Morgan and crew

**18/19 Nov** *1740-0135*
BERLIN
FO G S Morgan and crew

**22 Nov** *1702-2335*
BERLIN
FO G S Morgan and crew

**26/27 Nov** *1719-0135*
BERLIN
FO G S Morgan and crew

## 576 SQUADRON

**4 Dec** *0000-0720*
BERLIN
WO C C Rollins
FS J R Henningham
Sgt E D Roff
FO H L Rees
Sgt J Rutter
Sgt R Hammond
Sgt L S Sumak
Sgt M A Frost

**16 Dec** *1625-2339*
BERLIN
FO G S Morgan and crew
Sgt A C Blackie (2P)
Sgt D Roberts in,
Sgt Greenwood out

**20 Dec** *1703-2246*
BERLIN
FO G S Morgan and crew
Sgt R E Rogers in,
Sgt Roberts out

**24 Dec** *0020-0735*
BERLIN
FO G S Morgan and crew
Mr B Frazier (press)
Sgt R Harris in, Rogers out

**29 Dec** *1700-2330*
BERLIN
FO G S Morgan and crew
Sgt A Newman in, Sgt Harris out

## 1944

**2 Jan** *0020-0745*
BERLIN
Sgt D G Mann
Sgt J Anderson
Sgt R Mosley
FO B N J Price
Sgt F D Robbins
Sgt P T Lalor
Sgt R McManus RCAF

**2/3 Jan** *2330-0800*
BERLIN
FO G S Morgan and crew
FO K J Risi RCAF in, Newman out

**6 Jan** *0000-0930*
STETTIN
FL C A B Johnson
Sgt G B Valentine
FO H Gerus RCAF
Sgt N H Morris
Sgt R W Owen
Sgt J P Duns

**14 Jan** *1635-2220*
BRUNSWICK
FO G S Morgan and crew

At the end of the war, ED888 is 'awarded' a Bar to her DFC, painted on by the Station Commander.

**20 Jan** *1610-2325*
*BERLIN*
FO G S Morgan and crew
Greenwood back, Risi out

**21/22 Jan** *1940-0230*
*MAGDEBURG*
FO G S Morgan and crew

**28/29 Jan**
*BERLIN*
PO E H Childs
Sgt V E T White
Sgt R E Johnstone RCAF
Sgt E Bardsley
Sgt H R Bowles
Sgt C M Brewster
Sgt C A Gifford
(Damaged a Do217)
(lost 30/31 Jan; White and Bardsley
PoWs, rest KIA. Bardsley killed by
Allied aircraft, 19 April 1945)

**30 Jan** *1704-2345*
*BERLIN*
Sgt R R Read (DSO)
Sgt A Taylor
Sgt M A Sarak RCAF
FO G Hallows
FO W Murphy
Sgt G A Coon RCAF
Sgt Hodson

**24/25 Feb** *1820-0220*
*SCHWEINFURT*
FL P E Underwood
Sgt R J A Boon
FO E C Espley
Sgt J A Hildreth
Sgt A E Evans
Sgt H E Lawrence
Sgt L Washer

**25/26 Feb** *1820-0220*
*AUGSBURG*
FL P E Underwood and crew

**18/19 Mar** *1910-0125*
*FRANKFURT*
FS V A Sheerboom
Sgt H R Piper
FS R J Tinsley
FO W Woodfine
Sgt C E Harris
Sgt L V C LaBelle
Sgt J G DelaMothe

**26/27 Mar** *2000-0115*
*ESSEN*
FS C G Wearmouth (DFC)
Sgt D R Willis
Sgt J W Carter
FO H T Wilson
Sgt A MacDonald
Sgt J Graham
Sgt S J Bott
(shot-up by Ju88)

**24/25 Apr** *2150-0420*
*KARLSRUHE*
PO J S Griffiths (DFC)
Sgt J D Hawkeswood (FE)
Sgt D C Bint (BA)
Sgt T Atherton (N)
Sgt W J McCarthy (WOP)
Sgt D W Langmead (RG)
Sgt T Jago (MU)

**26/27 Apr** *2307-0356*
*ESSEN*
PO J S Griffiths and crew

**27/28 Apr** *2144-0650*
*FRIEDRICHSHAFEN*
PO J S Griffiths and crew

**3/4 May** *2222-0422*
*MAILLY-LE-CAMP*
PO J S Griffiths and crew

**7/8 May** *2145-0305*
*RENNES / ST JACQUES*
PO J S Griffiths and crew
Sgt D S Low in, Jago out

**9/10 May** *2240-0140*
*MARDYCK*
PO J S Griffiths and crew
Sgt S S Greenwood in, Lowe out

**11/12 May** *2206-0156*
*HASSELT*
PO J S Griffiths and crew
WO R S Pyatt RCAF in,
Greenwood out

**19/20 May** *2200-0255*
*ORLÉANS M/YARDS*
PO J S Griffiths and crew
Jago back

**21/22 May** *2235-0325*
*DUISBURG*
PO J S Griffiths and crew

**22/23 May** *2230-0330*
*DORTMUND*
PO J S Griffiths and crew
FL C F Keninson RCAF in,
Bint out

**25 May** *0020-0440*
*AACHEN*
PO J S Griffiths and crew
Bint back

**27/28 May** *2359-0445*
*AACHEN*
PO J S Griffiths and crew

**6/7 June** *2220-0345*
*VIRE M/YARDS*
PO J S Griffiths and crew

**10 June** *0025-0545*
*FLERS AIRFIELD*
PO J S Griffiths and crew

**12/13 June** *2240-0315*
*GELSENKIRCHEN*
PO J S Griffiths and crew

**14/15 June** *2025-0025*
*LE HAVRE*
PO J S Griffiths and crew

**16/17 June** *2305-0350*
*STERKRADE*
PO J S Griffiths and crew

**17/18 June** *2345-0410*
*AULNOYE*
PO J S Griffiths and crew

**22 June** *1350-1715*
*MINOYECQUES*
PO J S Griffiths and crew

**23/24 June** *2145-0525*
*SAINTES*
PO J S Griffiths and crew

**25 June** *0125-0515*
*FLERS – V1 SITE*
PO J S Griffiths and crew

**28 June** *0115-0450*
*CHÂTEAU BERNAPRE*
PO J S Griffiths and crew

**29 June** *1130-1515*
*DOMLÉGER – V1 SITE*
PO J S Griffiths and crew

**30 June** *0540-0940*
*OISEMONT – V1 SITE*
WO H D Murray
Sgt C C Addams
Sgt R Lee
Sgt D A Barnes
Sgt F Thackeray
Sgt P J Taylor
Sgt W O Kenyon
(all lost 26/27 Aug)

**2 July** *1155-1540*
*DOMLÉGER – V1 SITE*
PO J S Griffiths and crew

**4/5 July** *2159-0400*
*ORLÉANS M/YARDS*
PO J S Griffiths and crew

**5/6 July** *2100-0615*
*DIJON*
PO J S Griffiths and crew

**7 July** *1920-2230*
*CAEN*
PO J S Griffiths and crew

**12/13 July** *2115-0700*
*RÉVIGNY*
PO J S Griffiths and crew

**14/15 July** *2100-0525*
*RÉVIGNY*
PO J S Griffiths and crew
(shot down Ju88)

**20 July** *1925-0525*
*WIZERNES*
PO J B Bell (DFC)
Sgt H C Gore (FE)
Sgt T E Seabrook (BA)
Sgt R Hughes (N)
Sgt R E Badger (WOP)
Sgt S G Parry (MU)
Sgt P Turton (RG)

**23/24 July** *2245-0355*
*KIEL*
PO J B Bell and crew

**30 July** *0645-1035*
*CAHAGNES*
PO J B Bell and crew

**31 July** *1810-2140*
*LE HAVRE*
PO J B Bell and crew

**1 Aug** *1855-2150*
*BELLE CROIX*
FO J B Bell and crew
(aborted – cloud over tgt)

**3 Aug** *1140-1615*
*TROSSY ST MAXIMIN*
FO J B Bell and crew

**5 Aug** *1430-2230*
*BLAYE*
FO J B Bell and crew (fighter escort)

**7/8 Aug** *2110-0115*
*FONTENAY*
FO J B Bell and crew

**10 Aug** *0910-1415*
*DUGNY*
FO J B Bell and crew

**11 Aug** *1345-1745*
*DOUAI*
FO J B Bell and crew

**25 Aug** *2005-2355*
*RÜSSELSHEIM*
FO J B Bell and crew
(abort, rear turret u/s)

**26/27 Aug** *2000-0200*
*KIEL*
FO J B Bell and crew

**29/30 Aug** *2055-0540*
*STETTIN*
FO J B Bell and crew

**31 Aug** *1300-1725*
*AGENVILLE*
FO J B Bell and crew

**3 Sep** *1535-1920*
*EINDHOVEN*
FO J B Bell and crew

**5 Sep** *1625-1955*
*LE HAVRE*
FO J B Bell and crew

**6 Sep** *1705-2035*
*LE HAVRE*
FO J B Bell and crew

**8 Sep** *0620-0920*
*LE HAVRE*
FO J B Bell and crew

**10 Sep** *1630-2020*
*LE HAVRE*
FO J B Bell and crew

**12/13 Sep** *1820-0135*
*FRANKFURT*
FO J B Bell and crew

**17 Sep** *0025-0355*
*LEUWARDEN AIRFIELD*
FO J B Bell and crew

**17 Sep** *1623-1910*
*FLUSHING GUN*
FO J B Bell and crew (fighter escort)

**20 Sep** *1455-1820*
*CALAIS GUN*
FO J B Bell and crew

**23 Sep** *1825-2345*
*NEUSS*
FO J B Bell and crew

**24 Sep** *1645-1935*
*CALAIS*
FO J B Bell and crew

**27 Sep** *0850-1200*
*CALAIS*
FO J B Bell and crew

**3 Oct** *1300-1600*
*WESTKAPELLE*
FO J B Bell and crew

**5/6 Oct** *1800-0045*
*SAARBRÜCKEN*
FO J B Bell and crew

**14 Oct** *0640-1055*
*DUISBURG*
FO J B Bell and crew

**14/15 Oct** *2235-0340*
*DUISBURG*
FO J B Bell and crew

**19/20 Oct** *2120-0400*
*STUTTGART*
FO J B Bell and crew

**22 Oct** *1605-2200*
*ESSEN*
FL H Leyton-Brown (DFC)
Sgt R A Hawkins
FS G Paterson

Sgt L Peters
Sgt E Johnson
Sgt J P McCullen
Sgt G Lester

**25 Oct** *1250-1755*
*ESSEN*
FO R N Crowther
Sgt R F H Wilshire
Sgt W Thorpe
Sgt H L Basson
Sgt B T Wilmot
Sgt B Rink RCAF
FS J R Scarfe RCAF

**30 Oct** *1740-0000*
*COLOGNE*
FO R N Crowther and crew

## 103 SQUADRON

**6 Nov** *1146-1712*
*GELSENKIRCHEN*
PO A J Mosley RCAF
Sgt P L Thompson
Sgt G Marriott
FO K C Dunn RCF
Sgt R J Evans
Sgt L A Wolstenholme
Sgt R E Ward

**9 Nov** *0741-1314*
*WANNE-EICKEL*
FO A V J Vernieuwe
Sgt W N Wells (FE)
FO R H Seaton RCAF (BA)
FS G H A Othem (N)
FS W J M Baillie RAAF (WOP)
Sgt G HG Self (MU)
Sgt T I Quinlan (RG)

**16 Nov** *1304-1745*
*DÜREN*
FL R A Butts RCAF
Sgt A D Berndt
FS B C McGregor RCAF
FO C E Kramer RCAF
Sgt D H Penny RCF
FS W D Stuckey RCAF
FS J R Murphy RCAF

**18 Nov** *1551-2222*
*WANNE-EICKEL*
WO W J McArthur RCAF

Sgt H Canoy
FS M H Horne RCAF
Sgt M Greenstein RCAF
FO R J Lougheed
Sgt D J McAuley RCAF
Sgt D F Campbell RCAF

**21 Nov** *1544-2212*
*ASCHAFFENBURG*
PO G W Henry RAAF
Sgt K Foster
Sgt M M Bertee RAAF
FO H S Mitchell RAAF
FS K C McGinn RAAF
FS H J Porter RAAF
FS J W Grice RAAF

**27 Nov** *1548-2303*
*FREIBERG*
FS J C Cooke RCAF
Sgt E W McGrath
FO G T Mortimore
FS J A Goff RCAF
WO F R Hill RCAF
FS J M C McCoubrey RCAF
FS M O Orr RCAF

**29 Nov** *1152-1742*
*DORTMUND*
FL R A Butts and crew

**4 Dec** *1641-2304*
*KARLSRUHE*
FO A S Thomson
Sgt R C Pain
Sgt J M Peace
Sgt W H Tromp
Sgt A J Crampin
FS J C Rochester RCAF
FS D G Kyle

**24 Dec** *1448-2100*
*COLOGNE*
FL S L Saxe RCAF
Sgt J J Bent
FS J A Wright
FO H Shatsky RCAF
FS J C Benadetto RCAF
Sgt A C Clark
FS R C Snell RCAF

*Mike-Squared* – 140 not out!

# ED905
# FOX/AD EXTREMUM!

The early days of ED905 showing crossed British and Belgian flags and 21 bomb symbols. It was mostly flown by Belgian FO F V P van Rolleghem of 103 Squadron. John Lamming, who painted on the insignia, is third from left, sitting on a 'cookie'.

A Manchester-built Mark III, ED905 came off the production line in early 1943 and was sent to 103 Squadron at Elsham Wolds, Lincolnshire, the day after ED888 went there – 21 April 1943. Given the squadron code letters PM and individual letter X for X-Ray, she began operations in May.

Her first captain was a Belgian pilot, one of the relatively few who flew in Bomber Command – Flying Officer F V P van Rolleghem – so it is no surprise to note that during the aircraft's period with 103, X-Ray had crossed Belgian and British flags painted on the nose, painted by artist LAC John Lamming. Two rows of bombs were painted beneath the cockpit, the third symbol being a vegetable under a parachute, denoting a 'Gardening' sortie (mine-laying).

Florent "Rollo" van Rolleghem was a regular officer in the Belgian air force from 1933 and escaped to England, via Spain, in 1942. In his diary on 6 May 1943 he wrote: 'I receive a brand new Lancaster III coded X-Xray. I shall keep her during my tour ..' Their first trip was on 12/13 May. On 18/19 May the canopy escape hatch blew away on take-off but Rolleghem carried on his first mining trip. ED905 was damaged on 1 June, not by enemy action, but by being hit on the ground by a tractor, but she was back in action on the 12/13th, as Rolleghem recorded:

'At 23,000 feet I am coned by 50 searchlights and the flak is all around. One engine is hit, a stream of oil and smoke pours from it and I lose control. Vic [Sgt P O Vickers] does an emergency

# ED905 FOX/AD EXTREMUM!

FO F V P van Rolleghem received the DFC from AVM E A B Rice CBE MC, AOC 1 Group, on 17 August 1943.

With a new insignia, and now showing 70 bomb symbols, PO D A Shaw and his crew pose for the camera, August 1944.

David Shaw and crew.

feathering in vain. We have no more control on the engine or propeller. The WOP panics and suggests I jettison the bombs. At that time I see the red TI [markers]. We drop the bombs and the searchlights disappear. I am frightened the kite will catch fire. Suddenly the engine stalls, lack of oil I think.

'I lose 5,000 feet and the control of the Lanc. At 18,500 feet, I regain control and set course for Great Britain. The kite is desperately slow and heavy. I ask Vic the maximum power on the three remaining engines …

'[After landing] .. inspection of the kite: there are 21 holes and one engine u/s. Nothing too serious ..'

Despite the control problem, van Rolleghem got his crew home and decided not to land until it became light. 'At 4 am I decide to land. I keep extra height and airspeed in hand and I succeed. Full brake as soon as possible and reduce the speed and stop before the end of the runway.' ED905 was ready by that evening, with a new engine.

Thirty-year-old van Rolleghem received the DFC for this night's effort. (Gilbert Harry Agar later received the DFM.)

The Lancaster was hit by flak again on the 25/26th, on the homeward flight from Gelsenkirchen. The navigator, Sergeant G H Agar, received a large cut to his right arm, and Vickers was hit in the palm of his hand, otherwise they were lucky. Lucky? There were 125 holes in ED905, 17 of them in the pilot's canopy. The crew flew another op in ED905 on 7/8 August, and in his diary afterwards, van Rolleghem wrote that he was to receive a new 'X' (LM335) while ED905 was undergoing an overhaul and would then be coded $X^2$. She was to be away for three weeks.

We now have a possible recording error. Van Rolleghem's diary states that he was never happy with LM335 and was delighted on 28 July to fly again his old 'X'. 'I fly my old X which is back and I am happier than a kid. The kite is faster, better and lighter than the other.' He flew her again the next day. In the ORB the squadron records that van Rolleghem flew LM335 to Hamburg on 29/30 July and again on 2/3 August. However, his diary note says for the 29th: 'Take-off 22.05 … the kite is really wonderful.' It looks, therefore, as if the keeper of the Form 541 simply recorded LM335 instead of the re-instated ED905 for these two trips. After all, he now flew ED905 on a further nine raids, including Peenemünde, although he lost his brakes on landing and had to abandon ED905 on the taxi-track.

Finishing his tour, van Rolleghem went on to complete three bomber tours totalling 65 ops and received the DSO. The last time he mentioned ED905 in his diary was in May 1944, while it was having a major inspection, and he went to see her. He noted the two flags were still in place and in addition there was the head of a Sioux (Indian). Van Rolleghem remained in the Belgian air force, retiring as an Air Marshal in 1972. He died in 1982.

Van Rolleghem is down with 20 ops in ED905 – probably 22 if his diary is indeed correct – and his last on 6/7 September to Munich, was ED905's last trip with 103 Squadron. At this time C Flight of 103 became the nucleus of 166 Squadron, the Lancaster being one which was moved to the new unit. Her code letters were changed to AS but she retained her individual 'X'. She had a quiet start but soon the adventures with enemy defences and other problems started once again.

Over Düsseldorf on 3/4 November she was attacked by a night fighter, sustaining considerable damage and, although both gunners opened up, they made no claims. Returning to duty after this damage, the next trip was to Berlin on 29 December, with Pilot Officer J Horsley in command, flying his own 22nd op. Forty miles inside the Dutch coast the starboard engine failed but they continued on. Upon reaching Berlin they found the bomb-doors would not open, so they had to make a second bomb-run but again the bombs failed to release, so they finally jettisoned them during a third run.

Over the Big City the port engine was then hit by flak, caught fire and had to be feathered, while the artificial horizon and directional gyro both went u/s. Horsley had to drop to below 5,000 feet to fly home and although they were worried by flak and searchlights when they reached the Dutch coast, they got home – two hours after their ETA. Joe Horsley and his navigator Ken Cornwell both received Immediate DFCs. These two men along with the rest of the crew failed to return from another Berlin raid on 28 January 1944 (in ND382) flying on their 29th sortie, and all were killed.

Oddly enough, the Berlin raid of 28 January was when ED905 was next on the duty roster after repairs, Flight Sergeant R B Fennell completing this trip in the aircraft, but he then failed to return from the ill-fated Nürnberg raid on 30/31 March. Shot down by a night fighter, all except the bomb aimer were killed.

The next trip – yet another to Berlin – on 30 January, had to be abandoned as both turrets went u/s, and a raid to Stuttgart on 1 March was also aborted due to losing the starboard-outer engine. In between, on 24/25 February, Flight Sergeant R V F Frandson and crew had to jettison a 'cookie' as they were unable to gain operational height, but carried on afterwards and dropped their load of incendiaries on target. After yet another Berlin trip on

Heading down the runway, 2 November 1944.

ED905 roars by, off on her 100th – and last – mission, 2 November 1944.

24/25 March, ED905 was off ops until the beginning of May, although it is unclear where she was.

On 3/4 May, shortly before bombing the military camp and dump at Mailly-le-Camp, with Pilot Officer P J Wilson DFC in command, the aircraft was attacked by a Me110 night fighter. They had just been ordered to orbit the rendezvous point by the controller as the 110 was spotted by the rear gunner, Sergeant C G M Meadows. He yelled to the captain to dive to port and both bomber and fighter opened fire simultaneously – the mid-upper, Pilot Officer B W G Felgate, joining in. The 110 was trying to follow the diving curve but after more gunfire it was seen to pour smoke, going down out of control and on fire, to crash below.

Philip Wilson had earned his DFC on the Nürnberg raid, during which he received the unwelcome attentions of a night fighter. Later, with 156 Squadron, he won a Bar to his DFC. Barclay Felgate received the DFC for the May action, and also a Bar with 156.

Due for a major service, ED905 went to 54 MU on 26 May, but again the dates seem odd, van Rollegham seeing her on the 24th, although he doesn't say where exactly. And where had that Sioux head come from?

After the work, ED905 was sent to 550 Squadron on 10 June 1944, where she became BQ-F. F for Fox (shortened from the more usual F-Foxtrot), the previous 'F' (ME556) had failed to return from a sortie on D-Day. By this time the Lancaster had undergone a new paint job, the twin flags and original bomb log having been painted out. The flags were replaced by a colourful crest and the motto 'Ad Extremum!' beneath it. The crest appears to be a shield on which there are two fox heads, a lady's face and a foaming pint mug of beer! There also seems to be the cross of St Andrew on an inner shield.

Fox's 'new' bomb symbols were now marked in rows of 15 under the cockpit, back-dated, but omitting the parachute/vegetable. The 45th op would indicate the Lanc's first daylight sortie as it is in a lighter colour (yellow?), the others being in red. Although at this time ED905 had done over 70 trips, it is difficult to reconcile the changes in colours. Above the rows of bombs was also stencilled an RAF catch-phrase of the period: 'Press on Regardless'.

The 45th operation and the first daylight trip was an attack on a V1 site in the Pas de Calais, flown on 22 June. On her next raid Fox lost the port-outer engine and the

Gee apparatus, but the crew carried on and bombed. On their return the port-inner began to run rough but they made it back.

*Fox's* next light and dark coloured bombs do not appear to tie-up, but the day ops were against V1 rocket sites in France. Whatever was happening, the bombs were increasing regularly over the summer and *Fox's* more-or-less regular pilot now was Pilot Officer D A Shaw. However, Flight Lieutenant R P Stone flew her on 14 August, a daylight to Fontaine-le-Pin. Robert Stone was to fly three Ton-Up Lancs, ED905, EE139 and PA995. He remembered:

'My log-book entry states: Caen-Falaise Road. For the third time we set out to assist the Canadian Army in their attempt to break out and capture Falaise. We bombed through thick cloud from a height of 14,000 feet. After bombing we dropped down to ground level and the gunners fired at any German troops seen moving.

'There was a sequel to this attack in that it was decided that we had been brought down too low to bomb. Some aircraft received minor damage from the bombs exploding not very far beneath their wings. I believe that the wing commander leading the attack was reprimanded. I also read later that the target had been marked with coloured TIs. Inexplicably when the Canadians started to advance their officers signalled using Very Pistols firing the same colour cartridges. There was quite a large number of casualties from friendly fire when some of the Lancs bombed the Canadian signal lights.'

Celebrating the 100th on the morning of 3 November, although the 100th 'bomb' has yet to be painted on the nose. Shaw is fifth from left and FL J P Morris is sixth (he was killed on his next op). SL B J Redmond DFC, OC B Flight, is far right, and to his right is the I/O, FL Murray. FL R P Stone is on the far left.

In all ED905 is supposed to have flown 100 sorties – the 100th being noted in some records as being flown on 4 November 1944, with Flying Officer V B Ansell at the controls, the target Bochum. However, there is a photograph of Shaw sitting in *Fox's* cockpit with 99 bombs on the nose and another picture of the Lanc supposedly taking off for her 100th trip – with David Shaw – which is also dated 4 November. Clearly both pilots didn't take *Fox* to Bochum and it is more likely that Shaw would have done so, but not on the 4th! It would seem more likely that the 100th was in fact flown on 2 November – to Düsseldorf – with Shaw in command, but taking a new crew that night. Shaw was at the end of his tour (he received the DFC soon afterwards and later a Bar) and no doubt would have asked, if not insisted, that

he take ED905 on its 100th, and one way would have been to take a 'sprog' crew on one of their first trips. The 4 November raid to Bochum is noted as being flown in aircraft 'F' but the serial number shows this to be NG250, which could have been a replacement 'F'. The crew Shaw took on the 100th survived for a month, failing to return on 6/7 December.

Retired from operational flying, ED905 went to 1 LFS at Hemswell on 4 November – note the date! – then, on 10 November, to 1656 CU. Here the aircraft spent its last days, bringing its flying hours to over 628, but on 20 August 1945, a pilot allowed the old girl to swing on landing; the undercarriage collapsed and a crash followed. Written-off as at that date, ED905 passed into history.

## 103 SQUADRON
### 1943

**12/13 May** *2352-0510*
DUISBURG
FO F V P van Rolleghem
Sgt G H Agar (N)
Sgt W Carling (BA)
Sgt T Proctor (WOP)
Sgt P O Vickers (FE)
Sgt R White (MU)
PO R K McLeod (RG)

**13/14 May** *2337-0504*
BOCHUM
FO F V P van Rolleghem

**18/19 May** *2152-0553*
GARDENING – BIARRITZ
FO F V P van Rolleghem

**23/24 May** *2225-0315*
DORTMUND
FO F V P van Rolleghem

**25/26 May** *2341-0418*
DÜSSELDORF
FO D W Finlay
Sgt J H McFarlane
Sgt I D Fletcher
Sgt A S Wheeler
Sgt R H J Rowe
FS R J F Vivers
Sgt W C Gillespie

**11/12 June** *2300-0341*
DÜSSELDORF
FO F V P van Rolleghem

**12/13 June** *2229-0353*
BOCHUM
FO F V P van Rolleghem
(hit by flak)

**14/15 June** *2207-0411*
OBERHAUSEN
FO F V P van Rolleghem

**16/17 June** *2210-0400*
COLOGNE
FO F V P van Rolleghem

**21/22 June** *2259-0310*
KREFELD
FO F V P van Rolleghem

**22/23 June** *2258-0314*
MÜLHEIM
FO F V P van Rolleghem

**24/25 June** *2259-0419*
WUPPERTAL
FO A H Langville
PO E L G Grant
PO C B Reynolds
PO D Towers
Sgt R L Hollywood
Sgt G J Wallis
PO J H Addison

**25/26 June** *2300-0330*
GELSENKIRCHEN
FL F V P van Rolleghem
(hit by flak)

**29/30 Jul 1943** *2205-*
HAMBURG
FL F V P van Rolleghem

**2/3 Aug 1943**
HAMBURG
FL F V P van Rolleghem
(believed to have flown in ED905)

**7/8 Aug** *2052-0515*
TURIN
FL F V P van Rolleghem

**29/30 Jul** *2205-*
HAMBURG
FL F V P van Rolleghem

**2/3 Aug**
HAMBURG
FL F V P van Rolleghem
(believed to have flown in ED905)

**9/10 Aug** *2329-0558*
MANNHEIM
Sgt J E Thomas
Sgt W G Bell
Sgt D J Edwards
Sgt E M L Davies
Sgt J J Robshaw
Sgt A V Collins
Sgt W W O'Malley

**10/11 Aug** *2223-0607*
NÜRNBERG
Sgt J E Thomas and crew

**14/15 Aug** *2053-0619*
MILAN
PO R Atkinson
Sgt G F Bruce
Sgt R J H Littlejohn
Sgt A L Norman
Sgt H K Garewal
Sgt C Campbell
FS R L Taggart

**17/18 Aug** *2113-0354*
PEENEMÜNDE
FL F V P van Rolleghem

**22/23 Aug** *2104-0358*
LEVERKUSEN
FL F V P van Rolleghem

**23/24 Aug** *2015-0228*
BERLIN
FL F V P van Rolleghem

**27/28 Aug** *2100-0228*
NÜRNBERG
FL F V P van Rolleghem

**30/31 Aug** *2350-0413*
MÜNCHEN-GLADBACH
FL F V P van Rolleghem

**31 Aug/1 Sep** *2001-0524*
BERLIN
FL F V P van Rolleghem

**3/4 Sep** *1946-0346*
BERLIN
FL F V P van Rolleghem

**5/6 Sep** *1937-0204*
MANNHEIM
FL F V P van Rolleghem

**6/7 Sep** *1944-0335*
MUNICH
FL F V P van Rolleghem

## 166 SQUADRON

**23/24 Sep** *1856-0156*
MANNHEIM
FS C E Phelps
Sgt E P F Hillyard
FS W Mitchell
FS E D Nesbitt
Sgt R Winder
Sgt W H Clarke
Sgt H R Gibson

**27/28 Sep** *1937-0044*
HANNOVER
SL B Pape (DFC)
FS R Somerset
FO F E Claydon
Sgt E S Brown
Sgt H Fewster
FS A Barnes
Sgt D R Taylor

**29 Sep** *1820-2306*
BOCHUM
1/Lt J C Drew USAAF
Sgt K S Lewis
FS P W Lees
PO H Ellis
Sgt S A Pett
FO H G Cook
Sgt D Lowe

**1 Oct** *1821-2346*
HAGAN
1/Lt J C Drew and crew

**2/3 Oct** *1821-0234*
MUNICH
1/Lt J C Drew and crew

**7/8 Oct** *2006-0345*
STUTTGART
SL B Pape and crew
FO H Mitchell (2P)

**18 Oct** *1711-2214*
HANNOVER
SL B Pape and crew

**20/21 Oct** *1746-0020*
LEIPZIG
FO H Mitchell
Sgt P G Edyvean-Walker
Sgt F F Clarke
FO J D Maddox
WO E Merralls DFM
Sgt D G B Day
Sgt C Cushing
(all except Clarke and Cushing, KIFA 17 Nov)

**22 Oct** *1807-2351*
KASSEL
FO H Mitchell and crew

**3 Nov** *1721-2156*
DÜSSELDORF
FO R J Robinson
Sgt A R Bird
PO F F Denney
Sgt C E Clarke
Sgt D J Stoken
Sgt N O Jones
PO B O Wright
(night fighter attack,
Lanc damaged)

# ED905 FOX/AD EXTREMUM!

**29/30 Dec  1649-0151**
*BERLIN*
PO J Horsley (DFC)
Sgt A W E Pilgrim (FE)
Sgt W G Morgan (BA)
PO K F Cornwell (N) (DFC)
Sgt M Smith-Crawshaw
Sgt J R McCourt
Sgt J Davies
(badly damaged by flak,
landed on two engines)

## 1944

**29 Jan  0019-0807**
*BERLIN*
FS R B Fennell
Sgt W G S Pettis (FE)
FS W J C Keigwin (BA)
FS J Smyth (N)
Sgt L Parker RAAF
Sgt W Jones (MU)
Sgt W J Allen RAAF (RG)
(all lost 30/31 Mar, except
Keigwin (PoW) and Parker –
not on op)

**30 Jan  1712-1953**
*BERLIN*
FS R B Fennell and crew
(abandoned, turrets u/s)

**24/25 Feb  2010-0515**
*SCHWEINFURT*
FS R V G Frandson
Sgt K L Pile
Sgt R G Leevers
Sgt J W Latham
Sgt D V Randall
Sgt H V Reed
Sgt W V Francis

**15/16 Mar  1900-0335**
*STUTTGART*
FS J Gagg
Sgt A R Branson
Sgt P A Jessop
FS H J Vinden
Sgt H M McCann
Sgt L Morgan
Sgt L A Irvine

**18/19 Mar  1900-0035**
*FRANKFURT*
FS J Gagg and crew

**22/23 Mar  1830-0115**
*FRANKFURT*
FS J A Sanderson RNZAF
Sgt F J Soloman (FE)
Sgt C Farley (BA)
Sgt R G Marks (N)
Sgt W T Violett (WOP)
Sgt J T Cockburn (MU)
Sgt J A W Bodsworth (RG)
(lost 3/4 May;  Violett evaded, both
AGs killed, rest PoWs)

**24/25 Mar  1825-0209**
*BERLIN*
FS J A Sanderson and crew

**3/4 May  2200-0350**
*MAILLY-LE-CAMP*
PO P J Wilson DFC (*) RCAF
FS H R Moncrieff (2P)
Sgt F Reed
FO P N J Noble RCAF
WO G W Knowles RCAF
Sgt P J Hardiman
FO B W G Felgate (DFC)
Sgt C G M Meadows RCAF
(shot down Me110 in flames)

**21/22 May  2235-0335**
*DUISBURG*
PO T W Boyce

Shaw in the cockpit with 99 bombs showing.

Sgt J D Carter
FO M A Monks
FO A B Leonard
Sgt S Aldis
Sgt H Rothwell
Sgt I M Rose
(abandoned over tgt)

## 550 SQUADRON

**12/13 June  2308-0319**
*GELSENKIRCHEN*
PO S C Beeson
Sgt K J R Hewlett (FE)
FS A R McQuarrie RCAF (N)
Sgt D Neall (BA)
Sgt J K Norgate (WOP)
Sgt H S Picton (MU)
Sgt J A Trayhorn (RG)

**16/17 June  2321-0400**
*STERKRADE*
PO J Lord
Sgt K W C Down
FS R Sebaski RCAF
Sgt A A Vass RCAF
PO J Elliott
Sgt A J Schemberg RAAF
Sgt P J Sculley

**22 June  1415-1718**
*PAS DE CALAIS – V1 SITE*
PO D A Shaw  (DFC*)
Sgt C A Bunce (FE)
Sgt R N Harris (N)
Sgt S Gartland (BA)
Sgt L L llanwarne (WOP)
Sgt E J Griffiths (MU)
Sgt H A Buckingham (RG)

**23/24 June  2229-0645**
*SAINTES*
PO D A Shaw and crew
(bombed on 3 engines)

**25 June  0134-0505**
*V1 SITE*
PO D A Shaw and crew

**27 June  0134-0518**
*V1 SITE*
PO D A Shaw and crew

**29 June  1153-1501**
*DOMLÉGER – V1 SITE*
PO D A Shaw and crew

**30 June  0558-0954**
*OISEMONT – V1 SITE*
PO D A Shaw and crew

**2 July  1213-1553**
*PAS DE CALAIS – V1 SITE*
PO D A Shaw and crew

**5/6 July  2115-0552**
*DIJON*
PO D A Shaw and crew

**6 July  1849-2235**
*PAS DE CALAIS – V1 SITE*
PO L W Hussey RCAF
Sgt E Elliott
FO M DeGast RCAF
FO H S W Nelson RCAF (BA)
Sgt M H Collings
Sgt A G Sale
Sgt R L Holmgreen RCAF

**7 July  2017-2322**
*CAEN*
PO D A Shaw and crew

**12/13 July  2121-0656**
*RÉVIGNY M/YARDS*
PO D A Shaw and crew
FO L N B Cann (2P)
(abandoned by MB)

**18 July** *0320-0732*
SANNEVILLE
FO L N B Cann (DFC)
Sgt C Shaw
FL K MacAleavey (N) (DFC)
Sgt N I E Ostrom
FS J Lyons
FO H Yates
Sgt J L R Remilard RCAF

**19/20 July** *2328-0313*
SCHOLVEN
PO C Beeson and crew

**20 July** *1914-2247*
WIZERNES – V1 SITE
FO L N B Cann and crew
Sgt R V Fisher (N) in

**23/24 July** *2247-0402*
KIEL
FO L N B Cann and crew

**24/25 July** *2135-0630*
STUTTGART
FO L N B Cann and crew

**25/26 July** *2132-0612*
STUTTGART
PO D A Shaw and crew

**28/29 July** *2128-0544*
STUTTGART
PO D A Shaw and crew

**30 July** *0629-1031*
CAHAGNES
PO D A Shaw and crew

**1 Aug** *1808-2129*
LE HAVRE
PO D A Shaw and crew
FS R Hofman RAAF (2P)

**2 Aug** *1854-2148*
BELLE CROIX
FO L N B Cann and crew
(aborted by MB – cloud)

**3 Aug** *1143-1606*
TROSSY ST MAXIMIN
PO D A Shaw and crew

**3 Aug** *1703-2032*
LE HAVRE
PO D A Shaw and crew

**4 Aug** *1330-2126*
PAUILLAC
PO D A Shaw and crew

**5 Aug** *1426-2240*
PAUILLAC
FO L N B Cann and crew

**8/9 Aug** *2111-0030*
FONTENAY
PO D A Shaw and crew

**10 Aug** *0906-1438*
DUIGNY
PO D A Shaw and crew

**11 Aug** *1302-1743*
CAMBRAI MIYARDS
PO D A Shaw and crew

**12 Aug** *1122-1814*
BORDEAUX
PO D A Shaw and crew
(shrapnel hole in windscreen)

**14 Aug** *1328-1725*
Fontaine-le-Pin
FL R P Stone
Sgt G E White (FE)
FS C W Sayers RCAF (N)
FS E W Holliday (BA)
Sgt D E Norgrove (WOP)
Sgt L G B Wartnaby (MU)
FS F Wright (RG)

**15 Aug** *1006-1327*
LE COULOT AIRFIELD
FL D A Shaw and crew

**17/18 Aug** *2104-0502*
STETTIN
FL D A Shaw and crew

**19 Aug** *1918-2244*
LA NIBBLE – V1 SITE
FO J C Cameron
Sgt D Eldridge
FO J R Rigby
Sgt G C Sutherland
FS J W White
Sgt J F Piertney
Sgt F E Popple

**25/26 Aug** *2016-0508*
RÜSSELSHEIM
FO R Purvis (DFC)
Sgt G L Grant
Sgt T Stoddart
Sgt K R Scholefield
Sgt L W Guthrie
Sgt J Wright
Sgt V S B Scoble

**26/27 Aug** *2013-0138*
KIEL
FL D A Shaw and crew

**29/30 Aug** *2117-0646*
STETTIN
FO H Dodds
Sgt A R Brown
FS R J Moran RAAF
FO L O Browning (BA)
FS C W Beckingham RAAF
Sgt A Laidlaw
Sgt H Lewis
(lost 14 Oct, except Moran
and Browning, not on op)

**31 Aug** *1301-1702*
AGENVILLE – V1 SITE
FO H Dodds and crew

**5 Sep** *1634-2012*
LE HAVRE
FO H S Vaughan
Sgt R W Metcalfe
FO L C Davies
FS C Porter
Sgt T Elliott
Sgt W Watson RCAF
Sgt L D Purser

**6 Sep** *1722-2053*
LE HAVRE
FL D A Shaw and crew
PO F B Ansell (2P)
FS V R Farmer in (N)

**10 Sep** *1654-2041*
LE HAVRE
FO J J W Dawson
FL G T Pyke (2P)
Sgt E W C Edmunds
FS W F Wilmer (N)
FS D W Holliday RCAF
Sgt J M Palmer
Sgt J Earnshaw
FS W H Harkness

**12/13 Sep**
FRANKFURT
FL G T Pyke (DFC)
Sgt G Iddles-White
Sgt D E H Hellings
Sgt A G Peters
Sgt L Adams
Sgt D S Eldred
Sgt A T Ellemont

**16/17 Sep** *2147-0146*
STEENWIJK AIRFIELD
PO J Harris
Sgt C H Simpkins
FS J W Eppal RAAF
WO J C Conway RAAF
FS R G Bickford RAAF
Sgt W P Waddell
Sgt B S P Barby

**20 Sep** *1520-1908*
SANDGATTE
FO S H Hayter
Sgt L A Bassman
FO T Y Thomas
FO R R Bradshaw RNZAF
Sgt A J Pearce
Sgt E M Watkins
Sgt F E Self

**23 Sep** *1847-2355*
NEUSS
PO J Harris and crew

**25 Sep** *0717-1041*
CALAIS
FL D A Shaw and crew
Sgt A Cross in (N)
(aborted by MB – weather)

**26 Sep** *1047-1411*
CALAIS
FL D A Shaw and crew

**28 Sep** *0804-1150*
CALAIS
FO H L Rose and crew
(abandoned – weather)

**3 Oct** *1301-1615*
WALCHEREN
FL D A Shaw and crew

**5 Oct** *1856-2040*
SAARBRÜCKEN
FL D A Shaw and crew
FS W R Wilkins RAAF (N)
(abort; Gee u/s)

**7 Oct** *1159-1320*
EMMERICH
FL D A Shaw and crew
WO D M Stephen RCAF (N)
(abort – port-inner u/s)

**14 Oct** *0650-1118*
DUISBURG
FO J C Adams RCAF
Sgt W P Scott
Sgt Sterman
FO W R Elcoate
Sgt F Papple
PO F S Renton
Sgt K D Winstanley

**14/15 Oct** *2221-0431*
DUISBURG
FO J C Adams and crew
(aborted)

**23 Oct** *1616-2132*
ESSEN
FL D A Shaw and crew
FL E Keuffling (N)

**25 Oct** *1235-1719*
ESSEN
FL D A Shaw and crew

**28 Oct** *1319-1821*
COLOGNE
FL D A Shaw and crew
Sgt R W Harris (N)

**30/31 Oct** *1739-0004*
COLOGNE
FO F E Bond RCAF
Sgt C C Mortimer
FO H K Leigh RCAF
Sgt B R Smith RCAF
FS R C Bowling RAAF
Sgt H F Sullivan RCAF
Sgt J H Udink RCAF

**31 Oct** *1737-2326*
COLOGNE
FL D A Shaw and crew
FO E H Luder RAAF (2P)

**2 Nov** *1615-2326*
DÜSSELDORF
FL D A Shaw
FL J P Morris (2P)
Sgt A G Furber (FE)
FO A Leonard
Sgt H J Bailey
Sgt J R Byrne
Sgt G C Dennis
Sgt T J Hooper
(Morris and crew all killed 6/7 Dec
except Byrne, not on op)

# EE136
# SPIRIT OF RUSSIA

Part of Contract No.69274/40, this was a Mark III Lancaster with four Merlin 28 engines built in early 1943. Once ready for service life, it was assigned to 9 Squadron at Bardney, Lincolnshire (the same squadron from which W4964 was flying), on the last day of May. Given the squadron code letters of WR, its individual letter became 'R'. There was a good deal of pro-Russian feeling in the mid-war years, no doubt encouraged by our war leaders, Russia being our only European ally fighting from its own motherland. This was evidenced too in Bomber Command which had several bombers named with Russian themes. We have already seen *Uncle Joe* with ED611, and now this Lancaster was given the name *Spirit of Russia* and soon the bomb symbols painted on its nose began to mount.

These symbols were painted a little more forward of the cockpit than on some other Lancasters, probably due to the name being in the more usual bombs position, and were painted in rows of ten. Once the ten rows were completed, the 11th row was started to the right of the name.

EE136's first operation was flown on 11 June 1943, a trip to Düsseldorf with Sergeant J H S Lyon RAAF in the captain's seat. He and his crew became her regular team until September, and most of the crew were decorated, including the DFC for James Lyon – now commissioned. DFMs went to Ken Pack, Henry Jeffrey, Alexander Fielding and Alf Denyer. Although the aircraft had a few minor problems, by and large it had become a reliable machine.

At some stage two tiny white swastikas appeared beneath the name, presumably for the aircraft's two encounters with German night fighters. The first came on 14/15 August during a sortie to Milan.

At 18,500 feet, to the west of Paris on the way home, a Me109 attacked from astern and below, first seen at 500 yards by Sergeant C R Bolt, the rear gunner in Sergeant W W W Turnbull's crew. As William Turnbull began to manoeuvre to port, Cyril Bolt opened fire and the 109 broke away and disappeared. A second 109 then attacked from the starboard side above but was engaged by the mid-upper, Sergeant James Michael, and this too disappeared. Both gunners later received DFMs and Turnbull the DFC after being commissioned. Sergeant Joe Waterhouse, navigator, and Brian Owen, WOP, also received DFMs at the end of their tour. Waterhouse's citation mentions nine trips to Berlin and on his last sortie the bomber was attacked by a fighter, the engagement lasting for 15 minutes.

On 5 September, during a trip to Mannheim with Pilot Officer J McCubbin in command, EE136 was attacked by a night fighter near the target, whose fire almost destroyed the port tailfin, damaged the R/T and mid-upper turret,

A good shot of EE136 with 17 ops recorded, although the 'ice-cream cones' denoting Italian targets, do not tie-up with actual raids. The pilot is Jimmy Lyon (DFC), who took EE136 on its first operations. Flight Engineer Ken Pack (DFM) sits on the canopy, third from left.

PO J McCubbin and crew. From left to right, back row: -?-, -?-, K J Dagnall, McCubbin, B J Sherry, A M Smith and Norman D Owen. September 1943.

and wounding the gunner in the head and shoulder. They were at 20,000 feet and the rear gunner first saw the single-engine fighter following them. The pilot was informed and he began a corkscrew but the fighter closed in and opened up with a long burst from 400 yards. The mid-upper, Flight Sergeant C J Houbert, fired a few rounds before he was wounded.

The fighter next came in from the starboard-quarter, firing several bursts into the Lanc; the rear gunner, Flight Sergeant J L Elliott, returning fire all the time. In the final attack, Elliott's fire scored hits and the fighter burst into flames and dived beneath the starboard wing leaving a trail of fire behind it, seen by both the flight engineer and bomb aimer. EE136 was badly damaged, with too many bullet holes to even to start count. Norman Owen was the flight engineer:

'The fighter which attacked us was a FW190. Its initial attack was from the starboard quarter, followed by four further attacks, breaking away to starboard after the fifth and climbing. At that moment he suddenly burst into flames and

EE136 with 100 bomb symbols up, flown by 9 and 189 Squadrons.

EE136's insignia and score-board, showing two swastikas for night kills.

exploded. We were told later the bullet holes in the Lancaster were too numerous to count, and the hole in the port fin just above its junction with the tail-plane was quite frighteningly large! I was surprised that fin and tail-plane were still attached.

'That trip ended our first tour for pilot, navigator, WOP and myself. The bomb aimer did two more as the CO's B/A. Charlie Houbert's tour also ended, due to his shoulder wound and partial loss of sight to his right eye. After hospital treatment, I believe, he eventually went home to Rhodesia, as it was then.

'The rear gunner, "Geordie" Elliott, survived the war. I met him in the RAF Club at a 9 Squadron reunion in about 1960. We found ourselves in adjacent toilets! The crew were awarded two DFCs and four DFMs and five survived a second tour also!'

Jim McCubbin and Barclay John Sherry received DFCs, Andy Smith, Norman Owen, Dagnall and Jim Elliott got DFMs. Both McCubbins' original gunners had been hit in another night fighter attack – a Ju88 – in an earlier mission in August, the mid-upper being killed instantly. The bomb aimer, Ken Dagnall, had manned the front turret and drove the Junkers off, for which he later received the DFM.

The damage put EE136 out of action until November, but once back in service it operated during the Battle of Berlin that winter, going to the Big City 11 times, plus one aborted sortie, the aircraft losing its port-inner engine due to loss of oil pressure. Overall EE136 proved to be generally reliable and she flew on the night of D-Day, against V1 sites, and during the Caen break-out, with its regular skipper Pilot Officer R C Lake. When he finished his tour in August 1944, Roy Lake received the DFC and of his crew, his two gunners, Stan Major and Robert Kerr received the DFM and DFC respectively. Their award citations mention successful combats on 21 May, 21 June and 24 June, the latter resulting in one of three Ju88s being shot down. Robert Baird, the flight engineer, later received the DFC too, having completed 45 operations. John Peterson also won the DFC and later, following an extended tour, a Bar. George Watts collected a DFC too.

In October 1944, EE136 went to 189 Squadron which was formed at Bardney before moving to Fulbeck in November. It was a little strange that 9 Squadron should

allow EE136 to be re-assigned, considering it had, by this time, flown 93 sorties. Perhaps the aircraft was getting too old and the chance of a new Lancaster was too good to miss, but one still has to wonder why, for generally a squadron which had a veteran aircraft of strength, especially one approaching 100 ops would hang on to it. They knew publicity and a morale boost would follow.

It has been recorded that EE136 flew 97 ops with 9 Squadron but this total is open to question. Firstly, by counting up the trips listed in the 541 it is impossible to get to 97, so there has to be another reason. By the time EE136 was taken off ops, it had 109 bombs painted on her nose, so we can assume this was more or less correct. By subtracting the 12 it was supposed to have carried out with 189 – again from that unit's 541 – we are left with 97. However, the 12 are not correct. Someone listed the trips flown with 189, but there are four other ops that either list no serial number at all (2) or show EE126 (2). Because EE126 was a Lancaster with 207 Squadron, it is obvious there is a typing error. Thus she did 16 with 189, and so her 9 Squadron total was around 93.

Once with 189 she was coded CA but remained 'R'. Crews had come in from a number of squadrons to form the new unit. Flying Officer D M S van Cuylenburg from 44 (Rhodesian) Squadron took EE136 on her first mission on 1 November. The aircraft had no regular skipper although Flight Lieutenant E J Abbott, formerly of 61 Squadron, took her on seven of her 16 missions. Strangely enough, there was a man who was reunited with her, as wireless operator Dick Revill revealed to me:

'A little odd item that may interest you about EE136. We took it to Munich on 7/8 January 1945. Our mid-upper was a Londoner on his second tour – Alf Denyer DFM. On his first trip of his first tour he went with Sergeant Lyon to Düsseldorf on 11/12 June 1943, nearly two years before. I recall him telling us about it at the time. [When we flew her] she creaked in the joints a bit, but who wouldn't!'

EE136 made her last sortie on 2/3 February, to Karlsruhe, after which she became Cat B. Sent to 1659 CU and then on 2 April 1946 to 20 MU, she became 5918M at 1 Radar School, Cranwell. EE136 ended up at the RAF Fire School, Sutton on the Hill, in the early 1950s where the hulk was used for fire-fighting practice – an ignominious end to such a fine lady.

# 9 SQUADRON
## 1943

**11/12 June** *2345-0434*
DÜSSELDORF
Sgt J H S Lyon (DFC)
Sgt K Pack (FE) (DFM)
Sgt R W Corkill (BA) (DFC)
Sgt H W E Jeffrey (N) (DFM)
Sgt A Fielding (WOP) (DFM)
Sgt A G Denyer (MU) (DFM)
Sgt G Clegg (RG)

**14/15 June** *2246-0332*
OBERHAUSEN
Sgt J H S Lyon and crew

**8/9 July** *2216-0414*
COLOGNE
Sgt J H S Lyon and crew

**9/10 July** *2251-0518*
GELSENKIRCHEN
Sgt J H S Lyon and crew

**12/13 July** *2227-0807*
TURIN
Sgt W W W Turnbull RCAF (DFC)
Sgt J Wellings
Sgt J Waterhouse (N) (DFM)
Sgt J McMasters
Sgt B Owen (WOP)
Sgt J Michael (MU)
Sgt C R Bolt (RG)

**27/28 July** *2230-0309*
HAMBURG
FS J K Livingstone (DFC)
Sgt F Parsons
Sgt F T Watson (N) (DFM)
Sgt H C Brewer
Sgt J Prendergast (WOP) (DFM)
Sgt R N Browne
Sgt T C Taylor

**29/30 July** *2300-0404*
HAMBURG
Sgt C Payne
Sgt C A Gilbert
PO K W Armstrong
Sgt S C Young
Sgt J B Robinson
Sgt N D Bennett
Sgt P A S Twinn

**30/31 July** *2212-0254*
REMSCHEID
FS J H S Lyon and crew
Sgt F L Chipperfield and FS
C J Houbert in; Sgts Corkill
and Denyer out

**2/3 Aug** *2329-0439*
HAMBURG
PO K Painter
Sgt T Deacon
Sgt R C Saunders
Sgt J E Bacon
Sgt T Andrews
Sgt S P Hone
Sgt D W Angell
(abandoned – weather)

**7/8 Aug** *2107-0531*
MILAN
FS J H S Lyon and crew
Denyer back, Houbert out

**9/10 Aug** *2310-0521*
MANNHEIM
Sgt W W W Turnbull and crew
FS C J Houbert in, Bolt out

**10/11 Aug** *2144-0507*
NÜRNBERG
FS J H S Lyon and crew

**12/13 Aug** *2136-0110*
MILAN
Sgt W W W Turnbull and crew
(returned early – Gee failed)

**14/15 Aug** *2122-0610*
MILAN
Sgt W W W Turnbull and crew

**15/16 Aug** *2026-0415*
MILAN
FS J H S Lyon and crew

**17/18 Aug** *2126-0407*
PEENEMÜNDE
FS J H S Lyon and crew

**22/23 Aug** *2112-0146*
LEVERKUSEN
Sgt W W W Turnbull and crew

**27/28 Aug** *2119-0146*
NÜRNBERG
FS J H S Lyon and crew

**31 Aug** *0006-0508*
MÜNCHEN-GLADBACH
FO W English
Sgt Mitchell
PO J E Evans
Sgt L V Fussell
Sgt L G Lane
Sgt D R Carlisle
Sgt P W Hewitt

**31 Aug/1 Sep** *2016-0343*
BERLIN
FO W English and crew

**3/4 Sep** *2002-0425*
BERLIN
FS J H S Lyon and crew

**5/6 Sep** *2021-0259*
MANNHEIM
PO J M McCubbin (DFC)
Sgt N D Owen (FE) (DFM)
PO B J Sherry (N) (DFC)
FS K J Dagnall (BA)
FS A M Smith (WOP)
FS C J Houbert (MU)
FS J L Elliott (RG)
(damaged by night fighter
and wounded Houbart)

**10/11 Nov** *2054-0446*
MODANE
PO W E Siddle
Sgt A R Wilson
FS M C Wright
FS N Machin
Sgt J W Culley
Sgt J C Parker
Sgt C C Moore

**18/19 Nov** *1741-0127*
BERLIN
PO H Blow
Sgt F S Colman
Sgt S W A Hurrell
Sgt H P Smith
Sgt R O Smith
Sgt Hartley
Sgt W E Miller

**22 Nov** *1711-2346*
BERLIN
PO W J Chambers
Sgt W E Hayward
FL J Beeston
Sgt J Hannon
Sgt Mulcock
Sgt A Steward
FS J Campbell

**26/27 Nov** *1724-0115*
BERLIN
PO J G R Ling
Sgt L Moss
Sgt H Laws

Sgt J Fletcher
Sgt E A Gauld
Sgt E J Rush
Sgt I Prada

**20 Dec** *1704-2258*
FRANKFURT
PO J G R Ling and crew
Sgt J N Carter in, Laws out

**24 Dec** *0032-0803*
BERLIN
PO W E Siddle and crew
PO J W Hearn in, Wright out

**29/30 Dec** *1649-0004*
BERLIN
PO W E Siddle and crew
FS C A Peak (2P)
Sgt S Greenwood in,
Hearn out

## 1944

**2 Jan** *0006-0802*
BERLIN
PO R W Mathers (DFC)
Sgt A Ball
Sgt T A Cave
FO W E Pearson
Sgt J R Donaldson
PO R R Nightingale RAAF
Sgt A P Bartlett

**6 Jan** *0008-0930*
STETTIN
PO W E Siddle and crew
PO E Singer (2P)
Sgt R T C Lodge in,
Greenwood out

**14 Jan** *1638-2202*
BRUNSWICK
PO W Singer and crew

**20 Jan** *1627-2336*
BERLIN
FL L G Hadland (DFC)
GC N C Pleasance (2P)
Sgt A W Cherrington
FO C R Brown
Sgt J Gaskell
Sgt A D Tirel
FS G C Moore

**21/22 Jan** *2019-0258*
MAGDEBURG
FS C A Peak RAAF
Sgt E W Kindred
Sgt T W Varey
F/O J E Wilkes USAAF
Sgt V W G Torbett
Sgt J W Nelson
Sgt J Hogan
(all lost 10/11 April)

**27/28 Jan** *1734-0231*
BERLIN
FS C A Peak and crew

**29 Jan** *0029-0822*
BERLIN
PO R W Mathers and crew
Sgt J Thomas and FS D A
Keeble in, Ball and Pearson out

**15/16 Feb** *1745-0026*
BERLIN
PO R W Mathers and crew
Sgt W Wilson and FS H F
Robinson in, Nightingale
and Bartlett out

**19/20 Feb** *2327-0715*
LEIPZIG
PO R W Mathers and crew

**21 Feb** *0002-0716*
STUTTGART
PO R W Mathers and crew

**24/25 Feb** *1854-0235*
SCHWEINFURT
PO H Forrest
Sgt A W Hutton
Sgt S Harwood
FS R D Hassell
Sgt D McCauley
Sgt F M Corssman
Sgt D B Pinchin

**9/10 Mar** *2043-0619*
MARIGNANE
PO R W Mathers and crew
Bell back, Thomas out

**15/16 Mar** *1917-0302*
STUTTGART
PO R W Mathers and crew

**22/23 Mar** *1905-0037*
FRANKFURT
PO R W Mathers and crew

**24/25 Mar** *1854-0151*
BERLIN
PO R W Mathers and crew
Sgt C W Howe in, Bell out

**21/22 May** *2301-0341*
DUISBURG
PO R C Lake (DFC)
Sgt R W Baird
FS J A Peterson RCAF
Sgt G B Watts RCAF
Sgt G E Parkinson
Sgt S G D L Major
Sgt R D Kerr RCAF
(Nav error, bombed SW
München-Gladbach)

**22/23 May** *2243-0507*
BRUNSWICK
PO R C Lake and crew

**27/28 May** *2256-0443*
NANTES
PO R C Lake and crew

**31 May/1 June** *2334-0513*
SAUMUR
PO R C Lake and crew

**3/4 June** *2313-0248*
CHERBOURG
PO R C Lake and crew

**6/7 June** *2321-0323*
ARGENTAN
PO R C Lake and crew

**8/9 June** *2315-0616*
RENNES
PO R C Lake and crew

**12/13 June** *2239-0456*
POITIERS
PO R C Lake and crew

**14/15 June** *2234-0345*
AUNAY-SUR-ODON
PO R C Lake and crew

**15/16 June** *2123-0415*
CHÂTTELLERAULT
PO R C Lake and crew

**21/22 June** *2320-0342*
GELSENKIRCHEN
PO R C Lake and crew

**23/24 June** *2254-0543*
LIMOGES
PO L J Wood
Sgt M T Gordon
FS N Oates
Sgt R L Lutwyche

# EE136 SPIRIT OF RUSSIA

Sgt D C Mumford
Sgt N Hannah
Sgt J E Shuster RCAF

**24/25 June** *2248-0225*
*PROUVILLE – V1 SITE*
PO R C Lake and crew
(Ju88 Shot down)

**27/28 June** *2202-0630*
*VITRY-LE-FRANCOIS*
PO L J Wood and crew
(abandoned by MB)

**4/5 July** *2330-0335*
*CREIL*
PO G A H Langford
Sgt C G Fenn
Sgt J L Wright
FS S M Mitchell RAAF
Sgt I Feldman
Sgt J Wright RCAF
FO G T Baseden
(Langford, Fenn and Mitchell
PoWs 7/8 July, rest KIA)

**7/8 July** *2248-0314*
*ST LEU D'ESSERENT*
PO G B Scott
Sgt J E Simpkins
Sgt L A Harding
Sgt L W Langley
Sgt E M Hayward
Sgt F A Saunders
Sgt L J Hambly

**12/13 July** *2202-0603*
*CULMONT CHALANDRY*
FO R C Lake and crew
Sgt J R Gunnee in, Baird out

**15/16 July** *2212-0530*
*NEVERS*
FO R C Lake and crew
Baird back

**17 July** *0410-0759*
*CAEN*
FO W J Sheppard
Sgt R Johnstone
FO J G Glashan RCAF
FS J Mulhearn
FS W J Toomey
FS W J Harris
WO B S Dean RCAF

**19 July** *1925-2321*
*THIVERNY – V1 SITE*
FO R C Lake and crew

**20/21 July** *2305-0225*
*COURTRAI M/YARDS*
FO R C Lake and crew

**24/25 July** *2233-0355*
*DONGES*
FL E H M Relton
Sgt F W Johnson
FS C H Edwards RAAF
FS J K Scott RAAF
FS C T Scott RAAF
FS D W McConville RAAF
FS W R Andrews (RG)
(all lost 13 Aug, except RG)

**28/29 July** *2202-0553*
*STUTTGART*
FO R C Lake and crew

**30 July** *0626-1044*
*CAHAGNES*
FO G B Scott and crew
(abandoned by MB – cloud)

**31 July** *1746-2253*
*JOIGNY-LA-ROCHE*
FO W D Tweddle
Sgt C G Heath
FS E Shields

Sgt J W Singer RCAF
Sgt A Carson
Sgt J A Foot
Sgt K Mallison

**1 Aug** *1640-2127*
*MONT CANDON – V1 SITE*
FO R C Lake and crew
(abandoned by MB – cloud)

**2 Aug** *1430-1912*
*BOIS DE CASSAN – V1 SITE*
FO R C Lake and crew

**11/12 Aug** *2046-0438*
*GIVORS*
FL G C Camsell RCAF
Sgt W Andrews
Sgt R P Askin
FO R H Thomas
Sgt D Beevers
Sgt W J Herbert RCAF
Sgt A E Boon RCAF

**16 Aug** *1628-2301*
*LA PALLICE*
FO C Newton RCAF
Sgt W Gregory
Sgt P Grant
Sgt R Flynn RCAF
Sgt L G Kelly
Sgt E H Cooper RCAF
Sgt R S Stevens RCAF

**18 Aug** *1123-1745*
*LA PALLICE*
FS S F Bradford
Sgt J W Williams
Sgt R W Cooper
FO A P Hull
Sgt L G Roberts
Sgt W Brand
Sgt D Winch

**24 Aug** *1227-1547*
*IJMUIDEN*
FO A F Jones RAAF
Sgt A E W Biles
Sgt S Scott
FO R L Blunsdon
FS R L Birch RAAF
Sgt R Glover
Sgt J E Johnson

**27 Aug** *1410-1846*
*BREST*
FS A L Keeley
Sgt A E Wotherspoon
Sgt W Chorney RCAF
Sgt L W Tanner
Sgt S D Chambers
Sgt C H Cornwall
Sgt J E Johnson

**27 Sep** *0057-0744*
*KARLSRUHE*
FO R W Ayrton RAAF
Sgt H K Huddlestone
Sgt M J Herkes
FS N Bardsley
Sgt W Scott
Sgt D K Chalcroft
Sgt J A W Davies

**27/28 Sep** *2144-0432*
*KAISERSLAUTERN*
FO R W Ayrton and crew

**5 Oct** *0801-1230*
*WILHELMSHAVEN*
FO E I Waters RNZAF
Sgt C Booth
Sgt R Miles
Sgt S Coxon
FS E French RNZAF
Sgt G Jones
FL W T G Gabriel

**6 Oct** *1753-2241*
*BREMEN*
FO W G Rees
Sgt H Mayhew
Sgt G A Hammond
FS D A MacIntosh
Sgt T A Morrow
Sgt W L King
Sgt G M Heppell

**7 Oct** *1150-1454*
*FLUSHING*
FS A L Keeley and crew

**11 Oct** *1314-1612*
*FLUSHING*
FO H Anderson
Sgt W D Loakes
FS A B Vivian
Sgt E Sumner
Sgt A Cornfoot
Sgt K A Ashworth
FS G M Young RCAF

**15 Oct** *0638-1148*
*SORPE DAM*
FS A L Keeley and crew

**19/20 Oct** *1725-0103*
*NÜRNBERG*
FS A L Keeley and crew
Sgt Rogers and PO S E
Evans in, Sgt Chambers
and Cornwall out

## 189 SQUADRON

**1 Nov** *1416-1807*
*HOMBERG*
FO D M S Van Cuylenburg
Sgt G H Thomson
WO A C R Havers
Sgt N E Goodland
Sgt F W Ostopovitch RCAF
Sgt A Smith
Sgt K Pursehouse

**11 Nov** *1643-2150*
*HARBURG*
FL E J Abbott
Sgt H Henderson
FS J F Charlton
FS J D Rowan
Sgt W Ashford
FL W R Kennedy
Sgt J C Oberneck

**16 Nov** *1236-1744*
*DÜREN*
FO A D D Brian
Sgt L C Boyle
FO D W Deubert
FS C Morgan
Sgt L W H Lambert
FO J D Constable
Sgt D C Wainwright

**4 Dec** *1648-2332*
*HEILBRONN*
FO A D D Brian and crew
FO J Gilmour RCAF (2P)
Sgt E White in, Kennedy out

**6 Dec** *1710-2342*
*GIESSEN*
FL E J Abbott and crew

**8 Dec** *0916-1346*
*HEIMBACH DAM*
FO I V Seddon RAAF
FL J A Skilton (FE)
FS L A Laurence
Sgt W Helliker
Sgt A Tuthill
FS H B Hodder
Sgt G R White

**17/18 Dec** *1607-0216*
*MUNICH*
FO I V Seddon and crew

**18/19 Dec** *1726-0311*
*GDYNIA*
FL E J Abbott and crew

**21/22 Dec** *1652-0303*
*PÖLITZ*
FL E J Abbott and crew

**31 Dec** *0358-0817*
*HOUFFALIZE*
FO I V Seddon and crew
Sgt J H Sands in (FE),
Skilton out

## 1945

**5 Jan** *0123-0744*
*ROYAN*
FO S J Reid RCAF
Sgt F N Benson
FO T J Nelson RCAF
FO H G Harrison
Sgt R McCormack
Sgt M R Bullock RCAF
Sgt C F Caley RCAF

**7/8 Jan** *1725-0240*
*MUNICH*
FO J S Fenning
Sgt A E Veitch
FO H Loggin RCAF
FS R B Revell
WO A G Denyer (DFM)
FS W Langmaid
FS J Brown

**13/14 Jan** *1700-0301*
*PÖLITZ*
FO P Glenville
Sgt F Pallister
FS L S Harper
WO C J Gallagher RNZAF
Sgt J L Nolan
FO D P Hammersley
Sgt L Moore
(all lost 21/22 Feb except
Nolan (PoW) and Harper, not on op)

**14/15 Jan** *1639-0214*
*MERSEBURG*
FO P Glenville and crew

**1 Feb** *1611-2236*
*SIEGEN*
FL E J Abbott and crew
Sgt S J Joyner in, Oberneck out

**2/3 Jan** *2027-0344*
*KARLSRUHE*
FL E J Abbot and crew

# EE139
# PHANTOM OF THE RUHR

EE139 BQ-B at North Killingholme, 1944.

If it had been a coincidence that a crew member had flown in EE136 nearly two years after flying in her on her first operation as we read in the previous section, then we have another one here. EE139 flew her first operation on the same night and the same target as EE136 – Düsseldorf, 11/12 June 1943. And their flight times that night were within minutes of each other too, taking off and landing, despite their bases being some 30 miles apart.

Coming off Avro's production line not long after EE136, this Mark III Lancaster had four Merlin 28 engines and was assigned to 100 Squadron at Waltham, near Grimsby, Lincolnshire, on 31 May 1943.

It received the squadron code letters of HW and initially its individual letter was 'A' but in July became R-Roger. EE139 completed at least 29 sorties with 100 Squadron, which seems correct as there is a very slight change in the design of the bomb symbols beginning with the 30th, painted on by the new squadron ground crew. The bomb symbols were in rows of 15 and eventually there were eight of them (120) plus one more, to make a total of 121.

The bomber was given the name *Phantom of the Ruhr* painted on its nose by its first flight engineer, Sergeant Harold Bennett, just forward of where the bomb log would go. Above the legend a grim-looking painting of a ghoulish skeleton figure dressed in a hooded garment, reaches over some clouds while dropping one bomb and holding another in readiness. Just in front of this was the mustard-coloured circular gas detection patch which appeared on aircraft of 1 Group, Bomber Command.

The *Phantom's* first captain was Sergeant J R Clark, whom we have already met at the beginning of this book (The Tour). He recalled the *Phantom's* origins:

'The painting on the nose of the aircraft was executed by "Ben" Bennett, who says that he may have had feelings of revenge after suffering frequent bombing raids as a ground engineer in Fighter Command earlier in the war. Geoff Green, our rear gunner, adds that I was influenced by the film *Phantom of the Opera* showing at that time. The grand operatic Teutonic sagas of the British and the Germans performed nightly over the Fatherland, should have been accompanied by the music of Siegfried. I felt afterwards that something a little less ghoulish would have been more appropriate.'

Robert Stone flew EE139 on 3 August 1944, one of 29 ops he flew with 550 Squadron. Seen here in *Bad Penny II* (LL811) in which he flew most of his missions.

The *Phantom's* first raid, as mentioned above, came on the night of 11/12 June 1943 and its fifth one month later was to Turin, denoted on the bomb-log not by a bomb but by an ice-cream cone, an unofficial marking often used by Bomber Command to show a raid on an Italian target. Thus it is that the *Phantom's* 12th, 15th and 16th symbols were also cones, for trips to Genoa, and two to Milan. This marking process gives a clear indication of how some aborted ops were counted, for EE139's second op – to Oberhausen on 14/15 June – only lasted two hours, 38 minutes, the crew coming back after the R/T failed, jettisoning their bombs into the North Sea. It was not counted.

A second abort, on 2/3 August, due to intense predicted flak, severe electrical storms and icing in the Elbe area, made getting rid of the bombs essential, the crew dumping them over Bremen, a last-resort target. When they raided Berlin, which they did on three occasions (the *Phantom* went there 15 times in all), the bombs on the nose were marked in red.

Ron Clark and company flew the *Phantom* on 24 trips (23 plus a half to Hamburg which was later upgraded), and were close to 'buying it' over Mannheim on 23/24 September. They were coned by searchlights and hit by flak which damaged the starboard elevator, another shell going through the bomb-bay and out through the top of the fuselage, narrowly missing the wireless operator, Sergeant L J "Lish" Easby. The Lancaster went into a dive and while still held in the searchlight beams was attacked by a fighter, but the flight engineer ably assisted his pilot to pull the Lanc out of the dive. It was their last trip in the *Phantom* which was out of action until early November. However, both Ron Clark and Ben Bennett were decorated for the Mannheim trip with the DFC and DFM respectively.

This had not been EE139's first brush with enemy aircraft. On the ground it was being directed into its dispersal on one occasion as a German intruder aircraft attacked the airfield. The airman guiding the Lanc's pilot rapidly dropped his torch and got clear, but a couple of rounds hit the *Phantom*.

Towards the end of November 1943, C Flight of 100 Squadron became the new 550 Squadron, EE139 being transferred to the new unit and re-coded BQ-B for Baker. The Lanc had already completed six raids on Berlin prior to leaving 100 Squadron, and continuing with the Battle of Berlin, the *Phantom* went to Berlin on nine more occasions with 550. Its usual skipper now was a Canadian, Flight Sergeant Vernon J Bouchard, who flew her on 13 ops before he became tour expired in May, was commissioned, and received the DFC. Of his crew, David Knight RCAF and John Knox RCAF won DFCs.

They would have flown more but EE139 went off for a major inspection on 15 March 1944 and when she returned, her new pilot became Flight Sergeant T M Shervington, who also flew her 13 times until he and his crew failed to return on the night of D-Day, in ME556 'F'.

Bombing-up *Phantom of the Ruhr*. 95 ops showing and a DFC ribbon.

FO J C Hutcheson and crew flew EE139's 100th operation, although the bomb tally has not caught up with actual missions flown – September 1944.

The *Phantom* missed being part of D-Day because she had been damaged by a night fighter on 3/4 June, attacked by a FW190 which appeared to be a decoy for a Me110. EE139 was on the bomb-run as all this developed, but the mid-upper probably damaged the 190, while the rear gunner returned the 110's fire, both German machines breaking off and not coming back.

Returning to operational status on 17 June, Pilot Officer J C Hutcheson now took the *Phantom* over during the V1-site raids and attacks in support of the invasion forces. He also piloted the Lanc to Le Havre on 5 September, recorded as the 100th trip. Joe Hutcheson was a Scot from Troon, Ayrshire, and by this date had flown 25 of the crew's 26 sorties in the *Phantom* and went on to fly four more to complete the tour.

Hutcheson had been a chemist pre-war, and had his own share of excitement with the *Phantom*. On 12/13 July they had lost an engine but carried on to the target – even dodging a night fighter. On 24/25 July he again brought her back from Germany on three engines. No doubt Hutcheson got on well with the *Phantom's* ground crew who were mostly Scots: Sergeant Cuthbertson, the

NCO in charge, came from Kilmarnock, her fitter was LAC R Taylor from Dollar, near Stirling, and the rigger was LAC J Birney, from Glasgow. Hutcheson's crew was the usual mix of nationalities: Smithy, his navigator came from Harrow, London, the flight engineer from Liverpool, and both bomb aimer and wireless operator hailed from Sydney, Australia. The rear gunner came from Sale, Cheshire, the mid-upper – another Scot – from Dundee. Both Hutcheson and the *Phantom* received DFCs, the latter's ribbon being painted to the right of the first row of bombs.

As Hutcheson left to become an instructor at 17 OTU, the *Phantom* had a variety of skippers but one to mention is the pilot who was to fly three of our Ton-Up Lancs, Robert Stone, who we met when dealing with ED905.

'I flew EE139 on 3 August 1944 and I can remember nearly every minute of this trip. The target was Le Havre. As we went down the runway on take-off the cockpit began to fill with smoke. We got off the ground ok and the wireless

EE139 preparing to take off.

operator quickly moved into the navigator's compartment and traced the smoke to the G-box which had apparently burnt out. My navigator promptly told me that he could not go on but I replied that we were not turning back and that he was a qualified navigator who could get us to the target without a G-box. All seemed to go well for a couple of hours until my wireless operator told me that R___ had left his desk and was lying down on the bed. Leaving my flight engineer at the controls – he could fly straight and level but no more – I went back to have a look. It was quite obvious that R___ had done no work on his charts for over an hour and intended to take no further part in the war. I had no idea where we were and the only thing to do was to try and get home. It would not do to jettison our bombs if we were over France.

'We identified the English coast at Lyme Regis and made our way up to Lincolnshire. When the flight engineer saw our station beacon flashing I returned to the controls. Thoroughly browned off, tired and a bit disorientated, I landed at the next 'drome down the way from North Killingholme. Some time wasted explaining things and taking off again for home.'

*Phantom's* last sortie was to the Aschaffenburg marshalling yards on 21 November, flown by one of the flight commanders on 550 Squadron, Squadron Leader W F Caldow AFC DFM, who had arrived on 13 November. Caldow had won his DFM following a tour with 142 Squadron, then became an instructor although he flew a few raids between tours. Finally he instructed on Lancasters with 1656 CU receiving the AFC for his work. He would receive the DSO in 1945 while with 100 Squadron. Willie Caldow:

'I recall quite clearly the circumstances surrounding EE139's last operational sortie. I was posted to 550 Squadron as A Flight Commander and flew the first sortie of my second tour on 18 November with my all-officer crew, all very experienced, and all with one complete tour behind them on various 1 Group squadrons.

'Between that and my next sortie, my deputy flight commander, Flight Lieutenant George Pyke, came to me and said that he was a bit concerned that EE139 wasn't behaving very well. So, with nearly 900 hours experience on Halifax and Lancasters (about 800 on the latter) as an instructor, I considered myself qualified to pass judgement on the aircraft so decided to take it on the next sortie.

'On the way to Aschaffenburg I felt very sorry for the pilots who'd been flying it and George's concern was completely justified because with a full bomb load, EE139 wallowed around the sky. The trim had to be adjusted constantly; one of its engines kept over-heating and the aircraft was very tiring to fly. The sortie was 6½ hours of extreme discomfort.

'After the trip, I spoke to both the squadron engineering officer and then the squadron commander, recommending that the aircraft be taken off operational flying and replaced.

Although it handled better without a bomb load it wasn't a good aircraft of the type. Rumour has it that it was found to have a slightly twisted fuselage too.'

Leaving 550 Squadron with 121 ops to her name, EE139 moved to 1656 CU on 1 December, became Cat AC on 19 February 1945 and was sent to 58 MU. Back it came to 1656 CU on 5 June, then was assigned to 1660 CU on 17 December. The aircraft became Cat AC again on 12 January 1946 and was finally made Cat E and Struck off Charge on 19 February.

## 100 SQUADRON
## 1943

**11/12 June** *2313-0438*
*DÜSSELDORF*
Sgt J R Clark (DFC)
Sgt H Bennett (FE) (DFM)
Sgt J H Siddell (N)
Sgt D Wheeler (BA)
Sgt L Y Easby (WOP)
Sgt L R Simpson (MU)
Sgt W G Green (RG)

**12/13 June** *2310-0429*
*BOCHUM*
Sgt J R Clark and crew

**14/15 June** *2302-0140*
*OBERHAUSEN*
Sgt J R Clark and crew
(aborted – r/t u/s)

**16/17 June** *2247-0320*
*COLOGNE*
Sgt J R Clark and crew

**8/9 July** *2306-0413*
*COLOGNE*
Sgt J R Clark and crew

**12/13 July** *2202-0853*
*TURIN*
Sgt J R Clark and crew

**24/25 July** *2255-0352*
*HAMBURG*
Sgt J R Clark and crew

**25/26 July** *2237-0232*
*ESSEN*
Sgt J R Clark and crew

**27/28 July** *2235-0406*
*HAMBURG*
WO J R Clark and crew

**29/30 July** *2205-0324*
*HAMBURG*
WO J R Clark and crew

**30/31 July** *2213-0250*
*REMSCHEID*
WO J R Clark and crew

**2/3 Aug** *2313-0250*
*HAMBURG*
WO J R Clark and crew
(bombed Bremen due to weather, icing and flak)

**7/8 Aug** *2105-0602*
*GENOA*
WO H Wright
Sgt J S Henderson
PO W Bentley

Sgt O'Dea
Sgt T S McCleod
Sgt S O Hodges
Sgt J McKean

**9/10 Aug** *2310-0545*
*MANNHEIM*
FS E C Bagot
Sgt S F May
PO F Lampin
Sgt C E Webster
Sgt A Head
Sgt J J Lloyd
Sgt A Neal

**10/11 Aug** *2206-0555*
*NÜRNBERG*
WO J R Clark and crew

**12/13 Aug** *2109-0556*
*MILAN*
WO J R Clark and crew

**14/15 Aug** *2107-0630*
*MILAN*
FS E C Bagot and crew

**17/18 Aug** *2108-0401*
*PEENEMÜNDE*
WO J R Clark and crew
FO K J Wilson in (RG),
Simpson out

**22/23 Aug** *2142-0232*
*LEVERKUSEN*
WO J R Clark and crew
Sgt M R Shear (RG),
Wilson out

**23/24 Aug** *2041-0313*
*BERLIN*
WO J R Clark and crew
Sgt E Gordon in, Shear out
(saw Ju88 shot down by flak)

**31 Aug** *0025-0417*
*MÜNCHEN-GLADBACH*
WO J R Clark and crew
Sgt McRae in, Rodgers out

**31 Aug/1 Sep** *2001-0322*
*BERLIN*
WO J R Clark and crew

**3/4 Sep** *1942-0329*
*BERLIN*
WO J R Clark and crew
Simpson back

**5/6 Sep** *1933-0155*
*MANNHEIM*
WO J R Clark and crew
FS Hardman (2P)

**6/7 Sep** *1940-0347*
*MUNICH*
WO J R Clark and crew

**22/23 Sep** *1850-0032*
*HANNOVER*
WO J R Clark
Sgt R J Cook (2P)
Sgt D Brown
Sgt J Berger
Sgt V H Thompson
Sgt R Henderson
Sgt R V Waller
Sgt J Ringwood
(twice evaded Ju88)

**23/24 Aug** *1840-0136*
*MANNHEIM*
WO J R Clark and crew
(hit by flak and attacked by fighter in searchlights – but evaded)

**3/4 Nov** *1732-2135*
*DÜSSELDORF*
WO T V Hayes
Sgt P L Ashenden (FE)
Sgt S L Emmett (N)
Sgt W Kondra RCAF (BA)
Sgt G R Jenkins (WOP)
Sgt K W Kemp (MU)
Sgt J W Nash (RG)

**10/11 Nov** *2045-0437*
*MODANE M/YARDS*
WO G F Peasgood
Sgt S Sykes
Sgt W P Morris
Sgt G Walker
Sgt S J Richards
Sgt S O Jones
Sgt P P Clarkin

**18/19 Nov** *1714-0100*
*BERLIN*
WO G W Brook
Sgt L B Martin
WO M B Wareham
Sgt W H Ferdinands
Sgt J J McAnanay
Sgt J Godsave
Sgt J Flynn

**23 Nov** *1719-2345*
*BERLIN*
PO D C Dripps RAAF
Sgt J C Scott (FE)
PO J E Stewart RCAF (N)
Sgt W T Sibley (BA)
Sgt D Campbell (WOP)
PO R A Van Walwyk (MU)
Sgt D P Lawrence (RG)

## 550 SQUADRON

**26/27 Nov** *1708-0106*
*BERLIN*
FS V J Bouchard RCAF (DFC)
Sgt R Binney
FS D H Knight RCAF
Sgt J H Knox RCAF
Sgt E J Baker
Sgt C A Rann
Sgt J J H Galvin

**2 Dec** *1704-2358*
*BERLIN*
FS V J Bouchard and crew

**4 Dec** *0010-0823*
*LEIPZIG*
FS A H Jeffries (CGM)
Sgt E C W Bull
Sgt H Simpson
Sgt D S Jeffrey
Sgt S A Keirle
Sgt E Brennan

SL Willie Caldow AFC DFM took EE139 on her 121st and last sortie, 21 November 1944, then had to 'sideline' the veteran.

Sgt J W Whitely
(shot down 30/31 Mar: Jeffries, Simpson and Whitely KIA, Jeffrey and Keirle PoW – others not on op)

**16 Dec** *1608-2342*
*BERLIN*
FS V J Bouchard and crew

**23/24 Dec** *2338-0745*
*BERLIN*
FS V J Bouchard and crew

**29 Dec** *1654-2337*
*BERLIN*
FS V J Bouchard and crew

## 1944

**2 Jan** *0002-0813*
*BERLIN*
FS V J Bouchard and crew

**14 Jan** *1652-2230*
*BRUNSWICK*
Sgt C G W Kenyon
Sgt J N Ellis
PO P C Sharp
Sgt W R J Maroney
FS C E Duncan
Sgt G K Logan
Sgt L M Collicutt

**20 Jan** *1615-2326*
*BERLIN*
FS V J Bouchard and crew

**27/28 Jan** *1737-0142*
*BERLIN*
FS V J Bouchard and crew

**30 Jan** *1704-2325*
*BERLIN*
FS V J Bouchard and crew

**19/20 Feb** *2351-0654*
*LEIPZIG*
FS V J Bouchard and crew
FL A D McConnel (2BA)

**20/21 Feb** *2328-0707*
*STUTTGART*
FS V J Bouchard and crew

**24/25 Feb** *1854-0431*
*SCHWEINFURT*
FS V J Bouchard and crew

**25/26 Feb** *1815-0245*
*AUGSBURG*
FS V J Bouchard and crew

**18/19 Apr** *2154-0200*
*ROUEN M/YARDS*
FS T M Shervington
Sgt A Small
FS J R Mawhinney RCAF
Sgt K R Ansell
Sgt E R Hall
Sgt A C Griffiths
Sgt R G Dennett
(all lost 6/7 June)

**20/21 Apr** *2353-0425*
*COLOGNE*
FS T M Shervington and crew

**22/23 Apr** *2239-0346*
*DÜSSELDORF*
FS T M Shervington and crew

**24/25 Apr** *2134-0407*
*KARLSRUHE*
FS T M Shervington and crew

**26/27 Apr** *2256-0350*
*ESSEN*
FS T M Shervington and crew

**27/28 Apr** *2134-0301*
*FRIEDRICHSHAFEN*
FS T M Shervington and crew
(abort – port outer u/s)

**30 Apr/1 May** *2135-0215*
*MAINTENON*
FS T M Shervington and crew

**3/4 May** *2150-0328*
*MAILLY-LE-CAMP*
FS T M Shervington and crew

**7 May** *0032-0505*
*AUBIGNÉ-RACAN*
FS T M Shervington and crew

**7/8 May** *2141-0253*
*RENNES AIRFIELD*
FS D C Barton
Sgt R O G Ashby
FO W H Twitchell RCAF
FS A H Lingham
Sgt S Sulley
Sgt S G Reeve
Sgt K Coleman

**9/10 May** *2247-0126*
*MARDYCK GUN*
Sgt H C White
Sgt D D G Pryce
FS W E Megaw RCAF
FO C Garner (BA)
Sgt F D Mason
Sgt H W Jamieson RCAF
Sgt M H A Campbell

**11/12 May** *2154-0218*
*HASSELT M/YARDS*
FS T M Shervington and crew
(recalled)

**19/20 May** *2158-0242*
*ORLÉANS M/YARDS*
FO K B Bowen-Bravery (DFC)
F/O G P Fauman USAAF

Sgt L A Thompson (FE)
PO G L Thomas
FS J H Fyfe
WO P E E R Keeley
Sgt R Blackburn
Sgt R A Thomson

**21/22 May** *2241-0313*
*DUISBURG*
FS T M Shervington and crew

**22/23 May** *2232-0142*
*DORTMUND*
FS T M Shervington and crew
(abort – tech troubles)

**24/25 May** *2354-0431*
*AACHEN M/YARDS*
2/Lt G P Fauman USAAF
Sgt W J Killick
FS A E Stebner RCA
FO M S Merovitz RCAF
Sgt P E Cooksey
Sgt J A Ringrow
Sgt W A Drake

**27 May** *0005-0425*
*AACHEN M/YARDS*
FS T M Shervington and crew

**3/4 June** *2347-0305*
*WIMEREAUX GUN*
PO N D Holdsworth
Sgt H Mimmack
Sgt V Kirby
Sgt C E Venebles
Sgt J A S Steer
Sgt W Johnston
Sgt H Granger
(combat with FW190 and a Me110)

**22 June** *1411-1721*
*PAS DE CALAIS – V1 SITE*
PO J C Hutcheson (DFC)
Sgt S Wright (FE)
Sgt D F Smith (N)
FS J K Francis RAAF (BA)
WO W Y Smith RAAF (WOP)
Sgt A T Tosh (MU)
Sgt E C Hodgson (RG)

**23/24 June** *2230-0551*
*SAINTES*
PO J C Hutcheson and crew

**24 June** *0127-0537*
*PAS DE CALAIS – V1 SITE*
PO J C Hutcheson and crew

**27 June** *0128-0514*
*PAS DE CALAIS – V1 SITE*
PO J C Hutcheson and crew

**29 June** *1206-1514*
*DOMLEGER – V1 SITE*
PO J C Hutcheson and crew

**30 June** *0557-0953*
*OISEMONT – V1 SITE*
PO J J W Dawson
Sgt E W Edmunds
Sgt F W Willmer
FS K P Brady RAAF
Sgt J M Palmer
Sgt J Earnshaw (MU)
Sgt W A Harkness RCAF

**2 July** *1212-1551*
*PAS DE CALAIS – V1 SITE*
PO J C Hutcheson and crew

**4/5 July** *2206-0407*
*ORLÉANS M/YARDS*
PO J C Hutcheson and crew

**5/6 July** *2114-0551*
*DIJON*
PO J C Hutcheson and crew

**6 July** *1845-2226*
*PAS DE CALAIS – V1 SITE*
PO J J W Dawson and crew

**7 July** *1935-2330*
*CAEN*
PO J J W Dawson and crew

**12 July** *2118-0637*
*RÉVIGNY M/YARDS*
PO J C Hutcheson and crew

**14/15 July** *2109-0610*
*RÉVIGNY M/YARDS*

PO J C Hutcheson and crew
(abandoned by MB)

**18 July** *0335-0724*
*SANNERVILLE*
PO J C Hutcheson and crew

**19/20 July** *2252-0318*
*SCHOLVEN-BAUR*
PO J C Hutcheson and crew

**20 July** *1925-2241*
*WIZERNES – V1 SITE*
PO J C Hutcheson and crew

**23/24 July** *2259-0354*
*KIEL*
PO J C Hutcheson and crew

**24/25 July** *2122-0554*
*STUTTGART*
PO J C Hutcheson and crew

**28/29 July** *2124-0214*
*STUTTGART*
PO J C Hutcheson and crew
(abort – tech failure)

**30 July** *0638-1027*
*CAHAGNES*
PO J C Hutcheson and crew

**1 Aug** *1811-2150*
*LE HAVRE*
FO L N B Cann
Sgt C Shaw
Sgt R V Fisher
Sgt N I E Ostrom
FS J Lyons
FO H Yates
Sgt J L R Remilard RCAF

**3 Aug** *1716-2043*
*LE HAVRE*
FL R P Stone
Sgt C E White (FE)
Sgt _____ (N)
FS E W Holliday RCAF
Sgt D E Nargrove (WOP)
Sgt L G B Wartnaby (MU)
FS F Wright (RG)

Caldow's crew: Jim Cassidy, Derrick Gear, Jack Marston, Caldow, Sam Squires, Steve George.

**4 Aug** *1341-2138*
*PAUILLAC*
WO W H S Wright
FS G W Battersby
FO C R Cameron RCAF
FO I H R Hood
Sgt A Anderson
Sgt E W Parker
Sgt O Tabuteau

**5 Aug** *1435-2230*
*PAUILLAC*
FO L W Hussey RCAF
Sgt E Elliott
FO M DeGast RCAF
FO H S W Nelson RCAF
FS F E Dawson
Sgt A G Sale
Sgt R L Holmgreen RCAF

**8/9 Aug** *2121-0129*
*FONTENAY*
FO H G Manley RAAF
Sgt R Hughes
FO R O George
FS G E Hill
FO G P Brown
Sgt G B Ward
PO J K MacDonald
(abandoned by MB)

**10 Aug** *0920-1407*
*DUIGNY*
FO J C Hutcheson and crew
(hit by flak; FS Francis
slightly wounded in the leg)

**11 Aug** *1303-1741*
*DOUAI*
FO J C Hutcheson and crew
FS S E Card in (BA)

**13 Aug** *0009-0357*
*FALAISE*
FO H G Manley and crew

**14 Aug** *1326-1718*
*FONTAINE-LE-PIN*
FO J C Hutcheson and crew
FL C W Peek in (BA)

**17/18 Aug** *2107-0513*
*STETTIN*
Sgt G H Town
Sgt G Hope
FS D J T Slimming
FS J H Windsor
FS P D Probert
PO E C Ball
WO J Teasdale

**19/20 Aug** *2216-0117*
*GHENT*
FO J C Hutcheson and crew
Sgt B R Jones in (BA)

**25/26 Aug** *2015-0444*
*RÜSSELSHEIM*
FO J C Hutcheson and crew
FO W F Cox in (BA)

**26/27 Aug** *2012-0133*
*KIEL*
FO J C Hutcheson and crew
FL C W Peek in (BA)

**29/30 Aug** *2107-0555*
*STETTIN*
FO J C Hutcheson and crew
Sgt A Sutherland in (BA)

**3 Sep** *1558-1910*
*GILZE-RIJEN AIRFIELD*
FO J C Hutcheson and crew
FO A F W Nelson in (BA)

**5 Sep** *1604-1947*
*LE HAVRE*
FO J C Hutcheson and crew

FO L O Browning in (BA)

**6 Sep** *1716-2056*
*LE HAVRE*
FO J C Hutcheson and crew
FS W Windsor in (BA)

**8 Sep** *0636-1025*
*LE HAVRE*
FO J C Hutcheson and crew
FS Gartland in (BA)
(abandoned by MB)

**10 Sep** *1653-2036*
*LE HAVRE*
PO V P Ansell
Sgt C P Sythes
Sgt T D Rogers
Sgt L Trudgian
FS H A Elderfield
PO G J Horsfall
Sgt S J H Adams

**12/13 Sep** *1814-0341*
*FRANKFURT*
PO V P Ansell and crew
(slight damage from Me109)

**16/17 Sep** *2152-0126*
*STEENWIJK AIRFIELD*
FO H A Shenker RCAF (DFC)
Sgt J Faren
Sgt G H Lennox RCAF
Sgt L M Johnson RCAF
FS R J Emmett RAAF
Sgt P A Lander RCAF
Sgt A Ingram RCAF

**17 Sep** *1632-1923*
*BIGGE-KERKE GUN*
FO H A Shenker and crew

**20 Sep** *1525-1833*
*SANDGATTE*
FO J C Hutcheson and crew
FS Hutcheson RCAF in (BA)

**23 Sep** *1845-2320*
NEUSS
FO J C Hutcheson and crew

**11 Oct** *1524-1819*
*FORT FREDERIK HENDRIK*
FO F E Bond RCAF
Sgt C C Mortimer
FO H K Leigh RCAF
Sgt B R Smith RCAF
FO R C Boweling RAAF
Sgt H F Sullivan RCAF
Sgt J H Udink RCAF

**12 Oct** *0622-0945*
*FORT FREDERIK HENDRIK*
FO F E Bond and crew

**14/14 Oct** *2217-0428*
*DUISBURG*
FL M F A Martin
Sgt G N Raynes
FI J D Nelson RCAF
FS G B McGhee RCAF
Sgt G King
Sgt V Montague
Sgt R C Dyke

**19/20 Oct** *2132-0429*
*STUTTGART*
FO K F Sidwell
Sgt J Allen
Sgt J W Hewett
Sgt J L Banks RCAF
Sgt J F Chapman
Sgt F W E Woodley
Sgt D G Whitmarsh

**25 Oct** *1254-1748*
*ESSEN*
FO W P F Daniels
Sgt J G Woodall
Sgt R G Roberts
Sgt R Wright
Sgt F R Easton RCAF
Sgt A E Baker

Sgt W F Baker

**28 Oct** *1324-1853*
*COLOGNE*
FO W P F Daniels and crew

**30 Oct** *1745-2346*
*COLOGNE*
FO W P F Daniels and crew

**31 Oct** *1755-2257*
*COLOGNE*
FO W P F Daniels and crew

**4 Nov** *1732-2218*
BOCHUM
FO L O Williams
Sgt W Aspinall
FS C W Jones RCAF
FS W E Reed
FS P E Binder
FS W M Johnson
FS D L Marke

**6 Nov** *1145-1615*
*GELSENKIRCHEN*
FO W P F Daniels and crew

**16 Nov** *1242-1750*
*DÜREN*
FO E A Stevenson RCAF
Sgt W T Woodhams
FS D T Morrison RCAF
FS W W Fitch
FS E N Pearson
FS M O Olsen RCAF
Sgt C Copperthwaite

**21 Nov** *1531-2208*
*ASCHAFFENBURG MIYARDS*
SL W F Caldow AFC DFM (DSO)
FO S P George DFM (FE) (DFC)
FL J Cassidy DFC RAAF (N) (*)
FO D E Sloggett (BA)
FO D Gear (WOP)
FO C Squires (MU) (DFC)
FO J H Marston (RG) (DFC)

Post-war reunion: "Sam" Squires, Jim Cassidy, Willie Caldow, Derrick Gear, Jack Marston, Steve George ("Reg" Sloggett died in 1988).

# EE176
# MICKEY THE MOOCHER

Another Manchester-built Mark III Lancaster fitted with Merlin 28 engines, EE176 was part of Contract No.B69274/40 and came off the production line in the spring of 1943. It was assigned to 7 Squadron at Oakington, Cambridgeshire, on 11 June, but within ten days it had been moved to 97 (Straits Settlements) Squadron at nearby Bourn. It did not physically move, for the squadron flights were detached to three bases; C Flight, to which this bomber went, was also at Oakington.

With 97 Squadron it carried the code letters OF, its individual letter being 'N', possibly a legacy from 7 Squadron, but by early August this had been changed to 'O'. Her first operation was to Cologne on 3/4 July, and once more we see the not unusual sequence of a new aeroplane being used by various crews for the first few weeks, before a regular crew becomes evident – in this case Flying Officer D Moodie. However, after 15 ops, which included the famous raid on Peenemünde, three to Hamburg, one to Milan and two to Berlin, EE176 was moved again, this time to 61 Squadron at Syerston, Nottinghamshire, on 20 September. Here it became QR-M.

Aircraft lettered 'M' were usually known as Mother or Mike, but one of EE176's crew called it *Mickey* and later, Walt Disney's character Mickey Mouse, walking along pulling a bomb-trolley on which lay a bomb, was painted on the nose. Beneath this was the name *Mickey the Moocher*, an obvious parody of the popular song of the time, 'Millie the Moocher' sung by Cab Calloway. Mickey is walking towards a sign-post upon which was written '3 Reich' and 'Berlin'. Bomb symbols began to appear in rows of ten behind *Mickey* and after five such rows, a second column began aft of the first, although, oddly, after the first ten, the second row only had eight bombs, the next three having just five. There is a suggestion that the Lanc eventually had 115 marked on her nose. How, or if, its accredited 128 ops were shown is not known. Perhaps at some stage the short rows were filled with ten bombs each, but that would only make 100.

One crew to fly *Mickey* just twice was that of Flight

Norman Webb and crew. Back, from left to right: Jack Bailey, John Brown, Pat Walkins, Bluey Purcell. Front: Bert Collingwood, Webb, Roy Westcott.

Lieutenant Norman Webb RNZAF (DFC), to Stuttgart on 7/8 October and Berlin on 18/19 November. During his tour his mid-upper was wounded. Navigator Pat Walkins recalls:

'Purcell was injured by a stray bullet (friendly fire!) which just missed his lung. Later he came back to 61 Squadron and visited the dispersal point to wish us "All the best." We had a little trouble replacing "Bluey" Purcell. After many spare rear gunners the skipper decided on Roy Chapman, but I understand that Frank Emerson was offered to Webb after a number of others were tried. Emerson had been a member of Jock Reid's (VC) team that got badly shot-up by a night fighter. He later joined the army.'

On 24/25 February 1944, Webb's crew were on their 29th op, but an upwards-firing night fighter set them on fire. The pilot managed to keep the bomber straight and level

EE176 with air and ground crew; 91 bomb symbols showing.

do so, but then, when just 1,000 feet from the ground – actually the sea – Forrest regained control and quickly landed at the nearest base he could locate.

Although an immediate search was made, neither of the two men who had baled out were found. Harry Pronger was a married man, aged 33, while Len Darben was only 20. John Forrest was to die in action on another mission on 24/25 June, together with J R S Wood, D C Newman and J Macfie of his original crew.

until everyone got out. Six of the crew survived, with just the bomb aimer killed. The rear gunner was still Flight Sergeant A F Emerson (DFM), and as Pat Walkins recalled: 'He was the first out of the aircraft when we were shot down.' Pat also remembers EE176's markings: 'The title of *Mickey the Moocher* was never used in our day, nor were any number of bomb symbols shown on "M". These must have been a later idea.'

With 61 Squadron EE176 became the regular aircraft for Flight Lieutenant J E R Williams and crew, who took it to Germany 13 times between October 1943 and February 1944, out of its first 28 sorties with the squadron. During this period *Mickey* went to Berlin 15 times, although it had to abort the mission on 1/2 January as the starboard-outer engine suddenly caught fire. John Williams (DFC) then went to 617 Squadron and two captains, Pilot Officer J A Forrest RAAF and the flight commander, Squadron Leader S J Beard DFC, began to fly her.

On the fateful Nürnberg raid of 30/31 March, under the captaincy of Forrest, the aircraft was flown well north of track owing to wrong winds being broadcast and petrol began to get low. Near Hannover they ran into a hail and sleet storm. Reaching the North Sea, Forrest headed for Coningsby only to meet violent electrical storms off the Norfolk coast. The Lanc was hit by lightning, the shock passing right through the machine, stunning and temporarily blinding Forrest who lost control. Believing they had already crossed the coast he ordered the crew to bale out and EE176 dived earthwards. The WOP and mid-upper gunner were the only two to recover sufficiently to

In May Pilot Officer D E White RCAF and Sidney Beard shared most of *Mickey's* ops, Beard flying the aircraft on D-Day. *Mickey* flew all through the summer of 1944, attacking V1 sites and transport areas, Beard taking the Lanc on the Caen raid that heralded the Allied break-out from Normandy.

On 29 June, the target was Beauvoir but the main hydraulic system burst and it was thought the bomb-doors would not open. White had his engineer bandage together the pipe and then drain as much fluid as possible from the front turret and in this way they got the bomb-doors open as the target was reached. Both White and John Lyon were decorated with the DFC and DFM respectively. In all the aircraft had very few aborts due to mechanical problems and by August it was fast approaching the 100th trip. This appears to have been flown on 12/13 August by Delbert White, to Rüsselsheim. In all White flew 28 sorties in *Mickey*, while Beard completed 17, receiving a Bar to an earlier DFC.

*Mickey* encountered a night fighter going to Rheydt on 19/20 September. It opened fire at 600 yards, closing to 200, from the starboard quarter. Both gunners returned fire and the fighter broke away to port and was not seen again. German night fighter pilots didn't like crews who appeared awake!

Flying Officer Norman Hoad, who had flown several trips in ED860 – see earlier – took *Mickey* to the Dortmund-Ems Canal on 23/24 September, noting: 'Bombed from 7,800 feet to attain accuracy needed to hit this precision target.' He also had to take evasive action from a Ju88 which attempted an attack, although the enemy fighter did not get into a firing position. This was

EE176's 110th trip. Hoad and his crew failed to return from Brunswick in ME595 on 14/15 October, Hoad ending up as a prisoner of war.

*Mickey's* last combat took place on this same trip to Brunswick, with Flying Officer F A Mouritz RAAF in command. Nearing the target the mid-upper spotted a fighter approaching from the port quarter above but it then appeared to side-slip into position behind the bomber. He ordered the pilot to corkscrew as he began to fire, while also giving the rear gunner the fighter's position and who, upon seeing it too, also opened fire. The fighter dived quickly away, the mid-upper giving it a final burst as it disappeared.

On 9 November the veteran *Mickey* was flown to Netheravon by Mouritz. Along with a Halifax and a Stirling she was to be loaded with Red Cross parcels in order to find out how many each type could carry for relief flights for liberated prisoners on the continent once the war ended. Mouritz returned to Netheravon on the 30th to bring *Mickey* back, and within a day or so she left for good.

EE176 left the squadron in early December (?) going to 1653 CU where it was marked H4-X but became Cat AC on 21 April 1945. In May it became 5260M at BOAC, Whitchurch, and was converted to an instructional airframe.

It is not certain just how many ops EE176 carried out. After Norman Hoad noted the 23/24 September trip as being her 110th, the aircraft went on another nine sorties, although the last two were frustrated by orders not to bomb, both because of cloud covering the target. However, the last raid, 6 November, Frank Mouritz recorded that they did bomb before the Master Bomber abandoned the raid. So the further nine raids may have been ten as in Frank Mouritz's log-book, he shows a trip to Bremen in 'M' on 11 November!

Thus it seems that *Mickey* made 119 trips although, as stated earlier, the Lanc seems to have had 115 bombs on its nose when it left the squadron, while other records show the aircraft as having gone on 128. The figure of 119 seems about right, although there is the possibility that it was 118, and over the years a typing error changed this to 128.

In February 2000, the Battle of Britain Memorial Flight at RAF Coningsby repainted its flying Lancaster (PA474) with the wartime markings of *Mickey the Moocher* and by late 2004 these markings remained in situ.

## 97 SQUADRON

**3/4 July** *2245-0340*
COLOGNE
FL J H Sauvage
Sgt W G Walker (FE)
FO H A Hitchcock (N)
PO F Burbridge (BA)
FS E Wheeler (WOP)
FO J E Blair (MU)
Sgt G W Wood (RG)

**24/25 July** *2209-0357*
HAMBURG
FL J H Sauvage and crew

**27/28 July** *2243-0354*
HAMBURG
FS V Baker
Sgt W J Vaughan
PO C W Webb RCF
Sgt A Davis
Sgt J Richards
Sgt G Lowden
Sgt P McC Edwards
(both gunners PoWs 10/11 Aug, rest KIA)

**2/3 Aug** *2317-0533*
HAMBURG
Sgt C S Chatten
Sgt C Baumber
Sgt L R Armitage
FO Webb
Sgt W A Reffin
FS J R Kraemer RAAF
Sgt D V Smith
(shot down by intruder 24 Aug, Kraemer KIA)

**10/11 Aug** *2227-0533*
NÜRNBERG
FO D McN Moodie RCAF (DFC)
Sgt L E Melbourne (FE)
Sgt J T Bundle (N) (DFM)
Sgt H W N Clausen (BA) (DFM)
Sgt T E Stamp (WOP)
Sgt L A Drummond (MU)
Sgt F A Hughes (RG)
(all lost 18/19 Oct except Clausen – PoW)

**12/13 Aug** *2109-0507*
MILAN
SL J M Garlick DFC(*)
Sgt J M Anderson
Sgt A G Boyd
Sgt E O Charlton (DFM)
Sgt J Kenny
Sgt M T Ward
Sgt F Edwards
(Garlick and Edwards KIA 2/3 Dec, rest PoWs, except Kenny, not on op)

**17/18 Aug** *2101-0430*
PEENEMÜNDE
FO W Richen
Sgt G Winter
Sgt H W Watts
Sgt E H Pack
Sgt J Wrigley
Sgt R W Rowe
Sgt F C Nordhoff

**22/23 Aug** *2137-0227*
LEVERKUSEN
FO D McN Moodie and crew

**23/24 Aug** *2051-0351*
BERLIN
FO D McN Moodie and crew

**27/28 Aug** *2132-0441*
NÜRNBERG
FO D McN Moodie and crew

**31 Aug** *0044-0429*
MUNICH
FO D McN Moodie and crew

**3/4 Sep** *2026-0436*
BERLIN
FO D McN Moodie and crew

**5/6 Sep** *2005-0222*
MANNHEIM
FO D McN Moodie and crew

**6/7 Sep** *2000-0343*
MUNICH
FO K M Steven
Sgt A C East
Sgt S B Stevenson
PO R R Brown
Sgt W C Gadsby
Sgt L A Drummond
Sgt K D Newman

**15/16 Sep** *2114-0220*
MONTLUÇON
2/Lt J E Russell
Sgt H J Lazenby
2/Lt R Wright
FS L W Golden
Sgt J P Dow
Sgt E W Bark
FS T N Maston

## 61 SQUADRON

**4/5 Oct** *1850-0101*
FRANKFURT
FL J E R Williams
Sgt W Beach (FE)
FO A J Talbot (N)
PO A J Walker (BA)
Sgt A E Potter (WOP)
Sgt R Blagdon (MU)
Sgt K S Jewell (RG)

**7/8 Oct** *2250-0411*
STUTTGART
FL N D Webb RNZAF (DFC)
Sgt J W Brown (FE)
Sgt P S Walkins (N)
Sgt J Bailey (DFM) (BA)
FS C J Collingwood (DFM)
FS L J Purcell RAAF (MU)
Sgt D J Chapman (RG)
(Brown KIA 24/25 Feb '44, rest PoW except Purcell, not on op)

**8/9 Oct** *2250-0411*
HANNOVER
FL J E R Williams and crew
Sgt J Soilleux in (FE)

**18 Oct** *1736-2345*
HANNOVER
FL J E R Williams and crew
FS A G Leslie in (BA)

**20/21 Oct** *1700-0037*
LEIPZIG
FL J E R Williams and crew

**22/23 Oct** *1811-0013*
KASSEL
FL J E R Williams and crew

*Mickey the Moocher*, now with 119 ops. Crew, from left to right: Jim Leith, Den Cluett, Pete Smith, Frank Mouritz (pilot), Arthur Bass, Laurie Cooper, Davy Bloomfield.

**3 Nov** *1717-2156*
DÜSSELDORF
PO R A Walker
Sgt H E Houldsworth (FE)
FS N J Cornell (N)
PO J Wells
Sgt R C Bailey
Sgt C K Taylor
Sgt D R Kelly
Sgt G M Ward (2N)

**10/11 Nov** *2053-0515*
MODAN
Sgt C J Gray
Sgt W J McCullouch
Sgt Ward
Sgt R Jones
Sgt L E Jackson
Sgt W M Morrison
Sgt D R Hay

**18/19 Nov** *1719-0040*
BERLIN
FL N D Webb and crew

**23/24 Nov** *1723-0040*
BERLIN
FL J E R Williams and crew

**26/27 Nov** *1719-0118*
BERLIN
FL J E R Williams and crew

**2 Dec** *1653-2359*
BERLIN
FL J E R Williams and crew

**4 Dec** *0018-0746*
LEIPZIG
PO R H Todd
Sgt S Robson
FO J Hodgkinson
Sgt V R Duvall
FS W Housley
Sgt S McClosky
Sgt J Cartwright

**16/17 Dec** *1619-0011*
BERLIN
Sgt C J Gray and crew

**20 Dec** *1720-2321*
FRANKFURT
Sgt L Cannon
Sgt K H Dean
FS G J Hull
Sgt R Stones
Sgt H Wyrill

Sgt H Sherliker
FS J M Green RAAF
(all lost 18/19 Mar '44)

**23/24 Dec** *2355-0803*
BERLIN
SL S J Beard DFC (*)
FS J K Burnside
FL J R Anderson DFM (DFC)
WO D C Davies
Sgt A E Wood
PO J C Hodgkins
WO J Graham

**29 Dec** *1647-2359*
BERLIN
FL J E R Williams and crew

# 1944

**1/2 Jan** *2334-0226*
BERLIN
FL J E R Williams and crew
(abort, std outer caught fire)

**2/3 Jan** *2324-0713*
BERLIN
FL J E R Williams and crew

**5 Jan** *1650-2242*
STETTIN
PO F J Nixon
Sgt W Craig
Sgt J W Devenish
FS A T Garrett
Sgt J E Chapman
Sgt H F Bore
Sgt H W Pain

**20 Jan** *1624-2324*
BERLIN
FL J E R Williams and crew

**21/22 Jan** *2039-0308*
BERLIN
PO H H Farmiloe
Sgt G N Whitby (FE)
Sgt T K Telfer (N)
Sgt K Vowe (BA)
Sgt E A Davidson (WOP)
Sgt H J Newey (MU)
Sgt R Noble (RG)

**27/28 Jan** *1735-0202*
BERLIN
PO H Wallis
Sgt T F Preston
FS L E Tozer

Sgt A Pardoe
FS K Sims
Sgt D J Brewer
FS E Bremner

**28/29 Jan** *0021-0739*
BERLIN
FL J E R Williams and crew

**30 Jan** *1725-2345*
BERLIN
PO F P Moroney
Sgt G N Whitley
FO M Jenkins
Sgt J Davies
Sgt D Dushman
Sgt C A Mills
FS J Bell

**15/16 Jan** *1723-0028*
BERLIN
FL J E R Williams and crew

**19/20 Jan** *2351-0721*
LEIPZIG
SL S J Beard and crew

**24/25 Jan** *2029-0432*
SCHWEINFURT
SL S J Beard and crew

**15/16 Mar** *1916-0248*
SUTTGART
PO L Cannon and crew

**18/19 Mar** *1900-0124*
FRANKFURT
FS C W J Newman
Sgt R C H Jones
Sgt C Trottner
Sgt E J Outram
Sgt R A Taylor
PO E A Alston
Sgt R C Gardner
(all lost 24/25 Apr except
Trottner who evaded)

**22/23 Mar** *1856-0102*
FRANKFURT
PO J A Forrest RAAF
Sgt A H Davies (FE)
Sgt J R S Wood (N)
Sgt D C Newman (BA)
Sgt L Darben (WOP)
FS H W Pronger RAAF
Sgt J Macfie (MU)

**24/25 Mar** *1857-0153*
BERLIN
SL S J Beard and crew

**26/27 Mar** *1943-0046*
ESSEN
PO J A Forrest and crew

**30/31 Mar** *2203-0600*
NÜRNBERG
PO J A Forrest and crew
(WOP and RG baled out
during storm. Forrest, Wood
Newman and Macfie KIA 25 June)

**5/6 Apr** *2034-0444*
TOULOUSE
SL S J Beard and crew
FL J Breakey (3AG)

**10/11 Apr** *2115-0429*
TOURS M/YARDS
SL S J Beard and crew

**11/12 Apr** *2038-0057*
AACHEN
FS J Kramer
Sgt N H Shergold
Sgt R W Burkwood
Sgt C W Greenaway
Sgt P Donoghue
Sgt A N Avery
Sgt R F Coleman

**18/19 Apr** *2059-0135*
JUVISY M/YARDS
PO J A Forrest and crew
FS E J Kemish (WOP) and
Sgt C C Scrimshaw (RG) in,
FL J Breakey in (3AG)

**20/21 Apr** *2255-0345*
PARIS M/YARDS
SL S J Beard and crew

**22/23 Apr** *2305-0533*
BRUNSWICK
SL S J Beard and crew

**26/27 Apr** *2121-0615*
SCHWEINFURT
SL S J Beard and crew
Sgt C W Saunders in (FE)

**29/30 Apr** *2214-0547*
ST MÉDARD
SL S J Beard and crew
FL I M Pettigrew in (FE)
Sgt C C Scrimshaw (3AG)

**1/2 May** *2202-0345*
MALINES
FS J G Gibbard RAAF
Sgt R F Saunders
Sgt C Michael
FS E J Roberts
Sgt F Gibbons
Sgt T M Blackie
Sgt C J Jackson
Sgt C C Scrimshaw (3AG)

**7 May** *0045-0552*
LOUAILLES
FS J G Gibbard and crew
Sgt H S Rosher in (3AG)

**8/9 May** *2124-0245*
BREST
PO F Norton
Sgt K Chapman
FS W H Webb
FS K W Clement
Sgt H J Eldrett
FS J H Tollitt
FS S Calver

# EE176 MICKEY THE MOOCHER

**10/11 May** *2156-0115*
*LILLE*
PO W North
FS H Crowley
Sgt L Martin
FS N E Jarvis RAAF
Sgt G I Monteith
Sgt D A Bartlett
Sgt P E O'Shea

**19/20 May** *2207-0442*
*TOURS M/YARDS*
PO D E White RCAF (DFC)
Sgt J A D Lyon (DFM) (FE)
WO M B Blackwood RCAF
FP P O Points
FS A F Harrow
Sgt D E Gibb RCAF
Sgt L C Anderson RCAF

**22/23 May** *2230-0515*
*BRUNSWICK*
PO D E White and crew

**27/28 May** *2228-0444*
*NANTES M/YARDS*
PO D E White and crew

**28/29 May** *2244-0205*
*ST MARTIN*
PO D E White and crew

**31 May/1 June** *2341-0454*
*SAUMUR*
SL S J Beard and crew

**3/4 June** *2309-0239*
*FERME D'URVILLE*
SL S J Beard and crew
Sgt P F Lewis in (FE)

**6 June** *0205-0702*
*ST PIERRE*
SL S J Beard and crew

**6/7 June** *2336-0336*
*ARGENTAN*
SL S J Beard and crew
Sgt B F Rowland in (FE)

**10/11 June** *2245-0353*
*ORLÉANS M/YARDS*
PO D E White and crew

**12/13 June** *2241-0435*
*POITIERS*
PO D E White and crew

**14/15 June** *2230-0307*
*AUNAY*
PO D E White and crew

**15/16 June** *2127-0405*
*CHÂTELLERAULT*
PO D E White and crew

**19/20 June** *2218-0010*
*WATTEN – V1 SITE*
SL S J Beard and crew
Sgt L Morton in (FE)
(recalled)

**21/22 June** *2316-0429*
*GELSENKIRCHEN*
PO D E White and crew

**23/24 June** *2245-0519*
*LIMOGES M/YARDS*
PO D E White and crew

**24/25 June** *2315-0157*
*PROUVILLE*
PO D E White and crew

**27/28 June** *2207-0522*
*VITRY*
PO D E White and crew

**29 June** *1250-1545*
*BEAUVOIR – V1 SITE*
PO D E White and crew
(hydraulic line burst but
carried on and bombed)

**4/5 July** *2303-0318*
*ST LEU D'ESSERENT*
PO D E White and crew

**7/8 July** *2217-0250*
*ST LEU D'ESSERENT*
PO D E White and crew

**12/13 July** *2203-0531*
*CULMONT CHALANDREY*
PO D E White and crew

**14/15 July** *2206-0451*
*VILLENEUVE*
PO D E White and crew

**15/16 July** *2224-0520*
*NEVERS*
PO D E White and crew

**18 July** *0337-0707*
*CAEN*
SL S J Beard and crew

**18/19 July** *2308-0418*
*RÉVIGNY*
PO D E White and crew

**20/21 July** *2301-0209*
*COURTRAI*
PO D E White and crew

**24/25 July** *2225-0356*
*DINGES*
FO G M Taylor RCAF
Sgt G Gaunt
Sgt A F Niven
FO J Meek
Sgt S Adair
Sgt J H Jebb
FS H S Grahn

**25 July** *1750-2201*
*ST CYR AIRFIELD*
FO R F Heath
Sgt P Davis (FE)
FO A A Lorton (N)
FO F J Kelly RCAF (BA)
Sgt C E Ruane
Sgt E D Fisher
Sgt J Ryan

**28/29 July** *2200-0543*
*STUTTGART*
FO R J King
Sgt W N Heritage
FO M C Macfarlane RCAF
FO C H Oliver RCAF
FO R R Collard
Sgt F W Futter
Sgt E G Cutting

**30 July** *0556-1045*
*CAHAGNES*
FO R J King and crew
(abandoned by MB)

**31 July** *1720-2220*
*RILLY-LA-MONTAGNE*
PO D E White and crew

**1 Aug** *1645-2113*
*MONT CANDON – V1 SITE*
PO D E White and crew
(abandoned by MB)

**2 Aug** *1440-1920*
*BOIS DE CASSAN – V1*
PO D E White and crew

**3/4 Aug** *2115-0105*
*TROSSY ST MAXIMIN*
SL S J Beard and crew
Sgt M Kelly (FE), FS

C C Scrimshaw (MU) and
FS R R Langley in (RG)

**5 Aug** *1055-1530*
*ST LEU D'ESSERENT*
PO D E White and crew

**7/8 Aug** *2115-0105*
*SECQUEVILLE*
PO D E White and crew
(abandoned by MB)

**9/10 Aug** *2027-0250*
*CHÂTELLERAULT*
PO D E White and crew

**11 Aug** *1200-1937*
*BORDEAUX*
PO D E White and crew

**12/13 Aug** *2134-0303*
*RÜSSELSHEIM*
PO D E White and crew

**14 Aug** *1734-2229*
*BREST*
PO D E White and crew

**15 Aug** *1002-1343*
*GILZE-RIJEN AIRFIELD*
FO J S Cooksey
Sgt D E Rose
Sgt E P Meaker
Sgt T Stephenson
Sgt A R Marshall
Sgt S J Scarrett
Sgt N W Elliott

**5 Sep** *1558-2037*
*BREST*
FO H L Inniss (DFC*)
Sgt H T Ansell (FE) (DFM)
FO J T O Dickinson
FO J R Morrison RAAF
Sgt K F Moseley
Sgt J Aldridge
FS R R Langley

**10 Sep** *1507-1916*
*LE HAVRE*
FO J F Boland RAAF
Sgt L Muir
Sgt J Boon
Sgt J A Fitzgerald
Sgt L E Welch
Sgt H Cave
Sgt J L Jones

**11 Sep** *0358-0906*
*LE HAVRE*
FO J F Boland and crew

**11/12 Sep** *2056-0257*
*DARMSTADT*
FO M L Hunt RNZAF
Sgt F Askew
FS A T Harvey RNZAF
FS A T Bell RAAF
Sgt R Nesbit
Sgt S H H Jobson
Sgt J W H Harrison

**17 Sep** *0755-1113*
*BOULOGNE*
SL H W Horsley
PO L A Cawthorne
FO J C Webber
FO J P Wheeler
FS G Twyneham
Sgt H W Jennings
Sgt R T Hoskisson

**18 Sep** *1821-2318*
*BREMERHAVEN*
FO S E Miller
Sgt G McChrystal
FO H A Hunt
Sgt R T Galloway
FS D C Mummery RAAF

Sgt L A Hay
Sgt J E Norcutt

**19 Sep** *1855-2358*
*RHEYDT*
FO S E Miller and crew
(night fighter combat)

**23/24 Sep** *1859-0012*
*DORTMUND-EMS CANAL*
FO N E Hoad
Sgt C S Webb (FE)
FO K O W Ball (N)
FO W H Pullin (BA)
Sgt G P Boyd (WOP)
Sgt N England (MU)
Sgt G V Embury (RG)
(Ju88 encountered)

**27 Sep** *0100-0716*
*KARLSRUHE*
FL H B Grynkiewicz
Sgt W M Ratcliffe
Sgt J L Jones
Sgt E W Gibb
Sgt E J Day
Sgt G E Gwalter
Sgt K W Browne

**27/28 Sep** *2150-0410*
*KAISERSLAUTERN*
FO M L Hunt and crew

**5 Oct** *0750-1315*
*WILHELMSHAVEN*
FO C A Donnelly
Sgt A H Steers
FL J H Vincent
FS F D Green
Sgt R G D Brock
Sgt L Ayres
St T J Kerrigan

**6 Oct** *1743-2215*
*BREMEN*
FO M L Hunt and crew

**14/15 Oct** *2257-0622*
*BRUNSWICK*
FO F A Mouritz RAAF
Sgt A J Leith (FE)
FS L A Cooper (N)
FO P M R Smith (BA)
FS D C Bloomfield RAAF
Sgt A G B Bass (MU)
Sgt D C Cluett (RG)
(night fighter attack)

**19/20 Oct** *1730-0051*
*NÜRNBERG*
FO F A Mouritz and crew

**23 Oct** *1439-1735*
*FLUSHING*
FO F A Mouritz and crew

**28/29 Oct** *2210-0544*
*BERGEN*
FO T Bain
Sgt P G Lee
Sgt H G Harding
Sgt T Morgan
WO N G McKenzie
Sgt J H Hodgkins
Sgt J Casey
(aborted due to cloud)

**6 Nov** *1635-2228*
*GRAVENHORST*
FO F A Mouritz and crew
(aborted due to ground smoke)

# JB138
# JUST JANE

*Just Jane* was JB138 of 61 Squadron with a possible 123 operational sorties to her name – and form!  Plus one swastika for a night combat.

Part of an order for 550 Lancasters placed with Messrs A V Roe in 1941, JB138 – a Mark III – rolled off the production line in the early summer of 1943 and was sent to 61 Squadron at Syerston on 22 August.  Being given the code letters QR and individual letter J eventually helped shape the aeroplane's name of *Just Jane*.  Shape is right, for the artist who painted the name and motif on the Lanc's nose produced a very buxom nude stretched out on a bomb; undoubtedly inspired by the popular *Daily Mirror* newspaper cartoon character Jane.

Unlike most Lancaster bomb tallies, *Jane's* was not marked in neat rows of the more usual ten but in rows of 30.  The photograph – believed to have been taken in about July 1944, and reproduced here – shows the tally of 64 bombs, and she went on to make the 100th trip in early October.  *Jane* has been variously credited with 113 ops or even as high as 123, although records from the 541 would indicate something in the region of 120, so the higher figure may well be correct;  and 113 was either a typing error or a purely arithmetical error.

*Jane's* first operation was to Nürnberg on 27/28 August 1943, with an experienced crew.  Flying Officer N F Turner DFM was on his second tour, having completed 37 ops on his first with 61 in early 1942.  He flew some 15 ops in *Jane*, his second tour being completed in May 1944, for which he received the DFC.

*Jane* was just in time to fly during the upcoming Battle of Berlin that autumn and winter.  The aircraft went to the Big City eight times but the only problem occured on the trip on 1/2 January 1944.  Her pilot, Howard "Tommy" Farmiloe, had to land at the US 8th Air Force base at Molesworth due to a low fuel state.  Edward Davidson (WOP) recalls this sortie and the crew's first on 29/30 December:

'On 29/30 December we bombed on the red TIs from 22,000 feet, the glow of the fires being seen through the clouds for a considerable time as we headed for home.  This was our first operation.

'It was back to Berlin on 1/2 January.  Tommy

reported seeing route markers at the pinpoint, and we bombed on three Wanganui flares from 22,000 feet. One Electrical Direct Circuit unit was overcharging and failed entirely on leaving the target, which put the rear turret u/s. Then the main petrol feed line became partly blocked causing the starboard-inner engine to overheat. The Gee also failed.

'We landed at the American base at Molesworth and while Tommy was whisked off to the officers' mess, the rest of us NCOs had to spend the night sleeping in armchairs in a room, which we didn't find amusing. Their 'class' system was far worse than ours ever was. The Americans were fascinated by our Lancaster, but at least they put a guard on it overnight.'

Howard Farmiloe and crew crash-landed another Lanc at Little Snoring coming back from Berlin on 24/25 March. He received an Immediate DSO, while Ed Davidson and the bomb aimer received DFMs for another raid in March.

*Jane* was attacked by night fighters on several occasions, the first on the night of 29 September 1943, by no fewer than three of them, right in the target area of Bochum. Over Hannover on 8/9 October, flying under a half-moon at 19,000 feet, 20 miles south of Bremen, a fighter was spotted by the rear gunner making for another Lanc to starboard and opened fire, although no results were seen. Reaching the target a FW190 attacked from the starboard beam. The rear gunner again opened fire, the 190 breaking away to port as the Lanc went into a diving turn to starboard. Hits were observed by both gunners and the Focke Wulf was claimed as damaged.

Early in 1944, with the squadron CO Wing Commander R N Stidolph in command, *Jane* was attacked by a Me210 on the Stettin raid of 4/5 January. 'Monica' (see page 67) picked up the approaching bogey but neither gunner saw it until it began firing, closing in very fast. Both gunners fired back and saw the Messerschmitt break to port and climb, the gunners continuing to fire as it went. It was then seen to dip a wing in preparation for another attack but then smoke could be seen pouring from its starboard engine as it turned away and went down. It was claimed as destroyed. The 210 had, however, scored hits on *Jane* – a large hole had been blasted in the port fin and a smaller hole punched through the elevator. The port-outer engine

was set on fire and the wing holed too, while cannon splinters went through the port-side fuselage and mid-upper turret, but without injuring the gunner, Sergeant E A Gardener. The rear turret, powered by the now feathered engine, became u/s. The gunner was Pilot Officer J H Pullman, who was on his second tour.

Wing Commander Stidolph also discovered the Gee, visual Monica and R/T all u/s and to add to his problems, the aircraft became virtually unmanageable on three engines, so they had to return on just the two inner-engines at maximum boost and revs, and with the starboard-outer throttled right back. They landed at Matlaske with just 8½ gallons of petrol left after nearly ten hours of flying. Reginald Stidolph received an Immediate DFC for this effort, which must have been very immediate for it was gazetted on 25 January. John Pullman was also a recipient of the DFC.

After this night's damage, *Jane* was declared Cat AC for almost a month but was back on duty by 5 February but did not fly ops until March. On 10/11 March, Turner followed their bombs down and saw them hit the target, then heading back actually had his gunners shoot-up an airfield with machine-gun fire at zero feet! Pilot Officer Frank Norton became her more regular skipper, flying over 20 ops in her. Some of her captains at this time were pilots who had flown another 61 Squadron veteran, EE176, notably Squadron Leader S J Beard, Flight Lieutenant D E White and Flying Officer H L Innes.

*Jane* operated on both nights of D-Day, despite a lucky escape a few nights earlier just after midnight on 1 June. The crew had just set course when the bomber was hit by lightning. The machine stalled and as the port wing dropped, *Jane* went into a partial spin. Pilot Officer D C Freeman recovered and flew back to base, setting course again, but the aircraft's stability was very bad so they were forced to abort.

Her last combat occurred on 11/12 September, when returning from Darmstadt. A Me109 came in from behind shortly after leaving the target area, the rear gunner saw it and started firing, followed by the mid-upper. As the pilot, Flying Officer A P Greenfield RAAF, put the Lanc into a corkscrew and strikes were seen on the 109's fuselage, it was claimed as damaged. Albert Greenfield was awarded the DFC later, having completed most of his tour in *Jane*.

Her next major problem might well have been fatal, for on a daylight sortie to Düren on 16 November the aircraft was hit by a falling bomb and lost an engine! Flying Officer H R Smith RCAF was flying JB138 for the second time – and last. *Jane* was quickly repaired at 54 MU and was back by 2 December. However, the Form 541 notes her as flying three operations in late November which must be suspect, and it is likely that these entries are clerical errors, *Jane's* number being repeated without checking what actual aircraft was being flown.

Flying Officer F A Mouritz RAAF flew her to bomb the Gravenhorst canal on 1 January, having flown a couple of ops in EE176 during October/November, including its last trip. This was made on 14/15 January 1945 and on 2 February the aircraft was sent to 5 LFS. On 22 April she went to 4 School of Technical Training where she became 5224M and converted to an instructional airframe. JB138 was finally Struck off Charge on 16 October 1946.

## 61 SQUADRON
### 1943

**27/28 Aug** *2050-0435*
NÜRNBERG
FO N F Turner DFM (DFC)
Sgt G A Turnbull (FE)
Sgt J Barr (N)
Sgt R Freeth (BA)
WO R J Russell (WOP)
PO M Root-Reid (MU)
Sgt E A Walker (RG)

**30/31 Aug** *0002-0519*
MÜNCHEN-GLADBACH
FO N F Turner and crew

**31 Aug/1 Sep** *2018-0406*
BERLIN
FO N F Turner and crew

**3/4 Sep** *2002-0436*
BERLIN
PO P H Todd
Sgt S Robson
PO J Hodgkinson
Sgt V R Duvall
Sgt W Housley
Sgt Pattrick
Sgt J Cartwright

**6/7 Sep** *2008-0344*
MUNICH
PO H Wallis
Sgt T A Cooksey
Sgt I Tozer
Sgt A Holbrook
Sgt K Sims
Sgt D T Brewer
Sgt E Bramner

**22/23 Sep** *1858-0054*
HANNOVER
PO R A Walker
Sgt H E Houldsworth
Sgt N J Cornwall
PO J Wells
Sgt R C Bailey
Sgt C R Taylor
Sgt D R Kelly

**23/24 Sep** *1907-0150*
MANNHEIM
PO R A Walker and crew

**27/28 Sep** *1912-0044*
BOCHUM
FO N F Turner and crew

**29 Sep** *1844-2324*
HAGAN
FO N F Turner and crew
WO M R Braines in (MU)

**2/3 Oct** *1825-0235*
MUNICH
SL E A Benjamin DFC(*)
PO J J Stephenson
FO H L Hewitt
Sgt F W Steed
Sgt H D Dinsdall
Sgt J Fawley
PO M Root-Reid (RG)

**3/4 Oct** *1853-0046*
KASSEL
FO J E Williams
Sgt G N Whitley
PO A J Talbot
PO A J Walker
Sgt A E Potter
Sgt R Blagdon
Sgt K S Jewell

**4/5 Oct** *1825-0029*
FRANKFURT
FO N F Turner and crew
Sgt R S Brown in (MU)

**7/8 Oct** *2018-0240*
STUTTGART
FO N F Turner and crew
PO S R Hughes in (MU)

**8/9 Oct** *2247-0404*
HANNOVER
FO K R Ames
Sgt V R Biggerstaff
PO A J Wright
Sgt T H Savage
FS H Glasby
Sgt S P Nicholas
Sgt R S Parle
(EA attacked on bomb-run, hit by RG)

**18/19 Oct** *1701-0041*
LEIPZIG
FO N F Turner and crew
PO H H Farmiloe (2P)

**22/23 Oct** *1809-2102*
KASSEL
FO N F Turner and crew
(ASI failed, returned early)

**3 Nov** *1700-2131*
DÜSSELDORF
WC R N Stidolph (DFC)
Sgt H J Anthony
FO J H Dyer
FO G F Aley
Sgt J D Barnes-Moss
Sgt E A Gardener
PO J H Pullman (DFC)

**10/11 Nov** *2101-0455*
MODAN
PO F J Nixon
Sgt W Craig
FS J W Devenish
Sgt A T Garrett
Sgt J E Chapman
Sgt W Leary
Sgt H F Bore

**18/19 Nov** *1737-0055*
BERLIN
FO N F Turner and crew
FO G E Sharpe (2P)
FS J S Cook in (BA)
Sgt G A Davey in (MU)

**22 Nov** *1636-2315*
BERLIN
SL E A Benjamin and crew

**2 Dec** *1655-2335*
BERLIN
FO N F Turner and crew

**20 Dec** *1712-2000*
FRANKFURT
SL S J Beard DFC(*)
FS J K Burnside
FL J R Anderson
WO D C Davies
Sgt J D Barnes-Moss
PO J C Hodgkinson
WO J Graham
(abort – std-inner failed)

**29/30 Dec** *1712-0004*
BERLIN
FO H H Farmiloe (DSO)
Sgt G A Jerry (FE)
Sgt T K Telfer (N)
Sgt K Vowe (BA)
Sgt E A Davidson (DFM)
Sgt A Sherliker (MU)
Sgt R Noble (RGG

### 1944

**2 Jan** *0008-0830*
BERLIN
PO H H Farmiloe and crew
Sgt W M Morrison in (MU)

**6 Jan** *0002-0955*
STETTIN
WC R N Stidolph and crew
(Badly damaged by Me210, which was shot down by gunners)

**1/2 Mar** *2324-0712*
STUTTGART
FL N F Turner and crew
FS C J Woolnough (2P)
FS R A Bunyan in (WOP) and
Sgt H J Silzer RCAF in (MU)

**10/11 Mar** *1958-0133*
CHÂTEAUROUX
FL N F Turner and crew
FL G L Dunstone (WOP);
WO W Mainwaring in (3AG)
(strafed airfield)

**15/16 Mar** *1904-0237*
STUTTGART
FL N F Turner and crew
FO J G Cox (2P)

**24/25 Mar** *1840-0109*
BERLIN
FL N F Turner and crew

**26/27 Mar** *2006-0038*
ESSEN
FL G A Berry RCAF
Sgt F C Astell
FS A G Williams
FO R T Reid RCAF
Sgt E F Sutton
Sgt L G Brand
Sgt R W Levett

**30/31 Mar** *2201-0503*
NÜRNBERG
PO F Norton (DFC)
Sgt K Chapman
FS W Webb
FS K Clement
FS H Eldrett
FS J Tollitt
FS S Calver

**5/6 Apr** *2037-0403*
TOULOUSE
PO F Norton and crew
FS N Audley (3AG)
(front hatch blew off on bomb-run and had to make second run)

**10/11 Apr** *2231-0422*
TOURS M/YARDS
FS J Kramer RCAF
Sgt N H Shergold
Sgt R W Burkwood
Sgt C W Greenaway
Sgt P Donaghue
Sgt A N Avery
Sgt R F Coleman

**11/12 Apr** *2046-0039*
AACHEN
FL G A Berry and crew
(lost std-inner over tgt)

**18/19 Apr** *2057-0111*
JUVISY M/YARDS
FL N F Turner and crew

**20/21 Apr** *2305-0327*
PARIS M/YARDS
FL N F Turner and crew
FS O Baldwin in (MU)

**22/23 Apr** *2324-0538*
BRUNSWICK
PO F Norton and crew
PO G A Davey (3AG)

**24/25 Apr** *2057-0610*
MUNICH
PO F Norton and crew

**26/27 Apr** *2148-0613*
SCHWEINFURT
FO D Paul (DFC)
Sgt J Bosworth
PO H Griffin
Sgt J Millar
Sgt F R Brazzier
Sgt S Billington
Sgt P McGierney

**28/29 Apr** *2250-0616*
ST MÉDARD-EN-JALLES
PO F Norton and crew
(abandoned by MB)

**1/2 May** *2126-0530*
ST MARTIN-DU-TOUCH
PO F Norton and crew

"Target coming up, Skipper!"

**3/4 May** *2150-0339*
*MAILLY-LE-CAMP*
PO F Norton and crew
FS R Coxon (3AG)

**7 May** *0034-0535*
*LOUAILLES*
PO F Norton and crew
FS C Baldwin (3AG)

**24/25 May** *2305-0122*
*EINDHOVEN*
PO F Norton and crew
(abort – eng trouble)

**27/28 May** *2240-0350*
*NANTES M/YARDS*
PO F Norton and crew

**31 May/1 June** *2328-0350*
*SAUMUR*
PO D C Freeman
Sgt P E Cook
Sgt E J Coe
FS J W Morris
Sgt J H Heasman
Sgt D Gordon
Sgt I C Whitehead
(aborted after two attempts
following lightning strike)

**3/4 June** *2315-0301*
*FERME D'URVILLE*
PO D C Freeman and crew

**6 June** *0241-0648*
*ST PIERRE DU MONT*
PO D C Freeman and crew

**6/7 June** *2357-0343*
*ARGENTAN*
PO R H Passant RAAF
Sgt T E Hunt
Sgt P Uren
Sgt A M Frew
FS G E Nash RAAF
Sgt C Howard
Sgt D Copson

**8/9 June** *2316-0645*
*RENNES*
PO W North
Sgt L Morton
FS H Crawley
FS N E Jarvis
Sgt G I Monteith
Sgt D A Bartlett
Sgt E W Ravenhill

**10/11 June** *2218-0345*
*ORLÉANS M/YARDS*
PO F Norton and crew

**12/13 June** *2215-0434*
*POITIERS*
FL F Norton and crew

**14/15 June** *2212-0250*
*AUNAY*
FL F Norton and crew
FO H L Inniss (2P)

**19/20 June** *2215-0117*
*WATTEN – V1 SITE*
FL F Norton and crew
(recalled)

**21/22 June** *2304-0205*
*GELSENKIRCHEN*
FL F Norton and crew
(abort, std-inner caught fire)

**23/24 June** *2222-0505*
*LIMOGES M/YARDS*
FL F Norton and crew
FS C Baldwin in (RG)

**24/25 June** *2252-0203*
*PROUVILLE*

FL H L Inniss
Sgt H T Ansell
FO J T Dickinson RAAF
FO J R Morrison
Sgt K Moseley
Sgt J Aldridge
Sgt R R Langley

**27/28 June** *2204-0514*
*VITRY*
FL F Norton and crew
FS J Slome in (FE)

**29 June** *1153-0514*
*BEAUVOIR*
FL F Norton and crew
Sgt G A Jerry (FE)

**4/5 July** *2309-0325*
*ST LEU D'ESSERENT*
FL F Norton and crew

**7/8 July** *2221-0248*
*ST LEU D'ESSERENT*
FL F Norton and crew
(abort, port-inner u/s)

**12/13 July** *2153-0616*
*CULMONT*
FL F Norton and crew

**15/16 July** *2219-0523*
NEVERS
FL F Norton and crew
FS J K Burnside (FE)

**18 July** *0353-0749*
CAEN
FL F Norton and crew
Jerry and Calver back

**18/19 July** *2303-0411*
RÉVIGNY
FS S Parker
FS J K Burnside
Sgt H J Richardson
Sgt J H Wellens
Sgt K G West
Sgt K Smith
Sgt C H Stothard

**20/21 July** *2326-0242*
COURTRAI M/YARDS
FL F Norton and crew
FS J K Burnside (FE)

**24/25 July** *2219-0350*
DINGES
FO R F J Heath
Sgt P Davis
FO F J Kelly
FO A A Lorton
Sgt C F Ruane
Sgt E D Fisher
FS R Richardson

**26/27 July** *2113-0635*
GIVORS
FL F Norton and crew
FS R G Poulter (FE)

**30 July** *0617-1134*
CAHAGNES
FO R F J Heath and crew
(abandoned by MB)

**31 July** *1741-2252*
JOIGNY
FO R F J Heath and crew

**1 Aug** *1509-1926*
SIRACOURT
FO R F J Heath and crew
(aborted by MB)

**2 Aug** *1440-1920*
BOIS DE CASSAN
FO R F J Heath and crew

**3 Aug** *1208-1625*
TROSSY ST MAXIMIN
FO R F J Heath and crew

**5 Aug** *1108-1515*
ST LEU D'ESSERENT
FL H L Inniss and crew

**7/8 Aug** *2116-0134*
SECQUEVILLE
FL F Norton and crew
(aborted by MB on run-up)

**9/10 Aug** *2028-0245*
CHÂTELLERAULT
FL F Norton and crew
Sgt Scrimshaw (3AG)

**11/12 Aug** *2040-0436*
GIVORS
FL F Norton and crew
FS J F Boland RAAF (2P)

**12/13 Aug** *2128-0313*
RÜSSELSHEIM
WO A P Greenfield RAAF (DFC)
Sgt F F Fraser
Sgt W J A Gibb
Sgt W J Haddon
WO V P Smith
Sgt J P King
Sgt S D P Goodey

**13 Aug** *1631-2341*
BORDEAUX
FO J S Cooksey
Sgt D E Rose
Sgt I P Meaker
Sgt T Stephenson
Sgt A R Marshall
Sgt S J Scarrett
Sgt N W Elliott

**14 Aug** *1744-2239*
BREST
WO A P Greenfield and crew

**15 Aug** *1010-1347*
GILZE-RIJEN AIRFIELD
WO A P Greenfield and crew

**16/17 Aug** *2102-0526*
STETTIN
FS J F Boland RAAF
Sgt J Boon
Sgt L Muir
Sgt J A Fitzgerald
Sgt L E Welch
Sgt H Cave
Sgt J L Jones

**18 Aug** *1126-1554*
BORDEAUX
WO A P Greenfield
Sgt F F Fraser
FO A A W Larton
FO F J Kelly
FS A C R Brydges
FS J Ryan
Sgt E D Fisher

**19 Aug** *0524-1152*
LA PALLICE
FS J F Boland and crew

**25/26 Aug** *2033-0508*
DARMSTADT
FL D E White
Sgt A Lyon
PO M B Blackwood
FO A E Jones
WO H F Harrow
FS L E Gibb
FS L G Anderson

**26/27 Aug** *2006-0702*
KÖNIGSBERG
FL H L Inniss and crew

**31 Aug** *1609-2000*
ROLLENCOURT
Sgt M L Hunt RNZAF
Sgt F Askew
FS A T Harvey
FS A T Bell
Sgt R Nesbitt
Sgt S H H Jobson
Sgt J W Harrison

**5 Sep** *1604-2038*
BREST
FO W A Greenfield and crew

**10 Sep** *1513-1852*
LE HAVRE
FO W A Greenfield and crew

**11 Sep** *0403-0950*
LE HAVRE
FO N P Blain RCAF
Sgt F T Nicholls
Sgt R E Fulcher RCAF
FO K S Porte
Sgt K C Alder
Sgt A E Smith
FS D G Clements RCAF

**11/12 Sep** *2043-0300*
DARMSTADT
FO W A Greenfield and crew
(Me109 damaged in combat)

**17 Sep** *0743-1120*
BOULOGNE
FO W A Greenfield and crew

**18 Sep** *1805-2302*
BREMERHAVEN
FO W A Greenfield and crew

**19 Sep** *1831-2233*
RHEYDT
FO W A Greenfield and crew
(abort r/t u/s)

**23/24 Sep** *1904-0043*
MÜNSTER
FO W A Greenfield and crew

**27 Sep** *0054-0724*
KARLSRUHE
FO W A Greenfield and crew

**27/28 Sep** *2233-0414*
KAISERSLAUTERN
FO W A Greenfield and crew
(bomb load hung-up)

**5 Oct** *0738-1326*
WILHELMSHAVEN
FO A R Goodbrand
Sgt F C Sayer
FO S A Rogers
Sgt W Devine
Sgt E A Tyler
Sgt A H Siddom
Sgt P D Tointon

**6 Oct** *1753-2219*
BREMEN
FO C A Donnelly RAAF
Sgt A H Steers
FL J H Vincent RAAF
FS Green
Sgt R G D Brock
Sgt L Ayres
Sgt T J Kerrigan

**11 Oct** *1337-1713*
FLUSHING
FO C A Donnelly and crew

**14/15 Oct** *2233-0155*
BRUNSWICK
FO W A Greenfield and crew
(abort – pilot ill)

**19/20 Oct** *1730-0055*
NÜRNBERG
FO R Edwards
Sgt J R Owen
Sgt A S Madden
Sgt A Grant
FS C Brooker
Sgt J Clarke
Sgt J Rogers

**23 Oct** *1436-1749*
FLUSHING
FO W A Greenfield and crew

**28/29 Oct** *2221-0500*
BERGEN U/B PENS
FO W A Greenfield and crew

**1 Nov** *1340-1833*
HOMBURG
SL H W Horsley
FS L Morton
FS S Fleet
FS R J Sawyer
FS J Chapman
FS H A Graham RCAF
Sgt R Hoskisson
(saw markers too late to bomb)

**2 Nov** *1629-2144*
DÜSSELDORF
FO R A Lushey RAAF
Sgt G Goodier
Sgt J W A Brewster

Sgt L Brewin
Sgt H A Parsons
Sgt R L Humphries
Sgt W A Fox

**4 Nov** *1743-2222*
LADBERGEN CANAL
FO J F Swales RAAF
Sgt A J M Davies
FO C H Saunders
Sgt R Taylor
FS D M Easton
Sgt T Torney
FS H P L Hardy

**6 Nov** *1648-2232*
GRAVENHORST CANAL
SL H W Horsley and crew
FL E A Vale (FE), FL G L P Dunstone
(WOP) and FS A A Sherriff (MU) in
(failed to bomb)

**11 Nov** *1613-2155*
HARBURG
FO H R Smith RCAF
Sgt R Harris
Sgt R A Williams
Sgt M Gibson
FS R Schmidt RAAF
FO G R Bennett RCAF
FO G Bobenic RCAF

**16 Nov** *1255-1745*
DÜREN
FO H R Smith and crew

## 1945

**1 Jan** *1637-2105*
GRAVENHORST CANAL
FO F A Mouritz
Sgt A J Leith (FE)
FS L A Cooper (N)
FO P M R Smith (BA)
FS D C Bloomfield (WOP)
Sgt A Bass (MU)
Sgt D C Cluett (RG)

**5 Jan** *0045-0749*
ROYAN
FL W A Greenfield and crew
Sgt F C Sayer (FE) and FS
G A Robson (BA)

**6 Jan** *0054-0538*
HOUFFALIZE
FO R Edwards and crew
Sgt D S Tandy and Sgt A McQuilken
in, Brooker and Clarke out

**7/8 Jan** *1649-0307*
MUNICH
FL W A Greenfield and crew
Sgt L Muir in (FE)

**13 Jan** *1643-1847*
PÖLITZ
FO E W Hutchins
Sgt E Cleave
Sgt N C Shepherd
FS G F Burmaster
Sgt P W Scholey
FS A G Brookes
FS W G Webb
(abort, MU turret u/s)

**14/15 Jan** *1609-0223*
MERSEBURG
FO E W Hutchins and crew

# JB603
# TAKE IT EASY

This Mark III Lancaster came off the production line in the autumn of 1943, part of Contract No.1807, built at Manchester, with four Merlin 38 engines. Assigned to 100 Squadron on 3 November, at Waltham, near Grimsby, Lincolnshire, it was given the squadron code letters of HW and the individual letter E-Easy.

From this it was named *Take it Easy*, the legend appearing below a large flying bird painted beneath the cockpit. Ahead of this, rows of bomb symbols in tens began to appear regularly, the bombs being slightly angled rather than the more traditional vertical ones on other aircraft.

*Easy* arrived on the squadron just as the Battle of Berlin was warming up, and in fact,

100 Squadron's *Take it Easy* – JB603 – failed to return from her 111th operation, 5/6 January 1945.

of its first 15 raids, no fewer than 12 were to the German capital. These brought moments of excitement. On its second trip heavy flak scored a hit in the main-plane whilst flying over Hannover, then on trip number five its crew had a scrap with a night fighter that the gunners claimed as destroyed. Then on the first raid of 1944 the inner-starboard petrol tank and inner-engine cowling were holed by machine-gun fire, believed to have come from another Lancaster!

These first ops had Pilot Officer Franklin Tritton as skipper, and he received the DFC, as his tour finished. His WOP, Harry Hinderwell, received the DFM. Over the next month or so *Easy* had various skippers and this was not helped by crew and mechanical problems which led to aborted missions. This was followed by a trouble-free month until an anti-aircraft shell went through the starboard wing between the inner-engine and fuselage during a trip to Friedrichshafen on 27/28 April. The fuel had to be emptied from No.1 tank in that wing. The flight engineer, Sergeant Harry Widdup, received the DFM for this mission, although his citation causes two problems. One, was the sortie indeed completed, and two, what was the actual cause of the damage?

'Sergeant Widdup has now completed 15²/₃ operational sorties and has experienced much opposition from the most difficult and heavily defended targets. He possesses coolness and displays exceptional fearlessness in the face of danger, setting his mind on the task in hand in carrying out his responsible work with great skill under the most trying conditions. On one particular occasion when approaching the distant target of Friedrichshafen, one of the main petrol tanks was badly holed by a bomb falling from above and all petrol in that tank was lost. Sergeant Widdup maintained complete presence of mind and manipulated all his controls with such skill that the aircraft was enabled to regain its base. He is well deserving of the award of the DFM.'

It is not very often shown that someone had flown two-thirds of a mission, and one has to wonder if it was this raid that resulted in this 'shortened' trip. The squadron diary says it was flak but the citation says a falling bomb, but perhaps the cause is not as important as the actions that followed.

This was not Flight Sergeant T F Cook's first trip in JB603 but on this night he took a new crew out. In all he and his crews flew *Easy* 22 times and he was commissioned. Terry Cook received the DFC later, while members of his crew, Eric Norman (N), and Joe Stewart RCAF (BA) were also recipients, as was rear gunner Harold Pawsey, who had completed a second tour. Cook seems to have had several crew changes during his tour and a few times took new pilots on their first trips.

As JB603 was one of three Lancaster veterans to operate with 100 Squadron, it was almost inevitable that crews who flew in her would also have flown in the others. So occasionally familiar names are in the crew lists. Pilot Officer D W Lee was one pilot that flew *Easy* a great deal after Cook became tour-expired. In fact he did 20 trips in her, including the last of his tour on 5/6 October 1944, which was *Easy's* 85th. Dick Lee RNZAF was a recipient of the DFC.

During this period *Easy* had flown twice on D-Day, operated over V1 sites and supported the armies in France following the invasion, all with a minimum of fuss and breakdowns. The only problems seemed to come from flak, with the Lanc being hit over Essen in daylight on 25 October, which damaged its wings, tail-plane and bomb-doors, and again on a daylight to Dortmund on 11/12 November.

*Easy's* last regular captain was Flying Officer L T Harris, who did 18 ops in the aircraft between September and December 1944. Again it is not possible to be exact as to when she flew her 100th op, although it had to be about mid-November, but a couple of mechanical aborts confuse the picture somewhat.

However, by early 1945 *Easy* was into her second hundred, some records noting that the aircraft flew a total of 112 operations, while the squadron diary notes that it failed to return from Hannover on 5/6 January, flying her 111th sortie. *Easy* was being piloted on this fateful occasion by Flying Officer Reg Barker and crew, all of whom were killed and are buried at Gorssal Parish Cemetery, near Deventer, Holland. They had crashed at 23.00 near the hamlet of Haarbroek, Gelderland. 1 Group HQ had received the crew's target attack message at 22.06 hours – then silence.

## 100 SQUADRON
## 1943

**18/19 Nov** *1726-0111*
*BERLIN*
PO F H Tritton (DFC)
Sgt K Wright (FE)
WO A Selman (N)
Sgt G Hopkins (BA)
Sgt H O Hinderwell (DFM)
PO T D Seager (MU)
Sgt J C Knox (RG)

**22 Nov** *1648-2307*
*BERLIN*
PO F H Tritton and crew
(flak damage)

**23 Nov** *1744-2332*
*BERLIN*
PO F H Tritton and crew

**26/27 Nov** *1655-0055*
*BERLIN*
PO F H Tritton and crew

**2/3 Dec** *1644-0037*
*BERLIN*
FS C W Henderson
PO C N Waite
FO J M Ogilvie
Sgt C H Hendry
Sgt N Bowman
Sgt R D Stoneman
Sgt D Sissons
(claimed a fighter destroyed)

**4 Dec** *0009-0758*
*LEIPZIG*
FS E E Tunstall
Sgt J Wunderley
Sgt J C Sharp
PO J A Honey
Sgt J J Green

Sgt W Essar
Sgt R Allison

**16 Dec** *1617-2334*
*BERLIN*
WO T V Hayes (DFC AFC)
Sgt P L Ashenden (FE) (DFC)
Sgt S E Emmett (N) (DFM*)
Sgt W Kondra RCAF (BA) (DFM)
Sgt G R Jenkins (WOP)
Sgt K W Kemp (MU) (DFM)
Sgt J S Ross (RG)

**20 Dec** *1708-2233*
*FRANKFURT*
WO T V Hayes and crew

**23/24 Dec** *2330-0739*
*BERLIN*
FS J A Crabtree
Sgt R T Davies
FO M O Rees
Sgt J W Knight
Sgt F Holm
Sgt J J Whelan
Sgt T S Sanders

**29 Dec** *1650-2314*
*BERLIN*
WO T V Hayes and crew

## 1944

**2 Jan** *0022-0724*
BERLIN
WO T V Hayes and crew
(aircraft damaged)

**21/22 Jan** *2023-0018*
*MAGDEBERG*
FO D F Gillam
Sgt K Talbot
FS K Drury
Sgt D C Gemmell

Sgt W Moffatt
Sgt H R Crompton
Sgt G H Warren
(abort – Gee u/s)

**27/28 Jan** *1756-0210*
*BERLIN*
Sgt K W Evans RAAF
Sgt J J Lapes
Sgt P Atha
Sgt D Francis
Sgt J Armstrong
Sgt S C Brookes
Sgt F Whitehouse

**30 Jan** *1729-2344*
*BERLIN*
FS T F Cook (DFC)
Sgt H Widdup (FE) (DFM)
FO E W Norman (N) (DFC)
Sgt J C Stewart RCAF (DFC)
Sgt H P Peachey (BA)
Sgt A K Burchell (MU)
FO H G D Pawsey (RG) (DFC)

**15/16 Feb** *1735-0005*
*BERLIN*
FS T F Cook and crew

**19/20 Feb** *2350-0710*
*LEIPZIG*
FS T F Cook and crew
Burchell out, Pawsey (MU),
Sgt J Hewitson in as RG
(port-outer damaged)

**24/25 Feb** *1810-0210*
*SCHWEINFURT*
FS T F Cook
Sgt E R Belbin (2P)
Sgt R A Cassell (FE)
FO E W Norman (N)
FS K G Wilde (BA)
Sgt F T Baldwin (WOP)

Sgt E T Duckett (MU)
Sgt J R Truman (RG)

**1/2 Mar** *2330-0740*
*STUTTGART*
FS T F Cook and crew
(main oil pipe for r/t burst)

**15 Mar** *1855-2205*
*STUTTGART*
FS T F Cook and crew
(abort – RG elec suit failed)

**18/19 Mar** *1905-0100*
*FRANKFURT*
FS T F Cook
Sgt R W Pryce (FE)
FO E W Norman (N)
FO J Spector RCAF (BA)
Sgt A J Alcott (WOP)
Sgt F Parish (MU)
FO H G D Pewsey (RG)

**22/23 Mar** *1915-0055*
*FRANKFURT*
FO E L Eames
Sgt R W Pryce
FS D S Kirkwood RCAF
FO J Spector RCAF
Sgt A J Alcott
Sgt F Parish
Sgt C Bird

**24/25 Mar** *1900-0210*
*BERLIN*
FS J Littlewood
Sgt C McCartney
FS D A Tovell RCAF
Sgt J G Hughes
Sgt R W Gilbey
Sgt S C Smith
Sgt J Taylor

# JB603 TAKE IT EASY

**26/27 Mar** *2015-0115*
*ESSEN*
FO E L Eames and crew

**30/31 Mar** *2220-0525*
*NÜRNBERG*
FS D T Fairbairn
Sgt H R Tufton
FO F Tovery
FO J M Wilder
Sgt L Gibbons
Sgt G Tunstall
Sgt J G Wookey

**9/10 Apr** *2135-0555*
*GARDENING – GDYNIA*
FS T F Cook and crew

**10/11 Apr** *2330-0450*
*AULNOYE M/YARDS*
FS T F Cook and crew

**11/12 Apr**
*AACHEN M/YARDS*
PO E D King
Sgt R W Bland
FO L H Scott
Sgt F W Cheetham
Sgt S Beardsall
Sgt D Ralston
Sgt D W Young

**18/19 Apr** *2105-0355*
*GARDENING – BALTIC*
FS T F Cook and crew

**20/21 Apr** *2335-0359*
*COLOGNE M/YARDS*
FS T F Cook and crew

**22/23 Apr** *2230-0309*
*DÜSSELDORF M/YARDS*
FS T F Cook and crew

**24/25 Apr** *2209-0432*
*KARLSRUHE*
FS T F Cook and crew
PO R P Anderson in (FE)

**26/27 Apr** *2300-0310*
*ESSEN*
FS T F Cook and crew
Widdup back

**27/28 Apr** *2200-0610*
*FRIEDRICHSHAFEN*
FS T F Cook
PO J A Orr (2P)
Sgt H Widdup (FE)
FO E W Norman (N)
Sgt J M Campbell (BA)
Sgt W J Strange (WOP)
Sgt H W K Welsby (MU)
FO H G D Pawsey (RG)
(damaged by flak)

**3/4 May** *2155-0320*
*MAILLY-LE-CAMP*
FO E L Eames and crew

**7/8 May** *2140-0250*
*BRUZ*
PO J D Rees (DFC)
Sgt M J Dunphy
FS J Amory
FO E Jackson
Sgt A Palmer
Sgt T L Daly
Sgt V E Locke

**9/10 May** *2155-0105*
*MERVILLE GUN*
PO T F Cook and crew
PO T G Page RNZAF (2P)
Sgt D M Jones (2BA)
Sgt D Henderson (FE)
Sgt R Watson (RG)

*Easy's* crew on three Berlin trips were, from left to right: Tom Hayes DFC AFC, Peter Ashenden DFC, Sid Emmett DFM & Bar, William Kondra DFM, Glynn Jenkins, Ken Kemp DFM and Jock Ross.

**10/11 May** *2235-0140*
*DIEPPE GUN*
FL E L Eames and crew
FO T Slater in (BA)

**21/22 May** *2245-0305*
*DUISBURG*
PO T F Cook and crew

**22/23 May** *2240-0250*
*DORTMUND*
PO T F Cook and crew

**24/25 May** *2235-0105*
*LE CLIPTON GUN*
PO T F Cook and crew
FS R W W Pye in (MU)

**27/28 May** *2345-0323*
*MERVILLE GUN*
PO T F Cook and crew

**28/29 May** *2224-0200*
*EU GUN*
PO W Kay
Sgt H Dale
Sgt F H Fulsher
FO J Frink
Sgt E Harrop
Sgt T E Sharpley
Sgt W E Struck

**31 May/1 June** *0001-0421*
*TERGNIER M/YARDS*
PO W Kay and crew
Sgt W Everitt in, Struck out

**2/3 June** *2335-0310*
*BERNEVAL*
PO T F Cook and crew

**5/6 June** *2135-0310*
*ST MARTIN DE VARREVILLE*
PO T F Cook and crew
Pye (MU), Wookey (RG)

**6/7 June** *2155-0305*
*VIRE*
PO T F Cook and crew

**7/8 June** *2320-0400*
*FORÊT DE CERISY*
PO J H Shaw
FL C N Waite
Sgt J G Locke
FS B W Young
Sgt W J Jones
Sgt J G Gorman
Sgt W Everitt

**10/11 June** *2305-0400*
*ACHÈRES*
PO A J Orr
Sgt H Gibson
Sgt W Beet
Sgt J M Campbell
Sgt W J Strange
Sgt H W K Welsby
Sgt C H Barron

**14/15 June** *2045-0015*
*LE HAVRE*
PO J H Shaw and crew

**17 June** *0015-0405*
*DOMLEGER – V1 SITE*
FO O S Milne (DFC)
Sgt W H Lanning
Sgt R A D Newman
FO R B Hutchinson
Sgt B Nunely
Sgt H Taylor
Sgt K Yuelett

**7 July** *1950-2335*
*CAEN*
FO C M Stuart RCAF
Sgt H Prince
FO R H Rix
Sgt P Burnett RCAF
Sgt P W T Dunn
FO J F Insell RCAF
Sgt K S Kowal

**12/13 July** *2130-0400*
*TOURS M/YARDS*
FO C M Stuart and crew

**14/15 July** *2125-0500*
*RÉVIGNY M/YARDS*
PO D W Lee RNZAF (DFC)
Sgt F B Whitehouse (FE)
FS K G Braithwaite RAAF (N)
Sgt E Atherton (BA)
Sgt R Parkin (WOP)
Sgt L W Histed (MU)
Sgt E Spencer (RG)
(abandoned at 0156 am)

**18 July** *0355-0740*
*SANNERVILLE*
PO D W Lee and crew

**21 July** *0010-0310*
*COURTRAI M/YARDS*
PO D W Lee and crew

**23/24 July** *2305-0340*
*KIEL*
PO D W Lee and crew

**25 July** *0705-1050*
*COQUEREAUX – V1 SITE*
PO K I Cole RAAF
Sgt F Ritchie
Sgt J Jefferies
Sgt P A Paterson
Sgt A Plastow
Sgt K J Hamilton
Sgt G V George

**25/26 July** *2130-0545*
*STUTTGART*
PO J A Orr and crew
Sgt L Gibson in (RG)

**28/29 July** *2130-0535*
*STUTTGART*
PO D W Lee and crew

**30 July** *0630-1030*
*STUTTGART*
PO D W Lee and crew

**31 July/1 Aug** *2155-0055*
*FORÊT DE NIEPPE*
PO D W Lee
FO L S Bell (2P)
Sgt T A Kewley (FE)
FS K G Braithwaite (N)
FO R Watson (BA)
Sgt E A Pocock (WOP)
Sgt T Brennan (MU)
Sgt R Spencer (RG)

**3 Aug** *1135-1600*
*TROSSY ST MAXIMIN*
PO D W Lee and crew

**4 Aug** *1325-2125*
*PAUILLAC*
PO D W Lee and crew

**5 Aug** *1430-2245*
*PAUILLAC*
WO W T Ramsden (DFC)
Sgt E G Stubbings
Sgt S T Howard
FO R P Simpson
Sgt R M Chestnutt
Sgt R J Williams
Sgt N Crompton

**7/8 Aug** *2120-0125*
*FONTENAY LE MARMION*
FO L S Bell RCAF
Sgt T A Kewley (FE)
PO T M Shewring (N)
FO R Watson (BA)
Sgt E A Pocock (WOP)
Sgt T Brennan (MU)
Sgt C Barker (RG)

**10 Aug** *1030-1420*
*VINCLY – V1 SITE*
FS D W McKenzie RNZAF
Sgt R McLelland
Sgt F R Ford
FS W J D Allen RNZAF
WO H E Thornley
FS J F Malvern
Sgt C W Anderson RCAF
(abandoned – cloud)

**11 Aug** *1340-1735*
*DOUAI M/YARDS*
FO L S Bell and crew

**14 Aug** *1210-1600*
*FALAISE*
FO L S Bell and crew

**15 Aug** *1020-1240*
*VOLKEL AIRFIELD*
FS D W McKenzie and crew

**16/17 Aug** *2123-0520*
*STETTIN*
WO J Thompson RAAF
Sgt H R Tufton
FO J Honeyman
FO S C Hatfield
FS J R Lyons
FS E K Lindorff
FS J Roberts

**18/19 Aug** *2220-0120*
*RIEME*
PO D W Lee and crew
WO M S Paff in (N)

**25/26 Aug** *2005-0120*
*RÜSSELSHEIM*
PO D W Lee and crew
PO T Batley (2P)
Sgt D Clay (2BA)
Braithwaite back

**26/27 Aug** *2015-0120*
*KIEL*
PO D W Lee and crew

**29/30 Aug** *2125-0545*
*STETTIN*
PO D W Lee and crew

**31 Aug** *1235-1545*
*RAIMBERT*
PO D W Lee and crew

**3 Sep** *1610-2000*
*GILZE-RIJEN AIRFIELD*
PO L T Harris
Sgt A F Lambert
Sgt H G Roberts
FS C H Smith
FS B E Lawton RAAF
Sgt G S Gilbert
Sgt C A Daventry-Bull

**5 Sep** *1615-1930*
*LE HAVRE*
PO D W Lee and crew

**6 Sep** *1715-2035*
*LE HAVRE*
PO D W Lee and crew

**8 Sep** *0710-1045*
*LE HAVRE*
PO D W Lee and crew

**10 Sep** *1650-2015*
*LE HAVRE*
PO D W Lee and crew

**12/13 Sep** *1825-0130*
*FRANKFURT*
FO C M Stuart and crew

**20 Sep** *1524-1921*
*CALAIS*
FO L T Harris and crew

**23/24 Sep** *1850-0010*
*NEUSS*
FO L T Harris and crew

**25 Sep** *0735-1100*
*CALAIS*
FO L T Harris and crew
(abandoned)

**26 Sep**
*CAP GRIS NEZ*
FO L T Harris and crew

**27 Sep** *0830-1220*
*CALAIS*
FO L T Harris and crew
Sgt A G Tipple in (RG)

**5/6 Oct** *1845-0020*
*SAARBRÜCKEN*
PO D W Lee and crew

**7 Oct** *1210-1610*
*EMMERICH*
FO L T Harris and crew

**14 Oct** *0650-1055*
*DUISBURG*
FO F O Griffiths
Sgt A Dawson
FS A D Cozens
FS M A Kravenchuck
Sgt E McGuire
Sgt J I Morgan
Sgt C Nelson

**15 Oct** *0025-0545*
*DUISBURG*
FO F O Griffiths and crew
PO D M Ward (2P)
FO F C Squires (2BA)

**19/20 Oct** *1645-0000*
*STUTTGART*
FO L T Harris and crew

**23 Oct** *1620-2150*
*ESSEN*
FO L T Harris and crew

**25 Oct** *1250-1735*
*ESSEN*
FO L T Harris and crew
(flak damage)

**30 Oct** *1735-2325*
*COLOGNE*
FO L T Harris and crew

**31 Oct** *1750-2305*
*COLOGNE*
FO L T Harris and crew

**2 Nov** *1615-2130*
*DÜSSELDORF*
FO L T Harris and crew
FO W O Nobes (2P)
Sgt N L Warner (2BA)

**4/5 Nov** *1745-2220*
*BOCHUM*
FO L T Harris and crew

**6 Nov** *1155-1640*
*GELSENKIRCHEN*
FO C O P Smith RCAF
Sgt J Kieran
Sgt F G Dean RCAF
Sgt J Newlan RCAF
FS C Jones RCAF
Sgt G H Booth RCAF
Sgt A W Jenkins RCAF

**9 Nov** *0815-1300*
*WANNE-EICKEL*
FO C O P Smith and crew

**11/12 Nov** *1635-2125*
*DORTMUND*
FO R T Hoyle
Sgt P T Bickley
PO G S Charles
Sgt R A Ward
Sgt A E Law
PO L A Hoptroff
Sgt R Marshall
(flak damage)

**16 Nov** *1250-1800*
*DÜREN*
FO L T Harris and crew

**21 Nov** *1540-2220*
*ASCHAFFENBURG*
FO W O Nobes RCAF
Sgt J G Kerr
FO J H Kimpton
Sgt N L Warren
Sgt R Doherty
Sgt C L Taylor
Sgt L A Schofield

**27 Nov** *1610-2250*
*FREIBERG*
PO D N Shrimpton
Sgt C W Overton
Sgt J B Booth
Sgt R Livingstone
Sgt H J Cleghorn
Sgt R A Tilly
Sgt C Reilly

**29 Nov** *1210-1610*
*DORTMUND*
FO L T Harris and crew
(abandoned, eng trouble)

**3 Dec** *0755-1220*
*URFT DAM*
FO L T Harris and crew
(abandoned – cloud)

**6/7 Dec** *1640-0040*
*MERSEBURG*
FO C O P Smith and crew

**12 Dec** *1615-2200*
*ESSEN M/YARDS*
FO L T Harris and crew

**15 Dec** *1440-2110*
*LUDWIGSHAVEN*
FO L T Harris and crew

**17 Dec** *1515-2300*
*ULM*
FO L T Harris and crew

**21 Dec** *1455-2055*
*BONN*
FO L T Harris and crew

**28 Dec** *1545-2120*
*MÜNCHEN-GLADBACH*
FO J A Scholey RCAF
Sgt G Grundy
FO D H Lennox RCAF
FO A F Amies RCAF
FO A A Templeton
FS W L O'Shea RCAF
FS J A E Willis RCAF

**29 Dec** *1510-2115*
*GELSENKIRCHEN*
FO J A Scholey and crew

## 1945

**2 Jan** *1520-2340*
*NÜRNBERG*
WO W H Evans
Sgt J J Paxton
Sgt J L Pearson
Sgt A W Dack
Sgt J G Sutherland
Sgt K W J Hodges
Sgt F Burdett

**5/6 Jan** *1910-*
*HANNOVER*
FO R Barker
Sgt A S Gordon
FS F S Elliott
FS A A Law
PO J M C Wilson RAAF
Sgt E Gillen
Sgt B G Aldred
(failed to return – all lost)

# JB663
# KING OF THE AIR

JB663 – *King of the Air* – flew her 100th operation on 4 November 1944. It was denoted by a 'big' bomb symbol. Some of the flight's ground crew smile for the camera.

Named *King of the Air*, JB663 came off Avro's Woodford production line with four Merlin 38 engines in the autumn of 1943. This Mark III was then assigned to 106 Squadron based at Syerston, Nottinghamshire, on 15 November, where it was marked with the squadron code letter of ZN and given the individual letter A-Able.

The Battle of Berlin was raging when JB663 began ops, and the first trip on 26/27 November was to the Big City, followed by eight more, plus a spoof raid to Magdeburg, while the Main Force hit Berlin again on 21/22 January 1944.

JB663 was flown by senior and junior ranks alike, including the Squadron Commander, Wing Commander R E Baxter DFC, the Flight Commander, Squadron Leader

A R Dunn – the latter ten times – and later his replacement, Squadron Leader E Sprawson. Eric Sprawson flew this aircraft once only, but he had an unusual experience a month afterwards. Shot down on the night of D-Day he and his bomb aimer evaded and reached Allied positions in Normandy the following month. Albert Dunn and Sprawson each won the DFC.

One of JB663's more regular skippers was Pilot Officer B F Durrant, who first flew her in April and then completed 28 of his 34 trips in her by July. Brian Durrant received the DFC. Another senior airman to fly in her was the Station Commander, Group Captain W N McKechnie, holder of the George Cross who, of course, had no need to fly ops at all. Unhappily William Neil McKechnie was killed in action in another Lanc on 29 August 1944.

JB663's next regular captain was Flight Lieutenant S H Jones who took the aircraft on eight trips, including one with a BBC reporter aboard, on 18 August 1944, but Jones failed to return in ND686 on 23 September. He was the sole survivor. After a variety of skippers, Flying Officer L P Bence RAAF flew her on her last 11 ops beginning on Armistice Day 1944, although two of these had to be abandoned by the bombing controller, while a third had to be aborted following a glycol leak in the starboard-inner engine.

On occasion 106 Squadron acted as Pathfinders and, on 10/11 March 1944, Wing Commander Baxter flew in JB663, although Albert Dunn was the pilot, Baxter acting as leader and Pathfinder Controller in an attack on the Michelin factory at Clermont-Ferrand, France, by 33 Lancs from 5 Group. Frank Mycoe was the navigator and received the DFM for his part in the attack and for earlier operations:

'Flight Sergeant Mycoe as Navigator has taken part in 26 successful sorties against targets in Germany and Italy. This NCO is possessed of exceptional technical skill and is outstanding among the Navigators in the squadron. On the night of 10th March 1944, he was the Navigator of the aircraft which led the successful attack on Châteauroux/Deouls. His operational coolness and devotion to duty has contributed in a large measure to the successes obtained by his crew. He has proved himself to be an outstanding member of his crew and I consider his skill and fine record fully merit the award of the DFM.'

On the night of 23/24 March JB663 dropped flares continually to illuminate 617 Squadron's attack on an aero-engine factory at Lyons. Flight Lieutenant D U Gibbs was the pilot but when all the flares had gone down there were none left for his own attack. Gibbs dropped two green target indicators (TIs) from low level to help guide 617 further but the target could not be located so 617's leader gave the order to abandon the raid, fearing French civilian casualties.

*King of the Air* flew on both night ops of D-Day with Brian Durrant in command, then against V1 sites during June and transport centres in July. The Lanc's ground crew consisted of Sergeant G W Vidgen, Corporal W Black, Leading Aircraftmen L A Smith, J Picker and A Hirst, and Aircraftman First Class R J Roberts.

Following its earlier Pathfinder role, the squadron finally became part of PFF in September 1944 and its crews were given the opportunity of volunteering for PFF work (which usually meant a longer tour of ops) or they could go to other Main Force squadrons. Flight Lieutenant Jones was among those who stayed but failed to return before the month was out, as stated above, although he survived as a prisoner.

JB663's 100th mission was recorded as 4 November 1944, a raid on Ladbergen – Dortmund-Ems Canal, with Flying Officer F E Day in command – his one and only sortie in JB663! The following morning a huge bomb was painted on the aircraft's nose, next to the 99 bombs already there, put there in five neat, slanting rows of 20 and one of 19. Above the impressive scoreboard with wings outstretched was an eagle, looking much the same as the RAF eagle, above which were the words, *King of the Air.*

In all she flew around 111 operational sorties, and statistics compiled on this particular aircraft note that it flew 985 hours, covered 150,000 miles and carried over 600 tons of bombs and incendiaries to targets in Germany and France. Its final trip was a seven-hour sortie to a synthetic oil plant at Brux in Western Czechoslovakia.

JB663 became Cat B on 11 April 1945 at 24 MU, where she had gone after her final sortie. She was eventually based at 15 MU in August 1946 and Struck off Charge on 26 October of that year.

## 106 SQUADRON
### 1943

**26/27 Nov** *1730-0120*
BERLIN
FL M I Boyle
Sgt A T Cox (FE)
Sgt H Dixon (N)
FS D R Waddell (BA)
Sgt M Webb (WOP)
Sgt J H Higdon (MU)
Sgt M P Butler (RG)

**5 Dec** *0001-0805*
LEIPZIG
SL A R Dunn (DFC)
Sgt T E Eddowes
Sgt F Mycoe (N) (DFM)
FL R L Wake (BA)
FS E G King
Sgt R Nightingale
Sgt D Pinckard (RG) (DFM)

**16/17 Dec** *1625-0020*
BERLIN
FL M I Boyle and crew

**20 Dec** *1705-2320*
FRANKFURT
FL M I Boyle and crew
Sgt R Edwards (WOP) in, Webb out

**23/24 Dec** *2335-0735*
BERLIN
SL A R Dunn and crew
Sgt E Fortune (BA) in, Wake out

**29/30 Dec** *1620-0020*
BERLIN
FO J B Latham (DFC)
Sgt H Weinow
FL W Williamson
FO R T Martins
Sgt T E Witts
Sgt D J Crowley
Sgt H Burn

### 1944

**1/2 Jan** *2359-0740*
BERLIN
SL A R Dunn and crew

**6 Jan** *0010-0850*
STETTIN
FO J B Latham and crew

**14 Jan** *1650-2210*
BRUNSWICK
FO W B Jardine
Sgt J P Olive
FO G H Wright
Sgt A Dunae
Sgt J T Whitehead
Sgt J J Phillips
FO J W Paige

**20 Jan** *1635-2345*
BERLIN
FS G S Milne RCAF (DFC)
Sgt P J Butcher
FS J B Bevan
FS S J Halvorsen RCAF (BA)
Sgt M J Kimber RCAF
Sgt S S Harris
FS G Whittaker

**21/22 Jan** *2000-0425*
MAGDEBURG
PO D U Gibbs (DFC)
Sgt W R Mason
FS R Appleyard (DFM)
FO D L Cramp (DFM)
Sgt H Stubbs
Sgt J E Charnock
Sgt R F Birch

**27/28 Jan** *1750-0155*
BERLIN
FO E R F Leggett
Sgt E F Windeatt
FS A G Mearns (N) (DFM)
FO F B Chubb
Sgt T H Jones
PO S W Payne
Sgt J C Harrison

**30 Jan** *0050-0520*
BERLIN
FS G S Milne and crew
(abort – engine trouble)

**30/31 Jan** *1715-0005*
BERLIN
FO E R F Leggett and crew
FOs A E Bristow (N) and
A I Johnson (BA) in

**15/16 Feb** *1710-0040*
BERLIN
SL A R Dunn and crew

**19/20 Feb** *2345-0700*
LEIPZIG
SL A R Dunn and crew
FO E L Sharp (N under training)

**20/21 Feb** *2355-0450*
STUTTGART
FO E R Penman
Sgt R N Johnson
FO E L Sharp (N)
FO E O Aaron RCAF
Sgt S R Patti
Sgt R F Stubelt RCAF
Sgt J A Roberts
(abandoned – pitot-head
cover not removed)
(lost 7/8 May)

**24/25 Feb** *1830-0230*
SCHWEINFURT
WC R E Baxter DFC
and Dunn's crew

**25/26 Feb** *1830-0215*
AUGSBURG
SL A R Dunn and crew

**1/2 Mar** *2310-0720*
STUTTGART
SL A R Dunn and crew

**10/11 Mar** *2000-0140*
CHÂTEAUROUX / DEOULS
SL A R Dunn and crew
WC R E Baxter (Controller)

**15/16 Mar** *2100-0155*
METZ
SL A R Dunn and crew

**16/17 Mar** *1915-0220*
CLERMONT FERRAND
SL A R Dunn and crew

**18/19 Mar** *1940-0215*
BERGERAC
FL D U Gibbs and crew
Sgt T Monteith in (MU)

**20/21 Mar** *1910-0135*
ANGOULÊME
FL D U Gibbs and crew
Sgt M P Monton in (MG)

**22/23 Mar** *1905-0045*
FRANKFURT
FO E R Penman and crew

**23/24 Mar** *1925-0225*
LYONS
FL D U Gibbs and crew

**25/26 Mar** *1930-0305*
LYONS
FL D U Gibbs and crew
FS R J Smith (MU) and
Sgt E Long (RG) in

**26/27 Mar** *1950-0020*
ESSEN
FL D U Gibbs and crew
Monton back (MU)

**5/6 Apr** *2040-0410*
TOULOUSE
PO B F Durrant (DFC)
Sgt F R Broad
Sgt J C Pittaway (N)
FS A Buchanan RCAF
Sgt N H Jones
Sgt W Martin
Sgt K N Warwick

**9/10 Apr** *2120-0615*
GARDENING – BALTIC
FO E R Penman and crew

**10/11 Apr** *2235-0400*
TOURS
FO E R Penman and crew

**18/19 Apr** *2100-0135*
JUVISY M/YARDS
PO B F Durrant and crew

**20/21 Apr** *2310-0405*
LA CHAPELLE M/YARDS
PO B F Durrant and crew

**22/23 Apr** *2325-0240*
BRUNSWICK
PO B F Durrant and crew
(abandoned – eng failure)

**24/25 Apr** *2055-0655*
MUNICH
PO B F Durrant and crew

**26/27 Apr** *2130-0620*
SCHWEINFURT
PO B F Durrant and crew

**1/2 May** *2135-0530*
TOULOUSE
SL E Sprawson (DFC)
FL A W Williams (2P)
Sgt K Anderton (FE)
FO R R C Barker (N)
FO E L Hogg (BA)
Sgt W D Low (WOP)
FO P S Arnold (MU)

Marshalling yards were important targets prior to and after D-Day. These are the yards at Orléans 19/20 May 1944, photographed from ND898. The pilot is W/C Brooks, OC 635 Sqn, while the Master Bomber was FL Denis Linacre (DFC) who flew ops in Lanc ND709.

Sgt E E J Wiggins (RG)
(shot down 6/7 June; Arnold and
Wiggins KIA, Anderton and Low
taken prisoner, rest evaded)

**3/4 May** *2205-0325*
MAILLY-LE-CAMP
FL S J Houlden
Sgt R H Cosens
WO T H Whyte RAAF
FS K T Millikan RAAF
FS H Pringle RAAF
Sgt R C Hulme
FS S N Kelly

**7/8 May** *2205-0405*
SALBRIS
FS P C Browne (DFC)
Sgt G A Gray
FS R E Carmichael RCAF
Sgt W J Markey RCAF
Sgt C Tate
Sgt E A Stead
Sgt W A Greenwood

**9/10 May** *2220-0235*
GENNEVILLERS
PO B F Durrant and crew

**11/12 May** *2215-0145*
BOURG LÉOPOLD
PO B F Durrant and crew
FO P H George in (N),
Pittaway out

**19/20 May** *2215-0335*
TOURS
PO B F Durrant and crew
FS A R Kitto RNZAF (2P),
Pittaway back

**5/6 June** *0235-0645*
ST PIERRE DU MONT
PO B F Durrant and crew

**7 June** *0035-0500*
CAEN BRIDGE
PO B F Durrant and crew

**8/9 June** *2310-0345*
RENNES M/YARDS
PO B F Durrant and crew

**10/11 June** *2200-0405*
ORLÉANS M/YARDS
PO B F Durrant and crew
FO L C W Boivin (2P) – who
was lost 29/30 Aug

**12/13 June** *2230-0420*
POITIERS M/YARDS
PO B F Durrant and crew

**14/15 June** *2230-0235*
AUNAY-SUR-ODON
PO B F Durrant and crew

**15/16 June** *2130-0345*
CHÂTELLERAULT
PO S M Wright RAAF
Sgt W S McPhail
Sgt H Smith
Sgt W R Knaggs
FS L McGregor RAAF
Sgt A T Clarke
FS W Beutel RAAF

**19/20 June** *2250-0110*
WATTEN – V1 SITE
PO S M Wright and crew
(abandoned – weather)

**21/22 June** *2315-0330*
GELSENKIRCHEN
PO S M Wright and crew

**24/25 June** *2220-0150*
POMMERVAL – V1 SITE
PO B F Durrant and crew

**27/28 June** *2155-0515*
VITRY M/YARDS
PO B F Durrant and crew

**29 June** *1220-1530*
BEAUVOIR – V1 SITE
FO G S Mather RCAF
Sgt L T Lucas
PO A E Power
FO J S Kingston RCAF
Sgt W Stewart
Sgt W A Waldren RCAF
Sgt J Crawford RCAF
(abandoned – weather)
(all lost 7/8 July except Power
who was not flying)

**4/5 July** *2315-0310*
ST LEU D'ESSERENT
PO B F Durrant and crew
Sgt E C Bumford (2P)

**7/8 July** *2240-0255*
ST LEU D'ESSERENT
PO B F Durrant and crew

**12/13 July** *2150-0550*
*CULMONT M/YARDS*
FO B F Durrant and crew
FO H E Sayeau RCAF (2P)

**14/15 July** *2215-0445*
*VILLENEUVE ST GEORGE*
FO B F Durrant and crew

**15/16 July** *2200-0515*
*NEVERS M/YARDS*
FO B F Durrant and crew

**19 July** *1925-2315*
*THIVERNY*
FO B F Durrant and crew

**20/21 July** *2310-0205*
*COURTRAI M/YARDS*
FO B F Durrant and crew

**23/24 July** *2255-0335*
*KIEL*
FO B F Durrant and crew

**24/25 July** *2145-0535*
*STUTTGART*
FO B F Durrant and crew

**25 July** *1750-2135*
*ST CYR AIRFIELD*
FO B F Durrant and crew

**26/27 July** *2120-0600*
*GIVORS M/YARDS*
FO B F Durrant and crew

**28/29 July** *2200-0600*
*STUTTGART*
FL S H Jones
Sgt D Levene
FO G G Bryon RCAF
Sgt H I Shepherd RCAF
Sgt R H Julien
Sgt J F W Clark RCAF
Sgt K A McLaughlin RCAF
(all lost 23/24 Sep, except
Jones – PoW)

**30 July** *0600-1045*
*CAHAGNES*
FL S H Jones and crew
(abandoned by MB)

**31 July** *1725-2215*
*RILLY-LA-MONTAGNE*
GC W N McKechnie GC
FO B R Marks (2P)
SL G Crowe DFC (N)
Sgt R S Howarth (FE)
Sgt J C Burns (2N)
FO K M Render RCAF (BA)
Sgt H H Beard (WOP)
Sgt J A Monk
Sgt R Baldwin
(McKechnie lost 29/30 Aug)

**2 Aug** *1420-1850*
*TROSSY ST MAXIMIN*
FO P C Browne and crew

**3 Aug** *1145-1600*
*TROSSY ST MAXIMIN*
FO P C Browne and crew
(hit by flak)

**5 Aug** *1040-1525*
*ST LEU D'ESSERENT*
FO P C Browne and crew

**6 Aug** *1735-2250*
*LORIENT*
FO P C Browne and crew

**7/8 Aug** *2140-0050*
*SECQUEVILLE*
FO P C Browne and crew

**9/10 Aug** *2055-0300*
*CHÂTELLERAULT*
FO P C Browne and crew

**11 Aug** *1155-1940*
*BORDEAUX*
FO P C Browne and crew

**12/13 Aug** *2120-0250*
*BRUNSWICK*
FL S H Jones and crew

**14 Aug** *1205-1550*
*QUESNAY*
FO H E Sayeau RCAF (DFC)
Sgt S A Coucill
FS M H Moore RCAF
FS L P Mason RCAF
Sgt A W Stewart
FS A P Fontaine RCAF
FS M Waite RCAF

**15 Aug** *1005-1340*
*GILZE-RIJEN AIRFIELD*
Sgt J R Ford
Sgt W A Ambrose
Sgt R C Fondt
Sgt A T Worthington
Sgt P J O'Brien RNZAF
Sgt F S Williams
Sgt J B Dandy

**16/17 Aug** *2130-0455*
*GARDENING – STETTIN CANAL*
FL S H Jones and crew

**18 Aug** *1130-1610*
*FORÊT DE L'ISLE ADAM*
FL S H Jones and crew
Mr I Wilson (BBC)

**25/26 Aug** *2050-0515*
*DARMSTADT*
FL S H Jones and crew

**26/27 Aug** *2015-0615*
*KÖNIGSBERG*
FL S H Jones and crew

**29/30 Aug** *2040-0650*
*KÖNIGSBERG*
FL S H Jones and crew

**31 Aug** *1535-2000*
*AUCHY-LES-HESDIN*
FS W E Brunton RNZAF
Sgt W Dyson
Sgt H H Harris
FS W S Sutherland RAAF
Sgt F N Evans
Sgt M J Mehan
Sgt A Gray

**3 Sep** *1535-1915*
*DEELEN AIRFIELD*
FO B R Marks and crew

**10 Sep** *0245-0710*
*MÜNCHEN-GLADBACH*
FO R G Waterfall
Sgt D D Jones
Sgt E Kindley
Sgt G Dixon
Sgt F J Swindly
Sgt J J Campbell
Sgt S E Cunningham

**11 Sep** *0605-0905*
*LE HAVRE*
FO A M Dow
Sgt J Chamberlain
FO R A Muddle
FO H A Orrell
FO G R Willey
Sgt H F Brittain
Sgt W E McNeill

**11/12 Sep** *2105-0235*
*DARMSTADT*
FO A M Dow and crew

**12/13 Sep** *1910-0150*
*STUTTGART*
FO R B Sexton
Sgt R C Aird
PO I G Martin
FO H J Milne
Sgt R Jeavons
Sgt W R Orr
Sgt R Burtenshaw

**17 Sep** *0820-1105*
*BOULOGNE*
FO W D Kelley RAAF
Sgt J Howarth
Sgt F J Turkentine
Sgt A James
FS J H Grubb
Sgt F Cawlishaw
Sgt R F Dyson

**18 Sep** *1830-2315*
*BREMERHAVEN*
FO W D Kelley and crew

**19 Sep** *1900-2350*
*RHEYDT*
FO W D Kelley and crew

**23 Sep** *1915-2115*
*DORTMUND-EMS CANAL*
FO W D Kelley and crew

**26 Sep** *0100-0725*
*KARLSRUHE*
Lt P A Becker SAAF
Sgt R C Osman
FS W M Ching RNZAF
Sgt V P Tomei
Sgt C G Lees
Sgt N T Deacon
Sgt A R Roselt

**27/28 Sep** *2215-0400*
*KAISERSLAUTERN*
Lt P A Becker and crew

**5 Oct** *0755-1305*
*WILHELMSHAVEN*
FO W D Kelley and crew

**6 Oct** *1740-2205*
BREMEN
FO K R Simpson
Sgt R C Witcombe
FO A Stott
FS G H Lloyd
FO W D Mitchell
Sgt N D Reynolds
Sgt C Powell

**14/15 Oct** *2255-0555*
*BRUNSWICK*
FO A M Dow and crew

**19/20 Oct** *1740-0050*
*NÜRNBERG*
FO A M Dow and crew

**24/25 Oct** *1720-0205*
*SILVERTHORNE*
FO E Barratt
Sgt J F Emerson
Sgt A Berry
Sgt E C Towle
FS C P Calvert
Sgt R E Day
FS W D Lloyd

**30 Oct** *1040-1325*
*WALCHEREN*
FL A C Burden
Sgt S Routh
Sgt J N W King
FO F S Rowbory
Sgt J F Richards
PO A C R Udson
Sgt J W Jones

**1 Nov** *1350-1805*
*HOMBERG*
FO G F Laidlaw RAAF
Sgt G A Cryer
FO C S Oliver RAAF
FS C W Kineen RAAF
FS R Beardsley RAAF
PO W P O'Shaunessy
Sgt K J Mitchell

**2 Nov** *1700-2150*
*DÜSSELDORF*
FO G F Laidlaw and crew

**4 Nov** *1750-2205*
*LADBERGEN*
FO F E Day
WO N K Whitby DFM (FE)
FO A J Henington
FO H Jones RNZAF
Sgt J O'Donnell
Sgt E Harrison-Owen
Sgt R J Robertson

**6 Nov** *1630-2150*
*GRAVENHORST CANAL*
FO G F Laidlaw and crew
(abandoned by MB)

**11 Nov** *1630-2210*
*HARBURG*
FO L P Bence RAAF
Sgt F Raine
FS R E Tolley RAAF
Sgt T Donovan
Sgt R B Taylor
Sgt R S Marchant
Sgt K F Judd

**16 Nov** *1300-1805*
*DÜREN*
FO L P Bence and crew

**21 Nov** *1740-2330*
*LADBERGEN*
FO L P Bence and crew

**22/23 Nov** *1605-0315*
*TRONDHEIM*
FO L P Bence and crew
(abandoned by MB)

**27 Nov** *0005-0915*
*MUNICH*
FO L P Bence and crew

**30 Dec** *0235-0745*
*HOUFFALIZE*
FO L P Bence and crew

## 1945

**1 Jan** *1700-2355*
*GRAVENHORST*
FO L P Bence and crew

**4 Jan** *0025-0750*
*ROYAN*
FO L P Bence and crew

**5 Jan** *0025-0325*
*HOUFFALIZE*
FO L P Bence and crew
(abandoned – oil leak)

**7/8 Jan** *1640-0200*
*MUNICH*
FO L P Bence and crew

**16/17 Jan** *1755-0300*
*BRUX*
FO L P Bence and crew

# LL806
# JIG

15 Squadron's LL806, LS-J, in flight.

One of the lesser-known of the top half-dozen century-plus Lancasters, LL806 was part of Contract No.239 awarded to Avro and built under licence by Armstrong-Whitworth. Produced as a Mark I, it came from the factory in late 1943 equipped with four Merlin 24 engines and on 22 April 1944 it was flown to 15 Squadron at Mildenhall, Suffolk. This squadron had only recently converted from Stirlings to Lancasters.

The squadron code letters LS were painted on LL806's fuselage as well as its individual letter 'J', to become J for Jig. The aircraft carried no nose art-work, but when it completed sorties, a regular tally of bomb symbols began to appear beneath the cockpit, in rows of ten. After eight such rows, a second column was started and by January 1945 it had topped the 100 mark.

In all, 134 bombs were painted in *Jig*, all straightforward, with no colour-coding for day or night trips. At the end of April 1945, *Jig*, along with other heavy bombers, was used to fly food drops to starving Dutch civilians, a task which was known as Operation Manna – a true manna from heaven as far as the Dutch were concerned. Although these sorties had the tacit

agreement of the occupying German forces, there was still an element of risk by some determined – or fanatical – Nazis, or a trigger-happy soldier, so these missions counted as ops.

*Jig* did three such trips followed by three Exodus trips, bringing released Allied prisoners of war back to Britain

LL806's crew prior to her 100th op, 5 January 1945. From left to right: ground crewman, Ken Dorsett, R H Hopper-Cuthbert, Don Inglis, Sid Lewis; in doorway: Bob Heatley and Wally Lake; on ladder: George Charlton.

The bomb symbols mount on LL806. Here the 113th is stencilled on.

from the Continent. These last six sorties were marked up on *Jig's* nose as three food sacks, and three running matchstick-men, making 140 operations in total. Although the aircraft completed 134 operational war sorties, plus six of these other trips, it could be argued that it did 140 in all, especially as other Lancasters were credited with these Manna and Exodus sorties bringing some of them into the 100 op-plus category by counting them. Thus *Jig* could stand next to ED888 as jointly holding the record of 140 operations.

However, this all started by LL806 replacing the previous 'J' – LL801 – which had been lost on 27/28 April 1944, against Wilhelmshaven. LL806's first sortie was flown on 1/2 May against the railway stores and repair depot at Chambly, France, although the aircraft had a 1,000-pounder hang-up. *Jig's* first pilot was Pilot Officer Mervyn J Sparks, from Christchurch, New Zealand, who would survive the war as a flight lieutenant DFC; his navigator, Lancelot Elias and bomb aimer Edward Spannier RCAF, also won DFCs.

Sparks went on to fly 18 ops in *Jig*, although he missed the D-Day sorties with the aircraft. A few days after D-Day, on 10/11 June, *Jig's* gunners shot down a Me109 night fighter. Flight Lieutenant B G F Payne, the pilot on this occasion, later received the DFC. *Jig* was fortunate to have few aborts due to mechanical problems and continued to plod on, flying regularly over the summer and autumn of 1944, including such famous raids on Caen on 18 July, and Falaise on 12 August.

Another crew to fly *Jig* at this time was Flight Lieutenant W Leslie's. During June to August they carried out ten ops. She must have left a lasting impression on one of the crew – Bill Grundy – for in the mid 1990s he developed a hip problem which forced him into an electric buggy in order to get around. He had a plate put on the buggy reading: LL806 LS-J.

*Jig's* 80th op was believed to have been flown on 2 December, Flying Officer L H Marriott RAAF – later DFC – taking her to Dortmund. The 100th operation came on 5 January 1945 with a raid on Ludwigshaven, piloted by Flying Officer R H Hopper-Cuthbert RAAF. This crew carried out some 18 sorties in *Jig*, including the night the Gee caught fire following an electrical failure. Ken Dorsett was the rear gunner in this crew:

'I cannot give a 'Dambuster-like' image of J-Jig, she was just an old lady who did her bit. I had done seven operations as a spare gunner when I met Hopper and crew, who came rear-gunner-less from LFS. We looked over this rather tired old Lanc and you could almost feel the thoughts going through our heads – will we or won't we finish this war together?

Doug Hunt took LL806 on two of her sorties: From left, Pat Russell, Paddy Kirane, Hunt, George Pitkin, John Shepherd.

'Well, much to our relief we did. J-Jig turned out to be a good old lady. She took a few chunks of flak, had her rivets strained to breaking-point by "corkscrews", and the landings (not quite Hopper's speciality) must have played merry Hell with her undercarriage. Nevertheless she got us through with the aid of Hopper (despite his landings) and Lady Luck sitting on our shoulders.

'She even finished with us on a long haul to Königsberg, now known as Kaliningrad, just to prove she could do it. Other than that, just an old bomber in the stream that made the 100.'

Ken Dorsett's citation for his DFM reads:

'Sergeant Dorsett has now completed a very successful tour consisting of 32 sorties. He has attacked targets deep in the Reich as well as those in support of the Army. He joined the squadron as a spare gunner and although he at first flew with several different crews, he displayed a consistent enthusiasm. When finally crewed with Flying Officer Hopper-Cuthbert, he proved a very valuable crew member. Both in the air and on the ground his work has been of the highest order. He is recommended for the award of the Distinguished Flying Medal.'

*Jig's* last bombing raid was to Bremen on 22 April 1945, then came those six Manna and Exodus trips already mentioned above. In June and July came some Ruhr trips, flights taking some of the squadron's ground personnel – both men and women – on daylight sight-seeing tours to see devastated German cities. It had been decreed that they should see what part they had taken in the defeat of Germany.

*Jig* remained with 15 Squadron until finally Struck off Charge on 6 December 1945.

## 15 SQUADRON
## 1944

**1/2 May** 2215-0200
CHAMBLY
PO M J Sparks RNZAF (DFC)
FO L B A Elias (N) (DFC)
Sgt J Tapping RCAF (WOP)
FS E G Spannier RCAF (BA) (DFC)
Sgt P Hartshorn (FE)
Sgt J Aimesbury (MU)
Sgt N Freeman (RG)

**8/9 May** 2238-0039
CAP GRIS NEZ
PO M J Sparks and crew

**10/11 May** 2201-0041
COURTRAI
PO M J Sparks and crew

**11/12 May** 2234-0119
LOUVAIN
PO M J Sparks and crew

**19/20 May** 2224-0312
LE MANS
PO M J Sparks and crew
FS S Mellers (2P)

**21/22 May** 2235-0330
DUISBURG
PO M J Sparks and crew
FO W Leslie (2P)

**24/25 May** 2350-0349
AACHEN
FL S Fisher
FO G Tipping (N)
FL F Wright DFC (WOP)
FO J Wastenays RCAF (BA)
Sgt N Berryman (FE)
Sgt E Tiplady (MU)
FL W Bossom (RG)
(Tipping lost with another crew 24/25 July)

**28 May** 0016-0243
BOULOGNE
FS W Ferguson

Sgt B Bond
PO H Thorp
FO B Harper RCAF
Sgt W Went
Sgt W Poole
Sgt C Stewart

**28/29 May** 1809-0148
ANGERS
FL S Fisher
FS F Grimshaw
Sgt J Crew
FO J Wastenays RCAF
Sgt E Tiplady
FS G Allen
Sgt N Berryman

**30/31 May** 2302-0058
BOULOGNE
PO M J Sparks and crew

**31 May/1June** 2355-0501
TRAPPES
FO W Leslie
FO F Frudd RCAF
Sgt J Rozier
FO E McNiece
Sgt E North
Sgt D Findlay RCAF
Sgt W Grundy

**3 June** 0112-0310
WISSANT
FS W Ferguson and crew

**4 June** 0040-0240
CALAIS
FL J P Ball
FO E Leah
PO G W Bovett
FO B H Wrenshall RCAF
Sgt D R Ward (FE)
Sgt A L Barkshire
Sgt G Morrison
(all lost 7/8 Aug)

**6 June** 0327-0704
OUISTREHAM
FS W Ferguson and crew

**6/7 June** 2349-0323
LISIEUX
FL J P Ball and crew

**8 June** 0045-0426
MASSY-PALAISEAU
FL M J Sparks and crew

**8/9 June** 2134-0221
FOUGÈRES
FL M J Sparks and crew

**10/11 June** 2310-0325
DREUX
FL B G F Payne (DFC)
Sgt P Hemming
Sgt D Brady
FO C Allan RCAF
Sgt F Lambert
Sgt T Blackburn
Sgt R Butterworth
(Me109 shot down)

**12/13 June** 2303-0308
GELSENKIRCHEN
FL M J Sparks and crew

**18 June** 0041-0434
MONTDIDIER
FL M J Sparks and crew

**21 June** 1804-2039
DOMLEGER – V1 SITE
FL M J Sparks and crew

**30 June** 1753-2126
VILLERS BOCAGE
FL M J Sparks and crew

**2 July** 1234-1625
BEAUVOIR – V1 SITE
FL M J Sparks and crew

**5/6 July** 2250-0135
WIZERNES – V1 SITE
FS A Barford
Sgt F Bolan RCAF
Sgt W Parks
FS P Whitehouse
Sgt W Day
FS E Marshall
Sgt E Thomas

**7/8 July** 2245-0328
VAIRIES
FL B G F Payne and crew

**9 July** 1218-1614
LINZEUX – V1 SITE
FL M J Sparks and crew

**10 July** 0330-0737
NUCOURT – V1 SITE
FL M J Sparks and crew

**12 July** 1735-2221
VAIRIES
FO B G F Payne and crew
(abandoned – cloud)

**18 July** 0356-0749
CAEN
FL W Bell DFC
PO A Hayden (N)
FS P Sweetman (WOP)
WO F Oakes (BA)
Sgt M Feit (FE)
Sgt J Brennan (MU)
Sgt T Brookfield (RG)

**18/19 July** 2224-0144
AULNOYE
FL W Bell and crew
Sgt T Pavey in, Feit out
(abandoned, std-outer failed)

**23 July** 0633-1015
MONT CANDON
FL M J Sparks and crew

**23/24 July** 2253-0357
KIEL
FS W Mason RAAF
Sgt A Douglas RAAF
FS P Elgar RAAF (WOP)
Sgt D Brown (BA)
Sgt H Leigh
Sgt N Bibbing
Sgt M Hathaway

**24/25 July** 2150-0519
STUTTGART
FL M Johnston RNZAF
FS E King

FS J Paine
FS C Morris
Sgt E Marsh
Sgt A Hartley
FS N Barker

**25/26 July** *2140-0558*
*STUTTGART*
FO S Stewart
FS J Burrett
FS N Herbert
FS W Turner RAAF
Sgt J Bax
FS D McFadden RAAF
FS K Girle RAAF

**28/29 July** *2144-0538*
*STUTTGART*
FO H Kelly
FS J Mason
FS J Watts RAAF
FS A O'Sullivan RAAF
Sgt J Brown
Sgt R Tweddle
Sgt J Bardsley

**30 July** *0523-0925*
*AMAYE-SUR-SEULLES*
FL B G F Payne and crew

**1 Aug** *1906-2158*
*COULON VILLERS – V1 SITE*
FL W Leslie and crew
(abandoned – fog)

**5 Aug** *1427-2250*
*BASSENS*
FL W Leslie and crew

**7/8 Aug** *2140-0135*
*ROCQUECOURT*
FL W Leslie and crew

**8/9 Aug** *2207-0117*
*FORÊT DE LEUCHEAUX*
FS L Marshall
Sgt R Bates
Sgt R Knight
FO L Ford RNZAF
Sgt D Kenny
Sgt J Kay
Sgt H Jackson

**9/10 Aug** *2146-0028*
*FORT D'ENGLOS – V1 SITE*
FO W Mason
Sgt B Rennie
FS C Dyer
Sgt K Logan
Sgt W Brockett
Sgt G Donaldson
Sgt R Faint

**11 Aug** *1349-1730*
*LENS*
FO H Cato RAAF
Sgt D Lee RAAF
FS J Hance RAAF
Sgt T Priddle
Sgt H Hounsome
Sgt K Knok
Sgt W Henderson

**13 Aug** *0039-0357*
*FALAISE*
WO A McDougall
FS R Keen
WO D Moore
Sgt I Howitt
Sgt K McKie
Sgt J McNee
Sgt T Hunter

**14 Aug** *1341-1808*
*ST QUENTIN*
WO A McDougall and crew

**15 Aug** *0955-1354*
*ST TROND AIRFIELD*
FO R D Jennings RAAF (DFC)
Sgt J Fawcett
FS G Johnson
FO J Watts
Sgt J Biddle (FE)
FS G Tregoning
FS R Banks RAAF

**16/17 Aug** *2103-0529*
*STETTIN*
FL W Leslie and crew

**18/19 Aug** *2138-0309*
*BREMEN*
FL W Leslie and crew

**26/27 Aug** *2017-0212*
*KIEL*
FL W Leslie and crew

**29/30 Aug** *2055-0700*
*STETTIN*
FL W Leslie and crew

**31 Aug** *1549-1953*
*PONT RÉMY*
FL W Leslie and crew

**3 Sep** *1521-1852*
*EINDHOVEN AIRFIELD*
WO A McDougall and crew

**5 Sep** *1643-2053*
*LE HAVRE*
FL W Leslie and crew

**6 Sep** *1616-2016*
*LE HAVRE*
FO R D Jennings and crew

**8 Sep** *0536-0901*
*LE HAVRE*
FO R D Jennings and crew

**17 Sep** *1022-1335*
*BOULOGNE*
FO R D Jennings and crew

**20 Sep** *1456-1818*
*CALAIS*
FO R D Jennings and crew

**23 Sep** *1852-2325*
*NEUSS*
FO R D Jennings and crew

**24 Sep** *1652-1927*
*CALAIS*
FO R D Jennings and crew

**27 Sep** *0728-1954*
*CALAIS*
FO R Marsh
FS V Stuckey RAAF
FS R Murray RAAF
FO S Tudor-Lee
Sgt J Swainston
Sgt L Garrett
Sgt J Wade

**28 Sep** *0714-1034*
*CALAIS*
FO R D Jennings and crew
Sgt J Munro (FE) in,
Biddle out

**5/6 Oct** *1905-0112*
*SAARBRÜCKEN*
FL P W Percy (DFC)
FO W Shakespeare
FO A A Aleandri (DFC)
FO T R Palmer (DFC)
WO P Shields
FS D King
FS S Mackie

**6 Oct** *1632-2250*
*DORTMUND*
FL P W Percy and crew

**7 Oct** *1109-1546*
*KLEVE*
FL P W Percy and crew

**14 Oct** *0652-1132*
*DUISBURG*
FL H Cato and crew

**14/15 Oct** *2303-0343*
*DUISBURG*
FL H Cato and crew

**15 Oct** *1738-2145*
*WILHELMSHAVEN*
FO R H Hopper-Cuthbert RAAF
FS W Lake
FS R Heatley
Sgt G Charlton
Sgt S Lewis
Sgt D Inglis (MU)
Sgt K T Dorsett (DFM) (RG)

**18 Oct** *0856-1318*
*BONN*
FL H Cato and crew

**19/20 Oct** *2157-0404*
*STUTTGART*
FO D Kelly RAAF
FS J Bishop
FO R Johnson
FO C Clay
Sgt J Taylor
Sgt T Pownell
Sgt C Rhodes

**22 Oct** *1322-1750*
*NEUSS*
FO B Jones
FS L Beren
FS G Sim RAAF
FS R Warman
Sgt D Lord
Sgt F Atkinson
Sgt P Acton

**23 Oct** *1632-2204*
*ESSEN*
FS L Hastings RAAF
FO R Smith
FS V Pearce
PO H Burns RAAF
Sgt J Munro
Sgt G Malyon
Sgt D McFadden

**25 Oct** *1212-1710*
*ESSEN*
FL P W Percy and crew

**28 Oct** *0844-1107*
*FLUSHING*
FO R Marsh and crew

**15 Nov** *1213-1721*
*DORTMUND*
FL I Buchanan RAAF
FO J Varey
WO A Kimlin RAAF
FO S Hawkins
Sgt J Crosbie
FS A Helyer
Sgt T Field

**16 Nov** *1312-1806*
*HEINSBERG*
FO R H H-Cuthbert and crew

**20 Nov** *1214-1503*
*HOMBERG*
FO R H H-Cuthbert and crew
(abort – elec failure, Gee caught
fire)

**21 Nov** *1223-1655*
*HOMBERG*
FO R H H-Cuthbert and crew

**23 Nov** *1224-1728*
*GELSENKIRCHEN*
FO R H H-Cuthbert and crew

**26 Nov** *0753-1351*
*FULDA*
FO R H H-Cuthbert and crew

**27 Nov** *1210-1700*
*COLOGNE*
FO R H H-Cuthbert and crew

**29 Nov** *0254-0737*
*NEUSS*
FO C Noble RAAF
PO T McQuaid
WO F Watson
FO C Bender RAAF
Sgt G Fox
Sgt L Brown
Sgt A Adams

**30 Nov** *1035-1447*
*BOTTROP*
FO C Noble and crew

**2 Dec** *1305-1732*
*DORTMUND*
FL L Marriott
FS E Lumsden RAAF
FS D Woon RAAF
FS C Dane
Sgt J Wyllie
Sgt P Kite
Sgt J Ferbrache

**4 Dec** *1150-1618*
*OBERHAUSEN*
FO R H H-Cuthbert and crew

**5 Dec** *0907-1339*
*SCHWAMMENAUEL DAM*
PO J Slaughter RAAF
Sgt H Bradbrook
FS B Philpot RAAF
Sgt J Seel
Sgt R Fearn
Sgt H Hill
Sgt G Lock
(abandoned, equip failure)

**6/7 Dec** *1653-0021*
*MERSEBURG*
FS B Giles RAAF
Sgt B Cooper
FS Henry RAAF
Sgt R Bonner
Sgt A Campbell
Sgt H Bosworth
Sgt E Chettoe

**8 Dec** *0844-1310*
*DUISBURG*
FS B Giles and crew

**11 Dec** *0828-1300*
*OSTERFELD*
FO N Clayton
Sgt J Graham
Sgt L Brown
FO K Robertson
FS E Prewers
Sgt K Hardy
Sgt A Fletcher

**12 Dec** *1113-1610*
*WITTEN*
FO N Clayton and crew

**16 Dec** *1131-1715*
*SIEGEN*
FO R H H-Cuthbert and crew

**19 Dec** *1243-1748*
*TRIER*
FO R H H-Cuthbert and crew

**21 Dec** *1221-1729*
*TRIER*
FO R H H-Cuthbert and crew

**23 Dec** *1120-1633*
*TRIER*
FO R H H-Cuthbert and crew

**24 Dec** *1513-2023*
*BONN*
FO S Bignall RAAF
FS J Lacey RAAF
FS C Russell
Sgt D Jones
Sgt K Keeble-Buckle
FS T Thoroughgood RAAF
FS W Wilkie RAAF

**28 Dec** *1212-1659*
*COLOGNE*
FO N Burns
Sgt S Duke
Sgt J Nicholson
Sgt E Doble
Sgt S Franks
Sgt E Davis
Sgt M Giddings

**29 Dec** *1216-1713*
*COBLENZ*
FO R H H-Cuthbert and crew

**31 Dec** *1148-1635*
*VOHWINKEL*
FO R H H-Cuthbert and crew

## 1945

**2 Jan** *1518-2300*
*NÜRNBERG*
FO R H H-Cuthbert and crew

**3 Jan** *1258-1748*
*DORTMUND*
FO S Bignall and crew

**5 Jan** *1127-1754*
*LUDWIGSHAVEN*
FO R H H-Cuthbert and crew

**6 Jan** *1544-2047*
*NEUSS*
FO S Bignall and crew

**7/8 Jan** *1825-0237*
*MUNICH*
FO L Gray RAAF
FL S Tinkler
FS A Archibald
FS G R Dykstra
Sgt R Rawson
Sgt J H Cooper
Sgt H C Ferguson

**11 Jan** *1146-1656*
*KREFELD*
FO R H H-Cuthbert and crew

**15 Jan** *1155-1654*
*ENKERSCHWICK*
FO R H H-Cuthbert and crew

**16/17 Jan** *2308-0432*
*WANNE-EICKEL*
FL C Hughes
FS V S Flower
WO D Leahy RAAF
FS D Green
FS C Houlgrave
Sgt J Byrne
Sgt A Welsey

**22 Jan** *1657-2205*
*STERKADE*
PO I McHardy
FS A Bolton
FS D Buchanan
FS J Surridge
Sgt K Ashbolt
FS J Hall
FS F Borrell

**28 Jan** *1010-1601*
*COLOGNE*
FO L Gray and crew
FS D Metcalf RAAF in,
Archibald out

**29 Jan** *1022-1548*
*KREFELD*
FS V Tenger RAAF
FO E James RAAF
FS A Turner RAAF
FS G Hay (BA)
Sgt E Fulton
Sgt K Brown
Sgt B Conroy

**1 Feb** *1312-1842*
*MÜNCHEN-GLADBACH*
FO D Hunt RAAF
Sgt J Shepherd
FS P Smeeton RAAF
Sgt D A Russell (BA)
Sgt R Rawson
Sgt J Cooper
Sgt H Ferguson

**3 Feb** *1621-2159*
*DORTMUND*
FS V Tenger and crew

**14 Feb** *2010-0409*
*CHEMNITZ*
FO N Burns and crew

**22 Feb** *1301-1757*
*BUER*
FO N Burns and crew

**23 Feb** *1135-1703*
*GELSENKIRCHEN*
FS A Meikle
FS F Jacobs
Sgt J Whitehouse
Sgt E Utting
Sgt J Palmer
Sgt W Nunn
Sgt D Cherry

**25 Feb** *0931-1513*
*KAMEN*
FS A Meikle and crew

**26 Feb** *1036-1610*
*DORTMUND*
FO D Hunt and crew

**27 Feb** *1120-1704*
*GELSENKIRCHEN*
FS A Meikle and crew

**28 Feb** *0852-1401*
*GELSENKIRCHEN*
FO C Ayres RAAF
FS E Risley
WO P Greane RAAF
FO W Forsyth
Sgt D Keichley
FO A Chambers
FO P Giradot

**1 Mar** *1149-1729*
*KAMEN*
FS A Meikle and crew

**2 Mar** *1251-1818*
*COLOGNE*
FO C Ayres and crew

**5 Mar** *1028-1555*
*GELSENKIRCHEN*
FS L Baxendale
FO M Vaughan
Sgt A Fisher
FS A Wright
Sgt S Salter
Sgt L Taylor
Sgt R Kerwan

The final tally for LL806: 134 raids, three Manna trips, plus three Exodus missions.

**7/8 Mar** *1649-0219*
*DESSAU*
FS A Wright RAAF
FO R Rees RAAF
FS J Walden
FS G Gibson RCAF
FS F Williams
FS J Smith
Sgt L Harries

**9 Mar** *1029-1549*
*DATTELN*
FS A MacDonald RAAF
Sgt W Roberts
Sgt W Orford
Sgt R Davis
Sgt A Maw
Sgt N Farmer
Sgt A Cooper

**10 Mar** *1218-1721*
*GELSENKIRCHEN*
FS A Wright and crew

**11 Mar** *1115-1707*
*ESSEN*
FS A Wright and crew

**12 Mar** *1248-1911*
*DORTMUND*
WO V Tenger and crew
FS G Naldrett in (BA)
Hay out

**14 Mar** *1320-1828*
*DATTELN*
FS A Meikle and crew

**22 Mar** *1054-1611*
*BOCHOLT*
FS W Sievers RAAF
Sgt A Clarkstone
Sgt D King
FO J Hunter
Sgt R Williamson
Sgt H Wells
Sgt T Blenkain (RG)

**27 Mar** *1040-1545*
*ALTENBOGGE*
WO V Tenger and crew

**4/5 Apr** *1827-0317*
*MERSEBURG*
WO W Woodman
Sgt G Relt
Sgt P Gennoy
FO J Moffatt RCAF (BA)
FS J Freemantle
Sgt T Hammond
Sgt T Dickinson

**5/6 Apr** *1947-0201*
*KIEL*
FS W Sievers and crew

**13/14 Apr** *2010-0210*
*KIEL*
FS W Sievers and crew

**14/15 Apr** *1824-0323*
*POTSDAM*
FS W Sievers and crew

**18 Apr** *1014-1502*
*HELIGOLAND*
FS W Sievers and crew

**22 Apr** *1531-2056*
*BREMEN*
FS W Sievers and crew
FO C Taylor in (RG),
Blenkain out

**30 Apr** *1638-1922*
*MANNA – ROTTERDAM*
FS L Baxendale and crew

**2 May** *1104-1334*
*MANNA – THE HAGUE*
FS W Sievers and crew

**7 May** *1110-1345*
*MANNA – THE HAGUE*
FO W Woodman and crew

**Three Exodus ops 11, 17 and 24 May**

# LL843
# POD

PO-D, LL843, 467 RAAF and 61 Squadrons, achieved 118 operations.

Built under contract from Avro as part of order No.239/C4, by Messrs Armstrong-Whitworth at Coventry, LL843 was another Mark I with four Merlin 24 engines. On 28 February 1944 it was assigned to 467 Squadron RAAF based at Waddington, Lincolnshire. Here it received code letters of PO and an individual letter 'D'. The letter 'D' also appeared on the two tail fins.

Operations began for LL843 on 9/10 March in the experienced hands of the B Flight Commander, Squadron Leader Arthur William Doubleday DFC RAAF, flying what was described as a 'Special Job' – a 5 Group attack on an aircraft factory at Marignane, near Marseilles. As can be imagined, it was a long sortie, LL843 taking nine hours, 37 minutes to complete. As well as the Lanc's seven-man crew, Waddington's Station Commander, Group Captain S C 'Sammy' Elworthy DSO DFC AFC, went along as eighth man. (He was later Marshal of the RAF, Lord Elworthy KG.) Doubleday's mid-upper was Sydney Gray-Buchanan DFM, who had won his medal with 148 Squadron in 1943 after completing 48 ops in Europe and the Middle East.

On 5/6 April, during a raid on an aircraft factory at Toulouse, *Pod*, with Squadron Leader Doubleday again in command, acted as the Windfinder aircraft, reporting

back the wind strengths to Group HQ. A few nights later, on the 18/19th, Flight Lieutenant J Colpus and crew had a 1,000 lb bomb hang-up – and then fall – onto the closed bomb-doors, but it was later jettisoned without further problems. Colpus had been second pilot in *Sugar* (R5868) back in October, then flown her a couple of times. Colpus was now flying *Pod* in April and May.

Pilot Officer J L Sayers RAAF took *Pod* out several times during May, and his gunners had a combat with a Me110 on the night of 22/23rd, the Lanc suffering some damage from a flak hit in a heavy searchlight belt running west to east from Emden. Sayers' gunners had another engagement on 21/22 June, two enemy fighters having a go at them, but one was hit and seen to go down with its port engine on fire, the Lanc suffering only minimal damage. Sayers and some of his crew later operated with 617 Squadron, John Sayers having won the DFC, adding a Bar while with 617 Dambuster Squadron.

LL843 saw operations during the D-Day landings, and against transport centres and V1 sites, also over Caen in July, which proved to be the aircraft's last sortie with the Australians. The next day she was assigned to 61 Squadron at RAF Skellingthorpe, Lincolnshire, and had

PO J L Sayers RAAF (far right) took LL843 on 20 trips. With him are FOs E W Warner and B P Parry, while with 617 Squadron, the latter also his rear gunner in 467 Squadron.

John Cooksey (DFC) took her out at least 18 times and Corewyn 13, but Corewyn and crew were lost in LM720 on coming back from Leuna on 14/15 January. They collided with a radar mast on Bord Hill and crashed near Langham airfield, Norfolk, everyone on board being killed.

LL843 completed her 100th op during March 1945 and is reported to have flown a total of 118 by the war's end. Whether any Manna or Exodus flights are included is not known as no record of these sorties was kept in the 541. The aircraft also suffered a couple more flak hits – on 2 August 1944 and 27 March 1945. During a sortie to Karlsruhe on 2/3 February 1945, with Cooksey, she was unable to reach the target on time due to an iced-up ASI and an unexpected cloud base being encountered. Just five minutes from the bomb-run the Master Bomber ordered 'Cease bombing', so the crew had to jettison the 'cookie' and then cut a corner off the return route so as to rejoin the bomber stream.

On 21 May 1945 LL843 was sent to 1659 CU and then in early September went to 279 (ASR) Squadron, but three weeks later the veteran bomber was transferred to 20 MU. She was finally sold to Messrs Cooley and Co, at Hounslow, Middlesex, for scrap, on 7 May 1947.

new codes of QR painted on. She also met up with an old friend, A W Doubleday, now a Wing Commander and CO of 61 Squadron, and about to receive the DSO.

Operations slowly mounted until on 12/13 August, during a raid on Rüsselsheim, an attack by two night fighters and a flak hit put LL843 out of action for several weeks. She was sent back to RIW on the 28th and did not return until one month later. During the winter of 1944-45 she settled down with two particular skippers, Flying Officers W G Corewyn and J S Cooksey.

## 467 SQUADRON
## 1944

**9/10 Mar** *2037-0614*
*MARIGNANE*
SL A W Doubleday DFC RAAF
Sgt J Sloane
FO F J Nugent DFC RAAF
FL R B G Murphy DFC RAAF
FO B Sinnamon RAAF
FO S B Gray-Buchanan DFM RAAF
PO A A Taylor (DFC) RAAF
GC S C Elworthy (passenger)

**15/16 Mar** *1913-0310*
*STUTTGART*
FL A B Simpson DFC RAAF
PO S W Archer
FS K W Manson RAAF
PO R C Watts DFC RAAF (N)
FS L T Watson
FS C A Campbell RAAF
FS H Thompson

**18/19 Mar** *1902-0057*
*STUTTGART*
FL A B Simpson and crew
PO T H Ronaldson (WOP)
and PO R A Weeden (RG) in

**22/23 Mar** *1904-0018*
*FRANKFURT*
SL A W Doubleday and crew
FO H C Ricketts (BA) and PO
G G Johnson (WOP) in

**26/27 Mar** *1944-0045*
*ESSEN*
SL A W Doubleday and crew
FL D A G Andrews (WOP) in
Johnson out

**30/31 Mar** *2144-0524*
*NÜRNBERG*
SL A W Doubleday and crew
FO G G Abbott (BA) in,
Ricketts out

**5/6 Apr** *2027-0403*
*TOULOUSE*
SL A W Doubleday and crew
Abbott out, Ricketts in

**10/11 Apr** *2239-0435*
*TOURS M/YARDS*
SL A W Doubleday and crew

**18/19 Apr** *2047-0115*
*JUVISY*
SL J A Colpus RAAF (DFC)
Sgt K Smith (FE)
FS S T Bridgewater (BA)

FO D J Stevens (N)
Sgt P Macdonald (WOP)
WO R H Mark RAAF (MU
Sgt E A Rutt (RG)

**20/21 Apr** *2251-0318*
*LA CHAPELLE*
SL J A Colpus and crew

**22/23 Apr** *2311-0501*
*BRUNSWICK*
SL J A Colpus and crew

**24/25 Apr** *2112-0634*
*MUNICH*
SL J A Colpus and crew

**1/2 May** *2141-0543*
*TOULOUSE*
PO S Johns RAAF
Sgt D K J Phillips
FS M J O'Leary RAAF
WO C E Langstrom
FS P B Molloy RAAF
FS E D Dale RAAF
FS J J Fallon RAAF

**3/4 May** *2152-0318*
*MAILLY-LE-CAMP*
PO S Johns and crew

**8/9 May** *2140-0210*
*BREST*
SL J A Colpus and crew

**10/11 May** *2201-0054*
*LILLE*
SL J A Colpus and crew

**11/12 May** *2231-0150*
*BOURG LÉOPOLD*
PO J L Sayers RAAF (DFC*)
Sgt G D Colquhoun (FE)
FS A G Weaver RAAF
FO E G Strem RAAF
Sgt F H Hawkins
Sgt R P Kent
FS B P Barry RAAF

**19/20 May** *2205-0349*
*TOURS*
PO J L Sayers and crew

**22/23 May** *2245-0447*
*BRUNSWICK*
PO J L Sayers and crew
Sgt V L Johnson in (FE)
Colquhoun out
(combat with Me110 and hit
by flak near Emden)

**24/25 May** *2307-0213*
*EINDHOVEN AIRFIELD*
PO J L Sayers and crew

Hazards of the night sky – this 55 Squadron Lanc had both its gunners killed by a night fighter after a raid on Berlin, 30 January 1944.

**27/28 May** 2257-0346
*NANTES*
PO J L Sayers and crew

**31 May/1 June** 2356-0446
*SAUMUR*
PO J L Sayers and crew
Colquhoun back

**3/4 June** 2319-0235
*FERME D'URVILLE*
PO J L Sayers and crew

**6 June** 0258-0655
*ST PIERRE DU MONT*
PO J L Sayers and crew

**6/7 June** 2357-0319
*ARGENTAN*
PO J L Sayers and crew

**8/9 June** 2303-0422
*RENNES*
PO J L Sayers and crew
FS V E Cockroft (BA) and
Sgt G T Tipping (MU) in

**10/11 June** 2225-0335
*ORLÉANS*
PO J L Sayers and crew

**12/13 June** 2222-0444
*POITIERS*
PO P W Ryan RAAF
Sgt G A Hays
FS V E Cockroft RAAF
WO C C Jones RAAF
FL L H Porritt RAAF
FS W D D Killworth RAAF
FS J P Steffan RAAF

**14/15 June** 2242-0302
*AUNAY-SUR-ODON*
PO P W Ryan and crew

**15/16 June** 2142-0346
*CHÂTELLERAULT*
PO P W Ryan and crew

**19/20 June** 2254-0128
*WATTEN – V1 SITE*
PO P W Ryan and crew
(recalled)

**21/22 June** 2309-0340
*GELSENKIRCHEN*
PO J L Sayers and crew

(combats – one EA shot down,
some slight damage to Lanc)

**23/24 June** 2234-0506
*LIMOGES*
PO J L Sayers and crew

**24/25 June** 2250-0208
*PROUVILLE – V1 SITE*
PO J L Sayers and crew

**27/28 June** 2153-0505
*VITRY*
PO J L Sayers and crew

**29 June** 1203-1529
*BEAUVOIR – V1 SITE*
PO J L Sayers and crew

**4/5 July** 2308-0319
*ST LEU D'ESSERENT*
PO J L Sayers and crew

**7/8 July** 2235-0250
*ST LEU D'ESSERENT*
PO J L Sayers and crew

**12/13 July** 2153-0638
*CULMONT CHALINDREY*
FO S C Carey RAAF
Sgt G G C Morrison
FS G E Fisher RAAF
FS L E Formby RAAF
FL W H Braun RAAF
FO L Anchem RAAF
Sgt A G McCoy

**14/15 July** 2221-0428
*VILLENEUVE*
FO J L Sayers and crew
FO A R Dyer (2P)

**15/16 July** 2222-0506
*NEVERS*
FO J L Sayers and crew

**18 July** 0344-0741
*CAEN*
SL L C Deignan
FS R J Mellowship (2P)
FS L S Smith
WO H R Goodwin
FS C Dean
FO A W Allison
PO L G Burden
PO R W Wishart

## 61 SQUADRON

**20/21 July** 2316-0206
*COURTRAI M/YARDS*
FL S Parker
Sgt J A Palin (FE)
Sgt H J Richardson (N)
Sgt J H Wellams (BA)
Sgt K G West (WOP)
Sgt K Smith (MU)
Sgt C E Stothard (RG)

**23/24 July** 2255-0337
*KIEL*
FO D G Bates
Sgt G Farrow
FS A N Hughes
FO G O Cameron
Sgt F W Cotton
PO J Fletcher
Sgt D Hancock

**24/25 July** 2150-0539
*STUTTGART*
FL S Parker and crew
Sgt R S Steele (FE) in,
Palin out

**25 July** 1711-2136
*ST CYR AIRFIELD*
WC A W Doubleday DFC
FS J Stone
PO J F Mills
FO F J Nugent RAAF
FS A C R Brydges
FO R K W Clover
FS C Scrimshaw

**26/27 July** 2126-0601
*GIVORS*
WC A W Doubleday and crew

**28/29 July** 2211-0541
*STUTTGART*
FO C N Hill
Sgt C L Gos
FO D Hayley
FO C H Machin
Sgt M R Vagnolini
Sgt G R Mildren
Sgt J V O'Neill

**30 July** 0609-1041
*CAHAGNES*
WC A W Doubleday and crew
(aborted over tgt – cloud)

**31 July** 1732-2303
*JOIGNY-LA-ROCHE*
FO H Brooker
Sgt W J Morgan
FO K Brown
Sgt D J Hector
Sgt L B Smith
Sgt W P Hunter
Sgt A D'Arcy

**1 Aug** 1655-2135
*SIRACOURT – V1 SITE*
FO H Brooker and crew
(abandoned by MB)

**2 Aug** 1450-1910
*BOIS DE CASSAN – V1 SITE*
FO H Brooker and crew
(hit by flak)

**5 Aug** 1030-1545
*ST LEU D'ESSERENT*
WC A W Doubleday and crew

**6 Aug** 0945-1430
*BOIS DE CASSAN – V1 SITE*
FO H Brooker and crew
(abandoned by MB)

**7/8 Aug** 2105-0056
*SECQUEVILLE*
WC A W Doubleday and crew
Sgt L Chapman (WOP) in,
Dunstone out

**9/10 Aug** 2058-0322
*CHÂTELLERAULT*
FO A D D Brian
Sgt L C Doyle
FO L W Deubert
FO J D Constable
FS C Morgan
Sgt D W H Lambert
Sgt D Wainwright

**11/12 Aug** 2047-0450
*GIVORS*
WO A P Greenfield RAAF (DFC)
Sgt F F Fraser
Sgt W J A Gibbs
Sgt W J Haddon
WO V P Smith
Sgt J P King
Sgt S D P Goodey
(lost 9 Apr, all KIA except
Fraser and Goodey – PoWs)

**12/13 Aug** 2138-0320
*RÜSSELSHEIM*
FO L A Davies
Sgt J E Jolly
Sgt B Webster
Sgt L G Simpson
FS E Oddy
Sgt L A Williams
Sgt J Watson
(attacked by 2 fighters,
damaged by flak)

**5 Oct** 0741-1301
*WILHELMSHAVEN*
FO N T Collins
Sgt W F Lake
Sgt S F Heaven
FO E R Bloomfield
FS R W Pratt
Sgt D J Everson
Sgt W J Scott

**6 Oct** 1746-2222
*BREMEN*
FO J S Cooksey (DFC)
Sgt D E Rose
FS E P Meaker
FS T Stapleton
FS S J Scarrett
Sgt A R Marshall
Sgt N W Elliott

# LL843 POD

**7 Oct** *1222-1514*
FLUSHING
FO D W Scholes
Sgt C J Freeman
FS D J Murray
Sgt R Mayall
FS J J Gardner
FS J W Jackman
FS G Allen

**11 Oct** *1328-1656*
FLUSHING
FL H B Grynkiewicz
Sgt W M Ratcliffe
Sgt J L Jones
Sgt E J Day
Sgt H H Davie
Sgt G E Gwalter
Sgt K W Browne
(all lost 16/17 Mar except
Davie – not flying)

**14/15 Oct** *2255-0555*
BRUNSWICK
FO W G Corewyn
Sgt P R Earl
Sgt R C Battersby
Sgt E J Boakes
Sgt S J James
Sgt J Douglas
Sgt R Richardson
(all KIFA 14 Jan 1945)

**19 Oct** *1734-2131*
NÜRNBERG
FO W G Corewyn and crew
(aborted – port-inner failed)

**23 Oct** *1442-1740*
FLUSHING
FO J S Cooksey and crew

**28/29 Oct** *2234-0506*
BERGEN – U/B PENS
FO J S Cooksey and crew
(abandoned, tgt not identified)

**1 Nov** *1344-1837*
HOMBURG
FO J S Cooksey and crew
(abandoned, tgt not i/d –
damaged by flak)

**2 Nov** *1638-2150*
DÜSSELDORF
FO J S Cooksey and crew

**4 Nov** *1740-2153*
LADBERGEN CANAL
FO W G Corewyn and crew

**6 Nov** *1636-2230*
GRAVENHORST
FO J S Cooksey and crew
(abandoned by MB)

**11 Nov** *1627-2145*
HAMBURG
FO J S Cooksey and crew
(bombs hung-up)

**16 Nov** *1248-1734*
DÜREN
FO W G Corewyn and crew

**21 Nov** *1725-2323*
DORTMUND-EMS CANAL
FO W G Corewyn and crew

**22/23 Nov** *1541-0258*
TRONDHEIM
FO W G Corewyn and crew
(cancelled by MB)

**26/27 Nov** *2344-0914*
MUNICH
FO J S Cooksey and crew

**4 Dec** *1642-2313*
HEILBRONN
FO J S Cooksey and crew

**6 Dec** *1646-2331*
GIESSEN
FO J S Cooksey and crew

**8 Dec** *0836-1321*
URFT DAM
FO F S Farren
Sgt N F Howard
FS T L Benson
Sgt J Sinclair
Sgt W S Tandy
Sgt A Lockett
Sgt N Peckham

**17/18 Dec** *1639-0201*
MUNICH
FO W G Corewyn and crew

**18/19 Dec** *1717-0253*
GDYNIA
FO W G Corewyn and crew

**21/22 Dec** *1621-0245*
PÖLITZ
FO W G Corewyn and crew

**27 Dec** *1229-1708*
RHEYDT
FO J P Friend RAAF
Sgt D M Bremner
Sgt N T Nuttall
Sgt P Sears
FS G A Robson
Sgt C J Yates
Sgt C J Bell

**31 Dec** *0210-0732*
HOUFFALIZE
FO W G Corewyn and crew

## 1945

**1 Jan** *1630-2328*
GRAVENHORST
FO W G Corewyn and crew

**5 Jan** *0112-0740*
ROYAN
FO P B Shaw
Sgt W E Higgins
FS F B Robinson
FO S Burns
FS E Stafford
Sgt E Robertson
FS T V G Dearing

**6 Jan** *0100-0605*
HOUFFALIZE
FO W G Corewyn and crew
WO J W Jones (FE) and
WO G G Donald (RG) in

**7/8 Jan** *1654-0213*
MUNICH
FO W G Corewyn and crew
Sgt P R Bell (FE) in

**14 Jan** *1623-2054*
MERSEBURG
FO J S Cooksey and crew
(abort – RG sick)

**16/17 Jan** *1758-0318*
BRUX
FO J S Cooksey and crew

**1 Feb** *1541-2215*
SIEGEN
FO J S Cooksey and crew

**2/3 Feb** *2000-0334*
KARLSRUHE
FO J S Cooksey and crew
(failed to reach tgt in time)

**7/8 Feb** *2105-0259*
LADBERGEN
FO J S Cooksey and crew

**8/9 Feb** *1634-0208*
PÖLITZ
FO J S Cooksey and crew
(heavy flak over Sweden; first
aircraft to bomb target)

**13/14 Feb** *1757-0410*
DRESDEN
FO R J Palmer
Sgt B Webster
FS J E Jolly
FS L G Simpson
FS E Oddy
Sgt Weaver
Sgt J Watson
(L A Davies' crew)

**14/15 Feb** *1654-0211*
ROSITZ
FO R J Palmer
Sgt J Monaghan
Sgt R R Grant
FS A C Shelstad
Sgt M T Plant
FO A Dunn
FS A L Knoke

**19/20 Feb** *2332-0812*
BÖHLEN
FO R J Palmer and crew

**20/21 Feb** *2158-0400*
MITTERLAND CANAL
FO R J Palmer and crew

**24 Feb** *1401-1907*
DORTMUND-EMS CANAL
FO E Roocroft
Sgt Hodges
Sgt N Fallows
Sgt T L Hargreaves
Sgt F Stanney
Sgt L F Aitken
Sgt D Harvey
(could not i/d tgt)

**3/4 Mar** *1835-0011*
DORTMUND-EMS CANAL
FO E Roocroft and crew

**5/6 Mar** *1718-0242*
BÖHLEN
FO J S Cooksey and crew

**6/7 Mar** *1813-0338*
SASSNITZ
FO J S Cooksey and crew

**7/8 Mar** *1753-0048*
HAMBURG
FO K W Ainsworth
FS L D Mills
FO R Breakwell
FO Merrett
FS A W Snelling
Sgt P Kitching
Sgt F M Lancaster
(all lost 20/21 Mar except
Merrett – not flying)

**11 Mar** *1226-1731*
ESSEN
FO K N Ainsworth and crew

**12 Mar** *1309-1857*
DORTMUND
FO J P Friend and crew
FL J H B Billam (N)

**14/15 Mar** *1655-0215*
LUTZKENDORF
FO J P Friend and crew

**16/17 Mar** *1732-0129*
WÜRZBURG
FO J P Friend and crew

**20/21 Mar** *2348-0804*
BÖHLEN
SL I J Fadden
WO J W Jones
FL W A B Martin
PO H W Knight
FO W R Brown
WO S H A Neill
WO G G Donald

**22 Mar** *1128-1619*
BREMEN
FL D G G Phillips
FS S B Watson
FS Woodward
FO J Munn
FO W A Green
Sgt G E Green
Sgt A Robinson

**23/24 Mar** *1931-0103*
WESEL
FO W J Lambert
Sgt L Allward
PO R H Powley
FO J S Ross
FS G F Cartwright
FS L A Sandiford
Sgt Hanna

**27 Mar** *1033-1518*
FARGE
FO E Roocroft and crew
(std-outer hit by flak)

**4 Apr** *0558-1218*
NORDHAUSEN
FL L A Davies and crew

**6 Apr** *0845-1215*
IJMUIDEN
WO P K Morrison
FS G W Lilley
FS W Haughney
FS R G P Snelling
FS H H Neilson
Sgt G E King
WO C J Renaud

**9 Apr** *1452-1942*
HAMBURG
WO P K Morrison and crew

**16/17 Apr** *2344-0720*
PILSEN
WO P K Morrison and crew

**18/19 Apr** *2315-0752*
KOMOTAU
FO H S Beckett
FS D M Moinalty
FO D T Mead
PO J D Ilott
FS N Jackson
Sgt K L Dean
Sgt R H Carr

**23 Apr** *1520-2055*
FLENSBURG
FO H S Beckett and crew

**25/26 Apr** *2013-0316*
TONSBERG
FO H S Beckett and crew

# LL885
# JIG

Another Mark I built under licence by Messrs Armstrong-Whitworth at Coventry, LL885 rolled off their production line in early 1944, fitted with four Merlin 24 engines. On 23 March it was sent to 622 Squadron at Mildenhall, Suffolk, where the squadron code letters of GI were applied to its fuselage, together with the individual letter J for Jig. (Oddly enough, GI-J is JIG spelt backwards.)

*Jig's* first sortie was flown on the fateful Nürnberg raid of 30/31 March 1944 which resulted in 97 RAF bombers failing to return. *Jig* might well have been one of them, for it was struck by a falling incendiary over the target which cracked the main spar, but Pilot Officer J M Lunn brought the aircraft and his crew home safely.

*Jig* was out of action until May but then slogged away solidly during the pre-invasion build-up and then flew on both D-Day nights and on into the V1 site and communication targets period, and also flew on the Caen break-out support raid of 18 July. Jack Lunn completed his tour of ops in July and received the DFC, having flown *Jig* 15 times during it.

Following the aircraft's hesitant start, *Jig* did not in fact sustain any further serious damage until the night of 28/29 July. On her way to Stuttgart, having reached Orléans, she was attacked by a night fighter which suddenly appeared out of the darkness. The pilot, Flight Lieutenant R G Allen, ordered the crew to put on parachutes but the mid-upper gunner must have misinterpreted this precautionary instruction for he immediately clipped on his 'chute and baled out!

John Gray, the rear gunner, related how dark the night was and that the first he knew about the attack was when shells and bullets began to lacerate the rear part of the fuselage, tail and elevators. There was a terrific smell of cordite and some flares were set on fire. John ordered a 'corkscrew' and Allen put the Lancaster into the manoeuvre, rising up, then plunging down earthwards. John heard the call to get parachutes, so disconnected the R/T and climbed back out of his turret. Reconnecting his radio in the fuselage he noticed the rear door was open, so knew the mid-upper had gone. He checked

with the skipper about what was happening, and was told to hang-on. Allen and the flight engineer were both struggling to pull the bomber out of its headlong dive, but they managed it, then jettisoned the bombs. They had lost the fighter, and the damaged Lancaster was turned for home.

Richard Allen received the DFC at the end of his tour, while John Gray, who completed 27 ops before being sent to the Central Gunnery School, also received the DFC.

Following repairs, *Jig* was back on ops by 25 August, but on the second raid after her return, the Lanc again received the attentions of a night fighter on the way to Kiel, on 26/27 August. This time *Jig* was not only damaged but the rear gunner, Sergeant Percy Stanley Withers, was killed in his turret.

*Jig's* pilot, Flying Officer A H Thompson RAAF, first saw the fighter – a FW190 – after it dropped a flare but it attacked unseen from the starboard bow of the Lanc. Thompson went into a corkscrew and the 190 attempted to follow, managing to rake the port side of the fuselage. Three bursts from the mid-upper and the fighter was not seen again. Withers had turned his turret to starboard as the fighter first attacked and received a bullet in the back. He must then have swung the turret to port as he was hit in the chest before he could fire. After the fighter had gone the bomb aimer went back and finding the lock on the rear turret doors smashed, had to chop his way in, he got Withers out but he was already dead. *Jig* was u/s until 20 September.

*Jig* then had a long period of relative safety on raids, although it did collect a hole in the port wing on a daylight trip to Osterfeld on 11 December. On 1 February 1945 a sortie to München-Gladbach had to be abandoned after the starboard-outer engine suddenly feathered itself and would not stay un-feathered. The bombs had to be jettisoned in the Frankfurt area and *Jig* was turned for home.

*Jig's* more prolific captains were Flying Officer H P Peck, who flew 21 ops in her and won the DFC, and Flight Lieutenant Ned Jordan RCAF who did 13, and also

*Jig* was LL885, serving with 622 Squadron and later 44 (Rhodesia) Squadron, notching up 113 missions.

received the DFC. Another Canadian, Flying Officer B Morrison RCAF, the pilot who had the engine un-feather itself, went on to fly 14 trips in *Jig*, including her 98th and 99th raids on 4 and 5 March 1945. (He also flew a Manna trip to The Hague carrying a passenger, Lieutenant-General Morgan, the US Military Attaché.) However, the 100th op was flown by Flying Officer C B Moore RCAF on 6 March, a daylight sortie against an oil refinery at Salzbergen.

March saw some flak damage sustained on the 14th and 21st but *Jig* carried on to complete 114 missions, then flew six Manna and three Exodus flights. These made a possible total of 123 missions overall.

LL885 went to 44 (Rhodesia) Squadron on 27 August 1945, then to 39 MU on 3 January 1946. She was eventually Struck off Charge on 4 March 1947.

# 622 SQUADRON
## 1944

**30/31 Mar** *2225-0555*
NÜRNBERG
PO J M Lunn (DFC)
FS H A Trennery (N)
Sgt W E Lister (WOP)
FS P J Halloran RCAF (BA)
Sgt W Wallis (FE)
Sgt J W Farrow (MU)
Sgt K C Hughes (RG)

**1/2 May** *2240-0225*
CHAMBLY
PO A R Taylor
PO E J Insull RNZAF (N)
FS R E Johnston
Sgt F Harriott
Sgt L H Gregson
Sgt L S Shaw
FS G Hutchinson

**8 May** *0055-0545*
CHÂTEAU BOUGET
PO J M Lunn and crew

**8/9 May** *2235-0035*
CAP GRIS NEZ
PO J M Lunn and crew

**10/11 May** *2205-0030*
COURTRAI
FL R G Godfrey RAAF
PO A H Stewart
PO F S Sewell RNZAF
FO C D Chirighin
Sgt A W Ryder
FS W Ross
FS G E G Gardner RNZAF
(all lost 7/8 June)

**11/12 May** *2250-0130*
LOUVAIN
PO J M Lunn and crew
FL Donovan (2P)

**19/20 May** *2200-0250*
LE MANS
FL R G Godfrey and crew

**21/22 May** *2250-0255*
DUISBURG
PO J M Lunn and crew

**22/23 May** *2310-0240*
DORTMUND
PO J M Lunn and crew

**25 May** *0015-0415*
AACHEN
PO J M Lunn and crew

**27/28 May** *2245-0425*
GARDENING – GIRONDE
PO J M Lunn and crew

**28/29 May** *1845-0215*
ANGERS
PO E H Cawsey
FS E Panton
Sgt I Waters
FO G Hayter
Sgt F N Poynter
Sgt W E Mayes
Sgt C Pratt

**31 May/1 June** *2340-0440*
TRAPPES – M/YARDS
FO A Smith
FS J Chigwidden
Sgt P Brandon
FO A Montgomery
Sgt R Lewis
Sgt A O'Connor
Sgt J Spencer

**6 June** *0315-0630*
OUISTREHAM
PO J M Lunn and crew

**7 June** *0010-0350*
LISIEUX
PO A B Robbins RAAF
FS E Sutton
Sgt A Eldridge
FS G Wachter RAAF
Sgt A Margenstern
Sgt J A Mann
Sgt G R Wilby

**8/9 June** *2155-0250*
FOUGÈRES
PO A B Robbins and crew

**12/13 June** *2300-0300*
GELSENKIRCHEN
PO J E A Pyle
FS P A MacGibbon
Sgt E Crowther
FS L Tomlinson
Sgt A H Hall
Sgt W H Pool RCAF
Sgt J L Spaven
(all lost 20/21 July)

**13/14 June** *2240-0330*
GARDENING – BREST
PO J M Lunn and crew

**14/15 June** *2300-0250*
LE HAVRE
PO J M Lunn and crew

**15/16 June** *2305-0215*
VALENCIENNES
FL R W Trenouth RAAF (DFC)
FS S West
FS W A Atkins
FO B L Good
Sgt R B Francis
Sgt C C Pulman
FS D C Harvey

**18 June** *0110-0450*
MONTDIDIER
PO J M Lunn and crew

**23/24 June**
L'HEY – V1 SITE
PO J M Lunn and crew

**30 June** *1825-2115*
VILLERS BOCAGE
PO J M Lunn and crew

**2 July** *1215-1605*
BEAUVOIR – V1 SITE
FL R G Allen (DFC)
FS W A Bishop (N)
Sgt J Paton (WOP)
FO C D J Pennington (BA)
Sgt J Barker (FE)
FL D B Mason (MU)
PO J T W Gray (RG) (DFC)

**9 July** *1210-1555*
LINZEUX – V1 SITE
PO J M Lunn and crew

**10 July** *0355-0800*
NUCOURT – V1 SITE
FO J W Stratton
FS M L Reilly RNZAF (N)
WO J McGuiness
FO E F Thurston RNZAF
Sgt H H Clifton
FS H G Summerton RAAF
Sgt R N Pittaway

**17 July** *1050-1420*
VAIRIES – V1 SITE
FL R W Trenouth and crew
(all aircraft recalled)

**18 July** *0335-0725*
CAEN
FO N V Gill
FS E Featherstonehough
FS R I Smith
FS J R Short
Sgt K J Humphries
Sgt H Harris
Sgt H P R Russell

**18/19 July** *2240-0230*
AULNOYE
PO A B Robbins and crew
FS D Smith (2P)

**20/21 July** *2310-0255*
HOMBURG
PO A B Robbins and crew

**23 July** *0645-1030*
MONT CANDON
PO A B Robbins and crew

**24 July** *0920-1305*
PROUVILLE
PO A B Robbins and crew

**24/25 July** *2150-0535*
STUTTGART
FO A T Wheate
FS W Leonard
FO D C Chapman
FO D W Findlay RNZAF

LL885 being waved off on another operation.

Sgt R Kestrell
Sgt H Elliott
Sgt R J Thornton

**25/26 July** *2120-0355*
*STUTTGART*
PO A B Robbins and crew

**28/29 July** *2155-0255*
*STUTTGART*
FL R G Allen and crew
(aircraft damaged by night
fighter – MU baled out –
bombs jettisoned)

**25/26 Aug** *2035-0525*
*RÜSSELSHEIM*
PO A B Robbins and crew

**26/27 Aug** *2005-0141*
*KIEL*
FO A H Thompson RAAF
FS W S Ward RAAF (N)
FS R W Aland RAAF
FS R J Dilley (BA)
Sgt K J Boulton
Sgt D Smith
Sgt B S Withers (RG)
(RG killed by night fighter)

**20 Sep** *1430-1740*
*CALAIS*
FO H P Peck RAAF (DFC)
FS J W Barchard
FO R T Cargill
FO A G Long
Sgt R C Bowyer
Sgt J Rumsey
Sgt D C Pudney

**23/24 Sep** *1920-0015*
*NEUSS*
FO H P Peck and crew

**24 Sep** *1710-1930*
*CALAIS*
FL J A Brignell
FO K C Lewis RAAF
FS J Harris
FO M J McDonnell
Sgt J Irving
Sgt M Davis
Sgt M Coles

**25 Sep** *0800-1050*
*CALAIS*
FO H P Peck and crew
(abandoned – cloud)

**26 Sep** *1020-1350*
*CALAIS*
FS G Myles
FS W D Aveyard

WO F G Mills RAAF
Sgt V Reilly
Sgt A F Crawford
FS H C Field
FS F J Schell

**27 Sep** *0720-1035*
*CALAIS*
PO M G Baxter
Sgt L G Parsons
Sgt G C Brooker
FS R Hopkinson RAAF
Sgt E J Rossiter
Sgt J W Schuler
Sgt F Ramsey

**5/6 Oct** *1845-0040*
*SAARBRÜCKEN*
FO H P Peck and crew

**6 Oct** *1650-2200*
*DORTMUND*
FO H P Peck and crew

**7 Oct** *1120-1540*
*KLEVE*
FO H P Peck and crew

**14 Oct** *0630-1055*
*DUISBURG*
FO H P Peck and crew

**14/15 Oct** *2240-0355*
*DUISBURG*
FO H P Peck and crew

**18 Oct** *0825-1330*
*BONN*
FO H P Peck and crew

**19 Oct** *1725-2355*
*STUTTGART*
FO N G Flaxman
FO M G Stewart
FO G K Soderberg
FO J Adamson
Sgt E Turley
Sgt W J Thurman
Sgt K F Sadler

**22 Oct** *1300-1725*
*NEUSS*
FO H P Peck and crew

**23 Oct** *1610-2130*
*ESSEN*
FO H P Peck and crew

**25 Oct** *1230-1720*
*ESSEN*
FO H P Peck and crew

**28 Oct** *1310-1745*
*COLOGNE*
FO H P Peck and crew

**30 Oct** *1745-2300*
*COLOGNE*
PO C D Bennett
Sgt H C Grimsay
FS J P Sullivan
FO E J I Hurditch
Sgt C G Staplehurst
FS L C Nichols
Sgt F Murrell

**4 Nov** *1130-1600*
*SOLINGEN*
FO R Curling RAAF (DFC)
FS J W H Murdin
WO T Hine
FS L W Middleditch
Sgt D S White
Sgt C W S Robinson
Sgt H Wallace

**5 Nov** *1020-1520*
*SOLINGEN*
FO H P Peck and crew

**8 Nov** *0805-1245*
*HOMBURG*
FO N G Flaxman and crew

**11 Nov** *0820-1300*
*CASTROP*
FO N G Flaxman and crew

**15 Nov** *1235-1750*
*DORTMUND*
FO H P Peck and crew

**16 Nov** *1300-1730*
*HEINSBURG*
FO H P Peck and crew

**20 Nov** *1240-1745*
*HOMBURG*
FO H P Peck and crew

**21 Nov** *1235-1640*
*HOMBURG*
FO H P Peck and crew

**23 Nov** *1245-1755*
*GELSENKIRCHEN*
FO H P Peck and crew

**26 Nov** *0750-1330*
*FULDA*
FO H P Peck and crew

**27 Nov** *1220-1715*
*COLOGNE*
FO R Curling and crew
WO T R Allen in, Hine out

**28 Nov** *0240-0720*
*NEUSS*
FO H P Peck and crew

**30 Nov** *1050-1510*
*BOTTROP*
FO W H Thorbecke (DFC)
FL A Westbrook
Sgt R A Adams
FO H S Villiers
Sgt T J Hogen (FE)
FSO J W Scouler (MU)
Sgt A Staele (RG)

**2 Dec** *1255-1715*
*DORTMUND*
FO W H Thorbecke and crew
Sgt A J Smith in, Scouler out

**8 Dec** *0825-1255*
*DUISBURG*
FS L Stille
Sgt J W Morgan
Sgt S G Hewett
Sgt N Brabazon
Sgt E Eastwood
Sgt H Dewey
Sgt E Jones

**11 Dec** *0835-1310*
*OSTERFELD M/YARDS*
FS L Stille and crew

**12 Dec** *1103-1600*
*WITTEN*
FO N G Flaxman and crew

**15 Dec** *1125-1415*
*SIEGEN*
FO N G Flaxman and crew
(recalled)

**16 Dec** *1120-1650*
*SIEGEN*
FO N G Flaxman and crew

**24 Dec** *1525-2010*
*BONN AIRFIELD*
FS G E Darville RAAF (DFC)
Sgt T Lisle
FS M J Keough RAAF
Sgt D Pearce
Sgt W S Godfrey
Sgt D F Dunn
Sgt H V Beckwith

**28 Dec** *1228-1715*
*COLOGNE*
FS G E Darville and crew

**29 Dec** *1223-1709*
*KOBLENZ M/YARDS*
FO N Jordan RCAF (DFC)
FS W M McDonald
Sgt Mc J Robinson
FO R S Riley
Sgt L Eyre
Sgt T H Gregory
Sgt P C Laymore

## 1945

**2 Jan** *1535-2305*
*NÜRNBERG*
FO W H Thorbecke and crew

**3 Jan** *1300-1820*
*DORTMUND*
FO N Jordan and crew

**5 Jan** *1135-1750*
*LUDWIGSHAVEN*
FO N Jordan and crew

**6 Jan** *1530-2040*
*NEUSS*
FO N Jordan and crew

**7/8 Jan** *1840-0250*
*MUNICH*
FO A E W Waigh
FO T S Briggs
WO T R Allen RAAF

R G Allen and crew. From left to right: D B Mason, J Paton, Allen, J T W Gray, W A Bishop, J Barker, C D J Pennington.

FO T M R Lister
Sgt E Evans (FE)
Sgt P J Simmonds
Sgt W A Mitchell

**29 Jan** *1005-1530*
KREFELD M/YARDS
FO N Jordan and crew

**1 Feb** *1324-1638*
*MÜNCHEN-GLADBACH*
FO B Morrison RCAF
Sgt J B Orr
Sgt L Totman RCAF
PO J Pollard RCAF
Sgt A G Chambers
Sgt T G Stock RCAF
Sgt D W S West (RG)
(abandoned, std-outer u/s)

**3 Feb** *1617-2142*
*DORTMUND*
FO B Morrison and crew
Sgt A J Smith in, West out

**7 Feb** *1138-1734*
*WANNE-EICKEL*
FL N Jordan and crew

**9 Feb** *0330-0823*
*HOHENBUDBERG*
FL N Jordan and crew

**13/14 Feb** *2132-0705*
*DRESDEN*
FL N Jordan and crew

**14/15 Feb** *2024-0442*
*CHEMNITZ*
FL N Jordan and crew

**15 Feb** *1635-2352*
*GARDENING – KATTEGAT*
FO W H Thorbecke and crew

**18 Feb** *1157-1708*
*WESEL*
FO B Morrison and crew

**19 Feb** *1313-1812*
*WESEL*
FO B Morrison and crew

**20/21 Feb** *2149-0412*
*DORTMUND*
FL N Jordan and crew

**22 Feb** *1246-1748*
*GELSENKIRCHEN*
FO A G Moore
Sgt R G Price
FS B G Dawson
Sgt L W Lund
Sgt C W A Forsey
Sgt J R Thompson
Sgt R H Davis

**1 Mar** *1140-1720*
*KAMEN*
FO B Morrison and crew

**2 Mar** *1300-1834*
*COLOGNE*
FO J S Cameron RCAF
FS D E Cameron RCAF
Sgt M W Guy RCAF
FS W M Leeming
Sgt E S J Seldon
FS K E Boone DFM
Sgt A D Falconer
(abandoned over tgt)

**4 Mar** *0935-1431*
*WANNE-EICKEL*
FO B Morrison and crew

**5 Mar** *1032-1613*
*GELSENKIRCHEN*
FO B Morrison and crew

**6 Mar** *0827-1413*
*SALZBERGEN*
FO C B Moore RAAF
FS H D Patterson RAAF
Sgt E H G Potkins
Sgt F G Cowap
Sgt R B Sutcliffe (FE)
Sgt P F Cochrane
Sgt D C Carter

**9 Mar** *1042-1604*
*DATTELN*
FS L W O'Connor RAAF
FS A O'Neill RAAF
FS K J McKenzie RAAF
FS W D Williamson
FS E Wiles
Sgt A Featherstone
Sgt A Goodall

**10 Mar** *1200-1717*
*GELSENKIRCHEN*
FO B Morrison and crew

**11 Mar** *1129-1719*
*ESSEN M/YARDS*
FS L W O'Connor and crew

**12 Mar** *1231-1856*
*DORTMUND*
FO B Morrison and crew

**14 Mar** *1325-1847*
*EMSCHER*
FL N Jordan and crew
FS T C S Dodd (WOP) in
(hit by flak)

**18 Mar** *1158-1718*
*HATTINGEN*
FO B Morrison and crew

**20 Mar** *0952-1534*
*HAMM M/YARDS*
FS C Malcolm
FS L J Lane
FS R G Winden
FS R A Robinson
Sgt W Webster (FE)
FS D H Shorter
Sgt K Wood

**21 Mar** *0942-1526*
*MÜNSTER*
FO B Morrison and crew
(hit by flak)

**27 Mar** *1031-1553*
*KÖNIGSBORN*
FL C B Moore and crew

**29 Mar** *1221-1919*
*HALLENDORF*
FO J W Armfield
Sgt R R Last
FS H J Atkins RAAF
Sgt G C Anyan
Sgt W J Ellison
Sgt G Rivett
Sgt L W Pavey

**9/10 Apr** *1929-0133*
*KIEL*
FL N Jordan and crew

**13/14 Apr** *2030-0241*
*KIEL*
FL N Jordan and crew

**14/15 Apr** *1809-0240*
*POTSDAM*
FO W M Scriven RAAF
Sgt R H Field
Sgt W B Wolfe
FS A McDonald
Sgt W F McLean
Sgt S Cadman
Sgt L T Hyde

**22 Apr** *1520-2041*
*BREMEN*
FO W M Scriven and crew

**1 May** *1319-1540*
*MANNA – THE HAGUE*
FO B Morrison and crew

**2 May** *1053-1313*
*MANNA – THE HAGUE*
FL C B Moore and crew

**3 May** *1123-1349*
*MANNA – THE HAGUE*
FO J H Fielding RAAF
FS D H A Elliott (N)
WO R D Fitch RAAF (WOP)
FS H J Doherty (BA)
Sgt E J Taylor (FE)
Sgt E Smith (RG)
Sgt L Hayward (Pass)

**4 May** *1221-1450*
*MANNA – THE HAGUE*
FO B Morrison and crew
Lt-Col Morgan (Pass)

**7 May** *1122-1403*
*MANNA – LEIDEN*
SL C A Ogilvy
FL G J Speed (N)
FO F M Gloyne (WOP)
FO J W Tanner (BA)
FS E A Barton (FE)
Sgt L D Watkins (RG)

**Another Manna trip on 8 May, then 3 Exodus ops 10, 11 and 13 May**

LL885 after being damaged by a night fighter, 28/29 July 1944.

# LM227
# ITEM

This was a Mark I Lancaster built under licence by Messrs Armstrong-Whitworth at Coventry as part of Contract No.239. It came off the production line with four Merlin 24 engines in the spring of 1944 and was assigned to 576 Squadron at Elsham Wolds, Lincolnshire, on 30 June. Coded UL, the aircraft became I for Item when given the individual identification letter 'I' (later I²).

*Item's* nose art consisted of a Saturn-like ringed planet surrounded by stars and a crescent moon, plus a falling star leaving a trail of tiny stars behind it. Later a swastika was added for a night victory and the aircraft's 21st trip was marked with a key on a parachute to start the third row of bomb symbols. The stars and other adornments were painted on by Norman Bryan, *Item's* engine fitter, and he remembered it took a few days to complete and he was anxious to get it done in case the Lanc failed to return before he had finished the task. He recalled:

'I was the engine fitter on this aircraft the day she arrived brand new, till some time after the war ended. A very good aircraft, it was a pleasure to work on. As far as the emblem, I can say it was all my own work; it was all very different to everyone else's.

'Among her regular skippers I recall Flying Officer Till. He and his crew were always pleased with her performance. The other two in our ground crew team were LACs Bernard Clixman (engines) and Tommy Cookson (rigger).'

*Item's* first pilot was Pilot Officer J R "Mike" Stedman, who took the aircraft to Orléans on 4/5 July 1944. He remembered:

'We joined 576 Squadron as a crew on 20 April after converting from Stirlings to Lancasters at 1 LFS, Hemswell. Being a "sprog" pilot and crew we were allocated spare aircraft for the first few ops. I²-Item was eventually given to us (I forget its number) later losing its letter to LM227 on or about 1 July.

'It was a great thrill to have a brand new aircraft, Packard Merlins with "paddle" props which gave us an extra few thousand feet of altitude. We also had H2S and "Fishpond" which picked up enemy night fighters and allowed us to play cat and mouse with them!

'The nose insignia had no particular meaning, I just thought it would be appropriate as I expected most of my ops would be at night. However, it turned out to be just 19 [night ops] out of 32.

'We were posted to Special Duties Flight, Binbrook, for a month, rejoining LM227 on our return to Elsham Wolds on 13 August. Our last trip with LM227 was a daylight to Le Havre on 10 September.'

LM227 of 576 Squadron about to take off on her first bombing mission, 4/5 July 1944.

George Tabner RCAF, navigator to Harold Guilfoyle, remembered LM227 arriving and also its first op:

'This new Lancaster arrived at Elsham Wolds …. with a very bad oil leak and repairs were immediately done by the ground crew. The Group Captain was concerned about the new aircraft so he personally air-tested her.

'On 4 July, with P/O Stedman and crew, she flew her first op to Orléans. On the second trip she returned to base with two engines burned out. These were replaced and she was air-tested by FL H B Guilfoyle.

'Liking her performance and in spite of his crew's protests, he made her their aircraft. With more speed by 5 knots, it had a better climb rate than their old 'B' for the last ten trips. Guilfoyle and crew went on to complete their tour in her, by which time she had 24 symbols on her nose, 23 for bombing and one for mine-laying.'

As the number of *Item's* raids mounted the bomb symbols, painted in rows of ten on the lower half of the nose, reached 50, and then a second five rows of ten were marked next to them. A DFC ribbon was also painted above the first row, while ahead of the bombs was the swastika, denoting a combat – no doubt the one *Item* had on 28 July when the gunners claimed a Me109 as probably destroyed.

After Mike Stedman had broken the new Lanc's duck, Flight Lieutenant H B Guilfoyle RCAF began to fly *Item*, completing 17 trips and like Stedman and his bomb aimer, went on to win the DFC. Harold Guilfoyle's Canadian rear gunner, Flight Sergeant Nick J Hawrelechko also received the DFM. The latter's citation read:

'Flight Sergeant Hawrelechko, a Canadian NCO, has flown on 30 operational sorties as the rear gunner of a Lancaster heavy bomber. The targets which he has attacked have frequently been heavily defended but Flight Sergeant Hawrelechko has always shown coolness when under fire. One night in July 1944, the aircraft in which this NCO was rear gunner was attacked by an Me109. Flight Sergeant Hawrelechko rose to the occasion by giving an accurate and clear commentary to his

Some of 576's ground crew. From left, Bill Honeywell (rigger), Johnny Cook (engine fitter), Norman Hall (engines), Norman Bryan (engine fitter to LM227 and nose artist), Paddy Bennett (rigger): in front: Ronnie Brett (engine fitter).

Captain to manoeuvre his aircraft so that the gunners could engage the enemy fighter and destroy it. Flight Sergeant Hawrelechko has shown a high degree of courage, skill and initiative and his outstanding ability and strong sense of duty have been a fine example to all. I strongly recommend him for the award of the Distinguished Flying Medal.'

Harry Guilfoyle's navigator again:

'Guilfoyle and crew did 17 trips in her. On the 24th we were detailed as Windfinders, and again on the 28th, in order to increase the number of aircraft over the target at marking. I dropped the bombs on H²S and we claimed a Me109, credited to Nick Hawrelechko.

'On 9 August we laid mines in the Antioche Straits – a trip of six hours, 15 minutes. We could see two other aircraft all the way to the target, near which some gunner on a ship opened up at us. Nick silenced him with the four guns from his rear turret. I dropped six mines, again on H²S.

'On our last op – 12 August, to Brunswick – we were again Windfinder aircraft and bombed on H²S. Winds broadcast to the Main Force were "Speed 99" although my actual winds were 125 mph. We sent this back, breaking code, but the attack was very scattered. We bombed from 22,000 feet after circling and climbing over the target for 20 minutes.

LM227 – bomb-doors open.

LM227 with 24 ops completed and one night victory recorded. Note the 21st trip is recorded as a key on a parachute – a 'gardening' trip.

'Our last two trips were extra for six of us as we volunteered to do two extra in order to finish off Nick, who had missed trips due to receiving two black eyes during a fight in London!'

Pilot Officer Ken L Trent flew six trips in LM227 between the end of August and mid-October. He was one of the few to fly in three Ton-Up Lancs, having already flown raids in LM594 and ME801. He won the DFC and Bar. On one sortie, despite having a defective engine, he helped to rescue a downed crew in a dinghy in the North Sea. A light had been seen and he circled and then directed ships to the spot, circling the area for half an hour. He was later with 625 Squadron.

*Item's* next regular skipper was Flying Officer D E Till. Derek Till piloted the aircraft on no fewer than 28 sorties. Tour length during this period on the squadron was generally 35 ops, and his tour was completed on 24 March 1945, although in another Lancaster. Derek Till also piloted one mission in another 100-op veteran on 576

Squadron – ME801. In fact he flew 37 raids in all, making two extra trips in order that his bomb aimer could complete his tour with him, having missed a couple of sorties. Derek Till, who received the DFC, related:

'*Item* had no mechanical throttle gate to tell you when you were up to 16 lb of boost. Usually there was a wire which you had to break to take it up to the emergency boost of plus 18 lbs. I remember the first time I ran up the engines on *Item* one morning at dispersal. Without realising it I took the port-inner up to plus 18 and the Flight Sergeant came roaring up and gave me hell; he was worried about burning out the exhaust stubs and, of course, it didn't do the engine any good.

'There were a couple of targets that were difficult, one being the oil refinery at Merseburg which was extremely heavily defended due to its importance. We were very nervous going off on that one because we had all been bombed-up ready to go the previous day but then it was scrubbed. Rumours were rife that the Germans would know about it and be ready for us and indeed the flak at the aiming point was incredible.

'On another trip I thought we had missed a course change but my navigator said everything was alright and we went on and on and on. Then my WOP came on the R/T to say Charlie had passed out. His oxygen tube had become disconnected and after writing down some things on his navigational log which was absolute nonsense, he'd fainted. He soon came-to but, of

The Guilfoyle crew. From left, Pete Dodwell, Jack Powell, George Tabner, Harry Guilfoyle, S C Wilkins, N S Cassidy, Nick Hawrelechko.

LM227's 100th op was a Manna sortie on 8 May 1945, piloted by FO B Simpson (centre). To his right are T E Melocke and J Ellis, his navigator and engineer.

The Till crew. From left, Kevin Oliver, John Shorthouse, Derek Till, Geoff Gripps, Charles Bray, Bob Hamilton, D E Holland.

course, we were late to the target and we felt very lonely being the last to bomb on that occasion.'

Apart from the probable victory over the 109 on 28 July, *Item's* rear gunner on a raid to Pforzheim on 23 February 1945 spotted a Ju88 just as it began firing into the Lanc from astern. This caused damage to the port wing but the gunner, Sergeant D Ranchuck RCAF, claimed he damaged it. *Item* had only just completed a major inspection and became Cat AC, returning to Avro's for repair, but she was back on the squadron by 3 March. Her main pilot at the end was Flying Officer B Simpson – ten trips, including her 100th.

At the end of April *Item* had flown 93 sorties, then completed six Manna and one Exodus trips to make the 100. By and large the recorded sorties correlate, although there are two that could be at variance. On 5 August 1944 Guilfoyle is noted as flying aircraft 'I' but it is shown as ME800. It has been assumed ME800 is incorrect,

although there was a Lanc with this number on the squadron. The other raid is on Essen dated 11 March 1945, where the aircraft number is not recorded but the pilot on that occasion had just previously flown on his 'second dickie' trip with Derek Till, and may well have flown *Item* on one of his first crew ops.

*Item* did not last long after the war, being wrecked and declared Cat E on 16 October 1945 before being Struck off Charge. Some time after the original book was published, I had a letter from Norman Bryan's son Peter, informing me that his father had died. He thought it strange that his father had been an engine fitter '… because Dad was never mechanically minded, never owning a car or motorbike, his only tool kit comprised a hammer, screwdriver, pliers and an adjustable spanner. He was called the old man being 23 when the war started and most of the others were 18/19.' Perhaps he's back working on *Item* in an ex-fitter's heaven?

## 576 SQUADRON
### 1944

**4/5 July** *2150-0400*
*ORLÉANS M/YARDS*
PO J R Stedman (DFC)
Sgt R S Porter (FE)
FO H A W Rumbelow (BA) (DFC)
Sgt E Swift (N)
Sgt W S Woolridge (WOP)
Sgt D W Waldron (MU)
Sgt E W Shreeve (RG)

**5/6 July** *2115-0615*
*DIJON*
PO J Archibald RNZAF
Sgt J R Cuthbert
FO P J Biollo RCAF
Sgt J E Kearney
FS L Fielding
WO T P Barry

Sgt A Milne
(all lost 28/29 July)

**7 July** *1930-2330*
*CAEN*
FL H B Guilfoyle RCAF (DFC)
Sgt S C Wilkin (FE)
FO P J Dodwell RCAF (BA)
FO G E Tabner RCAF (N)
FS J D Powell (WOP)
Sgt N S Cassidy (MU)
Sgt N J Hawrelechko (RG) (DFM)

**12/13 July** *2110-0620*
*RÉVIGNY*
FL H B Guilfoyle and crew

**14/15 July** *2110-0530*
*RÉVIGNY*
FL H B Guilfoyle and crew

**17 July** *0320-0715*
*SANDERVILLE*
FL H B Guilfoyle and crew
(Spitfire escort)

**18/19 July** *2305-0315*
*SCHOLVEN*
FL H B Guilfoyle and crew

**20 July** *1905-2230*
*WIZERNES*
FL H B Guilfoyle and crew

**23/24 July** *2230-0400*
*KIEL*
FS A D'L Greig (DFC)
Sgt N Mason
FO J R Jones
FS G G Henville RAAF
Sgt S A Johnson
Sgt H Walton
Sgt J Thresh

**24/25 July** *2110-0550*
*STUTTGART*
FL H B Guilfoyle and crew

**26 July** *0040-0425*
*BOIS DES JARDINS – V1 SITE*
FL H B Guilfoyle and crew

**28/29 July** *2105-0535*
*STUTTGART*
FL H B Guilfoyle and crew
(Me109 probably destroyed)

**30 July** *0625-1015*
*CAHAGNES*
FL V Moss (DFC)
Sgt R A Robertson
FO R E Power RCAF
Sgt M G Callaghan
Sgt T E Sinton
Sgt V L Oatley
Sgt R Stanton

**31 July** *1800-2125*
*LE HAVRE*
FL H B Guilfoyle and crew

**1 Aug** *1845-2140*
*BELLE CROIX*
FL H B Guilfoyle and crew
(abandoned over tgt)

**3 Aug** *1125-1535*
*TROSSY ST MAXIMIN*
FL H B Guilfoyle and crew

**4 Aug** *1325-2125*
*PAUILLAC*
FO F H Watts RCAF
Sgt C Douglas
FO I G D Mills RCAF (BA)
FO R Hughes-Games (N)
Sgt M R Swallow
Sgt W S Clatworthy RCAF
Sgt D H Laing RCAF
(fighter escort)

**5 Aug** *1400-2200*
*BLAYE*
FL H B Guilfoyle and crew

**7/8 Aug** *2055-0055*
*FONTENAYE*
FL H B Guilfoyle and crew

**9/10 Aug** *2130-0345*
*GARDENING – LA ROCHELLE*
FL H B Guilfoyle and crew

**10 Aug** *0920-1440*
*DUGNY*
FO S F Durrant
Sgt R E Pearce
Sgt C J Brady RCAF
FO J Johnstone
FS J R McIntyre RAAF
Sgt J G Mackey RCAF
Sgt D Spowart
(all lost 23/24 Sep)

**11 Aug** *1330-1730*
*DOUAI*
FL H B Guilfoyle and crew

**12/13 Aug** *2135-0240*
*BRUNSWICK*
FL H B Guilfoyle and crew

**14 Aug** *1315-1725*
*FONTAINE-LE-PIN*
FO J J Mulrooney
Sgt B Beale
Sgt D M Reid RCAF
Sgt F Doaker
Sgt A P J Gostling
Sgt J T Smith
Sgt P Rayner
(Mulrooney POW 2/3
Nov, on 29th op)

**15 Aug** *0950-1320*
*LE CULOT*
FO J R Stedman and crew

**16/17 Aug** *2125-0450*
*STETTIN*
FO J R Stedman and crew

**18/19 Aug** *2230-0230*
*RIEME*
FO L Arthur
Sgt J Hill (FE)
FO O J T Troy (BA)
FO R J Williams (N)
FS D T H Madell
Sgt E N Wood
Sgt E L Gidden

**25 Aug** *2005-2355*
*RÜSSELSHEIM*
FO J R Stedman and crew

**26/27 Aug** *1940-0115*
*KIEL*
FO J R Stedman and crew

**28 Aug** *1855-2150*
*CHAPELLE NOTRE DAME*
FO J R Stedman and crew

**29/30 Aug** *2120-0640*
*STETTIN*
PO K L Trent (DFC)
Sgt A R Dunford
Sgt J N Wadsworth
Sgt H B Reynolds
Sgt R L Skelton RAAF
Sgt C Dalby
FO G C Riccomini

**31 Aug** *1245-1645*
*AGENVILLE*
FO J R Stedman and crew

LM227's tally: 100 operations, one enemy aircraft and a DFC ribbon.

**3 Sep** *1520-1910*
*EINDHOVEN*
FO J R Stedman and crew

**5 Sep** *1555-1920*
*LE HAVRE*
FO J R Stedman and crew

**6 Sep** *1700-2025*
*LE HAVRE*
FO J R Stedman and crew

**10 Sep** *1620-2005*
*LE HAVRE*
FO J R Stedman and crew

**12/13 Sep** *1810-0200*
*FRANKFURT*
FO M T Wilson
Sgt R P Kimm
Sgt P E T Brooked
Sgt L N Hill
Sgt S Douglas
Sgt T A Russell
Sgt J H Addison

**15/16 Sep** *2150-0755*
*GARDENING*
FO M T Wilson and crew

**17 Sep** *0055-0420*
*LEUWARDEN AIRFIELD*
FO R A Boggiano
Sgt E V Taylor
Sgt A W Black
FO A Conor RCAF
Sgt S R Coe
Sgt K Holdsworth
Sgt G R Logan

**23 Sep** *1835-2355*
*NEUSS*
PO K L Trent and crew

**24 Sep** *1615-1935*
*CALAIS*
POP K L Trent and crew

**27 Sep** *0910-1245*
*CALAIS*
FO D E Till
Sgt D E Holland (FE)
FO J Shorthouse (BA)
FO C R Bray (N)
FO G W Griggs RAAF
Sgt K Oliver (MU)
Sgt R Hamilton (RG)

The squadron's ground crews also take a bow along with the engineering officer, following LM227's 100th op.

**5/6 Oct** *1820-0110*
*SAARBRÜCKEN*
PO K L Trent and crew

**7 Oct** *1200-1625*
*EMMERICH*
PO K L Trent and crew

**12 Oct** *0635-1000*
*FORT FREDERIK HENDRIK*
FO D E Till and crew

**14 Oct** *0610-1120*
*DUISBURG*
PO K L Trent and crew

**14/15 Oct** *2220-0425*
*DUISBURG*
FO D E Till and crew

**19/20 Oct** *2135-0415*
*STUTTGART*
FO D E Till and crew

**22 Oct** *1610-2210*
*ESSEN*
FO D E Till and crew

**25 Oct** *1255-1815*
*ESSEN*
FO D E Till and crew

**27 Oct** *1335-1930*
*COLOGNE*
FO D E Till and crew

**30 Oct** *1745-2030*
*COLOGNE*
FO D E Till and crew

**2 Nov** *1615-2105*
*DÜSSELDORF*
FO D E Till and crew

**4 Nov** *1735-2235*
*BOCHUM*
FL J W Acheson RCAF
Sgt R M Cameron
FO R A Flight
FS J R Tudhope RAAF
Sgt T R Bell
Sgt H Bukoski RCAF
Sgt I Lewis

**6 Nov** *1140-1620*
*GELSENKIRCHEN*
FL J W Acheson and crew

**9 Nov** *0830-1255*
*WANNE-EICKEL*
FO D E Till and crew

**11 Nov** *1550-2110*
*DORTMUND*
FO D E Till and crew

**18 Nov** *1605-2200*
*WANNE-EICKEL*
FO E L Saslove RCAF
Sgt R Hoyle
FO G Davies
FO M Chisick RCAF
Sgt R F Hood RCAF
Sgt A S B Campton RCAF
Sgt G W McClelland RCAF
(Saslove, Campton and
McClelland KIA 7/8 Jan;
others PoW)

**29 Nov** *1225-1725*
*DORTMUND*
FO D E Till and crew

**3 Dec** *0735-1200*
*URFT DAM*
FO D E Till and crew

**4 Dec** *1630-2300*
*KARLSRUHE*
FO D E Till and crew

**6/7 Dec** *1635-0035*
*MERSEBURG*
FO D E Till and crew

**12 Dec** *1610-2145*
*ESSEN*
FO O R Herbert
Sgt E Heller
Sgt D Thornwell RCAF
PO R F Scott RCAF
Sgt J A Stephens RCAF
FS E J Wise
WO R J Turley

**15 Dec** *1450-2055*
*LUDWIGSHAVEN*
FO D E Till and crew

**17 Dec** *1515-2240*
*ULM*
FO D E Till and crew

**22 Dec** *1510-2210*
*COBLENZ*
FO E J Pollard RAAF
Sgt E B May
Sgt A Preston (BA)
Sgt C V Dolan RCAF (N)
Sgt J Patteson
Sgt R M Goodfellow
Sgt Brown

**28 Dec** *1515-2105*
*BONN*
FO D E Till and crew

**29 Dec** *1515-2130*
*SCHOLVEN*
FO B H O'Neill RCAF
Sgt R J Durran
FO S W Haakstead RCAF
Sgt J G Ogilvie
Sgt F C Smith
Sgt A J W George RCAF
Sgt D Ranchuk RCAF

**31 Dec** *1450-2055*
*OSTERFELD*
FO D E Till and crew

## 1945

**5 Jan** *0159-0907*
*ROYAN*
FO H Benson
FO H Woolstenhulme
FO H G Mather
FO P C Milner
FO F Wilson
Sgt R C Griffiths
Sgt R Goldsbury

**7/8 Jan** *1825-0320*
*MUNICH*
FO E J Pollard and crew

**14/15 Jan** *1905-0315*
*MERSEBURG*
FO D E Till and crew

**22 Jan** *1650-2155*
*DUISBURG*
FO D E Till and crew

**28/29 Jan** *1953-0252*
*STUTTGART*
FO C T Dalziel
Sgt P R Montgomery
Sgt W E Bradbury
Sgt W E May
Sgt A Burns
Sgt G T Thorley
Sgt D O'Sullivan DSM
(Dalziel and Bradbury PoW
7/8 Mar; others all KIA)

**1 Feb** *1600-2235*
*LUDWIGSHAVEN*
FO D E Till and crew

**2/3 Feb** *2045-0250*
*WIESBADEN*
FO D E Till and crew

**3 Feb** *1631-2206*
*BOTTROP*
FO E J Pollard and crew

**23 Feb** *1600-2355*
*PFORZHEIM*
FO B H O'Neill and crew
(damaged by Ju88 but the
night fighter also damaged)

**7/8 Mar** *1710-0200*
*DESSAU*
FO D E Till and crew
FS Brookes in, FO
Shorthouse out

**8/9 Mar** *1700-0035*
*KASSELL*
FO D E Till and crew
FS P F Sattler (2P)
Brookes out, FO S Strand in

**11 Mar** *1145-1705*
*ESSEN*
FS P F Sattler RAAF
Sgt W E A Jeffrey
FO N Whiteley
Sgt P F G A Garner
Sgt W Walker
Sgt K G Durston
Sgt D F Wood
(Sattler, Garner and Whiteley
PoW 16/17 Mar; others KIA)

**12 Mar** *1315-1830*
*DORTMUND*
FO D E Till and crew

**15/16 Mar** *1715-0050*
*MISBURG*
FL F A Collins RCAF
Sgt K J Tamkin
FO C L Dalgetty RCAF
FO W A Smith RCAF
Sgt H C Cutler
Sgt W N Riley RCAF
Sgt W Millard RCAF

**16/17 Mar** *1720-0155*
*NÜRNBERG*
FO D K Sullivan
Sgt G Charlton
Sgt G A Atkinson
Sgt I A Heath
Sgt D Phillips
Sgt R Erskine
Sgt G F Chatterton

**19 Mar** *0030-0755*
*HANAU*
FO D K Sullivan and crew

**21 Mar** *0750-1205*
*BREMEN*
FO D E Till and crew

**22 Mar** *1120-1620*
*HILDESHEIM*
FO D E Till and crew

**27 Mar** *1450-1944*
*PADERBORN*
FO B Simpson
Sgt J Ellis (FE)
Sgt S J Hurford (BA)
FO T E Melocke (N)
Sgt R Ridley (WOP)
Sgt G A Perfect (MU)
Sgt C J Rabey (RG)

**31 Mar** *0630-1135*
*HAMBURG*
FO I L Scott
Sgt H W Batchelor (FE)
FO G R Cross

Sgt A F Marshall
Sgt S Hoskin
Sgt J A McDougall
Sgt C G Rayner

**3 Apr** *1321-1952*
*NORDHAUSEN*
FO B Simpson and crew

**10/11 Apr** *1815-0250*
*PLAUEN*
FO B Simpson and crew

**14/15 Apr** *1945-0058*
*CUXHAVEN*
FO J Everitt
FS J Kitchen
FS T Royle
Sgt B Gilbert
PO A Popp
Sgt A Johnson
Sgt A Ward

**18 Apr** *1006-1447*
*HELIGOLAND*
FO J C Hood
FS C F Lea (FE)
Sgt E A J Taylor (N)
Sgt R J Ashford (BA)
Sgt R A Lisk (WOP)
Sgt J W Harrow (MU)
Sgt W E Culshaw (RG)

**25 Apr** *0522-1324*
*BERCHTESGADEN*
FO B Simpson and crew

**29 Apr** *1147-1432*
*VALKENBURG AIRFIELD*
FO B Simpson and crew

**1 May** *1456-1806*
*MANNA – ROTTERDAM*
FO B Simpson and crew

**2 May** *1302-1548*
*MANNA – ROTTERDAM*
FO B Simpson and crew

**4 May** *1128-1422*
*MANNA – VALKENBURG*
FO B Simpson and crew

**7 May** *1217-1601*
*MANNA – ROTTERDAM*
WO F J Carter
Sgt C A Charman
Sgt J R Pratt
FS G M Roberts
Sgt J F Rowan
Sgt G D Cook
Sgt D F Inkpen

**8 May** *1205-1525*
*MANNA – ROTTERDAM*
FO B Simpson and crew

**Simpson flew an Exodus trip to
Brussels on 26 May**

# LM550
# BEER/LET'S HAVE ANOTHER

A Mark III with four Merlin 38s, LM550 was built by A V Roe at Yeadon, coming off the production line in early 1944 as part of order No.2010, being completed at Woodford. Sent to 166 Squadron at Kirmington, Lincolnshire, it was given the code letters AS and the individual letter 'B', thus becoming B for Beer. With this name, it is not surprising that the aircraft soon had a keg of beer painted on its nose and a beer mug being filled from its tap. Beneath this was a yellow heraldic scroll upon which was written 'Let's Have Another' in red. Below this came not rows of bomb symbols, but mugs of foaming ale – yellow ones for night sorties, white ones for day.

*Beer's* first pilot was Pilot Officer J F Dunlop RCAF who took her on the first seven ops, including two D-Day missions. James Dunlop recalled:

'The nose-artwork and slogan was designed by me and painted by one of the Kirmington ground crew. The barrel was brown with black hoops, the scroll yellow, with the words in red.

'Stan Parish, the mid-upper, flew 21 trips with us before becoming tour-expired, having flown 122 sorties in the Middle East and with us. We were in fact in the aircraft ready for our 20th op when a van pulled up and a stranger, parachute in hand, informed me that Stan was screened. I made some joke about it being tough luck but Stan made a remark about betting me a pound that he'd be back on ops before we finished.

'He then went off to gunnery school as an instructor. Then on our 30th and last trip, well-wishers were there to give us a send-off and Stan came back to wish us luck. On the return journey, coffee was served and this voice said, "Here's your coffee, Skipper – you owe me a pound!" It was Stan Parish, in best blue, no parachute or helmet. He had stowed away so he actually did 123 ops not 122 as the records show.

'We also had a photographer on a few trips,

Pilot Officer "Horse" Ashley, who in the beginning was reluctant to come along. Coming back from one sortie, Ashley lamented that he could have done a good job if I had put the aircraft where he wanted it. By this time we were close to the enemy coast when Cy Straw (RG) spotted another bomber stream on their way to another target. "Why don't we take old Horse in again?" said Cy. Everyone was in favour so I did a steep turn and back we went.

'This time we were light, with no bombs, so we could really manoeuvre well, and I was able to put the aircraft right where Horse wanted, even though this was a much hotter target with the flak really flying. We were late back, of course, and reported missing, but Horse got his pictures.'

Stan Parish was awarded the DFM, and the Base Commander wrote in support of the recommendation:

'Flight Sergeant Parish's courage, skill and determination in action have contributed largely to the success of his crew and have set a fine example to the other air gunners of the squadron. His splendid record and quiet but dogged determination is worthy of very high praise.'

On *Beer's* eighth sortie, but with another skipper, she was engaged by two Ju88 night fighters but

Beer mugs and a barrel signified LM550's insignia and raid tally, with the motto 'Let's Have Another'. The aircraft eventually had 118 mugs!

Bill Capper and some of his crew: Clockwise from top left: Capper, Graham Bale, Len Sparvell, Tom Morris and George Luckraft.

there was no damage to either side. *Beer's* first daylight – and the aircraft's first white mug – was not auspicious as she was hit by heavy flak over the target, but without serious damage. This was Stan Parish's last op, and he received a well earned DFM, for his sorties were not only a squadron record but it was thought possibly a group record too. His citation mentions only 101 ops in the Middle East and a further 12 with 166 Squadron, so 113 in total – but still a good number!

James Dunlop continued to fly *Beer*, completing his tour in the aircraft on 20 July 1944 to receive the DFC. In all he had flown the Lanc on 21 trips. He retired from the RCAF as a Colonel in 1974 and was later manager of Gimli Airport, Manitoba. Cy Straw, his rear gunner, also recalled some of their raids and the artwork origins:

'The artwork, I think, came about because of the Canadians' (we had three in the crew) love of "dirty black stuff" – the name they called a pint of mild. When we were allotted B-Beer, the idea of a beer barrel with pint glasses instead of bombs came naturally. It was painted on by one of the ground crew and one of the mugs had a swastika for a fighter kill. That happened with another crew when we were away on leave.

'On 5 June 1944 we went to Cherbourg to destroy large naval gun emplacements on the coast. We didn't know it was D-Day until returning over the Channel and seeing the huge armada of vessels launching the attack. We suffered heavy flak damage against Mimoyecques on 22 June, mostly to the tail area. The ammo ducts to the rear turret were damaged and the belts hit. Also a fragment went through the rear turret door and exited the top of the turret. I was the rear gunner and must have been leaning forward in that instance. The first I knew about it, apart from the noise, was a knocking on the turret doors. I seem to recall that it was our bomb aimer, Gordon Johnson. He told me the intercom was out. However, I could hear what was being said and was able to reply by using a signal light installed for just that purpose. The skipper was having trim problems and I could see damage to the tail fins.

'The official photographer flew with us to Caen on 7 July as well as before that date. I don't recall how many trips he flew with us. I do remember at Caen we flew over at low level – the second time – so that he could get more pictures. I remember seeing gun emplacements, wreckage on the beaches and our soldiers waving to us.'

Pilot Officer H S Schwass, a New Zealander, began to fly *Beer* in June and as Dunlop left, became the Lanc's regular skipper. On his second mission his gunners shot down a FW190 night fighter (4/5 July). Henry Schwass went on to complete 15 sorties in *Beer* and received the DFC when he became tour-expired in October. His rear gunner Gordon Reynolds won the DFM for shooting down the 190. Fellow New Zealander Norman Grant also received the DFC.

At the beginning of October 1944, 153 Squadron was formed (or more correctly re-formed) at Kirmington, taking aircraft and crews from 166 Squadron. LM550 was one, and re-coded P4-C. By this time she had 57 ops recorded and without a single abort due to mechanical failure. The same month the new squadron moved to Scampton and into 5 Group.

LM550 continued to keep a clean slate as far as mechanical problems were concerned, although the aircraft did became Cat AC on 14 October, returning to Avros for a refit, but was back by the 28th. Flying Officer W C "Bill" Capper RNZAF had started flying her in 166 Squadron and for a while he became the regular pilot in 153, flying 11 ops in all. Len Sparvell was the flight engineer:

A post-war reunion: George Luckraft, Tom Morris and Len Sparvell.

'What can I tell you about an aircraft that did 118 ops? When you think that 921 aircrew lost their lives on 166 Squadron alone in the two years 1943-45, it really shows you how lucky my crew and indeed LM550 was. Although we only did 11 trips in LM550 we completed our 30.

'However, LM550 wasn't so lucky for Len Nutt, our mid-upper, for when we returned from the Düren trip, he fell down the steps and broke his arm, so we had a different gunner for our last few ops. The nearest we came to trouble was when we returned from a fighter affiliation sortie on 22 November. One leg of the undercarriage wasn't showing down and locked. After trying it again and diving her up and down sharply several times, we were still unsuccessful and were told to take all emergency actions, which meant opening the upper escape hatches. This we did and they went sailing gracefully over the Lincolnshire countryside. The crew went to bracing positions leaving Bill Capper and myself to land at Scampton.

'Bill did a lovely job landing, touching down on the good leg of the undercarriage and hearing a click, took it the troublesome leg had come down; I am happy to say, it had. The engineering officer wasn't pleased at losing the escape hatches, even suggesting we should get on our bikes and find them!'

George Luckraft was the wireless operator, and he recalled:

'C-Charlie, LM550, was surely a charmed 'plane. It returned us safely from 11 raids on major German cities and in all survived 118 ops. We were twice coned by searchlights on the way to Düsseldorf and Bill had to dive the 'plane with a full bomb load; what a relief when she responded on being pulled out of the dive. Especially as another Lancaster ahead of us went into a dive and continued straight down into the ground and burst into a huge orange glow.

'Of all the ops we did, including those in LM550, we never had intercom failure caused by the diaphragms of the microphones freezing-up. Thanks to a WAAF at the parachute room who told me to go to the guard room and buy nine "French letters" [condoms], one for each crew member's oxygen mask, one for the spare mask – and another one for myself!!

'She showed me how to cut out a square of rubber from each one, which was then stretched over the diaphragm and the top of the microphone was screwed back on again. It then became moisture-proof and never became frozen-up.'

One of LM550's last regular skippers was Flying Officer H W Langford who took the aircraft on 15 raids (possibly including its 100th), plus one Exodus flight. He finished his tour of flying in July 1945, receiving the DFC. William remembered:

'The crew of which I was pilot, flew 17 operations between November 1944 and May 1945, the first being to Freiberg on 27 November. I have a photograph of "Charlie" taken just before setting out for Essen on 11/12 March 1945 (how is 12.3.45 for a date!). Since this was her 101st operation, we had "100 not out" chalked on her nose.

'I also have a record of a trip on 28 February, take-off 08.40, mission abandoned and landing back at 12.15, but it counted. I recall too bringing back the cookie from Nürnberg on 16 March, just couldn't get rid of it. That night 1 Group lost a number of aircraft, but we missed all the mayhem

LM550 on the morning of 13 March 1945, noting 100 ops 'not out', although the accuracy of the date is suspect. Standing, from left to right: FL J Trusler (passenger), FO B F Rea-Taylor, Sgt W D Thomson, FL H W Langford (pilot), FO D S McDonald, Sgt D W Hallam, Sgt K A Hawkins, Sgt T E Jones. In front, the stalwart ground crew.

having to go round a few times trying to unload it, thus coming home alone some time after the rest. "Charlie" was good for us.

'As for the beer mugs, these had been removed after her change of squadron and identity letter, but we had them restored towards the end of the war. There were 118, as far as I remember, at the end.

I was not at all surprised when, on the last operation of the war in Europe, to Berchtesgaden, the Squadron Commander took her, and she obliged him to turn back with some engine problem, the only time it happened. Although he was a first class man in all respects, it seemed she didn't like him.'

So when did LM550 reach 100 sorties? William Langford infers it was 8/9 March 1945 (the 101st occurred on 11 March). That means she went on to complete 122! Purely by counting the ops in the 541, the 100th should have come in late April. Her 101st would therefore have been the Berchtesgaden trip on a pure count. Then came four Manna and two Exodus trips, to bring the aircraft's total to 107. She is reputed to have flown 118 ops but as I have stated, this cannot be substantiated from the Forms 541. Only 108 can be found, but as both 166 and 153 Squadron records LM550 as flying on the night of 7 October 1944, this has to be reduced to 107. Perhaps someone added the supposed 57 ops with 166 and an equally supposed 51 with 153 and made it 118 instead of 108? Whichever – she still topped the 100 mark.

**1944**
**166 SQUADRON**

**21/22 May** *2220-0300*
*DUISBURG*
PO J F Dunlop RCAF
Sgt L O Stevinson (FE)
Sgt G R Johnson RCAF (BA)
Sgt R R Kerns (N)
Sgt N P Powell (WOP)
FS S A E Parish (MU)
Sgt C Straw (RG)

**22/23 May** *2220-0300*
*DORTMUND*
PO J F Dunlop and crew

**24/25 May** *2335-0420*
*AACHEN*
PO J F Dunlop and crew

**27/28 May** *2350-0435*
*AACHEN*
PO J F Dunlop and crew

**3/4 June** *2327-0250*
*BOULOGNE GUN*
PO J F Dunlop and crew

**5/6 June** *2105-0145*
*CHERBOURG GUN*
PO J F Dunlop and crew

**7 June** *0002-0420*
*ACHÈRES*
PO J F Dunlop and crew

**10/11 June** *2250-0410*
*ACHÈRES*
PO J McLaren
Sgt D R Summers
FO S T Broad
FO L H Ellerker
Sgt D F Paton
Sgt F J Collins
Sgt J T E Chalk RCAF
(two combats, no results)

**12/13 June** *2226-0251*
*GELSENKIRCHEN*
PO J F Dunlop and crew

**14/15 June** *2020-0005*
LE HAVRE
PO J F Dunlop and crew

**16/17 June** *2240-0315*
*STERKADE HOLTEN*
PO J F Dunlop and crew
PO W C Kuyser (2P)

**17/18 June** *2330-0400*
*AULNOYE*
PO J F Dunlop and crew
(abandoned by MB)

**22 June** *1400-1700*
*MIMOYECQUES*
PO J F Dunlop and crew
(damaged by heavy flak)

**25 June** *0120-0450*
*FLERS*
PO J F Dunlop and crew
FS D B W Gilbert in (MU),
Parrish tour expired

**28 June** *0115-0530*
*CHÂTEAU BERNAPRE*
PO J Double (DFC)
Sgt J Read
Sgt P Peck
FS E G Farrow
Sgt H D Kirkham
Sgt I E Onions
Sgt K R Dean

**29 June** *1145-1450*
*DOMLEGER – V1 SITE*
FO R L Graham
Sgt C Potter
Sgt R E Lakin
FO R W Bissonette RCAF
Sgt F A M Eade
Sgt J Wagstaff
Sgt W M G Falconer

**30 June** *0550-0935*
*OISEMONT*
PO H S Schwass RNZAF
Sgt P A Millett
Sgt D Angel
FO N J Grant RNZAF (N)
Sgt D J Carter
Sgt S J Padman RNZAF
Sgt G A Reynolds (RG)

**2 July** *1215-1555*
*DOMLEGER – V1 SITE*
FO R L Graham and crew

**4/5 July** *2155-0420*
*ORLÉANS M/YARDS*
PO H S Schwass and crew
(FW190 shot down)

**5/6 July** *2100-0525*
*DIJON*
PO J F Dunlop and crew

**6 July** *1845-2210*
*DIJON*
PO J F Dunlop and crew

**7 July** *1920-2315*
*CAEN*
PO J F Dunlop and crew
(slight flak damage)

**12/13 July** *2115-0644*
*RÉVIGNY*
PO J F Dunlop and crew

**14/15 July** *2125-0535*
*RÉVIGNY*
PO J F Dunlop and crew
(abandoned by MB)

**18 July** *0310-0745*
*CAEN – SANNEVILLE*
PO J F Dunlop and crew
plus PO Ashley (photographer)

**18/19 July** *2225-0310*
*SCHOLVEN*
PO J F Dunlop and crew

**20 July** *1905-2210*
*WIZERNES*
PO J F Dunlop and crew

**23/24 July** *2240-0325*
*KIEL*
PO H S Schwass and crew

**24/25 July** *2125-0605*
*STUTTGART*
PO H S Schwass and crew

**28/29 July** *2130-0540*
*STUTTGART*
PO H S Schwass and crew
FO W B J Sedgwick (2P)

**30 July** *0630-1024*
*CAHAGNES*
FO F E Elliott RCAF
Sgt J H Cromley RCAF (FE)
Sgt M L Oliphant RCAF (BA)
Sgt N W L Linton (N)
FO R B Melville RCAF (WOP)
Sgt G M Canning (MU)
FS K G Rhodes (RG)
(crashed 31 Aug; Melville,
Canning and Rhodes killed, the
others evaded)

**31 Aug** *1810-2145*
*LE HAVRE*
FO F E Elliott and crew

**1 Aug** *1845-2150*
*LA BELLE CROIX*
PO J G Davies
Sgt C L Caston
FO F Cameron
Sgt A Rollinson
Sgt W A Holt
Sgt L M Nutt
Sgt R Leigh
(abandoned by MB)
(lost 23/24 Sep, except Nutt
and Holt – not flying)

**2 Aug** *1650-2045*
*LE HAVRE*
FO F E Elliott and crew

**3 Aug** *1125-1615*
*TROSSY ST MAXIMIN*
FO F E Elliott and crew

**5 Aug** *1420-2255*
*PAUILLAC*
PO T Donnelly
Sgt C F Sadler
Sgt W Higgins
Sgt L C Sims
FS A S Dickson RAAF
Sgt R Neal
Sgt C Madden

**7/8 Aug** *2110-0115*
*FONTENAY*
PO W B J Sedgwick (DFC)
Sgt D C Finch
FO H Rempel RCAF
Sgt G Cann
Sgt A E Irvine
Sgt C Offord
Sgt J Fletcher

**10 Aug** *0925-1400*
*DUGNY*
PO H S Schwass and crew

**11 Aug** *1345-1725*
*DOUAI*
PO H S Schwass and crew

**12 Aug** *1120-1825*
*BORDEAUX*
FS K G Groves RAAF
Sgt E Clay
FS Selkirk RAAF
FS N D McDonnell RAAF
FS H B J Kirkby RAAF
FS W C Healy RAAF
FS W H J Foot RAAF

**13 Aug** *0016-0356*
*FALAISE*
PO J G Davies and crew

Sgts F E Forge and R B Ward,
and FS E J Sharpe in, Caston,
Holt and Nutt out

**15 Aug** *0955-1328*
*LE CULOT*
PO H S Schwass and crew

**18/19 Aug** *2215-0120*
*RIEME*
PO H S Schwass and crew
FS H W Cooper in (N),
Grant out

**25 Aug** *2005-0440*
*RÜSSELSHEIM*
PO H S Schwass and crew

**26/27 Aug** *2020-0115*
*KIEL*
PO H S Schwass and crew

**29/30 Aug** *2100-0600*
*STETTIN*
PO J G Davies and crew
FS P W Byers RAAF (WOP)
in, Sharpe out

**3 Sep** *1550-1850*
*GILZE-RIJEN AIRFIELD*
PO H S Schwass and crew

**5 Sep** *1555-1930*
*LE HAVRE*
PO H S Schwass and crew

**12/13 Sep** *1750-0125*
*FRANKFURT*
PO H S Schwass and crew

**16/17 Sep** *2145-0107*
*STEENWIJK AIRFIELD*
PO H S Schwass and crew

**23 Sep** *1855-2350*
*NEUSS*
FO A J E Laflamme RCAF
Sgt F Etherington (FE)
FO G J Monckton (BA)
FO G McArthur RCAF (N)
FS D H Schofield RCAF (WOP)
Sgt S Pollitt (MU)
Sgt F Toogood (RG)

**25 Sep** *0720-1040*
*CALAIS*
FO A J E Laflamme and crew

**26 Sep** *0955-1330*
*CALAIS*
FO A J E Laflamme and crew

**27 Sep** *0905-1215*
*CALAIS*
FO A J E Laflamme and crew

**3 Oct** *1250-1555*
*WESTKAPELLE*
FO W C Capper RNZAF
Sgt L W Sparvell (FE)
FS G B Beale RNZAF (BA)
FS T C Morris (N)
Sgt G Luckraft (WOP)
Sgt L M Nutt (MU)
Sgt J D Ramsey (RG)

**5/6 Oct** *1820-0100*
*SAARBRÜCKEN*
FO W C Capper and crew

## 153 SQUADRON

**7 Oct** *1140-1615*
*EMMERICH*
FO W C Capper and crew

**11 Oct** *1535-1810*
*FORT FREDERIK HENDRIK*
FO W Holman RCAF
Sgt S Martin

Sgt V S Reynolds RCAF
FO R C Taylor RCAF
Sgt H J Burton
Sgt E S Neil RCAF
Sgt A D Kall RCAF
(lost 20/21 Feb '45; Martin,
Burton and Neil killed, the
others all PoW)

**14 Oct** *0705-1135*
*DUISBURG*
PO J Searle
Sgt S Robinson
Sgt R P R Wavish
Sgt W Thomason
Sgt K G Hunt
Sgt W T Flavell
Sgt J Thomas

**28 Oct** *1335-1830*
*COLOGNE*
FO L M Taylor
Sgt J F Yearsley
FS J F Howe
Sgt A Allan
Sgt F S Thornton
Sgt S R Hurst
Sgt F G Hammacott

**30 Oct** *1745-2335*
*COLOGNE*
SL T W Rippingale DSO (DFC)
Sgt R C Taylor
FO H L Howling
FO H B Coxon
PO C I Edwards
Sgt D Lewington
Sgt W Craig

**31 Oct** *1800-2305*
*COLOGNE*
FP W C Capper and crew
PO P H Morris (2P)

**2 Nov** *1610-2130*
*DÜSSELDORF*
FO W C Capper and crew

**4 Nov** *1730-2240*
*BOCHUM*
FO W C Capper and crew

**6 Nov** *1150-1615*
*GELSENKIRCHEN*
FO W C Capper and crew
FL G E Dury (2P)

**9 Nov** *0820-1310*
*WANNE-EICKEL*
FO W C Capper and crew
FO E S Blackman (2P)

**16 Nov** *1310-1745*
*DÜREN*
FO W C Capper and crew

**18 Nov** *1545-2120*
*WANNE-EICKEL*
FO W C Capper and crew

**21 Nov** *1540-2220*
*ASCHAFFENBURG*
FL J P Holland
Sgt C H Beauchamp
FO E G Turner
Sgt R M Nattress
Sgt G Turner
FL T Burgoyne
FO C A Groves

**27 Nov** *1605-2315*
*FREIBERG*
FO H W Langford (DFC)
Sgt W D Thompson (FE)
FO B F Rea-Taylor (BA)
FO D S McDonald (N)
Sgt T W E Jones (WOP)
Sgt D W Hallam (MU)
Sgt K A Hawkins (RG)

# LM550 BEER/LET'S HAVE ANOTHER

The first crew to fly LM550 was captained by J F Dunlop. Forty years later four of them were photographed in front of an old wartime picture. From left to right: Gordon Johnson (BA), Jim Dunlop, Cy Straw (RG) and Casey Kerns (N).

**29 Nov** *1230-1725*
*DORTMUND*
FO W C Capper and crew

## 1945

**2 Jan** *1350-2330*
*NÜRNBERG*
FO G B Potter
Sgt G P Woolley
FO W H Thomas
FS J Boyle
FS J S Askew RAAF
Sgt D Smith
Sgt H J Hambrook

**4 Jan** *0220-0905*
*ROYAN*
FO K W Winder
Sgt D George
FO M A Smith RCAF
Sgt A K Rabin
Sgt R Evans
Sgt G B Hamilton RCAF
Sgt T O'Gorman

**7/8 Jan** *1805-0225*
*MUNICH*
FO G R Bishop RCAF (DFC)
Sgt J S B Syme (FE)
FO Z R Clerko RCAF (BA)
FO W A Jackson RCAF (N)
WO E W Lott RCAF
Sgt T F Bolak RCAF
FS R E Dash RCAF

**22 Jan** *1645-2225*
*DUISBURG*
FO H W Langford and crew

**28 Jan** *1925-2335*
*STUTTGART*
FO L A Wheeler
Sgt V P G Morandi
FO E C Durman RNZAF
FS E F Fish
WO W I A Turner RAAF

Sgt A Hodges
Sgt A Scott

**3 Feb** *1605-2200*
*BOTTROP*
FO H W Langford and crew

**8/9 Feb** *1910-0330*
*PÖLITZ*
FL W Holman and crew

**13/14 Feb** *2130-0740*
*DRESDEN*
FO K A Ayres (DFC)
Sgt W C Taylor (FE)
FO R Mains
FS R J McMinn (N)
FS D Head
Sgt R Wilson
Sgt R Cox
(all except Mains (PoW)
lost 12/13 March)

**21/22 Feb** *1940-0125*
*DUISBURG*
FO J Rhodes
Sgt M F Kingdom (FE)
FO D G Webb
FO P C H Clark (N)
FS J E Livick (WOP)
Sgt T J Bicknell
FS H Cuthbertson RCAF
(all lost 1 March)

**23 Feb** *1545-2350*
*PFORZHEIM*
FL A F McLarty RCAF
FS D Huddlestone
FO D S Crawford
FO J M Stevenson
Sgt J Calderbank
Sgt W Brear
Sgt C Peacock

**1 Mar** *1145-1805*
*MANNHEIM*
FL H W Langford and crew

**2 Mar** *0655-1220*
*COLOGNE*
FL H W Langford and crew

**8/9 Mar** *1700-0035*
*KASSEL*
FL H W Langford and crew

**11 Mar** *1130-1705*
*ESSEN*
FL H W Langford and crew
FL L A E Trusler (FE) in,
Rea-Taylor out

**12 Mar** *1255-1825*
*DORTMUND*
FL H W Langford and crew
Rea-Taylor back but FL
Trusler still in (for exp)

**13 Mar** *1720-2300*
*GELSENKIRCHEN*
FL H W Langford and crew

**15/16 Mar** *1700-0105*
*MISBURG*
FO V S Morton RCAF
Sgt D N Baker
Sgt N E Fenerty RCAF
FO J Essen RCAF
Sgt H C Hanwell
Sgt R Gray RCAF
Sgt J Weston

**16/17 Mar** *1720-0145*
*NÜRNBERG*
FL H W Langford and crew
Trusler out

**19 Mar** *0030-0815*
*HANNAU*
FS D W Veale RAAF
Sgt J H Harrison
FS L J Mountcastle
Sgt N Fraen
Sgt D S Stewart
Sgt T Keegan
Sgt F H Lloyd

**21 Mar** *0736-1222*
*BREMEN*
FL H W Langford and crew
Trusler back

**22 Mar** *1114-1642*
*HILDESHEIM*
FL H W Langford and crew

**3 Apr** *1312-1944*
*NORDHAUSEN*
FL J A McWilliams RCAF
FS J Howitt
Sgt H V Muddle
FO J F Arnoldi RCAF
FO E H Mulligan RCAF
FS W J Smith RCF
FO E Ruse RCAF
FS J W Stewart RCAF

**4/5 Apr** *2103-0518*
LUTZKENDORF
FL H W Langford and crew
PO J F Douglas (2P)

**9/10 Apr** *1916-0139*
*KIEL*
FL P H S Kilner
FS L O Spinks
Sgt G H Bridger
Sgt W G Corcoran
Sgt K P Barker
Sgt R S Mepstead
Sgt W A Pinkham

**10/11 Apr** *1829-0306*
*PLAUEN*
FL H W Langford and crew

**1 Apr** *0956-1433*
*HELIGOLAND*
FO J Searle and crew
Sgt J B Mitchell in,
Thomas out

**22 Apr** *1520-2012*
*BREMEN*
FL H W Langford and crew
(abandoned by MB)

**25 Apr** *0500-1159*
*BERCHTESGADEN*
WC G F Rodney DFC AFC
FS K H Dickson
FS V J Vaughan (BA)
FS F R C Melville
Sgt D T Davies
Sgt J Brady
FL J T G Weaver
(abandoned – std-inner
engine failed)

**29 Apr** *1140-1519*
*MANNA – THE HAGUE*
WO H Eckershall
Sgt E C Hawker
FO M Downes
FO W R Proctor RCAF
Sgt R J Taylor
Sgt N A J Webb
Sgt J Duffield

**2 May** *1243-1546*
*MANNA – ROTTERDAM*
WO E Eckershall and crew

**7 May** *1208-1532*
*MANNA – ROTTERDAM*
FL J A McWilliams and crew

**One Manna and two Exodus trips
made 8, 11 and 26 May**

# LM594
# A-ABLE

Built at Avros, Woodford, this Mark III Lancaster with Merlin 38 engines was produced in early 1944. In May it was assigned to A Flight of 576 Squadron at Elsham Wolds, Lincolnshire, and coded UI, with the individual identification letter $G^2$. This was later changed to $A^2$ (Able) in the summer. The previous two Lancasters marked $A^2$ were lost in July – LM532 on the 4th and PB253 on the 28th.

*Able* had an auspicious day on which to start operational life, Flying Officer V Moss taking the aircraft to Vire on the night of D-Day. One of *Able's* early pilots was the A Flight Commander, Squadron Leader B A

A-Able – LM594 – of 576 Squadron pictured after her 100th op.

Templeman-Rooke DFC – "Rookie" – who had been with 100 Squadron in 1943. He was awarded a Bar later in the year, and the DSO in March 1945, with a promotion to Wing Commander. In all he flew 64 ops, later adding an AFC to his impressive list of decorations. He died in July 2004.

"TR" as he was also known, was known for dropping empty beer bottles out over Germany once he discovered they made a haunting screech as they fell. With 576 Squadron he developed what he called his 'unorthodox tactics' – returning from raids at very low level in order to avoid night fighters and AA fire. In 1945 he took command of 170 Squadron.

By the summer, *Able's* regular skipper became Flight Sergeant Archibald D'Largy Grieg who would fly 18 trips in her before being commissioned and receiving the DFC. He was followed by Pilot Officer C F Phripp RCAF, who would fly 25 of his 32 sorties in *Able* before becoming tour-expired in January 1945, and also winning the DFC. He also flew two of the other Ton-Up Lancs, ME801 and LM227, while on the squadron, but not operationally. Frank Phripp recalled:

'Crews preferred to avoid "the old clapped out" aircraft and we were no exception, so how did we come to do most of our ops on old LM594 – and to grow to love her dearly? After our second op as a crew we were assigned a nearly new aircraft, $B^2$. Beginning with considerable delight we took it in five days on five practice flights and finally on one operation when we were heavily loaded, both engines on one side stopped dead just as we were lifting off the runway. Only the very fast action of Denis Cleaver, my flight engineer, and myself prevented catastrophe in a very dangerous situation – particularly on an op.

'In each case we were able to restart the engines and carry on normally for the rest of the flight – a very mystifying situation. Throughout those previous five days I was complaining bitterly to my flight commander asking for a different aircraft but we were constantly assured that the aircraft was OK. Following the frightening experience of the op. I flatly refused to fly that aircraft again.

'The central maintenance people finally accepted the situation as serious, disconnected and examined the inside of the main fuel line to the one side and found that the lining was separated and at full fuel flow conditions would lock across the line cutting all flow! We were assigned LM594: "A well proven aircraft," I believe were my flight commander's words. My request was granted and it took only a couple of ops for us to get to like reliable A$^2$.

'My gunners had considerable sport with night fighters and their warnings kept me very fit with the strenuous corkscrew exercise. I was always amazed that they apparently achieved hits on our attacker when they were undergoing such drastic manoeuvres. The Me163 encounter was of particular interest, especially later when I was test flying at Farnborough and we had a captured model, less rocket motor, on test. It was towed to altitude by a Spitfire and tested when gliding down like a brick.

'Our ground crew did a great job of keeping A$^2$ in good shape despite her age and aches and pains. I'm afraid I look back with a little guilt in that I took their good efforts as a given and only seldom thanked them. However, our Flight Engineer, "Ginger" Cleaver, was almost as much in the ground crew as the aircrew and spent many hours working along with them. As a result he knew the aircraft intimately and was always alert to every nuance of its operation.

'It was apparent to me at the time that the ground crew liked to have an aircrew regularly assigned to their aircraft. They were already possessive about the aircraft and grew somewhat that way about the aircrew as we persisted in returning and doing them the favour of bringing back their machine! Nevertheless they were very apprehensive of us not returning and guarded against too strong an attachment. An interesting bonus for the ground crew that came with each aircraft that completed many ops, was being spared from the change to a strange aircraft and new crew.'

Frank Phripp's reference to the Me163 concerned their raid on Zeitz-Troglitz – a synthetic-oil plant near

Frank Phripp and crew. From left, Bill Wilson, "Curly" Streatfield, Phripp, "Dusty" Poxon, 'Bonny' Norman, Keith Kerns, Dennis Cleaver.

Leipzig – on 16/17 January 1945. It was their last mission of their tour, but two jet fighters tried to make it a difficult one. *Able's* gunners succeeding in shooting down both, one being a Me163 rocket fighter, which was seen to go down and explode.

*Able's* last regular captain was Flying Officer I R Carter RAAF (DFC), he and his crew taking her on 15 trips. Her 100th sortie appears to have been a Manna trip in May 1945 and in all one can count 104 sorties, which includes five Manna and two Exodus missions.

After the war *Able* went to 1651 CU, then to 16 Ferry Unit, finally being Struck off Charge on 13 February 1947. One hundred bomb symbols appeared on *Able's* nose with what appears to be a walking figure in a striped jumper with the letter "A" on it, saluting and carrying a bomb.

Phripp (centre) with his crew and ground personnel.

Nürnberg, seen as the heart of the Nazi regime, was a hard target. This picture, taken in 1945, shows the tremendous destruction wrought by Bomber Command.

## 576 SQUADRON
### 1944

**6/7 June** *2220-0350*
*VIRE*
FO V Moss (DFC)
Sgt R A Robertson
FO R E Power RCAF
Sgt M G Callaghan
Sgt T E Sinton
Sgt R Stanton
Sgt V L Oatley

**10 June** *0010-0625*
*FLERS*
FO V Moss and crew

**12/13 June** *2230-0240*
*GELSENKIRCHEN*
SL B A Templeman-Rooke DFC
Sgt F N Ashton
FS S R Strand
FS W E Sollis
Sgt B G Holmes
Sgt J Boyd
Sgt F A West

**14/15 June** *2035-0055*
*LE HAVRE*
PO W R Ireland
Sgt F Davis
Sgt J P Broadey
Sgt J Southwell
Sgt W Logan
Sgt A Hubeman
Sgt G J Brain

**16/17 June** *2315-0415*
*STERKRADE*
PO J Archibald RNZAF
Sgt P J Cuthbert
FO P J Biolloi RCAF
Sgt J T Kearney
Sgt L Fielding
Sgt A Milne
WO R S Pyatt RCAF

**17/18 June** *2350-0420*
*AULNOYE*
PO A J Aldridge
Sgt A L Lewenden
Sgt A R Giles RAAF
Sgt R B Rennie
Sgt S Ormonroyd
Sgt N Costigan
Sgt M F Nelson

**22 June** *1410-1740*
*MIMOYECQUES*
PO J Archibald and crew

**23/24 June** *2205-0555*
*SAINTES*
PO J Archibald and crew

**27 June** *0135-0535*
*CHÂTEAUX BERNAPRE – V1*
PO J Archibald and crew

**29 June** *1155-1500*
*DOMLEGER – V1 SITE*
PO W R Ireland and crew

**2 July** *1209-1612*
*DOMLEGER – V1 SITE*
Flt Off R J Servis USAAF
Sgt A Balfour (FE)
Sgt J M Weir
Sgt J Coates
Sgt R T Garden RCAF
Sgt E Reed
Sgt R A Clark RCAF
(crashed in France 24/25
July; all safe but pilot lost)

**4/5 July** *2150-0335*
*ORLÉANS*
SL B A Templeman-Rooke
and crew

**5/6 July** *2055-0510*
*DIJON*
SL B A T-Rooke and crew

**7 July** *1910-2310*
*CAEN*
SL B A T-Rooke and crew

**12/13 July** *2100-0600*
*RÉVIGNY*
WC B D Sellick DFC* with
Templeman-Rooke's crew

**17 July** *0315-0710*
*SANDERVILLE*
SL B A T-Rooke and crew

**18/19 July** *2300-0305*
*SCHOLVEN BUER*
FL V Moss and crew

**20 July** *1850-2220*
*WIZERNES*
SL B A T-Rooke and crew

**23/24 July** *2235-0430*
*KIEL*
FO F H Watts RCAF
Sgt G Douglas
FO I G D Mills RCAF
FO R Hughes-Games (N)
Sgt M R Swallow
Sgt W S Clatworthy
Sgt D H Laing

**24/25 July** *2135-0545*
*STUTTGART*
SL B A T-Rooke and crew

**26 July** *0055-0420*
*BOIS DES JARDINS*
SL B A T-Rooke and crew

**28/29 July** *2130-0635*
*STUTTGART*
PO J B Bell
Sgt H C Gore
Sgt T E Seabrook
Sgt R Hughes
Sgt R E Badger
Sgt S G Parry
Sgt P Turton

**7/8 Aug** *2100-0110*
*FONTENAYE*
FS A D'L Grieg (DFC)
Sgt N Mason
FO J R Jones
FS G G Henville RAAF
Sgt S A Johnson
Sgt H Walton
Sgt J Thresh

**10 Aug** *0910-1420*
*DUGNY*
FS A D'L Grieg and crew

**11 Aug** *1400-1800*
*DOUAI*
FO C D Thieme
Sgt L G Playfoot
FO H S Ravenhill
Sgt H W Vine
FS O R Davison
Sgt J L Morgan
Sgt J O O'Shea

**12 Aug** *1125-1815*
*BORDEAUX*
FO C D Thieme and crew

**15 Aug** *0950-1320*
*LE CULOT*
FO C D Thieme and crew

**18/19 Aug** *2235-0155*
*RIEME*
FO C D Thieme and crew

**25/26 Aug** *2015-0520*
*RÜSSELSHEIM*
FO S F Durrant
Sgt R E Pearce
Sgt S J Brady RCAF
FO J Johnstone
FS J R McIntyre RAAF
Sgt J G Mackay RCAF
Sgt D Spowart
(all lost 23/24 Sep)

**26/27 Aug** *2020-0155*
*KIEL*
PO K L Trent (DFC)
Sgt A R Dunford (FE)
Sgt J N Wadsworth (BA)
Sgt H B Reynolds (N)
Sgt R L Skelton RAAF (WOP)
FO G C Riccomini (MU)
Sgt C Dalby (RG)

**29/30 Aug** *2145-0610*
*GARDENING – STETTIN*
FS A D'L Grieg and crew

**31 Aug** *1305-1645*
*AGENVILLE*
FS A D'L Grieg and crew

**3 Sep** *1530-1915*
*EINDHOVEN*
FS A D'L Grieg and crew

**5 Sep** *1615-1930*
*LE HAVRE*
FS A D'L Grieg and crew

**6 Sep** *1700-2030*
*LE HAVRE*
FS A D'L Grieg and crew

**8 Sep** *0615-1000*
*LE HAVRE*
FS A D'L Grieg and crew
(abandoned by MB – cloud)

**10 Sep** *1625-2015*
*LE HAVRE*
FS A D'L Grieg and crew

**12/13 Sep** *1830-0130*
*FRANKFURT*
FS A D'L Grieg and crew

**14/15 Sep** *2145-0635*
*GARDENING – PALLEAU*
FS A D'L Grieg and crew

**17 Sep** *0050-0440*
*LEUWARDEN AIRFIELD*
FO K F Mills
Sgt J Mills
Sgt A G Martin
FS G L McLean RAAF
FS R R Maxwell RAAF
Sgt W A Murray
Sgt D Massey

**17 Sep** *1620-1905*
*FLUSHING*
FS A D'L Grieg and crew

**20 Sep** *1450-1810*
*CALAIS*
FS A D'L Grieg and crew

**23 Sep** *1820-2325*
*NEUSS*
FS A D'L Grieg and crew

**24 Sep** *1610-2005*
*CALAIS*
PO C F Phripp RCAF
Sgt D K Cleaver (FE)
FO L A Poxon RCAF (BA)
Sgt K M Kerns RCAF (N)
Sgt W Wilson (WOP)

Sgt R E Streatfield (MU)
Sgt R Norman (RG)

**26 Sep** *c.0850-1220*
*CAP GRIS NEZ*
PO C F Phripp and crew

**27 Sep** *0905-1235*
*CALAIS*
PO C F Phripp and crew

**3 Oct** *1305-1610*
*WESTKAPELLE*
PO C F Phripp and crew

**5/6 Oct** *1830-0125*
*SAARBRÜCKEN*
PO C F Phripp and crew

**7 Oct** *1205-1615*
*EMMERICH*
PO C F Phripp and crew

**14 Oct** *0645-1055*
*DUISBURG*
PO C F Phripp and crew

**14/15 Oct** *2155-0355*
*DUISBURG*
PO C F Phripp and crew

**15 Oct** *1730-2205*
*WILHELMSHAVEN*
PO T C Dawson
Sgt W J Stockwell
Sgt E Gedling
Sgt J S M Shearing
Sgt A Stewart
Sgt G A Fergus
Sgt A G Murray

**19/20 Oct** *2115-0415*
*STUTTGART*
PO C F Phripp and crew

**26 Oct** *1720-2110*
*GARDENING – FRISIANS*
FO J J Mulrooney
Sgt B Beale
FO C W P Mortel RAAF
FS F J L Paton RAAF
WO J N Casey RAAF
FS F B McGrath RAAF
FS R S M Coventry RAAF

**27 Oct** *1310-1820*
*COLOGNE*
FO C A Rhude
Sgt J C Duncan
FO C D Goughnour
Sgt G F Fitzgerald
Sgt Blythe
Sgt G A Falleur
Sgt A G Murray

**29 Oct** *1130-1420*
*DOMBERG*
FO W A Stewart
Sgt W Boyle
Sgt A N Schuett RCAF
FO H R Stevenson RCAF
Sgt E A Dermont
Sgt L Thomas
Sgt J T Challenger

**30 Oct** *1720-2320*
*COLOGNE*
FO C F Phripp and crew

**2 Nov** *1630-2115*
*DÜSSELDORF*
FO C F Phripp and crew
(encounter with EA)

**4 Nov** *1720-2150*
*BOCHUM*
FO C F Phripp and crew

**6 Nov** *1155-1625*
*GELSENKIRCHEN*
FO C F Phripp and crew

**9 Nov** *0835-1245*
*WANNE-EICKEL*
FO C F Phripp and crew

**11 Nov** *1550-2100*
*DORTMUND*
FO C F Phripp and crew
(combat with FW190)

**16 Nov** *1250-1810*
*DÜREN*
FO H Benson
Sgt H Woolstenhulme
FO H G Mather
FO P C Milner
PO F Wilson
Sgt R C Griffiths
Sgt R Goldsbury

**18 Nov** *1540-2045*
*WANNE-EICKEL*
FO C F Phripp and crew

**27 Nov** *1610-2230*
*FREIBERG*
FO C F Phripp and crew

**29 Nov** *1210-1705*
*DORTMUND*
FO C F Phripp and crew

**4 Dec** *1635-2230*
*KARLSRUHE*
FO C F Phripp and crew

**6/7 Dec** *1635-0040*
*MERSEBURG*
FO C F Phripp and crew

**12 Dec** *1605-2205*
*ESSEN*
FO O R Halnan
Sgt W G Young
FO G T Shepherd RCAF
FO E N Weldon RCAF
Sgt F R Lait
Sgt H G C Farey RCAF
Sgt R H Gray

**28 Dec** *1530-2105*
*BONN*
FO F A Collins RCAF
Sgt K J Tamkin
FO G L Dalgetty RCAF
PO W A Smith RCAF
Sgt H C Cutler
Sgt W N Riley RCAF
Sgt W Millard RCAF

**29 Dec** *1515-2045*
*SCHOLVEN BUER*
FO C F Phripp and crew

**31 Dec** *1455-2100*
*OSTERFELD*
FO C T Dalzeill
Sgt P R Montgomery
Sgt W E Bradbury
Sgt W R May
Sgt A Burns
Sgt C T Thorley
Sgt D O'Sullivan

## 1945

**2 Jan** *1450-2300*
*NÜRNBERG*
FO C F Phripp and crew

**5 Jan** *0140-0845*
*ROYAN*
FO C F Phripp and crew
FS P E T Brookes in,
Poxon out

**7/8 Jan** *1855-0245*
*MUNICH*
FO C F Phripp and crew

**14/15 Jan** *1915-0315*
*MERSEBURG*
FO C F Phripp and crew
Poxon back

**16/17 Jan** *1730-0105*
*ZEITZ-TROGLITZ*
FO C F Phripp and crew
(last trip of tour; two jet
fighters engaged over tgt,
both shot down)

**2/3 Feb** *2130-0310*
*WIESBADEN*
FO I R Carter RAAF
Sgt D Mayer (FE)
FS C Townsend (BA)
Sgt S RE Overden (N)
FS H R Wilson RAAF (WOP)
Sgt F J Day (MU)
Sgt J E Davies (RG)

**3 Feb** *1618-2204*
*BOTTROP*
FO C T Dalzeill and crew

**8/9 Feb** *1910-0340*
*PÖLITZ*
FO R Carter and crew

**13/14 Feb** *2125-0540*
*DRESDEN*
FO R Carter and crew

**11 Mar** *1140-1655*
*ESSEN*
FL R M Crowther RCAF
FS J E Ryan RAAF (2P)
Sgt R F Wilshire
FS W Thorpe
FS H L Basson
FS B T Wilmot
FS B Rink RCAF
FS J R Scarfe RCAF
(Ryan lost 16/17 March)

**12 Mar** *1305-1830*
*DORTMUND*
FO R Carter and crew

**15/16 Mar** *1715-0050*
*MISBURG*
FO R Carter and crew

**16/17 Mar** *1715-0140*
*NÜRNBERG*
FO R Carter and crew

**19 Mar** *0110-0820*
*HANAU*
FS G A Abercrombie
Sgt R R Ewart
Sgt W Milburn
Sgt R J Gratton
Sgt V Serge
Sgt Weston
PO S H Braithwaite

**22 Mar** *1120-1630*
*HILDESHEIM*
FO R Carter and crew

**24 Mar** *1300-1810*
*DORTMUND*
FO R Carter and crew

**27 Mar** *1442-1933*
*PADERBORN*
FO R Carter and crew
Sgt D H Hogg (2P)

**31 Mar** *0614-1121*
*HAMBURG*
FO R Carter and crew

**3 Apr** *1323-2006*
*NORDHAUSEN*
Sgt D H Hogg
Sgt J R Reed (FE)

Sgt J W Forster (BA)
Sgt S Cranige (N)
Sgt J Tyrer (WOP)
Sgt W K Monksfield (MU)
Sgt H J Allen (RG)
(shot down 4/5 Apr; all
PoWs except Allen – KIA)

**4/5 Apr** *2113-0511*
*LUTZKENDORF*
FO R Carter and crew

**9/10 Apr** *1910-0131*
*KIEL*
FO R Carter and crew

**10/11 Apr** *1855-0225*
*PLAUEN*
FO R Carter and crew

**18 Apr** *0948-1421*
*HELIGOLAND*
FO R Carter and crew

**22/23 Apr** *1510-2004*
*BREMEN*
FO R Carter and crew

**25 Apr** *0526-1338*
*BERCHTESGADEN*
FO B Hinderks RCAF
Sgt J M Hallsmith
FO H McCarthy RCAF
FO C Porter RCAF
Sgt F White
Sgt J Hudson
Sgt D Currie RCAF

**29 Apr** *1149-1445*
*MANNA – VALKENBURG*
FO C A Titchener
Sgt W J Faulkner
Sgt A W Watson
Sgt F A Kesteron
Sgt P R Elkington
Sgt M V Jones
Sgt G W Somerville

**1 May** *1451-1742*
*MANNA – ROTTERDAM*
FO W N Holmes RCAF
Sgt D J Nimmo
FO F W Christisen RCAF
FO M K Scruton RCAF
Sgt W Brown
FS E C Grife RCAF
FS W W A Parsons RCAF

**3 May** *1020-1317*
*MANNA – VALKENBURG*
FL R W McCurdy RCAF
Sgt J Chisholm
FO W J Driscoll RCAF
FO G W Stevens RCAF
WO A G Little
Sgt J Nazarko RCAF
FS F A Parker RCAF

**4 May** *1134-1418*
*MANNA – VALKENBURG*
FL B H O'Neill RCAF
PO R J Durran
FO S W Haakstead RCAF
FS J G Ogilvie
FS F C Smith
PO A J W George RCAF
FS D Renchuk RCAF

**7 May** *1231-1546*
*MANNA – ROTTERDAM*
FO C A Titchener and crew

**Two Exodus trips flown 11 and
16 May by Titchener's crew**

# ME746
# ROGER SQUARED

ME746 reaches her 100th operation on 11 March 1945. Here the air and ground crews present the aircraft with a mock DSO, held between Harold Musselman DFC and Corporal Dennis Terry. Far right is the squadron CO, W/C J Vivian.

Produced at Metro Vickers, Manchester, as part of aircraft order No.2221, this Mark I Lancaster, fitted with four Merlin 24 engines, rolled out of Avro's works on 2 April 1944. The aircraft was assigned to 166 Squadron at Kirmington, Lincolnshire, on 14 April – just two weeks prior to the arrival of LM550, another 100-op veteran – and was given the same code of AS, and individual letter 'C', which was later changed to R². Gordon Rodwell DFM, who was Squadron Leader A S Caunt's bomb aimer, recalled:

'When ME746 arrived at Kirmington she was allocated to the flight commander, Stan Caunt. We air-tested it and then due to the un-serviceability of another aircraft it was "borrowed" the next night. It had the letters AS-C – Stan's initials – and was known simply as "Charlie".

'Stan finished his tour on 5 June and the headless crew was taken on by Wing Commander Garner and also lent to Wing Commander [D A] Reddick [DFC AFC], who worked at Group.'

David Reddick had previously commanded 101 Squadron.

Unlike LM550 with her beer barrel and beer-mug symbols, ME746 had nothing other than a steadily growing number of bombs on her nose, in neat rows of ten. The man who painted on all the bombs was Corporal Dennis Terry, the aircraft's fitter-airframes. He remembered painting on a DFC ribbon after H J Musselman was awarded this 'gong', and when the aircraft was itself 'awarded' the DSO after its 100th op, this was painted on too, by which time the aircraft had become R² – *Roger Squared*.

Harold Musselman and crew.

ME746's first operation was to Cologne on the night of 20/21 April, with Flight Sergeant F A Mander and crew. It was their only trip in this aircraft and they failed to return on 27 May, Fred Mander and crew being killed. ME746 then became the regular machine for Stan Caunt, who was to win the DFC, and the CO, Wing Commander Donald A Garner, who went on to win the DSO. Another pilot who was later to fly *Roger* early in his tour was Pilot Officer J F Dunlop, who was to fly LM550 B-Beer for most of the rest of his tour.

*Roger* operated on D-Day, against V1 sites and rail targets, on the Caen attack prior to the Allied break-out from the Normandy beach-head, and all the other summer raids that occupied Bomber Command. Flying Officer W C Hutchinson became another regular skipper during the summer, completing 18 trips and winning the DFC when his tour ended in August. Later ME746 flew on eight ops with Flight Lieutenant A P Gainsford DFC, a New Zealander (ex-150 Squadron).

ME746 collected the odd bit of flak damage and was even hit by fire from another Lancaster during a raid on Révigny on 12/13 July, but the Lanc was almost totally free of any mechanical problems and soon its total of ops rose towards the 100 mark. Her regular skipper by then had become Flying Officer Harold Musselman RCAF, who received an Immediate DFC in January 1945. His citation gives the story:

'In December 1944, this officer was pilot and captain of an aircraft detailed to attack an enemy target [29th – Scholven/Buer oil refinery]. On the outward flight the starboard-inner engine failed. Despite the loss of engine power, Flying Officer Musselman continued his flight. Some time later the port-outer engine became defective. Nevertheless, this resolute pilot went on to attack a target [Duisburg] at a lower level than planned. Much anti-aircraft was directed at his aircraft which sustained damage but Flying Officer Musselman flew it back to base. Although beset by many difficulties this officer was fully determined to make his mission a success. He set a very fine example.'

*Roger* had also been hit by AA fire in the starboard wing-flap and main-plane; the second engine had suffered an oil leak. The flight engineer, Sergeant James Ronald Coghill received the DFM for his efforts with the engines on this night, which had made the sortie a success. The latter part of his citation records the events on another raid:

'A further incidence of this NCO's ability was given on the night of 1st February 1945, when he was detailed to take part in an attack on Ludwigshaven. On route to the target, engine trouble developed and one engine had to be feathered, but so complete was the Captain's confidence in his Flight Engineer that it was decided to press on and a successful attack was delivered, again largely owing to Sergeant Coghill's skilful handling of his engines. It is significant to note that, no matter how heavy the opposition encountered over enemy territory Sergeant Coghill, with complete disregard for his personal safety, has calmly carried on with his task and has always discharged his duties with conspicuous success.'

*Roger* began showing her age in the new year. A raid on 22 January had to be abandoned as smoke from a fire filled the machine although nobody found where it came from. Then on 13 February the aircraft had to turn back due to almost total instrument failure. On a trip to Kassel on 8 March 1945 *Roger* had an inconclusive scrap with a night fighter, and the next sortie was the 100th op. This occurred on 11 March, a daylight to Essen with Musselman in command. Again Dennis Terry remembers

this event, as Musselman proceeded to beat-up the control tower at Kirmington upon his return. Terry and Corporal Sid Woodcock, ME746's engine fitter, cycled like mad to the airfield to see it, getting there just in time to watch the final low-level fly-by.

Pilot Officer S Todd was ME746's final more regular captain, taking the Lanc on 11 raids and five Manna trips. In all ME746 is supposed to have flown 116 operational sorties, but it also flew six Manna and three Exodus flights, so a possible 124 in all.

The aircraft continued to serve with the squadron until 3 September 1945 at which time it became Cat AC and went back to Avros for repair and overhaul. *Roger* returned to 166 on 22 September but when the squadron disbanded the Lanc moved to 103 Squadron on 12 November, then to 57 Squadron two weeks later. On 29 December it was on the strength of RAF Lindholme and on 21 February 1946 the aircraft was sold for scrap to Hestons Ltd, and Struck off Charge.

## 166 SQUADRON
## 1944

**20/21 Apr** *2340-0415*
COLOGNE
FS F A Mander
Sgt H J Evans (FE)
FS G J Overand RCAF (BA)
Sgt V L J Newall (N)
FS O P McFadden RCAF (WOP)
FO B A White (MU)
WO H Shaw (RG)
(all lost 27 May)

**22/23 Apr** *2230-0350*
DÜSSELDORF
SL A S Caunt (DFC)
Sgt D J Baveystock (FE) (DFM)
FO B L Thomson RAAF (N) (DFC)
FS G G H Rodwell (BA) (DFM)
FS E Ridout (WOP) (DFM)
Sgt A R Williamson (MU)
FS L Wayte (RG) (DFM)

**24/25 Apr** *2205-0510*
KARLSRUHE
SL A S Caunt and crew
FO C Squire in, Williamson out

**27/28 Apr** *2125-0555*
FRIEDRICHSHAFEN
PO J F Dunlop RCAF
Sgt L D Stevinson (FE)
Sgt G R Johnson RCAF (BA)
Sgt R R Kerns RCAF (N)
Sgt N P Powell (WOP)
Sgt C Straw (MU)
FS S A E Parrish (RG) (DFM)

**30 Apr/1 May** *2130-0210*
MAINTENON
PO J F Dunlop and crew

**3/4 May** *2155-0325*
MAILLY-LE-CAMP
WC D A Garner (DSO) with
SL Caunt's crew;
Sgt L V Robins (MU)

**9/10 May** *2240-0130*
MARDYCK
PO J F Dunlop and crew

**11/12 May** *2200-0120*
HASSELT
PO J F Dunlop and crew

**19 May** *2210-0305*
ORLÉANS
PO J F Dunlop and crew
PO H A Brown (WOP)

**21/22 May** *2235-0255*
DUISBURG
WC D A Garner and
Caunt's crew;
FL T R Danby DFC (MU)

**22/23 May** *2220-0255*
DORTMUND
SL A S Caunt and crew
Sgt A G Manuel DFM (MU)

**24/25 May** *2345-0435*
AACHEN
FO W I Warmington (DFC)
Sgt E Askey
FS G S Gissing RAAF
FO J A Clark (DFC)
Sgt D Oakley
Sgt O W Sansby
Sgt H Peterson RCAF

**3/4 June** *2332-0245*
BOULOGNE
WC D A Garner and crew
FS P Robins (MU)

**5/6 June** *2110-0150*
CHERBOURG
SL A S Caunt and crew
Sgt G L Nordbye RCAF (MU)

**7 June** *0005-0500*
ACHÈRES
FO R L Graham (DFC)
Sgt G Potter
Sgt R E Lakin

FO R W Bissonette RCAF
Sgt F A M Eade
Sgt J Wagstaff
Sgt W M G Falconer

**10/11 June** *2255-0400*
ACHÈRES
FO W I Warmington and crew

**12/13 June** *2231-0316*
GELSENKIRCHEN
FO W C Hutchinson (DFC)
Sgt N Harris (FE)
FS H R Heaton RCAF (BA)
WO A T Mathews RCAF (N)
Sgt E A Lummins (WOP)
Sgt R B Parry (MU)
Sgt D G Prescott (RG)

**14 June** *2015-2355*
LE HAVRE
WC D A Garner and crew
Sgt F Watson (MU)

**17/18 June** *2340-0440*
AULNOYE
FO R L Graham and crew
(abandoned, tgt not identified)

**22 June** *1410-1725*
MIMOYECQUES – V1 SITE
FO W C Hutchinson and crew

**23/24 June** *2210-0520*
SAINTES
FO W C Hutchinson and crew

**24 June** *0130-0500*
FLERS – V1 SITE
FO W C Hutchinson and crew

**28 June** *0130-0500*
CHÂTEAU BERNAPRE – V1
FO W C Hutchinson and crew

**29 June** *1140-1505*
DOMLEGER – V1 SITE
FO W C Hutchinson and crew

**30 June** *0600-0945*
OISEMONT – V1 SITE
FO W C Hutchinson and crew

**2 July** *1210-1540*
DOMLEGER – V1 SITE
WC D A Garner and crew

**4/5 July** *2150-0410*
ORLÉANS M/YARDS
FO W C Hutchinson and crew

**5/6 July** *2105-0550*
DIJON
FO W C Hutchinson and crew

**6 July** *1855-2230*
FORÊT DU CROC
PO D J Dickie RNZAF (DFC)
Sgt W L McDonald (FE)
FO E R Pickering
FO J Mason (N)
Sgt K E Corbutt
Sgt R Turner
Sgt S L Giles

**7 July** *1925-2345*
CAEN
FO W C Hutchinson and crew

**12/13 July** *2125-0625*
RÉVIGNY
FO W C Hutchinson and crew
(abandoned over tgt – damaged
by another Lancaster)

**14/15 July** *2115-0535*
RÉVIGNY
FO W C Hutchinson and crew
(abandoned by MB over tgt)

**18 July** *0315-0715*
SANNEVILLE
FO W C Hutchinson and crew
Sgt D G Hutchinson in (MU)

**18/19 July** *2235-0320*
SCHOLVEN
PO D J Dickie and crew

PO S Todd and crew with ME746 at the war's end. The two ground crew on the left are Corporals Dennis Terry and Sid Woodcock. The aircraft now sports DSO and DFC ribbons atop the first column of bombs, with another 25 on the right.

**20 July** *1910-2220*
*WIZERNES*
WC D A Garner and crew
FL J Barritt (MU)

**23/24 July** *2240-0330*
*KIEL*
FS R W Miller RCAF
Sgt W A Adams
FO D W Harding
FO E A F Hall
Sgt A H MacDonald
Sgt J R Scott RCAF
Sgt C A Pike RCAF

**24/25 July** *2120-0555*
*STUTTGART*
FS R W Miller and crew
Sgt Schafer RCAF (MU)

**25/26 July** *2115-0540*
*STUTTGART*
FO W C Hutchinson and crew

**26/27 July** *2310-0330*
*GARDENING – HELIGOLAND*
FO W C Hutchinson and crew

**28/29 July** *2120-0545*
*STUTTGART*
FO W C Hutchinson and crew

**30 July** *0635-1010*
*CAHAGNES*
FO W C Hutchinson and crew

**31 July** *1825-2120*
*LE HAVRE*
FO W C Hutchinson and crew

**1 Aug** *1850-2145*
*LA BELLE CROIX – V1 SITE*
FO F D Elliott
Sgt J H Comley
Sgt M L Oliphant

Sgt N W L Linton
FO R B Melville
Sgt G M Canning
Sgt K G Rhodes
(abandoned by MB)

**2 Aug** *1650-2020*
*LE HAVRE*
WC D A Garner and crew
Sgt A R Williamson (MU)
(Williamson KIFA 12 Oct)
(aircraft damaged by flak)

**4 Aug** *1245-2140*
*PAUILLAC*
FL A P Gainsford DFC (RNZAF)
FO F G Kitson
FS J E F Rowe
FS W R Williams RAAF
FS F E Bennett
FO H G Cook RCAF
Sgt G H Davidson RCAF

**5 Aug** *1425-2210*
*PAUILLAC*
PO A G S Watkins
Sgt I M Morganstein (FE)
Sgt D M Barr (BA)
Sgt H G Carson RCAF (N)
Sgt A P Maitland (WOP)
Sgt F D McCohan RCAF (MU)
Sgt F W Walker (RG)
(both AGs PoW 13 Sept, rest
were killed)

**7/8 Aug** *2105-0125*
*FONTENAY*
FL A P Gainsford and crew

**10 Aug** *0930-1430*
*DUGNY*
FO W L Shirley RNZAF
Sgt O O Evans
Sgt G B McFee RCAF

FO F D Hill
FS C J Mitchell RAAF
Sgt N W Sykes
PO C J Bush

**11 Aug** *1345-1735*
*DOUAI*
WC D A Reddick DFC AFC
with Garner's crew
(Reddick from 101 GP HQ)

**14 Aug** *1315-1719*
*Fontaine-le-Pin*
FS A G Graves RAAF
Sgt E Clay RAAF
FS Selkirk RAAF
FS N D McDonnell RAAF
FS H B J Kirkby RAAF
FS W C Healy RAAF
FS W H J Foot

**15 Aug** *0950-1350*
*LE CULOT*
FL A P Gainsford and crew

**17 Aug** *2055-0455*
*STETTIN*
FL A P Gainsford and crew

**25/26 Aug** *2005-0500*
*RÜSSELSHEIM*
FL A P Gainsford and crew

**26/27 Aug** *2010-0140*
*KIEL*
FL A P Gainsford and crew

**29/30 Aug** *2100-0605*
*STETTIN*
FL A P Gainsford and crew

**31 Aug** *1315-1645*
*AGENVILLE*
FL A P Gainsford and crew

**3 Sep** *1550-1950*
*GILZE-RIJEN AIRFIELD*
FO J G Davies
Sgt C L Caston
FO F Cameron
Sgt A Rollinson
Sgt G B Bawley
Sgt R B Ward
Sgt R Leigh

**20 Sep** *1520-1850*
*SANGATTE GUN*
WC D A Garner and crew

**25 Sep** *0710-1155*
*CALAIS*
FL A E Jones
Sgt J L James
Sgt C L Cullen
FS J J L McDonell RAAF
Sgt D L Williams
Sgt R V Trafford
Sgt A Simpson
(abandoned over tgt)

**27 Sep** *0905-1230*
*CALAIS*
FL A E Jones and crew

**5 Oct** *1310-1445*
*SAARBRÜCKEN*
FL A E Jones and crew

**11 Oct** *1445-1805*
*FORT FREDERIK HENDRIK*
FO J A Sherry RCAF
Sgt A Martin (FE)
FO D M Bennett RCAF (BA)
FO M Bernyk RCAF (N)
Sgt K Surman (WOP)
Sgt C Young RCAF (MU)
Sgt J C Daze RCAF (RG)
(abandoned over tgt by MB)
(all lost 31 Dec 1944)

**14 Oct** *0625-1110*
*DUISBURG*
PO N Appleton (DFC)
Sgt J W Lackie
FS R J Taylor
FO D N Bain
FS W L Ball
FS L J Denney
FS B H Cook

**19/20 Oct** *1700-0035*
*STUTTGART*
FO W B J Sedgdwick
FO W A J Underwood (DFC) (2P)
Sgt D C Finch
FO H Rempel RCAF
Sgt G Cann (N)
Sgt A E Irving
FS J Rees
FS H I Scott RCAF

**4 Nov** *1730-2320*
*BOCHUM*
FO D G Stuart (DFC)
Sgt L M Christie
Sgt K M Wilding
FO W H Ford RCAF
Sgt B Robinson
FO M D Woods RCAF
Sgt J E Horner

**6 Nov** *1150-1625*
*GELSENKIRCHEN*
FO E P Burke RAAF
Sgt T E Carr (FE)
FS J M Meggitt RAAF
Sgt A K E John (N)
FS G W Kirk (WOP)
Sgt G Anson (MU)
Sgt T R Wood (RG)
(Burke and Carr KIA 16/17
Jan '45 – rest all PoWs)

**9 Nov** *0750-1310*
*WANNE-EICKEL*
FO J C Parry RCAF
Sgt E W Ball
Sgt L O Kirton RCAF
Sgt C G J Mason
Sgt F R Cole RCAF
Sgt D G Peggs RCAF
Sgt D W Morrow RCAF

**11 Nov** *1600-2140*
*DORTMUND*
FO H J Musselman RCAF
Sgt J R Coghill (FE)
Sgt F Reid (BA)
FS H W Park RCAF (N)
Sgt R Williamson (WOP)
FS J M Donnelly RCAF (MU)
FS K Forrest RCAF (RG)

**16 Nov** *1230-1755*
*DÜREN*
FO H J Musselman and crew

**18 Nov** *1550-2230*
*WANNE-EICKEL*
FO H J Musselman and crew

**21 Nov** *1545-2200*
*ASCHAFFENBURG*
FO H J Musselman and crew

**27 Nov** *1600-2310*
*FREIBERG*
FO H J Musselman and crew

**29 Nov** *1155-1735*
*DORTMUND*
FS R N Dickson RCAF
Sgt D Ball
FS R C Caswell RCAF
FO D S Derbecker RCAF
Sgt R Gregg RCAF
Sgt H E Barker RCAF
Sgt D M Williams RCAF

**4 Dec** *1625-2305*
*KARLSRUHE*
FO J C Parry and crew

**6/7 Dec** *1635-0105*
*MERSEBURG-LEUNA*
FO H J Musselman and crew

**12 Dec** *1550-2200*
*ESSEN*
FO H J Musselman and crew
Sgt Mulcaster in (FE)

**17 Dec** *1515-2305*
*ULM*
PO R D Ritchie (DFC)
Sgt F O Mulcaster
FO J E Walker RCAF (BA)
FO M D Greene RCAF
Sgt S O Badcock
Sgt J E Anderson RCAF
Sgt L E Dunlop RCAF

**24 Dec** *1450-2045*
*COLOGNE*
FO H J Musselman and crew
Sgt J Perry in (FE)

**27 Dec** *1205-1715*
*RHEYDT*
FO E P Burke and crew

**28 Dec** *1545-2110*
*MÜNCHEN-GLADBACH*
FO H J Musselman and crew
Coghill back
(Std inner failed and flak dam)

## 1945

**7/8 Jan** *1830-0305*
*MUNICH*
FO H J Musselman and crew

**14/15 Jan** *1850-0340*
*MERSEBURG-LEUNA*
FL J Glenesk RCAF (DFC)
Sgt G G Anderton
FO W H Couch RCAF
FO D E Junker RCAF
Sgt D H Fenwick
FO J N West RCAF
FO C Mizzen RCAF (DFC)

**16/17 Jan** *1730-0150*
*ZEITZ*
FL J Glenesk and crew

**22 Jan** *1650-2010*
*DUISBURG*
FO H J Musselman and crew
(abandoned – fire on board)

**1 Feb** *1540-2220*
*LUDWIGSHAVEN*
FO H J Musselman and crew

**2/3 Feb** *2015-0250*
*WIESBADEN*
FO H J Musselman and crew

**3 Feb** *1630-2135*
*BOTTROP*
FO H J Musselman and crew

**7 Feb** *1900-2400*
*KLEVE*
FO H J Musselman and crew

**8/9 Feb** *1940-0325*
*PÖLITZ*
FO H J Musselman and crew

**13/14 Feb** *2125-2400*
*DRESDEN*
FL H J Musselman and crew
(abandoned – instrument failure)

**14/15 Feb** *1955-0445*
CHEMNITZ
FL H J Musselman and crew
PO S Todd RCAF (2P)

**20/21 Feb** *2135-0345*
*DORTMUND*
FL H J Musselman and crew

**21/22 Feb** *1940-0215*
*DUISBURG*
FO E J Jenkins
Sgt S Appleby
Sgt D S Struthers
Sgt R J Khoo
Sgt R Bradley
Sgt J W Inman RCAF
Sgt E J Hammond

**23 Feb** *1540-2350*
*PFORZHEIM*
FO E J Jenkins and crew

**1 Mar** *1145-1805*
*MANNHEIM*
FL H J Musselman and crew

**2 Mar** *c.0700-1215*
*COLOGNE*
FL H J Musselman and crew

**5/6 Mar** *1610-0215*
*CHEMNITZ*
FL H J Musselman and crew

**7/8 Mar** *1645-0215*
*DESSAU*
FL H J Musselman and crew

**8/9 Mar** *1700-0035*
*KASSEL*
FL H J Musselman and crew

**11 Mar** *1125-1655*
*ESSEN*
FL H J Musselman and crew

**12 Mar** *1250-1825*
*DORTMUND*
FL H J Musselman and crew

**13 Mar** *1720-2255*
*ERIN (Oil)*
FL H J Musselman and crew

**16/17 Mar** *1715-0210*
*NÜRNBERG*
PO S Todd RCAF
Sgt W A Hall (FE)
Sgt J Connell (N)
FO C N Dumbelton (BA)
Sgt J G Brame (WOP)
Sgt J M Torris
Sgt R L Edwards

**19 Mar** *0040-0805*
*HANAU*
PO S Todd and crew

**21 Mar** *0740-1230*
*BREMEN*
PO S Todd and crew
Sgt S Pryce in, Torris out

**22 Mar** *1120-1640*
*HILDESHEIM*
PO S Todd and crew

**24 Mar** *1255-1830*
*HARPENERWEG*
FS J L Briggs
Sgt J Christie
Sgt R A Fraser
Sgt K W Fortune
Sgt G A Cearns
Sgt F Tucker
Sgt S Pryce

**25 Mar** *0630-1225*
HANNOVER
PO S Todd and crew

**27 Mar** *1445-1945*
PADERBORN
FS E Farrington
Sgt J Nimmo (FE)
Sgt J C Roberts (BA)
Sgt S F Allen (N)
Sgt L P Carter (WOP)
Sgt G W W Goodyear
Sgt A N Peacock

**31 Mar** *0626-1145*
*HAMBURG*
FS E Farrington and crew

**3 Apr** *1312-2009*
*NORDHAUSEN*
FS T C Anderson RCAF
FS G R Cockerwill
FO A T McCulloch RCAF
Sgt R A Ruttan
Sgt D C Smith
Sgt H Pearce RCAF
Sgt T W Stevenson RCAF

**4/5 Apr** *2108-0526*
*LUTZENDORF*
FS N J Fletcher RAAF
Sgt W A Hall
Sgt L W J Parsons
FS W M Wilson
Sgt R B Berry
Sgt R N Thompson
Sgt A D Kerr

**9/10 Apr** *1933-0118*
*KIEL*
PO S Todd and crew

**10/11 Apr** *1812-0253*
*PLAUEN*
PO S Todd and crew

**18 Apr** *1022-1446*
*HELIGOLAND*
PO S Todd and crew

**22 Apr** *1507-2019*
*BREMEN*
PO S Todd and crew
(abandoned by MB over tgt)

**25 Apr** *0522-1328*
*BERCHTESGADEN*
PO S Todd and crew

**29 Apr** *1210-1458*
*MANNA*
PO S Todd and crew

**30 Apr** *1600-1900*
*MANNA*
FS T C Anderson and crew

**1 May** *1345-1704*
*MANNA*
PO S Todd and crew

**2 May** *1210-1501*
*MANNA*
PO S Todd and crew

**3 May** *1122-1420*
*MANNA*
PO S Todd and crew

**7 May** *1231-1606*
*MANNA*
PO S Todd and crew

**Three Exodus trips 10,11 and
26 May 1945**

# ME758
# NAN

Just twelve aircraft on from ME746, another 100-plus veteran, this Lancaster came off the production line at Metro Vickers with four Merlin 28 engines, also as a Mark I, in early 1944. Assigned to 12 Squadron at Wickenby, Lincolnshire, it was given the squadron code of PH and its individual letter N for Nan.

*Nan* began operations with Pilot Officer N Rollin and his crew with a raid to Lyons on 1/2 May, who then flew five more missions in her before they went off to join 156 Squadron of the PFF, where they were to fly some ops in another centenarian featured in this book – ND875.

Like most aircraft, ME758 had the usual variety of crews in the first few weeks on the squadron. With one skippered by Pilot Officer L Pappas RCF, it had a fight with a Me109 night fighter which her gunners shot down during a raid on Tergnier on 31 May/1 June. As it happened, Len Pappas and crew had another fight exactly one month later and shot down a second night fighter (Ju88), for which he received the DFC and his rear gunner, Sergeant Berthan Carl Swanson RCAF, the DFM – although this action was in another Lancaster.

After the Tergnier show, Sergeant G F Holbrook (later commissioned) and crew took over *Nan* and flew her on 25 ops. George Holbrook became tour-expired in September and received the DFC. His navigator, Alan Witty, also received the DFC and remembers:

'I flew in *Nan* on 25 ops of my tour out of her first 47. She was lucky to survive the tour, never mind the sixty after our time with her. On our 22nd op, *Nan's* 37th, on 24/25 July, we returned all the way from Stuttgart on three engines after being airborne for eight hours, 40 minutes.

'Then on 3 August we took part in a daylight attack on the flying bomb storage depot at Trossy St Maximin, where we had the undivided attention of the German flak in broad daylight at 11,000 feet on what seemed an unending run-in to the target. This happened because the main body of the "gaggle" cut the corner at the previous turning

G F Holbrook and crew, May 1944, who took ME758 on 25 ops during their tour. Standing: Jock Payner, Tom Gibb, Ron Witty, Stan Swaine; in front: Tom Crook, Fred Holbrook, Johnny Squires.

point of the route (Compiègne) and left us miles behind.

'We were extremely fortunate to survive, our aircraft suffering extensive flak damage amounting to 50-60 holes and one engine out of action. Two of the crew, the bomb aimer and the flight engineer, received minor injuries for which they received wound stripes as souvenirs. They thought it was worth it to show them off! We made the return journey on three engines and *Nan* was out of service for nine days. We went on leave.'

Alan Witty also recalls that their flight engineer – Squires – was well over 40 years-old having been a regular army officer but too old to take part in WW2. He reduced his age by ten years and joined the RAF, completing two operational tours!

There followed another period during which *Nan* had no regular crews, although Flying Officers E King, K T Wallace RCAF and Colin H Henry (DFC) RNZAF, flew her

The presentation of mock DSO and DFC to *Nan* (ME758) of 12 Squadron at Wickenby in April 1945. The bomb tally shows 106 trips, plus one swastika and two searchlights shot out. In the centre is Squadron CO WC Maurice Stockdale DFC and to his left, SL P Huggins, OC B Flight.

more often than not. Ken Wallace later flew with 156 Squadron PFF where he piloted ND875 as well and won the DFC.

*Nan* was almost totally free of mechanical problems, although towards the end of her career her starboard-outer engine caught fire on 2 February 1945 and the raid had to be abandoned. This was Flight Lieutenant W Kroeker RCAF's crew. This crew had flown 16 ops when lost on 4 April. Six of them had spent some months in Sweden having had to crash land there in January 1944. They had finally got back to the squadron in September.

Otherwise, *Nan* did all the usual trips during the last year of the war, including D-Day, Caen, V1 sites, and the raid on Dresden on 13/14 February 1945. Flying Officer Arthur J D Leach became a regular captain with *Nan* in 1945, flying 16 times in her and winning the DFC. However, it was Flying Officer E M Baird RCAF who took *Nan* on her 100th operation, a mining sortie off Oslo on

22/23 March, then flew her just once more. Ernest McNea Baird later received the DFC. Seven ops later, then Manna trips began at the end of April. *Nan* flew six such sorties plus two Exodus flights, so in all 108 bombing ops plus these eight to make a total of 116 ops.

When *Nan* had reached 106, on 18 April, someone must have realised what this bomber and her crews had achieved, for there was a ceremony to present her with both the DSO and DFC, mock medals and ribbons being made and hung from the cockpit window ledge (see above). Beneath them were the 106 painted bomb symbols, ten rows of them, with another 'block' being started with the other six. Above them was the swastika, representing the Me109 destroyed before the invasion, and two searchlight beams to show the two occasions on which she had been coned over Germany but had managed to escape. A press release dated 20 April noted:

'Today [sic] N-Nan completed 106 successful operations against the enemy in the service of B Flight, 12 Squadron. One enemy fighter has been shot down by her crews and she has been coned by enemy searchlights on two occasions. Already *Nan* has dropped over a million pounds of bombs. For the outstanding achievement in the history of 12 Squadron, *Nan* was presented with the token DSO and DFC.'

W/C Maurice Stockdale DFC presenting *Nan* with her two 'gongs'.

Like some of the other 100-op Lancs there could have been a slight mix-up in this particular bombing log. It had red bombs for night and yellow for day raids, and clearly the first yellow bomb is shown as the 19th. However, the 541 shows *Nan* flew her first daylight trip on 22 June 1944, which is thus recorded as her 22nd sortie. Perhaps whoever added up *Nan's* 'score' failed to notice that the first trip, whilst noted as ME758 with the letter 'M' next to it, and for two ops in early May, the letter 'N' was shown but with the serial numbers of ME759 and MG758. ME759 was a 9 Squadron aircraft and there is no such Lancaster serial as MG758, so both are errors.

To add to the confusion, *Nan's* 100th bomb is also yellow, but the mining sortie to Oslo was a night flight. A straightforward count might indicate its 100th was two raids later, 27 March, a daylight to Paderborn. This would at least make the last bombing sortie on 25 April *Nan's* 106th – the number this aircraft is usually credited with. However, these problems occur with almost all the 100-plus op Lancasters as already mentioned.

*Nan* lived to see out the war but did not survive long enough to outlast the first six months of peace. She was Struck off Charge on 19 October 1945 and 'reduced to produce'.

ME758 now has 108 bombs, and markings for six Manna trips. The crew depicted flew on the last Exodus sortie, 11 May 1945. Standing are K Bratby, SL P S Huggins DFC, Len Laing, Geoff Robinson, while kneeling are Len Jackson, Sam Pechet and Tommy Thompson.

## 12 SQUADRON
## 1944

**1/2 May** *2145-0441*
*LYONS*
PO N Rollin
FO W A Chmilar RCAF (N)
Sgt S Hudson (WOP)
Sgt J W Pollack (BA)
Sgt H G Phillips (FE)
Sgt E Murray (MU)
Sgt D W Hornesby (RG)

**3/4 May** *2138-0333*
*MAILLY-LE-CAMP*
PO N Rollin and crew

**7 May** *0034-0504*
*AUBIGNÉ-RACEN*
PO N Rollin and crew

**7/8 May** *2143-0249*
*BRUZ*
PO E K Farfan
FS J C Gordon
Sgt V Poole
FO T H Vansickle
Sgt G Neal
Sgt J D Rollason
Sgt J Bell

**9/10 May** *2157-0118*
*MERVILLE*
PO N Rollin and crew

**19/20 May** *2211-0316*
*ORLÉANS*
PO J Downing
FO E D Figg
Sgt J Alten
Sgt T C Clitheroe
Sgt S V Day
Sgt W C Porter
FS H Lavallee

**21/22 May** *2248-0353*
*DUISBURG*
PO J Downing and crew

**22/23 May** *2213-0253*
*DORTMUND*
PO N Rollin and crew

**24/25 May** *2330-0445*
*AACHEN*
PO J W Landon
FS M C Griffiths
Sgt J Goodlett
Sgt J O Davies
Sgt J D Anderson
PO J Longbottom
Sgt J M Nicol

**27/28 May** *2355-0425*
*AACHEN*
Sgt G F Holbrook (DFC)
FO A R Witty (N) (DFC)
Sgt J P S Payner (WOP)
Sgt T P Crook (BA)
Sgt I E Squires (FE)
Sgt S Swaine (MU)
Sgt T S Gibb (RG)

**31 May/1 June** *2348-0443*
*TERGNIER*
PO L Pappas RCAF (DFC)
FO L M McLean
Sgt K B Phipps
FO A L Garrick
Sgt C Anderson
Sgt R K Redmond
Sgt B C Swanson RCAF (DFM)
(shot down Me109)

**2/3 June** *2322-0337*
*BERNEVAL RADAR*
Sgt G F Holbrook and crew

**4/5 June** *0139-0434*
*SANGATTE*
Sgt G F Holbrook and crew

**5/6 June** *2130-0213*
*ST MARTIN DE VARREVILLE*
Sgt G F Holbrook and crew
Sgt J P S Reid in (WOP), Sgt Payner out

**7 June** *0007-0455*
*ACHÈRES*
Sgt G F Holbrook and crew
(abandoned by MB)

**10 June** *0101-0545*
*FLERS LANDING GROUND*
Sgt G F Holbrook and crew

**12 June** *0045-0509*
*ÉVREUX*
Sgt G F Holbrook and crew

**12/13 June** *2238-0302*
*GELSENKIRCHEN*
Sgt G F Holbrook and crew

**14/15 June** *2103-0036*
*LE HAVRE*
Sgt G F Holbrook and crew
Payner back

**15/16 June** *2114-0032*
*BOULOGNE*
Sgt G F Holbrook and crew

**17 June** *2316-0415*
*AULNOYE BRIDGE*
Sgt G F Holbrook and crew
(aborted by MB)

**22 June** *1358-1713*
*MARQUISE*
Sgt G F Holbrook and crew

**23/24 June** *2222-0529*
*SAINTES*
PO K A Underwood
Sgt H J Heavener
Sgt D W O'Brien
FO L C Boyes
Sgt J F Marshall
Sgt H Ball
Sgt G H Beevers

**24 June** *0126-0448*
*FLERS – V1 SITE*
PO J B Starr
PO J W Steuart
FS A C Knott
FS P C Barr
Sgt A T Vass
Sgt W D North
FS F Mills

**28 June** *0038-0509*
*VAIRIES M/YARDS*
PO J B Starr and crew

**29 June** *1200-1553*
*SIRACOURT – V1 SITE*
FS H H Turner
WO B E Vipond
Sgt H Idle
FS E Getty
Sgt W Marshall
Sgt J P Ewing
Sgt F A Forster

**30 June/1 July** *2215-0356*
*VIERZON JUNCTION*
FS H H Turner and crew

**2 July** *1220-1544*
*DOMLEGER – V1 SITE*
WO G F Holbrook and crew

**4/5 July** *2147-0345*
*ORLÉANS M/YARDS*
WO G F Holbrook and crew

**5/6 July** *2101-0515*
*DIJON M/YARDS*
WO G F Holbrook and crew

**7 July** *1913-2316*
*CAEN*
PO R G Hancox
PO T B Booth (N)
Sgt R G W Wareham (WOP)
WO W E Moore (BA)
Sgt D A Nelson (FE)
Sgt T E Hayes (MU)
Sgt H A Burt (RG)

**12/13 July** *2106-0327*
TOURS M/YARDS
WO G F Holbrook and crew

**18 July** *0404-0850*
*CAEN*
Sgt F B Small
Sgt G W Allen
FS A S D Brown
PO E Standing
Sgt N J Moore
Sgt A Wilson
Sgt R J Sharp

**18/19 July** *2311-0323*
*SCHOLVEN*
PO A E Lowry (DFC)
Sgt A D McPherson
Sgt A Hetherington
FO S A Bacon
Sgt Brackenbury
Sgt P B Potts
Sgt W R Classen

**20/21 July** *2338-0259*
*COURTRAI M/YARDS*
WO G F Holbrook and crew

**23/24 July** *2238-0336*
*KIEL*
WO G F Holbrook and crew

**24/25 July** *2125-0605*
*STUTTGART*
WO G F Holbrook and crew
(returned on 3 engines)

**30 July** *0602-1000*
*CAUMONT*
WO G F Holbrook and crew

**31 July** *2203-0137*
*FORÊT DE NIEPPE – V1 SITE*
FO A J Thompson (DFC)
Sgt V O Langdon
FO J Simpson
FS A A Wheatley (N)
Sgt J E D Squires
Sgt D H Moyer
Sgt E Jones

**2 Aug** *1547-1910*
*LES CATELLIERS – V1 SITE*
PO G F Holbrook and crew

**3 Aug** *1154-1615*
*TROSSY ST MAXIMIN*
PO G F Holbrook and crew
PO J Williams (2P)

**13 Aug** *0032-0403*
*FALAIS*
FO G S Whyte
WO L V Dredge
FS C S R Horne
WO J V Parkinson
Sgt R O Walters
Sgt T Gilmour
Sgt J G Kernhan

**15 Aug** *0936-1326*
*VOLKEL AIRFIELD*
FO D W McLean RAAF
WO J Phillips RAAF
FS J E Kelly

FS A B Llewellyn RAAF
Sgt F W Niblett RAAF
FS K H Rowley RAAF
FS I H Fleming RAAF*
*known as Hunter
(all lost 23 Oct)

**16 Aug** *2045-0517*
*STETTIN*
FO D W McLean and crew

**25/26 Aug** *1958-0457*
*RÜSSELSHEIM*
PO G F Holbrook and crew

**26/27 Aug** *2004-0136*
*KIEL*
PO G F Holbrook and crew

**31 Aug** *1325-1639*
*ST RIQUIER DUMP*
PO G F Holbrook and crew

**5 Sep** *1630-1947*
*LE HAVRE*
FO E King
Sgt L F Elms
Sgt W E Spilsbury
Sgt A R Bailey
Sgt G W Smith
PO H S Brown
Sgt C V Swann

**8 Sep** *0625-1019*
*LE HAVRE*
FO E King and crew

**12/13 Sep** *1835-0141*
*FRANKFURT*
FO C H Henry (DFC)
Sgt F H Hesketh (FE) (DFM)
FO N L V Chesson (FE)
Sgt G C Heywood (N)
Sgt J K Penrose
FS E D Martin
Sgt F W Kendall

**16/17 Sep** *2158-0120*
*HOPSTEN*
FO C H Henry and crew

**17 Sep** *1705-1943*
*WESTKAPELLE*
FL T Nisbett
Sgt J K Pinder
Sgt C K Spencer
Sgt R V Holt
FS V C Kirchner
PO C E Simons
PO E L Williams

**20 Sep** *1531-1849*
*CALAIS*
FL T Nisbett and crew

**23 Sep** *1851-2340*
*NEUSS*
FO E King and crew

**25 Sep** *0720-1045*
*CALAIS*
FS I L McIntyre
Sgt N L Woods
Sgt J F Craigen
FS J R Syratt
FS K W Tong
Sgt E Reed
Sgt C G Rutzou

**26 Sep** *1055-1355*
*CAP GRIS NEZ*
FO E King and crew

**5/6 Oct** *1847-0050*
*SAARBRÜCKEN*
FO E King and crew

**7 Oct** *1153-1612*
EMMERICH
FO E King and crew
FO A S Mallik in (BA)

**14 Oct** *0648-1127*
DUISBURG
FO K T Wallace (DFC)
Sgt R B Glasper (FE)
FO C L Carlson RCAF (BA)
FS W D Bonter RCAF (N)
Sgt H S Hoare (WOP)
Sgt S A Bedford (MU)
FS J S Ross (RG)

**15 Oct** *1730-2145*
WILHELMSHAVEN
FO K T Wallace and crew

**19 Oct** *1649-2348*
STUTTGART
FO K T Wallace and crew

**23 Oct** *1632-2224*
ESSEN
FO K T Wallace and crew

**28 Oct** *1300-1815*
COLOGNE
FO A J D Leach
Sgt W White (FE)
FS C W Young (BA)
Sgt J W Moore (N)
Sgt H M Powell (WOP)
Sgt A W Lush (MU)
Sgt A M Hiebert (RG)

**29 Oct** *1206-1441*
DOMBURG
FL A J Thompson
Sgt F W Mills (FE)
FL J E T Mansfield (BA)
FS A A Wheatley (N)
FS J Hyde (WOP)
Sgt M J McMillan (MU)
FS E Jones (RG)

**30 Oct** *1748-2355*
COLOGNE
FO C H Henry and crew

**31 Oct** *1749-2309*
COLOGNE
FO K T Wallace and crew

**2 Nov** *1635-2155*
DÜSSELDORF
FO L L Galbraith
Sgt G C Eaton (FE)
FO J C Blyth (BA)
FO W M Ogle (N)
Sgt D C Johnson (WOP)
Sgt E M Warren (MU)
Sgt B Gallagher (RG)

**4 Nov** *1741-2225*
BOCHUM
FO K T Wallace and crew

**6 Nov** *1150-1626*
GELSENKIRCHEN
FL A J Thompson and crew
WO D M Pugh and Sgt V C
Langdon in, Mansfield and
Hyde out

**9 Nov** *0743-1310*
WANNE-EICKEL
FL A J Thompson and crew

**16 Nov** *1244-1805*
DÜREN
FL J L Walters
Sgt J M Gibb (FE)
FS W Blythe (BA)
Sgt S R Harris (N)
FS K O Langham (WOP)
Sgt C Butler (MU)
Sgt M Boulding (RG)

**18 Nov** *1602-2124*
WANNE-EICKEL
FO J L Walters and crew

**21 Nov** *1515-2206*
ASCHAFFENBERG
FO C H Henry and crew

**27 Nov** *1604-2320*
FREIBERG
FO P C L Bird
Sgt G W Robinson
FS S Pechet
FS W N Thompson
WO E Bratby
Sgt L W Lang
Sgt L A Jackson

**29 Nov** *1217-1735*
DORTMUND
FO P C L Bird and crew

**4 Dec** *1644-2255*
KARLSRUHE
FO C H Henry and crew

## 1945

**16/17 Jan** *1746-0136*
ZEITZ
FO L L Galbraith and crew

**1 Feb** *1527-2248*
LUDWIGSHAVEN
FL A J D Leach and crew
FS Middleman in (WOP),
Powell out

**2/3 Feb** *2046-0032*
WIESBADEN
FO W Kroaker and crew
(abandoned, std outer
caught fire)

**13/14 Feb** *2131-0720*
DRESDEN
FO P C L Bird and crew

**14/15 Feb** *1956-0523*
CHEMNITZ
PO N A Wickes
Sgt C McCabe (FE)
FS R J White (BA)
Sgt E Parker (N)
FS T A Connolly (WOP)
Sgt F S Saunders (MU)
Sgt D G Horton (RG)

**20/21 Feb** *2145-0426*
DORTMUND
FL A J D Leach and crew
Powell back

**21/22 Feb** *1944-0204*
DUISBURG
FL A J D Leach and crew

**23 Feb** *1543-2337*
PFORZHEIM
FL A J D Leach and crew

**28 Feb** *0823-1136*
DÜSSELDORF
FL A J D Leach and crew
(abandoned due to weather)

**1 Mar** *1159-1808*
MANNHEIM
FL A J D Leach and crew

**2 Mar** *0709-1225*
COLOGNE
FL A J D Leach and crew

**5/6 Mar** *1641-0220*
CHEMNITZ
FL A J D Leach and crew

**7/8 Mar** *1711-0249*
DESSAU
FO K W Mabee
Sgt K W Clarke
FO A R Hovis
Sgt L E Rae
Sgt D W Debonnaire
Sgt M M Barker
Sgt T K Imperious

**8/9 Mar** *1700-0037*
KASSEL
FL A J D Leach and crew

**11 Mar** *1145-1721*
ESSEN
FO K W Mabee and crew

**12 Mar** *1300-1856*
DORTMUND
FL A J D Leach and crew

**13 Mar** *1724-2327*
DAHLEUSCH
PO N A Wickes and crew
Sgt E L Cullup (MU) in

**16/17 Mar** *1716-0156*
NÜRNBERG
FL A J D Leach and crew

**19 Mar** *0006-0733*
HANAU
FL A J D Leach and crew

**21 Mar** *0224-0645*
GARDENING – HELIGOLAND
FO F M Baird
Sgt G W G Monk
FO G B MacPherson
FO M Couse
Sgt J D'Arcy
Sgt D D Boyd
Sgt D J Duncan

**22 Mar** *0037-0646*
BRUCHSTRASSE
FO C Grannum
Sgt E J Wickes
Sgt A Babayan
Sgt J J Wakelam
Sgt F Gankrodger
Sgt W McCormick
FS J Green

**22/23 Mar** *2129-0400*
GARDENING – OSLO
FO F M Baird and crew

**25 Mar** *0654-2250*
HANNOVER
FO F M Baird and crew

**27 Mar** *1440-1946*
PADERBORN
FL W Kroeker RCAF
FS C Brooks (FE)
FO C E Modeland RCAF
FL W D Smith RCAF (N)
FS J F Woodcherry
FO C W G Biddlecombe
FO G T Wood
(all lost 4 April; apart from
Biddlecombe, all had been
interned in Sweden between
Jan and Sep 1944)

**4/5 Apr** *2051-0510*
LUTZENDORF
FL A J D Leach and crew

**9/10 Apr** *1944-0116*
KIEL
FL A J D Leach and crew
FO G F Sage (2P)

**10/11 Apr** *1806-0236*
PLAUEN
FL A J D Leach and crew

**18 Apr** *1010-1514*
HELIGOLAND
FL T MacPherson
Sgt J Harrison
Sgt M L White
FO S Borkowitz
FS J B Hosie
Sgt J J Picco
Sgt P B Adams

**22 Apr** *1532-2018*
BREMEN
FL T MacPherson and crew
(raid abandoned)

**25 Apr** *0507-1319*
BERCHTESGADEN
FO G F Sage
Sgt G Horridge
FO M P Shewring
FO T W Owen
FO K P C Smith
FO W Faulkner
FL R C Candy

**30 Apr** *1500-1809*
MANNA
FL W H Cumming
Sgt J C Steele
FS W J Booth
FO J O J Bates
FS L J Minchin
Sgt R T Diamond
Sgt E P Bryant

**1 May** *1243-1535*
MANNA – VALKENBURG
FO C Grannum and crew

**2 May** *1030-1312*
MANNA – VALKENBURG
FO C Grannum and crew

**3 May** *1220-1531*
MANNA – VALKENBURG
FO C Grannum and crew
FL H Bradbury (FE) in,
Wicks out

**4 May** *1314-1559*
MANNA – ROTTERDAM
FO J L Wallace
Sgt V Tracey
FO R Brooke
FO D M Harrison (N)
FS G Smith
FS R W Middlemass
Sgt M Briggs

**7 May** *1319-1707*
MANNA – ROTTERDAM
FO C Grannum and crew
FO C Sutcliffe (2P)
Wicks back

**9 May** *PM*
EXODUS – BRUSSELS
FO C Grannum and crew

**11 May** *PM*
EXODUS – BRUSSELS
SL P S Huggins
Sgt G W Robinson (FE)
WO S Pechet (BA)
PO W N Thompson (N)
WO E Bratby (WOP)
Sgt L W Laing (MU)
WO L A Jackson (RG)

# ME801
# NAN

Lancaster ME801 of 576 Squadron pictured after its 100th op, 15/16 March 1945.

Built at Metro Vickers, Manchester, as part of Contract No.2221, this Lancaster came off the production line in the spring of 1944 as a Mark I, equipped with four Merlin 24 engines. Assigned to 166 Squadron it was almost immediately sent to 576 Squadron at Elsham Wolds, south of Hull, on 18 May and given the code letters of UL and an individual letter C-Charlie until October, at which time it was changed to N². The previous 'N' – PD235 – had been lost on 24/25 September.

Pilot Officer S G Hordal RCAF took ME801 on its first outing, and indeed its first 15 trips between 21 May to 24 June – including D-Day – and during both day and night sorties. Stephen Hordal flew the aircraft just once more before he completed his tour and went to 1666 CU, receiving the DFC.

ME801 was then taken over by Pilot Officer James MacDonald who took the aircraft on 24 raids before he too completed his tour in October, also receiving the

DFC. He failed to bomb on one occasion, during a raid on Le Havre on 6 September, because the radio failed. He therefore did not receive orders to reduce height due to the weather, was unable to identify the target and had to bring his bombs back. A month earlier one of his crew had been slightly wounded by flak over Agenville.

Although fairly trouble-free, ME801 did have to return early from a trip to Duisburg on 14/15 October with engine trouble, but this was its only reported failure. When the aircraft became Nan, the squadron had just changed bases, from Elsham Wolds to Fiskerton, just east of Lincoln. It operated on the first raid the squadron mounted from Fiskerton, its skipper Flying Officer D Fletcher. Another crew this night, and who had flown ME801 on 30 July, failed to return in another Lanc. It was their 29th op (F/O J J Mulrooney PoW, his crew killed).

Fletcher made six raids during this period (he and his crew were killed in a crash in another Lanc at Manston, coming back from Bonn on 28 December.) ME801 was then taken over by Flight Lieutenant H Leyton-Brown who, on his first trip in *Nan*, actually led the daylight formation against the oil refinery at Wanne-Eickel. He made five sorties in *Nan* during November, then another three in January 1945. On a further sortie on 20/21 February, they played cat-and-mouse with a FW190 but it did not attack.

A few nights later, however, on the 23rd, *Nan* was attacked by a Ju88 night fighter shortly after bombing. They were at 8,000 feet with a bright moon off to port. The rear gunner, Warrant Officer J J Hiscocks, saw the Junkers as it crossed at a range of 400 yards from the dark part of the sky, across the fires of the target – Pforzheim – as it climbed slowly beneath the bomber stream. Hiscocks opened fire with a five-second burst and saw its starboard wing start to break up. He had just ordered the pilot to corkscrew to port, and in a final defiant gesture, the 88's pilot fired a quick but ineffectual burst at the Lanc. Hiscocks fired again, the fighter now at 300 yards range and saw it begin to disintegrate, then burst into flames, later exploding on the ground.

Flying Officer D E Till, who flew most of his tour in another centenarian – LM227 – did one trip in *Nan* and remembered:

'Chemnitz on 14 February 1945 was the longest trip we'd ever done up to that point and we were concerned about the route being fairly straight due to the fuel load which was kind of bad news, but we made it.

'Boredom was always a problem on long trips and if you didn't keep your gunners alert they might doze off. After all, on night ops we had all been up some hours before taking off. Like a lot of people, we had this practice of sticking the aircraft on its sides every ten minutes or so, to ensure nothing was going on underneath us. It was probably more something to do rather than anything useful because there was still quite a time gap between doing it, but it kept everyone occupied.

'We knew nothing then about night fighters having upward-firing guns but we knew we were vulnerable from below, so we adopted this tactic as soon as we got over enemy territory, this and a bit of weaving.'

Harold Leyton-Brown continued flying *Nan*, taking it on seven more ops, making 18 in all for him. The last, on 15/16 March 1945, was his 36th and last of his tour. It was also ME801's 100th operation. On this raid Leyton-Brown spotted a Ju88 just 20 yards away on his port beam over the target but apparently its pilot did not see them, at least he did not attack. Tour-expired, Leyton-Brown received the DFC.

Flying Officer Don Graham then took over *Nan* on ops 102 to 105, then assorted crews brought her total up to 109 by the end of April. The aircraft is recorded as flying 113 sorties in all, so these must include Manna ops, making in fact 114, plus three Exodus flights.

With the previous centenarian, ME578, we read that it was Struck off Charge on 19 October 1945. ME801 preceded this Lanc by three days, being SOC following a crash that left the machine Cat E. *Nan* had no known nose-art other than its rows of bomb symbols, a swastika for the Ju88, and a DFC ribbon.

## 576 SQUADRON
## 1944

**21/22 May** *2225-0315*
DUISBURG
PO S G Hordal RCAF
Sgt G B Valentine
FO H Gerus RCAF (BA)
FS A M Cambrin RCAF
Sgt F Sheppard
Sgt F B Edwards
Sgt D E Jones RCAF

**22/23 May** *2215-0245*
DORTMUND
PO S G Hordal and crew

**24/25 May** *2340-0410*
AACHEN
PO S G Hordal and crew

**27/28 May** *2350-0420*
AACHEN
PO S G Hordal and crew

**2/3 June** *2230-0245*
CALAIS
PO S G Hordal and crew

**5/6 June** *2120-0130*
ST MARTIN DE VARREVILLE
OP S G Hordal and crew

**6/7 June** *2150-0300*
VIRE
PO S G Hordal and crew

**10 June** *0005-0505*
FLERS
PO S G Hordal and crew

**12/13 June** *2230-0240*
GELSENKIRCHEN
PO S G Hordal and crew

**14 June** *2020-2350*
LE HAVRE
PO S G Hordal RCAF
Sgt G B Valentine
FO H Gerus
FS A M Cambrin
Sgt N C Stafford
Sgt J Armstrong
Sgt J S McGinn

**16/17 June** *2255-0320*
STERKRADE
PO S G Hordal and crew

**17/18 June** *2330-0330*
AULNOYE
PO S G Hordal and crew

**22 June** *1345-1655*
MIMOYECQUES – V1 SITE
PO S G Hordal and crew

**23/24 June** *2140-0505*
SAINTES
PO S G Hordal and crew

**25 June** *0115-0440*
FLERS – V1 SITE
PO S G Hordal and crew

**27 June** *0130-0540*
CHÂTEAU BERNAPRE – V1 SITE
FS H D Murray
Sgt C C Adams
Sgt R Lee
Sgt D A Barnes
Sgt F Thackeray
Sgt P J Taylor
Sgt W O Kenyon

**29 June** *1135-1445*
DOMLEGER – V1 SITE
PO S G Hordal and crew

**30 June** *0605-1005*
*OISMONT – V1 SITE*
PO J MacDonald (DFC)
Sgt J Beeson
Sgt J S Pym (BA)
Sgt J Fell
Sgt J Thomson
Sgt J F F McDonald RCAF
Sgt K A Grant RCAF

**2 July** *1220-1615*
*DOMLEGER – V1 SITE*
PO D F J Baxter RCAF
Sgt J Ponder
Sgt D Shoebridge RCAF
Sgt E J McLasky RCAF
Sgt A H Treadwell
Sgt R F Hillman
Sgt E W Bookhout

**5/6 July** *2120-0620*
*DIJON*
PO J MacDonald and crew

**7 July** *1945-2355*
*CAEN*
PO J MacDonald and crew

**12/13 July** *2130-0645*
*RÉVIGNY*
PO J MacDonald and crew

**14/15 July** *2115-0515*
*RÉVIGNY*
PO J Archibald RNZAF
Sgt J R Cuthbert
FO P J Biollo RCAF
Sgt J E Kearney
FS L Fielding
WO T P Barry
Sgt A Milne
(all except pilot killed
28/29 July)

**17 July** *0340-0740*
*SANNEVILLE – V1 SITE*
PO J MacDonald and crew

**18/19 July** *2320-0335*
*SCHOLVEN / BUER*
PO J MacDonald and crew

**20 July** *1910-2300*
*WIZERNES*
PO J MacDonald and crew

**23/24 July** *2230-0325*
*KIEL*
PO J MacDonald and crew

**24/25 July** *2130-0625*
*STUTTGART*
FL D J Masters (DFC)
Sgt H Wightman
FO W C Johnstone RCAF
FS B W Wakely
FS Donovan RCAF
Sgt R E Smith
Sgt A S Smart

**25/26 July** *2130-0550*
*STUTTGART*
FO J MacDonald and crew

**28/29 July** *2105-0305*
*STUTTGART*
FO J MacDonald and crew
(aborted with sick navigator)

**30 July** *0640-1145*
*CAHAGNES*
FO J J Mulrooney
Sgt B Beale (FE)
FO C W P Mortal RAAF (BA)
FS F J L Paton RAAF
WO J N Casey RAAF
FS F B McGrath RAAF
FS R S M Coventry RAAF
(failed to return 2 Nov; pilot PoW,

Mortal, Casey and Paton KIA, others
not flying; FO Mulrooney's 29th op)

**31 July** *1810-2140*
*LE HAVRE*
FL D J Masters and crew

**1 Aug** *1850-2210*
*BELLE CROIX – V1 SITE*
FS A D'L Grieg (DFC)
Sgt N Mason
FO J R Jones
FS F G Henville RAAF
Sgt S A Johnson
Sgt H Walton
Sgt J Thresh

**3 Aug** *1140-1620*
*TROSSY ST MAXIMIN*
FS A D'L Grieg and crew

**4 Aug** *1325-2125*
*PAUILLAC*
FS A D'L Grieg and crew

**5 Aug** *1445-2230*
*BLAYE*
FS A D'L Grieg and crew

**7/8 Aug** *2110-0120*
*FONTENAYE*
FO J J Mulrooney and crew

**10 Aug** *0925-1430*
*DUGNY*
PO N Layden (DFC)
Sgt S B Naftel
FS F H Lowing
FS J E Wright
FS H J G Sibley
Sgt H Elliott
Sgt E Smith

**11 Aug** *1400-1730*
*DOUAI*
FO S F Durrant
Sgt R E Pearce
Sgt C J Brady RCAF
FO J Johnstone
FS J R McIntyre RAAF
Sgt J G MacKay RCAF
Sgt D Spowart
(abort, intercom failure;
all lost 23/24 Sep)

**14 Aug** *1325-1730*
*FONTAINE-LE-PIN*
FO S F Durrant and crew

**15 Aug** *1005-1345*
*LE CULOT*
FO S F Durrant and crew

**16 Aug** *2100-0505*
*STETTIN*
PO N Layden and crew

**18/19 Aug** *2220-0235*
*RIEME*
PO J MacDonald and crew

**25/26 Aug** *2005-0455*
*RÜSSELSHEIM*
FO J MacDonald and crew

**26/27 Aug** *1950-0125*
*KIEL*
FO J MacDonald and crew

**29/30 Aug** *2110-0550*
*STETTIN*
FO J MacDonald and crew
PO L F Moore and Sgt S H
Barton in, Beeson out)

**31 Aug** *1305-1700*
*AGENVILLE*
FO J MacDonald and crew
Beeson back, others out;
Pym slightly injured by flak

**5 Sep** *1630-2015*
*LE HAVRE*
FO M T Wilson
Sgt R P Kimm
Sgt P E T Brooked
Sgt L N Hill
Sgt S Douglas
Sgt T A Russell
Sgt J H Addison

**6 Sep** *1702-2035*
*LE HAVRE*
FO J MacDonald and crew
(failed to bomb due to radio failure)

**8 Sep** *0640-1030*
*LE HAVRE*
FL P P Hague (DFC)
Sgt T E Allen
PO K D Clements RCAF
Sgt R Low
Sgt C C Routledge
Sgt H Henson
WO J W Sargent
(Hague DFC, 103 Sqn)

**10 Sep** *1630-2020*
*LE HAVRE*
FO J MacDonald and crew

**12/13 Sep** *1815-0135*
*FRANKFURT*
FO K L Trent (DFC)
Sgt A R Dunford
Sgt J N Wadsworth
Sgt H B Reybolds
Sgt R L Skelton RAAF
Sgt C Dalby
FO G C Riccomini

**15/16 Sep** *2220-0445*
*GARDENING*
FO K L Trent and crew

**17 Sep** *1625-1920*
*FLUSHING*
FO K L Trent and crew

**20 Sep** *1500-1820*
*CALAIS GUN*
FO J MacDonald and crew

**23 Sep** *1830-2345*
*NEUSS*
FO J MacDonald and crew

**25 Sep** *0720-1020*
*CALAIS*
FO J MacDonald and crew
(abort due to weather)

**26 Sep** *1055-1400*
*CAP GRIS NEZ*
FO J MacDonald and crew

**5/6 Oct** *1815-0100*
*SAARBRÜCKEN*
FO J MacDonald and crew

**14 Oct** *0645-1055*
*DUISBURG*
FO J MacDonald and crew

**14/15 Oct** *2230-0105*
*DUISBURG*
FO J MacDonald and crew
(returned early, engine trouble)

**22 Oct** *1605-2200*
*ESSEN*
FO H R McClelland RAAF (DFC)
Sgt A Rhodes
FS J A Kennedy RAAF
FO W R Courtis RAAF (N) (DFC)
FS N G McGill
FS M Chapman RAAF
FS J P Coe

**25 Oct** *1305-1815*
*ESSEN*
FO D Fletcher
Sgt P D Lake
Sgt C G Campbell
Sgt L J Bull
Sgt G Warren RCAF
Sgt J Norris
(all killed 28 December,
returning from Bonn)

**27 Oct** *1310-1815*
*COLOGNE*
FO D Fletcher and crew

**30/31 Oct** *1750-0030*
*COLOGNE*
FO D Fletcher and crew

**2 Nov** *1625-2200*
*DÜSSELDORF*
FO D Fletcher and crew

**4 Nov** *1725-2225*
*BOCHUM*
FO D Fletcher and crew

**6 Nov** *1200-1625*
*GELSENKIRCHEN*
FO D Fletcher and crew

**9 Nov** *0805-1250*
*WANNE-EICKEL*
FL H Leyton-Brown (DFC)
Sgt R A Hawkins (FE)
FS G Paterson (BA)
Sgt L Peters (N)
Sgt E Johnson (WOP)
Sgt P M McMillan (MU)
Sgt G Lester (RG)

**11 Nov** *1555-2105*
*DORTMUND*
FL H Leyton-Brown and crew

**16 Nov** *1245-1730*
*DÜREN*
FL H Leyton-Brown and crew

**18 Nov** *1550-2050*
*WANNE-EICKEL*
FL H Leyton-Brown and crew

**21 Nov** *1530-2145*
*ASCHAFFENBURG*
FL H Leyton-Brown and crew

**27 Nov** *1610-2235*
*FREIBERG*
FO D C Smith RAAF
Sgt K Warner
FS R G Collins RAAF
FS D K E Anderson RAAF
FS D K Rowe RAAF
Sgt C G R Jones
Sgt S V Lloyd RAAF

**29 Nov** *1210-1720*
*DORTMUND*
FO D C Smith and crew
(slight flak damage)

**3 Dec** *0735-1155*
*URFT DAM*
FL L Arthur
Sgt J Hill
FO O J T Troy
FO R J Williams
FS D T H Madell
Sgt N Woods
Sgt E L Gidden

## 1945

**5 Jan** *0209-0916*
*ROYAN*
FO E J Pollard RAAF
Sgt E B May

# ME801 NAN

Sgt A Preston
Sgt C V Dolan RCAF
Sgt J Patterson
Sgt R M Goodfellow
Sgt Brown

**7/8 Jan** *1825-0240*
MUNICH
FL H Leyton-Brown and crew
FS Hill (2P)

**14/15 Jan** *1920-0335*
MERSEBURG
FO H J Rowe RCAF
Sgt T Parkinson
FO G L Dunn RCAF
FO R F Brothers RCAF
Sgt J A F Demant
Sgt E A Lindberg RCAF
Sgt F A Chidley RCAF

**16/17 Jan** *1745-0135*
ZEITZ-TROGLITZ
PO R R J Young
Sgt K G Greathead
FO H N Cheeseman
Sgt G R James
Sgt D P Bannister
Sgt H E Ward
Sgt M W Webb

**22 Jan** *1650-2150*
DUISBURG
FL H Leyton-Brown and crew

**28/29 Jan** *1950-0239*
STUTTGART
FL H Leyton-Brown and crew

**1 Feb** *1600-2310*
LUDWIGSHAVEN
FL C D Thieme
Sgt K Wallis
WO J H Lowing RAAF
FS H W Vine
FS C B Robinson RAAF
Sgt L Hull
Sgt C N Crouch
(crashed 22 Feb '45; Vine, Robinson
and Hull killed - rest evaded)

**7/8 Feb** *1900-0010*
CLEVE
FL C D Thieme and crew

**8/9 Feb** *1905-0350*
PÖLITZ
FL C D Thieme and crew

**14/15 Feb** *2000-0440*
CHEMNITZ
FO D E Till (DFC)
Sgt D E Holland (FE)
FO J Shorthouse (BA)
FO C R Bray (N)
FO G W Griggs RAAF
Sgt K Oliver (MU)
Sgt R Hamilton (RG)

**20/21 Feb** *2135-0335*
DORTMUND
FL H Leyton-Brown and crew
WO J J Hiscocks in, Lester out

**21/22 Feb** *1930-0120*
DUISBURG
FL H Leyton-Brown and crew

**23 Feb** *1545-2325*
PFORZHEIM
FL H Leyton-Bown and crew
FO D B Graham (2P)
(R/G shot down a Ju 88)

**28 Feb** *0845-1005*
NEUSS
FL H Leyton-Brown and crew

**1 Mar** *1145-1755*
MANNHEIM
FL H Lewton-Brown and crew

**2 Mar** *0715-1220*
COLOGNE
FL Sleight
PO W B Hazel
PO C Hathaway
FL C Dyson
FO J Hatchard
FS B R Phillips
FO F H Taylor

**5/6 Mar** *1645-0150*
CHEMNITZ
FL H Leyton-Brown and crew

**7/8 Mar** *1700-0215*
DESSAU
FL H Leyton-Brown and crew

**8/9 Mar** *1700-0025*
KASSEL
FL H Leyton-Brown and crew

**11 Mar** *1150-1655*
ESSEN
FO W N Holmes RCAF
Sgt D J Nimmo
FO F W Christisen RCAF
FO J K Scruten RCAF
Sgt W Brown
FS E O Grife RCAF
FS W W Parsons RCAF

**12 Mar** *1325-1825*
DORTMUND
FL H Leyton-Brown and crew

**15/16 Mar** *1720-0045*
MISBURG
FL H Leyton-Brown and crew
(36th and final op for this crew)

**21 Mar** *0755-1250*
BREMEN
PO D K Sullivan
Sgt G Charlton
Sgt G S Atkinson
Sgt I A Heath
Sgt D Phillips

Sgt R Erskine
Sgt G F Chatterton

**24 Mar** *1305-1830*
DORTMUND
FO D B Graham
Sgt C R Huxtable (FE)
FS P Brookes (BA)
Sgt W Hatton (N)
Sgt S F Gascoigne (WOP)
Sgt E J Boniface (MU)
Sgt E J Moore (RG)

**31 Mar** *0625-1135*
HAMBURG
FO D B Graham and crew

**4/5 Apr** *2130-0520*
LUTZENDORF
FO D B Graham and crew

**9/10 Apr** *1910-0135*
KIEL
FO D B Graham and crew

**10/11 Apr** *1805-0300*
PLAUEN
FL J R Tile
Sgt P J Robinson (FE)
Sgt D L Howells (BA)
Sgt W Vaughan (N)
Sgt J R Currie
Sgt S H Wragg
Sgt D I Vicary

**14/15 Apr** *1935-0055*
CUXHAVEN
FS R C Sayers
Sgt J G Blair (FE)
Sgt P Patterson
Sgt K E Stott
Sgt L V Hayes
FS H E Bell RAAF
Sgt R J Hagger

**18 Apr** *1010-1450*
HELIGOLAND
PO K Fry
FS H W Parkins
FS H Woodliff
Sgt D G Smith (N)

FL H T Shewan
Sgt A G Younger
Sgt J L Watkins

**25 Apr** *0530-1345*
BERCHTESGADEN
FS R C Sayers and crew
Sgt J D Cormack in (FE),
Sgt Blair out

**29 Apr** *1150-1448*
VALKENBURG AIRFIELD
FO A Roberts
FS L A Piddington
FS B Rosario
Sgt J Smale (N)
Sgt R Briggs
Sgt S Davies
Sgt B Benson

**1 May** *1535-1818*
MANNA – ROTTERDAM
FO A Roberts and crew

**2 May** *1256-1549*
MANNA – ROTTERDAM
FO H Drew
Sgt G Booth
Sgt A W Stone
St A T Turton (N)
FS W Guthrie
Sgt L Cousins
Sgt J P Riley

**3 May** *1018-1315*
MANNA – VALKENBURG
FO H Drew and crew

**8 May** *1207-1528*
MANNA – ROTTERDAM
FO D B Graham and crew

**11, 16 and 26 May, 3 Exodus trips
by FO D B Graham and crew**

An almost identical shot of ME801 but a DSO ribbon has been added next to the DFC and the swastika. There is now a leek emblem forward of the bomb tally.

# ME803
# L FOR LOVE

Another Lancaster Mark I from batch No.2221, built by Metro Vickers, Manchester, ME803 had four Merlin 24 engines and rolled out of the factory in the spring of 1944. Assigned to C Flight of 115 Squadron at Witchford, Cambridgeshire, on 20 May, it initially carried the code letters A4-D and began flying ops on the night of 31 May/1 June in the hands of Flying Officer J G Sutherland RAAF.

Its second sortie was on the night of D-Day, again with Sutherland in command. In fact Sutherland was to be this Lanc's regular skipper until August, taking it on a total of 19 trips. ME803's next regular captain was Flying Officer F A Stechman, who flew the bomber on a further 18 sorties. Freddie Stechman received the DFC at the end of his tour as did John Sutherland.

A pilot who flew just two sorties in her (27 Sept '44 and 14 Apr '45) was Flight Lieutenant E W Talbot, who came to bombers via being a glider pilot instructor. Bill Talbot completed his tour and won the DFC, and, unusually, received a Bar to this decoration in 1958 flying with 84 Squadron in Aden against Yemeni forces.

In October ME803 changed codes to KO-D and by November had changed its individual letter to L (L-Love), which it would keep until the spring of 1945, the time C Flight changed its codes again, ME803 becoming IL-B.

ME803 flew regularly on operations with hardly a mechanical problem until it had to abandon a daylight mission to Nordstern on 23 November. On this raid the port-outer engine went u/s, by which time the aircraft had flown more than 60 ops. On the next daylight – to Cologne – ME803 had its first reported flak hit which caused slight damage to the mid-upper turret.

It now seemed as if this particular Lanc was starting to live on borrowed time. On yet another daylight, to Dortmund on 2 December, ME803 was nearly clobbered by falling bombs from another bomber overhead, and on 21 December, the aircraft lost its port-inner engine but the pilot, Flying Officer J P R Mason RCAF, flew on and bombed the target. On *Love's* first sortie of 1945 the Gee became u/s, the electrics failed and in consequence she could not drop her bombs.

On the next raid the aircraft was hit by flak in both wings and the undercarriage, on the following trip flak put holes in the port elevator and port wing. Shaking off these misfortunes *Love* continued to press on but on 3 February she was coned by searchlights for ten minutes during a raid on Dortmund and the crew bombed the wrong target – Botrop. Seeing TIs (Target Indicators) which appeared to be dummy ones, they took a dead-reckoning course to other TIs , then found they were over the wrong target, by which time it was too late to do anything else but bomb Botrop instead.

On 22 February *Love* was hit again, flak damaging a hydraulic pipe. However, that ended the run of bad luck but with her total ops just a couple short of the century mark, ME803 was sent to 54 MU on 15 March, having become Cat AC. Her last regular skipper was Flying Officer G P Pickering who flew the Lanc on 21 ops during its problem period, but Godfrey Pickering received the DFC. He recalled the move to 54 Maintenance Unit:

> 'Shortly after finishing our tour we had to take the "Old Girl" to Oakington for a major service. She was found to have a cracked main spar in the port wing. After having repairs completed she returned to active service and completed a few more ops before the war ended. Not bad for an "Old Girl."

Cliff Cunningham, Pickering's rear gunner, recalled the nose-artwork: 'We called the Lancaster *L for Love*. She had a naked lady painted on her and there was a growing number of bomb symbols, each representing a raid completed.' Unhappily, pictures I have seen of ME803 do not make a clear enough image to identify the naked lady.

Returning to the squadron on 22 March, *Love* became IL-B by mid-April but quickly took her total ops to 100 during that month. Not unusually there is controversy on the exact mission that constituted the 100th. Flight Lieutenant Roy Roberts said he took it on the 100th to

Ground crew of 115 Squadron's ME803 in front of their aircraft following her 100th operation. Unfortunately it is not clear what the nose-art depicts, other than it was supposed to be a 'lovely lady'.

Dortmund on 26 February, carrying one 4,000 lb 'cookie' and twelve 500 lb bombs, which were released from 19,000 feet. Someone else says Warrant Officer M J Carberry's crew flew the 100th – Wesel, 19 February. If 26 February is correct, then counting on from there, raid 105 came on 22 April to Bremen. With three Manna trips between 30 April and 4 May, it makes it 108. If 19 February is correct, then the total would be 110. As the saying goes, 'You pays your money .....' Oddly enough Bill Talbot's second op in ME803, on 14 April 1945, was to Potsdam and took nine hours. He and his crew were photographed in front of ME803 which clearly shows 100 bombs. One has to wonder if this was taken after the Potsdam trip, and if so, was it because Talbot was finishing his tour, or was it because he'd flown the 100th the previous night?! If so, then five operational flights later comes the last pre-VE day trip, and brings the total ops to 105!

On 21 May – after another post-war Manna trip and three Exodus flights, ME803 went to 1659 CU then to 39 MU on 18 September, from where she was Struck off Charge on 20 November 1946.

A close-up does not help!

## 115 SQUADRON
## 1944

**31 May/1 June** *0001-0445*
*TRAPPES WEST*
FO J G Sutherland RAAF (DFC)
FS V Catchlove RAAF (N)
Sgt A Wright (BA)
FS H Huddlestone RNZAF
Sgt C Wright (FE)
Sgt S Cooper (MU)
FS D Day RAAF (RG)

**6 June** *0337-0637*
*OUISTREHAM*
FO J G Sutherland and crew

**7 June** *0021-0256*
*LISIEUX*
FO J G Sutherland and crew

**10/11 June** *2307-0257*
*DREUX*
FL D W Martin
FO R Fisher (N)
FS J Waple (B)
Sgt T S Longhurst (WOP)
Sgt C Bridges (FE)
FS R Champion (MU)
FS L Johns RAAF (RG)

**11/12 June** *2355-0450*
*NANTES*
FL D W Martin and crew

**12/13 June** *2326-0241*
GELSENKIRCHEN
FO J G Sutherland and crew

**14/15 June** *2358-0218*
*LE HAVRE*
PO F Frankland
FO H H Skinner
FS Stewart-Smith (BA)
Sgt E Martin
Sgt F Rutter
Sgt R Bayly
Sgt J Doering RCAF

**15/16 June** *2316-0226*
*VALENCIENNES*
PO F Frankland and crew

**21 June** *1803-2028*
*DOMLÉGER – V1 SITE*
FL D W Martin and crew
(aborted due to cloud)

**23/24 June** *2308-0138*
*L'HEY – V1 SITE*
FO J G Sutherland and crew

**27/28 June** *2329-0209*
*DIENNES DUMP*
FL D W Martin and crew

**30 June** *1815-2105*
*VILLERS BOCAGE*
FO J G Sutherland and crew

**2 July** *1238-1548*
*BEAUVOIR – V1 SITE*
FO J G Sutherland and crew
FO D F O'Sullivan in (BA),
Wright out

FO J L Snyder and crew flew ME803 on three ops in late 1944. From left, M J Kehoe, Snyder, A Hammond, K G Logue, E Keate, Jock Guyan, L Walker.

**5/6 July** *2312-0132*
WATTEN – V1 SITE
FO J G Sutherland and crew

**10 July** *0425-0755*
NUCOURT – V1 SITE
FO J G Sutherland and crew
Wright back

**12 July** *1810-2205*
VAIRIES
FO J G Sutherland and crew
(abandoned due to cloud)

**15/16 July** *2210-0410*
CHÂLONS-SUR-MARNE
FO J G Sutherland and crew

**18 July** *0410-0710*
ÉMIÉVILLE
FO J G Sutherland and crew

**18/19 July** *2240-0205*
AULNOYE
FO J G Sutherland and crew

**20/21 July** *2324-0244*
HOMBERG
FO J G Sutherland and crew

**23/24 July** *2240-0350*
KIEL
FS B S Wadham
FO R C Halkyard RAAF (N)
FS H Ellis (BA)
FS H Evans RAAF (WOP)
Sgt R Walker (FE)
Sgt T Cheeseman (MU)
Sgt H Minns (RG)

**28/29 July** *2147-0537*
STUTTGART
FS B S Wadham and crew

**30 July** *0610-0905*
AMAYE-SUR-SHULLES
FO F A Stechman (DFC)
Sgt A Middleton
FS N Cottle
Sgt J Courley (WOP)
Sgt L Rowles (FE)
Sgt T Barr
Sgt T Winters

**1 Aug** *1614-1909*
COULONVILLERS
FS R Cooper
FO D M Curtis
Sgt T Webb
Sgt G Piper
Sgt J Bracey (FE)
Sgt J Herrod
FS T Moore RCAF
(abandoned over tgt – cloud)

**3 Ag** *1150-1545*
BOIS DE CASSAN
FL J G Sutherland and crew

**4 Aug** *1346-2110*
BEC D'AMBES
FO A J Osborne (DFC)
Sgt W McNeil RCAF (N)
Sgt P McGowen
Sgt J Simcox
Sgt H Edwards (FE)
Sgt D Castle
Sgt J Cowan

**5 Aug** *1430-2200*
BORDEAUX
FL J G Sutherland and crew

**7/8 Aug** *2159-0119*
MARE DE MAGNE
FL J G Sutherland and crew

**8/9 Aug** *2205-0145*
FORÊT DE LUCHEUX
FS J Perry
Sgt E Bennett
Sgt E Wood
Sgt J Lynch
Sgt H Clarke (FE)
Sgt N Atkins
Sgt N Elvish

**9/10 Aug** *2204-0004*
FORT D'ENGLOS
FL J G Sutherland and crew

**11 Aug** *1420-1730*
LENS
FO F A Stechman and crew

**15 Aug** *1012-1327*
ST TROND AIRFIELD
FO F A Stechman and crew

**16/17 Aug** *2120-0515*
STETTIN
FS B S Wadham and crew
FS J Perry (2P)

**18/19 Aug** *2150-0255*
BREMEN
FO A J Osborne and crew

**25/26 Aug** *2025-0510*
RÜSSELSHEIM
FS J Perry and crew

**26/27 Aug** *2010-0130*
KIEL
PO B S Wadham and crew

**29/30 Aug** *2120-0655*
STETTIN
PO B S Wadham and crew

**31 Aug** *1620-1945*
PONT RÉMY
FO F A Stechman and crew

**6 Sep** *1625-1940*
LE HAVRE
FL T W Miller RAAF
FS A Taylor RAAF
FS L Dickinson RAAF
WO D L Wood
Sgt F R Ruston (FE)
Sgt A Pavelyn
Sgt J McCue

**8 Sep** *0610-0945*
LE HAVRE
FO F A Stechman and crew
FO S C Josling (2P)
(abandoned over tgt by MB)

**10 Sep** *1550-1910*
ALVIS IV / LE HAVRE
FO F A Stechman and crew

**11 Sep** *1615-2030*
KAMEN
FO F A Stechman and crew

**12/13 Sep** *1855-0110*
FRANKFURT
FO F A Stechman and crew

**17 Sep** *1015-1255*
BOULOGNE
FO F A Stechman and crew

**18 Sep** *1920-2210*
ZALTBOMMEL
FL T W Miller and crew

**20 Sep** *1450-1745*
CALAIS
FO F A Stechman and crew

**23 Sep** *1935-2340*
NEUSS
FO F A Stechman and crew

**25 Sep** *0830-1125*
CALAIS
FO F A Stechman and crew
(abandoned by MB – cloud)

**26 Sep** *1135-1405*
CAP GRIS NEZ
FO S C Josling
FO L A Wood RCAF (N)
FS H G H Park
FO S J Sargent
Sgt F S Martin (FE)
Sgt W D Leitch
Sgt D G Hunt

**27 Sep** *0750-1025*
CALAIS
FL E W Talbot
WO R O Mackley RAAF
Sgt F L Bonar
FS L B Swifte RAAF
Sgt W J Tandy (FE)
Sgt A Byrne
Sgt F Hawkins

**5 Oct** *1720-2235*
SAARBRÜCKEN
FL F A Stechman and crew
FL L D Easterman (2P)

**6 Oct** *1703-2223*
DORTMUND
FL F A Stechman and crew

**7 Oct** *1259-1621*
EMMERICH
FL P G Brown RNZAF (DFC)
FO J A Willman
FS E J Banks
WO R Critchley
Sgt P R Spittle (FE)
FS D W Pratt
FO G B McDonald RNZAF (RG)

**14 Oct** *0650-1100*
DUISBURG
FL F A Stechman and crew
FL L W Thorne (2P)

**14/15 Oct** *2310-0341*
DUISBURG
FL F A Stechman and crew

**19/20 Oct** *2215-0410*
STUTTGART
FL F A Stechman and crew
PO J Palmer (2P)

**21 Oct** *1120-1415*
FLUSHING
FL F A Stechman and crew
FO Scott (2P)

**25 Oct** *1327-1717*
ESSEN
FO K V Gadd RCAF (DFC)
FS C Hawkins
FO W T Smith RCAF
FS R Bradfield
Sgt D Marsh
FS G Brown RCAF
FS D Miller RCAF

**31 Oct** *1800-2242*
COLOGNE
FO S M Grant RAAF (DFC)
FS W Parlett
FO B Keating RAAF (DFC)
FS R Browne RNZAF
Sgt G Parsloe
Sgt J Duthie
Sgt G Fry

**11 Nov** *0835-1255*
CASTROP RAUXEL
FO E G Fillimore
FS H Charlesworth RAAF
FO W Worster RCAF

FS J Breadner RAAF
Sgt N Bannister (FE)
Sgt A Dennis
Sgt C Bradshaw

**15 Nov** *1244-1719*
DORTMUND
FO G P Pickering (DFC)
Sgt P O'Reilly (N)
Sgt J Kielback RCAF (BA)
Sgt L Morgan (WOP)
Sgt T Patterson (FE)
Sgt S Clowes (MU)
Sgt C Cunnington (RG)

**20 Nov** *1246-1702*
HOMBURG
FO G P Pickering and crew

**21 Nov** *1227-1638*
HOMBURG
FO G P Pickering and crew

**23 Nov** *1244-1330*
NORDSTERN
FO G P Pickering and crew
(abandoned; port-outer u/s)

**27 Nov** *0259-0707*
NEUSS
FL G O Russell DFC
WO C Wilson (2P)
Sgt M C Preston
FS G Alexander RNZAF
FO J Currin (WOP)
Sgt E S Shaw
Sgt A MacIntyre
Sgt D J Whitehead

**30 Nov** *1034-1506*
OSTERFELD
FO J L Snyder RCAF
FO K G Logue RCAF
Sgt M J Kehoe RCAF
WO L Walker
Sgt A Hammond
Sgt E Keate RCAF
Sgt V Miller RCAF

**2 Dec** *1318-1716*
DORTMUND
FO J L Snyder and crew

**4 Dec** *1147-1622*
OBERHAUSEN
FO J L Snyder and crew

**12 Dec** *1103-1554*
WITTEN
FO G P Pickering and crew

**16 Dec** *1117-1655*
SIEGEN
FO G P Pickering and crew

**21 Dec** *1222-1705*
TRIER
FO J P R Mason RCAF
FO R I MacKay RCAF
FO L W P Barker
Sgt G L Taylor
Sgt B Balders
Sgt M M Nauss RCAF
Sgt T M Michaik RCAF
(lost port-inner but flew
on with 3 engines)

**27 Dec** *1251-1628*
TRIER
FO G P Pickering and crew

**28 Dec** *1223-1652*
COLOGNE
FO G P Pickering and crew

**31 Dec** *1140-1625*
VOEWINKEL
FO G P Pickering and crew
PO A H Dick (2P)

FL E W Talbot DFC (third from left) took ME803 on two ops.

## 1945

**1 Jan** *1629-2202*
VOEWINKEL
FO G P Pickering and crew
FO R Busbridge RCAF (2P)
(abandoned due to technical failures)

**2 Jan** *1527-2312*
NÜRNBERG
FO F H Graham RCAF
FO R E Valentine RCAF
FO H B Tims RCAF
Sgt J Haigh
Sgt D Squires
Sgt W H Dubois RCAF
Sgt R J Giesel RCAF
(flak damage, std wing)

**5 Jan** *1120-1721*
LUDWIGSHAVEN
FO G P Pickering and crew
(slight flak damage)

**13 Jan** *1139-1745*
SAARBRÜCKEN
FS D F Cameron
Sgt V Higgins
Sgt G H Scott
Sgt G Graham
FS H Somerville
Sgt R Davison
Sgt J Boyd

**16/17 Jan** *2326-0446*
WANNE-EICKEL
FO R L Burbridge RCAF
Sgt H E Harrison
FO C W Walker
Sgt P W Pollack
Sgt A W Fisher
Sgt H R Sidney
Sgt L Ireland

**22/23 Jan** *1701-2148*
DUISBURG
FL G P Pickering and crew
FS L Arakiel in (MU),
Clowes out

**29 Jan** *1015-1530*
KREFELD M/YARDS
FL G P Pickering and crew
PO J Corner (2P)

**1 Feb** *1259-1810*
MÜNCHEN-GLADBACH
FL G P Pickering and crew
Clowes back

**2/3 Feb** *2042-0249*
WEISBADEN
FL G P Pickering and crew
WO A H Gibbons (2P)

**3 Feb** *1618-2121*
DORTMUND
FL G P Pickering and crew
(bombed Botrop after delay due to searchlights)

**9 Feb** *0321-0832*
HOHENBUDBERG
FL G P Pickering and crew
Sgt J Buckley in (MU)

**13/14 Feb** *2151-0655*
DRESDEN
FL G P Pickering and crew
WO Gibbons (2P)
Clowes back

**14/15 Feb** *2022-0431*
CHEMNITZ
FL G P Pickering and crew

**16 Feb** *1236-1731*
WESEL
FL G P Pickering and crew

**18 Feb** *1201-1649*
WESEL
FL G P Pickering and crew
WP M J Carberry RAAF (2P)

**19 Feb** *1316-1902*
WESEL
WO M J Carberry RAAF
FS G G Shepphard
FS A L Johnson RAAF
FO A Tracey
Sgt K W Shepherd
Sgt J D Bollard
Sgt S J Cheetham

**22 Feb** *1233-1732*
OSTERFELD
FL G A Sherwood RCAF
FO T D Lees RCAF
FO L Ing (BA)
FS B S Jones
FS E Thompson
FS A D Lennox RCAF
FS W H Hole RCAF
(slight flak damage)

**25 Feb** *0930-1500*
KAMAN
FL O F Hill
FS R A Hurnell
FS A W Whitehead
FS E W Oakham
Sgt D N Clarke
Sgt B R Smith
Sgt A G Walker

**26 Feb** *1042-1634*
DORTMUND
FL R E Roberts
FS A K Oliffe
Sgt C E Searle
Sgt B W Forst (BA)
PO S Liston (under gnr)
Sgt R Strange (FE)
Sgt B D Smith (MU)
WO R S Groves (RG)

**27 Feb** *1126-1625*
GELSENKIRCHEN
FO C A Knapp
FS C L Denison RCAF
FS K Edginton RCAF
FS F C Vines
Sgt E Whitley
Sgt B C Treagus
Sgt E Spencer

**9/10 Apr** *1934-0131*
KIEL
FL O F Hill and crew

**14/15 Apr** *1803-0304*
POTSDAM
FL E W Talbot
PO R O Mackley RAAF
FO F L Bonar
PO L B Swifte RAAF
Sgt W J Tandy (FE)
Sgt F Hawkins (MU)
Sgt A Byrne (RG)

**18 Apr** *1021-1512*
HELIGOLAND
FO J Bettle RNZAF
FS I W James
FS C MacDonald
FS H H Judge
Sgt J Milby
Sgt J Galley
Sgt G Oliver

**22 Apr** *1540-2040*
BREMEN
FO H A Hernan
Sgt W Pollock
FS J Fowler RCAF
FO R H Leonard (WOP)
FS J E Milner (FE)
Sgt P Mitchell
Sgt A Bevan

**30 Apr** *1653-1938*
MANNA –ROTTERDAM
FO H A Hernan and crew

**1 May** *1407-1649*
MANNA – ROTTERDAM
FO N H Byers
FS H E Spencer RAAF
FO J L Dunbar
Sgt F Tomlinson
Sgt C H Wood
Sgt T Oram
FS H Burbridge

**4 May** *1205-1453*
MANNA – ROTTERDAM
FO B J Doucette RCAF
FS R G Chatfield
FS D Sutter RCAF
Sgt B B Ashford (WOP)
FS L Craven (FE)
Sgt C A Copp (RG)
(no M/U)

**7 May** *1215-1447*
MANNA – ROTTERDAM

**Three Exodus trips 10-12 May**

# ME812
# FAIR FIGHTER'S REVENGE

Built at Metro Vickers, Manchester, another as part of Contract No.2221, this Lancaster Mark I came off the production line in the spring of 1944. It was flown to 166 Squadron at Kirmington, Lincolnshire and given the code letters AS and individual letter 'F'. It flew its first op on the night of 3/4 June 1944 in the hands of Flight Sergeant S G Coole DFM, who had begun his tour of ops at the end of March.

The bomber had a female figure painted on her nose, holding a duelling sword, with the words: 'Fair Fighter's Revenge' forward of her and beneath the front gun turret. The bomb log which began beneath the cockpit soon increased until there were five rows of ten bombs, followed by another similar block next to the first. After seven night raids, which included both nights of D-Day, ME812 flew her first daylight op on 22 June. This and the Lanc's other daylight sorties were identified by having stars, and/or perhaps tiny suns, marked above the bomb symbols.

Sidney Coole, who had won an Immediate DFM in May, together with his mid-upper gunner, Sergeant Ray Scargill, for bringing their badly damaged bomber home for a crash-landing, after a fight in which Scargill shot down their attacker, took ME812 on 16 trips over the first months of her time on 166 Squadron, completing his tour in August. Coole later ran a public house and spent the last years of his life (he died in 1993) in a wheelchair following an attack in his pub.

Other pilots who flew the aircraft were men who had also flown other 166 veteran Lancs, namely, W C Hutchinson, Henry Schwass and Douglas Dickie, the latter two both New Zealanders who would complete tours and receive the DFC. In fact, Schwass and his crew actually shot down a FW190 during a sortie on 4 July flying in aircraft 'B'. Arthur Downs was Sid Coole's flight engineer and recalls how ME812 got her name:

'When we arrived at 166 Squadron we were given a new Lancaster, LM521, and because its letter was "F" it was agreed that we name her *Fair Fighter,*

Early days! Eight bombs on ME812.

hence the female holding the rapier. This aircraft served us well until our 11th operation when, after bombing Aachen on 27/28 May, we were shot-up pretty badly and set on fire over Belgium, by a Me110. The fighter was shot down by the mid-upper gunner and after putting the fire out we managed to get back to England but crashed in a wood at Woodbridge. The aircraft broke in half and was a write-off.

'We were then given another new Lancaster, code letter "F" (ME812). The same artwork was painted on the nose with the addition of one word – Revenge – and this is why it was called *Fair Fighter's Revenge.*'

In fact three of the crew received Immediate DFMs: Coole and Scargill following the Aachen raid, and Albert Manuel, the rear gunner, for an earlier feat of courage during the Nürnberg raid on 30/31 March. A 110 had attacked them and although Manuel shot it down, the

Coole and the Gang! ME812's first crew took her on 14 raids: Front: Charles Birtwhistle, Sid Coole, Bob Rennie. Rear: Ray Scargill, William Ansell, Alf Holyoak, Arthur Downs.

Flight Lieutenant Louis K Firth RCAF took her over and completed 24 ops by April 1945, and won the DFC.

Her 100th sortie was flown in early April 1945 and in total she was credited with 105 operational sorties, which included four Manna missions and at least one Exodus flight. The squadron was disbanded in September and ME812 went to 20 MU at Aston Down. The Lancaster was Struck off Charge in October 1946.

Lanc was set on fire. Manuel came out of his turret and put out the fire with his clothes and parachute despite exploding ammunition and some bad burns to himself. Upon completion of their tour the other four NCOs each received non-immediate DFMs, Arthur Downs, Bob Rennie, Charlie Birtwhistle and Alf Holyoak. All their citations note the Aachen trip.

*Fair Fighter's Revenge* flew steadily on during the summer and autumn of 1944, against all the usual targets assigned to Bomber Command, only having one recorded problem due to intercom trouble on 23 September, which caused the crew to abort. Arthur Downs remembered the trip to Révigny on 12/13 July which lasted nine hours, 30 minutes, of which they flew the last three hours thirty minutes on three engines.

Then, at the beginning of October, having completed some 53 ops *Fair Fighter's Revenge* was re-assigned to 153 Squadron when this unit was formed with crews and aircraft from 166 at Kirmington, and then the new unit moved to RAF Scampton.

With 153 Squadron the Lanc became P4-F, but within a month it became Cat AC following night fighter damage to the starboard aileron and wing, but the aircraft was back on duty before the month was out. In December

## 166 SQUADRON 1944

**3 June** *2324-0315*
*BOULOGNE*
FS S G Coole DFM
Sgt A W Downs (FE)
Sgt R S Rennie RCAF (BA)
FS C L Birtwhistle (N)
Sgt A G Holyoak (WOP)
Sgt R Scargill DFM (MU)
FS A G Manuel DFM (RG)

**5/6 June** *2105-0140*
*CHERBOURG*
FS S G Coole and crew

**6/7 June** *0005-0525*
*ACHÈRES*
FO W C Hutchinson
Sgt N Harris
FS H R Eaton RCAF
WO A T Matthews RCAF
Sgt E A Lummins
Sgt R B Parry
Sgt D G Prescott
(abandoned – weather)

**7 June** *0005-0430*
*VERSAILLES*
FO W C Hutchinson and crew

**10 June** *2250-0355*
*ACHÈRES*
FO W C Hutchinson and crew

**12/13 June** *2229-0304*
*GELSENKIRCHEN*
PO J McLaren
Sgt D Summers
FO S T Broad
FO L H Ellerker
Sgt D F Paton
Sgt F J Collins
Sgt J T E Chalk RCAF

**14/15 June** *2015-0010*
*LE HAVRE*
FS S G Coole and crew

**17/18 June** *2340-0355*
*AULNOYE*
PO J McLaren and crew
(abandoned over tgt – cloud)

**22 June** *1405-1730*
*MIMOYECQUES*
PO E Schwass RNZAF
Sgt P A Millett (FE)
Sgt D Angel (BA)
FO N J Grant RNZAF (N)
Sgt D J Carter (WOP)
FS S J Radham RNZAF (MU)
Sgt G Reynolds (RG)

**23/24 June** *2205-0540*
*SAINTES*
PO S G Coole and crew

**24 June** *0140-0530*
*FLERS – V1 SITE*
PO S G Coole and crew

**28 June** *0130-0510*
*CHÂTEAU BERNAPRE – V1*
PO S G Coole and crew

**29 June** *1155-1455*
*DOMLÉGER – V1 SITE*
PO S G Coole and crew

**30 June** *0555-1000*
*OISMONT – V1 SITE*
PO S G Coole and crew

**2 July** *1210-1545*
*DOMLÉGER – V1 SITE*
PO S G Coole and crew

**5/6 July** *2105-0535*
*DIJON*
PO S G Coole and crew

**7 July** *1925-2320*
CAEN
PO S G Coole and crew
PO F D Elliott RCAF (2P)
(hit by flak, hole in BA's Perspex)

**12/13 July** *2120-0646*
RÉVIGNY
PO S G Coole and crew
FS W H Ansell in (RG),
Manuel out

**18 July** *0310-0715*
SANNEVILLE-CAEN
PO S G Coole and crew

**20 July** *1910-2245*
WIZERNES
FS R W Miller RCAF
Sgt W A Adams
FO L W Harding
FO E A F Hall
Sgt A H MacDonald
Sgt J Schafer RCAF
Sgt C A Pike

**23/24 July** *2235-0340*
KIEL
PO S G Coole and crew
PO W L Shirley RNZAF (2P)

**24/25 July** *2115-0610*
STUTTGART
PO D J Dickie RNZAF (DFC)
Sgt W L McDonald (FE)
FO E R Pickering (BA)
FO T Mason (N)
Sgt K E Corbett (WOP)
Sgt R Turner (MU)
Sgt S G Giles (RG)

**25/26 July** *2120-0600*
STUTTGART
FO F D Elliott RCAF
Sgt J H Comley
Sgt M L Oliphant RCAF
Sgt N W L Lindon
FO R B Melville RCAF
Sgt G M Canning
Sgt K G Rhodes

**28/29 July** *2120-0550*
STUTTGART
PO D J Dickie and crew

**30 July** *0635-1025*
CAHAGNES
PO D J Dickie and crew

**31 July** *1805-2130*
LE HAVRE
PO D J Dickie and crew

**1 Aug** *1845-2145*
LA BELLE CROIX – V1 SITE
PO S G Coole and crew
(abandoned over tgt – fog)

**2 Aug** *1655-2025*
LE HAVRE
PO S G Coole and crew

**3 Aug** *1130-1550*
TROSSY ST MAXIMIN
PO S G Coole and crew

**4 Aug** *1335-2205*
PAUILLAC
PO D J Dickie and crew

**5 Aug** *1415-2210*
PAUILLAC
PO D J Dickie and crew

**7/8 Aug** *2105-0105*
FONTENAY
FO D J Dickie and crew

**10 Aug** *0925-1410*
DUGNY
FO D J Dickie and crew

**11 Aug** *1340-1740*
DOUAI M/YARDS
FO D J Dickie and crew

**12 Aug** *1120-1825*
BORDEAUX
PO D M C Jones
Sgt P R Jenkinson
Sgt E W Fletcher
Sgt J F Dormer
Sgt Milburn
Sgt J Coles
Sgt H Ferguson

**14 Aug** *1315-1715*
FONTAINE
PO D M C Jones and crew

**15 Aug** *0955-1340*
LE CULOT
PO D M C Jones and crew

**16 Aug** *2115-0450*
GARDENING – STETTIN BAY
FO D J Dickie and crew

**18 Aug** *2215-0120*
ERTVELDE-REIME
FO D J Dickie and crew

**25/26 Aug** *2000-0425*
RÜSSELSHEIM
FL R L Graham
Sgt G Potter
FS R E Lakin
PO R H W Bissonette
Sgt F A M Eade
Sgt W M G Falconer
Sgt J Wagstaff

**26/27 Aug** *2015-0120*
KIEL
FO D J Dickie and crew
FL M B French (2P)

**29/30 Aug** *2100-0540*
STETTIN
FL R L Graham and crew
SL T W Rippingdale (2P) –
A Flt Cdr (DSO DFC)

**3 Sep** *1545-1955*
GILZE-RIJEN AIRFIELD
FO W C Capper RNZAF
Sgt L W Sparvell (FE)
FS G B Bale RNZAF (BA)
FS T C Morris (N)
Sgt G Luckraft (WOP)
Sgt L M Nutt (MU)
Sgt J D Ramsey (RG)

**5 Sep** *1615-2000*
LE HAVRE
FO W C Capper and crew

**6 Sep** *1745-2050*
LE HAVRE
FO R H Williams and crew
(abandoned over tgt)

**8 Sep** *0655-1045*
LE HAVRE
FO A J E Laflamme RCAF
Sgt J Etherington (FE)
FO G J Monckton (BA)
FO G McArthur RCAF (N)
Sgt D H Schofield RCAF (WOP)
Sgt S Pollitt (MU)
Sgt F Toogood (RG)
(abandoned – low cloud)

**10 Sep** *1645-2020*
LE HAVRE
FO D J Dickie and crew
FS D M Pugh RAAF (BA)
in, Pickering out

33 ops up. August 1944.

**12/13 Sep** *1750-0130*
FRANKFURT
FO D J Dickie and crew
PO N Appleton (2P)

**16/17 Sep** *2140-0109*
STEENWIJK AIRFIELD
FO D J Dickie and crew

**20 Sep** *1520-1835*
SANGATTE
FO D J Dickie and crew

**23 Sep** *1840-2040*
NEUSS M/YARDS
FO D J Dickie and crew
(abandoned – r/t failure)

**26 Sep** *0950-1310*
CALAIS
FO D J Dickie and crew

**28 Sep** *0805-1145*
CALAIS
FO D J Dickie and crew
(abandoned over tgt)

**5/6 Oct** *1820-0040*
SAARBRÜCKEN
FO A J E Laflamme and crew

## 153 SQUADRON

**7 Oct** *1130-1615*
EMMERICH
FO A J E Laflamme and crew
PO G B Potter (2P)

**14 Oct** *0650-1120*
DUISBURG
FO W Holman RCAF
Sgt A Martin
FS V S Reynolds
FO P C Taylor RCAF
Sgt W J Burton
Sgt E S Neil RCAF
Sgt A D Kall RCAF
(shot down 20/21 Feb '45;
Holman, Taylor, Reynolds,
Kall, PoWs, rest killed)

**19/20 Oct** *2125-0425*
STUTTGART
FO A J E Laflamme and crew

**23 Oct** *1630-2205*
ESSEN
FL A E Jones
Sgt S S James
Sgt C J Cullen
FS J J L McDonald RAAF
Sgt D L Williams
Sgt R V Trafford
Sgt A Simpson

**30 Oct** *1740-2330*
COLOGNE
FO J Rhodes
Sgt M F Kingdom
FO D G Webb
FO P C H Clark
Sgt J E Livock
Sgt T J Bicknell
FS W J Baulk
(all except Baulk (not on op)
lost 1 March 1945)

**31 Oct** *1755-2315*
COLOGNE
FO J Rhodes and crew

**2 Nov** *1615-2145*
DÜSSELDORF
FO L A Wheeler
Sgt V P G Morandi
FO E C Durman RNZAF
Sgt F F Fish
FS W I H Turner
Sgt A Hodges
Sgt A Scott

**4 Nov** *1730-2230*
BOCHUM
FO L A Wheeler and crew
(damaged by night fighter)

**27 Nov** *1615-2325*
FREIBERG
FO A J E Laflamme and crew

**29 Nov** *1220-1740*
DORTMUND
FO A J E Laflamme and crew

**3 Dec** *0745-1150*
URFT DAM
FL M B French and crew
(abandoned by MB)

**4 Dec** *1625-2300*
KARLSRUHE
FO A J E Laflamme and crew

**6/7 Dec** *1635-0020*
LEUNA
FO A J E Laflamme and crew

**15 Dec** *1435-2055*
LUDWIGSHAVEN
FO A J E Laflamme and crew

**17 Dec** *1520-2310*
ULM
FO A J E Laflamme and crew

**22 Dec** *1515-2020*
COBLENZ
FO A J E Laflamme and crew

**28 Dec** *1525-2110*
BONN
FL L K Firth RCAF (DFC)
Sgt P Clowes
Sgt R W White RCAF
FO G Denbeigh RCAF
Sgt W A Jones
Sgt L E Laur RCAF
Sgt G L Lawrence RCAF

**29 Dec** *1510-2105*
SCHOLVEN
FL L K Firth and crew

**31 Dec** *1525-2050*
OSTERFELD
FL L K Firth and crew

## 1945

**2 Jan** *1520-2315*
NÜRNBERG
FL L K Firth and crew

**4 Jan** *0200-0910*
ROYAN
FL L K Firth and crew

**7/8 Jan** *1800-0325*
MUNICH
FO G P Potter
Sgt G P Woolley
FO W H Thomas
FS J Boyle
FS J S Askew RAAF
Sgt D Smith
Sgt H J Hambrook

**22 Jan** *1700-2155*
DUISBURG
FL W Holman and crew

**28/29 Jan** *1940-0300*
STUTTGART
FL L K Firth and crew

**1 Feb** *1545-2245*
LUDWIGSHAVEN
FL L K Firth and crew

**3 Feb** *1600-2205*
BOTTROP
FL L K Firth and crew

**7/8 Feb** *1855-0020*
KLEVE
FL L K Firth and crew

**8/9 Feb** *1910-0400*
PÖLITZ
FL L K Firth and crew

**13/14 Feb** *2115-0710*
DRESDEN
FL L K Firth and crew

**14/15 Feb** *2000-0500*
CHEMNITZ
FL H W Langford (DFC)
Sgt W D Thompson
FO B F Rea-Taylor
FO D S McDonald
Sgt T W Jones
Sgt D W Hallam
Sgt K A Hawkins

**21/22 Feb** *1940-0130*
DUISBURG
FL L K Firth and crew

**23 Feb** *1555-2345*
PFORZHEIM
FL L K Firth and crew

**1 Mar** *1140-1805*
MANNHEIM
FO E J Parker
Sgt J J Nevens
FO H J Lodge
FO G H Small RCAF
WO R Taylor RCAF
Sgt A W Preston RCAF
Sgt L C Williams RCAF

**2 Mar** *0645-1225*
COLOGNE
FO E J Parker and crew

**5/6 Mar** *1635-0215*
CHEMNITZ
FL A F McLarty RCAF
FS D Huddlestone
FO D S Crawford
FO J M Stevenson
Sgt J Calderbank
Sgt C Brear
Sgt W Peacock

**7/8 Mar** *1650-0230*
DESSAU
FL L K Firth and crew

**8/9 Mar** *1705-0035*
KASSEL
FL L K Firth and crew

**11 Mar** *1130-1700*
ESSEN
FL L K Firth and crew

**12 Mar** *1300-1835*
DORTMUND
FL L K Firth and crew

**13 Mar** *1725-2315*
GELSENKIRCHEN
FL L K Firth and crew

**16/17 Mar** *1720-0145*
NÜRNBERG
FL L K Firth and crew

**19 Mar** *0030-0230*
HANAU
FL L K Firth and crew
(aborted, std inner failed)

**21 Mar** *0757-1214*
BREMEN
FL L K Firth and crew

**22 Mar** *1109-1634*
HILDERSHEIM
FL L K Firth and crew

**24 Mar** *1306-1823*
HARPENERWEG
FO J M Sharp
Sgt D S Broughton
FO B Andrews
FS J A Butler RCAF

WO L P Youle RCAF
Sgt S Evans
FS W H McKnight

**27 Mar** *1433-1950*
PADERBORN
FL L K Firth and crew

**3 Apr** *1313-1946*
NORDHAUSEN
FO V S Martin RCAF
FO J A Heaton
Sgt D N Baker
FS N E Fenerty RCAF
FO J Eisen RCAF
Sgt H L Hauxwell
FS R Gray RCAF
Sgt J Weston

**4/5 Apr** *2109-0528*
LUTZENDORF
FL P N Speed
PO F P Wittingstall
FO C A Meadows
FO R H Bates RNZAF
FO C D Hill
Sgt R H Fowler
Sgt J B Mitchell

**9/10 Apr** *1907-0109*
KIEL
FL L K Firth and crew

**22 Apr** *1544-2044*
BREMEN
FL P H S Kilner
FS L O Spinks
Sgt G H Bridger
Sgt W G Corcoran
Sgt K P Baker
Sgt R S Mepstead
Sgt W A Pinkham
(abandoned due to cloud
and smoke)

**29 Apr** *1123-1503*
MANNA – THE HAGUE
WO D W Veale
FL J H Harrison
FS L J Mountcastle
Sgt B Farren
Sgt D S Stewart
Sgt T Keegan
Sgt F H Lloyd

**3 May** *1201-1455*
MANNA – ROTTERDAM
FO L Purvis
Sgt A Hardiman
WO Vollane
FO Burke
FS A Storey
Sgt J Crowther
FS A Woolmer

**4 May** *1304-1551*
MANNA – ROTTERDAM
FO R E Norris
WO G W Smith
Sgt L R Pearson
Sgt E G Learoyd
Sgt W Sullivan
Sgt P A Cox
Sgt J Davies

**7 May** *1212-1546*
MANNA – ROTTERDAM
PO J F Douglas
FS R W R Short
Sgt D H E Watson
FS S F Ward
Sgt J C Smith
Sgt J J Randall
Sgt V Simmonds

**One Exodus op 11 May**

Total now 104, May 1945.

170

# ND458
# ABLE MABEL

Part of an order for 600 Lancasters from A V Roe at Chadderton, ND458 was a Mark III with four Merlin 38 engines, produced at the end of 1943. On 10 January 1944 this bomber was assigned to 100 Squadron at Waltham, near Grimsby, Lincolnshire and given the code letters of HW. With the individual letter A for Able, the aircraft quickly became known as *Able Mabel*, and as its bomb symbols grew, painted in ten rows beneath the cockpit, it was soon apparent how apt this Lanc's name was. After eight rows had been achieved, a second block was started next to the first. The name *Able Mabel* was painted in front of the bombs and between the two blocks of symbols two swastikas indicated two successful actions against German night fighters.

ND458 started operating as the Battle of Berlin was in full swing and her first trip was to the Big City on 20/21 January in the hands of Australian Sergeant Pilot K W Evans. *Able Mabel* went to Berlin four times but was forced to abort a fifth trip due to H²S failure. On a trip to Stuttgart on 20/21 February the aircraft was hit by flak and had its bomb-doors damaged but otherwise she was fairly free of any problems.

*Able Mabel* had the usual variety of captains in her early days, although Warrant Officer P R M Neal and Sergeant E R Belbin both flew a few missions in her. Then in March Warrant Officer (later Flying Officer) J Littlewood began taking her out, having done his 'second dickie' trip in her on 24/25 February. He eventually completed 22 ops with her and received the DFC.

Jack Littlewood took *Able Mabel* on the D-Day sorties and after this event the Lanc raided V1 sites and communication centres during the summer. Its bomb-doors were again damaged on 2 July whilst bombing a V1 site, and five days after that there was a fault in the bomb-release mechanism and the bombs dropped onto unopened doors, then their weight pushed them through, so the doors sustained damage once again. This was obviously part of a dangerous period for *Able Mabel*, for on the last sortie in July the starboard wing was holed by AA fire, part of the trailing edge having later to be replaced.

*Able Mabel*: Jack Playford in the cockpit, ND458 showing 129 bombs and two swastikas. She eventually completed 132 ops.

One of her combats with enemy fighters took place on a raid on Rüsselsheim on 25/26 August. It was just about 01.30 am while flying at 16,000 feet not far off Luxembourg. The bomb aimer spotted a twin-engined Me410 above on the starboard bow. The rear gunner saw it too and ordered the skipper to corkscrew to starboard. The Messerschmitt and both ND458's gunners opened fire at the same time, the rear gunner seeing cannon and machine-gun blasts from the fighter. *Able Mabel* was hit and both turrets were put out of action but the fighter broke away to starboard and dived; it was later claimed as damaged.

*Able Mabel* had been severely damaged in the starboard elevator and rudder fin, hydraulics, R/T, as well as the turrets, but she and her pilot, Pilot Officer C D Edge RAAF, got the crew home. The bomber was out of action for almost a month, Cat AC. Charles Edge and crew later flew with 156 Squadron PFF and won the DFC, while his rear gunner, Fred Twist, got the DFM. This had been their third op in ND458. They completed more than 40 ops with 156, and the flight engineer, Norman Thorn, and navigator Arthur Lacey, also received DFMs, bomb aimer Warrant Officer Robert Steel the DFC.

The aircraft survived any further mishaps until some slight damage by flak on 4/5 November, by which time her ops total was rising fairly well. This topped the 100 mark on 1 February 1945 with a raid on Ludwigshaven. Her last raid on 25 April, to the barracks at Berchtesgaden, was *Able Mabel's* 125th trip, and as the aircraft followed these with the first ever Exodus flight on 27 April, then six Manna sorties, it made a possible total of 132.

Among her later pilots, Pilot Officer G K Veitch RAAF took her on ten ops, while Flight Lieutenant J D Playford RCAF, made 26, including the 100th. John (Jack) Playford had arrived on the squadron on 4 November although he went to 583 Squadron for a few days in mid-February 1945. He received the DFC in December.

*Able Mabel's* rival on the squadron was Lancaster ND644 N-Nan which would also achieve 100-plus ops shortly before *Mabel*, but which was destined to be lost in March. By early 1945 *Able Mabel* had enjoyed over 800 hours of virtually trouble-free flying. This was due in no small part to the efforts of its ground personnel, who kept the aircraft free of major mechanical problems. These men were Sergeant W Hearne, Corporal R T Withey, and LACs J E Robinson, J Hale and J Cowis.

## 100 SQUADRON
## 1944

**20/21 Jan** *1640-2344*
*BERLIN*
Sgt K W Evans RAAF
Sgt J J Lapes
Sgt P Atha
Sgt D Francis
Sgt A J Armstrong
Sgt C Brookes
Sgt F Whitehouse

**21/22 Jan** *2003-0220*
*MAGDEBURG*
WO P R M Neal
Sgt R Cull
Sgt C Starr
Sgt R G Evans
Sgt H A T Warner
Sgt J Mason
Sgt G R Dixon

**27/28 Jan** *1758-0200*
*BERLIN*
FS T F Cook (DFC)
Sgt H Widdup (FE) (DFM)
FO E W Norman (N) (DFC)
Sgt J C Stewart (BA)
Sgt H B Peachey
Sgt K Burchell
FO H G D Pawsey (DFC)

**29 Jan** *0025-0813*
*BERLIN*
FS T F Cook and crew

**19/20 Feb** *2330-0650*
*LEIPZIG*
WO P R M Neal and crew

**20/21 Feb** *2335-0705*
*STUTTGART*
WO P R M Neal and crew
(hit by flak)

**24/25 Feb** *1810-0220*
*SCHWEINFURT*
WO P R M Neal and crew
FS J Littlewood (2P)
Sgt J G Wookey in (RG)

**25/26 Feb** *2120-0430*
*AUGSBURG*
WO P R M Neal and crew
Sgt E J Duckett in (MU)

**1/2 Mar** *2345-0800*
*STUTTGART*
Sgt E R Belbin (DFC)
Sgt R A H Cassell (FE)
Sgt H A Merchant
FS K G Wilde RCAF (N) (DFC)

Sgt F T Baldwin
Sgt E T Duckett (MU)
Sgt J R Trueman

**15/16 Mar** *1905-0320*
*STUTTGART*
Sgt E R Belbin and crew

**18/19 Mar** *1910-0055*
*FRANKFURT*
Sgt E R Belbin and crew

**24/25 Mar** *1900-0205*
*BERLIN*
Sgt E Walton
Sgt R T Rutter (FE) (DFC)
FS J O'Loughlin
Sgt T E Sanders
Sgt R J Taylor
Sgt L Whitewood
Sgt J R Logan

**26/27 Mar** *2005-0100*
*ESSEN*
Sgt E R Belbin and crew
Sgt F S Gaywood in,
Cassell out

**30/31 Mar** *2200-0600*
*NÜRNBERG*
FS J Littlewood (DFC)
Sgt T McCartney (FE)
FS B A Tovell (N)
Sgt J G Hughes
Sgt R W Gilbey
Sgt A G Girton
Sgt J Taylor

**9/10 Apr** *2130-0545*
*GARDENING – GDYNIA*
WO E R Belbin and crew
Cassell back

**10/11 Apr** *2345-0445*
*AULNOYE M/YARDS*
WO E R Belbin and crew

**18/19 Apr** *2100-0420*
*GARDENING – BALTIC*
WO J Littlewood and crew

**20/21 Apr** *0006-0405*
*COLOGNE M/YARDS*
WO J Littlewood and crew
Sgt R P Anderson (FE) in,
McCartney out

**22/23 Apr** *2245-0314*
*DÜSSELDORF M/YARDS*
WO J Littlewood
PO M C Hennessey (2P)
Sgt J V Dew (FE)
FS R A Tovell (N)
Sgt W J Massey (BA)

Sgt J H Woodcraft (WOP)
Sgt S C Smith (MU)
FS M Biggs (RG)

**24/25 Apr** *2217-0407*
*KARLSRUHE*
WO J Littlewood and crew
Sgt J V Dew (FE) in

**26/27 Apr** *2300-0315*
*ESSEN*
WO J Littlewood and crew
McCartney out, FL C N Waite (FE) in

**27/28 Apr** *2140-0550*
*FRIEDRICHSHAFEN*
WO J Littlewood and crew
McCartney back

**30 Apr/1 May** *2136-0211*
*MAINTENON*
WO J Littlewood and crew

**3/4 May** *2150-0315*
*MAILLY-LE-CAMP*
PO E D King
Sgt W F Bloomfield (FE)
FO L H Scott
Sgt F W Cheetham
Sgt S Beardsell
Sgt D Ralston
Sgt D W Young

**7/8 May** *2140-0240*
*BRUZ DUMP*
PO E D King and crew
Sgt R G Crabb in (FE)
Bloomfield out

**9/10 May** *2155-0110*
*MERVILLE GUN*
PO E A Wainwright
Sgt R L Thomson
WO J M Rosborough RCAF
FS R A Brown RCAF
Sgt E H Wallington
Sgt L Cohen
Sgt J J O'Mara

**10/11 May** *2240-0140*
*DIEPPE GUN*
PO J Littlewood and crew

**21/22 May** *2235-0250*
*DUISBURG*
PO J Littlewood and crew

**22/23 May** *2245-0255*
*DORTMUND*
PO J Littlewood and crew

**24/25 May** *2240-0105*
*LE CLIPTON GUN*
PO J Littlewood and crew

**27/28 May** *2347-0322*
*MERVILLE GUN*
PO J Littlewood and crew

**28/29 May** *2233-0143*
*EU GUN*
PO T G Page
Sgt D Henderson
Sgt L C Roots
Sgt D M Jones
Sgt E W Hayley
Sgt J Todd
Sgt R Watson

**31 May/1 June** *0006-0415*
*TERGNIER M/YARDS*
PO J M Shaw
Sgt W S Johnson
Sgt J C Locke
Sgt B W Young
Sgt W J Jones
Sgt J G Gorman
Sgt W Everitt

**2/3 June** *2335-0305*
*BERNEVAL*
PO J Littlewood and crew
FL C N Waite in (FE)

**5/6 June** *2120-0130*
*ST MARTIN DE VARREVILLE GUN*
PO J Littlewood and crew
PO P R Anderson (FE) in

**6/7 June** *2200-0300*
*VIRE*
PO J Littlewood and crew
Waite back in

**7/8 June** *2335-0400*
*FORÊT DE CERISY*
PO J Littlewood and crew
FO A B Good in (N),
Tovell out

**10/11 June** *2320-0410*
*ARCHÈRES*
FO O S Milne
Sgt W H Lanning
Sgt R A D Newman
FO R B Hutchinson
Sgt B Nundy
Sgt H Taylor
Sgt K Yenlett

**12 June** *0115-0515*
*EVREUX M/YARDS*
FO O S Milne and crew

**12/13 June** *2300-0245*
*GELSENKIRCHEN*
PO J Littlewood and crew
Sgt H Widdup in (FE) and
Tovell back

**17 June** *0015-0355*
DOMLÉGER – V1 SITE
PO R G Page and crew

**22/23 June** *2250-0320*
REIMS M/YARDS
FO O S Milne and crew

**24/25 June** *1610-1915*
LES HAYONS – V1 SITE
FO O S Milne and crew

**28 June** *0055-0515*
VAIRIES M/YARDS
FO O S Milne and crew

**29 June** *1155-1500*
DOMLÉGER – V1 SITE
PO J Littlewood and crew

**30 June/1 July** *2205-0315*
VIERZON M/YARDS
PO J Littlewood and crew
FS J G Wookey in (RG),
Taylor out

**2 July** *1215-1540*
OISMONT – V1 SITE
FO O S Milne and crew
(flak damage)

**4/5 July** *2215-0400*
ORLÉANS M/YARDS
PO J D Rose (DFC)
Sgt M J Dunphy
FS J K Martin
FO J M Wilder
Sgt A Palmer
Sgt P L Daly
Sgt V E Locke

**6 July** *1855-2225*
FORÊT DU CROC – V1 SITE
PO J Littlewood and crew

**7 July** *1940-2310*
CAEN
PO J Littlewood and crew

**12/13 July** *2135-0320*
TOURS M/YARDS
PO J Littlewood and crew
Taylor back

**14/15 July** *2125-0554*
RÉVIGNY M/YARDS
FO J G Evans RAAF
Sgt J Leitch
FO D G Heath
Sgt G P Clark
FS W H Preece
Sgt C G McKenna
PO J C Costigan

**28/29 July** *2125-0540*
STUTTGART
PO G K Veitch RAAF
Sgt P Pearce
FS A R Martin
PO H L Hamblin
FS K McIntyre
Sgt J H Smith
FS T E Hall

**30 July** *0640-1045*
VILLERS BOCAGE AREA
PO G K Veitch and crew
(std wing holed by flak)

**4 Aug** *1335-2135*
PAUILLAC
PO J Littlewood and crew

**5 Aug** *1435-2250*
PAUILLAC
FL C Holland
Sgt C A Taylor
PO J H Boyle RCAF
PO K Balster RCAF
FS E J Clarke RAAF

Air and ground crew looking at a 4,000 lb 'cookie' that will be dropped on a German target tonight.

FS C Hill RAAF
Sgt J Thornton

**7/8 Aug** *2120-0130*
FONTENAY-LE-MARMION
FO H J Healy RAAF
Sgt E Kitchen
Sgt S Owen
FS A S G Wilson
Sgt R Morgan
Sgt C J Webb
Sgt J R Buchanan

**10 Aug** *1015-1140*
VINCLY – V1 SITE
FO C M Stuart and crew
(abandoned – weather)

**14 Aug** *1215-1610*
FALAISE
WO W T Ramsden
Sgt E G Stubbings
Sgt S T Howard
FO R P Simpson
Sgt R M Chestnutt
Sgt R J Williams
Sgt F Crompton

**15 Aug** *1020-1340*
VOLKEL AIRFIELD
PO C D Edge RAAF
Sgt N Thorn (FE)
Sgt A F Lacey (N)
FS R P Steel (BA)
FS J M Muller (WOP)
Sgt F Twist (MU)
Sgt A Taylor (RG)

**16/17 Aug** *2115-0450*
STETTIN
FO G K Veitch and crew
FO S Ross and Sgt I J
Duffett in, Hamblin and
Smith out

**18/19 Aug** *2230-0145*
ERTVELDE RIEME
PO C D Edge and crew

**25/26 Aug** *2030-0515*
RÜSSELSHEIM
PO C D Edge and crew
(attacked by night fighter which
was claimed as damaged; Lancaster
badly damaged too)

**23 Aug** *1840-2340*
NEUSS
FO T Batley
Sgt W J Williams
Sgt R J Perry
Sgt D Clay
WO D L Edgar
Sgt J E Fellows
Sgt H J Faulkner

**25 Sep** *0730-1125*
CALAIS
FO G K Veitch and crew
(abandoned by MB)

**26 Sep** *1035-1315*
CAP GRIS NEZ
FO G K Veitch and crew

**28 Sep** *0825-1140*
CALAIS
FO P J McVerry and crew
(abandoned)

**5/6 Oct** *1855-0035*
SAARBRÜCKEN
FO G K Veitch and crew

**7 Oct** *1220-1610*
EMMERICH
FL D M D Brown (DFC)
PO R P Anderson (N) (DFC)
FO S A Harvey
FO W Bathgate
Sgt A Halstead
FS W Bill
Sgt A G Tipple

**14 Oct** *0645-1115*
DUISBURG
PO R Barker
Sgt A S Gordon
Sgt F S Elliott
Sgt A A Law
WO J M C Wilson
Sgt F Gillen
Sgt B G Aldred

**15 Oct** *0030-0600*
DUISBURG
PO R Barker and crew

**23 Oct** *1615-2125*
ESSEN
FO G K Leitch and 9 crew
PO D Shrimpton (2P)

PO P R Bond (BA) in,
plus Sgt R Livingstone (2BA)

**25 Oct** *1255-1730*
ESSEN
FO R T Hoyle
Sgt P T Bickley
PO G S Charles
Sgt R A Ward
Sgt A E Law
PO D R Hoptroff
Sgt L Marshall

**28 Oct** *1320-1800*
COLOGNE
FO G K Veitch and crew

**30/31 Oct** *1750-2325*
COLOGNE
FO R T Hoyle and crew

**31 Oct** *1755-2305*
COLOGNE
FO R T Hoyle and crew

**2 Nov** *1620-2135*
DÜSSELDORF
FO F L Conn RAAF
Sgt A H Wilson
Sgt J R Hartshorne
FO J R Hughesdon
FS J Brady RAAF
Sgt F Hemmant (RG)
Sgt W F Hart

**4 Nov** *1745-2215*
BOCHUM
FO D M Ward RCAF
Sgt W Hunter (FE)
FO J R L Linn RCAF (N)
PO F C Squires RCAF (BA)
WO J Safaruk RCAF (WOP)
Sgt J I Griffith RCAF (MU)
Sgt W Humphrey RCAF (RG)
(flak damage)

**18 Nov** *1600-2120*
WANNE-EICKEL
FL J D Playford RCAF (DFC)
Sgt H M Hadley
FO J Menagh RCAF
FO W J Elrick RCAF
Sgt R Kemp
Sgt H C Rasmussen RCAF
Sgt R L McKay RCAF

Daylight ops showed the crews just how many aircraft were close-by!

**16 Nov** *1305-1730*
*DÜREN*
FO G K Veitch and crew

**27 Nov** *1615-2300*
*FREIBERG*
FL J D Playford and crew

**29 Nov** *1215-1725*
*DORTMUND*
FL J D Playford and crew

**3 Dec** *0800-1225*
*URFT DAM*
FO F L Conn and crew

**4 Dec** *1645-2310*
*KARLSRUHE*
FL J D Playford and crew

**6/7 Dec** *1640-0050*
*MERSEBURG*
FL J D Playford and crew

**12 Dec** *1630-2155*
*ESSEN M/YARDS*
FL J D Playford and crew

**15 Dec** *1450-2115*
*LUDWIGSHAVEN*
FO D H Shrimpton
Sgt G W Overton
FS J E Beath
Sgt R Livingstone
FS J H Gleghorn
Sgt R A Tilly
Sgt C Reilly

**17 Dec** *1515-2300*
*ULM*
PO R Barker and crew

**26 Dec** *1255-1725*
*ST VITH*
FL J D Playford and crew

**28 Dec** *1530-2110*
*MÜNCHEN-GLADBACH*
FL J D Playford and crew

**29 Dec** *1515-2130*
*GELSENKIRCHEN*
PO J A Seagroatt
Sgt M S A Wildman
PO H O Berger
FO S M Plaskett
FO D Costello
Sgt R Wadge
Sgt L Robinson
Sgt J Whittaker

## 1945

**2 Jan** *1505-2325*
*NÜRNBERG*
PO R Barker and crew
(All lost in JB603 5/6 Jan,
on its 112th op)

**5/6 Jan** *1410-0025*
*HANNOVER*
WO W H Evans and crew
(see JB603 – Baxter and Evans
swapped aircraft on this date)

**6 Jan** *1600-2200*
*HANAU M/YARDS*
FS  D W McKenzie RNZAF
Sgt R McLelland
Sgt F R Ford
FS W T D Allen RNZAF
FS J F Malvern
WO H E Thornby
Sgt C W Anderson RCAF

**7/8 Jan** *1835-0330*
*MUNICH*
WO W H Evans and crew

**14/15 Jan** *1945-0355*
*MERSEBURG*
FO F L Conn and crew
PO J O'Riordon in, Sgt
Hemmant out (RG)

**16/17 Jan** *1735-0120*
*ZEITZ TROGLITE*
FO P J Whyler
Sgt H Doughty
Sgt F C Warin
Sgt A Robinson
Sgt L G Cox
Sgt H G Jones
Sgt A R E Witt

**1 Feb** *1555-2235*
*LUDWIGSHAVEN*
FL J D Playford and crew

**7/8 Feb** *1844-2355*
*CLEVE*
FO K V Fraser RCAF
Sgt W H Cooke
FS D J Sawer
FS J Wright
FS J Riddell
FS W V Gosleigh RCAF
FS H S Withers RCAF

**13/14 Feb** *2150-0740*
*DRESDEN*
FL J D Playford and crew
FS C Daventry-Bull in (RG),
Rasmusson out

**14/15 Feb** *2010-0505*
*CHEMNITZ*
FL J D Playford and crew
FS K S Mitchell in (RG)

**20/21 Feb** *2155-0415*
*DORTMUND*
FL A R V Butler RCAF
Sgt W Daymont
FO T R Pryde
FS L Cox
FL R P Thompson
FS A R M Hart
Sgt J B Roadhouse

**21/22 Feb** *1920-0135*
*DUISBURG*
FL A R V Butler and crew

**1 Mar** *1150-1800*
*MANNHEIM*
FL J D Playford and crew

**5/6 Mar** *1705-0220*
*CHEMNITZ*
FL L Morrison RCAF
Sgt E Alvarez
FO A A Munro RCAF
FO D L Paterson RCAF
Sgt W B Stewart
Sgt C F Webb
Sgt H J Baker

**7/8 Mar** *1700-0250*
*DESSAU*
FL L Morrison and crew

**8/9 Mar** *1730-0050*
*KASSEL*
FO H Brown
Sgt J Wadsworth
WO J S Grabb
FS J S Metcalfe
Sgt R S Hall
Sgt W H McGough
Sgt A Lloyd

**11 Mar** *1140-1705*
*ESSEN*
WC T B Morton
Sgt A McDougall
FS W S Merrall
FO S McMichael
FS J Smith
FS S E Greenley
FS P Kenny

**12 Mar** *1330-1845*
*DORTMUND*
WO W H Evans and crew
Sgt A Hopley in (RG),
Burdett out

**13 Mar** *1705-2315*
*BRIN BENZOL*
FL J D Playford and crew
Rasmusson back

**15/16 Mar** *1705-0045*
*MISBURG*
FL J D Playford and crew

**16/17 Mar** *1730-0150*
*NÜRNBERG*
FO L Morrison and crew

**19 Mar** *0035-0750*
*HANAU*
FO L Morrison and crew

**22 Mar** *0045-0650*
*BRUCHSTRASSE*
FL J D Playford and crew

**23 Mar** *0720-1150*
*BREMEN*
FL J D Playford and crew

**25 Mar** *0645-1220*
*HANNOVER*
FO L Morrison and crew

**27 Mar** *1500-1935*
*PADERBORN*
FL J D Playford and crew

**31 Mar** *0625-1140*
*HAMBURG*
FO L Morrison and crew

**4/5 Apr** *2101-0531*
*LUTZENDORF*
FL J D Playford and crew

**9/10 Apr** *1936-0107*
*KIEL*
FL J D Playford and crew

**10/11 Apr** *1834-0315*
*PLAUEN M/YARDS*
FL J D Playford and crew

**14/15 Apr** *1749-0258*
*POTSDAM*
FL J D Playford and crew

**18 Apr** *0954-1444*
*HELIGOLAND*
FL J D Playford and crew

**22 Apr** *1512-2006*
*BREMEN*
FL J D Playford and crew
(abandoned over tgt – weather)

**25 Apr** *0509-1330*
*BERCHTESGADEN*
FL J D Playford and crew

**27 Apr** *1644-0957*
*EXODUS*
FL J D Playford and crew

**30 Apr** *1547-1842*
*MANNA – LEIDEN*
FL J D Playford and crew

**1 May** *1357-1730*
*MANNA*
WO P S Terry
Sgt H T Sharp
Sgt A Carr
FS T O Marsh
FS E E Boot
Sgt K H Eland
Sgt P F Fellows

**2 May** *1155-1503*
*MANNA*
WO P S Terry and crew

**3 May** *1146-1502*
*MANNA*
WO P S Terry and crew

**5 May** *0631-0933*
*MANNA*
PO R E M Chaplin
FS V Quinn
Sgt D H Lewis
Sgt S T Reeves
Sgt T Cook
Sgt E Jones
Sgt J Taylor

**7 May** *1249-1631*
*MANNA*
PO R E M Chaplin and crew

# ND578
# YORKER

Another A V Roe-built Lancaster from order No.1807, a Mark III with four Merlin 38 engines, which came off the production line at the end of 1943 or early '44. On 5 February ND578 was assigned to 44 (Rhodesia) Squadron at Dunholme Lodge, Lincolnshire, and marked with the squadron code letters KM. Its individual letter became 'Y' and soon she became known on the unit as Y-Yorker.

*Yorker's* first operation was a big one – Berlin – and in the hands of a pilot who had joined the squadron the previous October. This was Pilot Officer John Chatterton and he would eventually fly her on 15 ops, complete his tour and receive the DFC. John, who helped me with the original book, died recently, but had recalled:

John Chatterton and crew took ND578 on its first op and flew a further 15 in her. From left to right: John Davidson, Bill Champion, Bill Barker, John Chatterton, D J Reyland, Ken Letts, John Michie. Chatterton and Reyland received DFCs, the others all got DFMs.

'I shall always think of "Y" as my aeroplane. In those days a crew usually had their own – perhaps shared with one other crew – and the two of us pilots would "create" considerably if the flight commander let "odd-bods" fly it. Things were very different later when lots of crew were competing for aircraft.

'I well remember when joining 44 Squadron, Squadron Leader Jack Shorthouse, flight commander B Flight, said, "You'll be sharing Yorker with Knight but he is senior (he had done about six trips in her predecessor – W4993) so he'll take precedence if you are both on ops the same night." There was the slight matter of a taxying accident with the chimney of a tar-boiler left dangerously close to the peri-track for which Knight was sent on a disciplinary course at Sheffield. During the fortnight he was away I was the uncontested driver of Y, so much so that when he came back he only did a couple more in Y before going missing in Z.

'We soldiered on in W4933 until the new year when the squadron was re-equipped with H²S Lancasters. My log-book shows "acceptance test" for ND578 as 12 February 1944: rather a grand name for the first air-test but I wasn't likely to say NO to a new kite. I was a bit worried that I might have to share it with Sergeant Frank Levy who took her on his first op to Stuttgart on 20 February but fortunately for me he was posted to 617 Squadron, but was lost with them on the way back from the *Tirpitz* raid.

'Halfway through my tour and maybe getting a bit big-headed, I was considerably affronted when the new squadron commander, Wing Commander F W Thompson, called me in to his office and said he intended to share Y with me. A week or so later I realised what a tremendous favour he had done me – by keeping "my" aircraft out of the hands of a sprog crew, after all, the OC wasn't allowed to operate more than one in three or four weeks, so I would still be virtually the sole owner.'

John Chatterton and his rear gunner, Jock Davidson. The white number on the flying helmet are his 'last three' – a quick method of equipment identification.

On completion of their tour, John Chatterton and his crew were decorated. Apart from John's DFC, Jack Reyland also received the DFC, while Ken Letts, Jock Michie, Bill Champion, Jock Davidson and Mansel Scott each received the DFM. It was unusual for all seven men in a bomber crew to be decorated, but as John explained:

'There was a short period in our squadron when the entire crew were decorated – I think as a sort of encouragement to others in the bad old days. I recently met two old pals from 44 Squadron and the same thing happened to their crews.

'Occasionally we took new men on their first trips and, because second pilots usually got in the way of the smooth running of the flight-deck, I generally tried to wangle second navigators. There was plenty of room and he could actually be useful with the H²S set.

'We had a photo taken at the end of our tour and it is a great pity it doesn't show Scotty who was our faithful bomb aimer for most of the tour, but he had finished his 30 trips so we had Barker for the last two or three. Our original bomb aimer, Pete Lees, was lost with another crew early in our tour. We were stand-by crew one night when another captain's bomb aimer (Scotty) went sick, so Lees went with them and so we inherited Scotty.'

Wing Commander F W Thompson DFC AFC had already done a tour on Whitley bombers with 10 Squadron in 1941, and came from 1658 HCU to command 44 Squadron. As John Chatterton says, Thompson also flew Yorker as 'his' aircraft, which was perfectly natural. Thompson recalled:

Yorker's ground crew (rear row only): Jock Biggar (rigger and bomb painter), Harry Prior (engines), Palmer, Dick Pinning (engines), Sgt Alan Rubenstein (NCO i/c).

'I always regarded Y-Yorker as my own lucky aeroplane. We always tried to fly with the same crew and that applied to the Squadron Commander along with all the others, although, of course, sickness, leave, etc., did at times dictate otherwise.

'I got so attached to Y-Yorker that I took great pains to see that she was detailed for operations with my most reliable crews. One sortie I recall, on 7 May 1944, was against a munitions factory at Salbris. On this one I was controlling and Wing Commander Leonard Cheshire was marking. The factory consisted of those large sheds with gaps of some 12 feet between. We decided to mark the first gap.

'Cheshire called, "Mark!" on time but I could not see any mark so I reported, "No mark." Cheshire went round again with the same results, and then for a third time. By now he and I were both getting rather cross. He said he put all three down the gap – and he had – but they were not visible at the height I was flying so I said to put one on the top of the second shed which he did and I was able to proceed.

'On 4 July we attacked flying-bomb stocks and on 15 July mines in the Kiel Canal. 44 Squadron had a reputation for accurate mine-laying but only the most experienced crews were used. I also see I took Yorker on a daylight raid to Caen at the opening of the Caen operation. Apart from these operations I did quite a lot of flying, always choosing to use Y-Yorker if possible. We regarded Yorker as a very special aircraft.'

Wing Commander Tommy Thompson received the DSO during the summer. His usual navigator with 44 was Flight Lieutenant – later Squadron Leader DFC – Steve Burrows, who remembered:

'Whilst Master Bombing Brunswick, 22/23 May, we were coned for a long period together with the usual flak. Attacks from fighters were numerous and damage to the port-inner resulted in its loss.

'We often took additional crew members who had not flown on ops before to let them see the pretty lights! We also operated on D-Day, but as far as I can remember were not told about it, but the radar screen soon showed us different.'

A whole variety of crews in fact flew *Yorker*, only a few becoming more or less regular for short periods, such as Flying Officer Lister W Hayler (DFC), who went on to fly 31 ops in the aircraft, Flying Officer Ronald Thomson (DFC), six ops, and Flying Officer H V Parkin, 11 ops.

*Yorker* had few operational problems, although she did lose her port-outer 25 minutes after bombing Düren on 16 November, while the port-inner engine had a runaway prop on 22/23rd – then the engine seized. *Yorker* had a couple of skirmishes with night fighters, the first during her third sortie. Frank Levy was taking her to Stuttgart on 20/21 February 1944 and was at 23,000 feet.

A Me210 was spotted by the rear gunner slightly above on the port quarter and coming in on a curving approach. Levy took evasive action as the gunner opened fire at 600 yards. The 210 was hit on the tail, dived away and was not seen again. The mid-upper could not fire as his turret had frozen up.

Then on 4 November, over Düsseldorf at 19,000 feet, the rear gunner saw fighter-flares to port and then two FW190s in formation crossed astern. The enemy fighters turned in on the port quarter flying a parallel course, closing in to 800 yards. The pilot was 'asked' to corkscrew to port as the rear gunner began firing. One Focke Wulf fired a long burst but it was then lost in the manoeuvre. While this was going on, the mid-upper was keeping an eye on a twin-engined fighter astern, but it did not approach.

*Yorker* completed her 100th sortie on 2/3 February 1945, with Hayler as skipper, and went on to accomplish 123 ops by 17/18 April, although the actual total may only have been 121. The aircraft had no personal nose-marking other than the row of bombs, ten rows each of ten, with another block starting behind the first, by which time *Yorker* was operating from Spilsby. However, someone had obviously been to London Zoo and had 'liberated' a sign which was placed inside the cockpit windows on the starboard side, which stated: 'These Animals are Dangerous'.

*Yorker* became Cat AC on 18 May 1945 and went off to Avro's, Lincoln, for overhaul, returning on 24 May. She then went to 75 (New Zealand) Squadron on 2 July, also at Spilsby, but was finally Struck off Charge on 27 October.

By the early 1990s John Chatterton's son was a regular pilot of the Battle of Britain Memorial Flight's sole flying Lancaster (PA474) and continued this job until 1997. He also flew his father and a couple of the old crew in it.

KM-Y, 44 Squadron. Aircrew from left to right: Pete Roberts, Steve Burrows, M J Stancer, WC F W Thompson DFC (ninth), Bill Clegg (eleventh) FL G E Mortimer (gunnery leader) far right.

## 44 SQUADRON
## 1944

**15/16 Feb** *1713-2355*
*BERLIN*
PO J Chatterton
Sgt F K Letts (FE)
FO D J Reyland (N)
FS M M Scott (BA)
Sgt J Michie (WOP)
Sgt W H R Champion (MU)
Sgt J H Davidson (RG)

**19/20 Feb** *2355-0645*
*LEIPZIG*
PO J Chatterton and crew

**20/21 Feb** *2347-0730*
*STUTTGART*
Sgt P Levy
Sgt P W Groom
FO C L Fox
Sgt E S Peck
Sgt G M Maguire
Sgt A F McNally
Sgt D G Thomas (RG)
(combat with Me210)

**25/26 Feb** *1831-2010*
*AUGSBURG*
PO J Chatterton and crew
(aborted, r/t failure)

**1/2 Mar** *2259-0755*
*STUTTGART*
WC F W Thompson DFC AFC
FL S Burrows DFC (FE)
FO P F Young
Sgt E Craven
PO P F Roberts (WOP) (DFC)
FS E V Burden
FS J Hall

**10/11 Mar** *2013-0409*
*OSSUN*
WC F W Thompson DFC AFC
Sgt H W Carter
FO J L Gourlay
Sgt R B Taylor
PO R H Bennett
Sgt P Curtis
WO W Bowling

**15/16 Mar** *1937-0310*
*STUTTGART*
PO J Chatterton and crew
Sgt W G Singfield in,
Sgt Davidson out, plus FS W T
Freeman in (2N)

**18/19 Mar** *1941-0109*
*FRANKFURT*
PO J Chatterton and crew
Sgt J Shaw in (RG)

**22/23 Mar** *1849-0034*
*FRANKFURT*
PO J Chatterton and crew
Davidson back

**24/25 Mar** *1859-0153*
*BERLIN*
PO J Chatterton and crew
plus FO T S Calder (2N)

**26/27 Mar** *1942-0057*
*ESSEN*
PO J Chatterton and crew
plus FS A O Kennedy (2N)

**5/6 Apr** *2029-0330*
*TOULOUSE*
PO J Chatterton and crew

**9/10 Apr** *2121-0556*
*GARDENING – HELPOINT*
PO J Chatterton and crew
plus FS L J Mitchell (2N)

**10/11 Apr** *2309-0439*
*TOURS M/YARDS*
PO J Chatterton and crew

**11/12 Apr** *2033-0035*
*AACHEN*
SL S L Cockbain (DFC)
FS S J Cristow
FL P Waterboys
FO C H McKenzie (BA) (DFC)
FS A Dicken (WOP) (DFC)
FS A E Bracegirdle (MU) (DFM)
FS J S Dean (RG)

**18/19 Apr** *2025-0123*
*JUVISY*
PO J Chatterton and crew
plus FS R Riddoch (2N)

**20/21 Apr** *2146-0233*
*PARIS / LA CHAPELLE*
PO J Chatterton and crew
plus FS E H Greatz (2N)

**22/23 Apr** *2250-0511*
*BRUNSWICK*
PO J Chatterton and crew

**24/25 Apr** *2044-0632*
*MUNICH*
PO J Chatterton and crew
FS W H Barker in, Scott out

**26/27 Apr** *2123-0645*
*SCHWEINFURT*
FS G Baxter
Sgt D E Betterton
FS B A Rutherford
FS S Young
FS K Scholes
Sgt D A Taylor
Sgt D R Whitfield

**28/29 Apr** *2122-0514*
*OSLO KJELLER*
WC F W Thompson DFC AFC
FL S Burrows DFC (FE)
FS M J Shearer (N) (DFM)
FO W Clegg (BA)
FS A Dicken (WOP)
FL G E Mortimer
FS J Hall
FO F D R Hilbrew

**1/2 May** *2124-0550*
*TOULOUSE*
PO W J Hough
Sgt H D Hoare
Sgt L Priestley
Sgt J H Singer RCAF
Sgt H W Nichols
Sgt P Anderson RCAF
Sgt P S Hanna
(all except Hanna lost 15/16
July, with another gunner)

**7/8 May** *2148-0339*
*SALBRIS*
WC F W Thompson and crew
FO P F Roberts and FS E P
Burden in, Dicken, Hilbrew
and Mortimer out

**11/12 May** *2232-0206*
*BOURG LÉOPOLD*
SL S L Cockbain
FL J E White (2P) (DFC)
Sgt R P Haly (FE)
FL W Woodhouse DFM (N)
FO C H McKenzie (BA)
FL I Radmeyer DFC (WOP)
FS D Bracegirdle (MU)
FS J S Dean (RG)
(abandoned, tgt not properly
marked)

**19/20 May** *2304-0208*
*AMIENS*

Jock Biggar paints on bomb number 107, March 1945. FL L W Hayler
in the cockpit. Lister Hayler took ND578 on over 30 trips and won
the DFC.

WC F W Thompson and crew
FL J Lowry in, Clegg out

**21/22 May** *2252-0331*
*DUISBURG*
PO W J Hough and crew

**22/23 May** *2234-0502*
*BRUNSWICK*
WC W F Thompson and crew
FS A J Cole (2P)

**27/28 May** *2250-0300*
*MORSALINES GUN*
PO W J Hough and crew

**31 May/1 June** *2252-0312*
*MAISY*
WC F W Thompson and crew
(aborted due to weather)

**6 June** *0129-0600*
*LA PERNELLE*
WC F W Thompson and crew
FS Burden back, Hall out

**7 June** *0029-0503*
*CAEN*
WC F W Thompson and crew

**8/9 June** *2223-0301*
*PONTAUBAULT*
FL J E White (DFC)
Sgt A J Rickeard
FS R C M Jones
Sgt T E Jenkins
PO L F A Marston
Sgt W M H Burnett
Sgt G W Nicholson

**9/10 June** *2146-0220*
*ÉTAMPES*
WC F W Thompson and crew

**13 June** *0009-0445*
*CAEN*
FL J E White and crew
Sgt D H Watts in (RG),
Sgt Nicholson out

**14/15 June** *2222-0255*
*AUNAY*
WC F W Thompson and crew
PO J E P Oxborrow (2P)

PO S J Bristow (FE) in
(FL Oxborrow DFC and his crew
all lost 12/13 Sep)

**16/17 June** *2300-0251*
*WESSELING*
FL J E White and crew
PO K J Gowing (2P)
(Gowing and his crew lost
7/8 July; he and one other
were killed)

**24/25 June** *2211-0138*
*POMMEREVAL – V1 SITE*
PO D J Ibbotson
Sgt J R W Worrall
FS E H Greatz
FS I R Murray
Sgt K G Andrews
Sgt T W Whitehand
Sgt F A Wells
(shot down over France
25 July, all evaded except
Whitehand – KIA)

**27/28 June** *2314-0237*
*MARQUISE – V1 SITE*
FO W J Hough and crew

**7/8 July** *2225-0315*
*ST LEU D'ESSERENT*
WC F W Thompson and crew

**12/13 July** *2158-0630*
*CHALINDREY*
FO R G Boswell
Sgt R E Lewis
Sgt R L Meakin
FO W Creed
FS J H Hunt
Sgt B Merry
Sgt V E Leslie

**14/15 July** *2201-0512*
*VILLENEUVE ST GEORGES*
FO R G Boswell and crew

**15/16 July** *2235-0428*
*GARDENING – KIEL*
WC F W Thompson and crew
FL H R Clarke in (RG), Hall out

# ND578 YORKER

**18 July** *0355-0721*
*CAEN*
WC F W Thompson and crew

**19 July** *1925-2335*
*THIVERNY – V1 SITE*
SL G A Hildred (DFC)
Sgt V G Bender
PO N O W Turner
FS L C Treloar
FS J M Parker
FO I P Hourigan
FO P Bradshaw

**20/21 July** *2253-0233*
*COURTRAI M/YARDS*
WC F W Thompson and crew

**24/25 July** *2150-0605*
*STUTTGART*
FO K M Davey (DFC)
Sgt J H Rawcliffe
FL T H Grant
PO D J Roddle
Sgt J H Oliphant
FS S J Arnold
Sgt J Kerley

**25/26 July** *2121-0629*
*STUTTGART*
FO S F Gale
Sgt A S Buchanan
Sgt L E Patterson
Sgt K H Irwin
WO J Brosnahan
Sgt R Marshall
Sgt T E Fardoe

**26/27 July** *2101-0630*
*GIVORS*
FS C E Binion
Sgt D M Pearce
FS A O Kennedy
WO G M Gebhard
Sgt F W Stroud
FS A Micalchuk
Sgt H M Knox

**28/29 July** *2211-0602*
*STUTTGART*
FL B J Dobson (DFC*)
Sgt A T McKenzie
Sgt J B Knight
FS A K Johnstone
FS R J Edge
Sgt D M Wilton
Sgt W J Dry

**30 July** *0611-1124*
*CAHAGNES*
FO R G Boswell and crew
Sgt C E Loynd and Sgt R S Routledge
in, Lewis and Merry out

**31 July** *1725-2302*
*JOIGNY*
FO W C Freestone (DFC)
Sgt G J Post
FS D A Gage
FO F R Woollan (BA)
Sgt R H Taylor
Sgt D M Wilton
Sgt E E Herders

**29/30 Aug** *2027-0654*
*KÖNIGSBERG*
FO L W Hayler (DFC)
Sgt R B Tink
Sgt A E Hearn (N)
FO E E Winterburn
Sgt B A Nash
Sgt B E James
Sgt W S H Knight

**31 Aug** *1551-2023*
*AUCHY-LES-HESDIN*
FO L W Hayler and crew

**1 Sep** *1106-1655*
*BREST*
FO L W Hayler and crew

**3 Sep** *1518-1947*
*DEELEN AIRFIELD*
FO D S Lade RAAF
FS T Starkie
WO T Awcock RAAF
FO J A W McCallum DFC
WO M Danahar
FS H J Conquest RAAF
Sgt M Benjamin
(jettisoned bombs, due to
mechanical defects)
(all lost 11 Sep except Danahar,
who was not on this mission)

**10 Sep** *0236-0729*
*MÜNCHEN-GLADBACH*
FO R K Hart (DFC)
FO E Yaxley (2P)
Sgt E E Smith
Sgt R P Green
FS W G Bell
Sgt A W Codrai
Sgt J A Spiers
FS B R Lillywhite

**10 Sep** *1526-1914*
*LE HAVRE*
FO E Yaxley
Sgt J A M Davies
FO J F Woodcott
FO J H Alabaster
FO G H Evans
Sgt H Wilkinson
Sgt R J Wilder

**11/12 Sep** *2104-0248*
*DARMSTADT*
FO E Yaxley and crew

**12/13 Sep** *1858-0213*
*STUTTGART*
FO L W Hayler and crew

**17 Sep** *0725-1045*
*BOULOGNE*
FO P W Kennedy
Sgt E P P Olsen
FS J P Kelly
FO W J Jones
Sgt J E Short
Sgt C McBurney
Sgt G Cohen

**18/19 Sep** *1814-0012*
*BREMERHAVEN*
FO L W Hayler and crew

**19/20 Sep** *1849-2352*
*MÜNCHEN-GLADBACH*
FO F E Wilson
Sgt H V Brian
Sgt F J J Dawe
Sgt E R Culley
Sgt R F Jenkins
Sgt S H Knight
Sgt W E Landsdowne

**23/24 Sep** *1848-0023*
*HANDORF*
FO L W Hayler and crew
FO R S Biggs in (N),
Hearn out
(ordered not to bomb)

**27 Sep** *0043-0732*
*KARLSRUHE*
FO M G Peel
Sgt G S W Saxby
Sgt J J Hall
Sgt S E Martinez
Sgt J A Mitchell
Sgt J A F Knowles
Sgt R Jackson

**27/28 Sep** *2109-0429*
*KAISERSLAUTERN*
FO L W Hayler and crew
FO P F Young (N) in,
Biggs out

**5 Oct** *0812-1309*
*WILHELMSHAVEN*
FO L W Hayler and crew
FS J P Kelly in (N),
Young out

**6/7 Oct** *1721-2219*
*BREMEN*
FO W D Barlow (DFC)
Sgt A H Thornalley
Sgt A E Simmonds
FS M R Fox
Sgt B S Clements
Sgt T H White
Sgt A J Wilkes

**7 Oct** *1216-1447*
*WALCHEREN*
FO L W Hayler and crew
Young back as (N)

**11 Oct** *1321-1553*
*VEERE FLUSHING*
FO R G Boswell and crew

**14/15 Oct** *2301-0623*
*BRUNSWICK*
FO L W Hayler and crew
Sgt J Swaffield (N)

**19/20 Oct** *1710-0124*
*NÜRNBERG*
FO P W Plenderleith (DFC)
Sgt L Burton
FO C E Digham
FO A F Nicholls
FS J A Rodda
Sgt J W Syms
Sgt P W Dearman

**28/29 Oct** *2222-0545*
*BERGEN*
FO L W Hayler and crew
Hearn back
(abandoned, could not i/d
target)

**30 Oct** *1039-1318*
*WESTKAPELLE*
FO L W Hayler and crew
Swaffield (N)

**1 Nov** *1340-1814*
*HOMBURG*
FO R Thomson (DFC)
Sgt D G Thorn
Sgt A W S Humber
Sgt J Smith
Sgt P R Wicks
Sgt A Lee
Sgt J F Padgett

**2 Nov** *1631-2155*
*DÜSSELDORF*
FO L W Hayler and crew
FO Smith (2P)

**4 Nov** *1753-2302*
*LADBERGEN*
FO L W Hayler and crew

**6 Nov** *1623-2151*
*GRAVENHORST*
FO R Thomson and crew
(ordered not to bomb)

**16 Nov** *1249-1840*
*DÜREN*
FL L W Hayler and crew
(came back on 3 engines
after bombing)

Wing Commander F W Thompson DFC,
OC 44 Squadron.

Steve Burrows DFC (FE) and Maurice
Stancer (DFM) navigator in Tommy
Thompson's crew.

**21/22 Nov** *1746-0004*
*GRAVENHORST*
Capt G W Hirschfeld SAAF
Sgt A D Lorrain
FO P Yorke
FO D E Murphy RAAF
FS H S Jones RAAF
Sgt J Storr
Sgt J Mitchell
(all lost 4/5 Dec)

ND578 with 121 bombs up.

**6/7 Mar** *1830-0319*
*GARDENING – SASSNITZ*
FL L W Hayler and crew

**7/8 Mar** *1822-0059*
*HARBURG*
FO D M R Piggott
Sgt J C Cousins
FS J P Madley
FO T A V Russell
FO V G Carpenter
FS I G Evans
WO D Pinckard

**11 Mar** *1212-1744*
*ESSEN*
FO H V Parkin and crew

**12 Mar** *1339-1907*
*DORTMUND*
FO H V Parkin and crew

**14/15 Mar** *1700-0221*
*LUTZENDORF*
FO H V Parkin and crew

**16/17 Mar** *1738-0212*
*WÜRZBURG*
FO R Thomson and crew

**20/21 Mar** *2344-0832*
*BÖHLEN*
FO R Thomson and crew

**23/24 Mar** *1929-0140*
*WESEL*
FO H V Parkin and crew

**7/8 Apr** *1834-0315*
*MOLBIS*
FO H V Parkin and crew

**8/9 Apr** *1758-0228*
*LUTZENDORF*
FO H V Parkin and crew

**10/11 Apr** *1826-0246*
*LEIPZIG*
FO H V Parkin and crew

**17/18 Apr** *2352-0829*
*CHAM M/YARDS*
FO H V Parkin and crew

**22 Nov** *1554-2340*
*TRONDHEIM*
FL L W Hayler and crew
(aborted with engine trouble
and bomb-site u/s)

**26/27 Nov** *2351-0904*
*MUNICH*
FL L W Hayler and crew

**4 Dec** *1615-2320*
*HEILBRONN*
FL L W Hayler and crew

**6/7 Dec** *1703-0004*
*GIESSEN*
FO H V Parkin
Sgt C A Green
Sgt E W Rowbottom
FS S H Henry
FS D W Kelman
Sgt L G Barker
Sgt G J Bredenkamp

**11 Dec** *1217-1732*
*URFT*
FO K A Smith
Sgt J Dent
FO R S Winters
FO A D Long
FS J R Pugh
Sgt D R Hall
Sgt R D James
(raid called off)

**17/18 Dec** *1614-0154*
*MUNICH*
FO R Thomson and crew

**18/19 Dec** *1652-0259*
*GDYNIA*
FL L W Hayler and crew

**21/22 Dec** *1705-0222*
*PÖLITZ*
FL L W Hayler and crew

**31 Dec** *0224-0734*
*HOUFFALIZE*
FO H V Parkin and crew

## 1945

**1/2 Jan** *1701-0009*
*GRAVENHORST*
FO H V Parkin and crew

**5 Jan** *0110-0751*
*ROYON*
FL L W Hayler and crew

**6 Jan** *1614-2131*
*GARDENING – SPINACE*
FO B T F Coventry (DFC)
Sgt A Shuttleworth
Sgt K W Ayre (N)
FS G Gibson
Sgt J O Wood
Sgt F T Perkins
Sgt G Lewis
(aborted with H²S u/s)

**13/14 Jan** *1639-0304*
*PÖLITZ*
FL L W Hayler and crew

**14/15 Jan** *1620-0209*
*MERSEBURG*
FO H V Parkin and crew

**16/17 Jan** *1753-0301*
*BRUX*
FO H V Parkin and crew

**1 Feb** *1607-2314*
*SIEGEN*
FL L W Hayler and crew

**2/3 Feb** *1951-0258*
*KARLSRUHE*
FL L W Hayler and crew
FO H L Maltos (2P)

**7/8 Feb** *2106-0335*
*LADBERGEN*
FO B T F Coventry and crew
Sgt A E Hearn (N) in, FO
F R Woollen (AB)

**8/9 Feb** *1658-0252*
*PÖLITZ*
FO H V Parkin and crew

**13/14 Feb** *1803-0404*
*DRESDEN*
FL L W Hayler and crew
FL H A B Symons (2P)

**19/20 Feb** *2345-0802*
*BÖHLEN*
FL L W Hayler and crew
FL D M Allen (2P)
FL L H Edwards (N) in,
Hearn out

**20/21 Feb** *2147-0414*
*GRAVENHORST*
FO L T Gardiner (DFC)
Sgt J A C Ludlow
FS E J MacDonald
WO G C Beaton RCAF
Sgt T E Burroughs
FS H A Walsh
FS L S Van Niekerk

**21 Feb** *1659-2335*
*GRAVENHORST*
FL L W Hayler and crew
FS H Symons in (N)

**24 Feb** *1406-1830*
*LADBERGEN*
FL L W Hayler and crew
FO R S Biggs in (N)

**3/4 Mar** *1841-0145*
*LADBERGEN*
FL L W Hayler and crew
Hearn back

**5/6 Mar** *1708-0253*
*BÖHLEN*
FL L W Hayler and crew
FL A J MacKay (2P)

ND578 KM-Y, Spilsby 1944-45. Note the letters now have white edging.

# ND644
# NAN

ND644 HW-N, 100 Squadron, showing 112 ops. From left to right: AC F Turrell and LAC J Atkinson (both fitter-engines), FL H G Topliss, Sgt H W Williams (NCO i/c), LAC B Gorst (fitter-airframes).

Built at A V Roe's Chadderton factory as part of order No.1807, ND644 was a Mark III with four Merlin 38 engines, coming off the production line in early 1944. On 20 February it was assigned to 100 Squadron at Waltham, near Grimsby, Lincolnshire, and given the code letters HW. With an individual identification letter 'N' painted on her fuselage, the aircraft became N-Nan.

*Nan* began operations with a trip to Augsburg on 25/26 February but it was not an auspicious start for she had to abort over France due to the starboard-outer engine failing. Sorting this out, she set off on the next op on 1/2 March, and although the target was reached, the wireless became u/s and *Nan* landed at RAF Ford on the south coast of England rather than home base.

The Lancaster then began an almost trouble-free tour

of duty, although it did lose another engine – the port-outer – on 3/4 May, but saw action on D-Day and over Caen, plus all the other summer targets Bomber Command had to deal with before going back to Germany.

The first regular captain was Flight Lieutenant Peter Sherriff. He took *Nan* on 23 ops and received the DFC at the end of his tour, which he completed in mid-June before moving to instruct at 28 OTU. The next regular skipper was Pilot Officer W Castle who took over the captaincy in June. He had flown his 'second dickie' trip with Sherriff on 9/10 May and went on to pilot 20 missions in *Nan* before being tour-expired in August, following Sherriff to 28 OTU.

*Nan* then had the usual variety of pilots during August

and September, but then Flying Officer P C Elliff began to fly her regularly, recording 19 ops. Unfortunately on the last sortie together – Stuttgart, 28/29 January 1945 – *Nan* was hit by flak in the starboard wing and inner-engine, the latter having to be feathered on the way back after the coolant had seeped away from a damaged pipe. Philip Elliff had made two runs over the target and perhaps he had been in the flak too long, but nevertheless he brought ND644 home safely. Elliff became tour-expired in February, received the DFC and was another to go off to 28 OTU.

Originally *Nan* had what has been described as 'a large painting of a lovely lady' on the front, along with the bomb symbols in neat rows of ten; the 'lady' seems to have been removed or over-painted when the Lanc went off for a major inspection on 5 August, returning on 2 September.

As can be seen from the crew lists below, 156 Squadron had a different policy from other units in that rather than taking a new pilot on his first trip with an experienced crew, the complete embryo crew and pilot went with just the experienced captain. It may have had some advantages but a pilot possibly nearing the end of his tour had the added strain of flying a mission with a wholly untried crew – which must have had its moments. Other times part of a new crew went, such as 9/10 May 1944. Peter Sherriff not only had five of his own crew but a new pilot, Castle, and Castle's flight engineer and bomb aimer – nine men in all!

As far as is known, *Nan* was the only one of these 100-op veterans to land in France during the war.

This occurred on 4 December following a raid on Karlsruhe, the aircraft running short of fuel, so Flying Officer H G Topliss RCAF landed at Juvincourt to refuel before returning across the sea to England. Hamilton Topliss flew *Nan* three times and had the well-known photograph taken with her ground crew following her 112th op. As, supposedly, this op came in March 1945 and he had not flown her since 5/6 January, it does not help to confirm ND644's total number of sorties.

If the final score of 115 ops is correct, then *Nan* reached her 100th in January 1945, although it could have been in December following a straight count from the Form 541. If the photograph is supposed to follow the last time Topliss flew the aircraft, then a further count puts *Nan's* total nearer to 128. However, 115 seems correct, and it has also been said that the 100th came on 16/17 January with Flight Sergeant F F Wright RCAF in command. Fred Wright won an Immediate DFC in March.

Whatever the count, *Nan* was the pride of her ground crew, who consisted of Sergeant H W Williams, LACs J Atkinson (fitter-engines), B Gorst (fitter-airframes) and AC F Turrell (fitter-engines). The aircraft had flown over 800 hours by March but she failed to return from a raid on Nürnberg on the night of 16/17 March together with the crew of Flying Officer George A O Dauphanee RCAF. They were shot down near Kraftshof, about eight kilometres from the target city's rail station. All the crew died except Flying Officer D B Douglas RCAF and Pilot Officer R S Bailey. Both these men were wounded, Douglas being repatriated to Canada. It was their second trip in ND644.

**100 SQUADRON 1944**

**25 Feb** *1825-2335*
AUGSBURG
Sgt A R Oxenham
Sgt D J Fuller (FE)
Sgt E Blackburn (N)
Sgt H Goodall (BA)
Sgt R J Willis (WOP)
Sgt J Barber (MU)
Sgt D A Goggin (RG)
(aborted with std outer u/s)

**1/2 Mar** *2335-0640*
STUTTGART
Sgt A R Oxenham and crew
(landed at Ford – radio u/s)

**15/16 Mar** *1915-0325*
STUTTGART
FL J H Inns
Sgt C C Davies
Sgt E Usher
FO G C Tincler
Sgt K Pearton
FO F J Blute
Sgt H Flint

**18/19 Mar** *1925-0105*
FRANKFURT
PO A J T Armon
Sgt D B Cox
FO R F Weadon
Sgt G R Boxell
Sgt D Jones
Sgt L D Burton
FS M Robertson

**22/23 Mar** *1900-0020*
FRANKFURT
FL P Sherriff (DFC)
Sgt J D Gray (FE)
FO J Galloway (N)
FO R H L Girvan RCAF (BA)
Sgt T A Hammill (WOP)
Sgt G R Dixon (MU)
Sgt G H Warren (RG)

**24/25 Mar** *1850-0130*
BERLIN
FL P Sherriff and crew

**26/27 Mar** *1955-0040*
ESSEN
FL P Sherriff and crew

**30/31 Mar** *2200-0535*
NÜRNBERG
FL P Sherriff and crew

**9/10 Apr** *2125-0535*
GARDENING – BALTIC
FL P Sherriff and crew

**10/11 Apr** *2330-0420*
AULNOYE
FL P Sherriff and crew

**18/19 Apr** *2225-0230*
ROUEN M/YARDS
PO E D King
Sgt R W Bland
FO L H Scott
Sgt F W Cheetham
Sgt S Beardsell
Sgt D Ralston
Sgt D W Young

**20/21 Apr** *2338-0412*
COLOGNE – M/YARDS
FL P Sherriff and crew

**22/23 Apr** *2244-0308*
DÜSSELDORF M/YARDS
FL P Sherriff and crew

**24/25 Apr** *2212-0404*
KARLSRUHE
FL P Sherriff and crew

**26/27 Apr** *2310-0320*
ESSEN
FL P Sherriff and crew
GC I B Newbigging (2P) (DFC)

**27/28 Apr** *2155-0545*
FRIEDRICHSHAFEN
FL P Sherriff and crew

**30 Apr/1 May** *2137-0205*
MAINTENON
PO E D King and crew

**3/4 May** *2155-0100*
MAILLY-LE-CAMP
PO E Wainwright
Sgt R L Thomsen
FS J M Rosborough
FO R A Brown
Sgt R H Wallington
Sgt L Cohen
Sgt J J O'Mare
(abandoned, port-outer engine u/s)

The men (and women) behind the crew; parachute packers, armourers, fitters and riggers.

**7/8 May** *2150-0255*
*BRUZ – DUMP*
FO J C Kennedy RCAF
Sgt T T Bligh
FO A T Sparks
FO A D Hennessy
Sgt A Aveyard
Sgt F Shuttleworth
Sgt K Owst

**9/10 May** *2150-0105*
*MERVILLE GUN*
FL P Sherriff
PO W Castle (2P)
Sgt E Bruce (FE)
FO F Tovey (N)
FO R H L Garvan (BA)
FO E Grundy (2BA)
Sgt R L Onions (WOP)
Sgt G R Dixon (MU)
Sgt H A G Kneller (RE)

**10/11 May** *2235-0125*
*DIEPPE GUN*
FL P Sherriff and crew

**21/22 May** *2235-0245*
*DUISBURG*
FL P Sherriff and crew

**22/23 May** *2250-0245*
*DORTMUND*
FL P Sherriff and crew

**24/25 May** *2235-0055*
*AACHEN*
FL P Sherriff and crew

**27/28 May** *2340-0315*
*MERVILLE GUN*
FL P Sherriff and crew

**28/29 May** *2235-0139*
*EU*
FL P Sherriff and crew

**31 May/1 June** *2345-0423*
*TERGNIER M/YARDS*
PO W L Smith
Sgt J E Connolly
FO R V Bennett
FO H D Muir
Sgt J E Whiteside
Sgt D Stott
Sgt F J Graham

**5/6 June** *2120-0120*
*CAISBECQ*
FL P Sherriff and crew
FL C N Waite (FE) and FS L H
Gladman (N) in, Gray and
Galloway out

**6/7 June** *2220-0310*
*ACHÈRES*
FL P Sherriff and crew
plus FO O Towers (2BA)

**7/8 June** *2330-0345*
*FORÊT DE CERISY*
FL P Sherriff and crew
FS R W Pye (MU) in,
Dixon out

**10/11 June** *2255-0340*
*ACHÈRES*
FL P Sherriff and crew

**11/12 June** *0115-0510*
*ÉVREUX*
FL P Sherriff and crew

**14/15 June** *2050-0005*
*LE HAVRE*
PO W Castle
Sgt E Bruce (FE)
Sgt E Palfreyman (N)
FO E Grundy (BA)
Sgt R L Onions (WOP)
Sgt A Melrose (MU)
Sgt H A G Kneller (RG)

**17 June** *0020-0405*
*DOMLÉGER – V1 SITE*
PO W Castle and crew

**22/23 June** *2245-0310*
*REIMS M/YARDS*
FO H H Reid RCAF
Sgt D Judson
FO W J Smith RCAF
Sgt W H MacDonald RCAF
Sgt K Nottage
Sgt S Krawchuck RCAF
Sgt C W Martens RCAF

**24/25 June** *1600-1920*
*LES HAYONS – V1 SITE*
FO H H Reid and crew

**25 June** *0740-1045*
*LIGESCOURT – V1 SITE*
FO H H Reid and crew

**28 June** *0050-0235*
*VAIRIES M/YARDS*
FO H H Reid and crew

**29 June** *1145-1510*
*DOMLÉGER – V1 SITE*
PO W Castle and crew

**30 June/1 July** *2205-0335*
*VIERZON*
PO W Castle and crew

**2 July** *1220-1530*
*OISEMONT – V1 SITE*
PO W Castle and crew

**4/5 July** *2220-0410*
*ORLÉANS M/YARDS*
PO W Castle and crew

**6 July** *1855-2225*
*FORÊT DU CROC – V1 SITE*
PO W Castle and crew

**7 July** *1940-2320*
*CAEN*
PO W Castle and crew

**12/13 July** *2120-0340*
*TOURS M/YARDS*
PO W Castle
PO J R Jones (2P)
Sgt T I Scott (FE)
FO E Grundy (BA)
FS A Roxby (2BA)
FS A H Lawry (WOP)
Sgt A Melrose (MU)
Sgt J M McCarthy (RG)

**18 July** *0335-0725*
*SANNEVILLE-CAEN*
PO W Castle and crew

**18/19 July** *2315-0305*
*SCHOLVEN*
PO W Castle and crew

**20/21 July** *2350-0305*
*COURTRAI M/YARDS*
PO W Castle and crew

Heading out.

**25 July** *0700-1035*
*COQUEREAUX – V1 SITE*
PO W Castle and crew

**25/26 July** *2135-0600*
*STUTTGART*
PO W Castle and crew

**28/29 July** *2125-0540*
*STUTTGART*
PO W Castle and crew

**31 July/1 Aug** *2205-0124*
*NIEPPE*
PO W Castle and this crew
FO D M D Brown (2P)
Sgt J K Wood (FE)
Sgt E Palfreyman (N)
FO W Bathgate (BA)
Sgt R L Onions (WOP)
Sgt W Tipple (2MU)
Sgt A Melrose (MU)
Sgt H A G Kneller (RG)

**3 Aug** *1130-1605*
*TROSSY ST MAXIMIN*
PO W Castle and crew

**4 Aug** *1330-2130*
*PAUILLAC*
PO W Castle and crew

**5 Aug** *1430-2230*
*PAUILLAC*
FO H Hassler RAAF (DFC)
Sgt W F Dorman
FO H W Craig
Sgt J H Challis
Sgt H Christopher
Sgt A Mills
Sgt D Nathan

**7/8 Aug** *2105-0027*
*FONTENOY*
PO W Castle and crew

**10 Aug** *1015-1420*
*VINCLY*
WO W T Ramsden (DFC)
Sgt E G Stubbings
Sgt S T Howard
FO R S Simpson
Sgt R A Chestnutt
Sgt R J Williams
Sgt F Crompton
(aborted due to weather)

**12 Aug** *1125-1745*
*LA PALLICE*
FO I S Bell RCAF
Sgt T A Kewley
PO T N Shewring RCAF
FO R Watson RCAF
Sgt E A Pocock RCAF
Sgt T Brannon
Sgt C Barker

**15 Aug** *1000-1325*
*VOLKEL AIRFIELD*
FO H Hassler and crew

**5 Sep** *1655-2030*
*GILZE-RIJEN AIRFIELD*
FO J R Copeland RNZAF
Sgt D G Bayliss
Sgt K Martin
FS H Taylor
Sgt G A Lavings
Sgt K Sawkins
Sgt E Sapsed

**6 Sep** *1730-2110*
*LE HAVRE*
FO P C Elliff (DFC)

Sgt F W Tompkins
FO W B Hartnett (DFC)
FO N P G Wallace RCAF
PO R P Hughes
Sgt V C Kite
Sgt K F Adams

**8 Sep** *0635-1015*
*LE HAVRE*
PO P C Elliff and crew
(abandoned due to weather)

**10 Sep** *1700-2030*
*LE HAVRE*
FO F O Parkinson (DFC)
Sgt S Goodfellow
FO W A Cotton
FS C W Knight
Sgt E T P Reardon
Sgt W Robertson
Sgt C L Wood

**12/13 Sep** *1840-0145*
*FRANKFURT*
FO J R Copeland and crew

**16/17 Sep** *2145-0125*
*HOPSTEN AIRFIELD*
FO H Hassler and crew

**17 Sep** *1625-1915*
*FLUSHING*
FO H Hassler and crew

**20 Sep** *1505-1850*
*CALAIS*
FO C D Edge
Sgt N Thorn
FS P Lacey
FS R P Steel
FS J M Muller
Sgt F Twist
Sgt A Taylor

**23 Sep** *1840-2350*
*NEUSS*
FO J R Copeland and crew

**25 Sep** *0735-1105*
*CALAIS*
FO P C Elliff and crew
(abandoned by MB)

**26 Sep** *1025-1345*
*CAP GRIS NEZ*
FO P C Elliff and crew

**27 Sep** *0850-1210*
*CALAIS*
FO P C Elliff and crew

**28 Sep** *0820-1130*
*CALAIS*
FO P C Elliff and crew
(abandoned – weather)

**5/6 Oct** *1840-0045*
*SAARBRÜCKEN*
FO P C Elliff and crew

**7 Oct** *1210-1610*
*EMMERICH*
FO P C Elliff and crew

**14 Oct** *0625-1100*
*DUISBURG*
FO P C Elliff and crew

**15 Oct** *0020-0535*
*DUISBURG*
FO P C Elliff and crew

**15 Oct** *1745-2140*
*WILHELMSHAVEN*
FO P C Elliff and crew

**19 Oct** *1710-2315*
*STUTTGART*
FO E A Jackson (DFC)
Sgt H W Cooke (FE)
FS C J Collier
Sgt J Irwin
Sgt P A Hopkins
Sgt J C Haggerty
Sgt J Hulsman

**23 Oct** *1635-2205*
*ESSEN*
FO E A Jackson and crew

**25 Oct** *1250-1710*
*ESSEN*
FO P C Elliff and crew

**28 Oct** *1320-1825*
*COLOGNE M/YARDS*
FO P C Elliff and crew

**30 Oct** *1755-2350*
*COLOGNE*
FO P C Elliff and crew

**31 Oct** *1755-2255*
*COLOGNE*
FO P C Elliff and crew

**2 Nov** *1625-2145*
*DÜSSELDORF*
FO O Lloyd-Davies (DFC)
Sgt K P Doughty
FO R Robinson
FS B Sandberg
WO R S Porter
Sgt E Sutherland
Sgt S R Vickers

**4 Nov** *1725-2210*
*BOCHUM*
PO E Smith
Sgt E R Aldridge
Sgt E Barnett
FS P Evans
Sgt J Moores
Sgt E C Turner
Sgt J Hodgkins

**6 Nov** *1200-1630*
*GELSENKIRCHEN*
FO F J Truman (DFC)
Sgt E J Motley
PO S L Caddey
FS T A Patterson
Sgt J E Hedley
Sgt W F Taylor
Sgt J Smart

**11 Nov** *1550-2130*
*DORTMUND*
FO F J Truman and crew

**18/19 Nov** *1550-2115*
*WANNE-EICKEL*
FO E A Jackson and crew
Sgt J G A Isaac (FE) in

**21 Nov** *1535-2210*
*ASCHAFFENBURG*
FS H Brown (DFC)
Sgt J Wadsworth
FS J S Grubb
FS B S Metcalfe
Sgt R S Hall
Sgt H McGough
Sgt A Lloyd

**27 Nov** *1605-2305*
*FREIBERG*
FO F T Quigley RCAF
Sgt F Stovell
Sgt R G Roller RCAF
FO W M Chapman RCAF
Sgt J Guy
Sgt M McMaster RCAF
Sgt J B Gibbons RCAF

**29 Nov** *1220-1725*
*DORTMUND*
FO H G Topliss RCAF (DFC)
Sgt H G Crowley (FE)
FL P V Knight
Sgt D L Fahey RCAF (N)
Sgt A L Pheiffer RCAF
FO J T Rock RCAF
Sgt V R Mason RCAF
Sgt G W McIntosh RCAF

**3 Dec** *0740-1210*
*URFT DAM*
FO P C Elliff and crew
(abandoned by MB)

**4 Dec** *1640-2205*
*KARLSRUHE*
FO H G Topliss and crew
(landed at Juvincourt – short
of fuel)

**6/7 Dec** *1645-0045*
*MERSEBURG*
FO P C Elliff and crew

**12 Dec** *1655-2225*
*ESSEN M/YARDS*
FO L A M Fludder RAAF
Sgt L T A Williams
Sgt F B Barnes
FS G V Armstrong
FS C G Mazlin
FS I J Duffett
Sgt J Eveleigh

**17 Dec** *1535-2310*
*ULM*
PO H C Smith RCAF
FO H O Berger (FE)
FS W S Merrall RCF
FO S McMichael RCF
Sgt J Smith
FS S E Greenley
FS P Kenny

**21 Dec** *1500-2040*
*BONN*
FO P C Elliff and crew
FS F F Wright (2P)
Sgt A F Smith (2BA)

**24 Dec** *1435-2010*
*COLOGNE*
FO F T Quigley and crew
(attacked by night fighter
– no damage)

**26 Dec** *1310-1725*
*ST VITH*
FL C S Johnson
Sgt C Albutt
FO W Hancock
FO T G Campion
Sgt R C Vicker
Sgt R J Barnham
Sgt R W Cousins

**28 Dec** *1540-2140*
*MÜNCHEN-GLADBACH*
PO H C Smith and crew
Sgt A McDougall (FE) in,
FO Berger out

**29 Dec** *1500-2125*
*GELSENKIRCHEN*
FO P M Brown
Sgt D J J Timm
FO R J Holford
FO R E Marsh
Sgt J E Benton
Sgt R Poulson
Sgt W Muir

## 1945

**5/6 Jan** *1900-0010*
*HANNOVER*
FO H G Topliss and crew

**16/17 Jan** *1745-0120*
*ZEITZ TROGLITZ*
FS F F Wright RCAF (DFC)
Sgt K N Whitney
Sgt A Gibbons
Sgt A F Smith
Sgt R D Davies
Sgt J C Wallace RCAF
Sgt G R Youngs

**28/29 Jan** *1945-0250*
*STUTTGART*
FL P C Elliff and crew
(damaged by flak, lost std-inner
engine, two runs over target)

**1 Feb** *1610-2255*
*LUDWIGSHAVEN*
FO M A Austin RNZAF
Sgt K R Noble
Sgt C Firth
FO T E Girling RCAF
Sgt K O Whittingham
Sgt A Hopley
Sgt L W Bruce

**2/3 Feb** *2045-0335*
*WIESBADEN*
FL C S Johnson and crew

**13/14 Feb** *2125-0700*
*DRESDEN*
FL W O Nobes RCAF
Sgt J D Kerr
FO J Kimpton
FS N L Warner
FS R A Doherty
FS C D Taylor
FS J Mitchell

**14/15 Feb** *2000-0510*
*CHEMNITZ*
FL C S Johnson and crew

**20/21 Feb** *2130-0410*
*DORTMUND*
FL C S Johnson and crew

**21/22 Feb** *1925-0150*
*DUISBURG*
FL C S Johnson and crew

**23/24 Feb** *1600-0005*
*PFORZHEIM*
FO H C Smith and crew

**1 Mar** *1145-1815*
*MANNHEIM*
FL C S Johnson and crew

**5/6 Mar** *1650-0150*
*CHEMNITZ*
FL C S Johnson and crew

**8/9 Mar** *1730-0105*
*KASSEL*
FO G A O Dauphanee RCAF
FS M R Jeffrey
FO D B Douglas RCAF
FO W R Vale RCAF
PO R S Bailey
FS W H Johnson RCAF
FS L E Bedell RCAF

**11 Mar** *1145-1655*
*ESSEN*
FO F F Wright and crew

**12 Mar** *1300-1742*
*DORTMUND*
FO F F Wright and crew
(abandoned, lost port inner
over French coast)

**15/16 Mar** *1720-0115*
*MISBURG*
FO G McTavish RCAF
Sgt F Hurt
FO S N Lipsey RCAF
FO B Y Sisson RCAF
WO P N Leveille RCAF
Sgt A R Brooks RCAF
Sgt A H Boswell RCAF

**16/17 Mar** *1755-*
*NÜRNBERG*
FO G A O Dauphanee and crew
(failed to return)

# ND709
# FLYING KIWI

Another Chadderton-built Mark III, part of A V Roe's order No.1807, ND709 came out of the factory in early 1944, equipped with four Merlin 38 engines. It moved to 32 MU at Wyton on 2 March and from there flew to 35 Squadron (PFF) at Gravely, Huntingdonshire, on the 7th. Coded TL-M she flew just two operations as a 'supporter' aircraft then, along with eight other Lancasters, was re-assigned to 635 Squadron which was formed on 20 March from 35 Squadron's B Flight. She was now at Downham Market, Norfolk, with new code letters – F2 – and a new personal letter of J, although a faded 'M' remained visible just ahead of the port elevator.

Initially ND709's pilot on 635 Squadron, which was also part of 8 Group's Pathfinder Force, was Squadron Leader J R Wood, but his first trip in the aircraft had to be aborted due to the starboard-outer engine failing. On her next sortie she succeeded in reaching the target, but Warrant Officer J M Bourassa had to fly back on three engines again.

As PFF squadrons generally had crews whose ranks were increased by one level above Main Force crews, ND709 could count senior ranks among her pilots, so that at the time she became the regular mount of the A Flight leader, D W S Clark DFC was of wing commander rank. Although David Clark was born in Surbiton, Surrey, he was a New Zealander, and had initially joined the RAF but was destined to transfer to the RNZAF in August 1944. He had already completed a tour of ops with 419 Squadron RCAF, flying Halifaxes, with whom he had won the DFC. He would gain a Bar with 635 Squadron.

It was Clark and his crew who thought up the emblem which was painted on the nose of 'J', consisting of a Kiwi with an Aldis sight attached to its beak (and a plaster on its behind!) astride a falling bomb. On the bomb was a maple leaf, which referred to Clark's Canadian bomb aimer. In fact his crew formerly had been that of Squadron Leader Wood, but Clark took them over when Wood completed his tour. Unlike most other Lancs, ND709's bomb-tally seems to have been painted on from the bottom upwards. The first three rows, each of 15

ND709 F2-J, 635 Squadron, still showing 'M' of 35 Squadron, with which she flew two trips. With the Lanc's new ground crew are David Coltman (DFC) and Denis Linacre (DFC).

bombs, were lower than normal and as the space was used up, so the subsequent rows were mounted on top. Therefore, as the aircraft eventually topped the 100 mark, the bomb-tally had risen to the front gun turret.

Wing Commander Clark had a memorable first trip in his *Kiwi*, a sortie to Duisburg on 21/22 May 1944. En-route to the target, they were fired on by a 'friendly' four-engined aircraft and both Clark and his Canadian navigator, Pilot Officer Harry P Laskowski RCAF, were wounded, although not so seriously that they could not carry on. Clark flew to the target, bombed it on time, then headed back only to have a tyre burst on landing, but they got away with it. Both men were taken to Ely Hospital, Clark with a bullet in the shoulder, Laskowski with bullet splinters to his back (he received the DFC).

Both men were back on strength a month later, Clark going on to complete 16 ops in ND709 (one at least acting as Master Bomber), including a raid on Stettin on 16/17 August, for which he received a bar to his DFC:

'One night in August 1944, this officer captained an aircraft detailed to attack Stettin. When over the target, anti-aircraft fire was directed at his

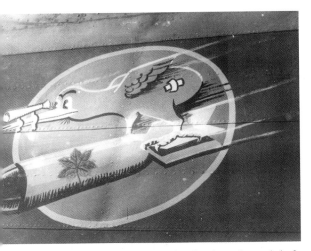

ND709's nose emblem, a flying Kiwi, with bomb sight, and a maple leaf on the bomb, representing the crew's New Zealand skipper and Canadian navigator.

There then followed a period of relative calm despite numerous sorties, but on 28 October, *Kiwi* was hit again, this time over Cologne, which damaged both starboard engines. With the port engines then beginning to overheat, Flying Officer R W Toothill decided to put down in Belgium (the only 100-op veteran to land in Belgium during the war). Despite the aircraft suffering from a frozen-up ASI both to and from the target, Reg Toothill got her down safely on the disused airfield at Moorsele. After repairs he flew back home on the 30th. At the end of his tour Toothill received the DFC, as did his navigator, John Luard, while his flight engineer, Syd Fortune and rear gunner, Frank Coombes, won DFMs.

By the new year, ND709's sorties were fast approaching the 100 mark. Squadron Leader P R Mellor took her to Oberfeld on 4 February, which was the 96th op, and the squadron commander, Wing Commander S Baker DSO DFC and Bar, flew as Master Bomber in *Kiwi* on the 7th, to Cleve – the 97th. The next op, being flown by Flying Officer J D F Cowden DFC, who flew her on 13 sorties, brought the aircraft up to 99; Peter Mellor and crew took her to Chemnitz on 14/15 February, *Kiwi's* 100th and final mission on 635 Squadron.

By one of those strange twists of fate, Cowden and crew flew in another Lancaster that night (PB287) and failed to return, shot down by a night fighter. It was a well-decorated crew and only the rear gunner survived as a prisoner. Duncan Cowden had won his DFC with 158 Squadron, and in all had flown 61 ops. Cowden may have been down to fly ND709, for in the Form 541 he and his

aircraft whilst it was illuminated in the searchlights. The bomber was hit. One engine was rendered useless and a second became erratic. Nevertheless, Wing Commander Clark flew safely to base and effected a masterly landing.'

They encountered some 20 searchlights over Stettin and their port-outer engine was the one hit. Clark had to order the marker flares jettisoned safe, but carried on to bomb on H²S. Only a few raids later *Kiwi* was hit again, this time over Soesterburg, a fairly large hole being blasted through the starboard side of the fuselage – but with another pilot.

WC D W S Clark DFC (left) and crew: Harry Laskowski, Denis Linacre, D A Tulloch, J Smith(?), David Coltman, J A Rayton.

SL P R Mellor and crew: Cliff "Gerry" Shaw (DFM) and Sam "Jock" Blair (DFM) (in doorway); Frank E Prebble (DFC), Peter Mellor (DFC), Lawrence Freeman (DFM), Arthur Rowbottom (DFM), and (in front) Ernest E Freake (DFM). Note the PFF insignia beneath their brevets.

1992 reunion: Messrs Prebble, Mellor, Rowbottom, Freake and Freeman

crew are listed as flying this machine, but obviously they did not. However, in the Form 540, Cowden is shown as being lost in aircraft 'T', while Mellor flew the 100th in 'J'.

According to the rear gunner, they had got aboard ND709 for the raid but were unable to get the starboard-outer to start. The crew took a vote and agreed to go on three engines. Before they could do so, the WingCo arrived in his car and ordered them to transfer to PB287. There was some moaning about this being a bad omen, and so it proved. There were two waves of attacking aircraft, Mellor taking ND709 on the second, by which time the wayward engine had been fixed. By such things do lives hang suspended.

Peter Mellor, who was to complete his tour and receive the DFC (all of his crew were also decorated), remembered:

'The [100th] operation itself was uneventful. It was a clear night until we approached the target where there was a thin overcast covering the aiming point and, as we could not identify it, we retained the markers and dropped the 4,000-pounder into the glow in the clouds, then returned home. The only opposition was some scattered AA fire. My main feeling on returning was one of relief that I had brought back the aircraft undamaged, as I seemed to act as a magnet for any pieces of scrap metal in the air.

'J was not really my aircraft, it had belonged to Wing Commander Clark, a New Zealander, who had a Canadian bomb aimer, hence the insignia. After he was tour-expired the aircraft became something of an orphan but it was treated with respect by those who flew it, which included myself. It was ironic that I had it then, because my aircraft –

FO J D F Cowden DFC.

LM524, "G" – was also in the nineties, so there was naturally some rivalry. As G was damaged beyond repair by fighters over Dresden on 7 March this could be considered a recompense.

'As far as celebrations were concerned, the only thing I recall was a toast in rum to J at debriefing but I don't doubt that the ground crew did some celebrating.'

Wing Commander "Tubby" Baker, who was about to receive a Bar to his DSO in early 1945 (and had himself completed 100 operational sorties during the war), remembered the Cleve sortie:

'The trip to Cleve with me as Master Bomber on 7 February 1945 was a very successful raid in close support of the Army, and Major Johnny Mullock flew with me to observe the flak. He was attached to HQ 8 (PFF) Group as Flak Liaison Officer, which may or may not have been his correct appointment title.

'There were no press-boys around when ND709 returned from her 100th sortie, and the photos of her were taken by the station photographic section, probably the next day, with her ground crew.'

The liaison officer, Major John B Mullock of the Royal Artillery, had won the MC earlier in the war, and had only recently been awarded the RAF's DFC for flying on ops while doing his HQ job.

Several references to ND709 virtually end her story with the 100th sortie but following a brief respite, she was sent to 405 (Vancouver) Squadron RCAF, which operated out of Gransden Lodge, Bedfordshire. 405 Squadron was also part of 8 Group, so ND709 continued in her Pathfinder role. Re-coded LQ-G, she arrived on 19 March and flew her first sortie on the 22nd – exactly a year to the day she had first flown with 635 Squadron. In all she flew eight missions with the Canadians, then added two Manna and one Exodus flight, bringing her total to 111.

On 11 June 1945 *Kiwi* returned to 35 Squadron but on 27 July went to 1667 CU. Just before Christmas ND709 moved again, this time to 1660 CU where she served for nearly a year before moving once again, to 1653 CU on 9 November 1946, coded now A3-U. On 9 May 1947 the veteran was delivered to 15 MU where the airframe was finally Struck off Charge on 28 August.

## 35 SQUADRON
### 1944

**15/16 Mar** *1932-0250*
STUTTGART
WO F G Tropman
FS R W Bullen
Sgt J L G Marshall
FS N W Curtis
FS J L Stevens
FS M E Ladyman
Sgt I K McGregor

**18/19 Mar** *1928-0036*
FRANKFURT
WO J M Bourassa
FS N Rowell
Sgt D Beaumont
Sgt R E Edie RCAF
Sgt R H Chapman
Sgt J B Fletcher

## 635 SQUADRON

**22 Mar** *1855-2245*
FRANKFURT
SL R P Wood
PO H P Laskowski RCAF (N)
FL G D Linacre RCAF (BA)
PO D G Coltman
FS J Smith
WO D R Tulloch
Sgt J A Rayton
(returned early, std-outer engine u/s)

**26/27 Mar** *1955-0045*
ESSEN
WO J M Bourassa and crew
(came home on 3 engines)

**30/31 Mar** *2200-0435*
NÜRNBERG
SL R P Wood and crew

**11 Apr** *0135-0545*
LÅON
FL C J K Ash
FS R J Birtles RAAF
FO C S Purkis
Sgt W C Vessey
Sgt W S Chapman
Sgt J J Leishman
PO T W Hone
(all lost 11/12 June)

**11/12 Apr** *2045-0015*
AACHEN
PO R W Beveridge
FO M I Massey
FO J G Irwin
Sgt J J Mather
Sgt J D Smith
FO J Allinson
Sgt A R Hall

**18/19 Apr** *2205-0220*
ROUEN
SL R P Wood and crew

**20/21 Apr** *2135-0115*
OTTIGNIES
SL R P Wood and crew

**22/23 Apr** *2120-0120*
LÅON
SL R P Wood and crew

**26/27 Apr** *2315-0115*
ESSEN
SL R P Wood and crew

**27/28 Apr** *2210-0535*
FRIEDRICHSHAFEN
FL H P Connolly
FS H S Troy
FO H J Morley
Sgt A Hambley
Sgt K A Harder
Sgt J McLaughlin
Sgt S L Conley

**1/2 May** *2225-0105*
MALINES
SL R P Wood and crew

**3/4 May** *2240-0210*
MONTDIDIER AIRFIELD
FL H P Connolly and crew

**7 May** *0050-0400*
MANTES / GASSICOURT
SL R B Roache DFC
FL G A Stocks
FO J C Wells
FS C Chadwick (WOP)
FS D H P Womar
FO C G Whittaker
FS E H Barry

**9 May** *0140-0440*
HAINES-ST-PIERRE
SL R P Wood and crew
FS H A Rudd in, Smith out

**19/20 May** *2300-0050*
ORLÉANS M/YARDS
FS D Griffiths
FS E J Waspe
FS E L C Howell
FS H P Whitehead
Sgt R Glass
FS W H Iball
Sgt A C Harding

**21/22 May** *2250-0300*
DUISBURG
WC D W S Clarke DFC
PO H P Laskowski RCAF (N)
FL G D Linacre RCAF (BA)
FS H A Rudd
FL J Highet
WO D R Tulloch
Sgt J A Rayton

**22/23 May** *2245-0221*
DORTMUND
FL J Billing
PO J E Moriarty
FS J Campbell
WO R D Curtis
PO J B Findlay
Sgt S L Edwards
PO T W Hope

**27/28 May** *2315-0408*
RENNES
FO J Caterer
Sgt M F Haberlin
PO W C Shepherd
Sgt H Scutt
Sgt W J Beeson
Sgt D Farrell
Sgt L Benson

**4 June** *0030-0225*
CALAIS
FO A L Johnson RAAF (DFC*)
WO J S Williams RAAF (DFC)
FS W O Paice RAAF (DFC)
PO J E L Liddle
PO E L Penman RAAF (DFC)
FS R E Harrop RAAF (DFM) (AG)
Sgt J Silburn (FE) (DFM)

Cowden and crew: Cowden, J R Donohue, J F Craik, R A Boddington, H Botterill, J T McQuillan, J S Davidson, W Gabbott. A highly decorated bunch with Cowden, Donohue and Craik having DFCs, the others (except) Davidson, all with DFMs, and Boddington the DFC and Bar.

**6 June 0300-0635**
LONGUES
FO A L Johnson and crew

**7/8 June 2340-0335**
FORÊT DE CERISY
FO A L Johnson and crew

**8/9 June 2200-0235**
ALENÇON
FO A L Johnson and crew

**9/10 June 0005-0500**
RENNES
FL H P Connolly and crew

**11/12 June 2146-0307**
TOURS
FO A L Johnson and crew

**16/17 June 2355-0245**
RENNESCURE – V1 SITE
FO A L Johnson and crew

**25 June 0025-0230**
MIDDLE STRAITS – V1 SITE
FS L J Melling (DFC)
FO R F Watkins (DFC)
FS L Bell
WO H R S Sullivan (DFC)
Sgt E G Ostime (DFM)
Sgt W H Hitchcock (DFM) (AG)
Sgt J E Blyth (DFM) (FE)

**4 July 1230-1550**
DOMLÉGER – V1 SITE
WC D W S Clark and crew
WO C W Newman in, Highet out

**5/6 July 2300-0125**
WIZERNES – V1 SITE
WC D W S Clark and crew

**6 July 1925-2245**
COQUEREAUX – V1 SITE
PO F L Boyd RCAF (DFC*)
Sgt H A Sygrove
FO E G Thomas (DFC)
FS C L Ransford
FO D W Taylor RAAF (DFC)
Sgt J MacLean
Sgt C H A Younger (DFM) (FE)

**7/8 July 2015-0005**
CAEN
WC D W S Clark and crew
SL B Moorcraft DFC in

**12 July 1805-2155**
VAIRIES – V1 SITE
WC D W S Clark and crew

**14/15 July 2155-0535**
RÉVIGNY
SL R B Roache DFC (bar) and crew
FS A D Morrison and FS D R
Patterson in, Stocks out – 8 crew)

**15/16 July 2345-0345**
NUCOURT – V1 SITE
WC D W S Clark and crew
(damaged by flak)

**18 July 0405-0715**
SANNEVILLE – CAEN
WC D W S Clark and crew

**18/19 July 2310-0253**
WESSELING
PO R L Vines (DFC*)
FO J D Hogg (DFC)
SL R G Goodwin
FO J G Ramsden (DFC)
FS J F Palen
Sgt W C Herrick (DFM) (FE)
Sgt J H Egan (DFM) (AG)

**20 July 1350-1635**
FERMES DE GRAND BOIX – V1 SITE
FO L A Johnson and crew

**24/25 July 2150-0545**
FERFAY – V1 SITE
FO A L Johnson and crew
(abandoned by MB over tgt:
Johnson was his deputy)

**25 July 0700-1000**
ARDOUVAL – V1 SITE
FO G S Henderson
WO R Pedrazzini
FS A T Till
Sgt J H C Ross
Sgt J H Morgan
FS F R Holledge
Sgt A V Urquhart

**27 July 1720-2050**
LES HAUT – V1 SITE
PO R M Clarke
FS W T Pethard
FS G K Hendy
Sgt C D Mountain
Sgt J H Watson
Sgt R E Catt
Sgt T Robertson

**28/29 July 2250-0335**
HAMBURG
WC W D S Clark and crew

**1 Aug 1930-2150**
LE HEY – V1 SITE
WC D W S Clark and crew
(abandoned by MB due
to fog and cloud)

**4 Aug 1100-1455**
TROSSY ST MAXIMIN
WC D W S Clark and crew
(hit by flak in fuselage and
starboard elevator)

**6/7 Aug 2155-0021**
SPECIAL OBS FLIGHT – CABOURG
SL F Smith DFC RAAF (DSO)
FL C G Whitehead DFC(*)
SL J R Dow DFC(*) RCAF (BA)
FL C J Fry
FS A H Mullard

FS C A Bradshaw
PO J A Wilson

**7/8 Aug 2140-0055**
SE CAEN
WC D W S Clark and crew
(did not bomb due to cloud)

**8 Aug 1915-2250**
FORÊT DE CHANTILLY
SL M M Henderson (DFC)
FO A H Emmott RCAF (DFC)
FL J F Craik (DFC)
FL J Highet DFM (DFC) (WOP)
FO W J Hanks DFC
FO A A Joseph (DFC)
WO R Gardner

**10 Aug 0945-1350**
DUGNY
FL I B Hayes (DFC)
FL W M Douglas (DFC)
PO J N Steel

The ground crew paint on the 100th bomb. Note the bombs were painted on in an upwards direction. ND709 then went to 405 Squadron RCAF and flew a further 11 ops.

The proud ground crew – A Flight 635 Squadron.

**15/16 Sep  2222-0212**
*KIEL*
FL J J Lowry
FO R F Watkins (DFC)
FL L Bell (DFC)
WO H R S Sullivan RAAF (DFC)
FS E G Ostime (DFM)
FS W H Hitchcock (DFM) (AG)
Sgt J E Blyth (DFM) (FE)

**26 Sep  1130-1338**
*CAP GRIS NEZ*
FL I B Hayes and crew

**27 Sep  0750-1240**
*CALAIS*
SL D T Wilt and crew

**6 Oct  1715-2211**
*DORTMUND*
FL L Henson (DC)
PO E J D Bill RCAF (DFC)
FO H S Davis
FL C J Fry
FL C A Harding
FS A H Mullard
PO J A Wilson

**12 Oct  0705-0920**
*FORT FREDERIK HENDRIK*
FO J D F Cowden (DFC)
PO J R C Donohue (N) (DFC)
FL J F Craik (DFC)
FL G R Hawes (DFC*)
FS H Botterill (DFM) (WOP)

FS J T McQuillan DFM (RG)
FL C G Whitaker (DFC) (MU)
FO W Gabbott (FE)

**14 Oct  0718-1115**
*DUISBURG*
FO P E Cawthorne
Sgt G Wilson
Sgt B G Roberts
FS T Reid
Sgt R V Moore
Sgt I J Kinney
Sgt J Goulbourn

**15 Oct  1725-2145**
*WILHELMSHAVEN*
FO R K Westhope
FO M H A Hawrylak
FO H E Odlam
Sgt A Newby
Sgt D W Beach
Sgt J Bromley
Sgt D E Darvell

**19 Oct  1741-2329**
*STUTTGART*
FL G W Johnson (DFC)
PO V Murphy
Sgt H M Smith
WO H Whittaker
FS L A W Howes
FS R B Benton
FS W Telford

FS R B Warner
FS J W Emms
FS A D Clayton
Sgt M R McMaster

**11 Aug  1415-1735**
*LENS*
WC D W S Clark and crew

**12/13 Aug  2145-0250**
*RÜSSELSHEIM*
SL D T Witt DFC DFM
SL P W G Lester (DFC)
FL R W Coutts (DFC)
WO S R J Harper (DFC)
FS R Stuart (DFM) (AG)
FS C Shaw (DFM) (AG)
Sgt P Cronin

**14 Aug  1240-1545**
*FALAISE*
WC D W S Clark and crew

**16/17 Aug  2115-0510**
*STETTIN*
WC D W S Clark and crew
FS G T King in, Linacre out
(a/c hit by flak on bomb-run)

**25/26 Aug  2055-0413**
*RÜSSELSHEIM*
FO F L Boyd and crew
plus FL J C Wells

**26/27 Aug  2015-0115**
*KIEL*
WC D W S Clark and crew
Sgt D L A Twaddle in, King out

**31 Aug  1325-1550**
*LAMBRES*

WC D W S Clark and crew
Sgt G Swindle in, Twaddle out
(abandoned over tgt – cloud)

**3 Sep  1605-1902**
*SOESTERBERG*
FL R D Williams
FS K O Handcock
FS F E Prebble
FS R Perry
Sgt J E Graham
Sgt J L W Robinson
(hit by flak in fuselage)

**6 Sep  1640-2000**
*EMDEN*
FL H McP Johnston DSO (DFC)
PO D L Venning (DFC)
PO R T Usher
PO R T Padden DFC (WOP)
FO C H Brown (DFC)
FS J H Ledgerwood DFM (RG)
FS G Williams

**10 Sep  1700-2004**
*LE HAVRE*
FL A L Johnson and crew
FO J V Watson and WO R Vere
in, POs Liddle and Penman out

**12 Sep  1137-1445**
*GELSENKIRCHEN*
FO J A Rowland RAAF (DFC)
FS C D McKenzie
FO H R Sindall
FO J R Donald
Sgt D A Jefferson
Sgt R Whybrow
Sgt W R Hill

WC S Baker DSO and Bar, DFC and Bar, flew ND709 on the Cleve trip, 7 Feb 1945.

**23 Oct** *1655-2210*
*ESSEN*
FL G W Johnson and crew plus
FS G Smith

**25 Oct** *1325-1710*
*ESSEN*
PO C L Ottaway RAAF (DFC)
FS A W Brown
FS S J Booth
FS W G Blackburn
FS J R Pierce
FS G M Cornett
Sgt R S Grist

**28 Oct** *1405-*
*COLOGNE*
FO R W Toothill (DFC)
Sgt J A Davies (BA)
FO J B Luard (N) (DFC)
Sgt W W Colvin (WOP)
Sgt F W Stone (MU)
Sgt F W Coombes (RG) (DFM)
Sgt S H Fortune (FE) (DFM)
(landed in Belgium with
damaged engines; ret'd on the 30th)

**4 Nov** *1757-2229*
*BOCHUM*
FO G A Thorne (DFC)
FO G N Rose (DFC)
WO R M H Keary (DFC)
FO B Bresshof
FO G M Suttie (DFC)
Sgt N M Scott (AG) (DFM)
Sgt T J A Rayment
Sgt J H Parker (FE) (DFM)

**16 Nov** *1335-1720*
*DÜREN*
FO J D F Cowden and crew
WO H A Rudd in, FL Whittaker
out, plus R A Boddington

**21 Nov** *1615-2140*
*WORMS*
FO R W Toothill and crew

**27 Nov** *1755-2205*
*NEUSS*
FO J D F Cowden and crew
FL J S Davidson in, Rudd out

**30 Nov** *1713-2143*
*DUISBURG*
FO J D F Cowden and crew

**2/3 Dec** *1815-0015*
*HAGEN*
FO J D F Cowden and crew

**4 Dec** *1705-2235*
*KARLSRUHE*
FL H T Paddison (DFC)
PO V A Murphy (DFC)
PO J D Bill RCAF (DFC)
FO G R Godfrey
FS C Shaw (AG) (DFM)
FS W C Telford (DFM) (AG)
FO G H Jones DFM (FE) (DFC)

**6 Dec** *1725-0015*
*MERSEBURG*
FL J A Rowland and crw
FO C F Jelley in, Jefferson out

**12 Dec** *1636-2122*
*ESSEN*
FL H T Paddison and crew
Sgt G E Muchmore and WO K W
Prior, FS R B Benton in; Bill and
Shaw out

**15 Dec** *1530-2130*
*LUDWIGSHAVEN*
FL H T Paddison and crew
SL F J Kelsh DFC in, Benton out

**17 Dec** *0320-0845*
*DUISBURG*
FO G A Thorne and crew
PO A H Mullard in, Scott out

**21 Dec** *1556-2026*
*COLOGNE*
FO G A Thorne and crew

**28 Dec** *1610-2110*
*MÜNCHEN-GLADBACH*
FO J D F Cowden and crew
FS C Duncan in, Rudd out

**29 Dec** *1606-2108*
*TROISDORF*
FO J D F Cowden and crew
WO G W Buttrick in, Duncan out

## 1945

**1 Jan** *1700-2120*
*DORTMUND*
FO J D F Cowden and crew
FS J S Davidson in, Buttrick out

**2 Jan** *1541-2245*
*NÜRNBERG*
FO J D F Cowden and crew

**5 Jan** *1700-2120*
*HANNOVER*
FO J D F Cowden and crew

**6 Jan** *1600-2130*
*HANAU*
FO G A Thorne and crew
Scott back

**7/8 Jan** *1900-0300*
*MUNICH*
FO G A Thorne and crew

**13 Jan** *1555-2125*
*SAARBRÜCKEN*
FO J D F Cowden and crew

**14/15 Jan** *1940-0410*
*MERSEBURG*
FO J D F Cowden and crew

**16/17 Jan** *1900-0050*
*MAGDEBURG*
FL G C Hitchcock RNZAF (DFC)
FS A R Chandler
FO T A King (DFC)
FO C W Spenceley
FS J Parkinson (WOP) (DFM)
FS A Purvis (AG) (DFM)
FS D C Dunkley (AG) (DFM)
Sgt W T N Trowhill (FE) (DFM)

**22/23 Jan** *2000-0030*
*GELSENKIRCHEN*
FL G C Hitchcock and crew
PO V G Marks in, Dunkley out

**1 Feb** *1641-2159*
*MAINZ*
FO J A Thrasher RCAF (DFC)
Sgt S E Sturgeon
FS D C Gray
WO F A Brunetta
FS H S Porter
FS A J Smith
FL L E Flatt DFC

**2/3 Feb** *2105-0236*
*WIESBADEN*
FL D B Jarvis (DFC)
FO C G Hale
FS A T Steele
FS R G Noakes
Sgt A Greeley
Sgt W S Bradford
Sgt F Murray

**4 Feb** *1815-2242*
*OBERFELD*
SL P R Mellor DFC
FL G Shaw (N) (DFC)
FO H L Coulter (2N)
FL F E Prebble RNZAF (BA) (DFC)
FS S Blair (WOP) (DFM)
FS A Rowbottom (FE) (DFM)
FS E E Freake (MU) (DFM)
FS L Freeman (RG) (DFM)

**7 Feb** *1933-2343*
*KLEVE*
WC S Baker DSO DFC*
FL R K Hawkins (DFC)
FS K E Glover (BA) (DFM)
FS A J R Teranzani
SL G R Hawes DFC (*)
Sgt W D Jones
FO J A Wilson RAAF (DFC)
Maj J B Mullock MC DFC RA

**8 Feb** *0335-0820*
*WANNE-EICKEL*
FL C H Hitchcock and crew
FL D Swaffield, PO V G Marks
and FL L E Flatt DFC in,
Chandler, Dunkley and
Trowhill out

**13/14 Feb** *1840-0215*
*DRESDEN*
FL J D F Cowden and crew

**14/15 Feb** *2043-0423*
*CHEMNITZ*
SL P R Mellor and crew
FS D Kirk in, Coulter out

## 405 SQUADRON RCAF

**22 Mar** *1150-1615*
*HILDESHEIM*
FO V R Norman RCAF
FO J M Davis RCAF (N)
FO P M Goffin RCAF
FO A L Jones RCAF (WOP)
FS A C Byers RCAF
FS R H Barker RCAF
Sgt G O'Hanlon RCAF

**27 Mar** *1516-1925*
*PADERBORN*
FL M S Fyte RCAF
FL W C Irwin (N)
FO J A Welch (WOP)
FO F C Fallon (BA)
FO B F Hobley (AG)
FO W Campbell (AG)
Sgt W A King (FE)

**31 Mar** *0642-1110*
*HAMBURG*
SL L G Neilly RCAF DFC(*)
FL R M Ferguson DFC(*) (N)
FL H G Windt (BA)
WO D Finley DFM (WOP)
PO K A C MacNair (DFC)
FO C B Legros (DFC)
PO A Warne (FE)

**4/5 Apr** *1912-0222*
*NÜRNBERG*
FL E Dereby
FO J B Miller
FO C W McClean
FS M F Botts
FS J R McCombe
FS S Young
Sgt G M Peters

**8/9 Apr** *1955-0046*
*HAMBURG*
FO R B Maxwell CGM (DFC)
FO M S Laidlow (DFC)
FO H W Cathron
PO J C Feasby

PO D Allan
PO E D Chisholm
FS H Jones

**10 Apr** *1442-2056*
*LEIPZIG*
FL J M Hall RCAF (DFC)
FO C A Weir (N)
FO J Lauley (BA)
FL E G Mader (WOP)
FS F Koroll (AG)
PO V Smith (AG)
Sgt H A Slater (FE)

**14/15 Apr** *1848-0222*
*POTSDAM*
SL L G Neilly and crew

**25 Apr** *0611-1301*
*BERCHTESGADEN*
FL J M Hall and crew
plus FO G H Gray (VB)

**30 Apr** *1550-1810*
*MANNA – THE HAGUE*
FL J M Hall and crew

**1 May** *1317-1529*
*MANNA – THE HAGUE*
SL C H Mussells RCAF (DFC)
PO E L Tempest
PO P Young
WO J L Larrimore
PO D T Dale
PO H L Eaton
PO C Ryan
FO R J H Littleton DFC

**9 May** *1055-1928*
*EXODUS*
FL J M Hall and crew
not Pauley

# ND875
# NUTS

ND875 on the occasion of reaching her 100th op, flown by SL P F Clayton (bottom right) and crew, 156 Squadron PFF, 24 March 1945.

Coming off the production line in early 1944 as part of aircraft order No.1807, this Avro-built machine was a Mark III, with four Merlin 38 engines. After some days at 32 MU commencing 9 April, it was assigned to 7 Squadron PFF on the 14th, but a week later re-assigned to 156 Squadron PFF at Upwood, Huntingdonshire, and coded GT-N.

ND875's operational tour began with a raid to Karlsruhe on 24/25 April, in the hands of Squadron Leader H F Slade DFC, who had with him that night the Squadron Navigation Leader, Squadron Leader A J Mulligan DFC (Mulligan was to receive the DSO in the summer). Herbert Slade flew the aircraft on 12 sorties before finishing his tour at the end of July, with a total of

58 ops with 156, for which he received an Immediate DSO in August. ND875 was also flown by the CO, Wing Commander T L Bingham-Hall DFC, who had come to the squadron in the same month as N-Nuts. Flight Lieutenant Hayden Jones was in Slade's crew and recalled:

'On [that first] Karlsruhe operation I was the Radar Navigator or Nav/B, so called, operating the $H^2S$ for navigation and bomb dropping. I expect we were PBMs as usual (Primary Blind Markers) if there was cloud. We bombed on $H^2S$ from about 20,000 feet on the majority of our trips.

'Slade died in Australia some years ago and

Tony Mulligan was lost on the ill-fated Avro Tudor [which was taking Sir Arthur Coningham to Bermuda on 30 January 1948] flying through the Bermuda Triangle; he was a wine sales rep by then.'

Among other notable pilots to fly *Nuts* were Squadron Leader A W G Cochrane, who would end the war with the DSO, DFC and two Bars, RNZAF, Squadron Leader T E Ison DSO DFC, Squadron Leader P F Clayton DFC, who arrived from 582 Squadron in August 1944 having been with 97 Squadron in 1943, and Squadron Leader Reg F Griffin DSO DFC. Cochrane had already flown a tour on Wellingtons and by February 1945 had himself completed 80 operations. He flew at least 14 of these as either Master or Deputy Master Bomber. His flight engineer, John Elder and rear gunner, Tom Drew, both received DFMs having completed 54 and 60 ops respectively. Drew's citation records:

'Flight Sergeant Drew has a fine operational record of 60 sorties, 35 of which have been with the Pathfinder Force, including 30 marker sorties. This NCO is a keen type of operational gunner who, until recently, flew with a crew who carried out Master Bomber duties. His keenness and vigilance have made him a valuable member of his crew and have on many occasions been responsible for the successful evasion of enemy aircraft. He is a resourceful and determined gunner who has now completed his second tour of operations. His loyalty and devotion to duty have been of a high order and I recommend that he be awarded the DFM.'

*Nuts* flew on D-Day, was shot-up by a night fighter on 23 June which knocked out the port-outer engine (becoming Cat AC), then flew over Caen as the Allied breakout came. On 7 October, to Cleve, Tom Ison flew a 'long-stop' mission, his duty being to ensure bombers did not overshoot the bomb-line and drop their loads onto Allied troops in the Nijmegen Salient. Another DFC winner who flew *Nuts* on a few raids was Flight Lieutenant Ken P C Doyle.

In total, Ison took ND875 on 17 trips, and Cochrane four – including one during which, acting as Master Bomber over Goch on 7/8 February 1945, they collided with another aircraft. Although the Lanc lost a chunk of its port wing, Cochrane continued to direct the bombing and stayed over the target until all had bombed. One interesting rear gunner Ison carried on 25 September was Squadron Leader D F Allen. As a sergeant he had won the George Medal in 1941 for rescuing three men from a crashed bomber and later won the British Empire Medal. He went on to win the DFC.

The 100th op was recorded as being flown on 24 March, with Squadron Leader Peter Clayton in command, on another 'long-stop' sortie for a raid against a Benzol plant near Dortmund. ND875 was credited with a total of 108 raids, although not all can be verified, but the aircraft certainly flew over the 100.

*Nuts* went to 1660 CU on 26 July, then to 1668 CU on 20 October, where she remained until 14 March 1946 when she returned to 1660 CU. Her final service was with 1653 CU with effect from 9 November and then she went to 15 MU on 9 May 1947, where she was Struck off Charge on 28 August.

## 156 SQUADRON
## 1944

24/25 Apr 2209-0407
*KARLSRUHE*
FL H F Slade DFC RAAF
SL A J Mulligan DFC (N)
FS T C Bower (BA)
FS B L Johnson DFM (FE)
FL H E Jones (WOP)
FS B H Andrews (MU)
PO H Toon DFM (RG)

26/27 Apr 2308-0301
*ESSEN*
FL D O Blamey
FS G H Clements
FS J Dillon
Sgt K Gilbert
FL J Booth
FS G W Gracey
WO D Pedder

2 May 0028-0140
*GHISLAIN*
2240-0140
FL H F Slade and crew
FS E A Jackson in, FS
Bower out

8 May 0028-0521
*NANTES AIRFIELD*
FL G C Hopton DFC RCAF
FL H D Gillis DFC
PO P J Moyes DFC
Sgt L E Gibbs
FL R B Leigh DFC
WO A R P Larkins
Sgt I Campbell
(all lost, except Leigh, 7/8
June; Hopton, by then a SL,
was on 46th op)

11/12 May 2215-0216
*HASSELT*

PO R H Samson
PO T W Kennedy
FS R J Andrew
Sgt R G Burton
WO A A Gilchrist
FS A G Bryant
FO S F Delongre

19/20 May 2303-0057
*MONT COUPLE – RADAR*
SL R F Slade DFC RAAF
FL G A R Undrell (N) (DFC)
PO C W Reeves (DFC)
PO A E Egan (DFC)
WO B L I Johnson DFM (FE)
WO B H Andrews (MU) (DFC)
SL J E Blair DFC DFM (RG)
(raid abandoned)

21/22 May 2252-0254
*DUISBURG*
SL R F Slade DFC RAAF

SL A J Mulligan DFC (N)
PO A E Egan
WO B L Johnson (FE)
FL G A R Undrell (2N)
WO B H Andrews (MU)
PO J H Detores (RG)

22/23 May 2250-0254
*DORTMUND*
FL R F Griffin DFC
FS L Proud
FS M N Finney
Sgt C F Pretlove
WO R E Bartleman
FS J J Corkery
FS F I Ide

27/28 May 2342-0325
*RENNES*
SL H F Slade and crew
Sgt G Edmond in (RG),
Detores out

A Lancaster drops its load: one 4,000 lb 'cookie' and a mass of incendiary bombs. The cookie smashes the target, the incendiaries set it alight.

**28/29 May** *2329-0111*
*MARDYCK*
SL H F Slade and crew
PO C W Reeves (N) in,
Mulligan out

**31 May** *0019-0402*
*TERGNIER*
WC T L Bingham-Hall DFC
Sgt R V Dickerson (N) (DFC)
FO H C Cavenagh (DFC)
Sgt H R Walker
FO J E Scrivener (DFC)
FS C R Alcock (DFC)
FS G R Green (DFM)

**6 June** *0258-0605*
*LONGUES BATTERY*
SL H F Slade and crew
Mulligan back, FS E Riley in,
Edmond out

**7 June** *0058-0333*
*FORÊT DE CERISY*
SL H F Slade and crew

**8/9 June** *2206-0215*
*FOUGÈRES*
SL H F Slade and crew
Reeves in, FS S Freeden in (RG)

**9/10 June** *2216-0235*
*LE MANS AIRFIELD*
SL H F Slade and crew
Sgt E C Bangs in, Freeden out

**11/12 June** *2147-0304*
*TOURS*
SL H F Slade and crew
FS E D Riley in, Bangs out

**14 June** *0210-0442*
*ST POL*
FO A McVitee in, Riley out;
FL J R Chislett in, Undrell out

**15/16 June** *2328-0210*
*LENS*
WC T L Bingham-Hall DFC
FO H Coker
FL H G M Robinson DFC RAAF
FL R E Manvell DFC DFM (FE)
FO F Holbrook (DFC)
FO F J Lockwood (DFC)

FO D Platana RCAF (DFC)
(Coker, Holbrook, Robinson,
Lockwood and Platana, all lost
in another crew, 14/15 July)

**16/17 June** *2358-0205*
*RENESCURE – V1 SITE*
PO K P C Doyle (DFC)
FS D Winslow
Sgt D K Green
Sgt T J Gedney
FS A Astle (DFC)
FS D J Hughes
PO J H Detores
(Doyle, Green and Astle KIA
24 Sept 1944)

**23/24 June** *2355-0221*
*COUBRONNES*
PO H T Griffin (DFC)
FL J A Turk (DFC*)
FS K J Negus
FS W J Norrys
FO E Dyson
FS P M Muir
FS J A McGregor
(damaged by fighter at 0112 hours)

**17 July** *1938-2205*
*MONT CANDON – V1 SITE*
FL A W G Cochrane DFC RNZAF
FO W J Evans
FO E E Court (DFC)
FS J B Elder (DFM) (FE)
PO H H Jenkins
FS L A Rookes
FS T E Drew (RG)
WO M Fleming RCAF (DFC)

**18 July** *0413-1720*
*SANNEVILLE – CAEN*
FL A W G Cochrane and crew

**19 July** *1412-1720*
*ROLLEZ – V1 SITE*
PO V B Temple (DFC)
WO H Graf
FS A E C Mundy
Sgt M J Waltham
FS A P Arnott
Sgt L E Reynolds
Sgt W V Cooper

**20 July** *1412-1731*
*FORÊT DE CROC – V1 SITE*
SL T E Ison DFC
FL H F Morrish (DFC)
Sgt L T Walton
Sgt C E Moss
FL F E Keighley (DFC)
PO A J Eley (DFC)
Sgt A Allen
FO J N Hough (DFC)
(Morrish KIA 24 Sept 1944)

**23/24 July** *2224-0324*
*DONGES*
SL T E Ison and crew
(Master Bomber)

**24/25 July** *2212-0521*
*STUTTGART*
FL R F Griffin and crew

**25/26 July** *2200-0601*
*STUTTGART*
SL T E Ison and crew

**28/29 July** *2251-0320*
*HAMBURG*
SL G C Hemmings DFC
FO S J Richards (N)
FL T J Pye (WOP)
Sgt A Green (FE)
FO P A Taylor (BA)
FO T H A Hill (MU)
PO G B Stone (RG)
(all lost 12 August)

**5 Aug** *1141-1403*
*FORÊT DE NIEPPE – V1 SITE*
SL T E Ison and crew

**6/7 Aug** *2141-0025*
*CABOURG*
SL T E Ison and crew

**7/8 Aug** *2127-0022*
*'TOTALIZE' – NORMANDY*
SL T E Ison and crew

**9/10 Aug** *2205-0039*
*FORT D'ENGLOS – V1 SITE*
FL K W Kitson (DFC)
FO B J L Dodd
Sgt J G Stewart
Sgt W G Taylor
FL J Booth
Sgt R O'Donnell
FS E G Gusway

**11 Aug** *1407-1708*
*SOMAIN*
SL T E Ison and crew

**12/13 Aug** *2158-0246*
*RÜSSELSHEIM*
FL P F Clayton DFC
FL F W Chandler
FO T G Greene (DFC)
FS R J Bruce
FO P B Kettle (DFC)
FO A G Lindsay
FO P O Bone DFC

**14 Aug** *1324-1625*
*'TRACTABLE' – NORMANDY*
SL T E Ison and crew

**16/17 Aug** *2122-0232*
*KIEL*
SL T E Ison and crew
FS W J Connolly (MU)

**18/19 Aug** *2140-0241*
*BREMEN*
SL T E Ison and crew

**25/26 Aug** *2106-0402*
*RÜSSELSHEIM*
FL P F Clayton and crew

**26/27 Aug** *2055-0119*
*KIEL*
FL A J Hiscock (DFC*)
FL J A Turk (DFC)
FS J S Turner
FO W N Bingham
PO C Wilson
FO J G Cooper
PO E W C Brackett

**26 Aug** *2125-0600*
*STETTIN*
FL H Rollin
FO W A Chmilar RCAF (N)
Sgt S Hudson (WOP)
Sgt M E Phillips (FE)
FS J W Pollock (BA)
Sgt E Murray (MU)
Sgt A W Hornsley (AG)

**31 Aug** *1419-1653*
*LUMBRES*
FL K P C Doyle
FS E F Hearn
FS D K Green
PO J A Brookes
PO A Astle
FO J A Noble
FO W A M Savill
(abandoned over tgt)

**3 Sep** *1600-1856*
*EINDHOVEN*
FL H Rollin and crew

**5 Sep** *1719-1856*
*LE HAVRE*
SL T E Ison and crew
(Deputy Master Bomber)

**9 Sep** *0700-0935*
*LE HAVRE*
SL T E Ison and crew
(abandoned – storms)

**10 Sep** *1537-1824*
*LE HAVRE*
SL T E Ison and crew

**11 Sep** *1652-2037*
*GELSENKIRCHEN*
SL T E Ison and crew

**12/13 Sep** *1859-0100*
*FRANKFURT*
FL W J Cleland DFC
PO G J Hudson
FS A J Wilson
FS J R Watson
FO N N Wray
FS W Appleby (DFM)
FS J A McGregor

**14 Sep** *1321-1535*
*HAGUE (DUMP)*
FL K P C Doyle and crew
WO E H Edinburgh (MU)
(Deputy Master Bomber)

**15/16 Sep** *2234-0350*
*KIEL*
FL K P C Doyle and crew

**17 Sep** *0740-0937*
*BOULOGNE*
FL K P C Doyle and crew

**20 Sep** *1520-1736*
*CALAIS*
SL T Ison and crew
(Master Bomber)

**25 Sep** *0935-1128*
*CALAIS*
SL T E Ison DFC
PO P T Kennedy (N)
FO N N Wray
Sgt F Gregory
PO A J Eley

FS W J Connolly (MU)
SL D F Allen GM BEM (RG)

**26 Sep** *0853-1124*
*CAP GRIS NEZ*
SL T E Ison DFC
FO A P Willoughby (N)
Sgt L T Walton
Sgt F Gregory
FL J R Chislett
FS W J Connolly (MU)
FO J Costigan (RG)

**5/6 Oct** *1921-0011*
*SAARBRÜCKEN*
FL L T R H Williams (DFC)
WO P A Robertson (DFC)
Sgt J Burgess
Sgt B A Butterfield (DFC)
FS H F Wilkinson
Sgt D Read
Sgt R J Heatrick

**7 Oct** *1206-1540*
*KLEVE*
SL T E Ison DFC
FL E T Cook (DFC)
FS L T Walton
Sgt F Gregory
FL J Booth
PO A J Eley
FS W J Connolly
FS J W Close
(Long-Stop op, to prevent
bombers bombing Allied
troops in Nijmegen salient)

**14 Oct** *am*
*DUISBURG*
FO F S Wallace (DFC)
Sgt G W Blick (N)
FS J T Barnes (WOP)
Sgt E Ogden
Sgt W I Davies (2N)
FO J M MacKrory RCAF
Sgt J Hayton

**15 Oct** *1727-2208*
*WILHELMSHAVEN*
FO F S Wallace and crew

**19 Oct** *1806-2354*
*STUTTGART*
FL A C Pope (DFC)
FO L E Munro RCAF (DFC)
Sgt K Antcliffe
Sgt G E Batten
Sgt E H Marlow
FO J F Aspinall
FS I W Kelly RCAF
FS R C Fletcher RCAF
(Pope, Munro, Antcliffe,
Marlow, Kelly and Fletcher
all lost 31 March 1945)

**23 Oct** *1707-2115*
*ESSEN*
FO A D Pelly (DFC)
FO D F Sinfield (N) (DFC)
FS W G Pearce RAAF
Sgt R Morgan (BA)
FO A J McLeod
FS L Ayres
FS T S Carr
(Sinfield and Carr KIA 20/21
Feb '45; rest, except Ayres
and Morgan PoWs)

**25 Oct** *1339-1707*
*ESSEN*
FL H Rollin and crew

**28 Oct** *1409-1751*
*COLOGNE*
FO J H Deremore-Denver (DFC)
FS S Carpenter (N)
WO J R Jones RAAF (WOP)

Sgt J C Bennett (FE)
FS R L Jacobs RAAF (N2)
Sgt J V McClosky (MU)
Sgt G MacQueen (RG)

**29 Oct** *1045-1301*
*WALCHEREN*
FO A B Pelly and crew

**1 Nov** *1800-2238*
*OBERHAUSEN*
FO F D Wallace and crew

**2 Nov** *1647-2120*
*DÜSSELDORF*
FO F D Wallace and crew

**4 Nov** *1749-2144*
*BOCHUM*
FO N Jackson
Sgt G W Blick
WO A Everest (WOP)
FS J S MacDonald
Sgt J Harvie
WO K K Muir
FS R R Willgoss

**16 Nov** *1330-1722*
*DÜREN*
FO A B Pelly and crew
Sgt J D Routledge (2N)

**27 Nov** *1759-2216*
*NEUSS*
FO F D Wallace and crew

**28 Nov** *0314-0745*
*ESSEN*
FO F D Wallace and crew

**30 Nov** *1718-2154*
*DUISBURG*
FO F D Wallace and crew

**3 Dec** *0813-1206*
*HEIMBACH*
FO F D Wallace and crew
FO F Reed (FE) in

**4 Dec** *1704-2229*
*KARLSRUHE*
FO F D Wallace and crew
PO R E Page (FE) in
(abandoned over target)

**5/6 Dec** *1828-0024*
*SOEST*
FO K T Wallace DFC RCAF
FS W D Bonter RCAF (N)
FL W Walker RAAF (WOP)
Sgt S B Glasper (FE)
FO C L Carlson RCAF (2N)
Sgt L A Bedford
FS E C Barnes

**17 Dec** *0350-0830*
*DUISBURG*
FO J H Deremore-Denver and crew
Sgt A M Gunton in as VM –
Visual Marker)

## 1945

**5 Jan** *1935-2357*
*HANNOVER*
FO M T Wilson
PO L N Hill (N)
PO E A Jackson RAAF (WOP)
Sgt R P Kimm (FE)
FO B W Munden RNZAF
FL S L Hyde
Sgt J H Addison

**7/8 Jan** *1918-0230*
*MUNICH*
FL N Jackson and crew
PO H J Scull in, Blick out;
WO H N Whitmore in,
FS Willgoss out

**2/3 Feb** *2110-0215*
*WIESBADEN*
SL A W C Cochrane DSO DFC
FO J Aaron RCAF (N)
FL R F Jenkins (WOP)
Sgt R E English (FE)
FL J R Burns RCAF (N2)
FO G K Dee RNZAF (VM)
FS D Reed
FO B W Felgate

**7/8 Feb** *1948-0140*
*GOCH*
SL A W G Cochrane and crew
(collided over target)

**17 Feb** *1230-1659*
*WESEL*
FL V M Todd
FO A B Walters RAAF
FO A Watson
FO J N Ashton
Sgt G S Kay
FO R L Martin
FS D J Price
FL J Jackson
(abandoned over tgt)

**20/21 Feb** *2215-0339*
*DORTMUND*
FL H G Hughes RCAF
FS F H Cripps (N)
FS P McEwen RAAF (WOP)
Sgt L Moody (FE)
FO G J Smith RCAF (VM)
Sgt P G Hinton
Sgt L Jackson

**21 Feb** *1720-2309*
*WORMS*
FL H G Hughes and crew

**1 Mar** *1227-1742*
*MANNHEIM*
FL I G Paull RAAF
PO S F Ladner RAAF
FO K T Glasziou RAAF
Sgt T L Pearson
FS V M Walsh RAAF
Sgt D R Haywood
Sgt D W D Riley

**5/6 Mar** *1725-0114*
*CHEMNITZ*
FL I G Paull and crew
PO J W Close RAAF – (MU)

**7/8 Mar** *1723-0154*
*DESSAU*
FL W J Taylor RAAF
FS E L Crispin RAAF
FS J E Ritchie RAAF
Sgt D A McLean
PO P S Green RAAF
FS K T Jones RAAF
FS R H Bennington RAAF

**8 Mar** *1846-2350*
*HAMBURG*
FL W E B Mason RCAF (DFC)
FO H J Collison RCAF (DFC)
FS C Saunderson (DFM) (WOP)
PO F V Walton
FS C S Fuller
FS H G Lee (DFM) (MU)
FS A S Orchard (RG)

**12 Mar** *1338-1828*
*DORTMUND*
FL I G Paull and crew
Sgt D S Breenbank (MU)
Sgt D R Haywood (RG)

**13 Mar** *1806-2302*
*DAHL*
FL W J Taylor and crew

**14 Mar** *1748-2243*
*HOMBURG*
FL W J Taylor and crew

**15/16 Mar** *1741-0018*
*HANNOVER*
FL I G Paull and crew

**16/17 Mar** *1810-0130*
*NÜRNBERG*
FL W J Taylor and crew

**18 Mar** *0109-0727*
*HANAU*
FL W E B Mason and crew

**20 Mar** *0207-0710*
*HEIDE*
FL H G Hughes and crew

**22 Mar** *1144-1616*
*HILDESHEIM*
FL H G Hughes and crew

**24 Mar** *1342-1813*
*HARPENERWEG*
SL P F Clayton DFC
SL F W W Chandler DFC
FL T G Greene DFC
WO R J Bruce
FL R J Burns RCAF
FO J F Aspinall
FS L E Reynolds
FO H Cornforth

**31 Mar** *0645-1129*
*HAMBURG*
FL H G Hughes and crew
FL R L Thomson RNZAF (2N)

**4/5 Apr** *2150-0505*
*LUTZKENDORF*
FL H G Hughes and crew

**8/9 Apr** *1928-0047*
*HAMBURG*
FL H G Hughes and crew

**9/10 Apr** *1947-0057*
*KIEL*
FL H G Hughes and crew

**10 Apr** *1434-2108*
*LEIPZIG*
FO C E Light
FO B B Coles
FO R J Grenfell
FS J T Thompson
Sgt G E Wilkes
Sgt D Greenbank
FS A J Greenacre

**11 Apr** *1208-1814*
*NÜRNBERG*
FL H G Hughes and crew

**13 Apr** *2031-0227*
*KIEL*
FL H G Hughes and crew

# NE181
# MIKE, THE CAPTAIN'S FANCY

*The Captain's Fancy* was NE181 of 74 (New Zealand) Squadron and is pictured here approaching her 100th sortie.

The last Lancaster of the 600 produced under order No.1807, NE181 was a Mark III that was built in the spring of 1944 with four Merlin 38 engines. Sent to 75 (New Zealand) Squadron based at Mepal, Cambridgeshire on 20 May it was probably given the squadron code of AA (A and B Flights), but it soon wore the code of C Flight – JN. NE181's individual letter became 'M' and from then on it was affectionately known as *Mike*.

The first sortie on 21/22 May was to Duisburg, with Pilot Officer C Crawford; the second was to Aachen one week later. *Mike* flew on both D-Day nights with Flight Sergeant J Lethbridge RNZAF as skipper and he piloted the Lanc on 26 trips during its first three months of operational duty. *Mike's* next regular captains were Flying Officer G Cuming, who took it on 14 raids, and Squadron Leader N A Williamson, seven ops. Even the squadron CO, Wing Commander R J A Leslie AFC did a couple.

On a raid in support of the imminent Arnhem operation, on the night of 16/17 September, 75 Squadron dropped not bombs but miniature dummy parachutists, near Moerdijk airfield, in order to create a diversion – NE181 being one of those who took part in this unusual mission.

Paddy McElligott, who was Gordon Cuming's rear gunner on this occasion also remembered the raid to Saarbrücken on 5 October:

'I recall we flew in formation low over France and in a vic formation before climbing in darkness to our bombing height of 14,000 feet. I saw one of the aircraft just behind ours dip and hit the ground in a ball of flame and smoke, as it collided with a Lancaster from 115 Squadron.

'This operation had personal connotations for me, for over the target we were attacked by a Junkers 88. To find an enemy fighter amongst the flak in the target area was unusual. I returned its fire and felt sure I had hit the fighter from the impression given by the tracer. The mid-upper gunner opened fire after me but soon his guns automatically cut-out when the turret was rotated towards our twin tail-fins. Thinking it was a stoppage he operated the manual over-ride, whereupon I became aware of tracer shooting over my turret.

'As I continued to fire, I called for the skipper

to corkscrew port, which he did, and the Ju88 went down to our starboard. I asked the mid-upper where the second fighter came from that was firing over my head and he calmly said it was him!'

Paddy McElligott also recalls a raid to Cologne on 31 October, when the Station Commander, Group Captain A P Campbell (aged 40) was with them:

'This was the second time we visited Cologne within 24 hours. The Group Captain flew with us as bomb aimer and Syd Sewell assessed his ability on this occasion as "shows promise"! I understand the Group Captain had already completed the requisite operational flying hours allocated to him for October, so by going as bomb aimer, he no doubt hoped his transgression would go un-noticed by Group HQ.

'On this raid we were "buzzed" on four occasions by a jet aircraft – presumably an Me262. On each occasion the jet climbed past us like a rocket but did not open fire. The encounters were so fast and abrupt we could not engage. We reported the incident at de-briefing.'

On 2 November, Jack Leslie took *Mike* to Homberg. "Tiny" Humphries was the crew's navigator:

'We had the misfortune to have one bomb hang-up and Leslie then announced he was going round again, but the bomb aimer couldn't release it manually on the second run. If anything was calculated to be foolhardy, going round again to drop one bomb over a place which had just been done over, that was! None of us wanted to fly with him again, but that was Jack Leslie. We got back somewhat late!'

*Mike* hardly recorded a single mechanical problem during the first seven months of operations. Not until 6/7 January 1945 did the aircraft lose an engine, during a mining sortie off Danzig, but the next raid, on 11 January, *Mike* lost its port-outer due to a coolant leak, while the port-inner gave the pilot, Squadron Leader J M Bailey DFC, indications of overheating.

John Bailey – or Jack as he was generally known – became *Mike's* regular pilot late in the Lanc's career, flying a total of 14 ops in this aircraft and ending his tour with a Bar to his DFC. Flight Lieutenant Alex Simpson also did a couple of trips in *Mike*, and recalled the aircraft, its nose-art painting, and Jack Bailey:

FO Gordon Cuming and crew. Rear: Paddy McElligott, Jack Christie, Bill Scott. Front: Jack Scott, Cuming, Syd Sewell.

Same crew 12 December 1944 – end of tour. Syd Sewell, Bill Scott, Paddy McElligott, Jack Lambert, Jack Christie, Jack Scott.

'When we went to Coblenz on 6 November, my log states we flew on three engines all the way. We cut a few corners on the route back because of our reduced flying speed, nevertheless we got back to Mepal fairly early, called up base but got no response. We soon realised our radio was u/s so climbed above the other orbiting aircraft and waited.

'Eventually the circuit lights went out and we were left alone in the darkness. Our only recourse was to fly in low over the airfield, fire a red Very cartridge and hope someone eventually got the message, which they did. The lights went on and we finally touched down some 1¹/₂ hours after everyone else!

'Sadly this was our last trip in *Mike*, though not of our tour – we still had eight to go. She was, in the terminology of the day, "a great old kite" – reliable and a proven operational veteran.'

'I had a lot of time for Jack Bailey. He was an Irishman of Southern Irish descent and had that delightful Irish sense of humour. He had tried very hard to get approval to fly *Mike* to New Zealand, being the first [and only] New Zealand heavy bomber to make 100 operations. He even went to the extent of soliciting aid from Bill Jordan, the New Zealand High Commissioner in London.

'We all knew *Mike* was getting near its 100th, in fact one of my arguments to Jack was that it was such a clapped-out old heap and I had my own aircraft in JN-K King, that I didn't want to fly it.

'I do not recall the background of naming *Mike, The Captain's Fancy*, other than knowing that the "Captain" as depicted on *Mike* was Captain Reilly-Foull from the wartime *Daily Mirror* cartoon strip.' [Captain A R P Reilly-Foull was a character in the *Just Jake* cartoon.]

Paddy McElligott remembered Reilly-Foull also had:

'… in his right hand a pint of beer and the inevitable dart, ready to be thrown, in his left hand. The cartoon invariably began with his expression – "Stap-me …!"

There was some confusion as to when *Mike* did the 100th trip. According to a press release, it was flown on 29 January 1945 which is in keeping with the Form 541 details. However, there must have been an earlier count of the ops, for initially it was thought the aircraft's 100th was due on 5 January. Jack Bailey, feeling superstitious about it, talked to his deputy flight commander, Alex Simpson, into flying the sortie, which he reluctantly did. Only after this had been flown was another count made, which indicated that Alex had in fact flown the 101st sortie. In the final event, that was only the aircraft's 96th. Therefore, *Mike* flew the 100th on 29 January – with Jack Bailey! It was his own 47th operation. His was a very good crew and the press release also noted the New Zealand pilot and his six English crewmen had, between them, flown a total of 294 ops. *Mike* managed one more sortie on 2/3 February before enough became enough for both the aircraft and any crews who might be assigned to fly her.

# NE181 MIKE, THE CAPTAIN'S FANCY

No doubt part of the confusion over the ops count was due to the existence of two aircraft lettered 'M' on 75 Squadron, the other being AA-M (ME752). In fact in the press release, this other aircraft was reported as flying the 99th trip on 22 January – whereas JN-M (NE181) did not fly that night. Undoubtedly too, the earlier confusion was due to someone counting up the 'M's but not taking notice of the serial numbers or the flight to which each Lancaster belonged.

*Mike* was retired after the 101st trip, and as authority finally thwarted the efforts to get the bomber sent to New Zealand, Alex Simpson (DFC) was detailed to fly it to Waterbeach on 17 February. Here, after a refit, she was assigned to 514 Squadron which operated from this base, on 19 July. 514 was disbanded in August so on 4 September *Mike* went to 5 MU where she was finally scrapped on 30 September 1947. The aircraft would have made a proud museum piece in New Zealand, but, alas, bureaucracy dictated that nothing could be done to get NE181 despatched to its far-off adopted country, where it could have represented the major contribution made by its airmen – both in the RAF and RNZAF – in WW2.

## 75 (NEW ZEALAND) SQUADRON 1944

**21/22 May** *2255-0320*
DUISBURG
PO C Crawford
FS E Rivers (N)
Sgt T Mason (BA)
Sgt T Feaver (WOP)
Sgt A Frost (FE)
Sgt N Heslop (MU)
Sgt R Phillips (RG)

**28/29 May** *1855-0210*
AACHEN
FS J D Perfrement RAAF (DFC)
Sgt W Hall
Sgt A Kirkham
PO J Craven
Sgt J Tomlinson
Sgt L King
FS D Trigg

**2/3 June** *0115-0355*
WISSANT
FS J Lethbridge RNZAF
Sgt P Crane
FO J Dickenson
WO C Newark
Sgt A Barnes
Sgt A Markham RNZAF
FS J Snodgrass RNZAF
(tgt not identified, did not bomb)

**4 June** *0035-0240*
CALAIS
FS J Lethbridge and crew

**5/6 June** *0330-0640*
OUISTREHAM
FS J Lethbridge and crew

**6/7 June** *2359-0355*
LISIEUX
FS J Lethbridge and crew

**10/11 June** *2310-0330*
DREUX
FS C G Nairne RNZAF
FS L C Perry RNZAF (N)
FS D A Kidby (BA)
Sgt A R Stannard (WOP)
Sgt R C Smith (FE)
Sgt S A G Woodford (MU)
FS P Falkiner RNZAF (RG)
(lost 30 July, all killed)

**11/12 June** *2350-0515*
NANTES
FS C G Nairne and crew

**14/15 June** *2340-0310*
GELSENKIRCHEN
FS C G Nairne and crew

Jack Bailey DFC took NE181 on her 100th sortie, 29 January 1945 and the 101st and last on 2/3 February.

**15/16 June** *2305-0230*
VALENCIENNES
FS C G Nairne and crew

**21 June** *1810-2040*
DOMLÉGER – V1 SITE
FS J Lethbridge and crew

**23/24 June** *2305-0130*
L'HEY – V1 SITE
FS J Lethbridge and crew

**24/25 June** *2330-0200*
RIMEUX – V1 SITE
FS J Lethbridge and crew

**30 June** *1810-2120*
VILLERS BOCAGE
FS J Lethbridge and crew

**2 July** *1257-1615*
BEAUVOIR – V1 SITE
FS J Lethbridge and crew

**5/6 June** *2307-0055*
WATTEN – V1 SITE
FS J Lethbridge and crew

**7/8 July** *2259-0329*
VAIRIES
FS A McKenzie
FS W Stoneham
FS T Bunce
WO J Wright
Sgt G Robertson
Sgt G McKellow
Sgt W Barker

**9 July** *1305-1606*
LIZIEUX – V1 SITE
PO F Timms RNZAF
Sgt W Morton
FO J Noble RNZAF
Sgt P McKerrel
Sgt R Woods
Sgt J Hindley
Sgt W Kemp

**10 July** *0420-0730*
NUCOURT – V1 SITE
FS J Lethbridge and crew

**12 July** *1811-2146*
VAIRIES
FS J Lethbridge and crew

**15/16 July** *2330-0225*
BOIS DES JARDINS – V1 SITE
FS J Lethbridge and crew

**18 July** *0440-0735*
CAGNY / CAEN
FS J Lethbridge and crew

**20/21 July** *2345-0250*
HOMBERG
FS J Lethbridge and crew

**23/24 July** *2244-0344*
KIEL
PO F Timms and crew

**25/26 July** *2140-0554*
STUTTGART
FL G R Gunn
FO F Smith (N)
FO A M Miller (BA)
FL W F M Naismith (WOP)
Sgt J H Bruce (FE)

# TON-UP LANCS

FO C Robertson (MU)
FO S Haines (RG)
(this crew crash-landed at RAF
Hawkinge 17 Sep '44; Gunn Dol
21st, Bruce also killed. Naismith
later PoW, 20 Nov)

**28/29 July** *2158-0543*
*STUTTGART*
FL G Gunn and crew

**30 July** *0605-1001*
*AMAYE-SUR-SEULLES*
FS J Lethbridge and crew

**1 Aug** *1913-2134*
*LE NIEPPE – V1 SITE*
FS J Lethbridge and crew

**3 Aug** *1156-1536*
*L'ISLE ADAM – V1 SITE*
FS J Lethbridge and crew

**4 Aug** *1335-2136*
*BEC D'AMBES*
FS J Lethbridge and crew

**5 Aug** *1422-2214*
*BASSENES – V1 SITE*
FS E O'Callaghan
FS C Busfield (N)
Sgt J Mitchell (BA)
FS S Matheson (WOP)
Sgt C Simpson (FE)
Sgt E Baines (MU)
Sgt A Shepherd (RG)

**7/8 Aug** *2157-0057*
*MARE DE MAGNE*
FS J Lethbridge and crew

**9/10 Aug** *2208-0019*
*FORT D'ANGLOS – V1 SITE*
FS J Lethbridge and crew

**11 Aug** *1428-1746*
*LENS*
FS J Lethbridge and crew

**12/13 Aug** *2244-0541*
*GARDENING – GIRONDE*
FS J Lethbridge and crew

**15 Aug** *0955-1331*
*ST TROND AIRFIELD*
FO J H Scott RNZAF
FS A H Scott RNZAF (N)
FS K P C Anderson RNZAF (BA)
FS E J F Howard RNZAF (WOP)
Sgt H M Thomas (FE)
Sgt J T Beardmore (MU)
Sgt J T Boyes (RG)
(all lost 4 Nov 1944)

**16/17 Aug** *2109-0516*
*STETTIN*
FS J Lethbridge and crew

**18/19 Aug** *2135-0309*
*BREMEN*
FS J Lethbridge and crew

**26/27 Aug** *2005-0153*
*KIEL*
FS P L McCartin RAAF
Sgt J Miles (N)
FO L A Martin (BA)
Sgt P F Smith RAAF (WOP)
Sgt W J Warlow (FE)
Sgt D G A Bryer (MU)
Sgt J N Gray (RG)
(all KIA on 20 Nov, except
Gray, taken prisoner)

**29/30 Aug** *2030-0555*
*GARDENING – DANZIG*
SL N A Williamson RNZAF
FO J Watts
FO G Coull
Sgt S Cook

FO S Moss (FE)
Sgt R Jones (MU)
FO J Tugwell (RG)

**31 Aug** *1630-1930*
*PONT RÉMY*
SL N A Williamson and crew
FS G Ellis RCAF in, Jones out

**5 Sep** *1739-2118*
*LE HAVRE*
FS P L McCartin and crew

**6 Sep** *1556-1943*
*HARQUEBOC / LE HAVRE*
FO G Cuming RNZAF
FS J G Scott (N)
FS S Sewell (BA)
FS J D Christie (WOP)
Sgt J C Lambert (FE)
Sgt W Scott (MU)
Sgt D P McElligott (RG)

**8 Sep** *0621-1046*
*DOUDELAINVILLE*
FS P L McCartin and crew

**12/13 Sep** *1847-0152*
*FRANKFURT*
FO G Cuming and crew

**14 Sep** *1300-1536*
*WASENAAR*
FO K Southward RNZAF
FO A F Thompson RNZAF (N)
PO B G Clare RNZAF (BA)
Sgt E W Vero (WOP)
Sgt D J Roberts (FE)
Sgt L Cooper (MU)
Sgt T Burnett (RG)
(shot down 6 Oct; pilot killed,
rest of crew taken prisoner)

**16 Sep** *2127-0019*
*MOERDIJK*
FO G Cuming and crew

**17 Sep** *1933-2235*
*EMMERICH*
FO G Cuming and crew

**20 Sep** *1429-1808*
*CALAIS*
SL N A Williamson and crew
Sgt D P McElligott in, Tugwell out

**5 Oct** *1730-2231*
*SAARBRÜCKEN*
FO G Cuming and crew

**6 Oct** *1652-2258*
*DORTMUND*
FO G Cuming and crew

**7 Oct** *2220-0614*
*EMMERICH*
SL N A Williamson and crew
Tugwell back

**14 Oct** *0650-1114*
*DUISBURG*
SL N A Williamson and crew

**14/15 Oct** *2239-0319*
*DUISBURG*
SL N A Williamson and crew

**15/16 Oct** *1827-0022*
*GARDENING – KATTEGAT*
FO E Robertson RNZAF
FS A Herrold RNZAF
FO S Richmond RNZAF
FS F Tibby RNZAF
Sgt F Thompson
Sgt R Maryan
Sgt P Smith

**19/20 Oct** *1737-2353*
*STUTTGART*
FO J A McIntosh RNZAF

NE181's ground crew paint on the 101st bomb. On the ladder are LAC Taylor and Thompson. Foreground, from left to right: Sgt Grantham, LAC F Woolerton, Jack Bailey, unknown.

FS R C Morgan RNZAF (N)
FS R W Newman RNZAF (BA)
FS R J Boag RAAF (WOP)
Sgt E Graves (FE)
Sgt C Brewer (MU)
Sgt E R Cooper (RG)
(all KIA 30 Nov, except Cooper,
PoW, and Graves – not flying)

**21 Oct** *1117-1410*
*FLUSHING*
FL T Waugh
PO C Woonton RNZAF
FS R Swetland
FS P Kidd
Sgt N Southgate
FS J Nickells RNZAF
FS D Sage RNZAF

**22 Oct** *1327-1733*
*NEUSS*
FL T Waugh and crew

**23 Oct** *1655-2148*
*ESSEN*
FO G Cuming and crew
Sgts J Huckle and A Weston in,
McElligott and Lambert out

**25 Oct** *1316-1722*
*ESSEN*
FO G Cuming and crew
Lambert back, WO R Powell in as RG

**26 Oct** *1304-1716*
*LEVERKUSEN*
FO G Cuming and crew
Powell out, WO I Cornfield in

**28 Oct** *1315-1746*
*COLOGNE*
SL J Bailey DFC RNZAF
FO J G Brewster (N)
FO J C Wall (BA)
Sgt R Pickup (WOP)
FO N Bartlett (FE)
FS T Gregory (MU)
PO J Bryant RAAF (RG)

**30 Oct** *0902-1335*
*WESSELING*
SL J Bailey and crew

**30 Oct** *1803-2318*
*COLOGNE*
FO E Butler RNZAF
FS H Holliday RAAF
FS H Stratford RNZAF
Sgt D Brazier
Sgt C Payne
Sgt J Heaton
Sgt J Messer

**31 Oct** *1820-2235*
*COLOGNE*
FO G Cuming and crew
McElligott back, G/Capt A P
Campbell in – passenger

75 Squadron Lancasters breaking formation over their base at Mepal 6 September 1944, returning from Harquebec. One of them is NE181!

**2 Nov** *1139-1544*
HOMBERG
WC R J A Leslie AFC
FS A L Humphries RNZAF (N)
FO E Holloway RNZAF (BA)
WO F Chambers RNZAF
FS S Cowen
FO R J Scott RNZAF (MU)
FS A McDonald (RG)

**4 Nov** *1129-1603*
SOLINGEN
SL J Bailey and crew
Cornfield in, Bryant out

**5 Nov** *1044-1459*
SOLINGEN
FO J McIntosh and crew
Sgt G Knight in, Graves out

**6/7 Nov** *1659-2144*
COBLENZ
FO G Cuming and crew

**8 Nov** *0752-1219*
HOMBERG
SL J Bailey and crew

**20 Nov** *1242-1720*
HOMBERG
FO J McDonald
FS C Aylott
WO E DeShaine
WO E Hughes
WO J Dunn
FS W Davies
FO H Campbell

**21 Nov** *1254-1656*
HOMBERG
WC R J A Leslie AFC and
FL Waugh's crew except
Swetland out, FO G Coull in

**23 Nov** *1249-1707*
GELSENKIRCHEN
FO J McDonald and crew

**27 Nov** *1228-1659*
COLOGNE
FO J McDonald and crew
Sgt J Messer in, Campbell out

**28/29 Nov** *0258-0712*
NEUSS
SL J Bailey and crew

**2 Dec** *1246-1705*
DORTMUND
FO J McDonald and crew
Campbell back

**4 Dec** *1217-1608*
OBERHAUSEN
FO D Williams RNZAF
FS D Sim RNZAF
WO G Duncan
WO O Harrison RNZAF
Sgt E Round
FS I Carrington RNZAF
FS R Smith RNZAF

**5 Dec** *0911-1347*
HAMM
SL J Bailey and crew
(bombed secondary tgt)

**6/7 Dec** *1708-0027*
MERSEBURG
FO A Simpson RNZAF
PO R Woodhouse
FS J Hemingway
Sgt A Dibbs
Sgt J Johnstone
FS E Thomas RNZAF
Sgt C Chippendale

**8 Dec** *0830-1243*
DUISBURG
SL J Bailey and crew

**11 Dec** *0842-1253*
OSTERFELD
SL J Bailey and crew

**12 Dec** *1112-1618*
WITTEN
FL L W Harrison RNZAF
FS H McLeod RNZAF
FO W Brizley RNZAF
FS W Jenkins RNZAF
Sgt P Yellin
Sgt R Williams
Sgt C Wilkinson

**16 Dec** *1118-1728*
SIEGEN
SL J Bailey and crew
FL A Creagh in (N), Brewster out

**21 Dec** *1226-1707*
TRIER
PO G S Davies RNZAF (DFC)
FS C C Greenhough RNZAF (N)
Sgt H E Chalmers (BA)
Sgt T M White (WOP)
Sgt I R H Evans (FE)
Sgt J J Maher (MU)
WO W Reavely (RG)
(all PoW 14 Feb '45; Chalmers
died of wounds 2 March; Reavely
not on that raid)

**23 Dec** *1200-1617*
TRIER
SL J Bailey and crew
Brewster back

**27 Dec** *1210-1646*
RHELDT
SL J Bailey and crew

**31 Dec** *1134-1629*
VOHWINKEL
FL L W Hanan and crew

## 1945

**1 Jan** *1603-2153*
VOHWINKEL
FL L W Hanan and crew

**3 Jan** *1232-1740*
DORTMUND
FL L W Hanan and crew

**5 Jan** *1136-1723*
LUDWIGSHAVEN
FO A D Simpson and crew

**6/7 Jan** *1618-0158*
GARDENING
FO D Clements
FO Hewitt
FO R Cato
FS T Hepard
Sgt W Richardson
Sgt J Wildish
Sgt F Watte
(returned on 3 engines)

**11 Jan** *1152-1647*
KREFELD
SL J Bailey and crew
(lost port-outer but
bombed target)

**16 Jan** *2316-0417*
WANNE-EICKEL
SL J Bailey and crew

**29 Jan** *1012-1558*
KREFELD
SL J Bailey and crew

**2/3 Feb** *2046-0231*
WIESBADEN
SL J Bailey and crew

# PA990
# BENNET'S BEAVERS

Robert Bennet and crew.  Standing:  Harry Hayton, Johnny Johnson, Bob Bennet, Gerry Smallshaw.
Front: Tommy Scales, Robbie Robson, Jim Thatcher.

Built at Avro's Woodford factory, PA990 was a Mark III with Merlin 38 engines, part of Contract No.1807 C4A. On 28 May it was sent to 300 Polish Squadron, according to the aircraft movement card, but the same date sees it assigned to 626 Squadron, at Wickenby, Lincolnshire. Coded UM, its individual letter was R, or to be correct, R², as all squadron aircraft had this ² after their letter, so that aircraft would not be confused with the 12 Squadron Lancs, who also used Wickenby. Several crews merely referred to PA990 as Roger Two.

PA990's first skipper was Flying Officer R C Bennet RCAF from Vancouver, and he took her on her first sortie on 2/3 June, against a radar site at Berneval, and then subsequently on the following two raids, but had to abort the fourth on instructions from the Master Bomber on D-Day. Bennet and his crew continued to be the regular operators throughout June and early July, although the Squadron CO, Wing Commander G F Rodney AFC – later DFC – and then Pilot Officer G Lofthouse had flights in her in early July. By this time PA990 had been named as *Bennet's Beavers*, painted on by Bob Bennet himself, assisted by Harry Hayton, his navigator. At any rate he held the paint brushes!

The motif was of a red-nosed backwoodsman wearing a racoon hat. Over his shoulder he carried an axe on which was perched a small bird. As to the colouring, the man had a yellow shirt, brown trousers, black shoes and belt, a black and yellow hat. The head of the axe was red with the cutting edge silver, and a brown shaft. He was superimposed on a green circle and the name lettering was in white.

It was positioned just below the pilot's window, and aft of it began the rows of bombs. The first block was seven rows of ten, red bombs for night and yellow for day ops. A second block was started behind the first.

An attack upon Gelsenkirchen on 12 June turned out lucky for the bomb aimer, Robbie Robson, due to his height – 5ft 5½ inches. Hit by flak while he was sitting in the front gun turret, a large piece of shrapnel (about the size of an ostrich egg he estimated) lodged just 3 inches about his head. Any taller and he would have been killed.

On 18/19 July PA990 was hit by flak again over Scholven and her bomb-doors were holed, but ops continued, with just a few other crews taking her out, until 18 August, the date of R C Bennet's last op in her, his 26th. He received the DFC. Bennet and Hayton both married mid-tour (July), Harry Hayton celebrating his 60th anniversary in 2004. Bob Bennet's DFC citation reads:

'As pilot and captain of aircraft this officer has taken part in many operational sorties. He has led his crew with gallantry and high courage, inspiring them with his own cheerful confidence in times of stress. In May 1944, while over enemy territory, he observed an enemy fighter attacking a Lancaster aircraft. Flying Officer Bennet immediately closed in, drew fire from the enemy and skilfully manoeuvred his aircraft to enable his gunners to drive off the enemy.'

Flying Officer B A Collens had started to fly her in August and went on to take her on seven trips, then there was no regular crew until Sergeant R C Yule flew to Saarbrücken

The other Bennett, with some of his crew who flew PA990 to Caen on 18 July 1944. From top to bottom: Ivor Billinge, Ron Bennett, K Lofts, E Cooper, L Paradise, J Slattery and J Reid.

Royan Yule seated in PA990, as she neared her 90th operation.

on 5/6 October. Flying Officer A H "Chippy" Wood flew PA990 on just one sortie, which he and his crew thought was their 30th and last operation of their tour. This was a raid to Bochum on 4 November. Douglas Joss, the rear gunner, recalls that they were happy and cheering as they returned, only to be advised by the 'boss' that as their bomb aimer, Don Wells, had missed one mission, he – and they too if they agreed – had to make Don up to 30 too! They took another Lanc to Gelsenkirchen on the 6th, and thus completed their tour.

On 29 December, with Flying Officer K G Hale as pilot, the Lancaster was hit in the starboard wing by flak, severing the hydraulics and pneumatic lines. Hale had to put down at the emergency strip at Woodbridge. The next trip, on 6 January 1945, was with Yule in command. On their way home they discovered a 500 lb bomb lying on the bomb-doors, which they quickly jettisoned.

Royan Charles Yule, from Aberdeen, became PA990's regular captain throughout the winter, being commissioned in December, although several other pilots flew odd sorties now and again, but Yule managed 18 during his tour, and won the DFC. Roy Yule lost his initial navigator after three trips but was fortunate enough to get Gus Marbaix, starting his second tour. He was the best navigator Roy ever had, and he too later received the DFC. Roy's last trip in PA990 was a mining sortie on 14/15

February 1945, at which time the number of her ops was in the mid-80s. Roy Yule recalls one operation:

'January 6, 1945. Fifteen of the squadron's crews were briefed to bomb the rail marshalling yards at Neuss, just west of Düsseldorf. In the event only ten of us got off, the armourers could not cope with such a short period. Roger 2 had been patched up from the flak damage sustained on 29 December and we took off at 3.30 pm.

'Nine-tenths cloud covered the target and Stan bombed red and green parachute flares five minutes after zero hour. We were at 20,000 feet and the flak was bursting mostly below us as I closed the bomb-doors and turned on to a westerly course. We had just crossed the battle lines north of Antwerp when there was a thump and a 500 lb bomb which had hung-up, dropped on to the bomb-doors. 4,000 lb blockbusters have three arming vanes, which revolve and drop off as they fall, but 500 and 1,000 lb bombs have a short cable and as they fall from their mounts, the safety pin is pulled out. Therefore, the bomb rolling about on our bomb-doors was live and if its detonator jarred, bye-bye life. I asked Gus how long before we were over the sea, and he said five minutes. The ominous rumble continued. I opened the bomb-doors and the bomb fell away. The chances of the bomb killing us was far greater than killing some farm workers on the Dutch-Belgian border.

'Bad weather had continued until 7 February, the date we were briefed for a night raid on Kleve. This operation was to prepare the way for the attack by the 15th Scottish Division across the German frontier near Reichswald. It was understood that the civilian population had been evacuated.

'We took off at 7 pm and at 10 pm approached the target on a heading of 060 degrees at 10,000 feet. There was a layer of thin cloud at 5,000 feet and we clearly heard the Master Bomber ordering the main force to come below cloud. The MB was Wing Commander [Tubby] Baker who was in a Mosquito circling wide round Kleve at 3,000 feet.

'To comply with the order I closed the throttles and put Roger 2 into a dive, getting under the cloud and levelling off at 4,000 feet. This turned out to be one hell of a bombing-run. Over half of the main force did not come below cloud and bombed the fires and flares which could be seen through the thin layer.

'The 140 or so Lancaster pilots that did obey the MB converged on to the tight bunch of target indicators. Stan gave "Bomb-doors open," then the clear casual voice of the MB, "Bomb to the starboard of the red T.Is." Then I had to dodge under a Lancaster coming from our port side. Looking up into its yawning bomb-bay with its rows of 500 lb bombs and a cookie, I jabbed left rudder to clear it. Stan, who could not see the other Lanc, had started his run-up patter giving me right, and shouted agitatedly, "Right, right, not bloody left!"

'The scene ahead was fantastic. Red and yellow tracer shells were criss-crossing from the flak batteries outside the town. They seemed to be coming from eight different positions and looked like 20 mm and 37 mm, which are nasty blighters at the height we were at. Strings of bombs were falling through the cloud from the Lancs above. Flashes from the exploding blockbusters on the ground were blinding.

A stricken Lancaster crashed on its run-in blowing up with its full bomb load. Large columns of black smoke rose from the town up to 3,000 feet.

'Stan gave, right, right, steady, bombs away, then Roger 2 was bucking and rearing as the pressure waves hit us. 4,000 feet was reckoned to be the absolute minimum height for dropping blockbusters. At last we were through the target and turning south over the Rhine where my stomach muscles started to relax.

'[At de-briefing] Frank said that a string of bombs with a wobbling blockbuster dropped past within a few feet of our starboard tail-plane as our own bombs were leaving. Tubby made us all laugh when he said he had his hands over his head and was shitting himself.'

In March her new skipper was Pilot Officer W F C Fanner, who flew her on 19 trips by the war's end. The name *Bennet's Beavers* remained but PA990 had *Fanner's Follies* substituted for the earlier name at or near the end. Her 100th sortie, by a reasonable count-up from the Form 541, suggests the raid on Berchtesgaden on 25 April, with Flying Officer A R H Warner RNZAF in command, and recorded as the Squadron's last bombing operation. No.101 appears to be a Manna trip by another pilot and then Fanner made another Manna sortie on 1 May which could be the 102nd. Each sortie flew and dropped 284 sacks of foodstuffs. Two more such sorties on the 3rd and 4th, and one on the last day of the war, the 7th, ended PA990's war with 105, or it has been suggested, 106 ops. One more Exodus flight was made on the 11th, Fanner bringing back 24 PoWs from B58 (Brussels-Melsbroek) to Dunsfold that morning.

Other than those mentioned already, several other pilots who flew PA990 were awarded the DFC: Gerald Lofthouse, Bernard Collens, Thomas Ford RCAF, Alfred Hicks, Gordon Hewitt RNZAF, William White RCAF, Brian Blennerhasset, Allan Wood, Ross Tierney RCAF and Frederick Benoit RCAF. Benoit did not have a good start for on his 'second dickie' trip on 31 December he had been shot down whilst flying with Pilot Officer R O Beattie RCAF and was lucky enough to land in friendly territory.

On 6 October, Flight Lieutenant R E Barnes flew her on a flypast over Leeds and York, probably one of her last flights. Ferried to 5 MU at Wroughton she was finally Struck off Charge on 18 August 1947.

Yule and crew in front of PA990.

## 626 SQUADRON
## 1944

**2 June** *2336-0348*
*BERNEVAL-LE-GRAND*
FO R C Bennet RCAF
Sgt T H Hayton (N)
Sgt H Johnson (FE)
Sgt A E Robson (BA)
Sgt A W J Scales (WOP)
Sgt J D Thatcher RCAF (MU)
Sgt G J Smallshaw RCAF (RG)

**4 June** *0158-0524*
*SANGATTE*
FO R C Bennet and crew

**5/6 June** *2134-0205*
*ST MARTIN VARNEVILLE*
FO R C Bennet and crew

**7 June** *0020-0517*
*ACHÈRES*
FO R C Bennet and crew
(aborted on instructions from MB)

**9 June** *0043-0519*
*FLERS*
FO R C Bennet and crew

**11 June** *0111-0540*
*EVREUX*
PO J Y N Wallbank RCAF
Sgt L A Sparrow RCAF (N)
Sgt E Shepherd (FE)
Sgt R N Purves (BA)

Sgt J M Dewar (WOP)
Sgt G M Derrington RCAF (MU)
Sgt T C Harris RCAF (RG)

**12/13 June** *2231-0311*
*GELSENKIRCHEN*
FO R C Bennet and crew

**14/15 June** *2018-0015*
*LE HAVRE*
FO R C Bennet and crew

**15/16 June** *2038-0104*
*BOULOGNE*
FO R C Bennet and crew

**17/18 June** *2339-0353*
*AULNOYE*
FO R C Bennet and crew

**22/23 June** *2220-0306*
*REIMS*
FO R C Bennet and crew

**24 June** *1545-1913*
*LES HAYONS – V1 SITE*
FO R C Bennet and crew

**25 June** *0723-1034*
*LIGESCOURT – V1 SITE*
FO R C Bennet and crew

**27 June** *0044-0459*
*VAIRIES M/YARDS*
FO R C Bennet and crew

**29 June** *1222-1530*
*STRACOURT – V1 SITE*
FO R C Bennet and crew

**30/31 June** *2220-0331*
*VIERZON*
FO R C Bennet and crew

**4/5 July** *2157-0356*
*LES AUBRAIS*
FO R C Bennet and crew

**6 July** *1840-2225*
*FORÊT DE CROC – V1 SITE*
WC G F Rodney AFC
Sgt J B Bright (N)
Sgt T E Jenkins (FE)
FS L S Curtain RAAF (BA)
FS O E Just RAAF (WOP)
Sgt J W Wood (MU)
Sgt W Whitehouse (RG)

**7 July** *1932-2318*
*CAEN*
PO G Lofthouse
FL L E T Cappi RAAF (N)
Sgt K W T Adams (FE)
WO E Peressini RCAF (BA)
Sgt K V Bettney (WOP)
FS R W Smith (MU)
WO R Roulston (RG)

**18 July** *0338-0739*
*CAEN*
FO R S Bennett RCAF
FO A V Clifford (N)

FS J P Slattery (FE)
FS L E Paradise (BA)
FS E S Cooper (WOP)
FS R S Heath (MU)
Sgt J M Reid (RG)
(lost 12 Aug; Reid was killed,
Bennett, Clifford, Paradise
and Slattery all PoW;  Cooper
and Heath not on that op)

**18/19 July** *2253-0307*
*SCHOLVEN*
FO R C Bennet and crew
PO W J Cook RCAF (2P)
(bomb-doors holed by flak)

**20/21 July** *2344-0308*
*COURTRAI M/YARDS*
FO R C Bennet and crew

**23/24 July** *2230-0337*
*KIEL*
FO R C Bennet and crew

**24/25 July** *2135-0525*
*STUTTGART*
FO R C Bennet and crew
(plus FS G T Ryan)

**30 July** *0617-1003*
*GAUMONT*
FO R C Bennet and crew

**31 July/1 Aug** *2145-0131*
*FORÊT DE NIEPPE*
FO G A Green RNZAF

FS W A Stephens RAAF
Sgt C W Farley (FE)
FS W A Dickson RAAF
FO K E F Taylor (BA)
Sgt W C Norman (MU)
FS G C Newton RAAF (RG)
(all KIA 4/5 Oct, except FS
Newton who was not flying)

**3 Aug** 1130-1556
*TROSSY ST MAXIMIN*
FO R C Bennet and crew

**4 Aug** 1342-2132
*PAUILLAC*
FO B A Collens (DFC)
FL J H Leuty (N)
Sgt H S Merry (FE)
FS W E Birch (BA)
Sgt K T Rainbird (WOP)
Sgt J Fulton (MU)
Sgt H Davy (RG)

**5 Aug** 1400-2216
*BLAYE*
FO R C Bennet and crew

**7/8 Aug** 2056-0122
*FONTENAY – NORMANDY*
FO J C Campbell RCAF
PO R Clouston RCAF
Sgt S L Akhurst (FE)
Sgt R Champagne RCAF
PO M H Hawkins
Sgt J G Reynolds
Sgt S J Cox

**8/9 Aug** 2148-0102
*AIRE-SUR-LYS*
FO R C Bennet and crew

**10 Aug** 1057-1412
*FERME-DU-FORESTAL – V1 SITE*
FO T H Ford RCAF (DFC)
Sgt J M Jackson (N)
WO H A S Tween
Sgt J C Payne
Sgt R A Wood
Sgt J C Moor
Sgt P L Potter

**11/12 Aug** 2054-0338
*GARDENING – GIRONDE*
FO R C Bennet and crew

**12/13 Aug** 2138-0251
*BRUNSWICK*
FO R C Bennet and crew

**14 Aug** 1207-1704
*FALAISE*
FL A C Hicks (DFC)
FS K J Brind (N)
Sgt S C King (FE)
FO P M Graves (BA)
FS J Saletto RAAF (WOP)
Sgt A B Jones (MU)
FO C M Bursey (RG)

**16/17 Aug** 2052-0506
*STETTIN*
FO R L Harris RCAF
FO H R Good RCAF
Sgt J A Purdue RCAF
FO J T Farrell RCAF
Sgt A Loveridge
Sgt J Keil
Sgt A C Kerr

**18 Aug** 1208-1500
*GHENT TERNEUZEN*
FO R C Bennet and crew

**29/30 Aug** 2123-0616
*STETTIN*
FO B A Collens and crew

**31 Aug** 1335-1650
*RIGUIER*
FL J Stewart
FO W M Mayr (N)
FS J S Wilson (FE)
PO A J Wilson (BA)
PO S J Nosworthy RAAF (WOP)
FS L R Smith (MU)
FS L F Vigar (RG)

**3 Sep** 1539-1926
*EINDHOVEN AIRFIELD*
FO G H Hewitt RNZAF (DFC)
PO J G Dickie
Sgt H J Dee
FS H J Bellinger (BA)
FS R H Rock
FS W Plummer
Sgt J Taylor

**6 Sep** 1707-2031
*LE HAVRE*
FO G Lofthouse and crew
PO R C McMillan RNZAF (N)
and FS F C Child (RG) in,
Cappi and Roulston out)

**8 Sep** 0650-1031
*LE HAVRE*
PO E W Parker RCAF
Sgt E H Arrowsmith
FS J D McPherson RAAF
Sgt J Tordoff
Sgt R H Westrop
Sgt W J Standen
Sgt G Hopkins
(Master Bomber abandoned
raid over target, bombs jett.)

**10 Sep** 1641-2049
*LE HAVRE*
FO R M Smith RCAF
FO J K Yeomans RCAF (N)
WO A H Kerr RCAF (WOP)
FO D Rymer RCAF (BA)
Sgt C J Lane (FE)
Sgt D G Crowe RCAF (MU)
Sgt E W Bock RCAF (RG)
(Bock killed by Ju88 22 Oct;
collided with another Lanc 7 Jan
'45 and Smith killed staying at
controls till crew baled out)

**11/12 Sep** 1937-0155
*GARDENING – KATTEGAT*
FO G A Green and crew

**12/13 Sep** 1841-0204
*FRANKFURT*
FO G A Green and crew
FO R J Tierney (2P)

**16/17 Sep** 2120-0136
*HOPSTEN*
FO G A Green and crew
FO J D Gilmore RCAF (2P)
FL W Whitehouse in, FS Newton out

**20 Sep** 1519-1828
*CALAIS*
FO B A Collens and crew

**23 Sep** 1839-2324
*NEUSS*
FO B A Collens and crew

**25 Sep** 0727-1050
*CALAIS*
FO B A Collens and crew

**26 Sep** 1012-1338
*CAP GRIS NEZ*
FO B A Collens and crew

**3 Oct** 1324-1600
*WESTKAPELLE SEA WALL*
FO B A Collens and crew
FO L Andrews (N)

**5/6 Oct** 1848-0115
*SAARBRÜCKEN*
Sgt R C Yule (DFC)
FO L Andrews (N)
FS G D Mayes RAAF (WOP)
WO E S Moore RAAF (BA)
Sgt G Leader (FE)
Sgt O F Fathers (MU)
Sgt A Clayton (RG)

**7 Oct** 1129-1624
*EMMERICH*
Sgt R C Yule and crew

**14 Oct** 0633-1125
*DUISBURG*
Sgt R C Yule and crew

**19/20 Oct** 1707-0005
*STUTTGART*
PO R O Beattie RCAF
FO A L Warren (N)
Sgt H Harrison (FE)
FO K H McWilliam RCAF
Sgt K H Austin (WOP)
Sgt J L Brown (MU)
Sgt T A Casey (RG)
(shot down 31 Dec; Austin,
Casey killed, others safe)

**23 Oct** 1615-2155
*ESSEN*
PO R O Beattie and crew

**28 Oct** 1333-1842
*COLOGNE*
FO W A T White RCAF (DFC)
FO J H Corsbie RCAF (N)
Sgt J W Anderson (FE)
FO M H Boyle RCAF (BA)
FO C Wright RCAF (WOP)
Sgt R J Jones RCAF (MU)
FS R Cunliffe (RG)

**29 Oct** 1153-1439
*DOMBURG*
FL B S R Blennerhassett (DFC)
FS R Raeburn (N)
Sgt F E James (FE)
FO W H Holland (BA)
Sgt D Jackson (WOP)
Sgt E U Scott (MU)
Sgt W T Phillips (RG)

**30 Oct** 1731-2345
*COLOGNE*
Sgt R C Yule and crew

**31 Oct** 1736-2244
*COLOGNE*
Sgt R C Yule and crew
FO G E H Marbaix (N) in,
Andrews out

**2 Nov** 1624-2141
*DÜSSELDORF*
Sgt R C Yule and crew

**4 Nov** 1725-2158
*BOCHUM*
FO A H Wood (DFC)
FS L S Hall (N)
Sgt J MacDonald (FE)
FS D S Wells (BA)
FS A Ward (WOP)
WO R S Pyatt RCAF (MU)
PO D A Joss (RG)

**6 Nov** 1115-1625
*GELSENKIRCHEN*
FO D Rodger
FO R W Donner (N)
Sgt H B King (FE)
FO T J O'Neill RCAF (BA)
Sgt C R Badger (WOP)
Sgt R Thomson (MU)
PO E R Poland (RG)
(all except Poland lost

21/22 Feb, whose place
was taken by WO Pyatt,
see Wood's crew above)

**9 Nov** 0832-1316
*WANNE-EICKEL*
FO R J Tierney RCAF
Sgt W E Potter RCAF (N)
FO E J Clark (FE)
FS A W Whitehead RCAF (BA)
PO G E Riddy RCAF (WOP)
FS D W Melnik (RG)

**11 Nov** 1613-2119
*DORTMUND*
FO D Rodger and crew

**18 Nov** 1550-2130
*WANNE-EICKEL*
Sgt R C Yule and crew

**29 Nov** 1222-1728
*DORTMUND*
Sgt R C Yule and crew

**3 Dec** 0735-1216
*URFT DAM*
PO R C Yule and crew

**4 Dec** 1632-2238
*KARLSRUHE*
PO R C Yule and crew

**6/7 Dec** 1648-0107
*MERSEBURG*
FO W N Patterson RCAF
FO J A Beck RCAF (N)
Sgt A T Dixon (FE)
FO J Crawford (BA)
Sgt K J Etherington (WOP)
Sgt T Whitby (MU)
Sgt H D Rutt (RG)

**12 Dec** 1625-2152
*ESSEN*
FO W N Patterson and crew

**15 Dec** 1437-2114
*LUDWIGSHAVEN*
FO J Cox
FO G Warren (N)
Sgt R Owen (FE)
FO S S Quinn RCAF (BA)
Sgt J W Williams (WOP)
Sgt D R Egan (MU)
FO D Menzies (RG)

**17 Dec** 1523-2305
*ÜLM*
FO J Cox and crew

**22 Dec** 1538-2223
*KOBLENZ*
PO R C Yule and crew

**28 Dec** *PM*
*BONN*
FO W A T White and crew
Sgt A F Brooks (RG) in,
FS Cunliffe out

**29 Dec** 1519-2046
*SCHOLVEN*
FO K G Hale
Sgt M D Middlemist (N)
Sgt W Rolley (FE)
Sgt W Dobson (BA)
FS R B Haydon RAAF (WOP)
Sgt W E Smith (MU)
Sgt A F Brooks (RG)
(damaged by flak, landed at
Woodbridge)

## 1945

**6 Jan** 1532-2132
*NEUSS*
PO R C Yule and crew

**7/8 Jan** *1818-0345*
MUNICH
PO R C Yule and crew

**14/15 Jan** *1931-0355*
MERSEBURG
FO F J Benoit RCAF (DFC)
FO K A Valentine RCAF (N)
Sgt K W Anstey (FE)
FO J C Crammond RCAF (BA)
Sgt D S Hyams (WOP)
FO K L Barker (MU)
FS P R Chambers (RG)

**28/29 Jan** *1953-0301*
STUTTGART
PO R C Yule and crew
FS A B M Warner RNZAF (2P)

**2 Feb** *1558-2305*
LUDWIGSHAVEN
PO R C Yule and crew

**2/3 Feb** *2029-0250*
WIESBADEN
PO R C Yule and crew

**3 Feb** *1623-2147*
BOTTROP
FO D Rodger and crew
WO R S Pyatt RCAF now
with crew, Poland out

**7/8 Feb** *1901-0042*
KLEVE
PO R C Yule and crew

**13/14 Feb** *2123-0650*
DRESDEN
PO R C Yule and crew

**14/15 Feb** *1803-0027*
GARDENING – ROSTOCK BAY
PO R C Yule and crew

**8/9 Mar** *1730-0118*
KASSEL
FO M J Enciso-Y-Seigler RCAF
FO J W Strachan RCAF (N)
Sgt G Butterfield (FE)
PO A J McMahan (BA)
Sgt A J Lloyd (WOP)
Sgt S Gardiner (MU)
Sgt E J Duncan (RG)

**11 Mar** *1201-1718*
ESSEN
PO R S Hyam
FO R V Wright (N)
Sgt P Davies (FE)
FO R Marshall (BA)
FO A R Jennings (WOP)
FS W L Robinson (MU)
Sgt T Jones (RG)

**19 Mar** *0029-0756*
HANAU
PO W F C Fanner
Sgt S Boyes
PO R G M Heath
FO D G K Williams
Sgt J C McCulloch (WOP)
Sgt G T Clavery (MU)
Sgt W K Storrie (RG)

**22 Mar** *0050-0706*
BRUCKSTRASSE
PO W F C Fanner and crew

**23 Mar** *0659-1158*
BREMEN BRIDGE
PO W F C Fanner and crew

**25 Mar** *0641-1225*
HANNOVER
PO W F C Fanner and crew

At the end of the war, PA990's name was changed to *Fanner's Follies*, this being painted where the previous name had been.

**27 Mar** *1432-2009*
PADERBORN
PO W F C Fanner and crew

**3 Apr** *1316-2001*
NORDHAUSEN
PO W F C Fanner and crew

**4/5 Apr** *2117-0535*
LUTZKENDORF
PO W F C Fanner and crew

**9/10 Apr** *1948-0017*
KIEL
PO W F C Fanner and crew
(abandoned; low oil pressure
caused port-inner to fail)

**14/15 Apr** *1752-0248*
POTSDAM
FO F J Benoit and crew

**18 Apr** *1025-1457*
HELIGOLAND
PO W F C Fanner and crew

**22 Apr** *1537-2047*
BREMEN
PO G A Gould
Sgt W E Hughes (N)
Sgt R W G Bizzell (FE)
Sgt T Cameron
Sgt R Pattern
Sgt T B Walker
Sgt R R Shaw
(abandoned over target by
Master Bomber; bombs jett.)

**25 Apr** *0501-1322*
BERCHTESGADEN
FO A R H Warner RNZAF
FO J W Foy RNZAF (N)
Sgt D F Locke (FE)
FS A G Rea RNZAF (BA)
FS A C Saywell RNZAF (WOP)
Sgt H Scott (MU)
Sgt F S Pearson (RG)

**30 Apr** *1500-1823*
MANNA
WO J McKenzie
FS F Rayner
FS L A Reeves
Sgt G O Long

Sgt D M Lamb
Sgt D Barnes
Sgt R W Hodgson

**1 May** *1246-1547*
MANNA
PO W F C Fanner and crew

**3 May** *1216-1533*
MANNA
PO W F C Fanner and crew

**5 May** *0618-0934*
MANNA
PO W A Gould and crew

**7 May** *1259-1648*
MANNA
PO W F C Fanner and crew

# PA995
# THE VULTURE STRIKES!

Robert Stone and crew flew PA995 for their first crew mission on 14/15 July 1944, which turned out to be a shambles. They flew her again on 25/26 July. From left to right: E W Halliday, C Sayers, D E Norgrove, Stone, L G B Wartnaby (with George, their bear mascot), C E White and F Wright.

Part of order No.1807/C4A, this Avro-built Mark III was produced in the spring of 1944 with four Merlin 38 engines. On 29 May it was assigned to 550 Squadron at Waltham, near Grimsby, Lincolnshire, where it became BG-K. The aircraft carried the letter 'K' until September after which it became V-Victor, but the 'V' soon took on other connotations, for a large vulture had been painted on her nose and the legend 'The Vulture Strikes!' was written above it.

PA995's bomb symbols began on 3/4 June following a raid to Wimereux, and at first these symbols were in neat rows of ten. After 43 bombs, the style changed to smaller, slanting bombs and a fifth row which had been started with three was completed with 11 of the slanting kind, making a row of 14. The next three rows were all of 13 (despite superstitions!) and then the original fourth row

had four more bombs added. All these can be seen in a well-known photograph of PA995 when she sported 98 bomb symbols, with Flying Officer G E Blackler in the cockpit. Although the picture shows 98 bombs, it was taken the morning after the 100th trip. Another photograph taken at the same time shows the Lanc surrounded by Blackler's men and the squadron's air and ground crews, plus the Station Commander, Wing Commander J C McWatters DFC.

George Blackler, who flew *Victor* on 27 raids, plus one abort and one recall out of his tour of 37 ops, remembered the vulture insignia as being black and yellow, edged in white. He also recalled that on the morning after the 100th op a tannoy message ordered everyone in B Flight to attend the aircraft, and on doing so photographs were taken to record the event. George

George Blackler in the cockpit of PA995 of 550 Squadron, 6 March 1945. Why the bomb symbols were changed is unknown.

arrived first and was thus photographed in the cockpit before the rest of the men arrived on the scene.

Flying Officer F S Steele RCAF had been PA995's first regular skipper back in mid-June 1944, flying at least 25 sorties in the aircraft and winning the DFC. When Steele completed his tour, George Blackler took over and he too received the DFC. In between, any number of pilots took her out over Germany.

Several crews that flew PA995 also flew EE139, another centenarian. One unusual pilot was an American on detachment from the US 8th Air Force, Flight Officer G P Fauman, who arrived on the squadron on 4 May 1944 and flew at least five ops in her, and two in EE139, before he returned to the USAAF in mid-September.

Another pilot, one we have met before, was Robert Stone, who flew PA995, EE139 and ED905:

'You have me down as flying [PA995] to Révigny on 15 July 1944 which is quite right. This was my first solo operation, and incidentally, I had been in the RAF for almost exactly three years before actually "going to war". As you may know the Révigny raids were a complete shambles. I returned that night confused. We lost our CO, Wing Commander Connolly, who was an excellent chap. My log-book shows that we were intercepted twice by night fighters; according to my upper and rear gunners by a Me110 and a Ju88. Your records would not show [they do now!] that two nights before I was the second pilot on the same aircraft on the first Révigny raid, the pilot being F/O Steele. It was the practice on 550 for a new pilot to accompany a seasoned crew as an introduction to operational flying. I remember at the first briefing (12 July) that our CO (P E G G Connolly) came over to me and said that he was glad that I had a nice quiet trip for my first op and that it wasn't a trip to the Ruhr. Of the 133 aircrew who attended that briefing, 21 were dead within 48 hours, including Connolly.'

PA995 had almost no mechanical problems of any note, although Steele did hit a tree on 18 July during the Caen breakout operation, which slightly damaged the H²S blister under the rear fuselage. Otherwise the aircraft flew on merrily and not until 19 October did it have to turn back from a mission, following a failure of the port-outer engine. Blacker took *Victor* to Chemnitz on 5/6 March 1945, recorded as the aircraft's 100th sortie, and then became tour-expired, going to 1656 CU. His mid-upper gunner was John Nicholson, who related:

'We carried out 27 ops in PA995. On our second in V-Victor we lost two engines on the first 100 miles or so and aborted. The aircraft was promptly overhauled, including two new engines, after which she behaved beautifully.

'We had our moments of excitement and anxieties. I shot down a Me163 rocket fighter on one sortie (I saw it explode), although I didn't know it was a 163 until after the war ended. It was never confirmed and was all but forgotten until our 1993 Squadron reunion.'

PA995's luck ran out on its very next sortie, the next day (7 March) – No.101 – a raid on Dessau, with Flying Officer C J Jones RCAF in command. In all 550 Squadron lost three Lancasters on this raid. The bomber was shot down by a Ju88 night fighter at 21.30 and crashed at Schauen, just south of Osterwieck. Jones and two of his crew died, the others taken prisoner. Of these, Sergeant M B Smith effected an escape in late March, succeeding in getting to the American lines, and returning to 550 in April. One of the other crews lost on the 7th was that of Flying Officer R D Harris RCAF, who had flown PA995 on 14/15 February.

George Blacker and his crew: Blacker, John Nicholson, W Ross, H P Nicholls, E Mozley, M McCutcheon, and Jack Bold in front.

Another crew to fly PA995 was that of the American, G P Fauman. From left to right: M S Merovitz, A E Stebner, W A Drake, Fauman, J A Ringrow. In front: W J Killick and P Cooksey.

## 1944
## 550 SQUADRON

**3/4 June** 2351-0243
*WIMEREUX*
FO K Bowen-Bravery (DFC)
Sgt L A Thompson (FE)
PO C E Thomas (N)
FS J P Fyfe (BA)
Sgt A Cleghorn (WOP)
Sgt R Blackburn (MU)
Sgt R A Thomson (RG)

**7 June** 0005-0457
*ACHÈRES*
SL P A Nicholas
Sgt J E Legg (FE)
FO W Dinney RCAF (N)
FS F C Wilkinson (BA)
FS C J Fuller (WOP)
Sgt W A Ansell (MU)
Sgt N S Smart (RG)
(aborted on orders of
Master Bomber)

**10 June** 0054-0527
*FLERS AIRFIELD*
SL P A Nicholas
Sgt W J Killick (FE)
FS A E Stebner RCAF (N)
FO M S Merovitz RCAF (BA)
FL A R Tippett (WOP)
Sgt J A Ringrow (MU)
Sgt W A Drake (RG)

**10/11 June** 2304-0407
*ACHÈRES*
FO M L Dubois RCAF

Sgt H Tulip
FO W F Cox RCAF
FO J C Young RCAF
Sgt H Wood
Sgt R Eves
Sgt L R R Haynes RCAF

**12/13 June** 2303-0311
*GELSENKIRCHEN*
Flt Off G P Fauman USAAF
Sgt W J Killick (FE)
FS A E Stebner RCAF (N)
FS M S Merovitz RCAF (BA)
FL A R Tippett (WOP)
Sgt J A Ringrow (MU)
Sgt W A Drake (RG)

**14/15 June** 2050-0009
*LE HAVRE*
Flt Off G P Fauman and crew

**16/17 June** 2307-0317
*STERKRADE*
Flt Off G P Fauman and crew

**22 June** 1405-1704
*MIMOYECQUES – V1 SITE*
FO F S Steele RCAF
Sgt R W E Walters
FO R G Fink RCAF
Sgt B R Railton-Jones
Sgt W Merrills
Sgt R G Roberts RCAF
Sgt E Smith RCAF

**23/24 June** 2228-0545
*SAINTES*
FO F S Steele and crew

**25 June** 0126-0501
*PAS DE CALAIS – V1 SITE*
FO F S Steele and crew

**28 June** 0124-0511
*PAS DE CALAIS – V1 SITE*
FO F S Steele and crew

**29 June** 1157-1459
*DOMLÉGER – V1 SITE*
Flt Off G P Fauman and crew

**30 June** 0602-0944
*OISEMONT – V1 SITE*
Flt Off G P Fauman and crew

**2 July** 1215-1552
*PAS DE CALAIS – V1 SITE*
FO F S Steele and crew

**4/5 July** 2203-0410
*ORLÉANS M/YARDS*
FO F S Steele and crew

**6 July** 1846-2227
*PAS DE CALAIS – V1 SITE*
FO F S Steele and crew

**7 July** 1930-2321
*CAEN*
FO F S Steele and crew

**12/13 July** 2127-0655
*RÉVIGNY M/YARDS*
FO F S Steele and crew
FL R P Stone (2P)
(abandoned over target
due to cloud)

**14/15 July** 2110-0615
*RÉVIGNY M/YARDS*
FL R P Stone
Sgt C E White (FE)
Sgt R F Ferry (N)
FS E W Holliday RCAF (BA)
Sgt D E Norgrove (WOP)
Sgt L G B Wartnaby (MU)
Sgt F Wright (RG)
(abandoned; target not identified;
Sqn CO lost on this raid)

**18 July** 0339-0729
*SANNERVILLE-CAEN*
FO F S Steele and crew
(damage to H²S blister in
hitting a tree)

**20 July** 1908-2239
*WIZERNES*
FO F S Steele and crew

**23/24 July** 2245-0334
*KIEL*
FO F S Steele and crew

**24/25 July** 2132-0606
*STUTTGART*
PO J J W Dawson
Sgt E W Edmunds
Sgt F W Wilmer
FS K P Brady
Sgt J M Farmer
Sgt J Earnshaw
Sgt W A Harkness

**25/26 July** 2143-0604
*STUTTGART*
FL R P Stone and crew

# PA995 THE VULTURE STRIKES!

Everyone turned out to celebrate PA995's 100th trip, but the Lanc failed to return from its 101st, on 7 March 1945.

**28/29 July** *2134-0215*
*STUTTGART*
FL R P Stone and crew
(aborted due to Gee u/s)

**30 July** *0639-1046*
*CAHAGNES*
PO L W Hussey RCAF
Sgt E Elliott
FO M A DeGast RCAF
FO H S W Nelson RCAF
Sgt P E Binder
Sgt A G Sale
Sgt R L Holmgren RCAF

**1 Aug** *1807-2130*
*LE HAVRE*
PO L W Hussey and crew

**2 Aug** *1848-2145*
*BELLE CROIX – V1 SITE*
PO L W Hussey and crew

**3 Aug** *1701-2028*
*LE HAVRE*
FO F S Steele and crew

**4 Aug** *1331-2139*
*PAUILLAC*
Sgt G H Town
Sgt G Hope
FS D J T Slimming
FS J H Windsor
FS P D Probert
PO E C Ball
WO J Teasdale

**5 Aug** *1425-2227*
*PAUILLAC*
FO F S Steele and crew

**8/9 Aug** *2109-0043*
*FONTENAY*
FO F S Steele and crew

**10 Aug** *0927-1440*
*DUGNY*
FO F S Steele and crew

**11 Aug** *1314-1735*
*DOUAI*
FO J J W Dawson and crew

**15 Aug** *1010-1330*
*LE COULOT AIRFIELD*
FL F S Steele and crew

**17/18 Aug** *2059-0528*
*STETTIN*
FL F S Steele and crew

**18/19 Aug** *2211-0121*
*GHENT TERNEUZEN*
Flt Off G P Fauman and crew

**25/26 Aug** *2020-0451*
*RÜSSELSHEIM*
FL F S Steele and crew

**26/27 Aug** *2020-0158*
*KIEL*
PO A Abrams RCAF
Sgt K W Nettleton (FE)
Sgt J W Brown RCAF (N)

Sgt R F Vennes (BA)
FS P L Brooker (WOP)
Sgt A P Soper (MU)
Sgt K R Salten
(all killed 14 Oct except
Abrams – PoW)

**28 Aug** *1800-2123*
*WEMAERS-CAPPEL – V1 SITE*
FL F S Steele and crew

**29/30 Aug** *2115-0618*
*STETTIN*
FL F S Steele and crew

**31 Aug** *1258-1654*
*AGENVILLE – V1 SITE*
FO L W Hussey and crew
FS J Fairclough in, Sgt Binder out

**3 Sep** *1600-1926*
*GILZE-RIJEN AIRFIELD*
FS R A Tapsell
Sgt F S Adley
PO D J K White
FO H Black
Sgt G E Collinson
Sgt J P Sheridan
Sgt p J Sculley

**5 Sep** *1626-2014*
*LE HAVRE*
FL F S Steele and crew

**6 Sep** *1717-2058*
*LE HAVRE*
FL F S Steele and crew

**8 Sep** *0640-1038*
*LE HAVRE*
FL F S Steele and crew

**10 Sep** *1649-2049*
*LE HAVRE*
FL F S Steele and crew
FO H A Shenker RCAF (2P)

**12/13 Sep** *1827-0144*
*FRANKFURT*
SL T D Misselbrook DFC
FO J Parr
FL K Keuffling
FL J P Blackie DFC
FO L A Cox
FO H Yates
FO H Cornforth

**16/17 Sep** *2159-0131*
*STEENWIJK AIRFIELD*
FO J J W Dawson and crew

**20 Sep** *1528-1901*
*SANGATTE*
FO G G Kennedy
Sgt G W Soundy
Sgt H Luxton
Sgt H H Powell
Sgt R T Wesley
Sgt A Frame RCAF
Sgt J Hogg

# TON-UP LANCS

**23 Sep** *1900-2338*
NEUSS
FO G G Kennedy and crew

**25 Sep** *0720-1059*
CALAIS
FO S H Hayter
Sgt L A Bassman (FE)
FO T Y Thomas (N)
FO R R Bradshaw RNZAF (BA)
Sgt A J Pearce (WOP)
Sgt Mills (MU)
Sgt F E Self (RG)
(all except Hayter and the
two gunners, KIFA 4 October)

**26 Sep** *1112-1409*
CALAIS
FO S H Hayter and crew
Sgt E M Watkins in, Mills out

**27 Sep** *0852-1212*
CALAIS
FO S H Hayter and crew

**28 Sep** *0803-1153*
CALAIS
FO G G Kennedy and crew
(raid abandoned over
target due to cloud)

**3 Oct** *1307-1609*
WALCHEREN
FL M L Dubois and crew

**5/6 Oct** *1847-0051*
SAARBRÜCKEN
FO G E Blackler
Sgt W R Ross (FE)
Sgt H P Nicholls (N)
FS J W Bold (BA)
Sgt E Mozley (WOP)
Sgt J Nicholson (MU)
Sgt M McCutcheon (RG)

**11 Oct** *1458-1813*
FORT FREDERIK HENDRIK
FO G W Bell RCAF
Sgt R J McElroy
FO D C R Hills RCAF
FO B H Lowen RCAF
Sgt J F Noonan
Sgt D E Hookham RCAF
Sgt R West RCAF

**14/15 Oct** *2220-0405*
DUISBURG
FO E S Allen
Sgt E T Smith
Sgt E B Dennison
Sgt G A Maginley
Sgt R W Lundy
Sgt E G Crump
PO J B M Sherreff

**19 Oct** *1704-2013*
STUTTGART
FO G E Blackler and crew
(aborted due to port outer u/s)

**23 Oct** *1628-2154*
ESSEN
FO G E Blackler and crew

**25 Oct** *1255-1800*
ESSEN
FO G W Bell and crew

**28 Oct** *1325-1827*
COLOGNE
FO R P Franklyn RAAF
Sgt S Dennis
Sgt R H Lucas
FS J A Dibley RAAF
FS K J Chester RAAF
Sgt K Sharp
Sgt P J James

**30 Oct** *1746-2356*
COLOGNE
FO J C Adams RCAF
Sgt W P Scott (FE)
FS B Sterman (N)
FO W R Elcoate RCAF (BA)
Sgt F Papple (WOP)
PO F S Renton (MU)
Sgt K D Winstanley (RG)
(all except RG lost 5/6 Jan '45)

**31 Oct** *1753-2327*
COLOGNE
FO G E Blackler and crew

**2 Nov** *1620-2147*
DÜSSELDORF
FO G E Blackler and crew

**4 Nov** *1729-2239*
BOCHUM
FO G E Blackler and crew

**6 Nov** *1127-1624*
GELSENKIRCHEN
FO G E Blackler and crew

**9 Nov** *0727-1317*
WANNE-EICKEL
FO G E Blackler and crew

**11 Nov** *1600-2126*
DORTMUND
FO G E Blackler and crew

**16 Nov** *1257-1830*
DÜREN
FO G E Blackler and crew

**18 Nov** *1539-2203*
WANNE-EICKEL
FO G E Blackler and crew

**27 Nov** *1548-2245*
FREIBERG
FO G E Blackler and crew

**29 Nov** *1119-1734*
DORTMUND
FO G E Blackler and crew

**4 Dec** *1631-2305*
KARLSRUHE
FO J C Adams and crew

**6/7 Dec** *1642-0037*
MERSEBURG
FO G E Blackler and crew

**12 Dec** *1623-2231*
ESSEN
FO C J Clarke RCAF
Sgt J T Tunstall
FS H E Meill RCAF
FO A L Coldwell RCAF
Sgt L O Precieux
Sgt F W Bradley RCAF
Sgt L A J Gauthier RCAF
(all lost 7/8 Jan '45 except
Coldwell – PoW)

**15 Dec** *1442-2143*
LUDWIGSHAVEN
FO C J Clarke and crew

**22 Dec** *1522-2200*
KOBLENZ
FO G E Blackler and crew

**24 Dec** *1439-2058*
COLOGNE
FO G E Blackler and crew

**29 Dec** *1500-0127*
SCHOLVEN-BUER
FO G E Blackler and crew

## 1945

**16/17 Jan** *1728-0127*
ZEITS
FO G E Blackler and crew

**22 Jan** *1659-2255*
DUISBURG
PO G E Mearns
Sgt F A Norris
FS W G Kelly RCAF
FS J F McKeown
Sgt D O'Neill
Sgt J Chambury
Sgt A G Slater

**1 Feb** *1533-2239*
LUDWIGSHAVEN
FO G E Blackler and crew

**7/8 Feb** *1838-0034*
KLEVE
FO G E Blackler and crew

**8/9 Feb** *1903-0356*
STETTIN
FO G E Blackler and crew

**13/14 Feb** *2136-0741*
DRESDEN
FL J Jarvis
Sgt I S Freeman
FO E B Hornsby
FS R W Richardson
FS P F Flux
FS Rees
RS R West RCAF

**14/15 Feb** *2010-0541*
CHEMNITZ
FO R D Harris RCAF
Sgt K J B Smith (FE)
FS D J Yemen RCAF
FO G J Nicol RCAF
Sgt G P Kelleher
Sgt W Towle
Sgt D J Hicks
(shot down 7/8 March; Harris,
Smith and another MU were
killed, Yemen, Nicol and Kelleher
all became prisoners)

**20/21 Feb** *2108-0351*
DORTMUND
FO G E Blackler and crew

**21/22 Feb** *1914-0131*
DUISBURG
FO G E Blackler and crew

**23 Feb** *1544-2341*
PFORZHEIM
FO G E Blackler and crew

**28 Feb** *0816-1044*
NEUSS
FO G E Blackler and crew
(abandoned on recall)

**1 Mar** *1137-1807*
MANNHEIM
FO G E Blackler and crew

**2 Mar** *0647-1220*
COLOGNE
FO G E Blackler and crew
PO R F Wallace RNZAF (2P)
(Wallace killed 15/16 March)

**5 Mar** *1635-0159*
CHEMNITZ
FO G E Blackler and crew

**7 Mar** *1659-*
DESSAU
FO C J Jones RCAF
Sgt S J Webb
FO J Buckmaster RCAF
WO L W Harvey RCAF (BA)
FS F M Main
Sgt M B Smith
Sgt S Pelham
(failed to return)

# PB150

PB150 CF-V is understood to have reached 100 ops with Manna and Exodus sorties. The Manna trips are recorded as tins of spam. The Kiwi wears a halo while standing on a bomb.

An Avro-built Mark III; part of order No.1807 C4A, this aircraft came off the production line in the spring of 1944, equipped with four Merlin 38 engines. The squadron code letters CV were painted on the aircraft's sides together with the individual letter 'V' when it was assigned to 625 Squadron at Kelstern, Lincolnshire. Operations began shortly after D-Day, taking in the full range of Bomber Command's summer targets of V1 sites, communication centres, ammo dumps and supporting the Caen breakout. Then came raids on German oil centres which became a priority in late 1944/early 1945.

PB150's first regular captain was a New Zealander,

Pilot Officer T G Wilson, who would take her on 22 sorties prior to finishing his tour in September 1944. Trevor Wilson RNZAF would receive the DFC, before going to 11 OTU as an instructor. Charles Callas, his mid-upper, received the DFM.

In support of his DFM, Callas by this time having flown over 30 trips, the Station Commander said:

'Throughout an arduous tour of operations, this NCO has proved to be an air gunner of outstanding ability. His coolness and courage under fire are exemplary and he has consistently

'100 NOT OUT' was chalked above the serial number of PB150, as was what appears to be a cat's rear end. The significance has not been discovered.

shown a very high standard of devotion to duty. He is strongly recommended for an award of the DFM. '

Wilson was followed by an Australian, Pilot Officer E P Twynam, who took her on 11 ops, but was then lost in PB154 'Y' on 4 November during a raid on Bochum. All the crew were killed. The last bombing sortie was against Hitler's personal complex at Berchtesgaden on 25 April 1945.

Although reputed to have achieved 100 operational sorties, photographs of PB150's nose-art show the number of bomb symbols to be 93, with seven further symbols depicting tins of spam for Manna flights; thus making 100. At that stage someone chalked up '100 NOT OUT!' under the 'tins', and also V for Victory, so one can assume this was done just after VE-Day. There also appears to be two ribbons painted below this, one a DFC,

the other possibly a DFM. Whether the latter had anything to do with Wilson and Flight Sergeant C E Callas is unknown.

At this same time someone had chalked the backside of an animal over the fuselage serial number. Exactly what it is, is not clear, perhaps a cat. It certainly has whiskers protruding and its tail is in the air. An obvious orifice beneath the tail would certainly have some connotation, not known to this author – which is perhaps just as well! Again, above this drawing is 100 NOT OUT.

The nose insignia is a Kiwi bird standing on a bomb, wearing a halo. This probably has reference to her first New Zealand skipper, Trevor Wilson. The bomb symbols are two-coloured (red and yellow?) depicting day or night sorties.

On 10 August 1945 PB150 went to 38 MU, then to 32 MU the following day, and back to 38 MU in March 1946, before finally being Struck off Charge on 22 May 1947.

**944**

**6/17 June** *0022-0350*
OMLÉGER – V1 SITE
O F Collett
gt N Jones (FE)
O W R Lott (BA)
O J Stephenson (N)
gt E Evison (WOP)
gt L Naylor (MU)
S W A Peterkin (RG)
ailed to return 28/29
uly, all taken prisoner)

**2/23 June** *2228-0310*
EIMS
O T G Wilson RNZAF
gt T H Howie (FE)
gt R L Baker (BA)
S D J Rant (N)
gt H Haine (WOP)
gt C E Callas RCAF (MU)
gt C E Tennant (RG)

**4 June** *1554-1919*
E HAYONS – V1 SITE
O T G Wilson and crew
gt G T Hagues in, Sgt Callas out

**5 June** *0732-1022*
IGESCOURT – V1 SITE
O T G Wilson and crew
L D W Webber DFC in,
gt Hagues out
Webber was sqn gunnery
officer – lost 12/13 Sep)

**27/28 June** *0025-0503*
AIRIES
O T G Wilson and crew
gt R Rimmer in, Webber out

**29 June** *1223-1539*
SIRACOURT – V1 SITE
gt A P Sims
gt F Brighton
gt D M Craig RCAF
gt S F Robertson
gt H Anderson
gt P M E Grandmaison
gt R J Farr

**30 June/1 July** *2214-0355*
VIERZON
FO W E B Mason RCAF
gt F V Walton
FO J A Noble RCAF
FO H J Collison RCAF
gt C Saunderson
gt H G Lee
gt K Steele

**2 July** *1211-1525*
OISEMONT – V1 SITE
PO F G Parker
gt L Brice
gt E C Williams
gt E J Coupland
PO D H Hutchinson
FO J A Knight
gt W Reed

**4/5 July** *2221-0403*
ORLÉANS M/YARDS
PO T G Wilson and crew

**6 July** *1849-2223*
FORÊT-DU-CROC – V1 SITE
PO T G Wilson and crew

**7 July** *1936-2322*
CAEN
PO T G Wilson and crew

**12/13 July** *2128-0352*
TOURS
PO T G Wilson and crew
Sgt R T Squire in, Rimmer out

**14/15 July** *2123-0534*
RÉVIGNY
PO T G Wilson and crew
(aborted by Master Bomber,
target not identified)

**18 July** *0339-0715*
SANNEVILLE-CAEN
PO T G Wilson and crew

**20 July** *1916-2238*
WIZERNES – V1 SITE
PO T G Wilson and crew
FS E W Sadler, Haine out

**23/24 July** *2247-0336*
KIEL
PO T G Wilson RNZAF
FO R M B Cairns (2P)
Sgt R D R Rees (FE)
Sgt R L Baker (BA)
PO P A C Ansell (N)
FS E W Sadler (WOP)
Sgt R T Squire (MU)
Sgt C E Tennant (RG)

**25 July** *0649-1032*
ARDOUVAL II – V1 SITE
FO R M B Cairnes
Sgt R D R Rees (FE)
Sgt J Crew
FO R J Cann
PO P A C Ansell (N)
Sgt R Perry
Sgt W Richie

**28/29 July** *2122-0601*
STUTTGART
PO T G Wilson and crew

**31 July/1 Aug** *2212-0145*
FORÊT DE NIEPPE – V1 SITE
FO E A Eckel RCAF
Sgt T Ord
FO K R Menzies RCAF
FS B G Little RCAF
Sgt W B Codd RCAF
Sgt F Onyski RCAF
Sgt R J Hammond RCAF

**3 Aug** *1137-1602*
TROSSY ST MAXIMIN
WO R B Pattison
Sgt R T Bryer
FS D P Ross RAAF
FS E G Russell
FS F G A McConnell
Sgt A Jacques (MU)
Sgt A Murray

**4 Aug** *1330-2125*
PAUILLAC
WO R B Pattison and crew
Sgt C Cletheroe in, Sgt Jacques out

**5 Aug** *1420-2218*
PAUILLAC
FL R Banks
Sgt M P Mary
FS J E Tooth
Sgt S T Kerr
Sgt R W Small
Sgt G T Hagues
Sgt W R Bates
(lost 12/13 Sept with FL Webber
(see 25 June))

**7/8 Aug** *2052-0113*
FONTENAY
FO E A Eckel and crew

**10 Aug** *1058-1450*
OEUF-EN-TERNOIS – V1 SITE
FO T G Wilson and crew

**11 Aug** *1352-1735*
DOUAI
PO J N Harvey RAAF

Sgt W A Edwards
FO J P M Brady RAAF
FS R T Williams RAAF
FS J W Smith RAAF
FS F J Allnutt RAAF
FS H R Brady RAAF

**12 Aug** *2119-2340*
BRUNSWICK
FO T G Wilson and crew
(aborted due to engine trouble)

**14 Aug** *1324-1721*
FONTAINE-LE-PIN (NORMANDY)
FO T G Wilson and crew

**15 Aug** *1008-1328*
VOLKEL AIRFIELD
PO J N Harvey and crew

**16/17 Aug** *2100-0455*
STETTIN
FO T G Wilson and crew

**18 Aug** *1915-2305*
VINCLY
PO E P Twynam RAAF
Sgt B H Fetch
FO G W Brown RAAF
Sgt D J Lincoln (N)
Sgt D Bousefield
Sgt A West
Sgt J Jones

**25/26 Aug** *2019-0457*
RÜSSELSHEIM
FO T G Wilson and crew

**26/27 Aug** *2013-0203*
KIEL
FO T G Wilson and crew

**29/30 Aug** *2111-0613*
STETTIN
FO T G Wilson and crew

**31 Aug** *1243-1600*
RAIMBERT
FO T G Wilson and crew

**3 Sep** *1544-1919*
GILZE-RIJEN AIRFIELD
FO T G Wilson and crew
FL R C Gordon DFM RNZAF
(BA) in; (DFC later)

**5 Sep** *1643-2013*
LE HAVRE
PO W Hutchinson
Sgt R A Greig
FL R C Gordon DFM (BA)
FS J Alcock (2BA)
PO J Ockieshaw
FS A A Solomon RAAF
Sgt J M Lehrie
Sgt K Hutchinson

**6 Sep** *1702-2039*
LE HAVRE
PO W Hutchinson and crew

**10 Sep** *1647-2017*
LE HAVRE
WC D D Haig DFC and Bar (DSO)
Sgt A L Robinson
FO H J Binns RCAF
FS J Davies
FO D J Travis
Sgt A Jacques
PO S A L Beacroft

**12/13 Sep** *1830-0136*
FRANKFURT
PO E P Twynam and crew

**17 Sep** *0050-0444*
RHEINE AIRFIELD
PO E P Twynam and crew
FO P L S Hathaway (N) in,
Lincoln out

**17 Sep** *1716-2011*
ELKENHORST
PO C D Mattingley RAAF
Sgt C E Bailey
FS A Fisher RAAF
PO R R Murr RAAF
FS R G Watson RAAF
FS N Ferguson RAAF
FS A J Avery RAAF

**20 Sep** *1514-1910*
CALAIS
PO L A Hannah RCAF
Sgt G Maynard
FS T M Baird RCAF
FS K R Strachen RCAF
Sgt J Soule
Sgt G E Way RCF
Sgt J H Loughran RCAF

**26 Sep** *1008-1323*
CALAIS
FO E A Eckel and crew
Sgt J E Cunliffe RCAF in,
Sgt Ord out

**3 Oct** *1234-1531*
WESTKAPELLE
PO E P Twynam and crew

**5 Oct** *1847-0150*
SAARBRÜCKEN
PO E P Twynam and crew

**7 Oct** *1152-1606*
EMMERICH
PO E P Twynam and crew

**14 Oct** *0624-1100*
DUISBURG
PO E P Twynam
FO C K Cochrane RCAF (2P)
Sgt T Ritchie (FE)
Sgt R Murphy (AB)
FS D J Lincoln (N)
WO R A Spencer RCAF (WOP)
Sgt B A Mead (MU)
Sgt J Jones (RG)

**15 Oct** *0031-0539*
DUISBURG
PO R A Court RCAF
Sgt P Garrison
Sgt E J Burke RCAF
Sgt G P Wright RCAF
FS G W H Smith RAAF
Sgt J W Gilpin RCAF
Sgt W F Larson RCAF

**20/21 Oct** *2113-0404*
STUTTGART
PO E P Twynam and crew

**25 Oct** *1249-1446*
ESSEN
FO J L Lane
Sgt T H Jakes
Sgt B J Mitchell
FO P R Talboys
FS E L M Bear RAAF
Sgt K Southwood
Sgt P J Kettle

**30 Oct** *1738-2307*
COLOGNE
PO E P Twynam and crew

**31 Oct** *1748-2248*
COLOGNE
PO E P Twynam and crew

**2 Nov** *1610-2128*
DÜSSELDORF
PO E P Twynam and crew

**4 Nov** *1734-2228*
BOCHUM
PO P H Allen
Sgt G K Williams

With 100 symbols, the Kiwi and also marked as '100 NOT OUT!'; a 'V for Victory' has also been added, to denote the end of the war. Also note the three dots and a dash, Morse code for 'V'.

Sgt W H Bell
Sgt D S Barker
Sgt C S Cathie
Sgt E G Whiteman
Sgt M Martin

**6 Nov** *1158-1612*
*GELSENKIRCHEN*
PO P H Allen and crew

**9 Nov** *0826-1241*
*WANNE-EICKEL*
FO A Fulbrook
Sgt E G E Philips
FS A E Napper
Sgt D W Tizard
Sgt W Magill
Sgt A R Huxtable
Sgt I S Goodman

**11 Nov** *1558-2123*
*DORTMUND*
FO W J Bulman
Sgt M Miles
FO J A Cottrell RCAF
FO R L Stevenson RCAF
Sgt E G Thale
Sgt L Smith
Sgt O R Sharman RCAF

**16 Nov** *1246-1733*
*DÜREN*
FO D R Ward RAAF
WC J L Barker (2P) (DFC)
Sgt M J Harris
FS J F Rudd
FO R H Thornton RAAF
FS R N Rowell RAAF
FS C Sykes
Sgt R Murcott

**18 Nov** *1605-2120*
*WANNE-EICKEL*
FL A B Fry (DFC)
Sgt A L Sykes
FO G G Davies
Sgt J Corrigan
FS J Soule
FO T A W Harper (MU)
FS K McCandlish (RG)

**21 Nov** *1550-2210*
*ASCHAFFENBURG*
FO J S Bray RCAF
Sgt E Foakes
FO H J Taylor
FO J Stevenson RCAF
Sgt R C Turner
FS D E Fumerton RCAF
FS B Ogrodnick RCAF

**27 Nov** *1631-2301*
*FREIBERG*
FO H W Hazell (DFC)
Sgt J O Pulford
FO M J Shenton
Sgt S Sellers
FS J Soule
Sgt A W Hall
Sgt W J Harrison
(shot down 14/15 Jan 1945;
Soule not in crew; only
Harrison survived as PoW)

**29 Nov** *1245-1721*
*DORTMUND*
FO W L Russell
Sgt S V Inwood
FO B J K Challes RCAF
FO W J Drysdale RCAF
Sgt J Gilchrist
Sgt G M Tulk RCAF
Sgt R F Cook

**4 Dec** *1635-2309*
*KARLSRUHE*
FL A B Fry and crew
FS J N Wadsworth (AB) and
FS D G McHardy (WOP) in

**6/7 Dec** *1639-0031*
*MERSEBURG*
FO T W Alexander RCAF
Sgt O C Lear (FE)
FO F R Chapman RCAF (BA)
FO W Petrashenko RCAF (N)
Sgt C W Morgan (WOP)
Sgt R Pyett (MU)
Sgt J V Williams (RG)
(all PoWs 5/6 March 1945 on
their 22nd operation)

**12 Dec** *1629-2200*
*ESSEN*
FO W L Russell and crew
Sgt G Attenborough (FE) and
FS G A Turner RCAF (RG) in

**15 Dec** *1438-2121*
*LUDWIGSHAVEN*
FO W L Russell and crew

**24 Dec** *1512-2004*
*COLOGNE*
PO J Jamieson
Sgt E J Cuthill (FE)
Sgt C G Aickin (BA)
FO E W O'Reilly (N)
Sgt D E Smith (WOP)
FS H W Elliott RCAF (MU)
Sgt E Wilson (RG)

**26 Dec** *1317-1713*
*ST VITH*
PO J Jamieson and crew

**28 Dec** *1533-2052*
*MÜNCHEN GLADBACH*
FL A B Fry and crew
FS J J McLeod (WOP), FS D O
O'Malley (MU), FS R R Job (RG)
in, Campbell and Harper out

## 1945

**2 Jan** *1436-2312*
*NÜRNBERG*
FL A B Fry and crew
FS K E Campbell (MU) back,
McClandish back, Job out

**5 Jan** *1913-0014*
*HANNOVER*
FL A B Fry and crew
FL J R W Orr (MU) in

**6 Jan** *1604-2206*
*HANAU M/YARDS*
PO J K English RCAF
Sgt J A Munday
FS T M Baird RCAF
FO H R Gottfried
Sgt M T Chalk
Sgt B A Thomas RCAF
Sgt G A Stowe RCAF

**14 Jan** *1908-0310*
*MERSEBURG*
FL A B Fry and crew
FO T A W Harper (MU) in,
Orr out

**16 Jan** *1733-0145*
*ZEITZ*
FO D R Paige RCAF
Sgt R B Bennett
FS J A Puttick
WO J P Sullivan RCAF
Sgt J Wallace
FS K E Campbell RCAF
FS J K McRorie
(survived a bale-out after hit
by falling incendiaries in PB815)

**7 Feb** *1915-0056*
*CLEVE*
PO C R Applewhite
Sgt R H T Winpenny
FS H G O Allan
FS C Wilson
Sgt A T Kaye
Sgt R E Edwards
Sgt C E H Cole

**8 Mar** *1732-0103*
*KASSEL*
FO B C Windrim RAAF
FS J E Platt
Sgt F S Tolley
FS W Porter
FS D E R Steen
Sgt S C Simmonds
Sgt J W Slater

**11 Mar** *1140-1706*
*ESSEN*
FL J R Forsythe
Sgt J W Stevens
FO K H Grindley
FO G Baker
FS W A Hughes
FP C E Jones DFM

**15 Mar** *1723-0109*
*MISBURG*
FL P Lennox
Sgt D Abbott
FO E J Harbord
FO M Brook
Sgt R G H Wilsdon
Sgt K Cowley
Sgt W Birkey

**16 Mar** *1745-0205*
*NÜRNBERG*
FL P Lennox and crew

**18 Mar** *0039-0747*
*HANAU*
FL P Lennox and crew

**22 Mar** *0108-0705*
*BRUCHSTRASSE*
FL P Lennox and crew

**23 Mar** *0745-1206*
*BREMEN*
FL P Lennox and crew

**3 Apr** *1328-1955*
*NORDHAUSEN*
FL P Lennox and crew

**4/5 Apr** *2121-0602*
*LUTZKENDORF*
FS N McDermott RAAF
Sgt E Fryer
Sgt D Johnson
Sgt G A Baillieu
Sgt C Wood
Sgt J Stock
Sgt E Stevens

**9/10 Apr** *1853-0200*
*KIEL*
FL P Lennox and crew

**14/15 Apr** *1808-0320*
*POTSDAM*
FL P Lennox and crew

**25 Apr** *0545-1353*
*BERCHTESGADEN*
PO K E Fife
FS J Flower
FS J G Morgan
FS F M Thomson
WO L W Keen
Sgt L D Coiner
Sgt H F Coakwell

**29 Apr** *1150-1520*
*MANNA – THE HAGUE*
PO K E Fife and crew

**2 May** *1236-1537*
*MANNA – ROTTERDAM*
PO K E Fife and crew

**3 May** *1215-1515*
*MANNA – ROTTERDAM*
PO W D Street
FS D F Gumbley
FS L C P Cheng RAAF
FS R D Given RAAF
Sgt W H G Bond
Sgt J R Jenner
Sgt J G King

**7 May** *1245-1613*
*MANNA – ROTTERDAM*
FS W J Norton
Sgt L Rickier
FO F W Wreggitt RCAF
Sgt E V Alkenbrack RCAF
Sgt T Langley
Sgt A Hutcheon
Sgt L J Clarkin

**8 May** *1108-1440*
*MANNA – THE HAGUE*
FO H J McMonagie
Sgt D J Kegan
FS W Fowler
FS E O Butts
FS D H Irvine
Sgt J Craig
Sgt A D Williams

# Narrative Index

# INDEX